Quick Guide

WRITE SOURCE

A BOOK FOR WRITING, THINKING, AND LEARNING

Written and Compiled by

Dave Kemper, Patrick Sebranek, and Verne Meyer

Illustrated by

Chris Krenzke

WRITE SOURCE®

GREAT SOURCE EDUCATION GROUP

a division of Houghton Mifflin Company
Wilmington, Massachusetts

Reviewers

Ilene R. Abrams
Cobb County School District
Marietta, GA

Dawn Calhoun Bray
Houston County School System
Warner Robins, Georgia

Doreen A. Caswell
Mary G. Montgomery
Semmes, Alabama

Tricia Dugger
St. Lucie County Schools District
Ft. Pierce, FL

Vallie J. Ericson
Sheboygan Area School District
Sheboygan, Wisconsin

Paula Denise Findley
Arkansas River Educational
    Cooperative
White Hall, Arkansas

Mary M. Fisher
Arlington Public Schools
Arlington, MA

Michelle Harden-Brown
Savannah-Chatham Southwest Middle
Savannah, Georgia

Kevin F. Harrington
Baldwin Middle School
Baldwin, New York

Beverly Canzater Jacobs
Solon City Schools
Solon, Ohio

Alissa Lowman
Hillside Middle School
Northville, Michigan

Elizabeth F. Manning
A.E. Phillips Laboratory School
Ruston, Louisiana

Rhea Mayerchak
Omin Middle School
Boca Raton, Florida

Steve Mellen
Prince George's County
    Public Schools
Temple Hills, Maryland

Diana L. Mooney
Lake Denoon Middle School
Muskego, Wisconsin

Ellen Nielsen
Clovis Unified School District
Clovis, California

Geraldine Ortego
Lafayette Parish
    District Office
Lafayette, Louisiana

Deborah Richmond
Ferry Pass Middle School
Pensacola, FL

Addie Rae Tobey
Shaker Heights
    Middle School
Shaker Heights, Ohio

Jodi Turchin
Silver Lakes Middle School
    Board of Broward County
North Lauderdale, FL

Bridget Wetton
Alpine Union School District
San Diego, California

Susan Wilson
South Orange/Maplewood
    School District
South Orange, New Jersey

Robert Wright
Sebastian River Middle
Sebastian River, FL

Peggy Zehnder
Bellingham School District
Bellingham, Washington

Technology Connections for *Write Source*

This series is supported by two Web sites:

The **Great Source iwrite** site is a writing resource that supports students, teachers, and parents. You'll find tutorials about the forms and traits of writing, as well as the latest articles, features, tips, and contests. Go to **www.greatsource.com/iwrite**.

The **Write Source** site features all the materials available from Write Source, as well as handy writing topics, student models, and help with research. You can even read about the history of Write Source. Go to **www.thewritesource.com**.

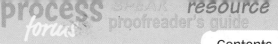

Using the Write Source Book

Your *Write Source* book is loaded with information to help you learn about writing. One section that will be especially helpful is the "Proofreader's Guide" at the back of the book. This section covers all of the rules for language and grammar.

The book also includes four main units covering the types of writing that you may have to complete on district or state writing tests. At the end of each unit, there are samples and tips for writing in science, social studies, and math.

The *Write Source* book will help you with other learning skills, too—study-reading, test taking, note taking, and speaking. This makes the *Write Source* book a valuable writing and learning guide in all of your classes.

Your *Write Source* guide . . .

With practice, you will be able to find information in this book quickly, using the guides explained below.

The **TABLE OF CONTENTS** (starting on the next page) lists the six major sections in the book and the chapters found in each section.

The **INDEX** (starting on page 751) lists the topics covered in the book in alphabetical order. Use the index when you are interested in a specific topic.

The **COLOR CODING** used for "Basic Grammar and Writing," "A Writer's Resource," and the "Proofreader's Guide" make these important sections easy to find.

The **SPECIAL PAGE REFERENCES** in the book tell you where to turn for additional information about a specific topic.

If at first you're not sure how to find something in the *Write Source* book, ask your teacher for help. With a little practice, you will find everything quickly and easily.

contents

The Writing Process

The Forms of Writing

DESCRIPTIVE WRITING

red juicy
big
delicious
EATEN!

EXPOSITORY WRITING

RESPONSE TO LITERATURE

CREATIVE WRITING

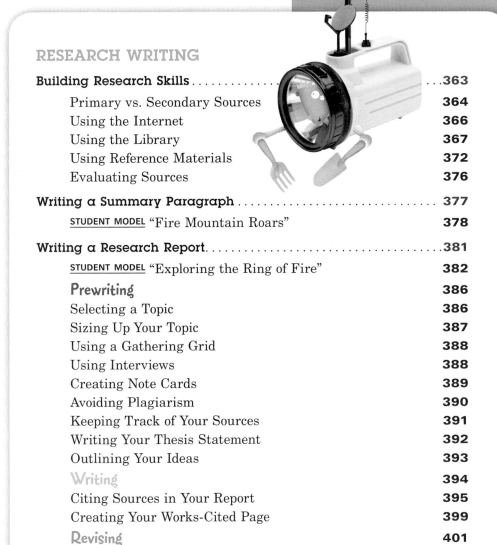

RESEARCH WRITING

The Tools of Learning

Basic Grammar and Writing

BUILDING EFFECTIVE SENTENCES

CONSTRUCTING STRONG PARAGRAPHS

A Writer's Resource

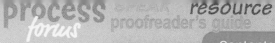

Proofreader's Guide

Test Prep!

The "Proofreader's Guide" includes test-prep pages to help you study for tests on punctuation, mechanics, usage, sentences, and the parts of speech.

Why Write?

This story by a middle school student will help answer this question.

Mr. Gibson made Randy my lab partner. I thought, "Great! I have to work with one of the biggest goof-offs in school."

One day my "partner" was absent. Mr. Gibson said that Randy and his older brother were beekeepers, and they were getting in a new shipment of bees. Randy, a beekeeper? I couldn't believe it.

That night I wrote about Randy in my journal. The more that I wrote, the more I began to understand him. He may not have liked school very much, but he still was learning a lot. He just did some of it in his own way.

Writing will do that. It can help you understand the people and the experiences in your life. What could be more important than that?

Maybe that's why you should write!

What's Ahead

- Reasons to Write
- Starting Points for Writing

Reasons to Write

Good things will happen if you write for the four reasons listed below. You will learn a lot about yourself and become a better writer.

1. To Explore Your Life

Writing in a personal journal helps you learn about yourself. All you have to do is set aside 10 or 15 minutes every day and write about people, places, and events in your life. (See pages 432–433 for more information.)

 Writing in a personal journal is great practice. You might already set aside time to practice a musical instrument or an athletic skill. Do the same with your writing.

2. To Understand New Ideas

Writing in a learning log helps you become a better student. In a learning log, you write about new ideas presented in your classes and in your reading assignments. Think of a learning log as your all-purpose study helper. (See pages 435–438 for more information.)

3. To Show Learning

Your teachers assign paragraphs, essays, and reports to see how well you are learning. To do well on these assignments, you must (1) understand the subjects you are studying and (2) use your best writing skills.

4. To Share Ideas

Write personal narratives (true stories), made-up stories, and poems. These forms of writing are meant to be shared with your classmates.

 Write to explore. Write nonstop for 5 to 8 minutes about something that happened to you yesterday or today. Write for the entire time. If you get stuck, write "I'm stuck" until something comes to mind. When you finish, you will have written a lot and learned something about yourself. Congratulations!

Starting Points for Writing

If you want to write, but you can't think of a good topic, review the ideas listed on this page. You're sure to find plenty of good starting points. (See pages 544–547 for more topics.)

Sample Topics

Describing *(telling what a topic looks like, sounds like, and so on)*

People: a neighbor, a friend, someone you wish you were like, a movie character

Places: an attic, an alley, the gym, a river, a church, a hideaway

Objects or things: a poster, a photograph, a stuffed animal, a hat

Narrating *(telling about something that happened)*

having a great day, making a mistake, showing friendship, moving, learning to _____ , getting hurt, doing something funny, learning a lesson

Explaining *(sharing information)*

How to . . . make your favorite food, make a friend, earn extra money, play a game, dress in style, fix something, clean a bedroom

The causes of . . . thunderstorms, earthquakes, erosion, the flu, baldness

Kinds of . . . music, friends, heroes, exercise, snack foods, diets, TV shows

Definition of . . . courage, faith, school, teamwork, love

Persuading *(expressing your opinion about a topic)*

dieting, dress codes, bicycle helmets, security officers in schools, curfews, recycling programs, movie or music reviews

 Find a topic. Write "Starting Points for Writing" at the top of a piece of paper. Then list these headings—Describing, Narrating, Explaining, and Persuading—down the left-hand margin. Leave space between each heading. Write two new writing ideas under each heading. Add other ideas throughout the school year.

4

Using the Writing Process

Understanding the Writing Process

You may already know about the writing process from experience. Just think of your best stories, reports, and essays. You probably worked very hard on each one, making many changes from one draft to the next. To do your best work, you must take your writing through a series of steps before sharing it. That is why writing is called a *process*.

The writing process is the key to unlocking your true writing potential. By taking a little time at each step along the way, you can become a stronger writer. You'll be amazed at the doors that writing can open for you.

This chapter will help you understand the writing process and build good writing habits along the way.

What's Ahead

- Developing Good Writing Habits
- The Writing Process
- The Process in Action
- Getting the Big Picture

Developing Good Writing Habits

To become a good writer, you must act like one. Following the tips listed on this page will help you do that.

Make reading part of your life.

Read lots of books, magazines, and newspapers. This will help you acquire an ear for good writing.

> Reading is to the mind what exercise is to the body.
> —Sir Richard Steele

Make writing part of your life.

Write as often as you can. Write early in the morning, late at night, or anytime in between. Just keep writing!

> Writing is not apart from living. Writing is a kind of double living.
> —Catherine Drinker Bowen

Write about topics that are important to you.

It's important for you to write about things you're interested in. Otherwise, it's like going out for softball when your favorite sport is track.

> When I speak to students about writing, I tell them to write about what they know.
> —Robert Cormier

Write about a quotation. Write nonstop for 3 to 5 minutes about one of the quotations on this page. Consider what it means to you.

The Writing Process

Experienced writers use the writing process to help them do their best work. The steps in the process are described below.

The Steps in the Writing Process

 Prewriting At the start of an assignment, a writer explores possible topics before selecting one to write about. Then the writer collects details about the topic and plans how to use them when writing.

 Writing During this step, a writer completes a first draft, using the plan as a guide. This draft is a writer's *first* chance to get everything down on paper.

 Revising After reviewing the first draft, a writer changes any ideas that are not clear or complete. A wise writer will ask at least one other person to review the draft, as well.

 Editing A writer then checks his or her revised writing for correctness before preparing a neat final copy. The writer proofreads the final copy for errors before sharing or publishing it.

 Publishing This is the final step in the writing process. Publishing is to a writer what an exhibit is to an artist— an opportunity to share his or her work with others.

 Assess your process. On your own paper, explain the process you used to complete your best piece of writing—what you did first, second, third, and so on. How similar was your process to the one described above?

The Process in Action

The next two pages show you the writing process in action. Use this information as a general guide for each of your writing assignments. This graphic reminds you that you can move back and forth between the steps in the writing process during an assignment.

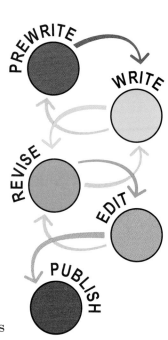

Prewriting Selecting a Topic

- Search for possible writing topics that meet the requirements of the assignment.
- Select a specific topic that really interests you.

Gathering Details

- Learn as much as you can about the topic before you start writing.
- Consider what to emphasize in the writing—either an interesting part of the topic or your personal feelings about it. This will be the focus, or thesis, of your writing.
- Decide which details you want to include in your writing. Also decide on the best way to organize the details.

Writing Developing the First Draft

- When you write your first draft, concentrate on getting your ideas on paper. Don't try to produce a perfect piece of writing.
- Use the details you collected and your prewriting plan as a general guide but feel free to add new ideas as you go along.
- Make sure your writing has a beginning, a middle, and an ending.

 Write on every other line and on only one side of the paper when using pen and paper. Double-space on a computer. This will give you room for revising, the next step in the process.

Revising **Improving Your Writing**

■ Review your first draft, but only after setting it aside for a while.
■ Use these questions as a general revising guide:
  - **Do I sound interested in my topic?**
  - **Do I say enough about it?**
  - **Are the ideas clear and in the right order?**
  - **Does the beginning draw the reader into the writing?**
  - **Does the closing remind the reader about the importance of the topic?**
  - **Are the nouns and verbs specific?**
  - **Are the modifiers (adjectives and adverbs) colorful?**
  - **Are the sentences varied? Do they read smoothly?**
■ Try to have at least one other person review your work.

Editing **Checking for Conventions**

■ Edit for correctness by checking for punctuation, capitalization, spelling, and grammar errors. Also ask someone else to check your writing for errors.
■ Then prepare a neat final copy of your writing. (See pages 24–26 for ideas.) Proofread this copy for errors before sharing it.

Publishing **Sharing Your Writing**

■ Share your finished work with your classmates, teacher, friends, and family members.
■ Decide whether you will include the writing in your portfolio.
■ Consider submitting your writing to your school newspaper or some other publication.

Consider the steps. On your own paper, list one new thing that you learned on pages 8–9 about each step in the writing process.

Getting the Big Picture

At this point, you may be wondering why writing has to be this involved. "Why can't I just sit down, write, and be done?" Well, you can, but your work won't be as good as it would have been if you had used the writing process.

Writers can't think of everything at once. They begin with the "big picture"—ideas, organization, and voice—and slowly sharpen their focus to look at individual sentences, words, and conventions (punctuation, spelling, capitalization, and grammar). These six qualities of writing are often called the six traits.

☐ Ideas

☐ Organization

☐ Voice

☐ Word Choice

☐ Sentence Fluency

☐ Conventions

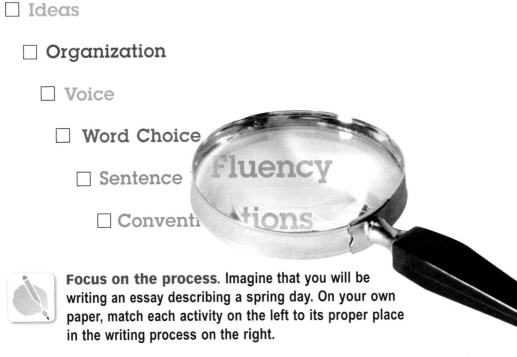

Focus on the process. Imagine that you will be writing an essay describing a spring day. On your own paper, match each activity on the left to its proper place in the writing process on the right.

___ 1. Check my writing for grammar, spelling, and punctuation.

___ 2. Gather details about what I would see, hear, feel, smell, and taste on a spring day.

___ 3. Move paragraphs so that they make more sense.

___ 4. Illustrate my description and post it on the fridge.

___ 5. Write a strong beginning, middle, and ending.

A. Prewriting

B. Writing

C. Revising

D. Editing

E. Publishing

One Writer's Process

Whether you want to tell a funny story, describe a roaring waterfall, or complain about something unfair, you have many things to write about. The challenge is writing down exactly what you want to say. The best way to express yourself is to use the writing process.

This chapter shows you how sixth-grader Reece King used the writing process to tell the story of meeting his closest friend. From the start, it was obvious how meaningful this event was to him. As he moved through the stages of the writing process, his story got better and better.

What's Ahead

- Previewing the Goals
- Prewriting
- Writing
- Revising
- Editing
- Publishing
- Assessing the Final Copy
- Reflecting on Your Writing

Previewing the Goals

Before Reece began writing, he looked at the goals for his narrative assignment, which are shown below. These goals helped him get started. He also previewed the rubric for narrative writing on pages 130–131.

Goals of Narrative Writing

Ideas

Use details and dialogue to tell about a specific experience or event. Make the reader want to know what happens next.

Organization

Open with a clear beginning that pulls the reader into the narrative. Then present ideas in the order in which they happened.

Voice

Write the narrative in a way that sounds natural—like the real you. Give the people in your narrative voice, too.

Word Choice

Use specific nouns, vivid verbs, and well-chosen modifiers.

Sentence Fluency

Use a variety of sentence styles that flow smoothly from one idea to the next.

Conventions

Be sure that your punctuation, capitalization, spelling, and grammar are correct.

 To understand the important goals for Reece's assignment, answer the following questions:

1. What types of ideas should he use to tell his story?
2. How should he organize his ideas?
3. How should his narrative sound?

Prewriting Selecting a Topic

Reece was asked to write a personal narrative about meeting a special friend for the first time. Since he has many friends, he used a cluster (also called a web) to decide which one to write about.

Cluster

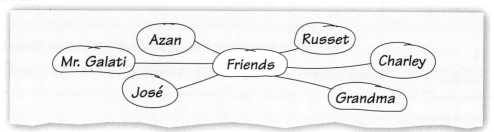

 Have you ever used a cluster? Try one now by clustering the names of your own friends. Could you write a story about a first meeting with one of the friends that you identified?

Gathering and Organizing Details

The time chart below helped Reece gather and organize details about meeting his dog, Russet. Reece focused on the five senses, personal feelings, and things that people said.

Time Chart

First ➜	Next ➜	Last
Mom said, "No pets until you're 12 years old." My Birthday. Waiting outside the animal shelter. Excited. Knew just what my dog would be like.	Looked for a golden retriever. Saw white terrier. Mean. Snarled. Old basset hound. Lots of mutts. Lots of barking.	Headache from all the barking. I tell Mom "HE'S NOT HERE!" I can see Russet in my mind. Then I saw him! His eyes were right!

 Have you ever used a time chart to gather details? What about a time line? (See page 548.) Use a graphic organizer to gather details about a first meeting with one of your friends. Were you able to collect a lot of details?

Writing **Developing Your First Draft**

Reece sat down to write his story. He used the ideas he had gathered and organized in his chart. His head was full of thoughts, and he wanted to get them all down on paper. (There are errors in Reece's first draft.)

The story starts with the problem and dialogue.

"For the last time Reece you can get your own dog when you turn twelve, and not a moment before" mom said. She set down my plate of hot pancakes.

That was disappointing to me.

A week later, my moment arrived. In exactly thirty seconds, the animal shelter would open. Mom stood beside me.

Details help create a clear picture.

"I hope they have the one I want," I said. I even knew his name: Russet. I had imagined the perfect dog. He'd be a retreiver puppy with a tale that wouldn't quit wagging. He'd be standing up at the gate of his cage, yipping. We'd know we were meant for each other. "Come on its a minute past!"

"Reece!"

Dialogue moves the action along.

The door was unlocked by a nice lady who came up to the other side of the door. I waited, and then I opened the door. I said "Good morning. We need a dog."

She said, "Why don't you go have a look."

PROCESS

Details appear in time order.

"Thanks!" I moved around the lady. I went to the door. The room beyond had cages. The moment my foot hit the cement, barking filled the air. There must have been thirty dogs in there. But which one was Russet?

The first dog was little. He growled at me. "I don't want you, either," I said and moved on. Next was a cute mutt. I kept going. Another dog and another, but where was my retriever?

I wandered the whole place twice. There wasn't a single retriever. I couldn't believe it. Maybe I missed it. After all, a puppy would be pretty small. While the dogs yapped, I searched their eyes. None of them was right.

Tension builds: What will happen?

"Have you decided?" Mom asked.

"He's not here, Mom!" I said. "I can't believe it. After all this waiting." Then I saw him! His outside was wrong, but his eyes were right. . . .

On page 13, Reece used a time chart to decide what he would say first, next, and last. Does his first draft follow this chart? Does he add any new details or leave any out? Explain.

Revising **Focusing on the Big Picture**

After Reece finished his first draft, he looked again at the goals on page 12 and used them as a revising guide. His thoughts tell you what changes he plans to make.

Ideas

Use details and dialogue to tell about a specific experience or event. Make the reader want to know what happens next.

"My overall idea is good, but I left out some important details from my time chart. I'll add some of those details."

Organization

Open with a clear beginning that pulls the reader into the story. Then present ideas in the order in which they happened.

"I shouldn't tell Russet's name before I describe him. I'll move that part."

Voice

Write the story in a way that sounds natural—like the real you. Give the people in your narrative voice, too.

"I could reword a few of my sentences so they sound more like me."

 Team up with a partner to review Reece's first draft. Write down at least two things that you like about the draft and one or two things that could be improved.

Reviewing Reece's First Revision

After Reece reviewed his first draft, he made the following revisions, or changes.

Reece adds dialogue to make his essay more interesting.

"For the last time Reece you can get your own

dog when you turn twelve, and not a moment before"
She repeated, "Not a moment before!"
mom said. She set down my plate of hot pancakes. ∧
"And not a moment after."
∧ ~~That was disappointing to me.~~
At last I was twelve years old.
A week later, my moment arrived. ∧ In exactly

thirty seconds, the animal shelter would open.
"Just hold on."
Mom stood beside me. ∧

To improve the essay, details are added, moved, and cut.

"I hope they have the one I want," I said. ⟨I even

knew his name: Russet.⟩ I had imagined the perfect

dog. He'd be a retreiver puppy with a tale that

wouldn't quit wagging. He'd be standing up at the

gate of his cage, yipping. We'd know we were meant

for each other. ∧ "Come on its a minute past!"

"Reece!"

The voice is improved by rewriting a boring sentence.

Finally,
~~The door was unlocked by~~ a nice lady ~~who came~~
unlocked ∧
~~up to the other side of~~ the door. I waited . . .

 Review Reece's changes. Find an idea or a detail that he added, one that he cut, one that he moved, and one that he rewrote.

Revising **Using a Peer Response Sheet**

One of Reece's classmates read his story. She used a rubric like the one on pages 130–131 and spotted more places that could use improvements. Reece's classmate wrote her comments on a "Peer Response Sheet."

Peer Response Sheet

Writer: *Reece King*   Responder: *Chiara Davidson*

Title: *"Looking at the Inside"*

What I liked about your writing:

* *You start right in the middle of the action.*

* *I like your voice. You sure wanted a dog.*

* *You use real-sounding dialogue.*

Changes I would suggest:

* *Could you add a few details in the beginning?*

* *What kind of retriever did you want?*

* *Sometimes, could you tell what the speakers are doing when they say something?*

 Review the classmate's suggestions for improvements listed above. Which one do you think is the most important? Explain. Also add one suggestion of your own. Focus on the ideas, organization, and voice in the writing.

Revising with a Peer Response

Using the comments made by his classmate, Reece revised his story again. The new details and quotations he used filled out his narrative.

> **Give more details in the beginning.**

"For the last time Reece you can get your own

dog when you turn twelve, and not a moment before"

mom said. She set down my plate of hot pancakes.

She repeated, "Not a moment before!"
  I started to spread the butter.
  ∧"And not a moment after."
                    It was Saturday, April 24 2008.
  A week later, my moment arrived∧At last I

was twelve years old. In exactly thirty seconds, the
                    her hand on my shoulder,
animal shelter would open. Mom stood beside me, ∧

"Just hold on."

> **Tell what kind of retriever.**

"I hope they have the one I want," I said. I had
                    golden
imagined the perfect dog. He'd be a∧retreiver puppy

with a tale that wouldn't quit wagging. He'd be

standing up at the gate of his cage, yipping. We'd

> **Tell what Mom was doing.**

know we were meant for each other. I even knew his
                    I said, knocking on the door.
name: Russet. "Come on its a minute past!"∧
            Mom pulled me back.
  "Reece!"∧. . .

Try It Have you ever used peer responding during a writing assignment? Discuss the experience with your classmates. Consider why peer responding is (or could be) helpful.

Revising Focusing on Words and Sentences

Once Reece had finished revising his ideas, organization, and voice, he began checking the style of his writing. He thought about what he had written and considered what he should change to make everything sound more effective.

Word Choice

Use specific nouns, vivid verbs, and well-chosen modifiers.

"Some of my words are kind of dull. I'll choose stronger nouns and verbs."

Sentence Fluency

Use a variety of sentence styles that flow smoothly from one idea to the next.

"Some parts are choppy. I'll put some sentences together and use transitions."

Try It Team up with a partner to review Reece's revised writing on page 19 for style. Identify two nouns, verbs, or adjectives that could be more specific, vivid, or colorful. Then find one or two sentences that could be improved.

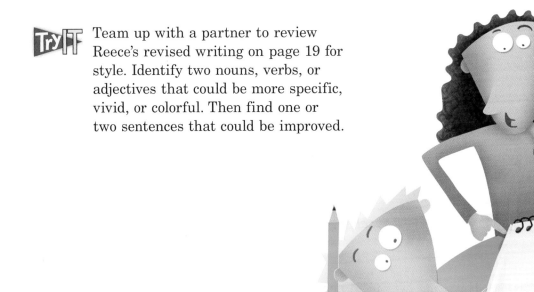

Checking Reece's Improvements in Style

Reece's next step was to concentrate on the style or sound of his ideas. He paid special attention to the effectiveness of the words and the sentences.

The word choice is improved, and choppy sentences are combined.

"For the last time Reece you can get your

own dog when you turn twelve, and not a moment

before" mom ~~said~~ *snapped*. She set down my plate of hot

pancakes. *and* ~~She~~ repeated, "Not a moment before!"

I started to spread the butter. "And not

a moment after."

A week later, my moment arrived. It was

Saturday, April 24 2008. *and* At last I was twelve years

old. In exactly thirty seconds, the animal shelter

would open *its doors*. Mom stood beside me, her hand on my

shoulder, "Just hold on."

Over the last five months,
"I hope they have the one I want," I said. I had

imagined the perfect dog. He'd be a golden retreiver

puppy with a tale that wouldn't quit wagging. He'd

be standing up at the gate of his cage, yipping.
The moment our eyes would meet,
We'd know we were meant for each other. . . .

Words are added at the beginning of sentences to vary the sentence style.

 Compare your comments about the style of Reece's writing (page 20) with the changes he actually made. How are they alike or different?

Editing Checking for Conventions

Once Reece was pleased with the way his story sounded, he checked his work for conventions. (Conventions deal with the rules for correct punctuation, capitalization, spelling, and grammar.)

Conventions

Be sure that your punctuation, capitalization, spelling, and grammar are correct.

> *"Spelling and punctuation are tough. I'll ask a classmate to help me catch everything."*

For help with writing rules, Reece turned to the "Proofreader's Guide" in the back of his *Write Source* book. He also used a checklist to help him look for errors.

Editing Checklist

PUNCTUATION

_____ **1.** Do I use end punctuation after all my sentences?

_____ **2.** Do I use commas correctly?

_____ **3.** Do I use apostrophes to show possession *(boy's bike)*?

CAPITALIZATION

_____ **4.** Do I start all my sentences with capital letters?

_____ **5.** Do I capitalize all proper nouns?

SPELLING

_____ **6.** Have I spelled all my words correctly?

_____ **7.** Have I double-checked words my spell checker might miss?

GRAMMAR

_____ **8.** Do I use correct forms of verbs *(had gone, not had went)*?

_____ **9.** Do my subjects and verbs agree in number?

_____ **10.** Do I use the right word *(to, too, two)*?

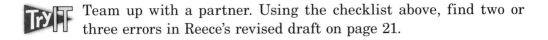 Team up with a partner. Using the checklist above, find two or three errors in Reece's revised draft on page 21.

Checking Reece's Editing for Conventions

Before writing a final copy, Reece checked his narrative for spelling, punctuation, capitalization, and grammar errors. (See the inside back cover of this book for a list of the common editing and proofreading marks.)

Punctuation mistakes are fixed.

Capitalization errors are corrected.

Use of numbers is corrected.

Spelling and usage errors are corrected.

"For the last time‸Reece‸you can get your own dog when you turn ~~twelve~~ 12, and not a moment before‸" ᵐom snapped. She set down my plate of hot pancakes and repeated, "Not a moment before!"

I started to spread the butter. "And not a moment after."

A week later, my moment arrived. It was Saturday, April 24‸2008, and at last I was ~~twelve~~ 12 years old. In exactly ~~thirty~~ 30 seconds, the animal shelter would open its doors. Mom stood beside me, her hand on my shoulder‸"Just hold on."

"I hope they have the one I want," I said. Over the last five months, I had imagined the perfect dog. He'd be a golden (retriever) *retriever* puppy with a ~~tale~~ *tail* that wouldn't quit wagging. He'd be standing . . .

 Review Reece's editing for conventions in the paragraphs above. Did you find some of the same errors when you reviewed page 21?

Publishing Sharing Your Writing

Reece used the tips below to help him write the final copy of his story. (See pages 25–26.)

Focus on Presentation

Tips for Handwritten Copies

- ■ Use blue or black ink and write neatly.
- ■ Write your name following your teacher's instructions.
- ■ Skip a line and center your title; skip another line and start your writing.
- ■ Indent every paragraph and leave a one-inch margin on all four sides.
- ■ Write your last name and page number on every page after page 1.

Reece King

Looking at the Inside

"For the last time, Reece, you can get your own dog when you turn 12, and not a moment before," Mom snapped. She set down my plate of hot pancakes and repeated, "Not a moment before!"

I started to spread the butter. "And not a moment after."

A week later, my moment arrived. It was Saturday, April 24, 2004, and at last I was 12 years old. In exactly 30 seconds, the animal shelter would open its doors. Mom stood beside me, her hand on my shoulder. "Just hold on."

"I hope they have the one I want," I said. Over the last five months, I'd imagined the perfect dog. He'd be a golden retriever puppy with a tail that wouldn't quit wagging. He'd be standing up at the gate of his cage, yipping. The moment our eyes would meet, we'd know we were meant for each other. I even knew his name: Russet. "Come on! It's a minute past!" I said, knocking on the door.

"Reece!" Mom pulled me back.

Finally, a nice lady unlocked the door and opened it. I said, "Good morning. We need a dog."

She replied, "Why don't you go have a look?"

"Thanks!" I dodged around the lady and rushed to the door marked "Kennel." The room beyond was lined with cages. The moment my foot hit the cement, barking filled the air. There must have been 30 dogs in there, and all of them were shouting, "Me! Me! Pick me!" But which one was Russet?

King 2

The first dog was a little terrier that growled at me. "I don't

---

King 2

Reece King

Looking at the Inside

"For the last time, Reece, you can get your own dog when you turn 12, and not a moment before," Mom snapped. She set down my plate of hot pancakes and repeated, "Not a moment before!"

I started to spread the butter. "And not a moment after."

A week later, my moment arrived. It was Saturday, April 24, 2004, and at last I was 12 years old. In exactly 30 seconds, the animal shelter would open its doors. Mom stood beside me, her hand on my shoulder. "Just hold on."

"I hope they have the one I want," I said. Over the last five months, I'd imagined the perfect dog. He'd be a golden retriever puppy with a tail that wouldn't quit wagging. He'd be standing up at the gate of his cage, yipping. The moment our eyes would meet, we'd know we were meant for each other. I even knew his name: Russet. "Come on! It's a minute past!" I said, knocking on the door.

"Reece!" Mom pulled me back.

Finally, a nice lady unlocked the door and opened it.

I said, "Good morning. We need a dog."

She replied, "Why don't you go have a look?"

"Thanks!" I dodged around the lady and rushed to the door marked "Kennel." The room beyond was lined with cages. The moment my foot hit the cement, barking filled the air. There must have been 30 dogs in there, and all of them were shouting, "Me! Me! Pick me!" But which one was Russet?

Tips for Computer Copies

- ■ Use an easy-to-read font and a 12-point type size.
- ■ Double-space and leave a one-inch margin around each page.

Reece's Final Copy

Reece felt great about his final story. It really captured the exciting day when he met his closest "friend."

Reece King

Looking at the Inside

"For the last time, Reece, you can get your own dog when you turn 12, and not a moment before," Mom snapped. She set down my plate of hot pancakes and repeated, "Not a moment before!"

I started to spread the butter. "And not a moment after."

A week later, my moment arrived. It was Saturday, April 24, 2004, and at last I was 12 years old. In exactly 30 seconds, the animal shelter would open its doors. Mom stood beside me, her hand on my shoulder. "Just hold on."

"I hope they have the one I want," I said. Over the last five months, I'd imagined the perfect dog. He'd be a golden retriever puppy with a tail that wouldn't quit wagging. He'd be standing up at the gate of his cage, yipping. The moment our eyes would meet, we'd know we were meant for each other. I even knew his name: Russet. "Come on! It's a minute past!" I said, knocking on the door.

"Reece!" Mom pulled me back.

Finally, a nice lady unlocked the door and opened it.

I said, "Good morning. We need a dog."

She replied, "Why don't you go have a look?"

"Thanks!" I dodged around the lady and rushed to the door marked "Kennel." The room beyond was lined with cages. The moment my foot hit the cement, barking filled the air. There must have been 30 dogs in there, and all of them were shouting, "Me! Me! Pick me!" But which one was Russet?

The first dog was a little terrier that growled at me. "I don't want you, either," I said and moved on. Next was a cute mutt. I kept going. A shepherd, a bulldog, a hound—but where was my golden retriever?

I wandered the whole place twice. There wasn't a single retriever. I couldn't believe it. Maybe I missed it. After all, a puppy would be pretty small. While the dogs leaped at their gates and yapped, I searched their eyes. None of them was right.

"Have you decided?" Mom asked, coming up behind me.

"He's not here, Mom!" I said. "I can't believe it. After all this waiting." Suddenly, I saw him. His outside was wrong, but his eyes were right. "Here! This is the one. This is Russet!"

Mom blinked at the puppy. "He's a beagle."

"You're looking at the outside," I said. I stuck my fingers in the cage. Russet bounced up to lick my hand. "You've got to look at his inside. He's the one."

That was the day I met my best friend. On that day, I learned that sometimes you need to look at the inside and not the outside. That beagle mutt sure turned out to be my Russet. I wouldn't trade him for any other dog in the world. And I doubt Russet would trade me for any other kid, either.

PROCESS

Assessing the Final Copy

Reece's teacher used a rubric like the one that appears on pages 130–131 to assess his final copy. A 6 is the very best score that a writer can receive for each trait. The teacher also included comments under each trait.

6 Ideas

What a creative twist, to write about a dog as your best friend! Your use of sensory details and dialogue makes the story so real. Well done.

5 Organization

Your story follows a clear time organization.

6 Voice

I can hear you speaking to me in every line!

5 Word Choice

Your use of strong verbs and specific nouns is good throughout.

4 Sentence Fluency

Though the first page is very smooth, the second page feels a little choppy. A few more transitions could help next time.

6 Conventions

Your story is error free. Great work!

Review the assessment. Do you agree with the comments and scores made by Reece's teacher? Why or why not? Explain your feelings in a brief paragraph.

Reflecting on Your Writing

After the whole process was finished, Reece filled out a reflection sheet. This helped him think about the assignment and plan for future narrative writing.

Reece King

My Personal Narrative

1. **The best part of my narrative is . . .**
   the voice. Even Mrs. Wilson says so. She said she can hear my voice in every line. That's great. Mrs. Wilson says that the voice is the personality in the writing.

2. **The part that still needs work is . . .**
   sentence fluency. I should have combined a few choppy sentences on the second page.

3. **The main thing I learned about writing a personal narrative is . . .**
   it's a process. If I'd quit after the first draft, my story never would've been what I wanted.

4. **In my next narrative, I would like to . . .**
   write about people instead of dogs.

5. **Here is one question I still have about writing a narrative:**
   What's the difference between a personal narrative and a story?

Peer Responding

Dancers practice in front of mirrors to see how well they are dancing. Writers don't have mirrors to tell them how well they are writing. To see their work from another angle, writers need the opinions of readers.

How do readers know what to look for in writing? One way is to use a rubric. A rubric can help them focus on the right traits at the right time. And how can readers share their reactions and suggestions? They can use a response sheet to organize comments, or simply talk about the writing in a group.

In this chapter, you will learn how to share your writing—and how to respond to the work of others. You'll do your reacting on paper and in small groups. Either way, a careful peer response can be just what a writer needs to improve a piece of writing.

What's Ahead

- Basic Rules of Peer Responding
- Writing-Group Guidelines

Basic Rules of Peer Responding

Learning how to respond well to other people's writing takes planning and practice. Whether you're working with a small group or with one other person, follow the basic rules below.

- **Make a plan.** Decide what steps you will follow for reading and responding to the piece of writing. (Find out about the assignment, review the rubric, read the piece once through, and so on.)

- **Listen and cooperate.** Encourage the writer by listening carefully and making positive suggestions.

- **Respond with respect.** Focus on the writing, not the writer, and think before you respond.

Using a Response Sheet

One of the best ways to react to someone else's writing is to complete a response sheet.

 As you read the following paragraphs about a special childhood object, focus on the writer's strengths and weaknesses. Then read the sample response sheet shown on the next page.

My Best Friend

Elmo is not a fancy guy, but he would definitely stand out in a crowd. His whole body is red, except for an orange, bulb-shaped nose and a pair of golf-ball-shaped eyes with black pupils. His hands have a few gigantic fingers, his feet have no toes, and his mouth spreads across his face in a huge smile. Staying in fashion has never been a problem for Elmo, because he doesn't wear clothes.

His voice sounds something like mine, but it's higher. It really gets shrill when he laughs. He can even sing, and his favorite tune is the "A, B, C" song. These days, he talks and sings less than he used to. Elmo doesn't have ears.

PROCESS

Peer Response Sheet

A classmate responded to the writing on the previous page using the following plan.

1 First he read the writing to get the overall picture.

2 Next he read the piece again, focusing on its strengths and weaknesses.

3 Then he filled out a response sheet.

Peer Response Sheet

Writer: *Lien*   Responder: *Dean*

Title: *"My Best Friend"*

What I liked about your writing:

  * *You were brave to write about Elmo. Lots of us liked*

    him when we were little, but we don't admit it now.

  * *You have lots of details telling how Elmo looks,*

    sounds, and feels. Nice job!

  * *Your voice is friendly and funny. It fits the subject.*

Changes I would suggest:

  * *Is the fact that Elmo doesn't have ears out of place?*

  * *The assignment asked you to tell why the object was*

    important to you. Why you care about Elmo?

Practice. Exchange a recent piece of writing with a classmate.

1 Read the writing once to get an overall feel for it.

2 Then read it again, focusing on what you like and what you might improve.

3 Fill out a response sheet like the one above.

Writing-Group Guidelines

You can read your writing out loud to a partner or a group and get immediate feedback. If you've never been in a writing group before, it might be helpful to work with a classmate first. You can take turns practicing the author's and the responder's roles.

The Author's Role

As the author, you need to choose a piece of writing that you want someone to review. The writing can be at any stage in the process. If possible, make a copy for each member of the group. Then follow these guidelines.

- **Introduce your writing** but don't say too much.
- **Read your writing out loud** or have people read it silently.
- **Ask others for comments** and listen to what they say.
- **Take notes** to help you remember what was said.
- **Be open and polite** when you explain your writing.
- **Ask your group for help** with any writing problems.

The Responder's Role

As the responder, you need to show interest and respect. Follow these guidelines.

- **Review the goals** for the form of writing you are responding to so that you will know what to listen for.
- **Listen carefully and take notes** to help you remember what you want to say.
- **Ask questions** if you are confused about something or want to know more.
- **Tell what works well** in the writing.
- **Tell what needs to be improved** by politely making specific suggestions.

Remember, don't just say, "Everything is great."

Understanding the
Traits of Writing

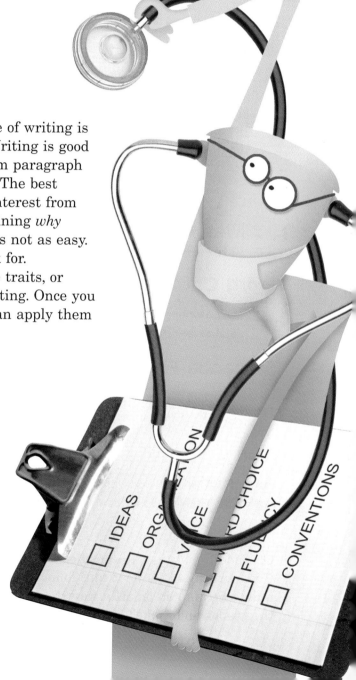

How can you tell if a piece of writing is good? One way is very easy: Writing is good when it keeps you reading from paragraph to paragraph. It's that simple. The best stories and essays hold your interest from start to finish. However, explaining *why* something keeps you reading is not as easy. You need to know what to look for.

This chapter identifies the traits, or qualities, found in all good writing. Once you understand these traits, you can apply them to everything you write.

What's Ahead

- Introducing the Traits
- Understanding Ideas
- Understanding Organization
- Understanding Voice
- Understanding Word Choice
- Understanding Sentence Fluency
- Understanding Conventions

Introducing the Traits

There are six main traits, or qualities, found in writing. You will do your best work if you keep these traits in mind when you write. This page introduces the traits. The next 10 pages provide a closer look at each one.

Ideas

Excellent writing has a clear message, purpose, or focus. The writing contains plenty of specific ideas and details.

Organization

Effective writing has a clear beginning, middle, and ending. The overall writing is well organized and easy to follow.

Voice

The best writing reveals the writer's voice—his or her special way of saying things.

Word Choice

Good writing contains strong words, including specific nouns and verbs. The words fit the audience and deliver a clear message.

Sentence Fluency

Effective writing flows smoothly from one sentence to the next. Sentences vary in length and begin in a variety of ways.

Conventions

Good writing is carefully edited to make sure it is easy to understand. The writing follows the rules for punctuation, grammar, and spelling.

One additional trait to consider is the **presentation** of your writing. Good writing looks neat and follows guidelines for margins, spacing, indenting, and so on. The way the writing looks on the page attracts the reader and makes him or her *want* to read on.

conventions ideas sentence fluency
VOICE organization word choice 35
Traits of Writing

Understanding Ideas

Nothing is more important than having great ideas in your writing. Just as a chef needs the best ingredients to make a delicious meal, a writer needs quality ideas to create a strong story or essay.

What is the key to good writing?

Good writing starts with a well-chosen topic or main idea—one that interests you and works well for your assignment. You must really care about a writing topic and know your audience.

What makes a writing topic good?

Effective writing topics provide the right amount of information for your assignments.

Sample Assignment: Recall an experience in which you learned something.

Possible Topics

- **Too Broad**   Things I've learned from Great-grandma
- **Too Narrow** Last night's e-mail message from Great-grandma
- **Just Right**   A memorable afternoon with Great-grandma

How should I write about a topic?

Good writing has a clear focus. It identifies a certain part of a topic or a feeling you have about it. Notice how the following statement brings a clear focus to the topic.

> **Focus statement:** *A memorable afternoon with Great-grandma* (topic) *taught me about her experiences in school* (a certain part).

 Practice choosing a good topic and a clear focus by following these directions: *Recall the hardest thing you have ever done. Then write a focus statement about this topic.* (Use the information on this page as a guide for your work.)

How can I use details to hold the reader's interest?

Details are what make writing worth reading. Writing that does not have enough details can be boring, like this idea: "Great-grandma told me what things were like when she was growing up." Including details such as facts, statistics, examples, and personal thoughts or feelings would make the idea more interesting. (See the following chart.)

Fact A fact is a detail that can be proved.

Great-grandma went to school in England.

Statistic A statistic is a fact that uses numbers.

In Great-grandma's day, nine out of ten boys wore shorts and knee-high socks to school.

Example An example is a detail that supports a fact.

Great-grandma said her teachers were very strict. *(fact)*

Students had to recite their lessons at the beginning of each class. If they couldn't, they had to stay after school. *(supporting example)*

Thoughts/Feelings Thoughts and feelings are the writer's own ideas and attitude about the topic.

Each morning, Great-grandma had to walk two-and-a-half miles to school. *(fact)*

It must have been a long walk, especially in bad weather. *(personal thought)*

 Choose one of your own narratives or essays or find a news story to review for details. Label any facts, statistics, examples, thoughts, or feelings that you find. (If the writing is long, label just the first few paragraphs.)

conventions ideas sentence fluency
VOICE organization word choice 37
Traits of Writing

PROCESS

Understanding Organization

Effective writing is built on a strong foundation, with a clearly developed beginning, middle, and ending. In addition, the details in a well-written essay or report follow a specific method of organization.

How can I write a strong beginning?

In the best essays, the beginning paragraph does two things. It (1) gets the reader's attention and (2) identifies the topic and focus of the paper. Here are several ways to get the reader's attention and introduce a topic.

Present interesting information about your topic.

When I perform a front wheelie on my stunt bike, people always say it looks easy.

Make a surprising statement.

I practiced the fox hop on my stunt bike hundreds of times before I got it right.

Ask a question.

Have you ever wished you could fly?

Share a brief story about the topic.

The very first time I rode a stunt bike, I hit a rut and broke my arm in two places.

Sample Beginning

The beginning paragraph below starts with a surprising statement. It then gives background information and states the topic.

I couldn't stand my front teeth! The rest of my face was fine—long brown hair, green eyes, freckled cheeks, and a dimpled chin. Unfortunately, when I smiled, all people saw were my crooked teeth. A week later, all they saw were my shiny new braces.

 Try It Share a strong beginning from something you have written or read. Explain how the beginning gets the reader's interest.

How can I organize details in the middle part?

The way the details are organized depends on the form of the writing. (Also see pages 534–537 and 550–551.)

Descriptive

Organize details by *location*.

> At the top of my closet, **you will find boxes of shoes and sweaters lining the shelf.** Below the shelf **is the clothes bar. Clothes are crammed together in this space.** On the floor, **there are piles of shoes and games that I just toss in.**

Narrative

Organize details *chronologically* (in time order).

> First **the orthodontist jammed metal bands around my molars.** Then **he glued sharp little squares of steel to all of my front teeth.** Next **he attached little wires to the squares.**

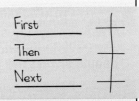

Expository

Organize details by *logical order* or *categories*.

> **What can we do to save our environment?** First of all, **we must stop littering.** In addition, **we must promote recycling.** Equally important, **we must reuse materials whenever possible.**

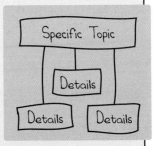

Persuasive

Organize details by *order of importance*.

> First of all, **letting students wear regular clothes saves money.** Second, **it sends the proper message.** Third, **and most importantly, it helps students become more responsible.**

Try It Complete a graphic organizer and write a short passage following one of the methods of organization above. Your writing should include at least three or four sentences.

conventions ideas sentence fluency
VOICE organization word choice 39
Traits of Writing

How can I write a strong ending?

You can write a strong ending paragraph by doing one or more of the following things.

Remind the reader about the paper's focus.

The school board may think study hall is a waste of time, but most students don't. Many of us struggle with our homework load. Without study hall, we'll be that much further behind. Ask your parents to call school board members and tell them to keep study hall.

Review the main points.

There are many things to consider before you make a dog part of your family. To choose the right dog, remember to find out the dog's age and notice its personality. Also remember that choosing to have a pet carries many responsibilities.

Emphasize the importance of one of the main points.

The East Bluff at Devil's Lake really is a great stone castle. Climbing the bluff is like attacking a fortress. With a lot of hard work, hikers reach the top. There they are treated to a view fit for a king or a queen.

Say something to keep the reader thinking about the topic.

The next time you see me landing a flip at the bike park, remember that I've carefully assembled my own bike. I know every inch of it. That gives me the confidence to try difficult stunts.

Sample Ending

The paragraph below reminds the reader about the topic and says something to keep the reader thinking.

Now when I look in the mirror, I'm glad I had braces. I use my new smile every day. Unfortunately, after the braces came off, I started to break out. Oh well! Maybe I'll look great by the time I'm 16.

 Share a strong ending from something you have written or read. Explain what types of information are included in this part.

Understanding Voice

Author Ralph Fletcher says, "Writing that has voice is writing that breathes." Voice gives writing energy and life. It is that special something that makes you say, "Hey, I like how that essay sounds."

How can I write with voice?

If you are truly interested in your topic, your writing will have voice. As writer Donald Graves says, "When a writer makes a good choice of a topic, voice booms through."

The writer isn't very interested in the topic, so this writing lacks voice.

One of my ancestors was born in Rhode Island. She was kidnapped when she was little. That's about all I know.

The writer is clearly interested, so this writing has voice.

I wonder if my great-great-grandma knew what was happening when she was kidnapped. She must have been scared. How did the kidnappers treat her? How was she able to pick up their language so fast?

How can my writing voice sound more natural?

The three tips below will help you write more naturally.

- Keep a personal journal.
- "Talk" to friends and relatives in friendly letters and e-mail messages.
- Begin writing assignments by freely recording your thoughts about your topic.

This writing sounds natural.

When we were walking, I looked up and saw the moon was out. It made the fog seem to glow. Off in the distance, I heard a dog bark and then a chorus of barks. I felt a shiver crawl up my spine. It was probably just the cold.

Write freely for 5 to 10 minutes about your day so far: *What has happened? How do you feel about what's happened?* Check your writing for voice by underlining words and phrases that sound like the real you.

conventions ideas sentence fluency
VOICE organization word choice **41**
Traits of Writing

PROCESS

Understanding Word Choice

Author Cynthia Rylant pays careful attention to word choice. "When I write," Rylant says, "I seek words; I chase after them." She knows that her writing will be only as good as the words that she uses.

What are the most important words?

When you write, every word is important—but your nouns and verbs are the most important. Study the passages below.

General Nouns **and Verbs**

> The boy cried **after the** accident.
> He went **to the** woman **in the** room.

Specific Nouns **and Verbs**

> The toddler sobbed **after he** pinched **his** finger.
> He ran **to his** mother **in the kitchen.**

Using Specific Nouns

In the chart below, the first words under each category are general nouns. The second set of words is *more* specific. The third set of words is *very* specific. These very specific nouns are the best ones to use.

Person	Place	Thing	Idea
woman	monument	food	system
writer	national monument	fruit	government
J. K. Rowling	Statue of Liberty	blueberry	democracy

Using Specific Action Verbs

Specific action verbs can make your writing more vivid. Action verbs like *glared* and *observed* say more than the overused, ordinary verb *looked*.

General verb: **Ms. Lang looked at the noisy students.**

Vivid verb: **Ms. Lang glared at the noisy students.**

 Make a chart like the one above and fill it in with your own nouns (a person, a place, a thing, and an idea). The nouns at the bottom of your chart should be very specific.

Understanding Sentence Fluency

Good writing is something that you can read without breaking a sweat. The sentences flow naturally, making the writing enjoyable from start to finish.

What does it mean to write fluent sentences?

Sentences are fluent when they flow smoothly from one to the next and follow these guidelines.

- Every sentence is important.
- A reader can easily follow the ideas.
- Short, choppy sentences have been combined to read smoothly.
- Transition words connect the ideas.

How can I improve my sentence style?

You can improve your sentence style by combining choppy sentences into longer, smoother ones. (See pages 512–514.)

Short, Choppy Sentences

Chinwe plans to go hiking. She will go hiking tomorrow.

Combining Using a Key Word

Chinwe plans to go hiking **tomorrow**.

Short, Choppy Sentences

My lazy cat takes long naps. It naps on top of the TV.

Combining Using a Prepositional Phrase

My lazy cat takes long naps **on top of the TV**.

Short, Choppy Sentences

Parnell picked up the flat stone. He examined its strange markings.

Combining Using a Compound Verb

Parnell **picked up** the flat stone and **examined** its strange markings.

What else can improve sentence style?

You can improve your sentences by using a variety of beginnings. If too many of your sentences begin in the same way, your writing will sound boring. (Also see page 522.)

Too Many Sentences Beginning in the Same Way

William looked at his science report. He picked it up and glued one more piece in place. He set it down. He thought, "Now, I am ready for the science fair."

Varied Beginnings

William looked at his science report. Then he picked it up and glued one more piece in place. After setting it down, he thought, "Now, I am ready for the science fair."

Another way to improve your style is to change the length of your sentences. If too many of your sentences have the same number of words, your writing will sound monotonous.

Too Many Sentences of the Same Length

Soccer is becoming more popular in the United States. Many schools have started soccer programs. Students are now able to play on organized teams. Soccer is a sport in which both boys and girls can play. They can easily play together on the same teams.

Varied Lengths

Soccer is becoming more popular in the United States. Since many schools have started soccer programs, more students are now able to play on organized teams. Both boys and girls can easily play together on the same teams.

 Choose one of your own narratives or essays or find a news story to review for sentence fluency. Do all of the sentences read smoothly? Do they have varied beginnings and lengths? (If the writing is long, review just the first few paragraphs.)

Understanding Conventions

Conventions are simply the rules of language. Punctuation, capitalization, grammar, and spelling all have special rules. When you follow these rules, the reader can focus on your ideas instead of being distracted by mistakes.

How can I make sure my writing follows the rules?

A conventions checklist like the one below can guide you as you edit and proofread your writing. When you are not sure about a certain rule, refer to the "Proofreader's Guide." (See pages 578–749.)

Conventions

PUNCTUATION

_____ **1.** Do I use end punctuation after all my sentences?

_____ **2.** Do I use commas correctly?

_____ **3.** Do I use apostrophes to show possession *(boy's bike)*?

CAPITALIZATION

_____ **4.** Do I start every sentence with a capital letter?

_____ **5.** Do I capitalize the proper names of people and places?

SPELLING

_____ **6.** Have I checked my spelling?

GRAMMAR

_____ **7.** Do I use correct forms of verbs *(had gone, not had went)*?

_____ **8.** Do my subjects and verbs agree in number?

_____ **9.** Do I use the right words *(to, too, two)*?

Using a Rubric

How do you become a good athlete? First, you learn the necessary skills. Then you compete as much as you can and evaluate each performance. In many ways, that's how you become a good writer, too. You learn the important skills, practice different types of writing, and evaluate each finished product.

This chapter explains a basic skill—using a rubric. **Rubrics** are charts that help you measure or evaluate your writing. This book includes rubrics for four important types of writing. Each rubric is organized according to the traits of writing.

What's Ahead

- **Understanding Rubrics**
- **Reading a Rubric**
- **Getting Started with a Rubric**
- **Revising and Editing with a Rubric**
- **Assessing with a Rubric**
- **Doing a Peer Assessment**
- **Assessing a Narrative**

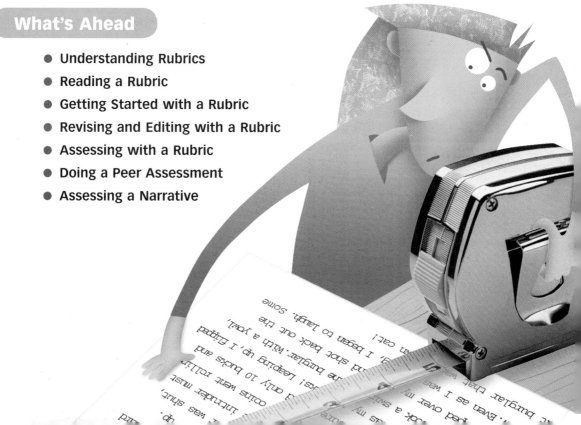

Understanding Rubrics

You already evaluate things in everyday life: "I give this song a 10!" "That movie gets four stars!" You can also evaluate writing using a rubric. The rubrics in this book evaluate writing using the following scale.

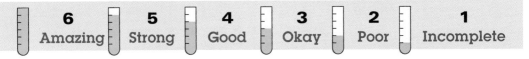

| **6** Amazing | **5** Strong | **4** Good | **3** Okay | **2** Poor | **1** Incomplete |

Your essays and stories can be evaluated for each of the main traits of writing—*ideas, organization, voice, word choice, sentence fluency,* and *conventions.* For example, in one of your essays, the ideas may be "strong" and the organization may be "good." That would give you a 5 for ideas and a 4 for organization.

Rating Guide

This guide will help you understand the rating scale.

A **6** means that the writing is truly **amazing**.
It goes way beyond the requirements for a certain trait.

A **5** means that the writing is very **strong**.
It clearly meets the main requirements for a trait.

A **4** means that the writing is **good**.
It meets most of the requirements for a trait.

A **3** means that the writing is **okay**.
It needs work to meet the main requirements for a trait.

A **2** means that the writing is **poor**.
It needs a lot of work to meet the requirements for a trait.

A **1** means that the writing is **incomplete**.
It is not yet ready to evaluate for a trait.

Reading a Rubric

For the rubrics in this book, each trait has its own color bar (green for *ideas*, pink for *organization*, and so on). There is a description for each rating to help you evaluate for a particular trait.

Rubric for Expository Writing

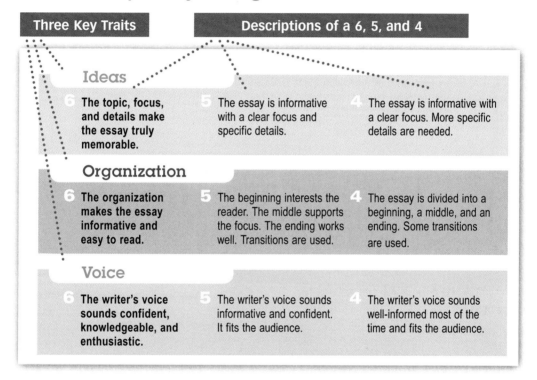

Three Key Traits	Descriptions of a 6, 5, and 4		
Ideas	**6** The topic, focus, and details make the essay truly memorable.	**5** The essay is informative with a clear focus and specific details.	**4** The essay is informative with a clear focus. More specific details are needed.
Organization	**6** The organization makes the essay informative and easy to read.	**5** The beginning interests the reader. The middle supports the focus. The ending works well. Transitions are used.	**4** The essay is divided into a beginning, a middle, and an ending. Some transitions are used.
Voice	**6** The writer's voice sounds confident, knowledgeable, and enthusiastic.	**5** The writer's voice sounds informative and confident. It fits the audience.	**4** The writer's voice sounds well-informed most of the time and fits the audience.

Guiding Your Writing

Learning how to use a rubric helps you . . .

- think like a writer—understanding your goal,
- make meaningful changes in your writing—using the traits of writing, and
- assess your final copies—rating their strengths and weaknesses.

Review the complete expository rubric. Review the rubric on pages 194–195 and list one thing that you learned from reviewing it and one question that you have about it. Share this information with your class.

Getting Started with a Rubric

At the beginning of each main writing unit, you will see a page like the one below. This page, which is arranged according to the traits of writing, explains the main requirements for developing the writing in the unit.

Understanding Your Goal

Your goal in this chapter is to write a well-organized, interesting essay that explains how to do or make something. The traits listed in the chart below will help you plan and write your how-to essay.

Traits of Expository Writing

Ideas

Select an interesting how-to topic, write a clear focus statement, and cover all the steps in the process.

Organization

Include an interesting beginning, a middle that explains all the steps, and a clear ending. Use transitions to help you organize.

Voice

Use an informative, confident voice that fits the audience.

Word Choice

Choose words such as specific nouns and specific action verbs that will make your essay informative.

Sentence Fluency

Make sure your sentences are complete and that they read smoothly.

Conventions

Check your essay for correct punctuation, capitalization, spelling, and grammar.

Get the big picture. Look at the rubric on pages 194–195. You can use this rubric to assess your progress. Your goal is to write an informative essay about how to do or make something.

PROCESS

A Closer Look at Understanding Your Goal

To use the "Understanding Your Goal" rubric at the beginning of each writing unit, follow these steps.

1 **Review the entire chart** to get the big picture about the form of writing.

2 **Focus your attention** on *ideas, organization,* and *voice* because these traits are so important at the beginning of a writing project. (See below.)

3 **Read the requirements** under each of these three traits. When you consider *ideas,* for example, try to do these things:
- Select an interesting topic.
- Write a clear focus statement.
- Include a lot of details.

4 **Make sure to talk to your teacher** if you have any questions about the requirements for the assignment.

A Special Note About the Traits

At each step in the writing process, certain traits are more important than others. Keep this point in mind as you use a rubric.

During **Prewriting** and **Writing**, focus on the *ideas, organization,* and *voice* in your writing.

During **Revising**, focus on *ideas, organization, voice, word choice,* and *sentence fluency.* (For some assignments, your teacher may ask you to concentrate most of your attention on one or two of these traits.)

During **Editing** and proofreading, focus on *conventions.*

When **Assessing** a final copy, use all six traits. (For some assignments, your teacher may ask you to assess a piece of writing for just a few of the traits.)

Write a paragraph. Review the rubric on page 48. Then write a short paragraph about an animal or a pet that you find interesting.

Revising and Editing with a Rubric

 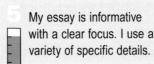

6 My topic, focus, and details make my essay truly memorable.

5 My essay is informative with a clear focus. I use a variety of specific details.

4 My essay is informative with a clear focus. I need to use a variety of specific details.

In each main writing unit, you will find a strip at the top of the pages dealing with revising and editing. Each strip covers one of the traits of writing and will help you improve your first drafts. The strip at the top of these two pages focuses on *ideas* for expository writing.

How can I use each strip to evaluate my first draft?

To use the strip, start by reading the number 5 description. Number 5 in the strip above says that your first draft should be informative, have a clear focus, and use a variety of specific details. Decide if your writing should get a 5 for ideas. If not, check the description for 6 or 4 and so on. Remember that a 5 means that the writing is *strong* for that trait.

Sometimes it's hard to know for sure if a first draft deserves a 6, 5, or another number for a trait. Just come as close as you can and revise your writing as needed.

 Review the sample paragraph below. Then rate the paragraph for ideas and explain your rating. (See pages 46–47 for help with rating a paper.)

My family has a guinea pig, and he is an interesting pet. Our pet, Gromit, is small, with red fur. Every time we bring him pellets and timothy hay, he greets us. All these things are interesting about my pet Gromit.

PROCESS

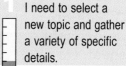

3 My focus needs to be clearer. I need more specific details.

2 I need to narrow or expand my topic, and I need many more specific details.

1 I need to select a new topic and gather a variety of specific details.

How can the strip help me revise my first draft?

After you find the proper rating on the strip for your paper, you will know what changes you should make. Here's what the writer of the paragraph on page 50 thought about ideas in her first draft.

- **Interesting topic:** I need to mention something about guinea pigs in general.
- **Clear focus:** Using Gromit to talk about all guinea pigs will work well.
- **Specific details:** I don't have enough details.

Making Changes

After deciding how to improve the ideas in her paragraph, the writer made the following changes.

Ideas	
The topic is made clearer.	*a short-earred animal that is really a type of rodent.* My family has a guinea pig, ~~and he is an~~ ^
	~~interesting pet.~~ Our pet, Gromit, is small, with red
A detail is added.	*He's a good singer, too.* fur. ^ Every time we bring him pellets and timothy hay,
	he greets us. All these things are interesting . . .

Revise **Revise your paragraph.** Review and revise the paragraph you wrote on page 49. Use the strip on these two pages as a guide.

Assessing with a Rubric

Follow the three steps below when you use a rubric—like the one on page 53—to assess a piece of writing.

1 **Create an assessment sheet.** On your own paper, list the key traits from the rubric (*ideas, organization,* and so on). Draw a line before each trait for your score and skip two or three lines between each trait for comments.

2 **Read the final copy.** Get an overall feeling for the writing to help you evaluate it.

3 **Assess the writing using the rubric.** To get started, read the descriptions for *ideas,* starting with the 5 rating. Decide which rating best fits the writing and put that number on your assessment sheet. Make comments as needed. Then go on to the other traits.

RESPONSE SHEET   Title: _____

_____ IDEAS

_____ ORGANIZATION

_____ VOICE

_____ WORD CHOICE

_____ SENTENCE FLUENCY

_____ CONVENTIONS

Evaluator: _____

 Assess your pet paragraph. Create an assessment sheet like the one above. Then evaluate your paragraph using the expository rubric on pages 194–195. Try to write something you did well and something you'd like to improve for each trait. (See the sample on page 55.)

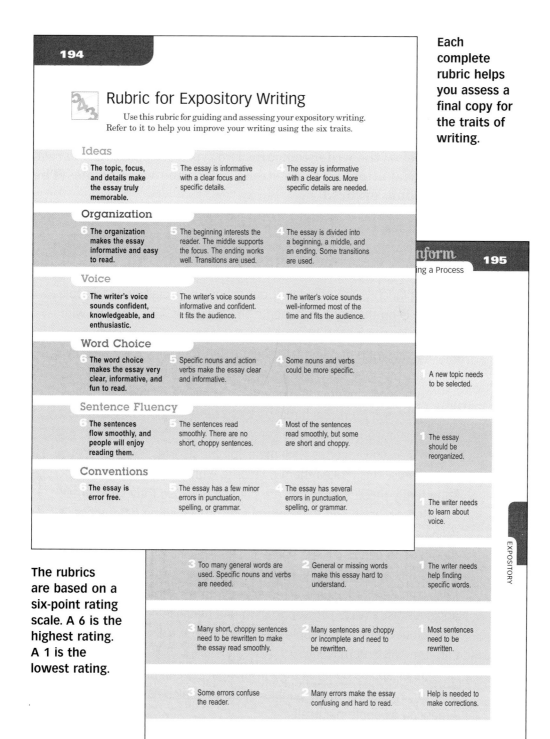

194

Rubric for Expository Writing

Use this rubric for guiding and assessing your expository writing.
Refer to it to help you improve your writing using the six traits.

Ideas

6 **The topic, focus, and details make the essay truly memorable.**

5 The essay is informative with a clear focus and specific details.

4 The essay is informative with a clear focus. More specific details are needed.

Organization

6 **The organization makes the essay informative and easy to read.**

5 The beginning interests the reader. The middle supports the focus. The ending works well. Transitions are used.

4 The essay is divided into a beginning, a middle, and an ending. Some transitions are used.

Voice

6 **The writer's voice sounds confident, knowledgeable, and enthusiastic.**

5 The writer's voice sounds informative and confident. It fits the audience.

4 The writer's voice sounds well-informed most of the time and fits the audience.

Word Choice

6 **The word choice makes the essay very clear, informative, and fun to read.**

5 Specific nouns and action verbs make the essay clear and informative.

4 Some nouns and verbs could be more specific.

Sentence Fluency

6 **The sentences flow smoothly, and people will enjoy reading them.**

5 The sentences read smoothly. There are no short, choppy sentences.

4 Most of the sentences read smoothly, but some are short and choppy.

Conventions

6 **The essay is error free.**

5 The essay has a few minor errors in punctuation, spelling, or grammar.

4 The essay has several errors in punctuation, spelling, or grammar.

---

nform **195**

ing a Process

1 A new topic needs to be selected.

1 The essay should be reorganized.

1 The writer needs to learn about voice.

3 Too many general words are used. Specific nouns and verbs are needed.

2 General or missing words make this essay hard to understand.

1 The writer needs help finding specific words.

3 Many short, choppy sentences need to be rewritten to make the essay read smoothly.

2 Many sentences are choppy or incomplete and need to be rewritten.

1 Most sentences need to be rewritten.

3 Some errors confuse the reader.

2 Many errors make the essay confusing and hard to read.

1 Help is needed to make corrections.

EXPOSITORY

Each complete rubric helps you assess a final copy for the traits of writing.

The rubrics are based on a six-point rating scale. A 6 is the highest rating. A 1 is the lowest rating.

Doing a Peer Assessment

Just as you can use a rubric to assess your own writing, you can also use a rubric to assess your classmate's writing.

Expository Essay

In the essay below, the writer compares two types of apples. As you read the essay, pay special attention to its strong points and weak points. **(The essay contains some errors.)**

Food for Thought

Bag lunches are populer at our school, especially when noodle surprise is on the hot-lunch menu. The basic bag lunch begins with a sandwich and ends with an apple. The apples in most lunch bags are Granny Smith and Red Delicious. These to apples have a lot in common, but they also have their differences.

Both apples are big in many ways. They are desplayed in all large grocery stores which makes them easy to find. They are stocked year round so people can always enjoy them. They can be eaten as snacks or as mini meals by themselves because they are so large. This makes them a favorite with everyone. And most importently these two apples are big hits because they taste great.

Granny Smith and Red Delicious also have some differences. A Granny Smith is green and has a tart taste. Because of the tartness the first bite can catch the eater by suprise. One of the things that makes this apple special is that it always seems to be crisp and fresh. The Red Delicious is a red apple with a sweet taste. This apple almost always lives up to its name because it delivers such a delicious taste. If this apple has a problem, it is its texture which can turn soft and mushey.

Other apples come and go from year to year. But it would be safe to say that for many people, these to apples have become as American as apple pie itself.

Sample Assessment

To complete the assessment of "Food for Thought," the evaluator used the rubric for expository writing on pages 194–195. Beneath each trait, he identified one strength (*1.*) and one weakness (*2.*) in the writing.

RESPONSE SHEET   Title: *"Food for Thought"*

5   IDEAS
1. The focus of the essay is clear.
2. A few of the details don't seem important (like where the apples are displayed).

5   ORGANIZATION
1. The essay has a beginning, a middle, and an ending.
2. More transitions could connect ideas.

4   VOICE
1. The writer sounds interested most of the time.
2. A personal comment or story would help.

4   WORD CHOICE
1. Most of the words are clear and easy to follow.
2. Some of the words are too general ("great," "big").

4   SENTENCE FLUENCY
1. Most of the sentences read smoothly.
2. Some sentence beginnings could be changed.

3   CONVENTIONS
1. The words are capitalized correctly.
2. There are some spelling and comma mistakes.

Evaluator: *Tim Smith*

Review the assessment. On your own paper, explain why you agree with the assessment above (or why you don't). Consider each trait carefully.

Assessing a Narrative

As you read through the personal narrative below, pay attention to the strengths and weaknesses in the writing. Then follow the directions at the bottom of the page. **(The essay contains some errors.)**

Squealer

I was so excited when I got first-chair trumpet in our middle school band. I even beat out Chuck, an eighth grader. That made him jealous, since I'd be playing all the trumpet solos.

For the spring concert, Mr. Moore handed out sheet music for "Summertime." It had a great trumpet solo, but it was really high. Chuck loaned me a "squealer" mouthpiece— extra small for playing really high notes. I learned the solo, and it worked great.

At dress rehearsal, the band played "Summertime," and I blew everyone away. Even Chuck said I rocked. I was so excited, I forgot to switch from the squealer to my regular mouthpiece for the next song, "I Love You, Porgy." It started with a real low solo. I tried to play it, but the squealer made every note blat and wobble. It was torture. Mr. Moore stared at me, pleading for just one good note, but I couldn't give it to him. Afterward, Chuck said I sounded like a bike tire losing air!

Well, I was embarrassed, but some good came of it. I asked Mr. Moore if Chuck could play the second solo. He said yes, and at the concert, we both sounded great.

Use a narrative rubric. Assess the narrative you have just read using the rubric on pages 130–131 as a guide. Before you get started, create an assessment sheet like the one on page 55 in this chapter. Remember to leave room after each trait for comments.

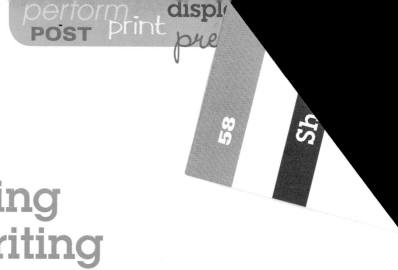

Publishing Your Writing

To publish or share your writing, you need an audience. This is true whether you are handing in a writing assignment in language arts class or sending an e-mail message to a relative. Before you share your writing with anyone else, you should be happy with it yourself.

Your writing is ready for publication when it says exactly what you want it to say and is as close to error free as you can make it. In other words, you've given it your best effort.

In this chapter, you will find information on a variety of ways to publish your work.

What's Ahead

- Sharing Your Writing
- Preparing to Publish
- Designing Your Writing
- Making Your Own Web Site
- Publishing Online

...aring Your Writing

Some publishing ideas are easy to carry out, like sharing your writing with your classmates. Others take more time and effort, like entering a writing contest. Try a number of these publishing ideas during the school year. All of them will help you grow as a writer.

Performing
- Sharing with Classmates
- Reading to Various Audiences
- Preparing a Multimedia Presentation
- Videotaping for Special Audiences
- Performing Onstage

In School
- School Newspapers
- Classroom Collections
- School Handbooks
- Writing Portfolios

Self-Publishing
- Family Newsletters
- Greeting Cards
- Bound Writings
- Online Publications

Posting
- Classroom Bulletin Boards
- School or Public Libraries
- Hallway Display Cases
- Business Windows
- Clinic Waiting Rooms

Sending It Out
- Local Newspapers
- Young Writers' Conferences
- Magazines and Contests
- Various Web Sites

Chart your publishing history. List the headings above on a piece of paper: *Performing, Posting, In School, Self-Publishing, Sending It Out.* Leave two or three lines between each heading. Under each heading, identify the publishing ideas that you have already tried. Then list and highlight those you would like to try.

Preparing to Publish

Your writing is ready to publish when it is clear, complete, and correct. Getting your writing to this point requires careful revising and editing. Follow the tips below to help you prepare your writing for publication.

Publishing Tips

- **Work with your writing.**
  Continue working until you feel good about your writing from beginning to end.

- **Ask for advice during the writing process.**
  Be sure your writing answers any questions your readers may have about your topic.

- **Revise the ideas, organization, and voice.**
  Every part of your writing should be clear and complete.

- **Check words, sentences, and conventions.**
  In addition, ask at least one classmate to check your work for these traits.

- **Prepare a neat finished piece.**
  Use a pen (blue or black ink) and one side of the paper if you are writing by hand. If you are writing with a computer, use a font that is easy to read. Double-space your writing.

- **Know your options.**
  Explore the many different ways to publish your writing.

- **Follow all publication guidelines.**
  Just as your teacher wants assignments presented in a certain way, so do the newspapers, magazines, or Web sites that review the writing you submit.

[
Save all drafts for each writing project. This will help you keep track of the changes you have made. If you are preparing a portfolio, you may be required to include early drafts as well as finished pieces.
]

Designing Your Writing

Whenever you write, always focus on content *first*. Then think about how you want your paper to look. You can follow the guidelines below.

Typography

- Use an easy-to-read font for both the body and headings.
- Use an appropriate title and headings. A title sets the tone for your writing, and headings break the writing into smaller pieces.

Spacing and Margins

- Double-space your writing and leave one-inch margins on all four sides of your paper.
- Indent the first line of every paragraph.
- Use one space after every period.
- Avoid awkward breaks between pages. For example, don't leave a heading or the first line of a paragraph at the bottom of a page.

Graphic Devices

- Create bulleted or numbered lists.
- Include a table, a chart, or an illustration if it can help make a point clearer. (See pages 574–575 for examples.)
- Keep each graphic small enough so that it doesn't dominate the page. A larger graphic can be put by itself on a separate page.

Share effective design. Find an article in a magazine, newspaper, or book that is well designed. Share the article with the class and identify the design features.

Computer Design in Action

The following two pages show a well-designed student essay. The side notes explain all of the design features.

The title is 18-point and boldfaced.

The main text is 12-point type.

Headings are 14-point.

Margins are at least one inch all around.

Will Lee

Wake Up the Wild Side!

"In each of you, there is a wild creature screaming to get out," Ms. Hillary tells the drama club at the start of each meeting. "It's the part of you that can be a star on this stage." Then she begins our warm-ups, which really get our bodies and minds in gear. They also help the group start working together. Some warm-ups are for individuals, and some are for partners. Ms. Hillary uses both types at every meeting.

Individual Warm-Ups

Every meeting begins with warm-ups to help individuals find their "centers." One is "Shake It Out," and the other is "Greet the Sun."

- **Shake It Out:** In this warm-up, people stand on tiptoes with their hands stretched over their heads and shake out all the tension from their bodies. Everyone ends up completely loose and relaxed.
- **Greet the Sun:** Then everyone lies on the floor and rises like a plant, growing toward the sun. Everyone ends up with faces lifted and hands out like leaves.

Lee 2

Partner Warm-Ups

After "Shake It Out" and "Greet the Sun,"
everyone gets a partner. Ms. Hillary then leads one
of the following warm-ups:

A bulleted
list helps
organize
the essay.

- **Setting:** She shouts out a setting—optometrist's
  office, Niagara Falls, detention room, whatever—
  and the pairs must act out a scene in that
  location.
- **Character:** She names two characters—a pizza
  cook and a superhero, a dog and a salesperson, a
  genius and a child—and each partner must play
  one role and create a scene between the
  characters.
- **Conflict:** She calls out a conflict—an argument
  over a goat, a staring contest, two couch potatoes
  with two TV remotes—and partners have to act
  out a scene that shows that conflict.

Ready to Act

Once the individual and partner warm-ups are
completed, the whole group is ready to act together.
With everyone's wild side fully awake, it's time to hit
the stage.

Design a page. Using the guidelines on page 60, create an effective design for an essay you've already written. Share your design with a classmate to get some feedback: Does your design help make your writing clear and easy to follow? Will any of it distract the reader?

Making Your Own Web Site

You can make your own Web site if your family has an Internet account. Ask your provider how to get started. If you are using a school account, ask your teacher for help. Then start designing your site. Use the questions and answers below as a starting point.

How do I plan my site?

Think about how many pages you want on your Web site. Should you put everything on one page, or would you like to have several pages? Check out other sites for ideas. Then plan your pages by sketching them out.

How do I make the pages?

Start each page as a text file using your computer. Many new word-processing programs let you save a file as a Web page. If yours doesn't, you will have to use Web page editing software or add HTML (Hypertext Markup Language) codes to format the text and make links to graphics and other pages. You can find instructions about HTML on the Net or at the library.

How do I know whether my pages work?

You should always test your pages. Using your browser, open your first page. Then follow the links to make sure they work correctly and that all the pages look right.

How do I get my pages on the Net?

You must upload your finished pages to the Internet. (Ask your Internet provider how to do this.) After the upload, visit your site to make sure it still works. Also check it on other computers if possible.

How do I let people know about my site?

Once your site is up, e-mail your friends and tell them to visit it!

 Keep a journal of Web pages that impress you. Answer these questions about each one: What is especially good about this page? What could be better? When designing your own pages, check your journal for ideas to use.

Publishing Online

The Internet offers many publishing opportunities, including online magazines and writing contests. The information below will help you submit your writing on the Net. (Always get a parent's approval first.)

How should I get started?

Check with your teacher to see if your school has its own Internet site where you can post your work. Also ask your teacher about other Web sites. There are a number of online magazines that accept student writing.

How do I search for possible sites?

Use a search engine to find places to publish. Some search engines also offer their own student links.

How do I submit my work?

Before you do anything, make sure that you understand the publishing guidelines for each site. Be sure to share this information with your teacher and your parents. Then follow these steps:

- **Send your writing in the correct form.**
  Some sites have online forms. Others will ask you to send it by mail or e-mail. Always explain why you are sending your writing.
- **Give the publisher information for contacting you.**
  However, don't give your home address or other personal information unless your parents approve.
- **Be patient.**
  A site should contact you within a week, but it may be several weeks before you hear whether your writing will be used or not.

Does Write Source have a Web site?

Yes. You can visit our Web site at www.thewritesource.com. The "Publish It" link lists Web sites that accept student submissions.

 Visit the Write Source Web site. Use the "Publish It" link. Find out what forms of writing the Write Source would like to see you submit. (Check for your grade level.) Also visit at least two of the other publishing sites that are listed. Find out their requirements for submitting work.

Creating a Portfolio

How can you judge your progress as a writer? One of the best ways is to put together a writing portfolio. A portfolio is a collection of your best writing completed during a semester or a grading period. With a portfolio, you can compare different pieces of writing to see how you have improved over time.

Think of a portfolio as a form of publishing your writing. Instead of sharing just one piece, a portfolio lets you share an entire "writing album." A portfolio presents a clear picture of you as a writer. It says, "This is who I am; this is what I can do."

What's Ahead

- Types of Portfolios
- Parts of a Portfolio
- Planning Ideas
- Sample Portfolio Reflections

Types of Portfolios

There are four types of portfolios you should know about: a showcase portfolio, a growth portfolio, a personal portfolio, and an electronic portfolio.

Showcase Portfolio

A showcase portfolio presents the best writing you have done in school. A showcase is the most common type of portfolio and is usually put together for evaluation at the end of a grading period.

Growth Portfolio

A growth portfolio shows your progress as a writer. It contains writing assignments that show how your writing skills are developing:

- writing beginnings and endings,
- writing with voice, and
- using specific details.

Personal Portfolio

In a personal portfolio, you save writing that you want to keep and share with others. Many professional people—including writers, artists, and musicians—keep personal portfolios. You can arrange this type of portfolio according to different types of writing, different themes, and so on.

Electronic Portfolio

An electronic portfolio is any type of portfolio (showcase, growth, or personal) available on a CD or a Web site. Besides your writing, you can include graphics, video, and sound with this type of portfolio. Now your writing can be available to friends and family members no matter where they are!

Select your best writing. Let's say you were going to create a showcase portfolio for your last two or three years in school. On your own paper, list four pieces of writing that you would include in this portfolio. Explain your choices.

Parts of a Portfolio

A showcase portfolio is one of the most common types of portfolios used in schools. It may contain the parts listed below, but always check with your teacher to be sure.

- A **table of contents** lists the writing samples you have included in your portfolio.
- A **brief essay** or **letter** introduces your portfolio—telling how you put it together, how you feel about it, and what it means to you.
- A **collection of writing samples** presents your best work. Your teacher may require that you include all of your planning, drafting, and revising for one or more of your writings.
- A **cover sheet for each sample** explains why you selected it.
- **Evaluations, reflections,** or **checklists** identify the basic skills you have mastered and those skills that you still need to work on.

Gathering Tips

- **Keep track of all your work,** including prewriting notes, first drafts, and revisions for each writing assignment. Then, when you put together a portfolio, you will have everything that you need.
- **Store all of your writing in a pocket folder.** This will help you avoid dog-eared or ripped pages.
- **Set a schedule for working on your portfolio.** You can't put together a good portfolio by waiting until the last minute.
- **Take pride in your work.** Make sure your portfolio shows you at your best.

 Reflect on your writing progress. Imagine that your teacher wants you to put together a portfolio, including a paragraph about your writing progress. Write such a paragraph, identifying your strengths and weaknesses as a writer. Also tell what types of writing you like to do best, what your favorite piece of writing is, and so on.

Planning Ideas

The following tips will help you choose your best pieces of writing to include in your portfolio.

1 Be patient.

Don't make quick decisions about which pieces of writing to include in your portfolio. Just keep gathering everything—including all your drafts—until you are ready to review all of your writing assignments.

2 Make good decisions.

When it's time to choose writing for your portfolio, review each piece. Remember the feelings you had during each assignment. Which one makes you feel the best? Which one did your readers like the best? Which one taught you the most?

3 Reflect on your choices.

Read the sample reflections on page 69. Then answer these questions about your writing:

- Why did I choose this piece?
- Why did I write this piece? (What was my purpose?)
- How did I write it? (What was my process?)
- What does it show about my writing abilities?
- What would I do differently next time?
- What have I learned that will make me a better writer?

4 Set future writing goals.

After putting together your portfolio, set some goals for the future. Here are some of the goals that other students have set:

I will write about topics that really interest me.

I will spend more time on my beginnings and endings.

I will make sure that my sentences read smoothly.

Plan a portfolio cover. On a piece of plain paper, design a creative cover for a portfolio folder. Include your name and an interesting title. Add sketches or photos related to your writing, your classes, your favorite pastime, and so on.

Sample Portfolio Reflections

When you take time to reflect on your writing assignments, think about the process that you used to develop each one. Also think about what you might do differently next time. The following samples will help you with your own reflections.

Student Reflections

The story about my ancestor in New York is my most interesting piece of writing, ever. I couldn't believe how much I learned about this person. All of my research was actually fun. Ms. Peña always tells us to write about topics that really interest us. Now I know just what she means.

—DeAndra Barker

One of our first assignments this year was to write about a life-changing experience. My narrative about playing in a basketball tournament turned out to be the best thing that I wrote all year. Instead of telling everything about the tournament, I focused on one important part. I wrote about my friend becoming ill and how his illness changed me. I like just about everything about this story, except that it could use more dialogue.

—Todd Ryan

Professional Reflections

I wrote *Mad Merlin* by combining legends of Camelot with histories and myths. As I look back at the novel, though, I see it is mostly about my own life. Good fiction is that way—creative in the details but otherwise full of truth.

—J. Robert King

With each book I write, I become more and more convinced that the books have a life of their own, quite apart from me.

—Madeleine L'Engle

SPECIFY

picture

Descriptive Writing

express

describe

portray

Descriptive Writing

Descriptive Paragraph

What animal has two points on the top of its head, big bright eyes, sharp claws, and an appetite for rodents? You might have said, "A cat, of course!" but what about an owl—or even the double-crested dinosaur called a Dilophosaurus? All three of these animals could easily fit the description.

When you write a description, you want to make sure your reader knows exactly what you are talking about. In this chapter, you will write a paragraph describing an interesting animal. Your goal is to tell about the creature's shape, size, and color, as well as the sounds it makes and the way it moves. With words alone, you can capture a wild animal!

Writing Guidelines

Subject: An animal you have seen

Form: Descriptive paragraph

Purpose: To describe an animal

Audience: Classmates

Descriptive Paragraph

A **descriptive paragraph** gives a detailed picture of a person, a place, a thing, or an event. It begins with a **topic sentence** that tells what the paragraph is about. The sentences in the **body** give all of the descriptive details about the topic. The **closing sentence** wraps up the paragraph. The paragraph below uses colorful details to describe a special bird of prey.

Night Visitor

Topic Sentence

In the glowing sunset, the great horned owl sat straight and still on top of the fence post. With pointed ears and a thick, long body, its shadow looked like a cat. The owl's head swiveled slowly from side to side like a security camera. Its ears listened for the softest sound. Its round, lemon-colored eyes looked for even the slightest movement. The owl's deep, sad voice haunted the darkness with *who-who-whooooooo.* Then the owl was ready to move on. It spread its wide, powerful wings, lifted from its perch, and glided away into the darkness.

Body

Closing Sentence

Respond to the reading. On your own paper, answer the following questions.

☐ Ideas (1) How is the topic introduced?

☐ Organization (2) What method of organization (time order, order of location, order of importance) did the writer use? Explain.

☐ Voice & Word Choice (3) What words or ideas make the animal seem real to the reader?

express describe portray
picture

Prewriting **Selecting a Topic**

To get started, you need to choose an animal that you've seen either in real life or in pictures. The animal should interest you. The writer of the paragraph on page 72 made the following list of possible topics using sentence starters.

List

> ### Animals I Have Seen
>
> *The most beautiful animal is . . . a toucan.*
>
> *The most mysterious is . . . a great horned owl.*
>
> *The ugliest animal is . . . an armadillo.*
>
> *The smallest animal is . . . a mouse.*
>
> *The scariest animal is . . . a black bear.*
>
> *The funniest animal is . . . a flying squirrel.*

Select a topic. Create your own list of animals by completing the sentence starters above. Then choose one that really interests you to describe in a paragraph.

Gathering Details—Show, Don't Tell

In a descriptive paragraph, the goal is to *show* readers something instead of *telling* them about it. Details that show are specific and colorful.

Collect your details. Answer the following questions to help you gather specific details about your animal.

- What does your animal's head look like?
- What does its body look like?
- What color and texture are its fur, feathers, or skin?
- What does it sound like?
- Where do you usually find it?
- What unusual or interesting things does it do?
- What can you compare this animal to?

DESCRIPTIVE

Writing Creating Your First Draft

The goal of a first draft is to get all of your ideas and details down on paper. Follow the guidelines below.

- Start with a topic sentence that catches your reader's interest.
- Arrange the descriptive sentences in the body according to location. Include the details that you gathered on page 73.
- End with a sentence that keeps the reader thinking about the topic.

 Write your first draft. Get your best ideas and details down on paper. Describe the animal from top to bottom or from left to right. Then give your paragraph a title.

Revising Improving Your Paragraph

When you revise, consider how well you've used ideas, organization, voice, word choice, and sentence fluency in your first draft.

 Review your paragraph. Use the following questions as a guide when you revise your paragraph.

1. Is my topic sentence clear?
2. Have I organized the details in my paragraph using order of location?
3. Do I sound interested in the topic?
4. Do I use specific nouns, verbs, and adjectives?
5. Do I use complete sentences that read smoothly?

Editing Checking for Conventions

Carefully edit your revised paragraph for punctuation, capitalization, spelling, and grammar. Then write a neat final copy.

 Edit and proofread your work. Use the following questions to check your paragraph for errors. Then write a neat final copy.

1. Do I use correct punctuation, capitalization, and spelling?
2. Do I use correct words *(to, two, too)* and grammar?

Descriptive Writing

Describing an Event

"This is Maylie Wilson reporting for the Safari Channel. I'm standing above a big old bullfrog in its natural habitat. Notice the tremendous strength of those hind legs. How about those bulging eyes? I think this bullfrog is ready to defend its territory against anyone, and I'm going to move out of range now!"

Describing an event is sort of like filming a documentary. Your job is to capture the moment so people anywhere in the world can experience it for themselves. In this chapter, you will write about an event—an animal in action—and take your readers on an animal safari!

Writing Guidelines

Subject: An event
Form: Descriptive essay
Purpose: To clearly describe an animal in action
Audience: Classmates

Descriptive Essay

In this sample essay, the writer describes a very natural event—two bullfrogs fighting. As you read the description, review the notes in the left margin. They explain the important parts of the writing.

The Face-Off

Beginning

The beginning puts the reader right into the middle of the action.

"Rom-rom-rom!" The booming song echoed across the murky river. I hurried to find its source. My toes squished through the sticky riverbank mud as I followed the song. I stopped. There it was, an olive green bullfrog at the edge of the river.

The bullfrog was a stone, sitting completely still. It had fixed its bulging eyes on a pile of branches in the water. "Hick!" it shrieked. From the middle of the branches came another "Hick," as the answering bullfrog disappeared into the dirty water.

Middle

The middle uses action verbs and vivid details to describe the bullfrogs in battle.

In a single motion, the first bullfrog used its long, powerful legs to leap into the river. It surfaced a few feet from the other bullfrog. For a split second, the two glared at each other. Then, in a flash, one leapfrogged the other with a huge splash.

All of a sudden, sounds of fighting filled the air. One frog chased the other until it was pushed against twigs and stones at the river's edge. It

DESCRIPTIVE

gripped the first bullfrog with its thumbs. If these bullfrogs were wolves, I'm sure I would have heard them snarling and growling at each other.

After wrestling near the surface, the frogs disappeared underwater. When they reappeared, they looked like a four-legged, two-headed monster. Then one frog pinned the other underwater. When the victim broke free, it escaped into the river. The other frog floated lazily in the now-calm water.

Ending
• • • • • • • • • • • •
The ending shares the writer's feelings about what he has seen.

I hadn't moved an inch during this amazing battle. I was still standing on the sticky riverbank. I never would have thought that funny-looking creatures like bullfrogs were really more like gladiators in disguise.

Respond to the reading. Answer the following questions about the essay.

☐ Ideas **(1) How is the topic introduced? (2) What two or three details do you especially like?**

☐ Organization **(3) How is the essay organized—by time, by location, or by both time and location?**

☐ Voice & Word Choice **(4) What words show that the writer is interested in the subject?**

Prewriting **Selecting a Topic**

The general topic for your essay is an animal. However, your specific assignment is to write about an animal in action. To get started, you need to think about different animals and what they do. A chart like the one below is a good way to brainstorm for ideas.

Topic Chart

Animal	Action
tiger	stalks prey
salmon	swims upstream to spawn
penguin	waddles clumsily onshore
blue jay	watches over a bird feeder
hunting dog	retrieves a duck
house cat	curls up to sleep

Create a topic chart. In the first column, list different animals that you would like to write about. In the second column, list an action or event related to each animal. When you complete your chart, select one animal for your essay. Pick one whose actions you can describe effectively.

Gathering Details

One way to gather details about a topic is to analyze it. (*Analyze* means to "think carefully about something.") Analyzing helps you consider a topic in several different ways.

Gather details. Answer the following questions to analyze your topic.

1 What does the animal look like? (Describe it from top to bottom or from front to back.)

2 What do I see, hear, smell, or feel when I see or think about this animal in action?

3 What is the animal similar to and different from?

4 What are its strengths and weaknesses?

Organizing Your Details

When writing about an animal in action, you may use two different methods of organization in your essay—time order and order of location.

▪ **Time order** *(first, second, third)*: You will use this method of organization to describe an event. For example, the writer of the essay on pages 76–77 uses time order. (See the list below.)

▪ **Order of location** *(top to bottom, front to back)*: You may also use this method if part of your essay describes the animal in detail.

List

1. *Follow the sound of a bullfrog*
2. *Discover the first bullfrog*
3. *Second bullfrog appears*
4. *Fight starts*
5. *Frogs disappear underwater*
6. *One escapes, fight ends*

Organize your details. Imagine you are a filmmaker creating a movie that shows an animal in action. List in order the scenes or details you want to share with your audience.

Using Figures of Speech

You can use figures of speech to make your descriptive writing clearer and more creative. Two common figures of speech are similes and metaphors. They both create special word pictures.

● A **simile** compares two different things using *like* or *as*.
   The owl swiveled its head from side to side like a security camera.

● A **metaphor** compares two different things without using *like* or *as*.
   The bullfrog was a stone, sitting completely still.

Write a simile and metaphor about your animal in action. If you like how either one turns out, include it in your essay.

Writing **Starting Your Descriptive Essay**

The beginning paragraph should introduce the event—your animal in action—in an exciting way. Here are two approaches.

Beginning Paragraph

■ **Put yourself in the description.** Tell where you were, what you were doing, or how you felt.

> **The writer makes a personal connection.**
>
> *When I was in preschool, we visited the zoo on Sunday afternoons. An enormous, mean peacock always roamed around near the main entrance. I imagined that it was a multicolored, screaming monster waiting to attack. It terrified me.*

■ **Observe the scene.** Focus your description on the animal, and not on your personal connection with it.

> **The writer focuses on the animal.**
>
> *The peacock at the local zoo was enormous and mean. It always roamed around near the main entrance. To some of the younger kids, it wasn't just a bird, it was a multicolored, screaming monster.*

Using an Engaging Voice

Voice is the special way that a writer expresses his or her ideas. A writer's voice shows that he or she really cares about the subject and the audience. Keep the following tips about your voice in mind as you write.

● Use a natural, sincere voice.
● Write as if you were sharing the description in a conversation.
● Show enthusiasm throughout your essay.

Write your beginning paragraph. Choose one of the approaches above to get started. If you don't like how your first attempt turns out, try another one.

DESCRIPTIVE

Developing the Middle Part

In the middle paragraphs of your essay, you should describe your animal in action. Your goal is to show the reader what happened in a clear and creative way. Use your organizing list from page 79 as a guide.

Middle Paragraphs

Here are two sample middle paragraphs. Each paragraph focuses on one specific scene or action. (The writer puts himself in the description.)

The paragraph describes one scene.

The paragraph describes a second scene that focuses on the two peacocks.

> One day without warning, the peacock jumped onto the sidewalk in front of me. It skipped from side to side almost as if it were trying to block my path. Then it spread its huge blue, green, and gold tail feathers. Suddenly, that bird was twice as big as I was! The peacock stretched its long neck and let out a high-pitched scream. I screamed right back and ran to my dad.
>
> Another time when our class visited the zoo, I saw the peacock attack another peacock. It put its head down and ran as fast as it could toward the other peacock. Its long tail was dragging across the grass. The second peacock did not know it was going to be attacked. It had a strange look on its face and jumped a foot or two off the ground. Then they both stretched their necks and danced around each other making screeching noises. Looking at those two screaming beasts made me want to get back on the bus.

Write your middle paragraphs. Create a clear, interesting, well-organized picture for your reader. Try to focus on one main scene in each paragraph.

Ending Your Essay

Your ending paragraph should wrap things up and say something to keep the reader thinking about your animal.

Ending Paragraph

> **The writer makes a final personal connection.**
>
> *Most people think that peacocks are beautiful, gentle birds. Not me. I think they are scary. Each feather on a peacock's tail has a design that looks like a weird, spooky eye. And all those eyes always seem to be watching me. That's why I avoid peacocks whenever I can.*

Write your ending paragraph. When you write your ending, make a final comment about the animal or event to help the reader remember it.

Revising and Editing

A first draft can always be improved. You may need to make an idea clearer or a detail more colorful. Consider these questions when you revise.

- ☐ **Ideas** Do I include enough descriptive details about the animal and its actions?
- ☐ **Organization** Do I use time order to organize the details?
- ☐ **Voice** Do I sound interested in my topic? Do I put myself in the essay as the narrator, or do I observe and report the action?
- ☐ **Word Choice** Do I use descriptive words and figures of speech? Do I use specific nouns and strong action verbs?
- ☐ **Sentence Fluency** Do my sentences flow smoothly when I read them out loud? Do I vary my sentence beginnings?

Revise your first draft. Revise your essay, using the questions above as a guide.

Edit your description. Use the checklist on page 128 when you edit. The checklist will help you look at punctuation, capitalization, spelling, and grammar. Then write and proofread your final copy.

Descriptive Writing
Across the Curriculum

Descriptive writing is often assigned in other classes. For example, in social studies, you may be asked to describe life in a different time. In math, you may be asked to describe a geometric shape. In science class, you may be asked to describe a common—or not so common—natural event.

To write strong descriptions, you need to know lots about your topic: what it looks like, how it works, where it occurs, what makes it special, and so on. If your description is a success, a reader will be able to picture the topic in his or her mind.

What's Ahead

- **Social Studies**: Describing a Scene in a Different Time
- **Math**: Describing Geometric Terms
- **Science**: Describing a Natural Event
- **Practical Writing**: Creating a Thank-You Note

Social Studies:
Describing a Scene in a Different Time

Descriptive writing is one way to share information about a different time and place. The student writer of the following essay puts herself back in time to bring to life a Colorado town during the gold rush.

Gold Rush Days

The **beginning** sets the scene.

It's 1891. The town of Cripple Creek, Colorado, has appeared almost overnight since gold was discovered nearby. Hundreds of people arrive by crowded trains and by dusty stagecoaches. Others also come on foot or by horseback to make their fortunes.

The **middle** describes the topic from a distance as well as up close.

Towering snowcapped mountains surround the town. Pikes Peak, one of the highest points in the Rocky Mountains, can be seen to the east. A muddy stagecoach trail follows the shoulders of the big peak and winds down toward the wild new town. The land all around Cripple Creek is full of tree stumps. The wood from these trees was used to build houses and mining tunnels. Hills above the town are dotted with piles of dirt from all the new mines.

Hotels, cafes, churches, and saloons line the dirt streets of Cripple Creek. People hurry along wood-plank sidewalks. Because of the gold, there's a lot of money here, but prices are very high. The people who sell the tools, food, and supplies that miners need are trying to get rich just like the miners.

The **ending** offers a final thought.

Cripple Creek is growing by leaps and bounds, but its future depends on the miners. If they strike it rich, who knows how big the town will get!

Writing Tips

Before you write . . .

- **Choose a different time and place that interests you.**
  Select a topic related to the subjects you are studying.
- **Do your research.**
  Learn as much as you can about your topic. Make sure to study any pictures that you can find.
- **Take notes.**
  Write down important details that will help you with your description.

Cluster

Details   Details

Famous Place

Details   Details

During your writing . . .

- **Write a clear beginning, middle, and ending.**
  In the beginning, set the scene. In the middle part, describe the place. End with a final thought about it.
- **Organize your thoughts.**
  When you describe a place, you may describe it from top to bottom, from left to right, or from far to near.
- **Use an engaging voice.**
  Your voice should sound as though you know a lot about your topic and are really interested in it.

After you've written a first draft . . .

- **Check for completeness.**
  Make sure that you have included enough information so that the reader can see your topic in his or her mind.
- **Check for correctness.**
  Proofread your essay to make sure there are no mistakes in punctuation, capitalization, spelling, or grammar.

DESCRIPTIVE

 Choose a time and place that interests you. Then write a creative and complete description about it to share with your classmates.

Math: Describing Geometric Terms

Descriptive writing can be used to write about geometric terms. In each paragraph below, notice how the student describes a geometric term.

The writer uses math words a reader should understand.

A Straight Angle

A straight line is just a line until a person learns more about it in a math class. A line is really a set of points lined up in a straight row. It goes on forever, but as soon as two end points are put on it, a line segment is formed. A line segment measured with a protractor measures 180 degrees. A line segment is also called a straight angle. There's more to a straight line than a person might think.

180°

Line Segment/Straight Angle

An illustration helps describe the term.

A Right Angle

It takes three things to form a right angle. It starts with two rays. A ray begins at a point and goes on forever in a straight line. Second, each of the rays must share one endpoint, or vertex. Third, the angle between the two rays must measure 90 degrees. It's as simple as that!

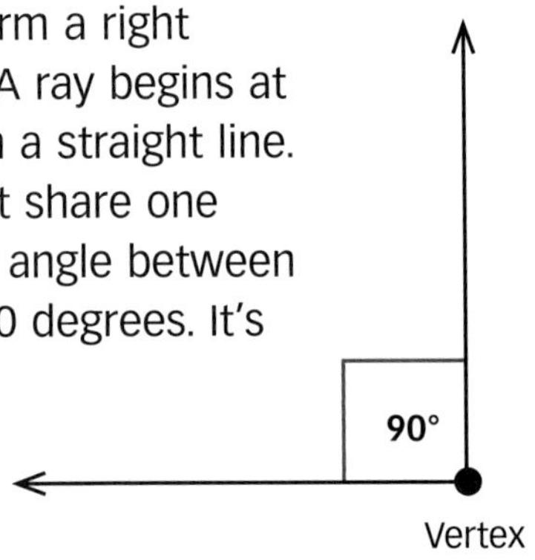

90°

Vertex

Writing Tips

Before you write . . .

- **Review the geometric term** you plan to describe.
- **Be sure you understand all of the vocabulary** that is needed to describe the term.
- **Make a plan,** starting with the simplest part of your description.
- **Jot down details** that will help you write a clear and interesting description.

Time line

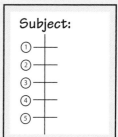

Subject:
① ━
② ━
③ ━
④ ━
⑤ ━

During your writing . . .

- **Study your basic plan.**
- **Describe everything very carefully** and be sure each sentence is clear.
- **Use math words your reader will understand** and explain any words that may be confusing.
- **Add details** in a logical order.
- **Include an illustration** if it helps describe the term.

After you've written a first draft . . .

- **Check for completeness.**
  Be sure that you used the correct vocabulary to describe your term.
- **Check for order.**
  Read through your description to make sure it is organized in a logical way.
- **Check for correctness.**
  Are the words spelled correctly? Are the sentences capitalized and punctuated correctly?

DESCRIPTIVE

Write your own description of a geometric term—possibly one of the polygons or triangles. Use the tips listed above. Share your description with your classmates.

Science: Describing a Natural Event

The world is filled with fascinating subjects to describe. Plants, landforms, animals, and weather all offer many excellent topics. In the following essay, a student describes what it is like to experience the arrival of fog.

Fog

The **beginning** gets the reader's attention.

Yesterday morning, I was standing by myself on the side of the road waiting for the school bus. A strange mist silently crept toward me just as daylight broke in our valley.

The **middle** describes the topic using specific details.

I first noticed the mist swallowing the mountains on the horizon. After that, it covered the woods behind our house. I saw the tall, white steeple vanish on the North Park Freedom Church, and then the church itself disappeared into the white vapor. My heart started beating faster as the thick, soupy cloud gulped my house and all the houses around it. It continued to float toward me! Then the sidewalk across the street slowly disappeared. Inch by inch, the street in front of me seemed to evaporate. All at once, I was inside a huge, wet cloud. Within seconds, I heard the roar of an engine and the high-pitched squeal of brakes. The school bus had come to my rescue.

The **ending** offers a final thought.

My imagination got the best of me that morning. Maybe I was still a little sleepy, or maybe the quiet affected me. Whatever the reason, I had almost forgotten that fog is really just warm, moist air traveling over the cold surface of the earth.

Writing Tips

Before you write . . .

- **Choose a topic that interests you.**
  If possible, select a natural event that you have seen or experienced yourself.
- **Research your topic.**
  Think about your experience with the topic and read about it. Take notes during your research.

During your writing . . .

- **Write a clear beginning, middle, and ending.**
  Grab your reader's interest in the beginning part. In the middle, describe your topic in the most interesting way you can. Close with a final thought about it.
- **Organize your thoughts.**
  Think about the organization of your description. The one on page 88 is organized from far away to very close. If there is a lot of action, you should probably organize your description according to time.
- **Use specific words.**
  A strong description contains specific nouns, vivid verbs, and modifiers (adjectives and adverbs).

After you've written a first draft . . .

- **Check for completeness.**
  Make sure that you have included all the details that the reader needs to understand your description.
- **Check for correctness.**
  Proofread your description for punctuation, capitalization, spelling, and grammar.

 Select a natural event to describe. Gather plenty of details about your topic. Then describe it in an essay using the tips above.

Practical Writing:
Creating a Thank-You Note

Descriptive writing appears in almost any form. Descriptions add life to letters, e-mail messages, notes, and greeting cards. The writer of this thank-you note describes a snowboard to his aunt.

❖ ❖ ❖ ❖ ❖ ❖ *Thank You* ❖ ❖ ❖ ❖ ❖ ❖

Dear Aunt Gloria,

The **beginning** identifies the reason for the note.

Thanks for the gift certificate you sent me for my birthday. I used it to buy what every kid here in Duluth wants, a freestyle snowboard!

The **middle** describes the topic.

The board I bought is called the Atomic Storm. If you stood it up next to me, you would see that it is almost as tall as I am. It is about 10 inches wide, which makes it a lot wider than an old-fashioned ski. The front is called the nose, and it is rounded, like the end of a paper clip. The design on it is awesome. Bright orange rows of flames spill all the way down the shiny black center. When you get to the back, or the tail, of the board, you find out that the fire is coming from a slick red race car. The tail of the board is rounded, just like the nose.

The **ending** gives some final thoughts.

I love my new board. It's perfect for getting big air at the snowboard park and doing spins and tricks like a pro. I'll send you some pictures of me using it.

Love,

Ty

Writing Tips

Before you write . . .

- **Select a topic.**
  Choose a topic for your thank-you note: a special gift that you received from a family member or friend.
- **List main ideas you want to include.**
  Since you are thanking someone for a gift, consider what it looks like, why you like it, and how you are using it.
- **Gather specific details.**
  List details to describe the gift.
- **Consider your feelings.**
  Ask yourself how you feel about the gift.

During your writing . . .

- **Organize your thoughts.**
  State the reason for the note in the beginning. Give the descriptive details in the middle part. Offer a final thought in the ending part.
- **Use colorful words.**
  Use specific nouns, strong action verbs, and colorful adjectives to describe the gift.

After you've written a first draft . . .

- **Check for completeness.**
  Keep your paragraphs fairly short. Are there enough details to make your description clear and fun to read? Do your sentences flow smoothly?
- **Check for correctness.**
  Proofread your note to make sure there are no mistakes in punctuation, capitalization, spelling, or grammar.

 Create a thank-you note for a family member or friend. Describe a special gift in your note. Use the tips above and the sample note on page 90.

tell
relate

Narrative Writing

narrate
remember
share

Narrative Writing

Narrative Paragraph

The next time you're with a friend, pay attention to what you say to each other. Maybe you talk about what happened on your walk to school, about a movie you saw last night, about the time Grandpa won the karate championship. . . . You and your friends tell all kinds of stories!

You can capture your storytelling talents on paper by writing a narrative. The following pages will help you write a narrative paragraph about a pleasant surprise.

Writing Guidelines

Subject:	A pleasant surprise that you experienced
Form:	Narrative paragraph
Purpose:	To entertain
Audience:	Classmates

Narrative Paragraph

Some of the most entertaining stories contain surprises. Perhaps your hamster escaped from his cage, but at school you opened up your backpack and discovered him chewing on your math assignment. Maybe you spiked your hair, thinking it was "Crazy Hair Day," when it was actually "Picture Day." These kinds of surprises make entertaining narrative paragraphs. The following narrative paragraph tells about a nighttime surprise.

Topic Sentence

Body

Closing Sentence

Things That Go Bump

One night last week, I was surprised by a thing that went "bump!" I was just drifting off to sleep when I heard a footstep in my dark bedroom. I gasped and sat up. Somebody was in the room with me. My door was shut, but the window was open. That's how the intruder must have gotten in. Something crashed, and coins went rolling all over the floor. My bank! Sure, I had only 10 bucks and some change, but it was my 10 bucks! Leaping up, I flipped on the light and took a swing at the burglar. With a yowl, Whiskers jumped over my fist and shot back out the window. Even as I was shaking, I began to laugh. Some cat burglar that was—my own cat!

Respond to the reading. Answer the following questions on your own paper.

- ☐ Ideas **(1) What ideas or details build suspense for the ending?**
- ☐ Organization **(2) How does the writer organize the events in the paragraph?**
- ☐ Voice & Word Choice **(3) What words or phrases show you that the writer enjoys this topic?**

Prewriting Selecting a Topic

Surprising things happen every day. The writer of "Things That Go Bump" used a cluster to write down some of his surprising experiences.

Cluster

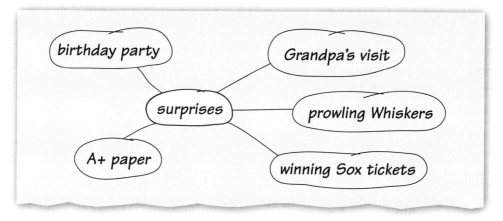

Create a cluster. In the middle of your paper, write the word "surprises" and circle it. Then create a cluster of four or five of your own surprising experiences. Choose one of these experiences to write about.

Gathering Details

To gather details, the writer of the sample paragraph on page 94 listed what happened first, what he expected to happen next, and what surprise actually happened.

Chart

What Happened First	What I Expected to Happen Next	What Surprise Actually Happened
heard a sound in my room at night	to see a burglar	saw my cat Whiskers

Chart your surprise. Make a chart like the one above. Write what happened first, what you expected to happen next, and what surprise happened.

NARRATIVE

Writing Developing the First Draft

A narrative paragraph has a topic sentence, a body, and a closing sentence. Each part serves a different purpose.

- The **topic sentence** introduces your story in an interesting way.
- The **body** uses sensory details to describe what happened.
- The **closing sentence** wraps up your paragraph.

 Write your first draft. Write your surprising story in your natural voice. Imagine you are telling your story to a classmate. If you get stuck, look back at the chart you used to gather details on page 95.

Revising Improving Your Writing

Once your story is on paper, you can revise it so that your readers will feel like they experienced it right along with you. Here are a few tips.

- **Show, don't tell.** Instead of telling readers "Nakita had a fit," show them by writing "Nakita waved her hands and hollered."
- **Check the order.** Tell the events in the order they happened.
- **Build up to a high point.** Increase the excitement as you lead up to the conclusion.
- **Check words and sentences.** Use strong nouns and verbs and make sure your sentences flow smoothly.

 Revise your paragraph. Check your ideas, organization, voice, word choice, and sentence fluency as you revise your narrative paragraph. Look for ways to improve your topic sentence, body, and closing sentence.

Editing Checking for Conventions

After completing your revised draft, check your story for correct use of punctuation, grammar, spelling, and so on.

 Edit your work. Use the following questions to make sure your narrative paragraph is free of errors.

1 Have I checked for errors in capitalization and grammar?

2 Have I checked my punctuation and spelling?

Proofread your story. Give your copy a final look.

Narrative Writing

Sharing an Experience

Like everyone else, you have stories to tell. Think about how many times you have said, "Guess what happened to me!" or "Do you know what I did?" Your life is full of stories. You took a trip, broke your arm, or finally got your own pet. Writing a personal narrative is a way to share one of your important stories. It's also a way for you to learn about yourself and your special place in the world.

Think about personal experiences that you could share with your classmates. You could write about something that happened to you, something you did, or someone you have a special relationship with. Here are some guidelines to help you get started.

Writing Guidelines

Subject:	**A personal experience**
Form:	**Personal narrative**
Purpose:	**To share a true experience**
Audience:	**Classmates**

Understanding Your Goal

Your goal in this chapter is to write an essay about an interesting personal experience. The traits listed in the chart below will help you plan and write your personal narrative.

Traits of Narrative Writing

Ideas

Use details and dialogue to tell about a specific experience or event. Make the reader want to know what happens next.

Organization

Open with a clear beginning that pulls the reader into the story. Then present ideas in the order in which they happened.

Voice

Write the narrative in a way that sounds natural. Use dialogue to give the people in your story voice.

Word Choice

Use specific nouns, vivid verbs, and well-chosen modifiers.

Sentence Fluency

Use a variety of sentence styles that flow smoothly from one idea to the next.

Conventions

Be sure that your punctuation, capitalization, spelling, and grammar are correct.

Get the big picture. Look at the rubric on pages 130–131. You can use this rubric to assess your progress. Your goal is to write an engaging essay about a personal experience.

Personal Narrative

In this personal narrative, the student author writes about a special person who taught her about turtles. The side notes point out the main parts of the narrative.

Turtle Lady

Beginning

The beginning catches the reader's attention and gives an idea of what the story is about.

When we first moved to Florida, Dad and I went to the ocean every week and enjoyed just taking walks on the beach. The beach was usually deserted, except for some seagulls and a few sand crabs. However, one night, we spotted a campfire way down the beach. We went to check it out. As we got closer, we saw someone sitting in the sand near the dying flames. The glow of the fire revealed an old woman wearing a long orange coat and a red bandanna.

"Stop right there! Don't move," the woman whispered loudly. Not far from where I stood, I made out the shape of a huge turtle digging in the sand. "That turtle needs her space right now."

"Why, what's wrong?" I whispered back.

Middle
The middle includes details and dialogue that introduce an important person in the story.

"She's digging out a nest, and she'll lay her eggs there tonight. When she's done, she'll go back to the sea."

"Who are you?" I whispered.

She came closer, and I smelled the campfire on her tattered clothing. "My name is Dolly Cripps, but you can call me Turtle Lady because I rescue turtles. Now if you two promise to be quiet, I'll tell you more about loggerheads." Then she began talking about the turtles.

Every week we hiked up the beach to visit Dolly, and every time she taught us more about the loggerheads. We'd sit in the sand near her fire, and Dolly would tell us about the turtles that she had helped. She must have been very

Middle
The middle includes details that tell what happened first, second, third, and so on.

Ending
• • • • • • • • • • •

The ending tells how the writer felt after her experience.

old because she knew turtles that were more than 100 years old!

After a couple of months, an amazing thing happened. The sand near the nest began to ripple and shake. A couple days later, dozens of little turtles tunneled their way out from under the sand and scrambled toward the sea. The waves tossed some of them back onto the shore. That's when Dolly, Dad, and I grabbed any baby turtles that landed upside down and couldn't get up. We quickly rescued them and gently placed them back in the ocean. If we had not been there, the hatchlings would have died, or they might have become some seagull's supper.

Rescuing those turtles was the coolest thing I've ever done. As quickly as the turtle rescue had begun, it was over. The turtles no longer needed us.

As the last turtle disappeared into the ocean, I turned to the turtle lady and asked, "Will we see you again next year?"

"Maybe," she answered. "Wherever my turtles are, that's where I will be."

Respond to the reading. Why is "Turtle Lady" such a good personal narrative? To find out, answer the following questions.

☐ **Ideas** **(1) What specific experience does the writer share?**

☐ **Organization** **(2) How does the writer organize the events in the story?**

☐ **Voice & Word Choice** **(3) What words and phrases show that the writer is interested in her topic?**

Prewriting

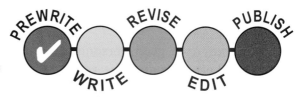

PREWRITE ✓ · WRITE · REVISE · EDIT · PUBLISH

Before you are ready to write your narrative, you need to choose a personal experience to write about. After selecting a topic, you will continue prewriting by gathering and organizing details.

Keys to Effective Prewriting

1. Select an experience that you know well and would like to share.

2. Make sure you can answer the 5 W questions about the experience.

3. Think about and describe the people in your narrative.

4. Put the events in order by using a quick list or a time line.

5. Gather details about sights, sounds, and other senses related to your narrative.

NARRATIVE

PROD. NO.   ROLL
SCENE   TAKE
SOUND

Prewriting Selecting a Topic

The key to a good personal narrative is finding an interesting topic—one that both you and the reader will enjoy. The chart below shows how one writer gathered story ideas by remembering different people, places, animals, and experiences.

Brainstorm Chart

People I Know	Places I've Been	Animals I Remember	Things I've Done
My brother Sam	The Liberty Bell	B. J., the dog	Marched in a parade
My friend Kenny	Cuba	Big raccoon	Met Tom Jones
Tyisha, the dancer	My uncle's wedding	Snake at the campground	Explored a cave

Brainstorm for topics. On your own paper, draw a chart like the one above. Use the same four headings for your categories. Then fill in the chart using the directions below.

1 Under each heading, list at least three possible story ideas.

2 Now go over your ideas and circle the topic that you think would make the best story. (You will use this topic in the next exercise.)

Focus on the Traits

Ideas Your topic does not have to be a complicated one. In fact, a short trip or a simple event can often make a great story. Think about important experiences that took place within a short period of time—a day, an hour, or even just a few minutes.

Sizing Up Your Idea

Now that you have a story idea, you must decide if it will make a good personal narrative. Your narrative should tell about an experience you had at a specific time and place. You can use the 5 W's to find out if your story idea has all of these details.

1. **Who** are the people in my story?
2. **What** main experience will I write about?
3. **When** and **where** did the experience take place?
4. **Why** did the experience change me?

 Prewrite **Size up your story idea.** Write your answers to the 5 W questions above. Review your answers. Do you have enough details to write a good story? If not, choose another idea from your chart (page 102).

Gathering Details About People

A personal narrative tells about your own experience, so you will be one person in your story. Other people and animals may appear as well. A personality web can help you gather details about the people in your story.

Personality Web

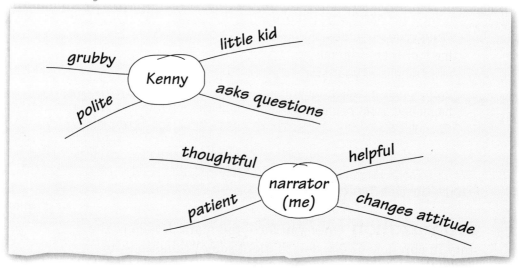

grubby

little kid

Kenny

polite

asks questions

thoughtful

helpful

narrator (me)

patient

changes attitude

 Prewrite **Make personality webs.** Create a personality web for each important person in your story. Write each person's name in a circle and include details about the person on the lines.

Prewriting **Putting Events in Order**

Once you've completed your personality webs, it's time to list the events in your story. Most narratives are organized in chronological (time) order. That means events appear in the order in which they happened. A quick list like the one below is one way to organize events.

Quick List

> ### My Friend Kenny
>
> – I thought little kids were a pain.
> – Uncle Eddie asked me to volunteer at bike camp.
> – There were tons of little kids at the camp.
> – I thought bike camp would be a drag.
> – I made friends with a neat little kid named Kenny.
> – I learned to like little kids.

Create your quick list. On your own paper, make a list like the one above. Write your story idea at the top. Then write the main details of your story in the order in which they happened, from beginning to end.

Focus on the Traits

Organization Once you have the main details of the story in chronological order, think of some transition words and phrases that could help tie your ideas together. (See pages 572–573.) You could add these words to your quick list.

Gathering Sensory Details

A good story has lots of colorful, specific details. Some of these details should relate to the senses. Then the reader is able to imagine not only what things look like but also how things sound, smell, taste, and feel.

Making a sensory chart, like the one below, is one way you can gather sensory details about your experience.

Sensory Chart

SENSORY DETAILS

I saw...	– little kids riding trikes – squirmy kids
I heard...	– Uncle Eddie – trike bells and bike horns
I smelled...	– chocolate on Kenny's clothes
I felt...	– Kenny's sticky little fingers – pain in my foot
I tasted...	– (could almost taste) the chocolate bar smeared on Kenny's face

Create a sensory chart. List the five senses with space after each one. Then recall your experience and fill in the chart as completely as you can. (It's all right to have many details for some senses and only a few or none for others.) You will use some of these details in your narrative.

Prewrite

Focus on the Traits

Voice The details and feelings you use in your writing are part of your natural voice. The words you choose to describe what you saw, heard, smelled, tasted, or touched are also part of your voice.

NARRATIVE

Prewriting Reviewing Your Details

Before you begin writing your story, look over your prewriting quick list, personality web, and sensory chart. Be sure you've collected enough details to write a good personal narrative.

 Read the paragraph below. Then answer these questions about the details used in "A Hair-Raising Experience."

1. Are the 5 W's (*who, what, when, where,* and *why*) answered?

2. What transitions show the time order of the paragraph?

3. What sensory details help create a clear picture?

A Hair-Raising Experience

1   One evening, my mom was downstairs doing the laundry.
2   As usual, she was trying to do 10 jobs at once when she grabbed
3   the wet clothes from the washer and tossed them into the dryer.
4   She slammed the dryer door, turned the timer, and started to
5   run upstairs. All of a sudden, a whining sound stopped her in her
6   tracks. The sound was coming from the dryer. She yelled for me.
7   As I raced downstairs, the sound grew louder and louder. I flung
8   open the dryer door. There to our surprise was Mica, our cat. He
9   looked like someone who had just gotten off a Tilt-A-Whirl ride. His
10   eyes bugged out, and his hair looked like a cartoon character with
11   a finger in an electric outlet. Mica darted out of the dryer and up
12   the stairs. After that, Mom always checked out the dryer before
13   slamming the door, and Mica stayed clear of the laundry room for
14   a long, long time.

 Examine your details. Review your prewriting activities before you begin to write your first draft. Use the following guidelines.

1 Be sure you can answer the 5 W's *(who, what, when, where,* and *why)* about your story.

2 Check your quick list to make sure the events are listed in the order that they happened.

3 Review the details in your sensory chart.

Writing

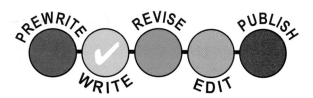

Now that you have gathered and organized your ideas, you are ready to write the first draft of your narrative. Focus on putting your ideas on paper in the best order. Use your own unique storytelling voice.

Keys to Effective Writing

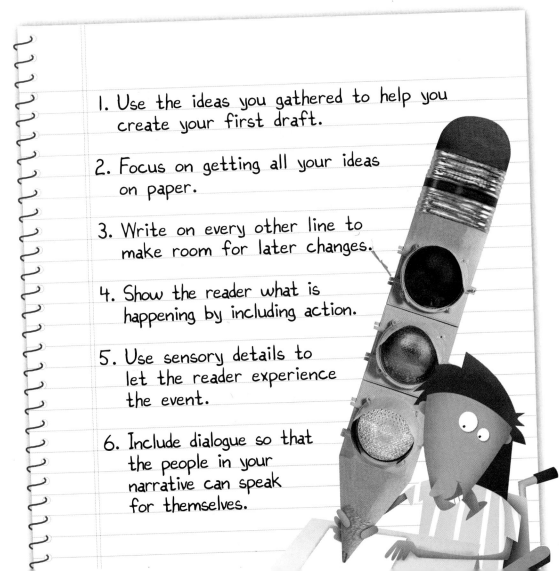

1. Use the ideas you gathered to help you create your first draft.

2. Focus on getting all your ideas on paper.

3. Write on every other line to make room for later changes.

4. Show the reader what is happening by including action.

5. Use sensory details to let the reader experience the event.

6. Include dialogue so that the people in your narrative can speak for themselves.

NARRATIVE

Writing **Getting the Big Picture**

The chart below shows how the parts of a personal narrative fit together. (The examples are from the narrative on pages 109–112.) You're ready to write your narrative once you . . .

- collect plenty of details about the experience.
- organize the details according to time.

Beginning

The **beginning** paragraph introduces the experience and makes the reader want to know what happens next.

Opening Sentences
Little kids are a pain—or so I thought. Then Uncle Eddie asked me to volunteer at bike camp . . .

Middle

The **middle** part gives details about what happened first, second, third, and so on. It also answers the *who, what, when,* and *where* questions.

When I arrived at bike camp . . .

My first job was to teach . . .

Kenny and I saw a lot . . .

By the end of camp, I wished . . .

Ending

The **ending** tells *why* or *how* you were changed because of this experience.

Closing Sentences
Little kids just don't know much yet. They need a big kid, like me, to give them some attention and answer their questions. . . .

Starting Your Personal Narrative

Once you have a plan for your story, you are ready to write your first draft. Write as though you were telling a friend your story. The first paragraph should catch your friend's interest and introduce your story. Here are several ways to begin your narrative.

- **Place yourself in the middle of the action.**
  When Uncle Eddie asked me to volunteer at bike camp, I said, "Sure." Secretly, I didn't want to because I thought little kids were a pain.

- **Begin with a surprising statement or fact.**
  Little kids can be a real pain!

- **Start with someone speaking (dialogue).**
  "Get off the field!" my friends and I yelled.

Beginning Paragraph

NARRATIVE

The writer catches the reader's interest with dialogue.

The writer introduces the story.

> *"Get off the field!" That's what my friends and I are always yelling at the little kids who get in the way when we are trying to have a game of softball. Little kids are a pain—or so I thought. Then Uncle Eddie asked me to volunteer at bike camp. The camp is a special Saturday when kids learn safety rules for riding their trikes and bikes. I didn't want to, but my family always helps run the camp, so I politely told Uncle Eddie, "Sure."*

Write your beginning. On your own paper, write the beginning of your story. Try using one of the three ways suggested on this page.

Writing **Developing the Middle Part**

Once you have your reader's attention, you want to keep it by adding interesting details. Don't tell everything, though. Tell just enough to capture the main event. Here are some things to remember as you write.

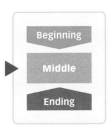

Beginning

Middle

Ending

- **Include a number of sensory details.**
- **Let the people in the narrative tell the story using their own words (dialogue).**
- **Share your feelings throughout the story.**

Middle Paragraphs

Strong sensory details (blue) let the reader "see and feel" the experience.

Dialogue makes the people seem real.

> *When I arrived at bike camp,* I heard the ringing ting-a-ling of trike bells and the constant beep, beep, beeping of bike horns. *The parking lot was a sea of little kids pedaling around and around and back and forth.* They looked like a bunch of ants rushing around but going nowhere.
>
> *"Kyle," Uncle Eddie said, "it looks like we have our work cut out for us today."*
>
> *"Yeah," I mumbled. I wasn't looking forward to this at all.*
>
> *My first job was to teach the squirmy little kids on trikes to watch out for hazards.* One grubby little five-year-old rode over my foot. *"What's a haz—zard?" he asked.* A chocolate bar was smeared in a brown mustache under his nose. *Suddenly he put his trike in reverse and rolled back over my foot.* A sharp pain shot up my leg.

"It is something dangerous," I said. I was talking very slowly so he couldn't tell how much my foot hurt. "A hazard is something that can hurt you or someone else," I answered. I was thinking to myself, "You are a hazard!"

"Boy, you sure are smart," said the little boy, whose name was Kenny.

> Personal feelings show how Kenny is changing the writer.

Kenny and I saw a lot of each other all day. He was full of questions, and he looked up to me as if I had all the answers. He became my talking shadow.

By the end of camp, I wished that I had a little brother just like Kenny. When he reached out to shake my hand, he said, "Thanks for helping me." I didn't even notice the chocolate on my hand until he was pedaling away to meet his dad.

NARRATIVE

Write your middle paragraphs. Before you start writing, read through the details you collected on your quick list (page 104) and on your sensory chart (page 105). Keep the following tips in mind.

Drafting Tips

- **Remember that your purpose** is to share a true personal experience with your classmates.
- **Relax and write freely.** Don't try to get everything perfect at this time.
- **Add any new ideas** that occur to you as you write.

Writing **Ending Your Personal Narrative**

After you share the most important moment, bring your story to a close in the final paragraph. Here are three ways for you to end your narrative.

- **Tell how the experience changed you.**

  By the end of bike camp, I decided that I was wrong about little kids. Kenny taught me that I should give them a break—and maybe some answers, too. The kids at camp learned a lot, but so did I. Now I can't wait for next year's camp.

- **Relate the experience to the audience.**

  I guess we all need to realize that we shouldn't make decisions about others until we get to know them. If we do, we could miss out on some neat experiences. Kids are people, too—just littler—and they can be a lot of fun.

- **Tell why the experience was important.**

Ending Paragraph

The writer tells why the experience was important.

> Did I say that little kids are a real pain? Well, I was wrong. Little kids just don't know much yet. They need a big kid, like me, to give them some attention and answer their questions. And maybe someday, when they're bigger, they'll remember and be nice to little kids, too.

Write your ending. Try one of the three ways listed above. Remember to keep it short and simple. It shouldn't go on too long.

Form a complete first draft. Put together a complete copy of your first draft. Then you will be ready to revise your writing.

Revising

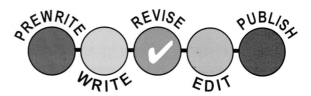

PREWRITE · WRITE · REVISE ✓ · EDIT · PUBLISH

When you revise, you improve your first draft in many ways. You might spice up descriptions, add dialogue, or experiment with different beginnings and endings. Revision can make even a ho-hum draft into something special.

Keys to Effective Revising

NARRATIVE

1. Set your narrative aside for a while so you can revise with a fresh perspective.

2. Read through your entire narrative to see how it works as a whole.

3. Check your beginning, middle, and ending to make sure each part works well.

4. Make sure your own unique storytelling voice comes through.

5. Check your words and sentences.

6. Use the editing and proofreading marks inside the back cover of this book.

Revising for Ideas

6 My narrative tells about one experience. The details make the reader want to read the whole story.	**5** My narrative tells about one experience. I use the 5 W's and sensory details.	**4** My narrative tells about one experience. More details would make it better.

When you revise for *ideas,* be sure you have focused on one experience. Check to see if you have answered the 5 W's and included sensory details. The rubric above will guide you as you work to improve your ideas.

Will readers understand my narrative?

Readers will understand your narrative if you include details that answer the 5 W's.

1. **Who** are the people in my narrative?
2. **What** events are included in this experience?
3. **When** do the events happen?
4. **Where** does my narrative take place?
5. **Why** is this experience important?

Once in a lifetime

 Try It Read the following paragraph and answer the *who, what, when, where,* and *why* questions.

1 Every other weekend, Mom drives me out to the family farm
2 where my older cousin, Buster, teaches me all kinds of new things.
3 He has taught me how to shoot arrows, fix an engine, and bale hay.
4 Usually, we spend the evenings in his workshop. The last time we got
5 together, Buster taught me how to carve a piece of wood into a
6 simple whistle. I really enjoyed carving and can hardly wait to start my
7 next project. I'd like to carve a figure of a wolf, but that may be too
8 hard for now. No matter what Buster teaches me, we have a great time
9 together.

 Check your ideas. Read through your first draft. Be sure your narrative includes details that answer the 5 W's.

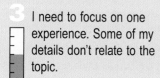

3 | I need to focus on one experience. Some of my details don't relate to the topic.

2 | I need to focus on one experience and answer the 5 W's.

1 | I need to choose a different experience to write about.

Have I included enough sensory details?

You have included enough sensory details if they help your readers use their imaginations—and their five senses—to connect with your experience.

 In the following paragraph, find and list at least five sensory details.

1   During the summer of 2005, my family lived on a busy street in
2 Cincinnati. During the daytime, buses rumbled and screeched right in
3 front of our second-floor apartment. The noise and oily exhaust from
4 these vehicles is something I will always remember. In the heat of
5 that summer, we passed the time playing hearts or rummy. My little
6 sister often sat in an old rocking chair and watched us. Mom always
7 made sure that there was a pitcher of sweet lemonade in the fridge.
8 Once in a while, she'd even surprise us with some fresh strawberries.
9 It may have been hot and noisy, but that summer was one of the best
10 ones ever.

Review your details. Have you included a variety of sensory details in your narrative. Do your details bring your narrative to life for your readers?

NARRATIVE

Ideas
A sensory detail and a detail that tells "where" are added.

When I arrived at bike camp, I heard the ringing
and the constant beep, beep, beeping of bike horns
ting-a-ling of trike bells. The parking lot was a sea of
around and around and back and forth
little kids pedaling. They looked like a bunch of ants

rushing around but going nowhere.

Revising for Organization

6 My organization makes my narrative enjoyable and easy to read.	**5** My events are in time order, and I use transitions well. I have a clear beginning, middle, and ending.	**4** My events are in time order. Most of my transitions are helpful. I have a beginning, middle, and ending.

When you revise for *organization,* use the rubric strip above to guide you. Check your narrative for a strong beginning, middle, and ending.

How do I check the beginning?

You check the beginning of your narrative by asking yourself the three questions below.

1. How does my beginning get the reader's attention?

2. What does my reader need to know to understand my experience?

3. What other way could I begin my narrative? (See page 109.)

 Reread your opening. Then answer each of the questions listed above. Make the changes that would improve your beginning.

How do I check the middle?

You check the middle by making sure you have arranged events in the order in which they happened. This is called chronological order, or time order. Transition words can help you move the reader through your story. Here are some transition words that **show time.** (See page 572.)

first	**while**	meanwhile	now	then
second	**then**	today	soon	next
third	**when**	tomorrow	later	as soon as

 Review for time order. Check the middle paragraphs of your narrative to make sure your events are in chronological order. Also make sure that you used transitions to move your reader easily through your story.

3 Some of my events are out of order. I need more transitions. My beginning or ending is weak.

2 I need to use time order and transitions in order to create a clear beginning, middle, and ending.

1 My narrative is confusing. I need to learn about time order.

How do I check the ending?

You check your ending by asking the following questions.

1. Does my narrative end soon after the most important event?

2. How will my reader know the experience was important to me?

3. What other way could I end my narrative? (See page 112.)

Check your ending. Use the questions listed above to see if you have written an effective ending.

Revise

NARRATIVE

Organization
One middle paragraph is reorganized as two paragraphs. (See page 111.)

Kenny and I saw a lot of each other all day.

He was full of questions, and he looked up to me

as if I had all the answers. He became my talking

When
shadow. He reached out to shake my hand, ~~and~~ *he*

said, "Thanks for helping me." I didn't even notice

the chocolate on my hand until he was pedaling

away to meet his dad. ¶ By the end of camp, I

wished that I had a little brother just like Kenny.

Revising **for** Voice

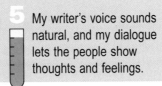
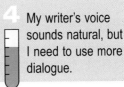

6 My writer's voice creates an unforgettable experience for the reader.

5 My writer's voice sounds natural, and my dialogue lets the people show thoughts and feelings.

4 My writer's voice sounds natural, but I need to use more dialogue.

When you revise for *voice,* check to see if your writing sounds natural, as if you were talking to someone. Also make sure you have used dialogue. The rubric above can guide you as you revise for voice.

Have I used a natural-sounding voice?

Your voice sounds natural if your reader can "hear" your personality in your narrative. You can check your voice by paying special attention to the way you use words. In each paragraph below, a different writer describes the same event. Notice how the personality and voice of each writer comes through in the writing.

Writer 1:

I flipped open my locker and jabbed my hand in. I got a fistful of fuzz. "Whoa. What's this critter doing in my locker!"

Writer 2:

I pulled open my locker and sighed. What a day! What could go wrong now? I reached in and felt something furry and alive. "Yikes! A rat!" I screamed.

 Write for 3 to 5 minutes about the experience below. Use your imagination to add lots of details. Your writing should sound like you're telling a story to a friend. When you finish, underline words and phrases that show your unique personality, or voice.

While cleaning up after a parade, I found a $50 bill on a littered street.

 Check your voice. Read through your personal narrative. Underline two sentences that show your unique voice. Then check the rest of your narrative for places where the voice can be improved. Revise as needed.

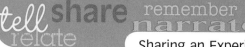
 Sometimes my writer's voice sounds natural, but I need to improve my dialogue.

 My writer's voice does not sound natural. I need to use dialogue.

1 I need to understand what a natural-sounding voice is.

How can dialogue improve my narrative?

Using dialogue in your writing helps you "show" instead of just "tell." Dialogue can make your narrative feel as if it is happening right now. As you write dialogue, remember that a five-year-old child would not speak like your English teacher. Here are some tips for writing dialogue. (See page 556.)

- Think about the people in your story and choose words that each of them would use.
- Make the words sound like everyday conversation.
- Indent each time a different person speaks.

 Write an exchange of dialogue between one of the pairs of people listed below.

- A coach and a player
- Two friends
- A clerk and a customer
- A brother and sister

 Read your narrative carefully. Make changes if your voice or the dialogue doesn't sound right.

Voice
Dialogue is changed to fit the little boy's age.

"A hazard is something that can hurt you or someone else," I answered. I was thinking to myself, "You are a hazard!"

"Boy, I ~~think~~ you sure are ~~intelligent~~ smart," said the little boy, whose name was Kenny.

Revising for Word Choice

When you revise for *word choice,* check to see if you used adjectives and adverbs to capture your experience. Also check to see if you have replaced overused words with synonyms. The rubric above can help you.

Have I used adjectives and adverbs well?

You have used adjectives and adverbs well if they help create a clear and interesting picture. Adjectives describe nouns or pronouns. Adverbs add meaning to verbs, adjectives, and other adverbs. The example below shows how a writer improved a basic sentence by adding adjectives and adverbs. (See pages 486–493.)

Basic Sentence

The cafeteria served sandwiches.

Improved Sentence

       adj.   adj. adj.   adv.

The school cafeteria served spicy sub sandwiches yesterday.

Try It Copy this paragraph and fill in the missing adjectives and adverbs. Compare your paragraph with a classmate's.

Our soccer team had practiced ___*(adverb)*___ to get ready for the championship game with our ___*(adjective)*___ rival. I arrived ___*(adverb)*___ on Saturday to find a flooded field, ruined by the ___*(adjective)*___ rain the night before. After running to the gym, I found our coach talking ___*(adverb)*___ to some other ___*(adjective)*___ players about postponing the game.

Revise for adjectives and adverbs. In your narrative, use adjectives and adverbs to help create a clear picture.

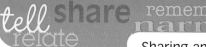

3 I need to add more adjectives and adverbs. I need to replace overused words with synonyms.

2 I don't use adjectives and adverbs. I keep using the same words again and again.

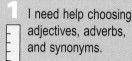
1 I need help choosing adjectives, adverbs, and synonyms.

Have I checked for overused words?

Writers often use synonyms—other words that mean almost the same thing—to replace overused or dull words. You can use a dictionary or a thesaurus to find just the right words for your writing.

Try It Write a synonym for each of the frequently overused words below. Then write a sentence using each synonym. The first one has been done for you.

1. mad

    angry: *I was angry after missing the bus.*

2. went   **4.** cold   **6.** good

3. bad   **5.** big   **7.** happy

Revise to replace overused words. Look at each sentence in your narrative. Make a list of words that you feel are dull or overused. Replace them with synonyms.

NARRATIVE

Word Choice

A synonym replaces the word "help."

Two adjectives and an adverb are added.

                        volunteer
Then Uncle Eddie asked me to ^help at bike camp.
        special   *safety*
The camp is a ^Saturday when kids learn ^rules for

riding their trikes and bikes. I didn't want to, but my
                              politely
family always helps run the camp, so I ^told Uncle

Eddie, "Sure."

Revising **for** Sentence Fluency

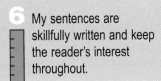 **6** My sentences are skillfully written and keep the reader's interest throughout.

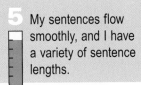 **5** My sentences flow smoothly, and I have a variety of sentence lengths.

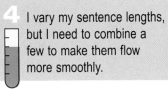 **4** I vary my sentence lengths, but I need to combine a few to make them flow more smoothly.

When you revise for *sentence fluency,* you need to check your writing for a variety of sentence lengths. You may need to combine some sentences to have a smoother flow. The above rubric will help guide you.

Are too many sentences of the same length?

You check your sentence lengths by counting the number of words in each sentence. When you speak, you automatically use sentences of many different lengths. This gives a natural flow to your sentences. When you write, you want to do the same.

 Read the following paragraph. Write down the number of words in each sentence. What did you discover about the sentence fluency of this paragraph?

(1) I see the shoe-shine man each morning. **(2)** He is always in the same spot. **(3)** He looks older than my grandpa. **(4)** Each day he wears green pants. **(5)** He has a red cap. **(6)** He has a long leather vest. **(7)** In its pockets are brushes and polish. **(8)** His stand is near the train stop. **(9)** He smiles at me every morning. **(10)** "Hello," he says, and nods. **(11)** We talk about my homework. **(12)** While we talk, he shines shoes. **(13)** He waves as I leave for school.

 Revise your paper for sentence lengths. Read through your narrative and check your sentences.

1 Write down the number of words in each of your first 10 to 15 sentences.

2 Do you have a variety of sentence lengths?

3 What did you discover about sentence fluency in your narrative?

3 I need to combine more sentences to have a better variety of lengths and a smoother flow.

2 My sentences are all the same length. I need to combine some of them.

1 Most of my sentences need to be combined or rewritten.

How do I combine sentences?

Two easy ways to combine short sentences are (1) creating compound sentences and (2) using a series of words. (Also see pages 512–514.)

Create Compound Sentences

I see the shoe-shine man each morning. He is always in the same spot.
I see the shoe-shine man each morning, and he is always in the same spot.

(Two sentences are combined using a comma and the conjunction *and*.)

Use a Series of Words

Each day he wears green pants. He has a red cap. He has a long leather vest.
Each day he wears green pants, a red cap, and a long leather vest.

(Three short sentences are combined into one using a series of words.)

 Below are two sets of sentences. Combine each of the sets, using the method given in parentheses.

1. I've always enjoyed reading about dinosaurs.
   I didn't realize that they had once lived in my neighborhood.
   (Create a compound sentence using a conjunction.)

2. My grandmother has taught me how to sew.
   She also showed me how to crochet and quilt.
   (Combine sentences using a series of words.)

 Combine sentences. Look at your word count (page 122). Combine some short sentences using the methods given above.

NARRATIVE

Sentence Fluency
Two sentences are combined.

                                    and
He was full of questions. He looked up to me as if I
had all the answers. He became my talking shadow.

Revising **Using a Checklist**

Check your revising. On a piece of paper, write the numbers 1 to 12. If you can answer "yes" to a question, put a check mark after that number. If not, continue to work with that part of your essay.

Ideas

_____ **1.** Do I tell about one important event?
_____ **2.** Do I answer all the 5 W's in my narrative?
_____ **3.** Do I include sensory details?

Organization

_____ **4.** Are my beginning, middle, and ending effective?
_____ **5.** Have I cut unnecessary details?
_____ **6.** Have I reorganized parts that were out of place?

Voice

_____ **7.** Does my voice sound natural?
_____ **8.** Have I used dialogue?

Word Choice

_____ **9.** Do my adjectives and adverbs make my narrative clearer?
_____ **10.** Have I replaced overused words?

Sentence Fluency

_____ **11.** Have I checked my sentence lengths?
_____ **12.** Have I used combining to vary my sentences?

Make a clean copy. When you've finished revising your essay, make a clean copy before you begin to edit.

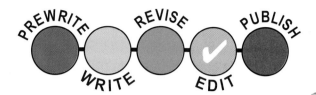

Editing

After you've finished revising your narrative, it's time to edit it for your use of conventions: punctuation, capitalization, spelling, and grammar.

Keys to Effective Editing

1. Use a dictionary, a thesaurus, and the "Proofreader's Guide" in the back of this book.

2. Check for any words or phrases that may be confusing to the reader.

3. Check your writing for correctness of punctuation, capitalization, spelling, and grammar.

4. Edit on a printed computer copy. Then enter your changes on the computer.

5. Use the editing and proofreading marks inside the back cover of this book.

NARRATIVE

Editing for Conventions

When you are editing for *conventions,* you need to check for spelling, grammar, capitalization, and punctuation errors. The rubric above and the information below can help you edit for dialogue.

Have I punctuated dialogue correctly?

To be sure you know how to correctly punctuate dialogue, review the following rules. (Also see page 556.)

- Commas are used to set off the words of the speaker from the rest of the sentence.

    "A raccoon crawled down the chimney," Laura announced, "and I think it's still in there."

- Sometimes an exclamation point or a question mark separates the speaker's words from the rest of the sentence.

    "Are you sure it went down the chimney?" Regina asked.

- The speaker's exact words are placed within the quotation marks.

    "I'm positive!" Laura replied.

 Copy and punctuate the following lines of dialogue.

1. Mom asked What time does the party start?
2. Ben said Right after supper.
3. You have to finish your homework first she reminded him.
4. He answered I'll start right now.
5. Later, his mom called up the stairs Tomas is here.
6. Great! Ben shouted.
7. I'll be right down he added because I just finished.

 Edit dialogue. Use the rules and examples above to make sure you have punctuated your dialogue correctly.

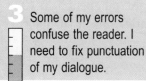

3 Some of my errors confuse the reader. I need to fix punctuation of my dialogue.

2 I need to correct many errors that make my narrative and dialogue hard to read.

1 I need help making corrections, especially with my dialogue.

NARRATIVE

How do I know when to indent dialogue?

As you write your narrative, remember that you need to indent and begin a new paragraph each time a different person speaks.

In the following paragraph, the dialogue runs together.

> "It's snowing!" cried my sister. "I hope it snows all night," I added. "Maybe we'll have a snow day, and we won't have to go to school tomorrow," she replied. "I hope so," I yelled. "Let's do a snow dance!"

To be correct, dialogue should be indented each time a new person speaks.

> "It's snowing!" cried my sister.
>
> "I hope it snows all night," I added.
>
> "Maybe we'll have a snow day, and we won't have to go to school tomorrow," she replied.
>
> "I hope so," I yelled. "Let's do a snow dance!"

Check the dialogue in your narrative. Have you started a new paragraph each time there's a new speaker? Use the paragraph symbol (¶) to mark each sentence that should begin a new paragraph. Make sure to indent these sentences.

Conventions
Quotation marks are added.

Dialogue is indented for a change in speaker.

"Kyle," Uncle Eddie said, "it looks like we have our work cut out for us today."

¶ "Yeah," I mumbled. I wasn't looking forward to this at all.

Editing **Using a Checklist**

Check your editing. On a piece of paper, write the numbers 1 to 12. If you can answer "yes" to a question, put a check mark after that number. If not, continue to edit for that convention of writing.

Conventions

PUNCTUATION

_____ ✓ **1.** Do I use end punctuation after all my sentences?

_____ **2.** Do I use commas after introductory word groups?

_____ **3.** Do I use commas after items in a series?

_____ **4.** Do I use commas in all my compound sentences?

_____ **5.** Do I use apostrophes to show possession *(boy's bike)*?

CAPITALIZATION

_____ **6.** Do I start all my sentences with capital letters?

_____ **7.** Do I capitalize all proper nouns?

SPELLING

_____ **8.** Have I spelled all my words correctly?

_____ **9.** Have I double-checked the words my spell-checker may have missed?

GRAMMAR

_____ **10.** Do I use correct forms of verbs *(had gone, not had went)*?

_____ **11.** Do my subjects and verbs agree in number? (She and I *were* going, not She and I *was* going.)

_____ **12.** Do I use the right words *(to, too, and two)*?

Creating a Title

- Use strong, colorful words: **A Weird and Wonderful Artist**
- Give the words rhythm: **My Little Buddy Kenny**
- Be imaginative: **Turtle Lady**

Publishing

Sharing Your Narrative

After you have worked so hard to improve your story, make a neat final copy to share. You may also decide to present your story in the form of an illustration, a skit, or a recording. (See the suggestions below.)

 Make a final copy. Follow your teacher's instructions or use the guidelines below to format your story. (If you are using a computer, see page 60.) Create a clean copy of your narrative and carefully proofread it.

Focus on Presentation

- Use blue or black ink and write neatly.
- Write your name in the upper left-hand corner of page 1.
- Skip a line and center your title; skip another line and start your writing.
- Indent every paragraph and leave a one-inch margin on all four sides.
- Write your last name and the page number in the upper right-hand corner of every page after the first one.

NARRATIVE

Illustrate Your Narrative

Pick an important part of your narrative and draw a picture of it. Post the picture and the story in your classroom.

Create a Skit

Read your narrative to a group of classmates. Decide who will play which parts. Then practice and perform the story for your class.

Record Your Storytelling

Record yourself telling your narrative. Play the recording back and think of ways to improve your storytelling. Keep trying until you are satisfied. Share the final recording with friends or family.

Rubric for Narrative Writing

Use this rubric for guiding and assessing your narrative writing. Refer to it whenever you want to improve your writing.

Ideas

6 | **The narrative tells about an unforgettable experience. The details make the story truly memorable.** | **5** The writer tells about an interesting experience. Details help create the interest. | **4** The writer tells about an interesting experience. More details are needed.

Organization

6 | **The organization makes the narrative enjoyable and easy to read.** | **5** The narrative is well organized, with a clear beginning, middle, and ending. Transitions are used well. | **4** The narrative is well organized. Most of the transitions are helpful.

Voice

6 | **The writer's voice creates an unforgettable experience for the reader.** | **5** The writer's voice sounds natural and creates interest in the story. Dialogue is used. | **4** The writer's voice creates interest in the story. More dialogue is needed.

Word Choice

6 | **The writer's exceptional word choice captures the experience.** | **5** Strong nouns and verbs and well-chosen modifiers create vivid, clear pictures. | **4** Modifiers are used. Strong nouns and active verbs would improve sensory images.

Sentence Fluency

6 | **The sentences are skillfully written and original. They keep the reader's interest.** | **5** The sentences show variety and are easy to read and understand. | **4** The sentences are varied, but some should flow more smoothly.

Conventions

6 | **The narrative is error free.** | **5** The narrative has a few minor errors in punctuation, spelling, or grammar. | **4** The narrative has several errors in punctuation, spelling, or grammar.

3 The writer needs to focus on one experience. Some details do not relate to the story.

2 The writer needs to focus on one experience. Details are needed.

1 The writer needs to tell about an experience and use details.

3 The order of events needs to be corrected. More transitions need to be used. One part of the narrative is weak.

2 The beginning, middle, and ending all run together. The order is unclear.

1 The narrative needs to be organized.

3 A voice can usually be heard. More dialogue is needed.

2 The voice is weak. Dialogue is needed.

1 The writer has not gotten involved in the story. Dialogue is needed.

3 Strong nouns, verbs, and modifiers are needed to create sensory images.

2 General and overused words do not create sensory images.

1 The writer has not yet considered word choice.

3 A better variety of sentences is needed. Sentences do not read smoothly.

2 Incomplete and/or short sentences make the writing choppy.

1 Few sentences are written well. Help is needed.

3 Some errors confuse the reader.

2 Many errors make the narrative confusing and hard to read.

1 Help is needed to make corrections.

Evaluating a Narrative

As you read the narrative below, focus on the writer's strengths and weaknesses. **(The essay contains some errors.)** Then read the student self-evaluation on page 133.

A Knotty Problem

"I'm sorry, Jessie, but I don't have time to show you how to knit right now," my mother was saying. "Why don't you just use your allowance money to buy Nana a scarf?"

"I think she should get a special, homemade scarf," I said.

My mother just sighed. So my Aunt Elena said she would show me how. She gave me some knitting needles. She showed me how to cast on the stiches. Then she was showing me some of the knitting patterns. They looked really hard. Then Aunt Elena took me to the craft store. We picked out some pretty yarn. It was Nana's favorite color.

I only had a couple of week's. Every day after I finished my homework I would try to knit the scarf. It did not go well. I got the yarn all knotted. Aunt Elena was really pateint. She would unravel the work and show me where I went wrong. After a few more days, the yarn was all dirty. We had pulled it out over and over again. I wanted to cry.

In the end Aunt Elena told me not to get upset and that we would try again. We put the yarn and a picture of the scraf in a box for Nana. When we went to the hospital. Nana was surprised when she opened the box. My mom was surprised too when she saw what was inside.

I told them that Aunt Elena promised to help me with a scarf. So until I finish the scarf, Aunt Elena and I will get together for Sunday afternoon knitting.

Student Self-Assessment

The assessment below shows how the writer of "A Knotty Problem" rated her own essay. First she used the rubric and number scale on pages 130–131 to rank each trait. Then she made two comments under each trait. The first tells about something she did well in the narrative. The second comment points out something that she feels she could have done better.

4 Ideas

1. *My narrative answers the 5 W's.*
2. *I could have used more sensory details.*

5 Organization

1. *My story has a clear beginning, middle, and ending.*
2. *In the ending, I could have told why the experience was important to me.*

4 Voice

1. *My voice sounds like me most of the time.*
2. *More dialogue could have helped me "show" instead of just "tell" my story.*

3 Word Choice

1. *I like my title.*
2. *I should have replaced overused words with synonyms.*

3 Sentence Fluency

1. *I combined a couple of sentences.*
2. *I could have combined more of the short, choppy sentences.*

4 Conventions

1. *The dialogue is punctuated correctly.*
2. *I forgot to check my spelling.*

NARRATIVE

Use the rubric. Assess your narrative using the rubric shown on pages 130–131.

1 On your own paper, list the six traits. Leave room after each trait to write one strength and one weakness.

2 Then choose a number (from 1 to 6) that shows how well each trait was used.

Reflecting on Your Writing

You've worked hard to write a narrative that your classmates will enjoy. Now take some time to think about your writing. Finish each sentence starter below on your own paper. Thinking about your writing will help you see how you are growing as a writer.

My Narrative

1. The best part of my narrative is . . .

2. The part that still needs work is . . .

3. The main thing I learned about writing a personal narrative is . . .

4. In my next narrative, I would like to . . .

5. Here is one question I still have about writing a narrative:

Narrative Writing
Biographical Narrative

"What happened when your friend got her new bike?" "What happened when your mother went to Puerto Rico?" "What happened when your older brother joined the soccer team?" If you sat down with a friend or family member and asked, "What happened when . . . ?" you would probably hear some great stories.

Writing about an important event in another person's life can help you and others understand that person. This type of writing is called a *biographical narrative,* and the next few pages will help you write one.

Writing Guidelines

Subject:	An event from someone else's life
Form:	Biographical narrative
Purpose:	To understand another person
Audience:	Classmates

Biographical Narrative

A biographical narrative tells the story of a single event in a person's life. The event should reveal something interesting about the person. Sharese, the writer of the biographical narrative below, tells a story about her father.

The Last Reckless Ride

Beginning

The beginning introduces the event.

Dad used to be a thrill seeker. He enjoyed extreme sports like bungee jumping and rock climbing, and he took lots of careless risks. But one day, when he was riding his mountain bike, things got too extreme—even for him.

Middle

Specific details move the story along.

It was a perfect day for riding. The sun was shining, the air was brisk, and people weren't yet crowding the high trails. Dad pumped the pedals of his mountain bike and climbed the gravel path. Once he reached the high point of the trail, he shot downhill. The rear tire of his bike sprayed gravel, and the front tire bounced down the path. He picked up speed and whooped as he tore around a corner.

Suddenly, something jumped up in the path ahead of him. It was a black bear!

Dad jammed on the brakes. He left a long skid on the path behind him and slid to within 10 feet of the bear.

It stared right at him and growled.

Rising Action

Dialogue adds to the rising action.

"Easy . . . easy," Dad said. There would be no way to ride past the bear. Dad glanced back over his shoulder. If he tried to turn around, the bear would just chase him down.

The bear stepped toward my dad.

That's when Dad got off the bike and lifted it like a shield. "Take it easy. We're both scared." He took a step back. "I'll go this way, and you go that way."

The bear took another step forward.

Dad's heart pounded. He should have had a noisemaker on his bike to scare off bears. His life was on the line because of his own carelessness.

High Point
· · · · · · · · · · · ·
At the high point, the reader is most concerned about what will happen.

Lifting his bike overhead, Dad said in a deep voice, "Back, you! Back, bear!"

The bear stopped in its tracks and sniffed. Then it turned and ambled off into the woods.

Dad trembled as he lowered the mountain bike. His legs felt like jelly. He turned and walked his bike back up the trail. Just to make sure he scared off any other bears, he sang at the top of his lungs.

Ending
· · · · · · · · · · · ·
The ending tells how the person changed.

That close call got Dad's attention. From then on, he was less reckless in his extreme sports.

NARRATIVE

Respond to the reading. Answer the following questions about the biographical narrative.

☐ Ideas **(1) What details make the story come alive?**

☐ Organization **(2) How does the writer begin the story? (3) How does she organize the middle? (4) How does she end her narrative?**

☐ Voice & Word Choice **(5) What words or phrases show that the writer enjoys this story?**

Prewriting Selecting a Topic

Think about your favorite people: family members, friends, teachers, or even famous people. What stories do you know about them?

Sharese, the writer of the sample biographical narrative, used a line diagram to list her favorite people and stories about their lives.

Line Diagram

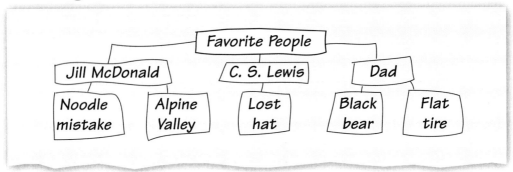

Choose your topic. Create your own line diagram. List favorite people and story ideas about their lives. Then choose the best story.

Gathering Details

To write a biographical narrative, you must learn as much as you can about the person's experience. Sharese used questions based on the 5 W's and H to interview her father.

5 W's and H List

1. *Who* was with you when you ran into the bear? *no one*
2. *What* did you do when you saw it? *skidded to a stop and held up my bike like a shield*
3. *Where* did this happen? *on a bike trail in the mountains*
4. *When* did it happen? *on a cool spring morning five years ago*
5. *Why* did it happen? *because I didn't carry a noisemaker*
6. *How* did the event change you? *was less reckless after that*

Use the 5 W's and H questions. If possible, interview the person you are writing about. Base your interview questions on the 5 W's and H.

Organizing Details

Narratives are usually organized by time. First one thing happens, and then another, and another, and so on. To organize her details, Sharese used a time line. Above the time line, she identified the most important actions. Below, she wrote details related to each action.

Time Line

Rode down trail	Met the bear	Used bike as shield	Shouted at bear
spraying gravel	skidded to a stop	heart pounded	turned back

Create a time line. Using the model above, organize the details of your biographical narrative in a time line.

Focus on the Traits

Organization The best narratives follow a pattern called a story line. The **beginning** grabs the reader's interest and starts the story. Next, **rising action** increases the excitement. The **high point** shares the story's most exciting part. Last of all, the **ending** wraps up the story.

Story Line

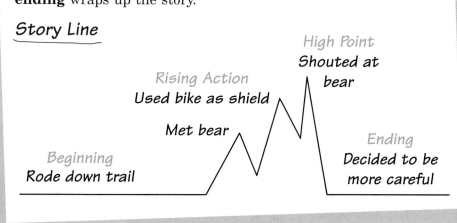

High Point
Shouted at bear

Rising Action
Used bike as shield

Met bear

Beginning
Rode down trail

Ending
Decided to be more careful

Writing Creating Your First Draft

Follow your time line as you write your first draft. Use the tips below to guide your writing.

Beginning Grab the reader's attention and start the story.

- **Begin with an interesting fact.** *My dad used to be a thrill seeker.*
- **Use a quotation.** *"I was careless the day I met a bear."*
- **Start in the middle of the action.** *My dad pumped the pedals of his mountain bike and climbed the gravel path.*

Middle Build the excitement in the narrative.

- **Be selective.** Tell only the important parts. Leave out anything that doesn't move the story along.
- **Use action and dialogue.** Show what happened and use dialogue.
- **Use sensory details.** Include sights, sounds, smells, textures, and tastes so that the reader can experience the story.
- **Build to a high point.** Use the action, dialogue, and sensory details to build to the most exciting part of the story.

Ending Bring your story to a close.

- **Describe the final action.** Write what happens after the high point.
- **Tell why the event was important.**
- **Focus on how it changed the person.**

Write the first draft. Use your time line from page 139 as a general writing guide but feel free to add new details as they come to mind. If you enjoy telling the story, your writing voice will be natural and interesting.

Revising **Improving Your Writing**

After you finish writing, set your narrative aside for a little while. When you are ready to revise, keep the following traits in mind.

- ☐ **Ideas** Add sensory details *(sights, sounds, smells, tastes, textures)* to parts that seem dull or unclear.

  > **The rear tire of his bike sprayed gravel, and the front tire bounced down the path.**

- ☐ **Organization** Check the time order of the action. Your story should flow from one action to the next.

  > **Dad jammed on the brakes. He left a long skid on the path behind him and slid to within 10 feet of the bear.**

- ☐ **Voice** Make sure the reader can "hear" your storytelling voice. Does it match how you feel at different parts in the story—excited, frightened, relieved, proud?

  > **My dad trembled as he lowered the mountain bike. His legs felt like jelly.**

- ☐ **Word Choice** Look for overused words that could be replaced by synonyms.

Overused	Lively
looked	glanced
pushed	jammed
walked very slowly	ambled

- ☐ **Sentence Fluency** Combine short, choppy sentences into longer sentences that flow smoothly.

Short, Choppy Sentences	Combined Sentence
The sun was shining. The air was brisk. People weren't yet crowding the high trails.	The sun was shining, the air was brisk, and people weren't yet crowding the high trails.

Revise your narrative. Add sights, sounds, smells, tastes, and textures. Rearrange any events that are out of order. Make sure your voice matches your feelings.

NARRATIVE

Editing Checking for Conventions

Once you have completed your revising, it's time to focus on editing your narrative. Keep the following trait in mind.

Conventions

Once your story sounds the way you want it to, check your punctuation, capitalization, spelling, and grammar. The following checklist can help you.

PUNCTUATION

_____ **1.** Do I use end punctuation after all my sentences?

_____ **2.** Do I use commas correctly?

_____ **3.** Do I use apostrophes to show possession *(boy's bike)*?

CAPITALIZATION

_____ **4.** Do I start all my sentences with capital letters?

_____ **5.** Do I capitalize all proper nouns?

SPELLING

_____ **6.** Have I spelled all my words correctly?

GRAMMAR

_____ **7.** Do I use correct forms of verbs *(had gone,* not *had went)*?

_____ **8.** Do my subjects and verbs agree in number?
(She and I *were* going, not She and I *was* going.)

_____ **9.** Do I use the right words *(to, too,* and *two)*?

Edit your biographical narrative. Make sure your words are lively and your sentences flow smoothly. Also proofread your narrative after writing a final copy.

Publishing Sharing Your Writing

Narratives are meant for sharing. They help us connect with people around us—friends, family members, and classmates.

Share your biographical narrative. Read your narrative to as many audiences as possible. You'll see how narratives bring people together.

Narrative Writing
Across the Curriculum

Writing narratives is a common activity in every one of your classes. For example, in social studies you may be asked to write journal entries or keep class minutes. In math, you may be asked to write story problems. In science class, you may be asked to connect a personal experience to a scientific concept.

To write strong narratives, no matter what the class, you must learn as much as you can about your topic and share the key details about it. If everything works out, your writing will help your readers understand as much as you do about your topic.

What's Ahead

- **Social Studies**: Writing Classroom Journals
- **Math**: Writing Story Problems
- **Science**: Writing an Anecdote
- **Practical Writing**: Recording Class Minutes

Social Studies: Writing Classroom Journals

Writing in a classroom journal can help you learn. When you write about what happens in class, you remember details better and gain a deeper understanding of the subject. The following journal entries are from a social studies class.

The date is given first.

The student reflects on events in class.

The student records details learned in class.

Monday, October 19: Today Mr. Henry showed us a video about Mexico City. It's huge! I thought New York City was big, but Mexico City has millions more people. It's the biggest city in the world.

The coolest part of the video showed the Plaza of the Three Cultures. It has ruins of an Aztec temple. Those ruins are 600 years old!

After the video, Mr. Henry told us what happened at the plaza. He said that on one day in 1521, the Aztecs and Cortez had a battle, and 40,000 Aztecs died. What a horrible day! Still, that was the beginning of Mexico.

Tuesday, October 20: Today Mr. Henry passed around postcards from his trip to Mexico. There sure are lots of beautiful places.

The most amazing pictures were from Chichen Itza. It's an ancient Mayan city. It has a gigantic pyramid called the Great Pyramid. The Mayans lived near it 1,300 years ago.

Writing Tips

Before you write . . .

- **Set up your journal.**
  Designate part of a notebook for your journal and also make sure to follow your teacher's guidelines.

During your writing . . .

- **Record the date.**
  Write the date of each journal entry.
- **React to what you are learning.**
  Record the most important facts. Also write your thoughts and any experiences that relate to the information you are studying.
- **Include sketches.**
  Make a sketch in your journal if your teacher shows you a picture of something interesting. Also copy and label any important diagrams. Pictures can help you remember as you look back at your journal.

The Great Pyramid

After you've written a first draft . . .

- **Reread your work.**
  Read the journal to help you remember what you're learning in class.
- **Review your journal for essay ideas.**
  Look through your journal whenever you need writing ideas.

NARRATIVE

 Write a journal entry about something you learned in social studies class. Remember to record the facts but also include your thoughts and feelings about them.

Math: Writing Story Problems

One way to create a story problem is to base it on a familiar fable, fairy tale, or nursery rhyme. In his math class, Alex wrote a story problem based on one of Aesop's fables.

The **beginning** summarizes the story.

The **middle** gives the variables, the problem to solve, and the story problem.

The **ending** shows the solution.

The Ant and the Grasshopper

One fine winter day, an ant was drying grain that he had collected in the summer. A hungry grasshopper came begging for food. The ant asked, "Why didn't you store food during the summer?" He replied, "I spent the summer singing." The ant said, "If you sing all summer, you go hungry in the winter."

Math Variables: Each day an ant
- gathers 6 grams of food, and
- eats 2 grams of food.

Problem to Solve: How many days must an ant work to gather enough food for a year?

Story Problem: An ant eats 2 grams of food every day of the year. He can gather 6 grams each day. How many days must he work to gather a year's supply of food?

1. First, find out how many grams of food the ant eats in a year. ($365 \times 2 = 730$ grams of food eaten in one year)
2. Then find out how many days it will take to gather 730 grams of food. ($730 \div 6 = 121.6$ days needed to collect the food)

Solution: The ant needs to work 121.6 days to gather enough food for a year.

NARRATIVE

Writing Tips

Before you write . . .

- Find a short fable, fairy tale, or nursery rhyme.
- Read the story and think of how you can include math variables. For example, the rates of speed could be one variable in the fable of the tortoise and the hare.

During your writing . . .

- Prepare a summary of the story.
- List the math variables.
- State the problem to be solved.
- Write the story problem.
- Explain each step that is used to solve the problem.

After you've written a first draft . . .

- Make sure your story summary and story problem are clear.
- Check your answer.
- Get a classmate to try to solve your problem.
- Check your writing for conventions.

 Write a story problem and solution using the following fable, math variables, and problem to solve. Revise and edit carefully.

Summary of story:

The Crow and the Pitcher

A thirsty crow saw a pitcher and flew to it. The pitcher contained so little water that the crow could not reach it. He flew off, brought back a stone, and dropped it in. One by one, the stones raised the water until the crow could finally take a drink.

Math variables:

- The pitcher contains 3 inches of water.
- Each stone will raise the water 5/8 of an inch.

Problem to solve: How many stones must the crow drop to raise the water level up to 8 inches?

Science: Writing an Anecdote

When you write an anecdote, you tell a brief story to help make an idea clearer. This type of writing is helpful for learning scientific ideas. In the sample below, a student used a personal experience to help explain the concept of buoyancy. (Also see page 558.)

The **beginning** paragraph sets up the story.

The **middle** explains the scientific concept and illustrates it.

The **ending** reflects on the story.

Oh, Buoyancy!

When Ms. Allard started teaching us about buoyancy, everybody said, "Huh?" Well, I understood right away because of my adventure in a canoe.

My sister Sarah took me canoeing, and I accidentally tipped over the boat. We flipped into the water, but our life jackets popped us up. Unfortunately, the metal canoe sank.

"Oh no! The canoe!" I shouted.

Sarah just laughed. "It'll come back up."

Sure enough, even though it was full of water, that metal canoe rose to the surface. "How did it do that?"

"It has buoyancy material in each end," Sarah said. "It's foam, like our life jackets."

We dumped out as much water as we could. Then we started bailing.

"Each time we throw a gallon of water out of the boat, the boat rises by a gallon."

"I get it. As the canoe weighs less, it sits higher."

"Right. That's buoyancy."

After that day, I'll always understand buoyancy. It's just too bad we had to get all wet in the process.

Writing Tips

Before you write . . .

- **Select a story that illustrates an idea or a concept.**
  Think about how the things you are learning in science relate to your everyday experiences. For example, when you're outside, have you ever noticed that frost sometimes remains in a shaded spot but has evaporated in the sunlit areas? That experience tells you something about freezing and evaporation.
- **Get your science facts correct.**
  Check into the scientific facts behind your story.

During your writing . . .

- **Let the story tell itself.**
  Have fun writing your story so the reader will have fun reading it.
- **Be clear and direct.**
  Make your explanation of the idea or concept as simple and clear as possible.

After you've written a first draft . . .

- **Revise your first draft.**
  Make sure that your story is complete, easy to follow, and interesting.
- **Check for accuracy.**
  Double-check your facts and details.
- **Edit for correctness.**
  Check for punctuation, spelling, capitalization, and grammar errors.

NARRATIVE

Think of an experience you have had that illustrates a principle of science. Use that experience and write an anecdote to help your classmates understand the concept.

Practical Writing: Recording Class Minutes

Class minutes tell the story of what happened in class. They can remind you about important information and help an absent classmate catch up. The following minutes were taken in a social studies class.

The **beginning** states the class information.

Social Studies, Third Period
Tuesday, November 17, 2009

<u>Absent</u>: Laura Parker and José Velasquez

<u>Topic</u>: Mississippi Mound Builders

<u>Handout</u>: Ms. Lindell handed out a fact sheet on mound builders (attached). She pointed out two things:
1. Mississippi Mound Builders built large mounds as temples, burial sites, and bases for government.
2. This culture lasted for 1,000 years, from 700 to 1700.

The **middle** identifies each activity in the order it happened.

<u>Video</u>: Ms. Lindell showed a video about Cahokia, IL.
1. Monk's Mound is 100 feet tall.
2. More than 100 other mounds are near Cahokia.
3. This was once a society of 40,000 people.
4. Builders hauled baskets of dirt on their backs.

<u>Discussion</u>: Ms. Lindell stressed two things:
1. The cities had complex government and trade.
2. Most mound builders died in the 1500s because of diseases from Europe.

The **ending** lists the assignment.

<u>Assignment</u>: Ms. Lindell had the class write journal entries about mound builders.

Writing Tips

Before you write . . .

- **Check the format.**
  Follow your teacher's guidelines for class minutes or use the model on page 150 as a guide.

During your writing . . .

- **Record the basic class information.**
  Make sure you note the day's topic and the students who are absent.
- **Be brief.**
  Write your minutes so that a reader can quickly tell what happened in class.
- **Write down the key points.**
  Consider what an absent person needs to know to keep up. Don't write down everything, but listen carefully to find out what the teacher considers most important.
- **Write neatly.**
  Make sure everyone can read your writing.

After you've written a first draft . . .

- **Double-check activities and assignments.**
  Make sure your information is complete. Ask a classmate to review the minutes to see if you missed anything.
- **Edit and proofread the minutes.**
  Correct any errors in your minutes. Other students may depend on them for makeup work, so it's important to be accurate.

NARRATIVE

 For class minutes in any subject area, follow the writing tips above. Record only the most important facts and examples.

Narrative Writing

Writing for Assessment

Many state and school writing tests ask you to write a response to a narrative prompt. A narrative prompt asks you to recall a personal experience or respond to a "what if" question. Study the following sample prompt and student response.

Narrative Prompt

Choose a day in your life that you would like to live over again. Would you like it to be the same or different? Write a story about what you would do on that day.

The **beginning** states the focus of the narrative (underlined).

"Tony, this is the last time that I'm going to tell you to get up and get ready for school." I hardly heard those words before falling back to sleep. This was a big mistake. If I could live yesterday over again, I would want it to be different, especially at the start.

Each **middle** paragraph covers one main point.

Most importantly, I would get out of bed early enough to make it to school on time. Then I'd be there to hear my math teacher go over the assignment instead of sitting in the principal's office. And I need all the help I can get in math.

have kept me from getting grouchy. Then I wouldn't have acted so stupid when I got home.

After school, I wouldn't have slammed our front door and blamed my mother for my bad day. I wouldn't have been sent to my room for being snotty. Instead, I would have relaxed and watched TV for a while before supper.

The **ending** paragraph reflects on the experience.

Yesterday could have easily been a better day, but I can't live my life over. I was surprised how much better it felt to get up right away this morning, have a good breakfast, and leave for school on time with a lunch in my hand. My mother felt much better about everything, too.

NARRATIVE

Respond to the reading. Answer the following questions about the sample response.

☐ **Ideas** **(1)** What is the focus of the writer's response? **(2)** How does the focus relate to the prompt? **(3)** What are some of the key details in the writing?

☐ **Organization** **(4)** How is the response organized?

☐ **Voice & Word Choice** **(5)** Do the writer's feelings come through in this writing? Give examples.

Writing Tips

Use the following tips as a guide when responding to a narrative writing prompt.

Before you write . . .

● **Understand the prompt.**
  Remember that a narrative prompt asks you to tell a story.
● **Plan your time wisely.**
  Take several minutes to plan your writing. Use a graphic organizer like a time line to help with planning your writing.

Time Line

Time Line
① ─┼─────
② ─┼─────
③ ─┼─────
④ ─┼─────
⑤ ─┼─────

During your writing . . .

● **Decide on a focus for your narrative.**
  Use key words from the prompt in your focus statement.
● **Be selective.**
  Tell only the main events in your story.
● **End in a meaningful way.**
  Reflect on the experience or story.

After you've written a first draft . . .

● **Check for completeness and correctness.**
  Present the events of your story in order. Delete any unneeded details and correct any errors as neatly as possible.

Narrative Prompts

■ One morning you open your front door, and there's a large package sitting outside. What's in it? Who put it there? What do you do with it? Write a story about the package.

■ Tell the story about the nicest thing you've ever done for someone else.

Plan and write a response. Respond to one of the prompts listed above. Complete your writing within the time limit your teacher sets. Afterward, list one part you like and one part you could improve.

Narrative Writing in Review

Purpose: In narrative writing, you *tell a story* about something that has happened.

Topics: An experience you have had
An event from someone else's life

Prewriting

Select a topic from your own life or interview other people about an episode in their lives. (See page 102.)

Size up your idea using the 5 W's to see if it will make a good personal narrative. (See page 103.)

Gather important details about the people involved and the order of events. List sensory details to use in the narrative. (See pages 103–106.)

Writing

In the beginning part, catch the reader's interest and introduce your story. (See page 109.)

In the middle part, tell the events of the story. Use sensory details and dialogue. Use your own words and show your feelings throughout the story. Bring the story to a high point. (See pages 110–111.)

In the ending, tell why the event was important, tell how it changed the people involved, or relate the experience to your audience. (See page 112.)

Revising

Review the ideas, organization, and voice first. Then check **word choice** and **sentence fluency.** (See pages 114–124.)

Editing

Check your writing for conventions. Review punctuation of dialogue. Ask a friend to edit the writing, too. (See pages 126–128.)

Make a final copy and proofread it for errors before sharing it with other people. (See page 129.)

Assessing

Use the narrative rubric to assess your finished writing. (See pages 130–131.)

NARRATIVE

describe

define

Expository Writing

solve

explain

inform

Expository Writing

Expository Paragraph

What can you do really well? Can you shoot a free throw or kick a soccer ball? Do you know how to wash a dog, make an omelet, or calculate the lowest common denominator? Think about what you know how to do and how you could explain it to someone else.

Writing that explains things is called *expository* writing. Most essays, reports, and newspaper articles are examples of expository writing. In each case, the writer knows something that he or she wants to explain to the reader.

In this chapter, you will write an expository paragraph about something you know how to do. You will become the teacher, sharing your knowledge with your classmates.

Writing Guidelines

Subject:	Something you know how to do
Form:	Expository paragraph
Purpose:	To share knowledge
Audience:	Classmates

Expository Paragraph

The expository paragraph is a basic form of writing. It almost always begins with a **topic sentence**, which tells the reader what the paragraph is about. The sentences in the **body** explain or support the topic sentence, and the **closing sentence** wraps up the paragraph. The paragraph below was written by a student who likes to cook her own breakfast.

Topic Sentence

Body

Closing Sentence

How to Make an Omelet

Anyone can make a delicious omelet, even if a person has never cooked before. For tools, all an omelet maker needs are a bowl, a hand beater, a frying pan, and a spatula. For ingredients, he or she needs two eggs, two tablespoons of milk, a quarter cup of grated cheese, a little salt and pepper, and a pat of butter. Then the person should follow these steps. First, break the eggs into a bowl and add the milk, salt, and pepper. Second, mix everything with the beater until it is foamy. Next, heat the frying pan and add the butter. Make sure the melted butter covers the whole bottom of the pan. When the butter begins to sizzle, pour the egg mixture into the pan and sprinkle the cheese over it. Let it cook until the eggs get firm around the edges. Then use the spatula to flip half of the omelet over the other half, like a taco. Give it another minute or so to melt the cheese and finish cooking the eggs. Finally, slide the omelet onto a plate to be enjoyed!

Respond to the reading. On your own paper, answer each of the following questions.

☐ Ideas **(1) What is the topic of the paragraph?**

☐ Organization **(2) How did the writer organize details in the paragraph (time order or order of importance)? Explain.**

☐ Voice & Word Choice **(3) What words or ideas show you that the writer is really interested in the topic?**

Prewriting Selecting a Topic

When it comes to choosing a topic, think of things you know how to do. Can you bunt a baseball? Do you know how to draw cartoons or care for a pet? Have you ever set up a tent or built a fort?

The writer of the sample paragraph on page 158 brainstormed a list of "Things I Know How to Do."

Brainstorm List

Things I Know How to Do

fix a flat tire	whistle	make balloon animals
make an omelet	knit	do a French braid
study for a test	juggle	play trombone

Brainstorm and select a topic. Using the list above as a guide, make your own list of things you know how to do. Then choose one that really interests you, one you could explain in a paragraph.

Writing a Topic Sentence

Write a sentence that tells the reader what your how-to paragraph will be about. A good topic sentence does two things: (1) It names the topic, and (2) it states your feelings about it. Here is a simple formula for writing good topic sentences:

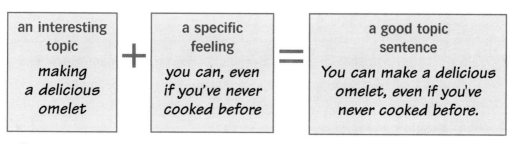

an interesting topic		a specific feeling		a good topic sentence
making a delicious omelet	+	you can, even if you've never cooked before	=	You can make a delicious omelet, even if you've never cooked before.

Write your topic sentence. Write a topic sentence for your paragraph. Use the basic formula shown above. You may have to try a couple of times before your sentence says exactly what you want it to say.

Writing Creating Your First Draft

When you write a first draft, your goal is to get all your ideas and details down on paper. Follow the suggestions below.

- Start with your topic sentence.
- Arrange the how-to steps in the correct order.
- End with a closing sentence that wraps up the instructions and shows your enthusiasm for the topic.

 Write your first draft. Try to get all of the important information down on paper, including the materials needed and the steps to follow.

Revising Improving Your Paragraph

When you revise your first draft, consider the effectiveness of the *ideas, organization, voice, word choice,* and *sentence fluency* in your paragraph.

 Review and revise your paragraph. Use the following questions as a guide when you revise.

1 Is my topic sentence clear?

2 Have I clearly explained all the steps in the correct order?

3 Do I sound interested in the topic?

4 Do I use specific nouns and action verbs?

5 Do I write complete sentences that read smoothly?

Editing Checking for Conventions

Carefully edit your revised paragraph for conventions.

 Edit your work. Use the following questions to check your paragraph.

1 Do I use correct punctuation, capitalization, and spelling?

2 Do I use correct word usage and grammar?

3 Have I checked the words my spell checker may have missed?

Proofread your paragraph. After making a final copy of your how-to paragraph, check it one more time for errors.

Expository Writing

Explaining a Process

How do you make spaghetti? How do you find the secret passage to the next level of your favorite video game? How do you skateboard or snowboard? The answers to questions like these may involve several steps. When you explain how to do or make something in an essay, you are doing expository writing.

In this chapter, you will write an expository essay. Your how-to essay should tell readers exactly what materials they will need and what steps they should follow. You will do your best writing if you choose a topic you care about—something you do well or enjoy doing.

Writing Guidelines

Subject: Something you know how to do or make

Form: How-to essay

Purpose: To explain how to do or make something

Audience: Classmates

Understanding Your Goal

Your goal in this chapter is to write a well-organized, interesting essay that explains how to do or make something. The traits listed in the chart below will help you plan and write your how-to essay.

Traits of Expository Writing

Ideas

Select an interesting how-to topic, write a clear focus statement, and cover all the steps in the process.

Organization

Include an interesting beginning, a middle that explains all the steps, and a clear ending. Use transitions to help you organize.

Voice

Use an informative, confident voice that fits the audience.

Word Choice

Choose words such as specific nouns and specific action verbs that will make your essay informative.

Sentence Fluency

Make sure your sentences are complete and that they read smoothly.

Conventions

Check your essay for correct punctuation, capitalization, spelling, and grammar.

 Get the big picture. Look at the rubric on pages 194–195. You can use this rubric to assess your progress. Your goal is to write an informative essay about how to do or make something.

Expository Essay

In the following expository essay, Lamarr explains how to give a dog a bath—step-by-step.

How to Give a Dog a Bath

Beginning

Beginning

The beginning introduces the topic and presents the focus statement (underlined).

If you or any of your friends have a dog, you know how much fun a pet can be. You also know that a dog can be a lot of work, especially if he is very active. It doesn't take long for a high-energy dog to look a mess and smell even worse. When that happens, it's time to gather up the dog shampoo and conditioner and freshen up your dog. If you follow these steps, bathing your dog can be easy and enjoyable.

To begin, get the bath ready and gather what you need. Use a nylon collar and leash (leather gets ruined by water) to control your dog during the bath. Your dog also needs something to stand on so he won't slip. A bath mat or towel will make him feel secure. Make sure the water is warm. Water that is too hot can burn a dog's skin. Cold water—especially from an outside hose—may scare your dog and send him running. Next, you'll need a way to get water all over your dog. A shower hose is the easiest method, but a plastic bucket can work well, too. You'll also need a special dog shampoo and conditioner because human shampoo is too strong for dogs. Of course, you'll need some big towels for the end of the bath.

Middle

The middle paragraphs include materials needed and provide a step-by-step explanation.

To continue, begin bathing your dog. Get your dog nice and wet. Then use enough shampoo to make a foamy lather on his coat. Talk to your dog all the time to help him relax.

EXPOSITORY

Middle
The middle paragraphs also provide important supporting details.

Ending
The ending offers some final thoughts.

Try to keep soapy water out of his eyes and ears. Then rinse your dog with fresh, warm water until his coat is shiny and free of soap. After that, you can rub some conditioner into his coat.

To finish, dry your dog as completely as possible. Use big towels and give your dog a complete rubdown. Dogs love this part! However, watch out because wet dogs like to shake. If you choose to use a hair dryer to dry your dog, keep it moving because holding it over one area too long could burn his skin. If you are outside, you'll discover that dogs like to roll when they're wet. After your dog shakes himself, play tag with him or offer him a chew treat—anything to keep him from rolling in the dirt!

If you treat your dog calmly and gently, giving him a bath should be fun. Dogs that get used to taking baths learn to enjoy them. Remember, whenever your dog starts smelling too doggy, it's time to gather your supplies and wash him until he's clean and huggable again.

Respond to the reading. After reading the sample essay, answer the following questions to discover how to use four important traits in your writing.

☐ **Ideas** (1) How does the writer get your attention?

☐ **Organization** (2) Is the essay organized by order of importance, time order, or order of location?

☐ **Voice & Word Choice** (3) List words and phrases that show the writer cares about the topic.

Prewriting

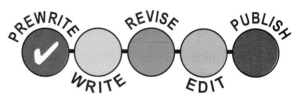

Prewriting is the first step in the writing process. It involves selecting a topic, gathering specific details, and organizing your ideas.

Keys to Effective Prewriting

1. Select a topic that you know well and want to write about.

2. Write a focus statement that clearly states the main idea of the essay.

3. Gather details that will make your explanation clear and interesting.

4. Organize your details using a cluster, chart, or gathering grid.

5. Use a list or an outline as a planning guide.

EXPOSITORY

PROD. NO.
SCENE   TAKE   ROLL
SOUND

Prewriting Selecting a Topic

The purpose of your essay is to explain how to do or make something. However, your essay should be more than just a list of directions. ("First, do this. Then, do this.") You also need to include details that will interest and inform the reader.

First, you need to think about things you know how to do or make. Making a cluster or web diagram like Soledad's below is one way to gather ideas for writing topics.

Cluster

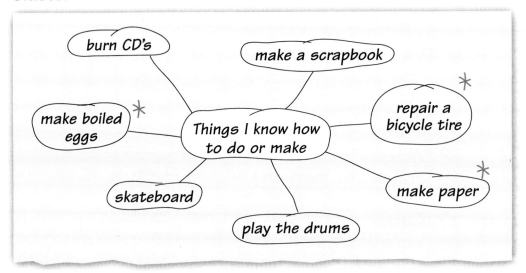

 Create your own cluster. Start your cluster with "Things I know how to do or make." List as many ideas as you can. Then put a star (✱) next to two or three of your favorite topics.

Focus on the Traits

Ideas You need a topic that has enough steps and details to keep your audience interested. You also need to understand the activity well enough to explain it clearly. Consider a topic that is especially fun, challenging, or unusual.

Sizing Up Your Topic

You will want to select a how-to topic that is just the right size—not too narrow and not too broad. Making a list of the steps can help you choose the right topic.

If you look at Soledad's lists below, you'll see that "Repairing a bicycle tire" may be too broad or complicated, while "Making boiled eggs" may be too narrow. "Making paper," however, has about the right number of steps.

Lists

Making boiled eggs
- *Put eggs in pot of water*
- *Bring to a boil*
- *Cover, shut off heat*
- *Let sit 15 minutes*

Making paper
- *Tear up newspaper*
- *Blend with water*
- *Pour pulp into a pan*
- *Strain pulp*
- *Tip onto felt*
- *Roll pulp between felt pieces*
- *Hang paper to dry*

Repairing a bicycle tire
- *Remove nails or glass*
- *Remove the wheel*
- *Push valve stem inside*
- *Pry tire edge over the rim*
- *Work the inner tube out*
- *Clean the puncture area*
- *Apply glue and let dry*
- *Press the patch over the puncture*
- *Pull the tube back into place*
- *Inflate the tube a little*
- *Work the tire into place*

Prewrite

Size up your topic. On your own paper, write the two or three starred topics from your cluster (page 166). Beneath each topic, list each of the necessary steps. Then ask yourself these questions about each topic:

1 Did I include all the necessary steps?

2 Is this topic too narrow? Too broad? About right?

3 Does the topic include interesting steps?

Choose your topic. After evaluating your topics, choose the best one.

Prewriting **Writing a Focus Statement**

Writing a focus (thesis) statement helps you explain the main idea of the essay and shows exactly what you will cover in your how-to essay.

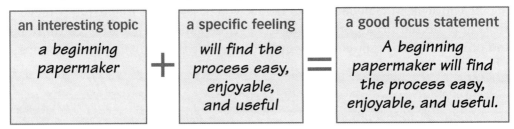

an interesting topic		a specific feeling		a good focus statement
a beginning papermaker	**+**	*will find the process easy, enjoyable, and useful*	**=**	*A beginning papermaker will find the process easy, enjoyable, and useful.*

Write your focus statement. Use the formula above to write your focus statement. Make sure you include a specific feeling about the topic.

Gathering and Sorting Details

The following chart lists the materials and steps needed to make paper.

Chart

Topic	Materials Needed	Steps
How to make paper	– old newspapers – blender and water – pan – piece of wire screen – two pieces of felt – rolling pin	*To begin* – Tear up newspaper – Mix with water *To continue* – Pour pulp into a pan – Strain pulp *To finish* – Tip onto piece of felt

Gather and sort your details. Create a chart like the one above for your own topic. Organize the "steps" under three headings: "To begin," "To continue," and "To finish."

Focus on the Traits

Organization Graphic organizers like the one above can help you organize the steps in your process. Also see page 170.

Planning Your Paragraphs

When you listed the steps for your how-to essay, you organized them into three parts: how the activity begins, how it continues, and how it ends. Each part can become a middle paragraph in your essay. For each middle paragraph, you will need to write a topic sentence.

Writing Topic Sentences

Each of your topic sentences can start with one of the following phrases: *to begin, to continue, to finish*. Then complete the sentence by telling what steps or information the paragraph will cover. Here are the topic sentences for the middle paragraphs in the essay on pages 163–164. Each one covers a different part of the dog-washing process.

■ ***To begin,*** get the bath ready and gather what you need.

■ ***To continue,*** begin bathing your dog.

■ ***To finish,*** dry your dog as completely as possible.

 Prewrite

Write your topic sentences. Use the steps you listed (page 168) and the points below to help you write these sentences.

1 What information is covered first?
Topic sentence: To begin,

2 What information is covered next?
Topic sentence: To continue,

3 What information is covered last?
Topic sentence: To finish,

EXPOSITORY

Focus on the Traits

Voice If you watch how-to shows on TV, you'll notice that the cooks or builders do more than just go through the steps one by one. They often talk about how they got involved in the project or why they enjoy it. This helps viewers stay interested. Sharing similar details in your writing will create a personal voice and keep the reader interested.

Prewriting Organizing Your Ideas

You next need to put these pieces of your essay in the best order. Below is an *organized list* for Soledad's essay. She used the directions to create her *organized list* of steps and topic sentences for her essay.

Directions   Organized List

Write your focus statement.

A beginning papermaker will find the process easy, enjoyable, and useful.

Write your first topic sentence.

1. *To begin, prepare the paper pulp.*

List any steps.

   - *Tear up paper*
   - *Put water in blender*
   - *Add shredded paper*
   - *Blend paper and water*

Write your second topic sentence.

2. *To continue, work with the pulp.*

List any steps.

   - *Pour into pan with clean water*
   - *Stir gently and cover screen*
   - *Lift screen to drain*

Write your third topic sentence.

3. *To finish, press the paper after it has drained.*

List any steps.

   - *Remove paper from screen*
   - *Squeeze out extra water*
   - *Hang to dry*

Make an organized list. To create your list, follow the directions above. You will use this list when you write your essay.

Writing

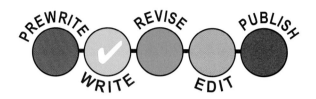

Once you've finished your prewriting, it's time to write your first draft. You're ready to write a first draft when you know enough about your topic and have written a clear focus statement.

Keys to Effective Writing

1. Use your organized list as a planning guide.

2. Get all your ideas on paper in your first draft.

3. Write on every other line for later changes.

4. Use a clear topic sentence for each paragraph.

5. Add clear, step-by-step details.

6. Use transitions to tie everything together.

EXPOSITORY

Writing Getting the Big Picture

The chart below shows how the parts of a how-to essay fit together. (The examples are from the sample essay on pages 173–176.) You're ready to write your essay once you . . .

- know enough about the steps in the process.
- state your topic in a clear focus statement.
- plan your paragraphs and write your topic sentences.

Beginning

The **beginning** introduces the topic and tells why the activity is important or interesting. It also gives the focus statement.

Focus Statement
After a few tries, I found that making paper is fun, easy, and useful.

Middle

The **middle** gives all the how-to information and a step-by-step explanation.

Three Topic Sentences
To begin, prepare the paper pulp.

To continue, work with the pulp.

To finish, press the paper after it has drained.

Ending

The **ending** may summarize the process and offer some final thoughts.

Closing Sentences
So have some fun, be creative, and save a tree. Give papermaking a try!

Starting Your Essay

In the first part of your expository essay, you should introduce the topic, say something interesting or fun about it, and state your focus.

You can also add voice to your essay if you begin with a personal story.

> Beginning
>
> Middle
>
> Ending

- **Share how you became interested in this process.**
- **Tell how you first learned this process.**
- **Show why the reader may like the activity.**

Beginning Paragraph

In the paragraph below, Soledad uses a story to capture the reader's attention. The focus statement gives the main idea of the essay—making paper is fun, easy, and useful.

The writer's interest is explained.

Materials are listed.

The focus statement is given (underlined).

> *On a class trip to the Natural History Museum, I saw paper that had been made by ancient Egyptians. It was beautiful, and I wondered if I could make paper, too. I discovered that if you want to make paper, you need the following items: old newspapers, a piece of wire screen, a bucket or pan, two pieces of felt, a rolling pin, a blender, and some water. After a few tries, I found that making paper is fun, easy, and useful.*

EXPOSITORY

Write your beginning paragraph. When you write your beginning paragraph, do the following three things:

1. Introduce your topic in an interesting way.
2. Include a clear focus statement.
3. Lead into your first middle paragraph.

Writing Developing the Middle Part

In the middle paragraphs of your how-to essay, you must explain the process step-by-step. Each paragraph should cover one main part of the process (1, 2, and 3 in your organized list from page 170). Look at how the steps are handled in the middle paragraphs on these two pages.

Beginning

Middle

Ending

Connecting Your Sentences

The following transitions can be used to connect sentences and to show chronological or time order in a how-to essay.

First	One	First of all	One way	To begin
Second	Then	Next	Another way	To continue
Third	Another	Finally	A third way	To finish

Remember: The last sentence of each paragraph should get the reader ready to move on to the next part of the process.

Middle Paragraphs

In the three middle paragraphs that follow, the underlined transitions help connect the sentences. The transitions move the reader from one step to the next.

Topic Sentence 1

Specific steps and details linked with transitions (underlined)

To begin, prepare the paper pulp. You can make pulp from newspapers, brown paper bags, magazine pages, or just about any other kind of paper. <u>First</u>, tear the paper into small strips. <u>Then</u>, pour two cups of water into the blender. <u>Next</u>, sprinkle in a few handfuls of the shredded paper. <u>Finally</u>, cover the blender, press the medium-speed button, and blend for a few seconds. When the mixture in the blender looks like thick potato soup, your paper pulp is ready.

Topic Sentence 2

Transitions (underlined)

     To continue, work with the pulp. Pour it into a flat pan with clean water and a piece of wire screen in it. <u>Now</u> is the time to add fun things like grass, flower petals, or glitter. <u>During this step,</u> keep the pulp from settling on the bottom by stirring it gently. <u>After that,</u> move the screen around so that the paper pulp settles onto it. Cover the screen as evenly as possible. <u>Then,</u> slowly lift it out of the water and let the water drain.

Topic Sentence 3

     To finish, press the paper after it has drained. Turn your paper-covered screen over onto one of the pieces of felt. The paper should fall off the screen easily. If it doesn't, just tap the back of the screen. <u>Next,</u> put the other piece of felt on top of the paper. Roll the rolling pin over the top layer of felt to squeeze out all the extra water. <u>Finally,</u> remove the damp paper from between the pieces of felt and hang it in a sunny place. In about three hours, you will have a sheet of paper.

EXPOSITORY

Write

Write your middle paragraphs. Using your organized list from page 170, write your middle paragraphs. Follow the "Drafting Tips" below.

Drafting Tips

- **If you have trouble getting started,** try writing as if you were talking to a friend about your topic.
- **If you have trouble continuing with your writing**, write for 3- to 5-minute spans with breaks in between. See what happens.

Writing **Ending Your Essay**

After you've explained all the steps, you may end your essay by summarizing the process and making some final comments about your topic. Your ending may also encourage the reader to try the activity.

Beginning

Middle

Ending

Ending Paragraph

End with an invitation to try the activity.

> *Papermaking is an easy, inexpensive hobby that is lots of fun. Your friends and family will love to get notes and cards on your homemade paper. You can also feel proud that you are helping to save trees by recycling paper. So have some fun, be creative, and save a tree. Give papermaking a try!*

Try It Read the three sets of final sentences below. Which one of these three endings do you think works the best? Why?

1. So have some fun, be creative, and save a tree. Give papermaking a try!

2. This recycling of paper creates more ideas. Besides that, you'll enjoy wrapping gifts or covering school books with your paper.

3. I, like the ancient Egyptians, can now make beautiful paper.

Write

Write your ending. Now write an ending for your essay that includes some final thoughts about the process. Encourage the reader to try it.

Form a complete first draft. Write a complete copy of your essay. Write on every other line to make room for your revising changes.

Revising

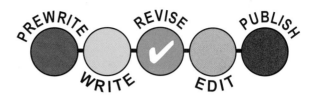

A first draft never turns out just right. One part may need more details. Another part may not be clear enough. To fix or improve these parts, you need to revise your first draft.

Keys to Effective Revising

1. Read through your entire draft to get a feeling of how well your essay works.

2. Make sure your focus statement states your topic clearly.

3. Check your paragraphs to make sure the steps and details are clear and in the right order.

4. Your essay should have a personal, yet confident voice.

5. Check your words and sentences.

6. Use the editing and proofreading marks inside the back cover of this book.

EXPOSITORY

Revising for Ideas

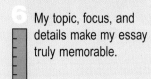 My topic, focus, and details make my essay truly memorable.

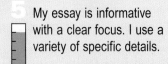 My essay is informative with a clear focus. I use a variety of specific details.

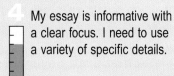 My essay is informative with a clear focus. I need to use a variety of specific details.

When you revise your essay for *ideas,* you check for these things: that your topic is the right size, your focus statement is clear, and your supporting details are specific. The rubric strip above will help guide you.

How can I add variety to my details?

You can improve your how-to essay by adding personal details. Here are three types of personal details and a chart prepared by the student who wrote the essay about making paper.

1. **Memory details** include personal memories about what happened as you learned to do or make something. The details might include how you became interested in the topic or the mistakes you made as you first learned the process.

2. **Reflective details** include personal thoughts about the process and why it is important to you.

3. **Sensory details** include descriptions of what the activity looks, feels, tastes, smells, or sounds like.

Memory details	Reflective details	Sensory details
I saw Egyptian paper in a museum. Once I added glitter.	I like recycling. People like notes on handmade paper.	Pulp looks like potato soup. It smells like a wet dog.

Revise

Check your details. Make a chart like the one above for your topic.

1 Write the three types of details across the top.

2 Then list several specific details under each type.

3 Checkmark any details that could make your essay more interesting.

My focus needs to be clearer. I need more specific details.

 I need to narrow or expand my topic, and I need many more specific details.

I need to select a new topic and gather a variety of specific details.

Are my details specific enough?

If your details paint a clear, vivid picture for your reader, they are specific enough. If your details are general and not very interesting, you need to make them more colorful. Using specific details makes the process easier to understand.

> **General Detail**
>
> **Next, add some paper.** *(How do you add it? How much? What kind?)*
>
> **Specific Detail**
>
> **Next,** sprinkle in a few handfuls of the shredded **paper.**

 Read the sentences below about making a sandwich. Rewrite the sentences, adding details that will make the process clearer and more complete. (To think of specific details, ask questions such as *what kind? how much?* and *how?*)

Take some bread. Put peanut butter and jelly on it.

 Review your writing. Look for places in your essay that need specific details. Have a partner read your essay and point out any parts that are unclear or incomplete. Add specific details wherever they are needed.

EXPOSITORY

Ideas
Specific details are added.

To begin, prepare the paper pulp. You can make
newspapers, brown paper bags, magazine pages, or
pulp from just about any other kind of paper. First,
tear the paper into small strips. Then, pour two cups
of water into the blender. Next, sprinkle in a few. . .

Revising for Organization

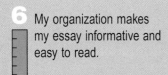

6 My organization makes my essay informative and easy to read.

5 My beginning interests the reader. The middle supports the focus. The ending works well, and I use transitions.

4 My essay is divided into a beginning, a middle, and an ending. I use some transitions.

When you revise for *organization,* check to see if your thoughts are organized into three main parts: a beginning, a middle, and an ending. Also check your transitions. Use the rubric strip above as a guide.

How do I check my overall organization?

You can check the overall organization of your how-to essay by making sure the details in each paragraph are in the right place. Use the chart below.

Beginning Paragraph	The **focus statement** states your topic. It belongs somewhere in the opening paragraph.

Middle Paragraphs	The **first topic sentence** begins the explanation of the process. The **second topic sentence** continues the explanation. The **third topic sentence** finishes the explanation.

Ending Paragraph	The **closing sentences** summarize the process and encourage the reader to try it.

Check your organization. Carefully check each part of your essay.

1 Underline the focus statement in your essay.

2 Place a **1** next to the first topic sentence, a **2** next to the second topic sentence, and a **3** next to the third topic sentence.

3 Then place a star (✱) at the beginning of the ending paragraph.

4 Compare your essay to the chart above. Fix any out-of-place parts.

3 My beginning or ending is weak. The middle needs a paragraph for each main point. More transitions are needed.

2 My beginning, middle, and ending all run together. I need paragraphs and transitions.

1 I need to learn how to organize my thoughts.

How can I use transitions?

In a how-to essay, the steps of the process must be clear and in the correct order. That's why transitions such as *first, second, next,* and *then* are so important. They help lead the reader step-by-step through your explanation.

You can also use prepositional phrases to show connections between the steps. The following prepositions can be used to help organize your essay. (Also see pages 494–495 and 742 for more information about using prepositions.)

Prepositions				
about	before	during	in	through
after	below	for	near	until
along	between	from	off	with

Prepositional Phrases

Cover the bowl and let the mixture rest for a while. After two hours, **add two teaspoons of salt and a little oil to the batter.** Along with the salt and oil, **add . . .**

Review for transitions. Read your paper. Are the steps easy to follow? If not, add transition words and prepositional phrases that will make your directions clearer.

EXPOSITORY

Organization
Two prepositional phrases are added.

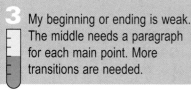

During this step,
^Keep the pulp from settling on the bottom by
                    After that,
stirring it gently.^Move the screen around so that

the paper pulp settles onto it. Cover the screen . . .

Revising **for** Voice

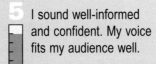

6 I sound knowledgeable, confident, and enthusiastic.	**5** I sound well-informed and confident. My voice fits my audience well.	**4** I sound well-informed, and my voice fits my audience.

When revising your essay for *voice,* check to see if you sound confident and enthusiastic. The words you use should fit your audience, purpose, and topic. The rubric strip above can guide you.

Does my voice fit my audience?

Your voice fits your audience when it matches the people—teachers, parents, or friends—you are talking to. In writing, your voice should also change depending on your audience and your topic. To check your voice, answer three questions:

1. Who is my audience?

2. How should I speak to that audience?

3. How should I present my topic to that audience?

Audience	Teacher	Classmates	Friends
Voice	formal, polite	informal, but respectful	very informal

 Number your paper from 1 to 3. Write which of the audiences listed above in red would fit the voice in each of the following sentences.

1. Would you hand me that pencil?

2. May I please borrow a pencil?

3. Hey, got a pencil I could use?

Voice
A phrase is changed to fit the audience.

. . . press the medium-speed button and blend for

a few seconds. When the mixture in the blender

like thick potato soup
looks ~~really gross~~, your paper pulp is ready.

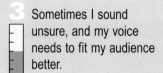

3 Sometimes I sound unsure, and my voice needs to fit my audience better.

2 I sound unsure. My voice needs to fit my audience better.

1 I need to figure out what voice is.

Is my voice too informal?

Your voice in an expository essay is probably too informal if it sounds like you're talking to a friend. The two explanations below are similar in many ways, but the two voices are very different. The first is too casual or informal for this topic. The second is just right.

Voice 1: Too Informal

First, grab a couple of eggs and whack 'em against the side of the bowl. Dump them into the bowl. Next, throw in a little milk, a pinch of salt, and a drop of vanilla for extra oomph. Whip it all up with a fork and pour it into a hot pan. Keep pushing everything around until all the raw stuff is gone. When it looks ready to eat, chow down!

Voice 2: Just Right

Select two large eggs. Crack them one at a time into a bowl. Add one tablespoon of milk for each egg, a quarter teaspoon of salt, and a drop of vanilla. Next, mix everything together with a fork. Then, empty the bowl into a sizzling, buttered pan. Stir the eggs until they firm up into a hot, golden heap. You're now ready to eat and enjoy.

EXPOSITORY

Compare the two explanations shown above. List four words or phrases that make "Voice 1" too informal for an essay.

Listen to your voice. Read your essay and listen to your voice. Is it "too informal" or "just right"?

1 Write down three words from your writing that fit your audience.

2 Then look for words from your writing that don't fit.

3 Replace the words that don't fit with ones that match the voice you want to create in your essay.

Revising for Word Choice

6 The words I use make my essay very clear, informative, and fun to read.

5 Specific nouns and action verbs make my essay clear and informative.

4 I use some specific nouns and verbs, but I could use more.

When you revise for *word choice,* check your nouns and verbs. Do you use specific nouns? Do you use action verbs? Do your words help the reader understand the steps in the process? The rubric strip above can guide you.

Do I use specific nouns?

If your nouns name a particular person, place, thing, or idea, they are most likely specific. (See the chart below.) In a how-to essay, specific nouns can make your directions much clearer. For example, the specific word "hammer" gives your reader a clearer picture than the general word "tool."

Specific nouns make your writing stronger and more interesting. In the chart below, the top row lists *general* nouns. The second row shows *specific* nouns, and the bottom row gives *very specific* nouns. (See pages 470–471.)

Person	Place	Thing	Idea
worker	building	food	sickness
cook	restaurant	fish	cancer
baker	delicatessen	salmon	leukemia

For each general noun listed below, write a specific noun. Then use that noun in a sentence.

1. cheese

1. cheese—mozzarella

Next, sprinkle the grated mozzarella on the pizza.

2. dog   **3.** tree   **4.** sport   **5.** fruit   **6.** feeling

Check your nouns. Replace the general nouns with more specific nouns wherever it will help make your writing clearer. (Remember that not all general nouns need to be replaced.)

3 I use too many general words. I need specific nouns and verbs.

2 I use general nouns and verbs and leave out words. My essay is hard to understand.

1 I need help finding the right words.

Do I use specific action verbs?

If your verbs tell precisely what is happening in a sentence, you are using specific action verbs. Specific verbs describe movement and action and make your explanation stronger. Use a thesaurus to find just the right word.

General Verb	Specific Verbs
put	place, slide, enter, press, draw, set, insert, include, add, pour

 Number your paper from 1 to 4. For each of the sentences below, choose a word from the above chart to replace the verb "put." (Each sentence contains clues for choosing a specific verb.)

1. Slice a potato in half and use a marker to *put* a design on it.
2. Next, *put* a knife alongside the outline and cut a shallow line around the design.
3. Then, *put* the knife in deeper and cut away the potato outside the line.
4. Finally, *put* your potato stamp on an ink pad and try it out.

 Examine your paper. Replace general or overused verbs in your essay with specific action verbs.

EXPOSITORY

Word Choice

General and overused verbs are replaced.

Then ~~put~~ *pour* two cups of water into the blender. Next, ~~add~~ *sprinkle* in a few handfuls of the shredded paper. Finally, cover the blender, press the medium-speed . . .

Revising **for** Sentence Fluency

 6 My sentences flow smoothly, and people will enjoy reading them.

 5 My sentences read smoothly. I don't have any fragments or choppy sentences.

4 Most of my sentences read smoothly, but I need to expand a few choppy ones.

When you revise for *sentence fluency,* begin by reading your sentences out loud. They should read smoothly. If you have used a lot of short sentences or fragments, your sentences will sound choppy and not very interesting. The rubric strip above can guide you.

How can I fix my choppy sentences?

If too many sentences in your essay are short and choppy, you may want to expand them by adding details. You can do this by answering the 5 W's and H *(who? what? where? when? why?* and *how?).*

Sentence: **Wipe the paintbrush.**

Where? Wipe the paintbrush **against the palette.**

When? **After dipping the paintbrush into paint,** wipe it against the palette.

Why? After dipping the paintbrush into paint, wipe it against the palette **to avoid drips.**

How? After dipping the paintbrush into paint, **gently** wipe it against the palette to avoid drips.

 Add specific details to the following sentences using some or all of the 5 W's and H.

1. Plant the marigolds.
2. Dribble the ball.
3. Mix the plaster.
4. Cut the paper.

 Expand your sentences. Use the 5 W's and H to expand some of the short sentences in your essay. Be careful, though, not to overload your sentences with too many words and details. Just pick the best ones.

3 Some of my sentences are choppy, and I need to fix some fragments.

2 I need to rewrite many of my sentences so they don't confuse my reader.

1 I need to rewrite most of my sentences.

How can I fix fragments?

A fragment is part of a sentence, but it doesn't express a complete thought. It can be fixed by adding a subject or verb or by combining the fragment with a sentence. (See pages 504–505.)

Fragment	Sentence
After we review the recipe,	**we gather the ingredients.**

Sentence	Fragment
Don't place a cake in the oven	**until the oven is hot enough.**

 Turn the fragment in each set below into a complete sentence by connecting it with the other sentence.

1. Add a handful of baking chips. If you like a sweeter cake.
2. Wear an oven mitt. While taking hot pans out of the oven.
3. When baking aromas fill the room. I feel hungry.

 Check for fragments. As you read your essay, make sure you used complete sentences. Correct any fragments.

EXPOSITORY

Sentence Fluency
A fragment is fixed, and a sentence is expanded.

Roll the rolling pin over the top layer of felt. ~~To~~

squeeze out all the extra water. Finally, remove
from between the pieces of felt
the damp paper ʌ and hang it in a sunny place.

A piece of paper will be ready in about . . .

Revising **Using a Checklist**

Check your revising. On a piece of paper, write the numbers 1 to 13. If you can answer "yes" to a question, put a check mark after that number. If not, continue to work with that part of your essay.

Ideas

_____ **1.** Do I focus on an interesting idea?
_____ **2.** Have I divided my idea into interesting topic sentences?
_____ **3.** Do I use enough specific details?

Organization

_____ **4.** Do I include a beginning, a middle, and an ending?
_____ **5.** Have I cut unnecessary details?
_____ **6.** Have I reorganized parts that were out of place?

Voice

_____ **7.** Do I show interest in—and knowledge of—my topic?
_____ **8.** Does my voice fit my audience? My purpose? My topic?

Word Choice

_____ **9.** Do I use specific nouns and active verbs?
_____ **10.** Do I use colorful adjectives and adverbs?

Sentence Fluency

_____ **11.** Have I written clear sentences and avoided fragments?
_____ **12.** Have I fixed any choppy sentences?
_____ **13.** Do I use a variety of sentence beginnings and lengths?

Make a clean copy. When you've finished revising your essay, make a clean copy before you begin to edit.

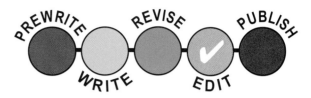

Editing

After you've finished revising your essay, it's time to edit your work for your use of conventions: punctuation, capitalization, spelling, and grammar.

Keys to Effective Editing

1. Use a dictionary, a thesaurus, and the "Proofreader's Guide" in the back of this book.

2. Check for any words or phrases that may be confusing to the reader.

3. Check your writing for correctness of punctuation, capitalization, spelling, and grammar.

4. Edit on a printed computer copy. Then enter your changes on the computer.

5. Use the editing and proofreading marks located inside the back cover of this book.

EXPOSITORY

Editing for Conventions

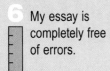 **6** My essay is completely free of errors.

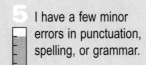 **5** I have a few minor errors in punctuation, spelling, or grammar.

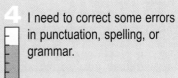 **4** I need to correct some errors in punctuation, spelling, or grammar.

When you edit for *conventions,* you need to check for capitalization, grammar, spelling, and punctuation errors. On this page and the next, you will edit for conventions in two ways: using commas with introductory word groups and using commas in a series. The rubric strip above can guide you.

Do I use commas with introductory word groups?

When you begin a sentence with an introductory word group—a phrase or a clause—you need to set it off with a comma. One word group that is often used to begin a sentence is a *prepositional phrase.* (See page 742.) The phrase below starts with a preposition (For) and ends with the object of the preposition (results).

Introductory Phrase

> For best results, **sprinkle the sand evenly across the section to be covered.**

In addition, when you begin a sentence with a clause that starts with a subordinating conjunction (After), you should set it off from the main sentence with a comma. (See page 744 for a list of subordinating conjunctions.)

Introductory Clause

> After you add the dye, **stir the sand quickly to spread the color throughout.**

 On your own paper, rewrite the following sentences. First, move the italicized phrase or clause to the front of each sentence. Then, punctuate each one correctly.

1. Sand paintings are unique *because of their soft colors.*
2. I often make sand paintings *for birthday or holiday gifts.*
3. Gently sprinkle on your first color *after you glue the board.*

 Check your essay. Find any introductory phrases or clauses in your essay. Be sure you punctuated them correctly.

3 Some of my errors may confuse the reader. I need to fix them.

2 I need to correct many errors that make my essay confusing and hard to read.

1 I need help making corrections, especially with my commas.

Do I use commas correctly in a series?

If you use commas to separate a series of three or more words, phrases, or clauses, you are using them correctly. See the examples below.

Commas to Separate Words

Gather together your glue, scissors, and fabric.

Commas to Separate Phrases

Fabric squares can be added to decorate wall hangings, to trim place mats, or to cover pillows.

Commas to Separate Clauses

Sue gives them as presents, Daniel displays them for decoration, and Ranell uses them as gift wrapping.

Practice using commas in a series. Copy the sentences below and place commas in the proper places.

1. Art allows you to have fun get involved and be creative.
2. In art, you can draw paint or sculpt.
3. You can work on your own with a partner or in a group.

Edit for commas. Check your essay to see that you punctuated words, phrases, or clauses in a series. Make any necessary corrections.

Conventions
Commas are used after an opening phrase and in a series.

After a few tries, I found that making paper is fun,

easy, and useful.

EXPOSITORY

Editing **Using a Checklist**

Check your editing. On a piece of paper, write the numbers 1 to 12. If you can answer "yes" to a question, put a check mark after that number. If not, continue to edit for that convention.

Conventions

PUNCTUATION

_____ **1.** Do I use end punctuation after all my sentences?

_____ **2.** Do I use commas after introductory word groups?

_____ **3.** Do I use commas after items in a series?

_____ **4.** Do I use commas in all my compound sentences?

_____ **5.** Do I use apostrophes to show possession *(boy's bike)*?

CAPITALIZATION

_____ **6.** Do I start all my sentences with capital letters?

_____ **7.** Do I capitalize all proper nouns?

SPELLING

_____ **8.** Have I spelled all my words correctly?

_____ **9.** Have I double-checked the words my spell-checker may have missed?

GRAMMAR

_____ **10.** Do I use correct forms of verbs *(had gone,* not *had went)*?

_____ **11.** Do my subjects and verbs agree in number?
(She and I *are* going, not She and I *is* going.)

_____ **12.** Do I use the right words *(to, too, two)*?

Creating a Title

Write a title for your expository essay, using any one of the following suggestions.

■ Create a word picture: **Making Amazing Maps**

■ Repeat a sound: **From Pulp to Paper**

■ Use action words: **Print with Potatoes**

Publishing

Sharing Your Essay

After you have worked so hard writing your essay, you'll want to proofread it and make a neat copy to share. You may also decide to present your essay as a demonstration, an online essay, or a poster. (See the suggestions below.)

Make a final copy. Follow your teacher's instructions or use the guidelines below to format your essay. (If you are using a computer, see page 60.) Create a clean final copy of your essay and carefully proofread it.

Focus on Presentation

- Use blue or black ink and write neatly.
- Write your name in the upper left corner of page 1.
- Skip a line and center your title; skip another line and start your writing.
- Indent every paragraph and leave a one-inch margin on all four sides.
- Write your last name and the page number in the upper right corner of every page after the first one.

Create a Poster
Make a poster based on your essay. List the steps in the process. Make sure the instructions are clear; then decorate your poster in an eye-catching way.

Give a Demonstration
In class, demonstrate the process you covered in your essay. (See pages 426–430 for more information about giving demonstrations.)

Post Your Essay Online
Search for an online bulletin board related to the subject of your essay. Post your work for others who have the same interest. (Get permission before posting your essay.)

EXPOSITORY

Rubric for Expository Writing

Use this rubric for guiding and assessing your expository writing.
Refer to it to help you improve your writing using the six traits.

Ideas

6 | **The topic, focus, and details make the essay truly memorable.**
5 | The essay is informative with a clear focus and specific details.
4 | The essay is informative with a clear focus. More specific details are needed.

Organization

6 | **The organization makes the essay informative and easy to read.**
5 | The beginning interests the reader. The middle supports the focus. The ending works well. Transitions are used.
4 | The essay is divided into a beginning, a middle, and an ending. Some transitions are used.

Voice

6 | **The writer's voice sounds confident, knowledgeable, and enthusiastic.**
5 | The writer's voice sounds informative and confident. It fits the audience.
4 | The writer's voice sounds well-informed most of the time and fits the audience.

Word Choice

6 | **The word choice makes the essay very clear, informative, and fun to read.**
5 | Specific nouns and action verbs make the essay clear and informative.
4 | Some nouns and verbs could be more specific.

Sentence Fluency

6 | **The sentences flow smoothly, and people will enjoy reading them.**
5 | The sentences read smoothly. There are no short, choppy sentences.
4 | Most of the sentences read smoothly, but some are short and choppy.

Conventions

6 | **The essay is error free.**
5 | The essay has a few minor errors in punctuation, spelling, or grammar.
4 | The essay has several errors in punctuation, spelling, or grammar.

EXPOSITORY

3 The focus of the essay needs to be clearer, and more specific details are needed.

2 The topic needs to be narrowed or expanded. Many more specific details are needed.

1 A new topic needs to be selected.

3 The beginning or ending is weak. The middle needs a paragraph for each main point. More transitions are needed.

2 The beginning, middle, and ending all run together. Paragraphs and transitions are needed.

1 The essay should be reorganized.

3 The writer sometimes sounds unsure, and the voice needs to fit the audience better.

2 The writer sounds unsure. The voice needs to fit the audience.

1 The writer needs to learn about voice.

3 Too many general words are used. Specific nouns and verbs are needed.

2 General or missing words make this essay hard to understand.

1 The writer needs help finding specific words.

3 Many short, choppy sentences need to be rewritten to make the essay read smoothly.

2 Many sentences are choppy or incomplete and need to be rewritten.

1 Most sentences need to be rewritten.

3 Some errors confuse the reader.

2 Many errors make the essay confusing and hard to read.

1 Help is needed to make corrections.

Evaluating an Expository Essay

As you read through Anna's expository essay below, focus on the strengths and weaknesses. **(The essay contains several errors.)**

Making Amazing Maps

For your next geography project, why not make a plaster map? All you need is a copy of a map, a bag of plaster, some water, vinegar, and a board for the map's base. It's fun. It's easy. It really gives you a better idea of geography.

The first thing you should do is copy the outline of the map onto your board. Make sure the board or piece of plywood is large enough to fit your map. Don't worry about mistakes. The drawing will be covered with plaster.

When your drawing is finished mix your plaster. Put about two cups of dry plaster into a bowl. Add a little water at a time until the mixture is like thick oatmeal. Use a few drops of vinegar to make the plaster dry slower. Rinse out the bowl as soon as you empty it so the plaster doesn't get hard.

Now it's time to shape your map. Pour some plaster onto your board. Check your map to see what the geography of the country is like. Shape the plaster—thinner along a coast and built up for mountains. Use your fingers or a wooden stick to create lakes. Use a toothpick to make rivers through the wet plaster. After your map dries use watercolors or food coloring to paint deserts, beaches, rivers, and grasslands.

Making plaster maps is great fun. You are creating something interesting and you are actually learning about an area's geography. You can feel the hills and rivers as well as see them. Your teacher will be impressed, and you will have a much clearer view of the world.

Student Self-Assessment

The assessment below includes comments by Anna, who evaluated her own essay (on page 196). Notice that she includes a positive comment first. Then she points out an area of her writing that could be improved. (The writer used the rubric and number scale on pages 194–195.)

_4_ Ideas

1. I'm pretty sure my topic will interest my classmates, and I've used some specific details about shaping the map.
2. My list of supplies isn't complete.

_5_ Organization

1. I wrote a clear topic sentence for each paragraph.
2. The tip about cleaning the bowl should be in the fourth paragraph.

_4_ Voice

1. It is clear that I enjoy making plaster maps.
2. I could have added a story about maps I have made.

_3_ Word Choice

1. I use a few strong action verbs.
2. I should have used the word "use" less.

_4_ Sentence Fluency

1. I didn't have any fragments.
2. Some short sentences could have been expanded or combined, and I could have used more transitions.

_4_ Conventions

1. I couldn't find any errors in spelling or capitalization.
2. In the future, I need to use commas more carefully.

Use the rubric. Assess your essay using the rubric on pages 194–195.

 1 On your own paper, list the six traits. Leave room after each trait to write one strength and one weakness.

2 Then choose a number (from 1 to 6) that shows how well you used each trait.

EXPOSITORY

Reflecting on Your Writing

Now that you've completed your expository essay, take a moment to reflect on it. Complete each starter sentence below on your own paper. These thoughts will help you prepare for your next writing assignment.

My Expository Essay

1. The best part of my essay is . . .

2. The part that still needs work is . . .

3. The main thing I learned about writing an expository essay is . . .

4. The prewriting activity that worked best for this essay was . . .

5. In my next piece of expository writing, I would like to . . .

6. Here is one question I still have about writing an expository essay:

Expository Writing

Classifi ca tion Essay

One way to explain a topic is to divide it into its parts. That's true whether you're talking about a sandwich, a bicycle, or the United States government. Knowing the different parts of a subject helps people understand the whole.

An expository essay that explains a subject in this way is called a classification essay. Often, teachers assign this kind of writing as a way of checking students' understanding of a subject covered in class.

In this chapter, you will learn how to write your own classification essay. You may choose to explain a topic that you know a lot about, or you may tackle a subject that you want to understand better.

Writing Guidelines

Subject: A topic with different parts

Form: Classification essay

Purpose: To explain

Audience: Classmates

Classification Essay

In the following student essay, Jana explains the main types of band instruments and tells why each type is different. She learned about the types of instruments by attending a band information night.

What Instrument Are You?

Beginning

The topic is introduced, and the focus statement names the types (underlined).

At the beginning of the school year, Riverview Middle School held a band information night. An incredible number of instruments were introduced, including four different sizes of saxophones. Some instruments have wooden reeds, and others have mouthpieces. There are even four different kinds of drums. It was hard to keep the instruments all straight. Then Mrs. Delgato clarified things. <u>Our band program uses just three types of instruments: brass, woodwinds, and percussion.</u>

Middle

Each middle paragraph explains one type of instrument.

Most brass instruments are made out of brass, of course, or some other kind of metal. They get their sound from blowing into the mouthpiece. The size of the mouthpiece and the length of tubing create different pitches. Cornets have small mouthpieces and short tubing, so they can play high notes. Trombones have medium mouthpieces and tubing, so they hit the middle range of notes. Tubas and sousaphones have huge mouthpieces and lots of tubing, which is why they sound so low.

Woodwinds get their name because they used to be made of wood and the sound comes

Middle

Each middle paragraph provides examples.

from blowing into them. Some clarinets, oboes, and bassoons are still made of wood. Flutes and piccolos are metal. These two woodwinds make sound by having the player blow air over an opening. Other woodwinds create sound with a vibrating wooden reed.

Percussion instruments make noise when one thing hits another thing. A drumstick hits a drumhead or wood block, or a mallet hits a bar on a xylophone. Surprisingly, a piano is actually a percussion instrument, too. It makes sounds when hammers hit metal strings! Most percussion instruments, like cymbals or bass drums, don't have an exact pitch. Others, like chimes and kettledrums, do.

Ending

The ending reflects on the ideas in the essay.

Once Mrs. Delgato explained the different kinds of instruments to us, no one felt so overwhelmed. Instead of walking out the door, most beginning band members checked out all the instruments and found the one that was just right for them. Now comes the real challenge, becoming a skilled trombonist or drummer.

Respond to the reading. On your own paper, answer the following questions about the sample essay.

☐ Ideas (1) Without looking, how many different instruments can you remember from the essay? (2) What details helped you remember these instruments?

☐ Organization (3) How does the writer organize her description of band instruments?

☐ Voice (4) How does she show her interest in this topic?

Prewriting Selecting a Topic

To choose a topic for a classification essay, think of topics that can be divided into different types, or groups. Jana wrote a list of things she had learned about recently. Then she chose a topic from that list.

List

types of clouds	<u>types of band instruments</u>
branches of government	the food pyramid
the respiratory system	planets in the solar system

Choose your topic. Write a list of topics you find interesting. (Try to write at least five.) Underline the topic you would like for your own essay.

Freewriting to Gather Details

To gather her thoughts about her topic, Jana decided to spend a few minutes freewriting. She wrote down whatever came to mind from the band information night she had attended.

Freewriting

> I sure love learning trombone. A slide is way cooler than valves or keys. Besides, there is no way I'd remember all the keys on a saxophone! There are so many instruments. The brass are the loudest, I think. Once we get all those cornets and trombones and tubas going, we'll blow the woodwinds away. Of course, drummers can make a lot of noise, too. Kettledrums are super loud, and what about the cymbals! But the flutes and clarinets have the prettiest sound. Like Mrs. Delgato says, "Never louder than lovely."

Gather details. Write freely for 5 to 10 minutes about your topic. Write whatever comes to mind. Get down on paper what you already know about your topic.

Organizing with a Line Diagram

To organize her thoughts, Jana made a line diagram. She began with her main topic—band instruments—and then listed its three divisions: brass, woodwinds, and percussion. Next, she listed instruments that belonged to each division.

Line Diagram

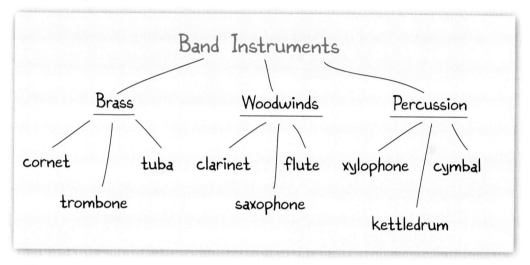

Organize your thoughts. Make your own line diagram to organize the parts of your topic.

Researching the Topic

Looking at her line diagram, Jana decided to gather more examples of instruments for her essay. She also wanted to include a few details about each one. She visited the band room again and jotted down notes.

> Sousaphone – brass, low pitch
> Trombone – slide is three feet long!
> Clarinet, oboe, bassoon – woodwinds made of wood
> Flute, piccolo – woodwinds made of metal

Do your research. Decide what details you still need to learn about your topic. Ask an expert or check the library. Take notes.

EXPOSITORY

Writing Creating Your First Draft

Using your notes and freewriting as a guide, write your first draft. Concentrate on explaining your topic in the best possible order.

- In your first paragraph, introduce your topic. Give the reader a reason to be interested in it, too.
- Each of your middle paragraphs should explain one part of your line diagram.
- Summarize your topic and end with an interesting thought. (Jana finishes by telling us that she thinks there is an instrument for everybody.)

 Write your first draft. Using the guidelines above, write a first draft of your own classification essay.

Revising Improving Your Writing

Keep the following traits in mind as you revise your first draft.

- ☐ **Ideas** Do I include enough details so that the reader will understand my topic?
- ☐ **Organization** Does the middle include a paragraph for each part of my topic? Do my ideas appear in a logical order?
- ☐ **Voice** Do the words and details I use show that I am interested in my topic?
- ☐ **Word Choice** Do I use specific nouns and strong verbs?
- ☐ **Sentence Fluency** Do my sentences read smoothly?

 Revise your writing. Carefully consider the questions above. Then revise your writing as needed to make it clear and interesting.

Editing Checking for Conventions

When your revising is completed, edit your paper for conventions.

- ☐ **Conventions** Have I checked spelling, capitalization, and punctuation? Have I also checked for commonly misused words *(to, too, two)* and other grammar errors?

 Edit your work. Edit your essay using the two questions above. Have someone else check it over, too. Then make a final copy and proofread it.

Expository Writing
Across the Curriculum

Expository writing is used to share information, so you will find it in every school subject. In social studies, you may be asked to take a survey and present the results. In science, you may write up an explanation of how something works. In math, you may have to explain a concept. In any class, you may be asked to write directions. All are forms of expository writing.

On the following pages, you will work with four types of expository writing for other classes. You will learn the form needed for each, along with tips for using the writing process. At the end of the chapter, you will have the chance to practice writing for an assessment test.

What's Ahead

- **Social Studies**: Creating a Survey
- **Math**: Explaining a Concept
- **Science**: Writing an Explanation
- **Practical Writing**: Drafting Directions

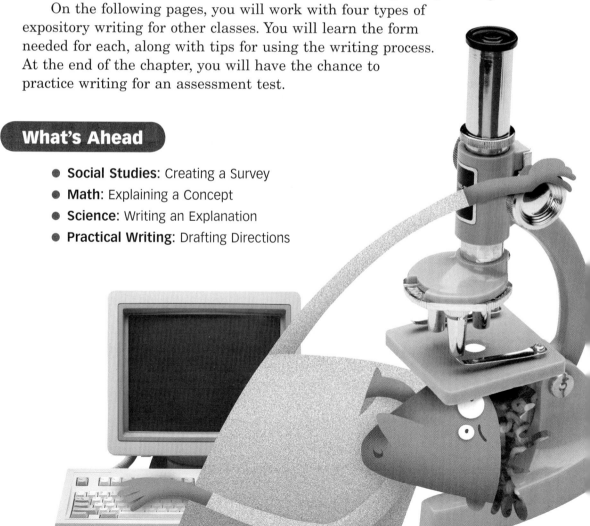

Social Studies: Creating a Survey

A survey is a set of questions or choices given to a group of people. Their responses show what the group thinks about a certain subject or issue. LaToya created the following survey, which asks students to help choose a new school mascot.

The **beginning** introduces the topic.

A call to action is made.

The choices are listed.

Elwood Mascot Survey

The students and staff of Elwood Middle School will be choosing a new mascot. Each choice below is an animal that has special qualities that would make it a great mascot.

You can help make this decision! Make your opinion count by checking the box next to the mascot you would most like to represent Elwood Middle School:

☐ **The Roadrunners:** Roadrunners are quick. They would race all over the field or the court. Who could catch a roadrunner?

☐ **The Bears:** Bears are big and strong. They would power their way to victory. Would you want to tackle a bear?

☐ **The Cougars:** Mountain lions are very fierce. That's what our opponents would think if they saw this mascot on helmets and jerseys. Wouldn't you like to be a cool cat?

☐ **The Wolverines:** Wolverines are the toughest animals in the woods. They would be tough on fields, tracks, and courts. Who could beat a wolverine?

Writing Tips

Before you write . . .

- **Understand your purpose.**
  Be sure you understand why you are creating this survey.
- **List your choices.**
  Decide which questions or choices you will use on the survey.
- **Compare your choices.**
  Provide enough details to give the reader plenty of good information about each choice.

During your writing . . .

- **Organize your thoughts.**
  Introduce the survey, explain how to complete it, and then list the choices.
- **Keep it fair.**
  Write each question or choice in the same way. For example, if you write two details about the first choice, you should write two details for all the others. If you end one choice with a fun question, you should end all the choices with a fun or interesting question.

After you've written a first draft . . .

- **Check for completeness.**
  Make sure you have included all of the information needed to answer the questions (or make the choices) on your survey.
- **Check for correctness.**
  Proofread your survey several times for punctuation, spelling, capitalization, and other conventions.

EXPOSITORY

 Write a survey asking your classmates about their favorite school lunch, TV show, restaurant, or musical group. Choose a topic your classmates will have opinions about.

Math: Explaining a Concept

One of the best ways to understand a topic is to explain it to someone else. In his math class, Josh was assigned to write an explanation of a math concept. He chose the concept of "rates of speed." He was surprised by how much more he knew about the concept after he finished his writing.

The beginning states the basic concept.

The middle part explains the concept.

The ending identifies ways to apply or use the concept.

Rates of Speed

In math, "rates of speed" are used to compare time to distance. For example, miles per hour (mph) is a very common way to describe the speed of cars, airplanes, and other machines.

Miles per hour is really just a ratio that tells how far something goes during a certain time. Other common rates of speed are feet per second (fps) and kilometers per hour (kph). A rate of speed used by scientists, especially astronomers, is the speed of light. It is 186,000 miles per second. It takes a ray of sunlight only about 8 minutes to travel the 93 million miles from the sun to the earth.

When figuring a rate of speed, ask these two questions: How far did it go? How long did it take? The first answer divided by the second is a rate of speed. So, if a train goes 120 miles in 2 hours, its rate of speed is $120 \div 2$, or 60 miles per hour.

Rates of speed are easy to use. To find out how far something traveled, multiply the time it traveled by its rate of speed. For example, if it took 60 seconds to read this essay, the light first used would be 11,160,000 miles away by now (60 seconds $\times$ 186,000 miles per second).

Writing Tips

Before you write . . .

- **Select a topic.**
  If you have not been given a topic, use your math textbook or your notes to find a concept that you can write about.

- **Study your topic.**
  Pick a few examples that will help you make your writing clear. In the sample explanation, the speed of light provides a clear and interesting example.

During your writing . . .

- **Organize your thoughts.**
  Decide on an order for the information. You could start with a definition and offer some examples. Then explain the concept and how it relates to the real world.

- **Use examples and comparisons.**
  In the sample essay, the writer uses miles per hour as a common example of a rate of speed.

- **Think of some questions.**
  Include some questions in your essay. Choose questions that you can answer using the math concept.

After you've written a first draft . . .

- **Check your sources.**
  Make sure you have explained the concept correctly.

- **Keep it simple.**
  Look for places where your explanation may be unclear. Try to make your explanation as simple as possible.

- **Check for correctness.**
  Review facts and figures, as well as grammar, punctuation, spelling, and other conventions.

EXPOSITORY

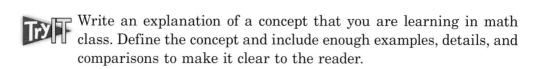 Write an explanation of a concept that you are learning in math class. Define the concept and include enough examples, details, and comparisons to make it clear to the reader.

Science: Writing an Explanation

Scientists often use expository writing to share their knowledge with readers. An essay that provides an explanation is a basic form of expository writing. Ravi's essay explains how and why a geyser erupts.

The beginning introduces the focus statement (underlined).

The **middle** part provides supporting details.

The **ending** concludes the explanation.

How a Geyser Erupts

Geysers are awesome eruptions of water or steam. Geysers can be found in many parts of the world and are often located near volcanoes. There are about 1,000 known geysers, and Yellowstone Park has more than half of them. In Iceland, people even use the steam that comes from geysers to generate electricity.

Geysers are created when water seeps down through the ground and touches hot molten rock called magma. The heat turns the water to steam. The trapped steam builds up pressure under more water. Finally, the steam and hot water blast up through a crack and out of the ground. The blast reduces the pressure, and then the geyser stops. The process is repeated, and when the pressure builds up, the geyser erupts again.

Different geysers act in different ways. Old Faithful in Yellowstone Park erupts almost every hour. Other geysers may go months, or even years, between eruptions. Geysers are one of the true wonders of nature.

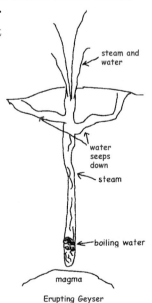

steam and water

water seeps down

steam

boiling water

magma

Erupting Geyser

Writing Tips

Before you write . . .

- **Do your research.**
  Make sure you understand the topic you plan to explain.
  Use different sources—textbooks, Internet sites, books
  in the library, and your own personal experiences.
- **Organize your thoughts.**
  Write a focus statement based on the details you have
  listed during your research.

During your writing . . .

- **Share specific details.**
  Choose details that will help explain the topic to the
  reader.
- **Use comparisons or illustrations.**
  Make comparisons to help the reader understand
  surprising or difficult facts about the topic. Also consider
  including drawings. In the sample essay, the writer uses
  a simple drawing to explain why geysers erupt.

After you've written a first draft . . .

- **Ask for another opinion.**
  Let several of your classmates read the essay. Do they
  understand it? Remember that the purpose of your essay
  is to write an explanation.
- **Check for organization.**
  Review each paragraph and sentence to make sure each
  thought leads naturally to the next thought.

EXPOSITORY

 Write an expository essay about a topic related to nature. Think of
things like weather, landforms, and the oceans. Research your topic
and write a short essay in which you share what you have learned
with your classmates.

Practical Writing: Drafting Directions

The key to writing directions is giving clear and complete information in the correct order. The following sample, written by the drum major of a middle school marching band, gives directions to a location where band members must meet.

How to Reach the Memorial Day Parade Route

The **beginning** identifies the directions.

Memorial Day is Monday, May 31, and the band will march in the city parade. All band members must attend. Band members will walk together to the parade route but should keep a copy of these directions in case they arrive late.

Band members should come to the Franklin Middle School band room by 8:00 on Monday morning, put on their uniforms, and prepare their instruments. By 8:15, Ms. Robertson will walk with the group to the parade's meeting place at the Lincoln statue on Jenkins Street. Here are the directions:

The **middle** states the steps.

1. Leave from the front door of the school and turn left on Evans Street.
2. Walk to the railroad tracks. Look for trains and cross the tracks.
3. Continue on Evans Street until it meets Randolf Street.
4. Turn left on Randolf Street.
5. Follow Randolf around a sharp curve and over a bridge.
6. Turn right on Jenkins Street. The Lincoln statue is on the right.
7. Wait in the parking lot just beyond the statue.

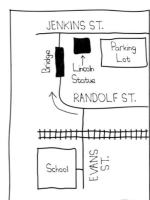

The **ending** gives the final information.

The total walk is one mile and should take about a half hour. Be ready!

Writing Tips

Before you write . . .

- **Think about the start and finish of the route.**
  If your readers are coming from different directions, think of a common starting point for everyone.
- **Check a map.**
  Trace the route from start to finish. Make sure that you choose a path that is direct, easy to follow, and safe. You might even include a basic map in your directions.

During your writing . . .

- **Provide specific street names.**
  Give the name of each street, as well as details about the street. ("Follow Randolf around a sharp curve.")
- **List landmarks.**
  Mention spots along the way that will help readers know they are on the right course. ("Walk to the railroad tracks" or "the Lincoln statue is on the right.")
- **Provide times and distances.**
  Tell readers how long the trip is. ("The total walk is one mile and should take about a half hour.")
- **Use left/right, north/south, east/west.**
  Explain which way to turn. ("Turn right on Jenkins Street.")

After you've written a first draft . . .

- **Follow your own directions.**
  If possible, walk the route to test your directions.
- **Check the details.**
  Double-check all the turns, streets, and landmarks carefully.

EXPOSITORY

 Write directions from your school to an important location in your city or town. Provide every detail that a stranger would need to make the trip. Then ask a classmate to read your work to see if the directions are clear.

Expository Writing

Writing for Assessment

Many state and school writing tests ask you to respond to an expository prompt. An expository prompt asks you to explain something or share information. Study the sample prompt and the student response below.

Expository Prompt

Learning respect is one of life's important lessons. Respectful actions such as sharing, cooperating, and following rules help people work together. Write an essay explaining how someone taught you about the value of respect, either through the person's words or actions, or both.

The **beginning** paragraph states the focus or thesis (underlined).

> My first grade teacher, Mrs. Kloften, made a big impression on me. In one important way, she was a lot like my mom because she taught me about getting along and respecting other people. <u>Everything we did in Mrs. Kloften's classroom centered around becoming respectful classmates.</u>

The **middle** paragraphs each address one kind of assignment.

> We had to share everything in her class. We shared crayons and markers and paper. On the playground, we had to share all of the equipment, and during classroom playtime, everyone got a chance to play with the best board games. At first, we may not have liked all of that sharing, but it helped us become better classmates and friends.

> When we played any outdoor games, especially kickball, Mrs. Kloften expected us to follow certain

EXPOSITORY

Vivid examples create a strong writing voice.

rules. Her main rule was, "Everyone who wants to play gets to play." Also, everyone got a chance to be pitcher and cover first base as well as to kick. If a student was caught making fun of someone, that person had to apologize or take a time out. With these rules, Mrs. Kloften was trying to teach us about being good sports.

Mrs. Kloften also wanted us to be polite, at all times. During class work, we had to be good listeners, and we had to wait our turn to talk. When we were given something, we had to say, "Thank you." When we left the room, we had to line up by the door without taking "cuts" and wait until everyone was quiet.

The **ending** cleverly refocuses the essay.

My first-grade teacher taught us a lot about reading and math, too. She also made science a lot of fun, especially when we studied animals. But the most important thing Mrs. Kloften taught us was how to act in class. She wanted to make sure that we became good classroom citizens, and I respect her for that.

Respond to the reading. Answer the following questions.

☐ Ideas **(1)** What is the focus of the writer's explanation? **(2)** What key words in the prompt also appear in the essay?

☐ Organization **(3)** What is the topic of each middle chapter?

☐ Voice **(4)** What details make the writer's voice vivid?

Writing Tips

Before you write . . .

- **Understand the prompt.**
  Remember that an expository prompt asks you to explain.
- **Plan your time wisely.**
  Spend several minutes planning before you start writing. Use a graphic organizer (cluster) to help you gather ideas.

Cluster

```
        Detail          Detail


              Person


        Detail          Detail
```

During your writing . . .

- **Decide on a focus for your essay.**
  Keep your main idea or purpose in mind as you write.
- **Choose carefully.**
  Use clear examples and explanations.
- **End in a meaningful way.**
  Remind readers about the importance of the topic at the end of your explanation.

After you've written a first draft . . .

- **Check for completeness and correctness.**
  Write your supporting details in logical order and correct any errors in capitalization, punctuation, spelling, and grammar.

Expository Prompts

- If your school could have only three rules for students, what would they be? Explain why these three rules are so important.

- Making friends is an important part of life. Write an essay explaining what makes a good friend.

 Plan and write a response. Respond to one of the prompts listed above. Complete your writing within the period of time your teacher gives you. Afterward, list one part you like and one part you could improve.

Expository Writing in Review

Purpose: In expository writing, you *explain something* to readers.
Topics: Explain . . .
> how to do or make something
> the causes of something
> the kinds of something
> the definition of something

Prewriting
Select a topic that you know a lot about or one that you want to learn about. (See pages 166–167.)

Write a focus (thesis) statement, telling exactly what idea you plan to cover. (See page 168.)

Gather the important steps or details and organize them according to time order or order of importance. (See pages 168–170.)

Writing
In the beginning part, introduce your topic, say something interesting about it, and state your focus. (See page 173.)

In the middle part, give the details or the steps that explain the focus. (See pages 174–175.)

In the ending, summarize your writing and make a final comment about the topic. (See page 176.)

Revising
Review the ideas, organization, and voice first. Then review for **word choice** and **sentence fluency.** Make sure that you have included the important details or steps. (See pages 178–188.)

Editing
Check your writing for conventions. Also have a trusted classmate edit your writing. (See pages 190–192.)

Make a final copy and proofread it for errors before sharing it. (See page 193.)

Assessing
Use the expository rubric to assess your finished writing. (See pages 194–195.)

EXPOSITORY

persuade

argue

Persuasive Writing

convince

support

Persuasive Writing
Persuasive Paragraph

If you could change one thing at school or at home, what would it be? How would you change it? Do you think you could convince other people to go along with the change?

Persuasive writing is your chance to get people to think the way you do about something. Advertisements, editorials, and even some letters are common kinds of persuasive writing.

In the next few pages, you'll write a persuasive paragraph about a change you'd like to make.

Writing Guidelines

Subject:	An important change
Form:	Persuasive paragraph
Purpose:	To convince readers to agree with you
Audience:	Classmates, parents, guardians, or school officials

Persuasive Paragraph

In a persuasive paragraph, the topic sentence states an opinion, the body sentences give reasons to support it, and the closing sentence restates the opinion. The following paragraph was written by a student concerned about access to the school stage.

Topic Sentence

Body

Closing Sentence

Ramp It Up!

Bryant Middle School needs to add a ramp to its auditorium stage. State law says that everyone has to have equal access to important parts of the school, and the stage is important. In this year's spring play, the student who is playing the Wizard of Oz is in a wheelchair. A ramp is needed so he can get up on the stage and also move down into the audience during performances. A ramp also would open drama to more students. That's the most important reason for it. Putting in a ramp isn't just about state laws or one student. The ramp would give more students the chance to perform.

Respond to the reading. Write answers to the following questions.

☐ **Ideas** (1) What reasons does the writer give to support the opinion?

☐ **Organization** (2) How is the paragraph organized—by time, by location, or by order of importance?

☐ **Voice & Word Choice** (3) What specific words or phrases make this paragraph persuasive?

Prewriting **Selecting a Topic**

Think about the places where you spend the most time. What important changes would you like to make in each of those places? A chart like the one that follows can help you think about important changes.

Chart

Home	School	Martin Luther King, Jr., Park
Less dish duty	Make stage accessible	Remove leash law
Get cable	Improve school food	Clean up graffiti

Think about important changes. Create a chart like the one above. Write down three places where you spend time. Under each one, list at least two changes you would like to make. Choose one change to write about in a persuasive paragraph.

Gathering Reasons

Everyone has opinions. To convince others to agree with your opinions, you need to provide strong support, or reasons. The writer of the sample paragraph on page 220 used listing to gather support for her opinion.

List

Bryant Middle School needs to build a ramp to the stage.

- *State law says important spots need to be accessible.*
- *The actor playing the Wizard of Oz has a wheelchair.*
- *Anybody who wants to be in drama should be able to get onto our stage.*

List your reasons. At the top of your paper, write the important change you chose to write about. Under it, write as many reasons as you can think of to support your opinion. Try to come up with at least three.

PERSUASIVE

Writing Developing the First Draft

Write the first draft of your paragraph. Use the following tips:

- Start with a sentence that clearly states your opinion.
- In the body, write sentences that give your supporting reasons.
- End with a sentence that restates your opinion.

 Write your first draft. When you write your first draft, include at least three good reasons to support your opinion.

Revising Improving Your Writing

After you complete the first draft of your paragraph, you are ready to revise it. Check your *ideas, organization, voice, word choice,* and *sentence fluency.*

 Revise your paragraph. Make the necessary changes to improve your first draft, using the questions below as a guide.

1. Does the topic sentence state a clear opinion?
2. What details should be added or removed?
3. Do I sound persuasive?
4. Have I used specific nouns and strong verbs?
5. Have I written complete sentences that flow smoothly?

Editing Checking for Conventions

Once you have revised your paragraph, check it for *conventions.*

 Edit your paragraph. Ask yourself the questions below.

1. Have I used correct spelling, punctuation, and capitalization?
2. Have I checked for errors in usage *(to, too, two; it's, its; there, their, they're)* and other grammar errors?

Proofread your paragraph. After making a neat final copy of your paragraph, check it one more time for errors.

Persuasive Writing

Promoting a Cause

"Save the whales!" "Alba Moreno for class president!" "Reuse and recycle!" Each of these statements identifies a cause. Like most people, you probably have worthy causes that you support, too. If you feel strongly enough about them, you will want to persuade others to support them as well.

Persuasive writing is one way to get others to think the way that you do. To do this, you must express a thoughtful opinion and give strong reasons to support it. In this unit, you will be asked to write an essay that persuades others to support one of the causes that you believe in.

Writing Guidelines

Subject:	A cause that you believe in
Form:	Persuasive essay
Purpose:	To persuade others to agree with you
Audience:	Classmates

Understanding Your Goal

Your goal in this chapter is to write a well-organized persuasive essay about a cause you believe in. The traits listed in the chart below will help you plan and write your essay.

Traits of Persuasive Writing

Ideas

Support your opinion about an important cause.

Organization

Create a smooth flow of ideas from the beginning through the middle to the ending.

Voice

Sound confident and sincere about your cause.

Word Choice

Use strong words and avoid repetition.

Sentence Fluency

Vary your sentence beginnings and the types of sentences that you use.

Conventions

Check your writing for errors in punctuation, capitalization, spelling, and grammar.

 Get the big picture. Look at the rubric on pages 256–257. You can use that rubric to assess your progress as you write. Your goal is to write a convincing persuasive essay about a cause that you believe in.

Persuasive Essay

The focus of the following persuasive essay is avoiding exotic pets, a cause that the writer feels strongly about. The writer begins by getting the reader's attention and stating an opinion. Then the writer supports the opinion with reasons and ends with a call to action.

Beginning

The beginning introduces the topic and states the opinion (underlined).

Middle

The middle paragraphs give reasons that support the opinion.

Avoiding Exotic Pets

Last year, a neighbor got a dingo. As a puppy, this Australian wild dog was very friendly. By the time it was six months old, though, the dingo was big and mean. After it attacked another dog, Animal Control had to take the dingo away. What if this neighbor buys a baby crocodile next? Exotic pets might be interesting, but they can also cause a lot of trouble. People should think carefully before buying unusual pets.

One problem is that owners often don't think about what will happen when the animal grows. For example, potbellied pigs are cute when they're little, but they can be hard to handle later on. In fact, pigs may turn over furniture or dig up the backyard looking for something to eat. Owners may become frustrated with their pet's behavior.

Another problem is that owners who grow tired of their exotic pets have trouble finding new homes for them. Often, shelters can't take these pets, so owners turn them loose. Releasing exotic animals can be very harmful to native animals and dangerous for people. For example, foreign fish that have been released into lakes

PERSUASIVE

and rivers are wiping out native fish like bass and trout. Scarier yet, when a woman in Wisconsin reached into her flower garden, a large tropical snake attacked her.

The most important reason is saved for last.

The most serious problem is that exotic pets may carry dangerous diseases. For instance, monkey pox has become a problem in this country because infected animals brought it here from Africa. Even worse, some imported pets could also carry the deadly Ebola virus to the United States. *opposing point*

Ending
. . . .

The ending summarizes the main points and makes a call to action.

Even though some owners are well prepared to keep exotic pets, most of these animals were never meant to be pets like dogs and cats. A big dog may cause some damage once in a while, but a pet wolf can chew through doors. Is it really worth it to keep an animal that can be destructive or even dangerous? For the sake of these animals and the environment, people should avoid having unusual pets.

Respond to the Reading. Answer the following questions, which focus on important traits in writing.

☐ Ideas (1) What is the writer's opinion about the topic? (2) What are the three reasons that support the opinion?

☐ Organization (3) How are these reasons organized?

☐ Voice & Word Choice (4) Does the writer sound confident and sincere? (5) What words or phrases tell you so?

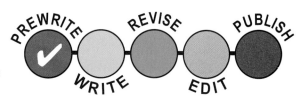

Prewriting

Prewriting is the first step in the writing process. It involves selecting a topic, gathering specific details, and organizing your ideas.

Keys to Effective Prewriting

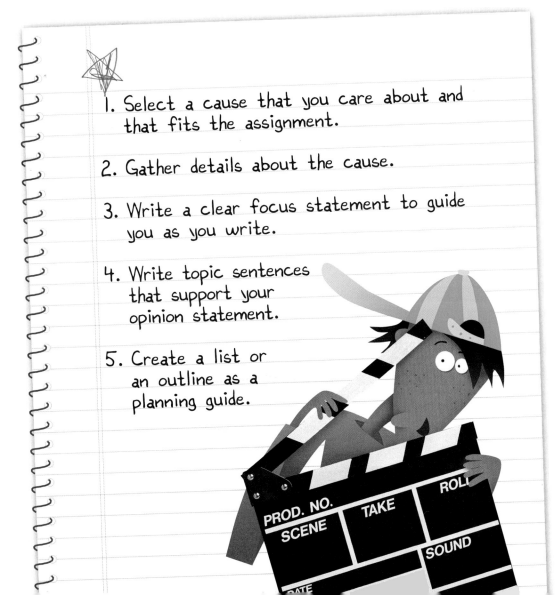

1. Select a cause that you care about and that fits the assignment.

2. Gather details about the cause.

3. Write a clear focus statement to guide you as you write.

4. Write topic sentences that support your opinion statement.

5. Create a list or an outline as a planning guide.

PERSUASIVE

Prewriting Selecting a Topic

To get started, think of a worthwhile cause to write about. For example, if your school district is thinking about dropping art classes, you might write an essay opposing this proposal.

A chart like the one below can help you find causes that you feel strongly about. Different causes are listed under four separate categories.

Chart

Animals	Community	Sports	School
Support animal shelters *Clean up after pets	*Build a skateboard park Improve the library	Add soccer teams Schedule games so parents can watch	*Keep art classes Expand school menus

Create a chart. Make a chart like the one above. Under each category (animals, community, sports, school), list causes you feel strongly about. When you finish, put a star (✱) next to two or three causes that interest you the most. Ask yourself the following questions about each one.

1 Why is this cause important to me?

2 Why would this cause interest my readers?

Choose a topic. After you have answered the questions above, choose your best topic and explain your choice using the following sentences.

I will write about _____ . I picked this topic because . . .

Focus on the Traits

Ideas Choose a cause that you feel strongly about so that you have plenty of convincing things to say about it. You will need at least three strong reasons to support your opinion.

Gathering Ideas and Information

Once you select a topic, the next step is to gather your first thoughts about it. The writer of the essay on pages 235–238 did this by answering three basic questions: *Why is this cause important to me? What do I already know about it? What else do I need to find out?* Review his answers below.

First Thoughts

CAUSE: KEEPING ART CLASSES

Why is this cause important to me?

- Art is one of my favorite subjects.
- Art allows me to use my imagination.
- It is a nice break from regular classes.

What do I already know about it?

- Art classes might be cut next year.
- The school board says that it doesn't have money for the program.
- When I asked the principal what I could do, she told me that parents should contact school board members.

What else do I need to find out?

- I need more background information about this topic.
- How can schools solve money problems?
- Are there other reasons why we should keep art?

Gather your thoughts. Answer the three questions above about your own topic.

1 Start by writing your cause on the top of a piece of paper.

2 Then list each question, leaving space after each one for your answers.

3 If you need more information, interview people about the cause and see what you can find in newspapers, in magazines, and on the Internet.

Prewriting Understanding Opinions and Facts

At this point, make sure that you are clear about the difference between facts and opinions. An opinion is a feeling or belief; a fact is a detail that can be used to support an opinion.

Opinion vs. Fact

Opinion: *School officials should keep art in our schools.*
(This statement expresses a feeling and cannot be checked.)

Fact: *The school administration has proposed to cut art classes.*
(This statement can be checked.)

 Number a piece of paper from 1 to 6. Then decide if each statement below is a fact or an opinion. Write "O" for opinion and "F" for fact.

1. Carlos should run for class president.
2. Carlos has a 4-point average.
3. Our band room is the size of a regular classroom.
4. Park Middle School needs a new band room.
5. Josie is the tallest player on our basketball team.
6. Josie is the best player on the team.

Writing an Opinion Statement

Your opinion statement must identify (1) your cause and (2) your feeling about it. Review the examples that follow.

Opinion Statements

People should think carefully (feeling) *before buying exotic pets* (cause).
Art classes (cause) *should be kept in our school* (feeling).

 Write an opinion statement. Remember that your opinion statement should express your true feelings about your cause. If your first statement doesn't work, write one or two more versions. Pick the best one.

Making a Plan

Once you have written your opinion statement, the next step is to list the main supporting reasons. See the reasons listed below.

Reasons List

Opinion Statement: *Schools in our district should keep art classes.*

First reason: *encourages creativity and trying new things*

Second reason: *fun way to learn about other subjects*

Third reason: *best place for many kids to make art*

Identify your supporting reasons. Write your opinion statement and then list at least three strong reasons that support your opinion.

Writing Topic Sentences

Each of your main reasons becomes a topic sentence for a supporting paragraph in your essay. Study the example that follows.

Reason: *encourages creativity and trying new things*

Topic sentence: *Art encourages people to be creative and try something new.*

Write your topic sentences. Turn each of your reasons into a strong topic sentence. Use the example above as a guide.

Focus on the Traits

Organization Think about the arrangement of your reasons. In persuasive essays, many writers either start with their most important reason or end with it.

PERSUASIVE

Prewriting Organizing Your Ideas

Once you've written your topic sentences, identify the facts and details needed to support each topic sentence. The directions below can help.

Directions   **Organized List**

| Write your opinion statement. | *Schools in our district should keep art classes.* |

| Write your first topic sentence. | *Art encourages people to be creative and try something new.* |
| List facts and details. | *– Have freedom to imagine*
– Able to experiment
– Make ceramics, paintings, and drawings |

| Write your second topic sentence. | *Art is a fun way to learn about other subjects.* |
| List facts and details. | *– Study Native American culture in social studies*
– In art, create Native American pouches |

| Write your third topic sentence. | *School is the best place for many kids to make art.* |
| List facts and details. | *– Need special supplies not found in most homes*
– Peers can offer support |

Make an organized list. To create your list, follow the directions above. You will use this list as a guide when you write.

Focus on the Traits

Voice In a persuasive essay, it's important to sound convincing, and you will sound convincing if you know a lot about your cause.

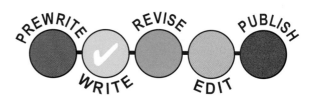

Writing

A first draft lets you get all your ideas down on paper. You're ready to write a first draft when you have written a clear opinion statement and gathered supporting details.

Keys to Effective Writing

1. Use your organized list or outline as a planning guide.

2. Get all your ideas on paper in your first draft.

3. Write on every other line to make room for later changes.

4. Write a clear opinion statement; use topic sentences in the middle paragraphs that support your opinion.

5. Add specific details to support your topic sentences and interest the reader.

6. Use transitions to tie everything together.

PERSUASIVE

Writing **Getting the Big Picture**

Once you have finished your prewriting, you are ready to begin the first draft of your persuasive essay. Remember, you are trying to convince the reader to agree with your feeling about a cause—and perhaps also to do something as a result.

The graphic below shows how the different parts of a persuasive essay fit together. (The examples are from the student essay on pages 235–238.)

Beginning

The **beginning** grabs the reader's attention and states the opinion.

Opinion Statement
Schools in our district should keep art classes.

Middle

The **middle** includes a paragraph for each supporting reason.

Topic Sentences
Art encourages people to be creative and try something new.

In addition, art is a fun way to learn more about other subjects.

Besides, school is the best place for many kids to make art.

Ending

The **ending** summarizes the argument and makes a call to action.

Closing Sentences
We need to stand together against this, or it might actually happen. I don't want to live in a world without art, do you?

Starting Your Essay

Once you have written an opinion statement and organized your thinking, you're ready to start writing your essay. In the beginning paragraph of a persuasive essay, you should grab the reader's attention and state your opinion. Here are several good ways to begin:

- **Give some interesting information about your topic.**
- **Ask a question.**
- **Quote someone.**
- **Share an experience.**

> Beginning
> Middle
> Ending

Beginning Paragraph

The writer of the following essay captures the reader's attention with a question and some interesting information and then shares an opinion statement (underlined).

The topic is introduced.

The paragraph ends with a clear opinion statement (underlined).

Can anyone imagine a world without art? Take away colorful paintings, metal sculptures, and beautiful photographs. Erase the artwork from book covers, magazine ads, and comic books. Who would want to live in a world without art? Students in Burnley might have to. The school board is planning to cut art class. But this is wrong. Schools in Burnley should keep art classes.

Write an opening. Write the beginning paragraph of your persuasive essay. Make sure that you grab the reader's attention and clearly state your opinion.

PERSUASIV

Writing Developing the Middle Part

After writing your opening paragraph, you are ready to develop the middle part of your essay. Each middle paragraph must present a reason that supports the opinion statement. Specific details are used to support each reason. As you move from paragraph to paragraph, be sure to use transitions like *besides, in addition,* and so on, to help the reader follow your argument. (See pages 572–573.)

The following middle paragraphs are from the persuasive essay about keeping art classes in school. Each paragraph has three parts:

1 The **topic sentence** (underlined) states a reason that supports the opinion statement. Transitions are often used in topic sentences to tie the paragraphs together.

2 The **body** provide details that support the reason, including **facts** and **examples**.

3 The **closing sentence** summarizes the information in the paragraph.

Middle Paragraphs

The topic sentence states a reason.	<u>Art encourages people to be creative and try something new.</u> In art, students make ceramics, paintings, and drawings. Even though art teachers give directions, students have the freedom to follow their imaginations. Students experiment and make mistakes as they try to capture their dreams using clay, paint, and paper. There is no better place for creative thinking than in an art class.
The body provides facts and examples.	
The closing sentence gives a summary.	
Topic Sentence	<u>In addition, art is a fun way to learn more about other subjects.</u> For example, students in

Body	social studies class study Native American culture by reading books and surfing the Internet. In art class, they work with leather to make pouches like Native Americans do. Students feel a personal connection with the Native American tribes they are studying.
Closing Sentence	Hands-on projects are an important way for students to learn more about other subjects.
Topic Sentence	Besides, school is the best place for many kids to make art.
Body	Some kinds of art require lots of special supplies like clay, glazes, canvases, paints, and brushes. These expensive materials and tools are provided in art classes. Many students can't afford to have these things at home.
Closing Sentence	It would be unfair to take away the students' chances to explore different kinds of art.

Write your middle paragraphs. Make sure that each paragraph includes one reason that is supported with facts and examples.

Drafting Tips

- **Follow your prewriting** plan as you begin to write.
- **Provide details** that support your opinion statement and topic sentences.
- **Use a voice** that sounds confident and positive.
- **Write freely** and focus on arranging your ideas in the best order.

PERSUASIVE

Writing **Ending Your Essay**

The ending of your persuasive essay may be a good place to address a possible concern or objection to your opinion. It's also a good place to restate your opinion and make a call to action. A call to action encourages the reader to do something or to think a certain way.

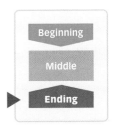

Examples of a call to action

- Help save our energy resources by walking or riding a bike.
- Join us at the rally to save music in our schools.
- Don't let your pet run loose.

Ending Paragraph

An objection is addressed (underlined), and the opinion is stated again.	*Everyone knows that the district has money problems. But instead of cutting subjects, the district should think of ways to raise money to keep art classes. Art connects everything else that is learned. It's hard to imagine a school dropping reading or math, but the school board plans to drop art class. Students need to stand together against this, or it might actually happen. No one wants to live in a world without art, do they?*
The call to action encourages the reader to think about the problem.	

Write your ending. Write the last paragraph of your essay. Remember to state your opinion again and make a call to action. Also try to include a strong final sentence.

Form a complete first draft. Write a complete copy of your essay. Skip every other line if you write it by hand or double-space if you use a computer. This will give you room for revising.

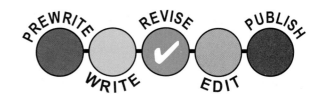

Revising

A first draft can usually be improved in a number of ways. Paragraphs may need to be shifted around, and parts of the argument may need to be clearer. You revise your writing in order to fix problems like these.

Keys to Effective Revising

1. Read through your entire draft to get a feeling of how well your essay works.

2. Make sure your focus statement states your topic clearly.

3. Check your paragraphs to make sure your topic sentences support your focus statement and your details support your topic sentences.

4. Fine-tune your voice to sound confident and convincing.

5. Check your words and sentences.

6. Use the editing and proofreading marks inside the back cover of this book.

PERSUASIVE

Revising **for** Ideas

6 The ideas in my essay inform and convince my reader.	**5** I persuade my reader by using qualifiers and avoiding fuzzy thinking.	**4** I use qualifiers, but I need to clear up some of my fuzzy thinking.

When you revise for *ideas,* you want to make sure your opinion and supporting reasons are sensible and can be supported. It's easier to support an opinion if you use *qualifiers*—terms such as *most* and *usually.* (See page 241 for more.) The rubric above can guide you.

How can I recognize "fuzzy thinking" in my writing?

You have used fuzzy thinking when an idea is misleading and cannot be fairly supported. Here are three types of fuzzy thinking to watch for.

Jumping to Conclusions

Avoid using one small fact to reach a big conclusion.

Last year, a kid got sick after lunch, so cafeteria food isn't healthy.

Bandwagoning

Avoid using a group's opinion as if it were the truth.

None of my classmates think that metal detectors make schools safer.

Take It, or Leave It

Avoid statements that don't leave room for discussion.

Either the pep band will sell 1,000 pizzas, or it will never play again.

 Read the following examples. Then identify the type of fuzzy thinking each one contains. How could it be improved?

1. Either the principal will remove the metal detectors, or this school will be a prison.

2. Our pep band didn't raise much money this year, so nobody appreciates us.

3. Everybody knows that restaurant food is healthier than cafeteria food.

 Revise fuzzy thinking. Review your essay and look for places where you have used fuzzy thinking. Revise your writing to fix whatever logic errors you find.

3 I need to use more qualifiers and improve my thinking.

2 I don't use qualifiers, and my thinking is not well supported.

1 I need to learn more about qualifiers and avoid fuzzy thinking.

How can qualifiers make my ideas easier to support?

Ideas that suggest "all" or "nothing" are difficult to support. That's why qualifiers are so important in persuasive writing. Read the two ideas below. Notice the qualifier in the second sentence.

Students in study hall can't work because of lunchroom noise.

Many **students in study hall can't work because of lunchroom noise.**

The qualifier "many" limits the idea, making it easier to support. Other helpful qualifiers include *most, often, usually, some,* and *in many cases.*

 Rewrite the following four statements. Add a different qualifier to each one.

1. Students think teachers assign too much homework.
2. Classrooms are crowded.
3. Students don't work hard.
4. Parents are too busy to help with homework.

 Revise "all-or-nothing" ideas. Look for ideas that are difficult to support. Add qualifiers to limit these ideas.

Ideas
Fuzzy thinking is fixed, and a qualifier is added.

~~When the school board~~ *is planning to cut* ~~cuts~~ art classes, *every*

~~student artist will quit,~~ But this is wrong.

in Burnley
Schools should keep art classes.

Art encourages people to be creative and . . .

PERSUASIVE

Revising **for** *Organization*

6 My organization makes my essay logical and convincing.

5 My transitions connect my reasons well from beginning to end.

4 I use some transitions within each paragraph, but I need to link my paragraphs.

When you check your essay's *organization,* look for a smooth flow of ideas both within each paragraph and from one paragraph to the next.

How can I check the transitions in my paragraphs?

To check a paragraph for transitions, read it carefully, making certain that each sentence moves logically into the next.

 Read both paragraphs below. The first paragraph does not have transitions; the second one does. The transitions in the second one help the reader understand how the details relate to each other.

Without Transition Words and Phrases

> Kids who grow up in the city should go to a wilderness summer camp at least once. Kids will learn survival skills. They will learn how to purify water, to keep warm, and to stay calm during an emergency. Camping in the wilderness gives kids many new experiences and teaches them that not all wildlife is dangerous. Kids will come to enjoy and respect the world of nature.

With Transition Words and Phrases

> Kids who grow up in the city should go to a wilderness summer camp at least once. <u>First of all</u>, kids will learn survival skills. <u>For example</u>, they will learn how to purify water, to keep warm, and to stay calm during an emergency. Camping in the wilderness <u>also</u> gives kids many new experiences and teaches them that not all wildlife is dangerous. <u>As a result</u>, kids will come to enjoy and respect the world of nature.

 Connect your sentences. Review each paragraph in your essay. Do you need to add a few transitions to show how your details relate to each other? Make any needed changes. See pages 572–573 for a list of transitions.

3 I need to use transitions within my paragraphs and between my paragraphs.

2 My beginning, middle, and ending run together. I need to create paragraphs.

1 My organization is unclear, and I need to learn how to use transitions.

How can transitions link my paragraphs?

Transitions can help show how the ideas in one paragraph are related to the ideas in others. Read the topic sentences below from a persuasive essay about improving a neighborhood playground. As you'll see, the transitions (in blue) show how the paragraphs' ideas are related.

To begin with, **the playground at 6th Street and Rio Grande is a health hazard.**

In addition, **the playground is an eyesore.**

Finally, **fixing up the playground will send a positive message to neighborhood kids.**

 Read the following topic sentences from a persuasive essay about tutoring. Rewrite them, adding transitions that help show how the ideas are related. Choose from the following transitions: *First of all, Also, In addition, As a result,* and *Lastly.*

1. A tutoring program could help struggling students.
2. Tutoring would give teachers a break.
3. The program would let advanced students share what they know.

Organization
A transition is added between paragraphs.

Besides,
⋀School is the best place for many kids to make art. Some kinds of art require lots of special supplies like clay, glazes, canvases, paints, and . . .

PERSUASIVE

Revising **for** Voice

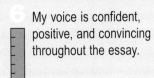

6 My voice is confident, positive, and convincing throughout the essay.

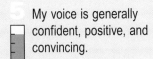

5 My voice is generally confident, positive, and convincing.

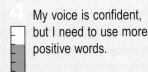

4 My voice is confident, but I need to use more positive words.

When you revise for *voice,* check to see how your essay sounds. You should try to sound confident and positive. The rubric above will guide you.

How can I make my voice sound confident?

You can make your writing voice sound confident by removing words that make you sound unsure about your ideas. Read the two examples below. The first one contains words (in blue) that make the writing sound unsure. The second example sounds much more confident.

Unsure Writing Voice

Probably it would be a good idea if **students could learn to swim before they graduate from high school.** It seems like **there are many reasons for learning how to swim. Swimming is** supposed to be **a great all-around exercise.**

Confident Writing Voice

Students should learn to swim before they graduate from high school. There are many reasons for learning how to swim. Swimming is a great all-around exercise.

Identify the words in the following sentences that make the writer sound unsure. Then rewrite each one to sound more confident.

1. Another possible reason for learning to swim would be that it can be an activity that might be enjoyable.

2. Probably you might be able to swim at a public pool for a cost that is hopefully reasonable.

Check your voice. Review your essay for words that make you sound unsure of yourself. Sometimes it is necessary to qualify your ideas, but using too many qualifiers will make you sound unsure.

3 At times my voice sounds confident, but I use some overly negative words.

2 I need to sound confident and avoid overly negative words.

1 I need to understand how to create a confident and positive voice.

How can I make my writing sound positive?

You can make persuasive writing sound positive by avoiding overly negative words. Always use strong, positive words to motivate your reader to agree with you.

 Find and replace negative words and phrases in each of the following sentences.

1. Our school doesn't give a rip about the marching band.
   Our school doesn't care enough about the marching band.
2. Kids who don't exercise will turn into blobs.
3. You're a dummy if you don't pay attention in school.
4. The rule against hats in school is ridiculous.

 Revise for voice. Review your persuasive essay for overly negative words. Replace those words and phrases that are so negative they change the voice of the essay.

Voice
Negative words are replaced, and uncertain words are cut.

Many students ~~are too broke~~ can't afford to have these things at home. ~~Maybe it might be a little bit~~ It would be unfair to take away the students' chances to explore different kinds of art.

Everyone knows that the district has money . . .

Revising **for** Word Choice

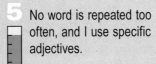

6 The words I use in my essay are strong and help persuade the reader.

5 No word is repeated too often, and I use specific adjectives.

4 No word is repeated too often, but I could use a few more specific adjectives.

When you revise for *word choice,* you want to make sure your words keep the reader's attention and express your persuasive message. Use the rubric above to help you revise the words in your essay.

Do I repeat any words too often?

To find out if you have repeated some words too often, carefully read your essay. You can replace repeated words by using pronouns and synonyms. As you read the paragraph below, notice the effect of repeating one word over and over again.

> **People can use computers to connect with the outside world. For example,** people (they) **can meet new** people (friends) **in chat rooms. People can also play games, like chess, with** people (other players) **all over the world**.

Now read the paragraph again, substituting the words in parentheses. Did you notice a difference?

 Read the following examples. Then copy the sentences on your own paper, replacing the boldfaced words with pronouns or synonyms.

1. The student council is sponsoring a mock election. Earlier this week, **the student council** handed out information sheets.

2. Pep band is exciting! Not only do the students get to choose **exciting** music, but they have an **exciting** time jamming.

3. The sixth graders gather toys for a holiday drive. They **gather** video games, action figures, and board games.

 Check for repeated words. Read your essay and look for repeated words. Replace them with pronouns or synonyms.

3 I need to replace some words with synonyms and pronouns. I could use more specific adjectives.

2 I repeat many words and use general adjectives. I need to replace them.

1 I need to learn how to use synonyms, pronouns, and specific adjectives.

Do I use too many general adjectives?

Your adjectives should help send a specific message to the reader. Try to avoid weak words like *nice, good,* and *bad.*

 Study the pairs of sentences below. Which sentence in each pair sends a clear, specific message? Explain your choices.

1. **a.** The morning announcements contain good information.
   b. The morning announcements contain valuable information.

2. **a.** That new girl is nice.
   b. That new girl is friendly.

3. **a.** The pencil sharpener made a bad sound.
   b. The pencil sharpener made a clawing sound.

4. **a.** Tanya's little brother is interesting.
   b. Tanya's little brother is clever.

 Check your adjectives. Replace any general adjectives with adjectives that send clear, specific messages.

Word Choice
A general adjective and repeated words are replaced.

Take away ~~good~~ colorful paintings, metal sculptures, and beautiful photographs. ~~Take away~~ Erase the artwork from book covers, magazine ads, and comic books. Who would want to live in a world without art? . . .

PERSUASIVE

Revising **for** Sentence Fluency

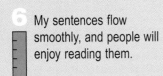 **6** My sentences flow smoothly, and people will enjoy reading them.

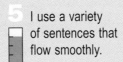 **5** I use a variety of sentences that flow smoothly.

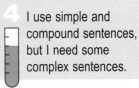 **4** I use simple and compound sentences, but I need some complex sentences.

When you revise for *sentence fluency,* you need to make sure you have used a variety of sentence types. If you use too many simple sentences, your writing may sound monotonous. The rubric above can help you.

Have I used a variety of sentence types?

You can check your writing for sentence variety by seeing how many simple, compound, and complex sentences you use. (See pages 515–517.)

- A **simple sentence** is a subject and predicate forming one complete thought.

     The school board is planning to cut art class.

- A **compound sentence** is two simple sentences joined by a comma and a coordinating conjunction such as *and, but, or, so, for,* or *yet.*

     I don't want to live in a world without art, but **I might have to.**

- A **complex sentence** is a simple sentence plus a clause beginning with a subordinating conjunction such as *when, after, because,* or *as.*

     Students experiment and make mistakes as **they try to capture their dreams using clay, paint, and paper.**

 Read the following sentences. For each one, identify whether it is simple, compound, or complex.

1. When people in the cafeteria are too noisy, students in study hall can't work.

2. Bellwood needs a different study hall.

3. It's hard to concentrate, and the smell of food is distracting.

 Check your sentence variety. Read each paragraph of your essay. How many simple, compound, and complex sentences do you have in each one? If too many simple sentences appear together, rewrite some of them as compound or complex sentences. (See pages 515–517.)

3 In some places, I use too many simple sentences. I need to combine some of them.

2 My writing has too many simple sentences. I need to combine many of them.

1 Most of my sentences need to be rewritten.

How can I improve my sentence variety?

You can improve your sentence variety by combining simple sentences in a number of ways. You can use a coordinating conjunction like *and, but, or, so, for,* or *yet* to form a compound sentence. You can also use a subordinating conjunction like *when, after, because,* or *as* to make a complex sentence.

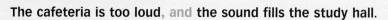
have to have all kinds

Two Simple Sentences

The cafeteria is too loud. The sound fills the study hall.

One Compound Sentence

The cafeteria is too loud, and the sound fills the study hall.

One Complex Sentence

When the cafeteria is too loud, the sound fills the study hall.

Try It Combine each pair of simple sentences using the first word in parentheses. Then combine the pairs again using the second word.

1. People in the cafeteria are rude. Students in study hall struggle to work. *(so, when)*

2. The principal is looking for solutions. She knows this is a problem *(for, because)*

Revise **Combine simple sentences.** If you have too many simple sentences together, combine a few into compound or complex sentences.

PERSUASIVE

Sentence Fluency
Two sentences are joined.

It's hard to imagine a school dropping reading or
*   but*
math. The school board plans to drop art . . .

Revising **Using a Checklist**

Check your revising. On a piece of paper, write the numbers 1 to 12. If you can answer "yes" to a question, put a check mark after that number. If not, continue to work with that part of your essay.

Ideas

_____ **1.** Do I focus on an interesting cause?
_____ **2.** Have I corrected any "fuzzy thinking" in my essay?
_____ **3.** Do I use qualifiers to make ideas easier to support?

Organization

_____ **4.** Do I include a beginning, a middle, and an ending?
_____ **5.** Do I use transitions within and between paragraphs?
_____ **6.** Have I reorganized parts that were out of place?

Voice

_____ **7.** Does my voice sound confident and positive?
_____ **8.** Does my voice fit my audience? My purpose? My topic?

Word Choice

_____ **9.** Have I replaced repeated words with synonyms and pronouns?
_____ **10.** Do I use strong adjectives and verbs?

Sentence Fluency

_____ **11.** Do I use different sentence types?
_____ **12.** Have I fixed short, choppy sentences by combining them?

Make a clean copy. When you've finished revising, make a clean copy before you edit. This makes checking for conventions easier.

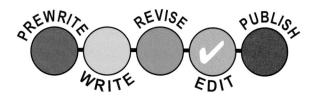

Editing

After you've finished revising your essay, it's time to edit it for your use of conventions: punctuation, capitalization, spelling, and grammar.

Keys to Effective Editing

1. Use a dictionary, a thesaurus, and the "Proofreader's Guide" in the back of this book.

2. Check for any words or phrases that may be confusing to the reader.

3. Check your writing for correctness of punctuation, capitalization, spelling, and grammar.

4. If you are using a computer, edit on a printed computer copy. Then enter your changes on the computer.

5. Use the editing and proofreading marks inside the back cover of this book.

PERSUASIVE

Editing **for Conventions**

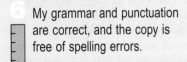
6 My grammar and punctuation are correct, and the copy is free of spelling errors.

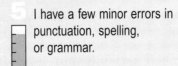
5 I have a few minor errors in punctuation, spelling, or grammar.

4 I need to correct some errors in punctuation, spelling, and grammar.

When you edit for *conventions,* you should focus on grammar, spelling, capitalization, and punctuation. Use the rubric above to guide your editing.

How do I check comparative and superlative words?

The comparative form of an adjective compares two people, places, things, or ideas. (Also see pages 487 and 734.4.)

- One way to create the comparative form is to add the suffix *er* to a word.

    Toshi has a big **dog, but Lupe's dog is** bigger.

- If the word has two or more syllables, add the word *more* to make it comparative.

    However, Lupe's dog is more annoying **than Toshi's.**

The superlative form of an adjective compares three or more people, places, things, or ideas. (See pages 487 and 734.5.)

- One way to make the superlative form is to add the suffix *est.*

    My sister has the biggest **gerbil I've ever seen.**

- If the word has two or more syllables, use the word *most* to create the superlative form.

    Ravi is the most enthusiastic **pet owner I've ever seen.**

Number your paper from 1 to 6. For each of the words below, write two sentences: one using its comparative form and one using its superlative form.

        wild   **difficult**   **quick**

Check for comparatives and superlatives. Edit your paper to make sure you used the proper form for any comparatives or superlatives.

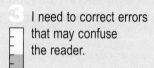

3 I need to correct errors that may confuse the reader.

2 I need to correct many errors that make my essay difficult to read.

1 I need help making corrections.

How do I know when to capitalize an adjective?

You need to capitalize proper adjectives, which are formed from proper nouns. The common noun it modifies is not capitalized. (See 618.1)

Proper Noun	Proper Adjective + Common Noun
Shetland Islands	Shetland pony
Yorkshire, England	Yorkshire terrier
Canada	Canada goose

If the adjective is not proper, it is not capitalized.

potbellied **pig**   bald **eagle**

 Number your paper from 1 to 4. In each sentence, if an adjective needs a capital letter, write the correction on your paper.

1. Anthony's pet python came from the amazon jungle.

2. He could have had a plain old garden snake.

3. Kylee wanted a tasmanian devil.

4. I'd be happy with an arabian horse for a pet.

Edit for conventions. Check your paper to make sure you have capitalized any proper adjectives.

Conventions
A proper adjective is capitalized.

Students feel a personal connection with the

native american tribes they are studying. Hands-
  ≡   ≡

on projects are an important way for . . .

PERSUASIVE

Editing Using a Checklist

 Check your editing. On a piece of paper, write the numbers 1 to 13. If you can answer "yes" to a question, put a check mark after that number. If not, continue to edit for that convention.

Conventions

PUNCTUATION

_____ **1.** Do I use end punctuation after all my sentences?

_____ **2.** Do I use commas after introductory phrases and transitions?

_____ **3.** Do I use commas between items in a series?

_____ **4.** Do I use commas in compound sentences?

_____ **5.** Do I use quotation marks around any direct quotations?

CAPITALIZATION

_____ **6.** Do I start all my sentences with capital letters?

_____ **7.** Do I capitalize all proper nouns and proper adjectives?

SPELLING

_____ **8.** Have I spelled all my words correctly?

_____ **9.** Have I double-checked the words my spell-checker may have missed?

GRAMMAR

_____ **10.** Do I form comparative and superlative forms correctly?

_____ **11.** Do I use correct forms of verbs *(had gone,* not *had went)*?

_____ **12.** Do my subjects and verbs agree in number? (She and I *are* going, not She and I *is* going)?

_____ **13.** Do I use the right words *(to, too, two)*?

Creating a Title

- Restate the call to action: **Shelter the Animals**
- Write a slogan: **Let's Band Together**
- Be creative: **Where Art Thou, Art?**

Publishing

PREWRITE · WRITE · REVISE · EDIT · PUBLISH ✓

Sharing Your Essay

After you have worked so hard to write and improve your essay, make a neat final copy to share. You may also present your persuasive essay as an editorial, a speech, or a multimedia presentation.

Make a final copy. Follow your teacher's instructions or use the guidelines below to format your essay. (If you are using a computer, see page 60.) Create a clean final copy of your essay and carefully proofread it.

Focus on Presentation

- Use blue or black ink and write neatly.
- Write your name in the upper left corner of page 1.
- Skip a line and center your title; skip another line and start your writing.
- Indent every paragraph and leave a one-inch margin on all four sides.
- Write your last name and the page number in the upper right corner of every page after the first one.

Submit to a Newspaper

Follow the paper's instructions for submitting an essay to your local or school newspaper.

Give a Speech

Present your persuasive essay to your classmates in the form of a speech. See pages 423–430 for more information about preparing a speech.

Create a Multimedia Presentation

Turn your persuasive essay into a multimedia presentation. See pages 411–415 for more information.

PERSUASIVE

Rubric for Persuasive Writing

Use the following rubric for guiding and assessing your persuasive writing. Refer to it whenever you want to improve your writing using the six traits.

Ideas

6 **The clear reasoning informs and convinces the reader.**

5 The essay has a clear opinion statement. Logical reasons support the writer's opinion.

4 The opinion statement is clear, and most reasons support the writer's opinion.

Organization

6 **The organization logically presents a smooth flow of ideas from beginning to end.**

5 The opening contains the opinion statement. The middle provides clear support. The transitions build strong connections.

4 The opening contains the opinion statement. The middle provides support. Some transitions do not work.

Voice

6 **The writer's voice is confident, positive, and completely convincing.**

5 The writer's voice is confident and helps persuade the reader.

4 The writer's voice is confident. It needs to persuade the reader.

Word Choice

6 **Strong, engaging, positive words contribute to the main message. Every word counts.**

5 Strong, positive words help make the message clear.

4 Strong, positive words are used, but some overused words need synonyms.

Sentence Fluency

6 **The sentences flow smoothly, and people will enjoy reading the variety of sentences.**

5 Variety is seen in both the types of sentences and their beginnings.

4 Varied sentence beginnings are used. Sentence variety would make the essay more interesting to read.

Conventions

6 **The essay is free of errors.**

5 Grammar and punctuation errors are few. The reader is not distracted by the errors.

4 Grammar and punctuation errors are seen in a few sentences. They distract the reader in those areas.

3	2	1
3 The opinion statement is clear. Reasons and details are not as complete as they need to be.	**2** The opinion statement is unclear. Reasons and details are needed.	**1** An opinion statement, reasons, and details are needed.
3 The beginning, middle, and ending exist. Transitions are needed.	**2** The beginning, middle, and ending run together.	**1** The organization is unclear. The reader is easily lost.
3 The writer's voice needs to be more confident and persuade the reader.	**2** The writer's voice sounds bored.	**1** The writer's voice can't be heard.
3 Many words need to be stronger and more positive.	**2** The same weak words are used throughout the essay.	**1** Word choice has not been considered.
3 Varied sentence beginnings are needed. Sentence variety would make the essay more interesting.	**2** Most sentences begin the same way. Most of the sentences are simple. Compound and complex sentences are needed.	**1** Sentence fluency has not been established. Ideas do not flow smoothly.
3 There are a number of errors that may confuse the reader.	**2** Frequent errors make the essay difficult to read.	**1** Nearly every sentence contains errors.

PERSUASIVE

Evaluating a Persuasive Essay

As you read through the persuasive essay below, focus on the writer's strengths and weaknesses. Then read the student self-assessment on the next page. **(The student essay below contains some errors.)**

Get Moving

Many students have televisions, stereos, and computers in their homes. They have cable channels to watch, stacks of CD's to listen to, and games to play. These things entertain them, but can cause problems if they do them to much. Friends, schoolwork, and health are things that can suffer because of to much home entertainment.

For one thing, to much time alone can hurt friendships. Not being in sports or other activities gets people in the habit of being by themselves. They sometimes become to shy. Because they spend to much time alone. Then they wonder why they don't have any friends.

In addition, coming home from school and turning on the TV or computer puts off getting started on schoolwork. Instead of doing assignments right after school, students might wait until there to tired to do a good job. Even worse, they might not do there homework at all. That is a big problem!

Even health can be a problem for those who sit around to much. Doctors say that young people are out of shape and overwieght. Bad habits that start early can cause problems later on. Almost everyone needs to be more active.

There probably are good shows to watch on TV and computer games that teach things. Sitting around the house to much is not good. Everyone needs to be careful about letting toys take to much of their time. If kids want to have more friends, think better, and feel better, they need to get moving!

Student Self-Assessment

The assessment that follows includes the student's comments about his essay on page 258. In the first comment, the student mentions something positive from the essay. In the second comment, the student points out an area for possible improvement. (The writer used the rubric and number scale on pages 256–257 to complete this assessment.)

5 Ideas

    1. *My opinion about my cause is clear.*
    2. *My paragraph on health effects could have more information.*

5 Organization

    1. *I talk about one problem in each paragraph.*
    2. *I could have used better transitions between paragraphs.*

4 Voice

    1. *My call to action is strong.*
    2. *I could have been more convincing overall.*

3 Word Choice

    1. *My audience will understand my words.*
    2. *I overused the words "problem" and "problems."*

4 Sentence Fluency

    1. *I used some complex sentences.*
    2. *I could have made my sentences flow more smoothly.*

3 Conventions

    1. *I used commas correctly in a series.*
    2. *I still get confused using "to" and "there."*

Use the rubric. Assess your essay using the rubric on pages 256–257.

  1 On your own paper, list the six traits. Leave room after each trait to write one strength and one weakness.

  2 Then choose a number (from 1 to 6) that shows how well you used each trait.

PERSUASIVE

Reflecting on Your Writing

Now that you've completed your persuasive essay, take a moment to reflect on it. Complete each starter sentence below on your own paper. Your thoughts will help you prepare for your next writing assignment.

My Persuasive Essay

1. The best part of my essay is . . .

2. The part that still needs work is . . .

3. The prewriting activity that worked best for me was . . .

4. The main thing I learned about writing a persuasive essay is . . .

5. In my next persuasive essay, I would like to . . .

6. Here is one question I still have about writing a persuasive essay:

Persuasive Writing

Pet-Peeve Essay

"I'm peeved" is an old-fashioned expression meaning "I'm irritated." A pet peeve may be something that bothers you a little bit more than it bothers others.

Writing about a pet peeve is another form of persuasive writing. In this form, a writer complains about something annoying but doesn't really expect to change it.

We all have pet peeves: people who chew gum with their mouths open, kids who always cut in line, parents who think they can rap. A pet-peeve essay gives you a chance to vent some frustration as you complain in a humorous way about something that irritates you.

Writing Guidelines

Subject:	Something that annoys you
Form:	A pet-peeve essay
Purpose:	To complain
Audience:	Classmates

Pet-Peeve Essay

The following pet-peeve essay was written by a student annoyed by the food served in the school cafeteria.

No More Mystery Meat

Beginning

The beginning introduces the pet peeve.

The cafeteria served "mystery meat" for lunch again today. At least, I think it was meat. It was chunky, brown, and coated with a yellow sauce. I've seen that stuff before. Sometimes the meat is served with noodles. Sometimes it's baked, and sometimes it's fried, but what it really is remains a mystery.

Now, I don't like to complain. Still, it seems to me that after we spend a long morning of working math problems and studying science, the school could at least give us something good to eat. Imagine getting a slice of steaming hot pizza, covered with lots of cheese! Picture some fried chicken or even a hot dog with all the fixings. We get these types of lunches at times, but not enough.

Middle

Humor keeps the reader's attention.

No, instead, we usually get something that doesn't even look like food. What is that

Middle
Specific details make the complaint interesting.

tough brown stuff? All I know is that it certainly doesn't look like lunch to me! But it keeps showing up on our trays, and we can either choke it down or go hungry. That's not much of a choice.

It seems like we have mystery meat at least once a week, or maybe even more. Now that I think about it, maybe they get a truckload of the stuff and just keep on serving it week after week until it's all gone. Unfortunately, they never seem to run out of it! They also try to disguise this mystery meat, but we always recognize it.

Ending

The last paragraph offers a humorous solution.

I have a better use for mystery meat. Next time it's served, I'll take it home to my dog, Jiggs. He likes chewing on old shoe leather like this.

Respond to the reading. On your own paper answer the following questions about the sample essay.

☐ Ideas (1) What complaint does the writer want to communicate?

☐ Organization (2) How did the writer organize the main ideas—by time, by location, or by logical order?

☐ Voice & Word Choice (3) What words and phrases show the writer's irritation?

Prewriting **Selecting a Topic**

To choose a topic for a pet-peeve essay, think of everyday annoyances—things that "bug" you. Does your brother or sister annoy you? Does riding the bus drive you crazy? Are the school lunches boring?

The writer of the sample pet-peeve essay used the freewriting below to discover a writing topic.

Freewriting

What bugs me? Let's see, I hate the way my sister follows me around. She always wants to meet my friends and talk to them. But I guess my friends kind of like her, and anyway, she's not that bad. The school bus! That's something I don't like. Well, except it's fun when José and Rick and I get the back seat and bounce over the railroad tracks. School isn't so bad, either. How about lunch—ack! What is that stuff? How come the cafeteria thinks we can eat fried shoe leather? . . .

Choose your topic. Freewrite about your life. Go through your day and think about things that irritate you. Keep going until you settle on a topic that you can complain about in a pet-peeve essay. If you have trouble getting started, answer the question "What things bug me the most?"

Adding Humorous Details

Humor makes a pet-peeve essay fun to read. These techniques can help.

- **Make comparisons.** Comparing your pet peeve with something else can emphasize your feelings. In the sample essay, the writer compares mystery meat to an old piece of shoe leather.

- **Use exaggeration.** A writer can add humor to an essay by exaggerating. In the sample essay, the writer suggests that the mystery meat comes by the truckload.

Create humorous details. Write at least one comparison and one exaggeration that you could use in your essay.

Writing **Organizing a Pet Peeve**

When you write a basic persuasive essay, order of importance is an effective way to organize your ideas. With order of importance, you tell the most important reason first or last.

However, you can also arrange the reasons in a way that simply makes the best sense, called *logical order*. With this order, one reason is no more important than the one before or after it. This is the type of organization that is used in the pet peeve on pages 262–263.

Using logical order is like fitting the pieces in a jigsaw puzzle. The graphic below shows how the three main reasons in the pet peeve fit together.

Logical Order

After a long morning, we need something good to eat.

But usually we get some tough mystery meat.

The cooks must have a truckload of the stuff.

Creating Your First Draft

Though an essay about a pet peeve is a lighter kind of persuasive essay, it still has a definite form. As you write your essay, follow these guidelines.

- **Introduce your pet peeve.** Maybe you could begin with a funny story about an annoying experience you had.

- **Discuss the pet peeve.** Help the reader understand why the topic annoys you. Remember to make comparisons and use exaggeration in your explanation. Organize your ideas in the best way. (See above.)

- **Close your essay by offering a solution.** Your solution might be reasonable: "It's time to start bringing my own lunch." It might be funny: "Next time I get mystery meat, I'll take it home to my dog, Jiggs. He likes chewing on just about anything."

Write your first draft. Use the information above as a guide. Try to keep your writing voice light and humorous.

Revising **Improving Your Writing**

Read over your first draft. Revise it by asking yourself the following questions.

- ☐ Ideas Have I stated my complaint clearly? Have I included any comparisons or used any exaggerations? Do I need to cut any details that are off the subject?

- ☐ **Organization** Are my paragraphs easy to follow? Are the points in the paragraphs in the best order?

- ☐ Voice What would make my writing voice stronger? Does my essay sound like me?

- ☐ **Word Choice** Have I used convincing words? What words could I replace to make my essay more effective?

- ☐ **Sentence Fluency** Have I used complete sentences? Do I vary the way my sentences begin?

Revise your writing. Improve your first draft, using the questions above as a guide. Make your changes and then create a clean copy for editing.

Editing **Checking for Conventions**

As you edit your essay, focus on the following questions.

- ☐ **Conventions** Have I carefully checked my work for punctuation, capitalization, and spelling errors? Have I also checked for errors in usage *(to, too, two; their, there, they're; its, it's)* and other grammar errors?

Edit your work. Use the questions above to decide how to edit your essay. After making your changes, create a final copy and check it one more time for errors.

Persuasive Writing

Across the
Curriculum

You can use the valuable skill of writing persuasively throughout the school day. For example, your social studies teacher may assign an editorial cartoon about a social problem. Your math teacher may require convincing proof for some mathematical fact. In science, you may need to argue for or against some scientific theory. In or out of school, you may need to write persuasive letters to convince others to take a certain action.

You may also need to be persuasive on writing tests. The model and tips at the end of this chapter will help you.

What's Ahead

- **Social Studies:** Creating an Editorial Cartoon
- **Math:** Presenting a Proof
- **Science:** Supporting a Theory
- **Practical Writing:** Drafting a Persuasive Letter

Social Studies:
Creating an Editorial Cartoon

A picture is worth a thousand words, especially when the picture is an editorial cartoon. An editorial cartoon is a drawing that pokes fun at a political or social problem.

The following editorial cartoon was created for a social studies class. While the paragraph explains the social problem, the cartoon does most of the persuading. What makes the cartoon persuasive? What makes it funny?

The paragraph explains the problem.

Social Problem: Some people think that oil companies should be allowed to drill for oil in some national parks and wildlife refuges. This is a bad idea. If it really is a wildlife refuge, animals ought to be able to live there safely and naturally. The cartoon expresses this opinion.

The drawing illustrates the problem.

Writing Tips

Before you write . . .

- **Choose a problem you care about.**
  Think of things that worry you about your city, the country, or the world.
- **Do your research.**
  Read articles and gather information.
- **Think of symbols.**
  Consider symbols to use in your cartoon. In the example, the oil well symbolizes the oil industry.
- **Use pictures as models.**
  Find a picture of an oil well, for example, if you need to draw an oil well.

During your writing . . .

- **Explain the problem.**
  Tell why the problem concerns you.
- **Draw your cartoon.**
  Concentrate on one or two images.
- **Write a caption below the cartoon, if necessary.**
  If your cartoon needs explaining, create a sentence or paragraph that will get your point across. This sentence is called a caption.

After you've written a first draft . . .

- **Review your opening explanation.**
  Make sure that all of your ideas are clear.
- **Study your cartoon.**
  Redraw any parts that could be better.
- **Improve your caption.**
  Make sure each word has a purpose.

PERSUASIVE

Create an editorial cartoon about a social problem that concerns you. Use the tips above as a guide.

Math: Presenting a Proof

The best way to show that a given math concept is correct is to prove it. This type of writing is called a "proof."

The beginning names the concept.

Long Division Is Short Subtraction

Concept: Division is a quick form of subtraction.
Proof 1: One way to solve 42 ÷ 7 would be to subtract 7 from 42 until the answer is 0.

$$42 - 7 = 35$$
$$35 - 7 = 28$$
$$28 - 7 = 21$$
$$21 - 7 = 14$$
$$14 - 7 = 7$$
$$7 - 7 = 0$$

The middle shows two proofs.

How many 7's would need to be subtracted to reach 0? The answer is 6. Of course, 42 ÷ 7 = 6.

Proof 2: Here is a harder problem: 209 ÷ 46 = ?.

$$209 - 46 = 163$$
$$163 - 46 = 117$$
$$117 - 46 = 71$$
$$71 - 46 = 25$$
$$25 - 46 = ?$$

The last subtraction would end with a negative number. That means 25 is the remainder. Then we count how many 46's were subtracted. The answer is 4, with a remainder of 25. Dividing it out brings the same answer (209 ÷ 46 = 4, remainder 25).

The ending restates the concept.

Conclusion: A division problem can be solved by using either division or subtraction.

Writing Tips

Before you write . . .

- **Choose a math concept.**
  Think of math concepts you understand well. Make a list and choose one.
- **Study the concept.**
  Review the idea until you thoroughly understand it.
- **Experiment with ways to prove it.**
  Recall how your teacher first taught the idea to the class. Think of how you could prove the concept. Check books and Internet articles for other ways.
- **Plan your proof.**
  List the steps for proving the concept.

During your writing . . .

- **Introduce the math concept.**
  State what you will prove.
- **Give the proof or proofs.**
  Present the information in a step-by-step process.
- **Summarize your proof.**
  Restate your concept.

After you've written a first draft . . .

- **Check for completeness.**
  Include all of the information the reader will need.
- **Check for correctness.**
  Make sure there are no errors in your math, spelling, punctuation, and grammar.

 Choose a math concept to prove. (Here is an example: An even number plus or minus another even number will always equal an even number.) Then follow the tips above to present your proof.

Science: Supporting a Theory

A scientific theory is an idea or group of ideas that explains an event. When you support a theory, you back your ideas with facts and reasons. The following essay supports one theory about how the dinosaurs became extinct.

What Happened to the Dinosaurs?

The **beginning** introduces the topic and the theory.

There are many mysteries about dinosaurs. One of the most interesting is this question: "Why did they become extinct?" Scientists have been arguing about this since the first fossils were discovered. The most popular theory says that the earth was struck by a gigantic meteor or asteroid when dinosaurs lived all over the world.

The **middle** paragraphs describe the theory.

According to the theory, the huge meteor caused a shock wave of heat and strong winds that killed many dinosaurs. A big cloud of dust darkened the skies for years. That made the world grow colder because the sun couldn't shine through all the dust. There wasn't enough light for plants to grow. Without plant life, the dinosaurs couldn't survive.

Research backs up this theory. Scientists have found a crater in the Gulf of Mexico that was caused by a huge force at about the time the dinosaurs disappeared. They also have found in many places a layer of dirt that is made up of materials found in meteors. This layer was probably formed when the huge dust cloud settled to the ground.

The **ending** summarizes the writer's support for the theory.

Right now, no one knows for sure why the dinosaurs died, but every day scientists dig up new clues. Someday they may be able to prove the meteor theory. For now, it seems like a good explanation.

Writing Tips

Before you write . . .

- **Choose a topic.**
  List scientific theories you are studying. Choose one to support.
- **Research your topic.**
  Read about the theory and make sure you understand it. Find strong reasons to support the theory.
- **Take notes.**
  Jot down facts, reasons, and examples.

Table Diagram

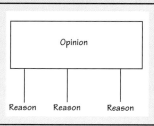

During your writing . . .

- **Introduce the topic and the theory.**
  Give the reader necessary background information.
- **Develop the middle paragraphs.**
  Explain how the theory works and support the explanation.
- **End your essay.**
  Summarize your support for the theory, adding any thoughts or final details.

After you've written a first draft . . .

- **Check for completeness.**
  Make sure you have clearly explained the theory with reasons, facts, and examples.
- **Check for conventions.**
  Make sure there are no errors in spelling, punctuation, and grammar.

PERSUASIVE

 Select a scientific theory that you agree with—for example, the theory of global warming. Your teacher may suggest other topics. Do some research and then write a persuasive essay supporting the theory.

Practical Writing:
Drafting a Persuasive Letter

A polite persuasive letter can influence people and get things done. This sample letter talks about a dangerous intersection and what should be done about it.

The letter follows the correct format. (See pages 276–277.)

1414 Johnson Street
Walvan, WI 53000
April 20, 2009

Mayor Phillip Smith
Walvan City Hall
111 Main Street
Walvan, WI 53000

Dear Mayor Smith:

The beginning introduces the writer and the problem.

I am a student at Parker Lane Middle School. At a city council meeting last October, I asked the council to put up a stoplight at the intersection of 34th Avenue and Cottage Street. That is two blocks away from our school.

The body of the letter explains the problem.

Six months later, cars are still going too fast on 34th Avenue. That makes it dangerous for kids trying to cross the street on their way to and from school. I think that the city should put up a stoplight before someone gets hurt on that corner.

The closing calls for action.

I am not the only one who thinks this corner is dangerous. I have enclosed a petition asking for a stoplight, signed by more than 400 students, teachers, parents, and neighbors. Mayor Smith, please vote for putting a traffic light at 34th Avenue and Cottage Street.

Sincerely,

Ruby Keast

Ruby Keast

Writing Tips

Use the following tips as a guide when you are asked to write a persuasive letter. (Also see pages 276–277.)

Before you write . . .

- **Choose a topic you care about.**
  Think of problems that you would like to solve.
- **Form your opinion.**
  Write freely about the topic to understand it better.
- **Gather information as needed.**
  Collect details and facts that support your opinion.
- **Consider your reader.**
  Learn as much as you can about the organization or person you are writing to.

During your writing . . .

- **Keep it short.**
  Stick to important details. The letter should not be longer than one page. If you have extra information, such as the petition in the example letter, include it on separate pages.
- **Stay on the topic.**
  Make sure every sentence supports your argument.

After you've written a first draft . . .

- **Check for completeness.**
  Add any important reasons you forgot to include.
- **Check for correctness.**
  Read the letter several times. If possible, have someone else read it as well. Make sure that your letter is free of errors and that all names are capitalized and spelled correctly.

PERSUASIVE

 Think of a problem in your community. Find out who could help solve it. Write a persuasive letter to that person, making a strong but polite argument.

Parts of a Business Letter

1 The heading includes your address and the date. Write the heading at least one inch from the top of the page at the left-hand margin.

2 The inside address includes the name, title, and address of the person or organization you are writing to.
- If the person has a title, make sure to include it. (If the title is short, write it on the same line as the name. If the title is long, write it on the next line.)
- If you are writing to an organization or a business but not to a specific person, begin the inside address with the name of the organization or business.

3 The salutation is the greeting. Always put a colon after the salutation.
- If you know the person's name, use it in your greeting.
  Dear Mr. Christopher:
- If you don't know the name of the person, use a salutation like one of these:
  Dear Store Owner:
  Dear Sir or Madam:
  Dear Madison Soccer Club:

4 The body is the main part of the letter. Do not indent your paragraphs; instead, skip a line between them.

5 The closing is placed after the body. Use **Yours truly** or **Sincerely** to close a business letter. Capitalize only the first word of the closing and put a comma after it.

6 The signature ends the letter. If you are using a computer, leave four spaces after the closing; then type your name. Write your signature between the closing and the typed name.

Turn to page 577 for more about writing letters, as well as a set of guidelines for addressing envelopes properly.

Business-Letter Format

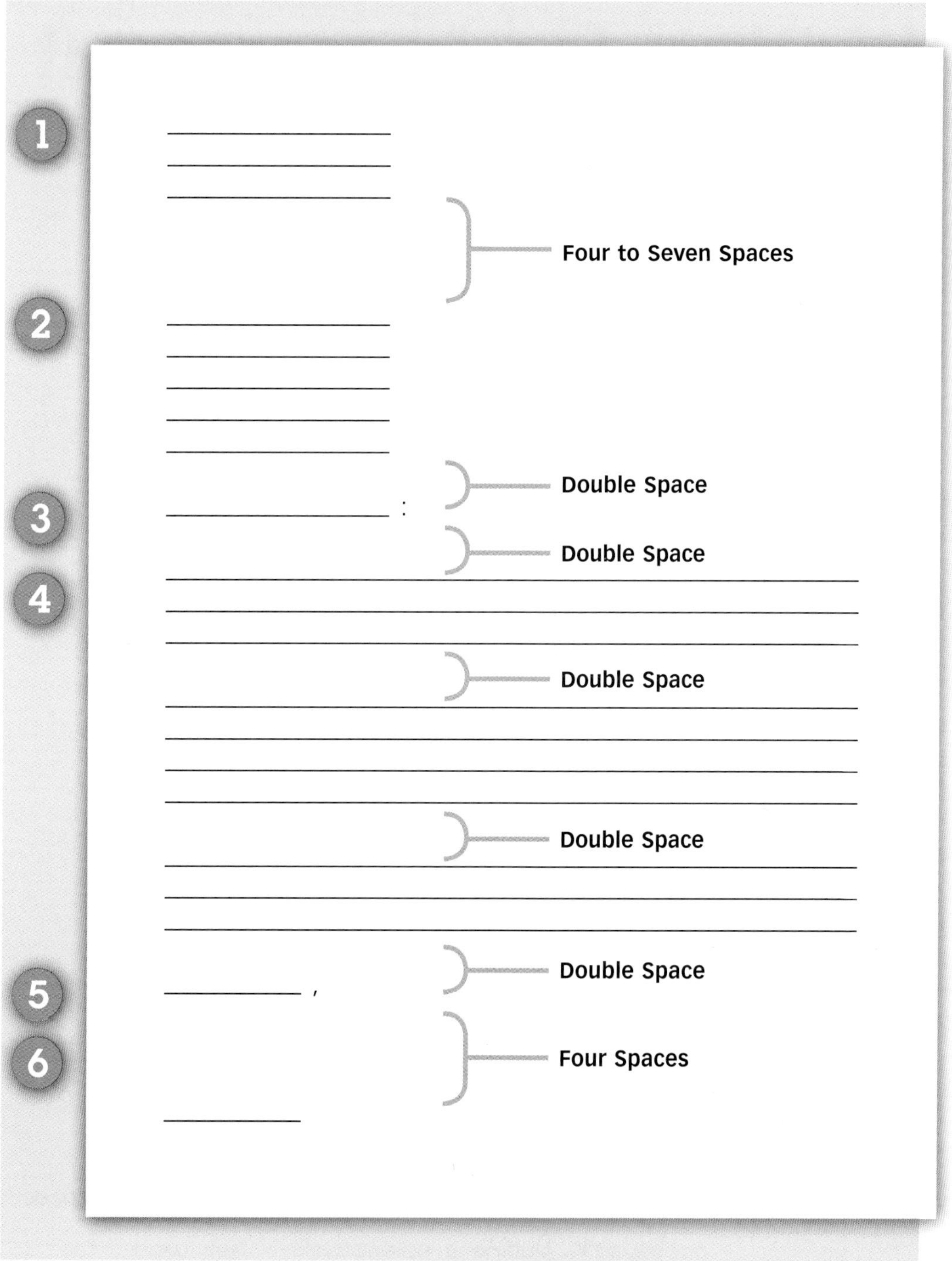

1

2

3

4

5

6

Four to Seven Spaces

Double Space

Double Space

Double Space

Double Space

Double Space

Four Spaces

PERSUASIVE

Personal Writing

Writing for Assessment

Many writing assessment tests include a persuasive writing prompt. A persuasive prompt asks you to state an opinion and support it with strong reasons. Study the following sample prompt and student response.

Persuasive Prompt

Some students complain about having too much homework. Do you agree or disagree with them? Write an essay convincing your teachers to give more or less homework.

The **beginning** includes the opinion statement (underlined).

Each **middle** paragraph gives a reason and details that support the opinion.

Students often complain about having too much homework. They say things like "It takes so long" or "I don't understand it." Some homework can help kids learn, but too much homework can make learning harder. Copeland Middle School students need less homework, not more.

Students at Copeland are already busy. School goes from 8:00 in the morning to 3:00 in the afternoon. Kids who ride the bus may spend an extra hour just getting to school and back home. Then some kids stay after school for an hour or two of sports. Add a couple of hours of homework, and that makes an 11-hour day!

Too much homework may cause students to do poor work. During a science video last week, two students fell asleep. They had always paid attention in class, but the night before, they stayed up late doing homework. Overloading kids with assignments can leave them too tired for school.

When there's too much homework, some kids feel like giving up. Teachers at Copeland might say that they give only 20 minutes of homework a day. Still, if six teachers each give just 20 minutes of homework, that's two hours of work. With all of that work, there's no time to relax.

Some homework is a good thing, but too much homework is not. It overloads kids who are already busy, makes it harder for some kids to learn, and can even make others want to give up. Teachers at Copeland Middle School should give less homework. Then maybe their students will learn even more.

The **ending** summarizes the essay and restates the opinion.

Respond to the reading. Answer the questions to learn about the student response.

☐ Ideas **(1) What is the writer's opinion? (2) What key words in the prompt also appear in the essay? (3) What are two of the reasons that the writer has used to support the opinion?**

☐ Organization **(4) How is the essay organized— by time, location, or point by point?**

☐ Voice **(5) How would you describe the writer's voice in this essay (humorous, serious, angry)?**

PERSUASIVE

Writing Tips

Before you write . . .

- **Understand the prompt.**
  Remember that a persuasive prompt asks you to state and support an opinion.
- **Use your time wisely.**
  Take a few minutes to plan your writing. Use a graphic organizer like a table diagram to help with your planning.

Table Diagram

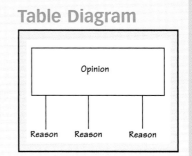

During your writing . . .

- **Form an opinion statement.**
  Think of an opinion that you can clearly support.
- **Build your argument.**
  Think of reasons to support your opinion.
- **End effectively.**
  Summarize your argument and restate your opinion.

After you've written a first draft . . .

- **Check for clear ideas.**
  Rewrite any ideas that sound confusing.
- **Check for conventions.**
  Correct errors in punctuation, spelling, and grammar.

Persuasive Prompts

- Some people say that children under 14 should be at home before 7:00 p.m. unless they are with an adult. Write an essay expressing your opinion about this idea.

- In a letter, convince your parents to take a family trip to a place you would like to visit.

Write a response. Respond to one of the prompts above. Complete your writing within the period of time your teacher gives you. Afterward, list one part of your essay you like and one part you could improve.

Persuasive Writing in Review

Purpose: In persuasive writing, you work to *convince people* to think the way you do about something.

Topics: Your opinion about something
An action you feel is important
A worthy cause

Prewriting

Select a topic that you care about, one that you can present confidently and that is appropriate for your audience. (See page 228.)

Gather ideas about your topic. (See page 229.)

Write an opinion statement that identifies your "cause + feeling." (See page 230.)

Organize your ideas in a list or an outline with your opinion statement at the top, followed by topic sentences with supporting facts or details beneath each. (See pages 231–232.)

Writing

In the beginning part, grab the reader's attention and clearly state your opinion. (See page 235.)

In the middle part, devote a paragraph to each reason with supporting facts and examples. (See pages 236–237.)

In the ending, restate your opinion and make a call to action. (See page 238.)

Revising

Review the ideas, organization, and voice first. Then check for **word choice** and **sentence fluency**. Avoid repeated words and general adjectives. Use a variety of sentence structures. (See pages 240–250.)

Editing

Check your writing for conventions. Ask a friend to edit the writing, too. (See pages 252–254.)

Make a final copy and proofread it for errors before sharing it with your audience. (See page 255.)

Assessing

Use the persuasive rubric as a guide to assess your finished writing. (See pages 256–257.)

PERSUASIVE

experience
answer

Response to Literature

evaluate
react
PREVIEW

Response to Literature

Response Paragraph

You're sitting in a movie theater, the lights dim, and the "Coming Attractions" begin. Each preview highlights a new movie. In a very short time, you know whether or not you want to see it.

A response to literature in the form of a paragraph is much like a movie preview. The writing must get right to the point and say something meaningful about the story. This type of response usually highlights an important event.

On the next page, you will read a sample paragraph that responds to a book. Then you will write a response paragraph of your own.

Writing Guidelines

Subject:	An important event in a book or short story
Form:	A paragraph
Purpose:	To respond to a story
Audience:	Classmates

Response Paragraph

When you write a paragraph about something you've read, it should focus on one event. The **topic sentence** identifies the story, the author, and the event. The details in the **body** of the paragraph describe the event, and the **closing sentence** tells why the event is important.

In the following response, Shandra writes about the book *Bridge to Terabithia*. She shares an event she thinks is very important.

Topic Sentence

Body

Closing Sentence

A Friendship Fort

The most important event in Katherine Paterson's *Bridge to Terabithia* is when Jess and Leslie build their fort. Jess is a shy boy who wants to be an artist, and Leslie is the new girl in the neighborhood. They don't fit in with other kids, but they get along with each other. Together, Jess and Leslie create Terabithia, a secret meeting place in the woods. To get there, they must cross a creek by swinging on an old rope. Jess and Leslie build a wooden fort in Terabithia and spend a lot of time there. Their little wooden fort takes them to a thousand places. The day Jess and Leslie create Terabithia is the day they begin to build their friendship.

Respond to the reading. On your own paper, answer the following questions.

☐ **Ideas** (1) What part of the story does the writer think is most important? (2) Why is it important?

☐ **Organization** (3) Is this paragraph organized by time, by order of importance, or by some other logical order?

☐ **Voice & Word Choice** (4) Does the writer sound knowledgeable about the story? (5) What words or phrases tell you so?

Prewriting **Selecting a Topic**

Your first step in writing a response to literature is choosing a book or short story to write about. Shandra began by listing novels and stories she had read. (See pages 600 and 602 for punctuation of titles.)

List

Books	Short Stories
Holes	"The Gift of the Magi"
The Cay	"The Bell"
Bridge to Terabithia	"The Legend of Sleepy Hollow"

 Prewrite **Choose a book or short story.** On your own paper, list some of your favorite books or short stories. Circle the one that interests you the most.

Focusing on an Important Event

Think about things that happen in the story you've chosen. Focus on events that affect the whole story. A cluster like the one below can help you find the important events.

Cluster

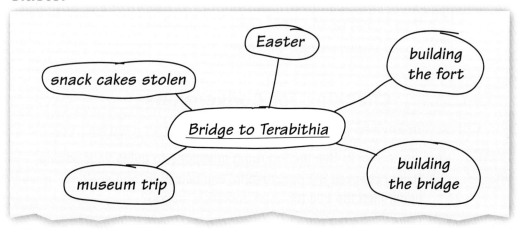

 Prewrite **Create a cluster.** In the center of your cluster, write the title of the book or short story. Around it, write a number of important events. Then choose one event for your paragraph.

Writing Creating Your First Draft

Remember that a paragraph has three main parts: a topic sentence, the body, and a closing sentence. (See the sample on page 284.)

- **Topic sentence:** Write a sentence that names the book or short story, its author, and the main event you will focus on.
- **Body:** Write sentences that describe the event.
- **Closing sentence:** End with a sentence that tells why the event is important.

 Write the first draft of your paragraph. Use the information above as a guide.

Revising Improving Your Paragraph

After you've written your first draft, you need to revise your paragraph for *ideas, organization, voice, word choice,* and *sentence fluency*.

 Review your paragraph. Use the following questions as a guide when you revise.

1 Have I written about an important event?

2 Do my sentences appear in the best order?

3 Does my interest in the story show in my voice?

4 Have I used specific nouns and strong verbs?

5 Do my sentences flow smoothly?

Editing Checking for Conventions

Check your revised paragraph for correct use of conventions.

 Edit your work. Use the following questions to guide your editing:

1 Have I checked my punctuation, capitalization, and spelling? Have I underlined the title (or used quotation marks)?

2 Have I used the right words *(to, two, too; who's, whose)*?

Proofread your paragraph. After making a neat copy of your final paragraph, check it one more time for errors.

Response to Literature

Writing a Book Review

Have you ever been carried away by a book? You start to read but soon lose track of where you are and what time it is. For a while, nothing exists outside of the story, and you and the book soar together on a flight of fancy.

Writing a response to a book helps you relive those flights of fancy. In this assignment, you will write about an insight you have discovered in a book or story. As you recap the important events, you'll soar once more.

Writing Guidelines

Subject:	**A book or a story**
Form:	**An essay**
Purpose:	**To share an insight**
Audience:	**Classmates**

Understanding Your Goals

How do you know what to include in your response? For starters, your response must clearly and concisely retell the story and develop an insight. The chart that follows lists all the key traits of writing a response to literature.

Traits of a Response to Literature

Ideas

Write a focus statement that tells what your insight is and support it with carefully selected details.

Organization

Organize your response using one of the organization patterns. (See page 551.)

Voice

Use a formal voice that fits the assignment and the audience.

Word Choice

Use active verbs instead of passive verbs and avoid too many modifiers.

Sentence Fluency

Vary sentence beginnings and avoid rambling sentences.

Conventions

Correct all errors in punctuation, capitalization, spelling, and grammar.

 Get the big picture. Look at the rubric on pages 318–319. You can use this rubric to assess your progress. Your goal is to write a book review that contains your personal insight about a book or short story.

Writing a Book Review

Bud, Not Buddy is the winner of the 2000 Newbery Medal and the 2000 Coretta Scott King Award. The following essay by student writer Jiang Li tells how the events in the story lead to her understanding and insight.

Bud, Not Buddy

Beginning

The beginning introduces the book and shows the writer's insight in the focus statement (underlined).

Bud, Not Buddy by Christopher Paul Curtis is a story about a young boy finding people who care about him. Bud knows that being cared for is a special thing. The "family" that Bud finds has some of the same qualities that a lot of families have today. This story shows that some members of a family may not be related, but they still care for each other.

When the story starts, 10-year-old Bud lives with his mother in Flint, Michigan. It is 1936, and the Great Depression is making life hard for most people. Times are very difficult, but they become more difficult for Bud after his mother dies. She never tells him who his father is. Bud thinks a man named Herman E. Calloway may be his father because of five posters his mother has kept through the years. The posters advertise a band named Herman E. Calloway and the Dusky Devastators of the Depression. Bud sets out to find Herman E. Calloway.

Middle

The middle paragraphs summarize the main events that lead to the writer's insight.

Many things happen to Bud as he searches. All of the situations that he comes across show readers what the Great Depression was like. For example, Bud spends time with other homeless people. He tries to leap into a boxcar of a moving train to get to another city. He also waits in food lines and eats at missions. We see how strangers help each other and become like the extended families we have today.

When Bud finally reaches Grand Rapids, he finds Calloway and tells him his story. Calloway says he is not Bud's father. However, he gives Bud jobs in exchange for room and board. Bud doesn't unpack the few things he owns: an old blanket,

LITERATURE

Middle
This paragraph shares details that continue to develop the writer's insight.

five smooth rocks with letters and dots written on them, the five posters, and a picture of his mother. Because Calloway is a grumpy, rather mean person, Bud thinks about moving on, but the band members are good to Bud. For one thing, they buy him an old saxophone. This is one of the ways they show Bud that they care. The band members know each other's weaknesses and skills. They are a family in many ways, and Bud likes being a part of their lives.

The five smooth rocks, not the posters, turn out to be the key to Bud's identity. When Bud discovers that Calloway has a collection of smooth stones in the glove compartment of his car, he tells Calloway, "I've got some of these, Sir." Calloway turns out to be his mother's father, not Bud's father, but this makes Calloway his grandfather.

Ending

The ending paragraph restates the writer's understanding of this story.

One of the best parts of the story is when Bud gets his old blanket out and remakes his bed. Now he knows this is the bed his mom slept in as a child. Readers know now that he isn't going to leave. Even though Bud never finds his father, he has found a "family" in the band members and a grouchy grandfather. Not all members of his family are related by blood, but they care for him as any family would.

Respond to the reading. Answer the following questions about the sample response.

☐ **Ideas** (1) What is the important insight stated in the first paragraph?

☐ **Organization** (2) What is the purpose of the four middle paragraphs? (3) How is the last paragraph like the first paragraph?

☐ **Voice & Word Choice** (4) Find some sentences and words that help to show the writer's voice.

Prewriting

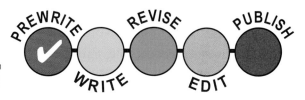

Prewriting is the first step in the writing process. It involves selecting a book or story to write about, listing important events in the plot, writing a focus statement, and planning your paragraphs.

Keys to Effective Prewriting

1. Select a book or story you have recently read and would like to write about.

2. Use a time line to list key events in the plot in the order that they happened.

3. Write a clear focus statement to guide your writing. If you are given a prompt, use it to write your focus statement.

4. Review your time line to find the most important events for your middle paragraphs.

5. Write topic sentences for each of your middle paragraphs.

PROD. NO. SCENE TAKE ROLL SOUND

LITERATURE

Prewriting **Selecting a Topic**

To choose a good topic, think of novels, short stories, or plays you have recently read. Consider those that you know well and enjoyed reading.

Chart your choices. Make a chart like the one shown below. In the first column, fill in three or four titles of stories you've read recently. In the second column, write a sentence that sums up the story.

Chart

Title	Story Summary
* The Talking Earth	Billie Wind travels alone through the Everglades.
"Zlateh the Goat"	Zlateh and Aaron save each others' lives.
The Miracle Worker	Annie Sullivan tries to teach Helen Keller to speak.

I choose The Talking Earth because I really like the story. It's different, but I think other students will like it, too.

Choose your topic. Review your chart and put a star next to the title you would like to write about. Beneath the chart, explain the reason for your choice.

Focus on the Traits

Ideas Each story that you read expresses important ideas about life. To learn about these ideas, pay careful attention to the main character's thoughts, feelings, and actions. In this way, you will develop an understanding or insight into the story.

Gathering Details

Once you select a story to review, the next step is to identify the important events in the plot. A time line like the one below allows you to list the events in the order in which they happened. After listing the events, you can use them to develop the insight you have about the story. An insight often centers around growing up or learning a lesson.

Time Line

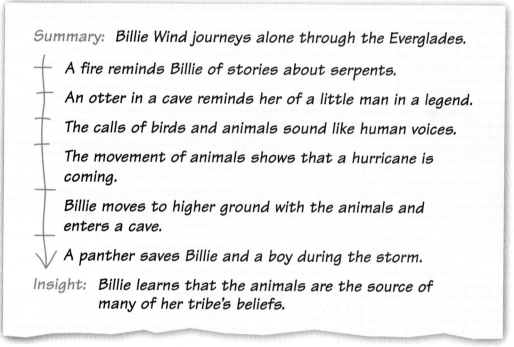

Summary: *Billie Wind journeys alone through the Everglades.*

A fire reminds Billie of stories about serpents.

An otter in a cave reminds her of a little man in a legend.

The calls of birds and animals sound like human voices.

The movement of animals shows that a hurricane is coming.

Billie moves to higher ground with the animals and enters a cave.

A panther saves Billie and a boy during the storm.

Insight: *Billie learns that the animals are the source of many of her tribe's beliefs.*

Prewrite **Make a time line.** List the key events in the order in which they happened. (Try to list five or six events.) Study the events to help you discover how they lead up to your insight about the story you've read.

Focus on the Traits

Voice There's a good chance your writing will have a confident, knowledgeable voice if you know and understand the story well. So make sure you carefully review your story.

Prewriting **Writing a Focus Statement**

In any story, the events will change the main character in some way. For example, the events in *The Talking Earth* teach Billie Wind to respect her tribe's beliefs.

In the time line you created (page 293), you listed the important events in the story. In your review, you will summarize these events and present your insight to the reader. Here is a formula that will help you write a two-part focus statement that will guide your book review.

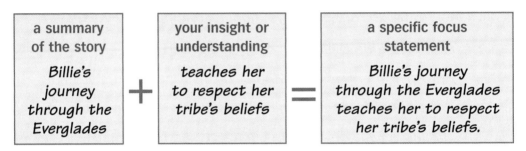

a summary of the story		your insight or understanding		a specific focus statement
Billie's journey through the Everglades	**+**	*teaches her to respect her tribe's beliefs*	**=**	*Billie's journey through the Everglades teaches her to respect her tribe's beliefs.*

Form a focus. Write a focus statement for your essay using the formula above. If you don't like how your first one turns out, write another.

Planning the Middle Part of Your Essay

Once you have written a focus statement, the next step is to plan the middle part of your essay. The first middle paragraph should cover events in your time line that happened early in the story. The second paragraph should cover the events that happened later on. (If you have a lot of events, you might need a third and even a fourth middle paragraph.)

Plan your middle paragraphs. Review your time line. Make sure you've listed all the important events.

1 Put one check next to the events that happen early in the story. (These events will be in your first middle paragraph.)

2 Put two checks next to the events that happen later on. (These events will be in your other middle paragraphs.)

3 Write topic sentences for your middle paragraphs. (See pages 552–553 for more information.)

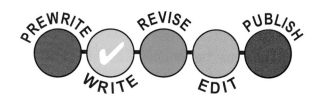

Writing

When you write your first draft, you turn your prewriting ideas into an essay. Your time line, focus statement, paragraph plan, and topic sentences will help you write your essay.

Keys to Effective Writing

1. Use your time line as a planning guide.

2. Get all your ideas on paper in your first draft.

3. Write on every other line to make room for later changes.

4. Let your focus statement and topic sentences guide you.

5. Add specific details to support your topic sentences and to interest the reader.

6. Use transitions to tie everything together.

Writing Getting the Big Picture

The chart below shows how the parts of a book review fit together. (The examples are from the essay about *The Talking Earth* on pages 297–300.) You're ready to write your review once you . . .

- know enough about the story,
- state your topic in a clear, two-part focus statement, and
- plan your paragraphs.

Beginning

The **beginning** paragraph introduces the story and states the writer's insight in a focus statement.

Focus Statement
Billie's journey through the Everglades teaches her to respect her tribe's beliefs.

Middle

The **first middle** paragraph covers early events in the story.

The **other middle** paragraphs cover events that occur later on.

Two Topic Sentences
During her travels, Billie sees and hears things that make her think of her tribe.

Billie has no way of knowing that a hurricane is coming soon.

Ending

The **ending** explains the writer's insight into the story.

Closing Sentences
She finally understands what her elders mean when they speak of "the talking earth," and now she can respect her tribe's beliefs.

Starting Your Review

The beginning paragraph should introduce the story and state your insight in a focus statement.

Beginning

Middle

Ending

Beginning Paragraph

Read the beginning paragraph below. Notice how this paragraph begins with a general introduction and ends with a specific focus statement. Also review the first paragraph of the model on page 289.

The first part introduces the story.

The focus statement includes the writer's insight (underlined).

The Talking Earth by Jean Craighead George is about a Seminole Indian girl named Billie Wind. She doubts the beliefs held by her people. The elders speak of great serpents in the swamp, little people underground, and talking animals. Billie says she doesn't believe in anything she can't see, so she decides to take a trip alone through the swamps. Billie's journey through the Everglades teaches her to respect her tribe's beliefs.

Retelling in the Present Tense

A book review can be written in the past or present tense. The verbs in the sample paragraph above are all in the present tense *(is, doubts, speak, says, decides)*. Because the events in a story happen again and again each time the story is read, it makes sense to discuss them in the present tense. In the essay you are about to write, you also should use the present tense.

Write your beginning. Write the first paragraph of your essay. Be sure to include information that introduces the story and state your insight in a focus statement.

LITERATURE

Writing Developing the Middle Part

The middle paragraphs should summarize the main events that lead to your insight. Start each middle paragraph with a topic sentence that introduces the events that follow. (Use your time line to help you with this part.)

> Beginning
>
> ▶ Middle
>
> Ending

First Middle Paragraph

The first middle paragraph tells about the important events in the first part of the story.

The topic sentence introduces the paragraph.	*During her travels, Billie sees and hears things that make her think of her tribe.* <u>*First*</u>*, a huge fire reminds her of a serpent because the flames are like the tongues of snakes.* <u>*Then*</u>*, in a cave, she mistakes a playful young otter for a little man like the one in her tribe's legends.* <u>*Later,*</u>
Transitions (<u>underlined</u>**) connect the events.**	*the calls of birds and animals begin to sound like human voices. She feels close to nature, but she still doesn't think that the beliefs of her elders are really true.*

Transitions

The transitions below show time. These words can help make the ideas in your essay easier to follow. (Also see pages 572–573.)

about	before	later	soon	tomorrow
after	during	meanwhile	then	until
as soon as	finally	next	third	when
at	first	second	today	yesterday

Second Middle Paragraph

The second middle paragraph tells about events that happen later in the story. You may write additional paragraphs as needed.

> **The topic sentence introduces the paragraph.**
>
> **Details about each event help develop the writer's insight.**

> Billie has no way of knowing that a hurricane is coming soon. <u>Then</u> she notices the unusual movement of the animals and follows them to higher ground. <u>Once again</u>, she finds shelter in a cave with a boy and young panther. <u>Later,</u> the wind quiets down. Billie and the boy start to go outside, but they notice that the panther is not budging from the cave. Billie and the boy decide to stay in the cave because the panther does. The panther saves their lives.

Write the middle of your review. Using the following tips, write the middle paragraphs of your essay. (Look again at the sample paragraphs.)

Drafting Tips

- **Talk about the story** with a classmate before you begin to write this part.
- **Review your time line** to make sure you've included all the significant events.
- **Include important details** that will help the reader understand your insight.
- **Write as freely as you can,** without being too concerned about neatness.

Writing **Ending Your Book Review**

Your focus statement introduced your insight into the story, and your closing paragraph should restate it. Ask yourself the following questions:

- What main events helped me gain an insight into the story?
- How does the change in the main character help my understanding of the story?
- How should I state my insight in the conclusion?

 Your insight is the message you want to leave with your readers. It often centers around *growing up* or *learning a lesson.*

Ending Paragraph

Read the ending paragraph below. The writer states that Billie learns an important lesson about nature and about her tribe.

The ending restates the writer's insight.

After her journey, Billie understands that nature speaks to everyone. She sees that the animals really have been talking to her all along because they have been showing her how to live. She finally understands what her elders mean when they speak of "the talking earth," and now she can respect her tribe's beliefs.

 Write your ending. In your last paragraph, be sure to explain how the change in the main character helped you develop your insight.

Form a complete first draft. Make a complete copy of your essay. Double-space to leave room for revising.

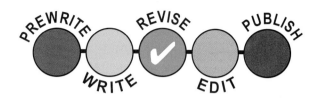

Revising

A first draft is never perfect. One of the paragraphs might be missing an important idea. Another might appear in the wrong place. Revising your essay can fix problems like these.

Keys to Effective Revising

1. Read through your entire draft to get a feeling of how well your essay works.

2. Make sure your focus statement clearly states your insight into the story.

3. Check your paragraphs to make sure the details support the topic sentences.

4. Work with your voice until it sounds personal and knowledgeable.

5. Check your words and sentences.

6. Use the editing and proofreading marks inside the back cover of this book.

Revising **for** Ideas

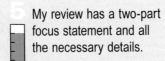
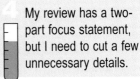

6 My focus statement and details show knowledge and real insight into the reading.	5 My review has a two-part focus statement and all the necessary details.	4 My review has a two-part focus statement, but I need to cut a few unnecessary details.

When you revise for *ideas,* you're focusing on the thoughts and details in your essay. The rubric above will help you revise your essay for this trait.

Does my focus statement work?

Your focus statement works if it clearly introduces the story and includes your insight. Be sure you have used the formula below to write your focus statement. (Also see page 294.)

Effective Focus Statement

> Billie's journey through the Everglades *(summary of the story)*
> teaches her to respect her tribe's beliefs *(a specific insight).*

Read each pair of focus statements below. For each pair, decide which statement works better. Be prepared to explain why.

1. a. **As Jody cares for his pony, he works really hard**.
   b. As Jody cares for his pony, he learns about love and loss.

2. a. **Buck's trials and challenges increase his courage and leadership qualities**.
   b. Buck tries hard, unlike his owners.

3. a. **Meg's journey to save her father makes her more confident**.
   b. Meg's journey to save her father is long.

4. a. **The team's efforts to make the finals were valuable**.
   b. The team's efforts to make the finals helped them realize that everyone has unique talents.

Review your focus statement. Make sure that your focus statement introduces the story and contains a specific insight. If you're unsure the focus statement works, ask your teacher or a classmate for help.

3 My focus statement has only one of the parts. I need to cut a few unnecessary details.

 2 I need an effective focus statement and better details.

 1 I need to learn how to write a focus statement and gather details.

Have I cut unnecessary details?

When summarizing a story, you should include only the key details. All other information should be cut. You should . . .

- delete anything that you repeated,
- cut unnecessary details, and
- drop unimportant personal thoughts and feelings.

 Write the paragraph below on your own paper. Using the list above as a guide, cut any details that are unnecessary. Afterward, share your work with a classmate.

1 "Dog's Eye View" is a pretty good story about a dog named
2 Moose. Lots of people give their pets funny names. One day, Moose
3 slips out of his owner's apartment and goes exploring. The story
4 follows Moose all around New York City. I love New York City. Moose
5 meets lots of interesting New Yorkers.

 Review your essay. Make sure your essay contains the main points and no unnecessary details. Revise your essay as needed.

Ideas
An unnecessary detail and personal comment are dropped.

The Talking Earth by Jean Craighead George,
~~who also wrote My Side of the Mountain,~~ is about a
Seminole Indian girl named Billie Wind. ~~I liked it.~~

LITERATURE

Revising for Organization

6 My opening, middle, and ending lead the reader smoothly through my essay.

5 My beginning is well organized. Transitions clearly connect sentences and paragraphs.

4 My beginning is organized. I use transitions to connect sentences.

When you revise for *organization,* focus on the way your writing is put together from beginning to end. Use the rubric above.

Is my beginning organized properly?

Your beginning paragraph for this essay should start with general information about your book and end with a specific insight or focus. Review the beginning paragraph below from the sample essay on page 289.

General ideas

Bud, Not Buddy by Christopher Paul Curtis is a story about a young boy finding people who care about him. Like all of us, Bud knows that having people who care for you is a lucky thing. The "family" that Bud finds has some of the same qualities that a lot

Specific insight or focus

of families have today. This story shows that some members of a family may not be related, but they still care for each other.

 Write a beginning paragraph using the following sentences. Put the sentences in order from general information to a specific focus.

- The story begins on a hot, dusty August day when Winnie wanders in the woods near her house.
- Just as Winnie is about to drink from the spring, her life changes, and she must make a big decision.
- The novel *Tuck Everlasting* by Natalie Babbitt is the story of 10-year-old Winnie Foster.
- After a while, she discovers a natural spring.

 Check your beginning. Carefully review your beginning paragraph to make sure that it is organized from general to specific.

3 My beginning should be better organized. I need to use transitions to connect sentences.

2 I need to reorganize my beginning and use transitions.

1 I need to learn how to organize my writing and connect my ideas.

What's the best way to connect my ideas?

One of the best ways to connect the sentences and paragraphs in your essay is to use transitions. Usually, you will use transition words that show time: *first, next, then, finally.* (See pages 572–573.)

 Read the paragraph below. On your own paper, write a revised version that adds a few more transition words or phrases. One transition word *(underlined)* has been added to get you started.

1   Gary Soto's story "The Drive-in Movies" is about a boy who
2   does chores for his mom so she will take him to a drive-in movie.
3   <u>First</u>, he makes his mother breakfast. He weeds the garden and
4   mows the lawn. He waxes their car with his brother's help. The
5   boy's mother takes the whole family to the movies, but he is so
6   tired from the chores that he falls asleep.

 Review your first draft. Check to make sure that you have included enough transition words and phrases in your essay. Be careful not to overuse them. Too many transition words can be a real distraction.

Organization
Transitions are added to make the ideas easier to follow.

First,
A huge fire reminds her of a serpent because the
Then,
flames are like the tongues of snakes. In a cave,
she mistakes a playful young otter for a little man
Later,
like the one in her tribe's legends. The calls of . . .

LITERATURE

Revising **for** Voice

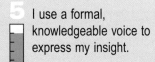 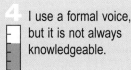

6 I use a formal, knowledgeable voice to express a clear insight and understanding of the story.

5 I use a formal, knowledgeable voice to express my insight.

4 I use a formal voice, but it is not always knowledgeable.

When you revise for *voice,* you check your essay's language for understanding and interest. Is your voice knowledgeable? Is it formal enough? The rubric above and the information that follows will help you revise your review for voice.

How do I know if my voice is knowledgeable?

A *knowledgeable* voice uses facts to build a specific insight. The voice in the first paragraph below does not use facts. It results in a general feeling and not a specific insight.

> **General Feeling**
>
> I really loved reading *Private Nobody.* At first, I was bored when the main character was joining the army. After all, who cares about the 1960s? Then I got a little interested because of all the fights. Those fights sure seemed real to me.

The voice in the next paragraph is knowledgeable because it focuses on facts that help the writer share a specific insight.

> **Specific Insight**
>
> *Private Nobody* by Greg Washington is about a young man named Larry who joins the United States Army in the late 1960s. He is sent to Vietnam and gets into lots of fights. However, the fights are with his fellow soldiers, not the enemy. The fights show that the young man was filled with anger even before he arrived in Vietnam.

Revise

Check for a knowledgeable voice. Review your essay, looking for places where you focus on your opinions or feelings instead of on facts and a specific insight. Revise to make your voice more knowledgeable.

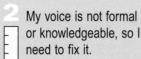

3 I need to use a more formal voice and be more knowledgeable.

2 My voice is not formal or knowledgeable, so I need to fix it.

1 I need to understand how to create a formal, knowledgeable voice.

How do I know if my writing is formal enough?

When you speak to close friends, you say things like "Hey, what's up?" A book review, however, should be more formal. One way to make your writing more formal is to avoid street talk or slang.

Read the following informal paragraph. On your own paper, list at least three words, phrases, or clauses that make the writing too informal. One phrase is underlined for you.

> 1   One night, Larry gets into a <u>giant smackdown</u>. He's on
> 2   guard duty when this one dude comes out of nowhere! Larry
> 3   tries to take off running, but he gets bashed. Larry wakes
> 4   up in an army hospital with this big humongous bandage on
> 5   his head and no memory at all. He can't even remember his
> 6   own name. He's like totally wacko. Letters from his mom and
> 7   girlfriend help him regain his memory, and eventually Larry gets
> 8   a Purple Heart medal.

Check your level of language. As you revise your book review, pay special attention to words and phrases that sound too informal.

Voice
The language is made more knowledgeable and formal.

understands that nature speaks to everyone.
After her journey, Billie ~~gets a clue. I think~~
~~this part is the coolest.~~ She sees that the
animals really have been talking to her all along . . .

LITERATURE

Revising for Word Choice

| 6 My clear word choice creates a response that engages the reader. | 5 I use active verbs and well-chosen modifiers to make the writing clear. | 4 I use active verbs whenever possible. A few modifiers need to be cut. |

When you revise your writing for *word choice,* you need to check your verbs to make sure most of them are active. Also, you should remove unnecessary modifiers. The rubric above will help you revise your word choice.

How can I make my verbs more active?

Sentences with active verbs are more exciting than those with passive verbs. A verb is active if the subject of the sentence is doing the action. A verb is passive if the subject is receiving the action. Below, the word *attack* is used as both a passive and an active verb. (See page 482.)

Passive Verb

> **The panther is attacked by the alligator.**
> (The panther receives the action.)

Active Verb

> **The alligator attacks the panther.**
> (The alligator is doing the action.)

 Read the following sentences that contain passive verbs. In each sentence, ask yourself who or what is doing the action. Then rewrite the sentence, changing the passive verb to an active verb.

1. The panther cub is saved by Billie Wind.
   1. Billie Wind saves the panther cub.

2. The men in the swamp are avoided by her.

3. Her friendship with Petang the otter is enjoyed by Billie.

4. Billie is helped many times by her animal friends.

 Check for passive verbs. Whenever necessary, change your passive verbs to active verbs.

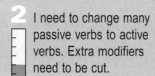

3 I need to change a few passive verbs to active verbs. Extra modifiers need to be cut.

2 I need to change many passive verbs to active verbs. Extra modifiers need to be cut.

1 I need help choosing both active verbs and modifiers.

Have I used too many modifiers?

Once Mark Twain wrote: "When you catch an adjective, kill it." He knew that too many adjectives and adverbs can make writing sound fake or unnatural. A sentence such as "Bilbo quite loudly shouts for greatly needed help" would sound clearer as "Bilbo shouts for help."

Read the following paragraph. Write down five adjectives or adverbs that should be removed. (Two have been removed.)

1   Bilbo Baggins has never been in such a ~~completely shadowy~~,

2   dark pit. He pulls out his wonderful sword, which glows really bright

3   in the big dark cave. On the floor of the cave, Bilbo sees a shiny,

4   gleaming piece of metal. It is a beautifully lovely ring. Bilbo grabs

5   the ring and quickly and rapidly puts it in his pocket. That's when

6   he hears a scary and frightening sound—the growl of the creature

7   Gollum.

Remove extra modifiers. Read through your essay and cut any unneeded adjectives and adverbs that you find.

Word Choice
Extra modifiers are removed, and a passive sentence is made active.

quiets down.
Later, the wind ~~gets so very much quieter and~~

~~quieter.~~ Billie and the boy start to go outside, but

they notice that
~~the fact that~~ the panther is not budging from the

cave ~~is noticed by them.~~ Billie and the boy decide . . .

Revising **for** Sentence Fluency

6 My sentences are skillfully written and keep the reader's interest.	**5** I avoid rambling sentences and use a variety of sentence beginnings.	**4** I avoid rambling sentences, but some subject-verb beginnings need to be changed.

When you revise for *sentence fluency,* you need to check the clarity, flow, and smoothness of your sentences. The rubric above will help you do that.

How many "and's" are too many?

You have used too many *and's* when they create a rambling sentence. A rambling sentence is a sentence that goes on *and* on *and* on. To fix a rambling sentence, you need to remove an *and* or two and start new sentences.

Rambling Sentence

Teen Business is about a girl who wants to start a baby-sitting service **and** first she asks her friends to help her, but her friends have no experience with kids **and** then she decides to start a business that teaches kids how to be baby-sitters **and** the business is soon very successful.

Improved Sentence

Teen Business is about a girl who wants to start a baby-sitting service. First, she asks her friends to help her, but her friends have no experience with kids. Then she decides to start a business that teaches kids how to be baby-sitters. The business is soon very successful.

 On your own paper, correct the rambling sentences below by taking out some of the *and's*. You may also need to change a word or two.

1. "Lenny's Mountain" is about a teenager named Lenny and he wants to be a mountain climber and the landscape is flat in the Midwest where he lives and he builds himself a fake mountain.

2. The main character, Lorne, is new in town and he wants to make friends and he hosts a big party and no one shows up and Lorne is crushed.

I need to fix a few rambling sentences and vary the beginnings. Many sentences begin the same way.

 I need to fix many rambling sentences and vary the beginnings.

1 My sentences show a number of problems. I need to learn more about sentences.

How do I begin my sentences?

If too many of your sentences begin in the same way, your essay will sound odd. The following paragraph has too many sentences that begin with a subject and verb. (See page 522.)

> Annie Sullivan tries **everything to help Helen.** Annie becomes **frustrated because of Helen's lack of understanding.** Annie **then** has **Helen fill a pitcher with water.** Annie signs **"water" in the palm of Helen's free hand at the same time.**

The paragraph has been rewritten below. Each sentence after the first one has been changed. Each new sentence begins with either a phrase or a transition word. To add even more variety, the pronoun "she" is used in place of "Annie" in the third sentence.

> **Annie Sullivan tries everything to help Helen. Because Helen lacks understanding, Annie becomes frustrated. Then she has Helen fill a pitcher with water. At the same time, Annie signs "water" in the palm of Helen's free hand.**

 Revise for sentence fluency. Check your writing carefully for rambling sentences. Then check how your sentences begin.

Sentence Fluency
A sentence beginning is changed, and a rambling sentence is fixed.

> Billie has no way of knowing that a hurricane
> is coming soon. Then ~~Billie~~ *she* notices the unusual
> movement of the animals and ~~she~~ follows them to
> higher ground,~~and~~ *Once again,* she ~~once again~~ finds shelter . . .

Revising Using a Checklist

Check your revising. On a piece of paper, write the numbers 1 to 13. If you can answer "yes" to a question, put a check mark after that number. If not, continue to work with that part of your essay.

Ideas

_____ 1. Have I included my insight in a clear focus statement?
_____ 2. Have I written informative topic sentences?
_____ 3. Have I cut unnecessary details?

Organization

_____ 4. Have I included a beginning, a middle, and an ending?
_____ 5. Do I use transitions to connect my ideas?
_____ 6. Do I present my ideas in the best possible order?

Voice

_____ 7. Do I show interest in—and understanding of—my topic?
_____ 8. Is my voice knowledgeable and formal?

Word Choice

_____ 9. Do I use specific nouns and active verbs?
_____ 10. Have I removed unnecessary modifiers?

Sentence Fluency

_____ 11. Do I write clear sentences and avoid fragments?
_____ 12. Have I fixed any rambling sentences?
_____ 13. Do I use a variety of sentence beginnings and lengths?

Make a clean copy. When you've finished revising your essay, make a clean copy before you begin to edit.

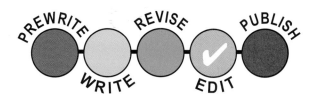

Editing

After you've finished revising your essay, it's time to edit it for your use of conventions: punctuation, capitalization, spelling, and grammar.

Keys to Effective Editing

1. Use a dictionary, a thesaurus, and the "Proofreader's Guide" in the back of this book.

2. Check for any words or phrases that may be confusing to the reader.

3. Check your writing for correctness of punctuation, capitalization, spelling, and grammar.

4. If you are using a computer, edit on a printed computer copy. Then enter your changes on the computer.

5. Use the editing and proofreading marks inside the back cover of this book.

LITERATURE

Editing for Conventions

6 My essay is correct from start to finish.

5 My essay has minor errors that do not interfere with the reader's understanding.

4 I need to correct some errors in punctuation, spelling, or grammar.

When you edit for *conventions,* you need to check your writing for grammar, punctuation, capitalization, and spelling errors. The rubric above will help you edit your essay for this trait.

How do I avoid shifts in verb tense?

When you write, you need to keep all your verbs in the same tense. For example, if you start a sentence in the present tense, you should not, later on, incorrectly switch to the past tense. This would be a shift in verb tense.

> **Shift in Verb Tense**
>
> **Maria, the main character,** travels **all over the world and never** settled **down.** ("Travels" is in the present tense. "Settled" is in the past tense.)
>
> **Consistent Verb Tense**
>
> **Maria, the main character,** travels **all over the world and never** settles **down.** (Both verbs are now in the present tense.)

 Number your paper from 1 to 5. Correct the shifts in verb tense by rewriting the following sentences in the present tense. (See the examples above.)

1. The story takes a different turn when Mike asked Serina for her help.
2. In the middle of the novel, Jason catches the flu, and a doctor gave him the wrong medicine.
3. At the end of the story, Sybil clears her throat and began to speak.
4. What happens after Billy received a mysterious e-mail message?
5. At the end of the novel, even though she is still angry, Lila forgave her sister.

3 I need to correct errors that may confuse the reader.

2 I need to correct many errors that make my essay confusing and hard to read.

1 I need help making corrections.

Have I checked for commonly misused words?

You need to check your "Proofreader's Guide" if you're not sure which commonly misused word is the one to use. In the paragraphs below, you will find six examples of this problem. The first one is corrected (in blue).

1   *Hatchet* is a book written by Gary Paulsen. It's a story about a 13-
2   year-old named Brian Robeson <u>whose</u> *(who's)* stranded in the Canadian
3   wilderness. When Brian is flying to visit his father, the small plain crashes.
4   Brian is left with the clothes he is wearing and the medal hatchet that his
5   mother gave him before he left on the trip. He must use everything he has
6   ever learned to survive this hole event.
7   During the flight, the pilot teaches Brian how to fly, but not how to
8   land. Than the pilot suddenly dyes of a heart attack. Brian reacts real fast
9   and grabs the controls. As the plane runs out of fuel, Brian must chose
10 where to land. He survives by crashing into a lake.

 On your own paper, write six words that are used incorrectly in the paragraph above. Next to each one, write the correct word.

 Edit for conventions. Pay special attention to any shifts in verb tense. Also correct any misused words.

Conventions
A usage error is corrected, and a tense shift is fixed.

After her journey, Billie understands that
nature speaks to everyone. She ~~seas~~ *sees* that the
animals really ~~had~~ *have* been talking to her all along . . .

LITERATURE

Editing **Using a Checklist**

Check your editing. On a piece of paper, write the numbers 1 to 13. If you can answer "yes" to a question, put a check mark after that number. If not, continue to edit for that convention.

Conventions

PUNCTUATION

_____ **1.** Did I punctuate titles correctly?

_____ **2.** Do I use commas after introductory word groups?

_____ **3.** Do I use commas after items in a series?

_____ **4.** Do I use commas in all my compound sentences?

_____ **5.** Do I use apostrophes to show possession *(boy's bike)*?

_____ **6.** Do I use quotation marks around any direct quotations?

CAPITALIZATION

_____ **7.** Do I start all my sentences with capital letters?

_____ **8.** Have I capitalized all proper nouns?

SPELLING

_____ **9.** Have I spelled all my words correctly?

_____**10.** Have I double-checked the words my spell-checker may have missed?

GRAMMAR

_____**11.** Do I use correct forms of verbs *(had gone,* not *had went)*?

_____**12.** Do I keep all my verbs in the same tense?

_____**13.** Have I used the right words *(to, too, two)*?

Creating a Title

- Use the title of the book: ***The Talking Earth***
- Describe the main idea: **Billie Finds Respect**
- Be creative: **Swamp School Lessons**

Publishing

Sharing Your Essay

After you have worked so hard to write and improve your essay, you'll want to make a neat-looking copy to share. You may also decide to present your essay in some other form: an illustration, a reading, or an online posting. (See the suggestions in the boxes below.)

Make a final copy. Follow your teacher's instructions or use the guidelines below to format your paper. (If you are writing with a computer, see page 60.) Write a final copy of your essay and proofread it for errors.

Focus on Presentation

- Use blue or black ink and write neatly.
- Write your name in the upper left corner of page 1.
- Skip a line and center your title; skip another line and start your writing.
- Indent every paragraph and leave a 1-inch margin on all four sides.
- Write your last name and the page number in the upper right corner of every page after the first one.

Illustrate Your Summary

Draw a picture that shows an important event in the story. Post your essay and illustration in your classroom.

Post Online

If you wrote about a book, go to a bookselling Web site and try to post your response. (Be sure to get permission first.)

Give a Recitation

Read aloud a part of the story in which an important event occurs. Then tell the class how the event helped you find an insight.

LITERATURE

Rubric for Response to Literature

Use this rubric for guiding and assessing your writing. Refer to it whenever you want to improve your writing using the six traits.

Ideas

6 The focus statement and related details show real insight into the reading.

5 The response has a clear focus statement and all the necessary details.

4 The response has a clear focus statement. Unnecessary details need to be cut.

Organization

6 The opening, middle, and ending lead the reader smoothly through the response.

5 The organization pattern fits the topic and purpose. All parts of the response are well developed.

4 The organization pattern fits the topic and purpose. A part of the response needs better development.

Voice

6 The writer's voice expresses interest and complete understanding. It engages the reader.

5 The writer's voice expresses interest and understanding.

4 The writer's voice expresses understanding of most of the reading.

Word Choice

6 Clear word choice creates a response that inspires the reader.

5 Specific nouns and active verbs make the response clear and informative.

4 Some nouns and verbs could be more specific.

Sentence Fluency

6 All sentences are skillfully written and keep the reader's interest.

5 No sentence problems exist. Sentence variety is evident.

4 No sentence problems exist. More sentence variety is needed.

Conventions

6 The response is correct from start to finish.

5 The response has minor errors that do not interfere with the reader's understanding.

4 The response has some errors in punctuation, spelling, or grammar.

3 The focus statement is too broad. Unnecessary details need to be cut.

2 The focus statement is not developed. Details are needed.

1 The response needs a focus statement and details.

3 The organization fits the response's purpose. All the parts need more development.

2 The organization doesn't fit the purpose.

1 A plan needs to be followed.

3 The writer's voice needs to express a clearer understanding.

2 The writer's voice does not express an understanding.

1 The writer needs to understand how to create voice.

3 Too many general words are used. Specific nouns and verbs are needed.

2 General or overused words make this response hard to understand.

1 The writer needs help finding specific words.

3 Sentence problems are found in a few places.

2 The response has many sentence problems.

1 The writer needs to learn how to construct sentences.

3 The response has errors that may confuse the reader.

2 The number of errors confuses the reader and makes the essay hard to read.

1 Help is needed to make corrections.

LITERATURE

Evaluating a Book Review

As you read through the following review, focus on the strengths and weaknesses. Then read the student's self-evaluation on page 321. **(There will be errors in the book review below.)**

"Zlateh the Goat"

The short story called "Zlateh the Goat" by Isaac Singer is about a village family that doesn't have enough money to celebrate Hanukkah. The father decides that selling Zlateh is the only way that the family can celebrate the holidays. He tells his son Aaron to take the animal to town. The journey to town helps Aaron, his family, and Zlateh realize how much they care for each other.

Zlateh looks at Aaron with trusting eyes and followed him down the long road from their village to town. Suddenly it starts snowing very hard. Aaron and Zlateh have trouble walking as the stuff piles up. Aaron and Zlateh get so tired they can hardly go on. Just when it looks like they will be buried by the blizzard they come to a big haystack.

The boy burrows into the haystack and pulls Zlateh inside his little cave. It snows for three days, and during that time Zlateh eats the hay and Aaron drinks the goat's milk. When the snow stops on the forth day, Aaron digs his way out and leads Zlateh back to his village.

After the storm Aaron's family is glad to see that he is safe. After Aaron tells them how Zlateh kept him warm and gave her milk, the goat is brought home to remain with the family. Aaron, his parents, and his sisters learn that they don't want anyone to get their goat.

Student Self-Assessment

The assessment shown below includes the student writer's comments about her review. In the first comment, she mentions something positive about her writing. In the second comment, she points out something she feels she can improve. (The writer used the rubric and number scale on pages 318–319 to complete this assessment.)

5 Ideas

1. I clearly stated my insight in a focus statement.
2. I could have told about the family's search for Aaron.

5 Organization

1. My writing contains a beginning, a middle, and an ending.
2. I could use transition words between paragraphs.

4 Voice

1. I understand the story, and my voice shows that.
2. My last line is funny, but maybe it shouldn't be.

4 Word Choice

1. I use active verbs.
2. I should have used different sentence beginnings.

4 Sentence Fluency

1. I don't have any rambling sentences.
2. I could have combined some of my sentences.

4 Conventions

1. I didn't make too many errors.
2. I should have fixed a shift in verb tense in my second paragraph.

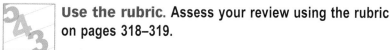

Use the rubric. Assess your review using the rubric on pages 318–319.

1 On your own paper, list the six traits. Leave room after each trait to write one strength and one weakness.

2 Then choose a number (from 1 to 6) that shows how well you used each trait.

Reflecting on Your Writing

Now that your book review is finished, you can think about it by completing each starter sentence below. These reflections will help you see how you are growing as a writer.

My Book Review

1. The best part of my book review is . . .

2. The part that most needs change is . . .

3. The main thing I learned about writing a book review is . . .

4. In my next book review, I would like to . . .

5. Here is one question I still have about writing a book review:

6. Right now I would describe my writing ability as . . . (excellent, good, fair, poor)

Response to Literature

Fictionalized Journal Entries

Stories can cast a powerful spell, letting you leap into other worlds. Perhaps you'll land on the deck of a pirate ship—or a galactic cruiser! You might imagine yourself as a warrior in ancient Japan or as a rat on the Zuckerman farm.

One way to imagine yourself into the stories you read is to write fictionalized journal entries. The following pages provide writing samples and guidelines to help you create your own journal entries.

Writing Guidelines

Subject: A book or short story that you have read and enjoyed

Form: Fictionalized journal entries

Purpose: To think and write like someone in the story

Audience: Classmates

Fictionalized Journal Entries

Writing fictionalized journal entries is one way to better understand the books you read. In the following student sample, the writer imagines that he is Templeton, the rat in the book *Charlotte's Web*. The side notes will help you understand how to write fictionalized journal entries.

Charlotte's Web

The writer imagines himself as a character in the book.

Friday, September 20: Wow, I have to admit that old sheep was right when she told me about all the tasty treats I'd find at this fair. I feasted on cheese, sandwiches, candied apples, popcorn, and any other pieces of food I could find.

Before I fell asleep, I told Wilbur that the pig next door had already won the blue ribbon. It's a tough break for Wilbur.

Each entry is dated.

Saturday, September 21: I woke up this morning and had to hold on. The crate was headed on another journey. The truck didn't go far before it stopped. I peeked out and saw hundreds of eyes staring right in my direction. Great, I thought, how can I make my escape?

The character's feelings are included.

Wilbur solved that problem. He fainted just as he was about to get a special medal. The Zuckermans panicked. I, once again, came to the rescue. With one mighty bite on Wilbur's tail, I had the little pig back up on his feet. Mission accomplished.

Each entry reflects on a particular part of the story.

Sunday, September 22: My day began with Wilbur rudely waking me up and tossing me into the air with his pudgy snout. He then loudly ordered me to do just one more favor for him. He kept grunting commands and telling me to hurry up.

I wasn't about to do another favor for him until he made me a promise I couldn't pass up. He guaranteed me first pickings from his trough for every meal of my life! 75

All I needed to do was climb up and get Charlotte's egg sac. The job sounded easy until I started chewing away at the threads. They were stickier than eating cotton candy and taffy at the same time. It took me forever to get that gooey stuff off my teeth.

Wilbur got so emotional when I gave him the sac. All I wanted to do was take a little nap, so I crawled back inside the crate. I'll be glad to get back to the farm and hear Wilbur tell how I saved Charlotte's family.

Respond to the reading. Answer the following questions about these traits in the sample journal entries.

☐ Ideas **(1) What main events does the writer talk about?**

☐ Organization **(2) Does the writer use time order, order of importance, or order of location?**

☐ Voice & Word Choice **(3) How does the writer create the character's voice?**

Prewriting Selecting a Novel

To begin your fictionalized journal entry, choose a book or story you would like to write about. Then think of a character that you would like to become in your writing. This could be a real character from the story or a different character that would fit in the story.

If you have trouble choosing a story, just start listing some that you've read and enjoyed. With a little effort, a favorite book or story will come to mind as you make your list.

List

> *The Giver*   *✱Charlotte's Web*
>
> *Locked in Time*   *Crispin*

List novels that you have read. Make a list of books or stories that you've enjoyed and would like to write about. Put a star (✱) next to the one that you liked the most.

Selecting a Character

Think about the book or story that you have starred. Consider which character is your favorite or which character you could add to the story.

Select a character and an event. On your own paper, make a chart like the one below. Name the character you will become in your journal and the parts of the story you will focus on. Give reasons for both choices.

Character-Event Chart

> *Character:* **Templeton**
>
> *Explain your selection:* **He's most like me.**
>
> *Parts of the story you will focus on:* **Going to the fair and getting Charlotte's egg sac**
>
> *Explain your selection:* **These were my favorite parts.**

Writing Creating Your First Draft

Remember to write your journal entries as if you were part of the action yourself. Consider the following points as you begin to write.

- **Focus on one event in each journal entry.**
  What does each event mean to the character you are playing?

- **Ask factual questions.**
  What important things happen during this time? Who does what? Who says what?

- **Ask sensory questions.**
  What do the characters see, feel, hear, smell, taste, or touch?

 Read the following part of a story. Imagine being Mario. Then write a short journal entry as if you were Mario and actually had this experience. Afterward, share your results with a classmate.

---

1   Mario trudged down the sidewalk in the park. Though the

2 night was still, his mind echoed with the shouts of his coach:

3 "If you're going to be on the track team, you've got to run!

4 Run! Run!" The words were almost a bark . . . and then Mario

5 realized it *was* a bark.

6   A big black dog came racing toward him down the sidewalk.

7 It seemed to gather up the shadows of the oak trees, growing

8 until it was the size of a charging rhino.

9   Mario turned and ran. He ran as never before. His coach

10 wouldn't have believed how fast he ran. Ahead stood a tree—

11 a tree Mario had climbed a hundred times. He hurled himself

12 to the lowest branches, caught on, and hauled his feet up.

13   With a monstrous snarl, the dog leaped and snapped at

14 Mario's heels. He scrambled higher, and the beast could not

15 reach him.

 Write your journal entries. After completing an entry from Mario's point of view, write two or three entries for the character that you selected on page 326. Use the three points at the top of this page to guide your writing. (Also review the sample journal entries on pages 324–325.)

Revising **Improving Your Writing**

After you finish the first draft of your fictionalized journal entries, you need to revise them for the following traits.

- ☐ **Ideas** Does each entry focus on one event or part of the book?

- ☐ **Organization** Have I dated each entry? Is the action in each entry easy to follow?

- ☐ **Voice** Do I sound like a character who actually experienced these things in the story?

- ☐ **Word Choice** Do I use strong nouns and verbs? Do I use words that my character would use?

- ☐ **Sentence Fluency** Are my sentences complete? Do they vary in length and in the way they begin?

Revise your writing. Ask yourself the questions above as you revise your journal entries.

Editing **Checking for Conventions**

When you edit your fictionalized journal entries, focus your attention on the conventions of writing.

- ☐ **Conventions** Have I checked punctuation and capitalization? Have I checked spelling and grammar?

Edit your work. Ask yourself the questions above to help you edit your journal entries. Also check the "Proofreader's Guide" (pages 578–749) for additional editing help.

Publishing **Sharing Your Writing**

Once you've finished your journal entries, it's time to share them with your classmates.

Write your final copy. Create a final copy of your journal entries. Proofread this copy carefully before sharing it with others.

Response to Literature

Across the Curriculum

In 1977, Earth sent two ambassadors to the stars. *Voyager 1* and *2* each carried a "golden record" that contained sounds from Earth. The records include greetings in 55 languages, whale songs, and animal calls. Any space travelers who find these records could learn about life in 1977 on our planet.

Literature is also a golden record. It tells about events long ago or far away. In social studies, you might read a biography about a person's life in another time and place. In science, you could read articles about distant worlds. Even a poster in your school hallway can open up new horizons for you.

After working with the different forms of response writing in the following pages, you will be able to practice responding to a timed test prompt and analyze what you have learned.

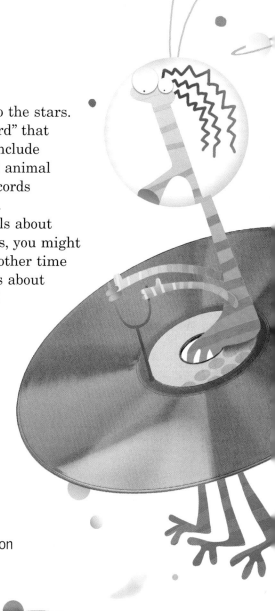

What's Ahead

- **Social Studies:** Reviewing a Biography
- **Science:** Summarizing an Article
- **Practical Writing:** Completing an Evaluation

Social Studies:
Reviewing a Biography

Social studies explores the way people have lived in different places and at different times. A good biography can teach you about both.

In his social studies class, Josh read a biography of Nelson Mandela. It told about what life was like for Mandela and other black Africans when South Africa was racially divided.

The **beginning** names the book and author.

The **middle** points out important events in the biography.

The **ending** tells about the importance of the person's life.

Freedom Fighter

Nelson Mandela, A Voice Set Free, by Rebecca Stefoff, tells about a man who fought discrimination in South Africa. The life story of Nelson Mandela shows that nobody should take freedom for granted.

When Nelson Mandela was young, South Africa had a system called "apartheid." It kept black Africans from getting good educations, jobs, or housing. Nelson protested this system by joining the African National Congress (ANC). This group fought for equal rights. Nelson was so successful that the government banned him from ANC activities. He kept working anyway.

In 1956, police arrested Nelson for treason. Four years later, he was found innocent. Police arrested him again in 1962, and this time he was found guilty. Nelson spent 27 years in prison but kept leading the fight for freedom. In 1990, he gained his personal freedom and helped to finally get rid of apartheid. He became South Africa's president in 1994 in the first free elections.

The life of Nelson Mandela shows that freedom is worth fighting for. It also shows that a person who won't give up can change the world.

Writing Tips

When you write about a biography, consider these tips.

Before you write . . .

- **Imagine being the person in this biography.**
  Think about what it must have been like to live in another time and place.
- **Think about why this person's life is important.**
  Ask yourself how the person's actions changed society, both in the past and in the present.

Cluster

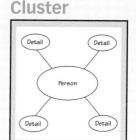

During your writing . . .

- **Focus on the person's important experiences.**
  Don't try to include everything.
- **Share interesting details.**
  Select details that show what the person was really like.

After you've written a first draft . . .

- **Revise for ideas, organization, and voice.**
  Make sure the details are well organized and that your voice is formal enough.
- **Double-check important facts.**
  Make sure that the names and dates in your review are correct.
- **Edit and proofread.**
  Check your review for punctuation, capitalization, spelling, and grammar. Then make a final copy of your work and proofread it for errors.

 Search the classroom, the library, or the Internet for a biography that interests you. Then read the biography and write a review of it using the information above as a guide.

LITERATURE

Science: Summarizing an Article

A summary paragraph captures the main idea of a longer piece of writing. The article on this page describes the possibility of life on one of Jupiter's moons, and the paragraph below it is a student's summary of the article.

Is There Life on Europa?

Scientists are planning to send a probe to one of Jupiter's moons to look for signs of life. The first inkling that the moon Europa might have life came in 1997 when the *Galileo* space probe flew past and photographed its frozen surface. The photographs revealed a possible sea under the ice and showed volcanic activity. Scientists theorize that where there is liquid water and a source of heat, life could exist.

Ironically, the very space probe that discovered the possibility of life on Europa became a threat to further missions. By 2003, the *Galileo* space probe was losing power. If it had accidentally crashed on Europa, it could have spread micro-organisms from Earth on the world. Then, if later probes found life, scientists wouldn't know whether the life originated on Earth. Instead of possibly "contaminating" Europa with terrestrial life forms, NASA scientists decided to steer *Galileo* into Jupiter, where it burned up.

If life does exist on Europa, it may be bacterial, such as life forms found in geothermal pools in Yellowstone. On the other hand, scientists have discovered six-foot-long tube worms living beside volcanic vents at the bottom of Earth's oceans. Perhaps larger life forms such as those could exist on Europa.

A NASA probe will be sent to Europa in the future. Until then, scientists will have to wait to find out whether Jupiter's satellite contains extraterrestrial life.

Extraterrestrial Life?

Topic Sentence

In 1997, the Galileo *space probe discovered that one of Jupiter's moons could have life on it.* The moon was Europa, and photos showed that under the moon's frozen surface there may be a sea and volcanoes. Life might exist where there is liquid water and heat. NASA wants to send a probe to find out if Europa has life.

Body

They even made Galileo burn up in Jupiter's atmosphere to avoid contaminating Europa with life from Earth. If life does exist there, it might be small like bacteria or big like a tube worm. **Scientists won't find out until the first NASA probe reaches Europa.**

Closing Sentence

Writing Tips

Before you write . . .

- **Read and reread.**
  Read the article to get an overall sense of it. Then reread the article, focusing on individual details.
- **Mark up the article and make notes.**
  Ask yourself, "What is the main idea of this article?" Write it down in a single sentence. Then underline important details that support the main idea.
- **Plan your paragraph.**
  Write a topic sentence that sums up the main idea of the article. Consider which facts you will use in the middle. Finally, decide on an interesting closing sentence.

During your writing . . .

- **Be brief.**
  Write a summary that is a third the size of the original— or even smaller. Focus on the main idea of the article and the most important details that support it.
- **Paraphrase the information.**
  Put details from the article into your own words. Avoid copying phrases and sentences from the original source.

After you've written a first draft . . .

- **Revise your paragraph.**
  Ask yourself whether you have summed up the main idea and provided the most important details. Revise parts that are incomplete or unclear.
- **Check your paragraph for correctness.**
  Make sure there are no mistakes in spelling, punctuation, or other conventions.

 Look for a science-related article in a newspaper or magazine, or use the article that your teacher hands out to you. Follow the tips above as you write a paragraph that summarizes the article.

LITERATURE

Practical Writing:
Completing an Evaluation

Posters use words and graphics to inform, persuade, or entertain. One student filled out the following form to evaluate this poster about "Tutoring."

What's Your Best Subject?
Math? Art? Science?
Reading? Band? Social Studies?
Share What You Know—
TUTOR!

Contact the office for details.

Poster Evaluation: Please complete this form by filling in the subject of the poster, circling its purpose, and rating its parts. Then add your overall comments at the bottom.

Poster Subject: *Tutoring*

Purpose: Inform (Persuade) Entertain

	1	2	3
Information:	(key facts missing)	(some facts missing)	(no facts missing)
Letter Style:	1 (too much variety)	(2) (a few problems)	3 (just right)
Letter Size:	1 (too small or too large)	(2) (a few problems)	3 (just right)
Colors:	(1) (too few or too many)	2 (some don't work)	3 (great choices)
Design (Words):	1 (words hard to read)	2 (some hard to read)	(3) (easy to read)
Design (Art):	1 (too empty or crowded)	(2) (some problems)	3 (very attractive)

The strong points: *The questions got my attention. The different letter styles make each subject stand out. The poster made me think about becoming a tutor.*

Possible improvements: *The words are crowded at the top of the poster, and the books are just floating there. There should be information about the person the reader should contact.*

Writing Tips

If you are asked to complete an evaluation form, use the following tips to guide you through the process.

Before you write . . .

- **Study the piece you are evaluating.**
  Review the form so that you know what specific things you are to judge.
- **Read the directions on the form.**
  Be sure you know how to complete the form.

During your writing . . .

- **Follow all the directions.**
  Complete the whole form.
- **Make your comments clear.**
  Give all the information that the form requests.

Try IT Review the evaluation form on page 334. Then study the soccer poster at the right. On your own paper, write at least two "strong points" and two "possible improvements" for the poster. (If your teacher supplies a blank evaluation form, review the tips above before completing the form.)

JOIN NOW!

Informational Meeting
Tuesday at 3:15
See a member for details.

Response to Literature

Writing for Assessment

On some assessment tests, you may be asked to read a story and write a response to it. The next two pages give you an example of such a test. Read the directions, the story, and the student's comments (in blue). Then read the student's response on pages 338–339.

Response to Literature Prompt

DIRECTIONS

- Read the following story.
- As you read, make notes. (Your notes will not be graded.)
- After reading the story, write an essay. You have 45 minutes to read, plan, write, and proofread your work.

When you write, focus on the author's message in the story. Show your insight into the characters and ideas. Use clear organization and support your focus with examples from the text.

Amazing

Tomas Mendez smiled as he rounded the turn from Prairie Street to Woodward Avenue. He had run a perfect marathon so far. He'd qualified to start in the top ten, averaged an impressive 5 minutes and 55 seconds per mile, and slowly pulled away from the pack. Now Tomas was alone in front, poised to win his third straight Beloit City Marathon. The homestretch lay ahead, and the crowds on both sides of the street cheered as Tomas came into view. Just 200 more yards . . .   *They both feel happy.*

Tomas's girlfriend, Stacy, stood by the red tape and screamed the loudest. In one hand, she gripped a water bottle, and in the other she waved a sign that said, "Threepeat!"

Seeing Stacy, Tomas kicked into high gear. His legs complained, and his lungs ached, but he wanted to give Stacy and all of them a real show.

The crowd went wild, signs flapping over their heads. One group was chanting something that sounded like "Do it! Do it! Do it!" When Tomas looked to Stacy, though, he saw that her sign hung limp at her side and her eyes were wide with disbelief.

Another runner thundered past Tomas.   *shock*

"What?" he gasped, straining for breath. Shock poured through him as he watched the runner pull away. The back of the guy's sweat-soaked shirt read, "Lewis."

That's what the crowd was shouting—not "Do it!" but "Lewis!"   *Crowd cheers Lewis.*

With a little cry, Tomas clenched his teeth and drove forward, but his legs were wet rags and his gut was a knot. He was still ten feet out when Lewis lunged across the   *No one* tape and snapped it. Leaving the sidewalk, the crowd   *notices* flooded into the street to surround the winner.   *Tomas.*

Unnoticed, Tomas jolted up to cross the line. He grabbed his knees, spat between his feet, and stood there, panting.

Stacy came up to him and patted his shoulder. "Good race."

Tomas shook his head and gasped. "That guy—Lewis— he beat me."   *disappointed*

"Yeah," Stacy said, smiling in admiration at the winner. "Amazing."   *angry*

"Why are you smiling?" Tomas reddened, feeling angry. "What's amazing?"

hero "It's amazing he can run at all. That's the guy who broke his back two years ago. They said he'd never walk again, but he said he'd run a marathon. Not only did he run, but he won. Amazing."

Straightening up and staring through the crowd, Tomas nodded, and he smiled, too. "Amazing." *They both smile.*

Student Response

The following essay shows a student response to the story "Amazing." Note how the student uses details from the story to support the focus.

Beginning

The first paragraph shares the focus of the essay.

Middle

The middle paragraphs support the focus with examples from the story.

In the story "Amazing," Tomas and his girlfriend Stacy think of only one thing, winning. They confidently hold on to this attitude until the surprising turning point in the story. "Amazing" shows that people can unexpectedly change how they feel about someone or something.

Tomas is running in a marathon and expects to win for the third time. Stacy is cheering for him. As Tomas rounds the final turn, he is thinking he "had run a perfect marathon." He is feeling great. He sees Stacy at the finish line. They both feel sure he will win.

Everything changes when a runner shoots past Tomas. Suddenly, he realizes that the crowd was not shouting, "Do it!" for him. They were shouting, "Lewis," the name of the runner who had just passed him.

Then the crowd surrounds the winner.
Tomas is exhausted and sees that no one
even notices as he crosses the finish line,
second. Of course, he feels disappointed and
embarrassed when Stacy says, "Good race."
He sees her smiling at the winner and hears
her say, "Amazing." That makes him angry.
Then Stacy tells Tomas that the winner
broke his back two years before.

Ending

The final
paragraph
explains the
meaning of
the story.

Suddenly, Tomas isn't thinking of himself.
He and Stacy are thinking about Lewis
and his struggle to win a marathon. Tomas
still wishes he had won, but in the end, he
sees that his opponent really is amazing.
The writer is trying to show that thinking
about other people is the first step to
understanding and respecting them.

Respond to the reading. Answer the following questions
about the sample prompt and student response.

☐ **Ideas** (1) What is the focus of the student's response?
(2) What feelings does this student describe?

☐ **Organization** (3) How did the notes on pages 336–337
help the student organize the response?

☐ **Voice & Word Choice** (4) Is the student's voice
objective or personal? (5) What words tell you so?

LITERATURE

Practice Writing Prompt

Practice a response to literature. Carefully read the directions to the practice writing prompt on the next two pages. Use 10 minutes at the beginning to read the story, make notes, and plan your writing. Also leave time at the end to proofread your work.

DIRECTIONS:

- Read the following story.
- As you read, make notes on your own paper.
- After reading the story, write an essay. You have 45 minutes to read, plan, write, and proofread your work.

When you write, focus on the author's message in the story. Show your insight into the characters and ideas. Use clear organization and support your focus with examples from the text.

Fishing

"You mean you're spending two whole days with Chad?" I laughed at the look on Jack's face. He had just told me he was going on a weekend fishing trip with none other than Chad Jones, the brainiest kid in class.

"It's not like I want to!" Jack growled. "Our dads are buddies, and they planned this father-son trip. I have to go!"

Chad was always on the edge of our group, eager to be accepted when he just wasn't a part of things. It's not like we were nasty to him. Still, we never went out of our way to include him in things like after-school hoops. He wasn't smelly or weird or anything. He just wasn't—like us.

The whole weekend, every time I thought about Jack and Chad stuck together in a boat, I had to chuckle. I could see Jack, silent and grumpy, while Chad talked his ear off about his dull ideas. I figured Jack would be ready to tip the boat and swim to shore just to get away from Chad.

Monday, I got to class early so I could kid Jack some more. He was already there, sitting next to Chad. A group of kids were clustered around them, listening. I moved closer to the group and could hear Chad talking about the fishing trip. Jack saw me and signaled me to come over.

"Hey, Max, c'mere!" he yelled. "You gotta hear about this trip. It was amazing! Chad's like the best fly fisherman I've ever seen." Chad blushed—he actually blushed!

"I've been fishing since I was little," he said modestly. "No big deal."

"No big deal?" Jack exploded. "He was amazing! He showed me how to tie flies—look at this one." He held up a delicate little fishing fly that looked enough like a dragonfly to take off around the room. "He made this! And he caught the biggest largemouth bass I have ever seen! Tell 'em about that one, Chad."

Chad started to talk about the fish. As he got more and more into the story, his face and eyes glowed from excitement. He made the fight with the fish sound exciting. I stood there, feeling really left out. Looking up at my reflection in the window, I saw the same look I had seen so often on Chad's face. I suddenly felt ashamed for the way I'd treated him.

"So what do you think of that, Max?" Jack asked.

"I think—" Chad was looking at me shyly, as if what I said really mattered. I smiled. "I think next time I want to go with you guys!" I sat down next to Chad.

"Let's shoot some hoops after school," I said. "You in, Chad?"

imagine

entertain

Creative Writing

show

create

discover

Creative Writing

Writing Stories

People have always told stories. Early on, they gathered around campfires and spoke of heroes and heroines, kings and queens, beasts and battles. Over time, people began writing their stories down, acting them out, and producing them for the screen. Stories entertain us, and they teach us about life.

Almost all stories use the same simple plan: There are *people* in a *place* doing some *activity,* and a *problem* occurs. Because of the many stories you have heard, read, or written, this simple plan has become part of your own thinking. As a result, writing a story will come naturally to you.

In this chapter, you will read a sample story about the future and then develop a story of your own to share.

Writing Guidelines

Subject:	Future event
Form:	Short story
Purpose:	To entertain
Audience:	Classmates

Short Story

In many stories, events change the main character in some way. The character may learn something new, gain a friend, achieve a goal, or lose a prized possession. The way a character faces a problem or challenge is what makes a story interesting.

Imagine an important event or challenge that you might face in the future. In the story below, Sarah imagined her journey up the slopes of Mount Everest and the problems she faced. The side notes identify the different parts of the story.

Journey to the Top of the World

Beginning

The beginning introduces the main characters and the setting.

I opened my eyes and stared up at the orange roof of my tent. The world was silent. What a wonderful sound! All night, winds had whistled and snow had pounded the tent walls. At last, the storm was over. Today I could head up from Camp 5 to the summit of Mount Everest.

After dressing in my gear and eating an energy bar, I came out of my tent. The sun shone brightly, and wind had carried away much of the snow. Even through the oxygen mask I wore, I could feel the cold, biting air.

"Ready for the climb?" asked Kami, our guide. She stood with the other team members near their tents.

I replied, "I've been ready since fifth grade."

Rising Action

The rising action adds a conflict and increases the suspense.

We slid on our backpacks, grabbed our ice axes, and started climbing. My boots bit into the snow, and I paused with each step. Even going slow, I had to fight for breath. I adjusted my oxygen mask and remembered the first time I'd worn one of these.

Just after turning 11, I had my first serious asthma attack. My parents took me to the hospital, and the doctor gave me oxygen and bitter medicine. That night, I saw a National Geographic special about climbing Mount Everest.

A flashback can tell about earlier events.

The people in the show were short of breath and wore oxygen masks just like me. I decided that someday I would climb Mount Everest. Today that dream would come true.

I looked up the trail. The peak looked so high and black, it made me dizzy. My legs felt like lead. Worst of all, my throat started to tighten up. I stopped walking and dropped to my knees. I couldn't breathe.

"Are you okay?" asked Kami, checking my oxygen mask. "Do you need to go back?"

I shook my head and closed my eyes. Just as I had learned to do in fifth grade, I calmed my heart and relaxed my throat. It took a minute, but I slowly got my throat to open again. "I'll be fine," I gasped.

High Point

At the high point in this story, the main character succeeds.

I stood up and began to walk. My feet soon fell into a regular pace, and my breathing did, too. One step at a time, I would make it to the top.

Just after 1:00 p.m., I stood at the top of the world. The sun couldn't fight off the bitter cold, but my heart burned with joy. The mountains all around me seemed small next to Everest.

Ending

The ending tells how the main character has changed.

Suddenly I knew I could do anything I set my mind to doing. I silently thanked my fifth-grade self for that long-ago decision. That's really when this amazing journey up the mountain began.

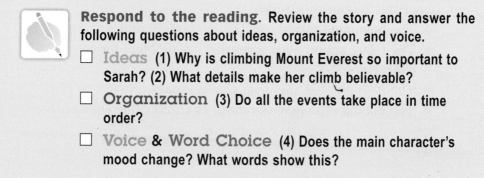

Respond to the reading. Review the story and answer the following questions about ideas, organization, and voice.

☐ **Ideas** (1) Why is climbing Mount Everest so important to Sarah? (2) What details make her climb believable?

☐ **Organization** (3) Do all the events take place in time order?

☐ **Voice & Word Choice** (4) Does the main character's mood change? What words show this?

Prewriting Selecting a Topic

It's fun to think about the future and imagine the things you might do. Sarah Silverton used freewriting to dream about her future. She kept writing until she found an interesting topic for her story.

Freewriting

I'm supposed to think about a future event. Well, if I became a vet, maybe I'd get to work with racehorses. I love horses. Or maybe I could be a forest ranger and help save spotted owls. I hope I'm not allergic to spotted owls. My allergies have been awful since that asthma attack last year. That's when I decided to climb Mount Everest. That might make a cool story. . . .

Prewrite

Freewrite to select a topic. Write freely about possible events in your future. Write until you discover a good topic for your story. If you have trouble getting started, follow Sarah's example above and write about careers you would like to try.

Focus on the Traits

Organization

The actions that take place during a story make up the plot line. Each part of the plot plays an important role in the story.

- The **beginning** introduces the characters and setting.
- The **rising action** adds a conflict—a problem for the characters.
- The **high point** is the most exciting part.
- The **ending** tells how the main character has changed.

Creating a Plot

Sarah thought about what it would be like to climb Mount Everest. She used a plot chart to organize the details for her story.

Plot Chart

Beginning	Rising Action	High Point	Ending
The story starts at the camp. I wake up and greet the team.	We start to climb. I remember why I want to do this: the bad asthma attack in fifth grade.	Suddenly I can't breathe! The guide checks my oxygen. I calm myself and keep going.	Victory! I know I can do anything I set my mind to doing.

Create a plot chart. Make a plot chart like the one above. Imagine what will happen in each part of your story from the beginning to the ending.

Gathering Sensory Details

A well-written story helps readers feel as if they are experiencing the events themselves. To do this, use plenty of sensory details. Sarah created the chart below to gather sensory details for her story.

Sensory Chart

See	Hear	Smell	Taste	Touch/Feel
orange tent, bright sun, tall mountain, rugged rock	whistling wind, snow hitting the tent	fresh air, oxygen mask	bitter medicine, energy bar	cold air, tight throat, spiky shoes, tired legs

Gather sensory details. Create a sensory chart like the one above. Write down the things you would see, hear, smell, taste, and feel throughout your story. Try to think of at least two details for each sense.

Writing Developing Your First Draft

You now have everything you need to begin writing your story. As you write, keep the following tips in mind.

1 **Begin in the middle of the action.**

Instead of . . . I always wanted to climb Mount Everest.
Write . . . I opened my eyes and stared up at the orange roof of my tent.

2 **Use dialogue to move the story along.**

Instead of . . . I said I would be fine, but it was hard to talk.
Write . . . "I'll be fine," I gasped.

3 **Show what happens instead of just telling about it.**

Instead of . . . I couldn't go on because of an asthma attack.
Write . . . I stopped walking and dropped to my knees. I couldn't breathe.

 Write your first draft. Use your plot chart and sensory chart as you write your first draft. Remember to *show* instead of *tell.* Use dialogue and specific nouns and verbs. Enjoy telling your story!

Revising Improving Your Writing

Once you finish your first draft, set it aside for a while. After taking a break, you'll be able to see what changes could make your story better.

☐ **Ideas** Do I tell about a future event? Do I use sensory details?

☐ **Organization** Have I followed my plot line?

☐ **Voice** Does the way I write reflect my personality?

☐ **Word Choice** Do I use specific nouns and past tense verbs?

☐ **Sentence Fluency** Do my sentences flow smoothly from one to the next? Do I vary the lengths and types of sentences?

 Revise your story. Use the questions above as a guide when you revise your first draft.

Editing   Checking for Conventions

Once you have completed your revisions, it is time to edit your story for *conventions.*

☐ **Conventions** Have I corrected any errors in spelling and capitalization? Have I included end punctuation for each sentence? Have I checked easily confused words *(to, too, two; your, you're)*?

Edit your story. Use the questions above to guide your editing. When you finish, use the tips below to write a title. Then write a final copy and proofread it.

Creating a Title

The title of your story should catch the reader's interest. Here are three strategies for writing story titles.

- Use words from the story: **Journey to the Top of the World**
- Use colorful words: **A Breathless Victory**
- Be creative: **Conquering Asthma in the Himalayas**

Publishing   Sharing Your Story

Here are three suggestions for sharing your story with others.

- **Hold a storytelling session.** Practice reading your story out loud. Then read it to others. Ask them to read their stories, too.

- **Act out your story.** Choose some friends to act out the story with you. Then present your skit to your class or family.

- **Post your story online.** Search for a Web page that accepts student writing and post your story there. Make sure to get permission from a parent or guardian before doing this.

Present your story. Choose one of the ideas above or make up your own. Then share your story.

Story Patterns

Here are brief descriptions of five story patterns. These popular patterns may give you ideas for stories of your own.

The Discovery	In a *discovery* story, the main character follows a trail of clues to discover a secret. Mystery and suspense novels use this pattern. **A young man discovers a mountain hideaway.**
The Quest	In a *quest,* the main character goes on a journey into the unknown, overcomes a number of obstacles, and returns either victorious or wiser. Many ancient myths follow this pattern, but so do many modern stories. **A young woman overcomes a severe leg injury so she can walk again.**
The Choice	The *choice* pattern involves the main character making a difficult decision. Suspense builds as the decision draws near. **A middle school student must decide between trying out for softball and helping her grandmother.**
The Rite of Passage	In the *rite of passage* pattern, a difficult experience changes the main character in a major and lasting way. These stories are also called "coming of age" stories. **A young soldier learns about courage while on the battlefield.**
The Reversal	The *reversal* pattern is one in which the main character follows one course of action until something causes him or her to think or act in a different way. **A young man lives for football until his best friend is seriously injured during a game.**

 Look back at the sample short story on pages 344–345. Decide which story pattern it follows. Explain your choice.

CREATIVE

Elements of Fiction

The following list includes many terms used to describe the elements or parts of literature. This information will help you discuss and write about the novels, poetry, essays, and other literary works you read.

Action: Everything that happens in a story

Antagonist: The person or force that works against the hero of the story (See *protagonist.*)

Character: A person or an animal in a story

Characterization: The way in which a writer develops a character, making him or her seem believable
Here are three methods:
- Sharing the character's thoughts, actions, and dialogue
- Describing his or her appearance
- Revealing what others in the story think or say about this character

Conflict: A problem or clash between two forces in a story
There are five basic conflicts:
- **Person Against Person** A problem between characters
- **Person Against Himself or Herself** A problem within a character's own mind
- **Person Against Society** A problem between a character and society, the law, or some tradition
- **Person Against Nature** A problem with some element of nature, such as a blizzard or a hurricane
- **Person Against Destiny** A problem or struggle that appears to be beyond a character's control

Dialogue: The words spoken between two or more characters

Foil: The character who acts as a villain or challenges the main character

Mood: The feeling or emotion a piece of literature or writing creates in a reader

Moral: The lesson a story teaches

Narrator: The person or character who actually tells the story, giving background information and filling in details between portions of dialogue

Plot: The action that makes up the story, following a plan called the plot line

Plot Line: The planned action or series of events in a story (The basic parts of the plot line are the beginning, the rising action, the high point, and the ending.)

- The **beginning** introduces the characters and the setting.
- The **rising action** adds a conflict—a problem for the characters.
- The **high point** is the moment when the conflict is strongest.
- The **ending** tells how the main characters have changed.

Point of View: The angle from which a story is told (The angle depends upon the narrator, or person telling the story.)

- **First-Person Point of View**

  This means that one of the characters is telling the story: "We're just friends—that's all—but that means everything to us."

- **Third-Person Point of View**

  In third person, someone from outside the story is telling it: "They're just friends—that's all—but that means everything to them." There are three third-person points of view: *omniscient, limited omniscient,* and *camera view.* (See the illustrations on the right.)

Protagonist: The main character or hero in a story (See *antagonist.*)

Setting: The place and the time period in which a story takes place

Theme: The message about life or human nature that is "hidden" in the story that the writer tells

Tone: The writer's attitude toward his or her subject (can be described by words like *angry* and *humorous*)

Total Effect: The overall influence or impact that a story has on a reader

Third-Person Points of View

Omniscient point of view allows the narrator to tell the thoughts and feelings of all the characters.

Limited omniscient point of view allows the narrator to tell the thoughts and feelings of only one character at a time.

Camera view (objective view) allows the story's narrator to record the action from his or her own point of view without telling any of the characters' thoughts or feelings.

Select one of the five types of conflicts on page 351. In one sentence, describe a conflict from a story you know. In another sentence, describe the setting for this story. Add a sentence that describes the protagonist.

Creative Writing

Writing Poems

Poets love words. They love the way words sound and the way they look on the page. They love the way words create pictures and unlock ideas. Today many poets write free-verse poems, which don't follow a regular pattern. With free-verse, writers can play with the sounds and arrangement of their words, as in the poem to the right.

In the following chapter, you will write a free-verse poem about an animal that you would like to be. You'll also find other types of poetry that you could try. The last pages of the chapter tell about special techniques you can use when writing poetry.

I stretch,
I stretch,
my ostrich
neck.
Crack!
Crack!
The kinks
are back!

Writing Guidelines

Subject:	An animal you would like to be
Form:	Free-verse poem
Purpose:	To entertain
Audience:	Classmates

Free-Verse Poem

Many free-verse poems contain sensory details. Sights, sounds, smells, and other sensations let the reader "experience" the topic of the poem. Caleb Carter wrote the following poem about the life of a firehouse dog.

White Flame

People call me White Flame.
I ride on a wailing fire truck
    as it roars down crowded streets.
I leap off to sniff the smoky air
    and face the blazing flames.
I splash through the hose's spray
    and sit by the little gray girl
    and lick the salty tears
    from her sooty cheeks.

repetion, line/breaks, sensory details

Respond to the reading. On your own paper, reflect on the ideas, organization, and voice of the free-verse poem.

☐ **Ideas** (1) List five details that refer to the senses.

☐ **Organization** (2) What words and letter sounds are repeated in this poem?

☐ **Voice** (3) Who is the speaker in the poem?

Prewriting **Selecting a Topic**

Poets are inspired by all sorts of things. You will be writing a poem about an animal you would like to be. Caleb used a cluster to think about his favorite animals.

Cluster

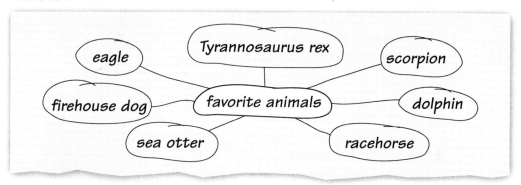

Create a cluster. Write "favorite animals" in the center of a sheet of paper. Around these words, cluster the types of animals you would like to be. Choose one to write about.

Gathering Details

Poems are full of sensory details. These details help create images in the mind of the reader. Caleb created the following sensory chart to help him think about being a firehouse dog.

Sensory Chart

See	Hear	Smell	Taste	Touch
black/white	barking	dog breath	biscuit	hot fire
gray	siren wailing	people smells	salty tears	cold water
fire truck	splash	ash		spray
flames	crying	smoke		

Gather sensory details. Create a chart like the one above and list sensory details about your topic. Include details about the animal and about the setting of your poem.

Prewriting Using Poetry Techniques

Poets play with the sounds of words. Two simple techniques will help you create poetic sounds as you write your free-verse poem.

■ **Onomatopoeia** (ŏn′ə-măt′ə-pē′ə) is using words that sound like the noises they name.

> I ride on a wailing fire truck
>   as it roars down crowded streets.
> I leap off to sniff the smoky air
>   and face the blazing flames.

■ **Alliteration** (ə-lĭt′ə-rā′shən) is repeating beginning consonant sounds.

> I splash through the hose's spray
>   and sit by the little gray girl
>   and lick the salty tears
>   from her sooty cheeks.

Use poetry techniques. Look back at your sensory chart. Circle any words that sound like the noise they name (onomatopoeia). Then underline words that start with the same consonant (alliteration). Add a few more of each kind of word.

Writing Developing Your First Draft

Now that you have gathered sensory details and learned two poetry techniques, you are ready to write the first draft of your poem. Follow these tips.

■ **Imagine being the animal.** What things do you sense? What thoughts do you think? How do you feel about your world?

■ **Tell your story.** What important things do you do? What will be happening in your poem? (Your animal should be doing something.)

■ **Play with words.** What words make the most interesting sounds? What words create the strongest images, or word pictures?

Write your first draft. Create the first draft of your poem. Write as if you were the animal, telling about something that happens in your life.

CREATIVE

Revising Improving Your Poem

Revise your first draft by thinking about these traits of writing.

- ☐ **Ideas** Do I include sensory details? Do I share thoughts and feelings?
- ☐ **Organization** Do I arrange my sentences or ideas in a special way?
- ☐ **Voice** Does my writing voice sound interesting (like the animal)?
- ☐ **Word Choice** Do I use onomatopoeia? Do I use alliteration?
- ☐ **Sentence Fluency** Do my lines flow smoothly? Do they have a pleasant rhythm?

Revise your writing. Ask yourself the questions above and decide what changes would improve your poem. Continue working with your poem until you like the way it looks and sounds.

Editing Fine-Tuning Your Poem

Focus on the conventions of writing as you edit your poem.

- ☐ **Conventions** Is my work free of spelling errors? Have I used punctuation and capitalization effectively? (In free-verse poetry, you do not have to capitalize the first word in each line.)

Edit your work. Edit your poem using the questions above as a guide. Make a final copy of your poem and proofread it again for spelling.

Publishing Sharing Your Poem

There are a number of ways you can share your poetry.

- **Perform it.** Read the poem to your classmates or to your family.
- **Post it.** Display your poem where people can read it—on a bulletin board, on a Web site, or on your refrigerator.
- **Send it out.** Submit your work to a local or student newspaper.

Present your work. Choose one of the presentation suggestions above or come up with one of your own.

Writing Haiku

Another form of poetry is *haiku*. This type of Japanese poetry presents a picture of nature, so an animal makes a perfect topic. A haiku poem is three lines long. The first line has five syllables, the second has seven, and the third has five. Guess what animal is described in each of the following haiku poems.

Mud smears on pink skin—
soft grunts rumble from its snout—
it loves to wallow.

Guards all dressed in black,
patrolling from the treetops,
nod and caw commands.

Huge gray beasts lift their
ears and eyes and nostrils from
muddy waterways.

Spreading hood and fangs,
it slithers from the basket
to the charmer's tune.

Writing Tips

- **Select a topic.** Think of an interesting animal.
- **Gather details.** List things about the animal that you would see, hear, smell, or feel.
- **Follow the pattern.** Make sure you use five syllables each in the first and last lines and seven in the middle line.

Create your haiku. Choose an animal and write your haiku poem. Make sure each line has the right number of syllables.

CREATIVE

Writing Other Forms of Poetry

Poems take many forms. Here are three other forms that work well for describing animals.

Limerick

A *limerick* is a humorous poem of five lines. Notice that the first, second, and last lines rhyme with each other, as do the third and fourth. Also notice that the first, second, and last lines have three accented syllables. The third and fourth have two.

A monkey named Joe plans to save
His money to purchase a shave.
But razors can't hack
All the hair on his back,
And barbers in town aren't that brave.

Name Poem

A *name poem* uses the letters in a name to begin each line.

Feline
Loudly
Utters her
Fierce but
Funny-sounding
Yowl

Phrase Poem

A *phrase poem* states an idea with a list of phrases.

Into the lake
with a swoosh
of flying water
over flapping wings
across bright feathers
with a sparkling splash

Write a poem. Choose one of the forms of poetry on this page and use the example as your model. Try the other forms at another time.

Using Special Poetry Techniques

On the next two pages, you will find a number of special techniques that poets use to develop poems.

Figures of Speech

Poets use the following techniques to create strong images in their poems. These techniques are called *figures of speech*.

- A **simile** *(sĭm´ə-lē)* compares two different things using the word *like* or *as*.

  The branch curved like a claw.

- A **metaphor** *(mĕt´ə-fôr)* compares two different things without using the word *like* or *as*.

  Her eyes were flashlights in the dark.

- **Personification** *(pər-sŏn´ə-fĭ-kā´shən)* gives human traits to something that is not human.

  The leaves gossiped among themselves.

- **Hyperbole** *(hī-pûr´bə-lē)* is an exaggeration.

  My heart hit the floor.

Sounds of Poetry

Poets use the following special techniques to add pleasing and interesting sounds to their poems. (Also see page 356.)

- **Alliteration** *(ə-lĭt´ə-rā´shən)* is the repetition of beginning consonant sounds.

  The kids rode a carousel of cartoon characters.

- **Assonance** *(ăs´ə-nəns)* is the repetition of vowel sounds in words.

  A green apple gleams at me from the tree.

- **Consonance** *(kŏn´sə-nəns)* is the repetition of consonant sounds anywhere within words.

  The angry eagle shrieked again.

CREATIVE

- **End rhyme** *(ĕnd\\rīm)* is the use of rhyming words at the ends of two or more lines.

    My country, 'tis of thee,
    sweet land of liberty . . .

- **Internal rhyme** *(ĭn-tûr´nəl\\rīm)* is the use of rhyming words within a line of poetry.

    The smoke could choke a chimney.

- **Onomatopoeia** *(ŏn´ə-măt´ə-pē´ə)* is the use of words that sound like the noise they name.

    The crackling bag crumpled in his fist.

- **Repetition** *(rĕp´ĭ-tĭsh´ən)* is the use of the same word, idea, or phrase for rhythm or organization.

    We ran above.
    We ran below.
    We ran where no one else would go.

- **Rhythm** *(rĭth´əm)* is the way a poem flows from one idea to the next. In free-verse poetry, the rhythm follows the poet's natural voice. In traditional poetry, a regular rhythm is created. Notice how the poet William Blake accented certain syllables to create a regular rhythm.

    Tiger, Tiger, burning bright
    In the forests of the night, . . .

Write a poem. In your poem, write about an amazing animal. Include at least one figure of speech and one other special poetry technique.

organize

NOTE

Research Writing

summarize

RESEARCH

cite

Research Writing
Building Skills

Research is a form of exploration. It can take you to remote corners of the world or down to the depths of the ocean. By using the right tools and digging into your subject, you can discover amazing things.

Of course, the tools of your research probably won't include a mini-sub. Instead, you'll use tools such as a computer catalog, *The Readers' Guide to Periodical Literature,* and Internet searches. But once you know how to use these tools of research, you will be ready to explore your world!

What's Ahead

- **Primary vs. Secondary Sources**
- **Using the Internet**
- **Using the Library**
- **Using Reference Materials**
- **Evaluating Sources**

Primary vs. Secondary Sources

Primary sources of information are original sources. They give you firsthand information. You're working with a primary source when you . . .

- visit a place to learn about your topic,
- ask people questions about your subject, or
- conduct a survey or an experiment.

Secondary sources contain information that has been gathered by someone else. Most nonfiction books, newspapers, magazines, and Web sites are secondary sources of information. You're working with secondary sources when you . . .

- read a magazine article about your subject,
- check out a reference book, or
- visit a Web site.

Primary Sources

1
Visiting a
health-food store

2
Interviewing
a vegetarian

3
Cooking a
vegetarian meal

Secondary Sources

1
Article about
vegetarians

2
Encyclopedia entry
on vegetarian diets

3
TV documentary
about vegetarians

 Decide whether each of the following is a primary or a secondary source of information.

    A Web-site review of a vegetarian cookbook

    A taste test of vegetarian foods

What other resources can you imagine for this topic? Think of one more primary or secondary source about vegetarianism.

REPORT

Types of Primary Sources

Primary sources of information provide you with firsthand details. Review the following list of primary sources.

Diaries, Journals, and Letters

Reading the diaries, journals, and letters of other people (especially historical figures) is an interesting way to gather information. You can find this sort of information in libraries and museums.

Presentations

Visiting historical sites or museums can provide you with firsthand information about your topic. You can also listen to guest speakers or watch live demonstrations.

Interviews

In an interview, you can talk with someone who is an expert on your subject. You can interview in person, over the phone, by e-mail, or through the mail.

Surveys and Questionnaires

You can also use a survey or questionnaire to gather firsthand information. Begin by making a list of the questions you would like answered. Then give copies of your questions to people who can answer them. Collect the completed surveys or questionnaires and study the results.

Observation and Participation

Observing people, places, and things is one method of gathering information. Taking part in an event also supplies firsthand details. For example, to research ethnic foods, be sure to taste some yourself.

 Gather information by observing students in your cafeteria. During lunch, make note of what is served and what students select and eat. Also make note of what they avoid. If possible, use this method of research when you do a research report.

Using the Internet

The World Wide Web allows people all around the world to publish information, making it a great place to do research. You can find many helpful Web sites, including online encyclopedias, that contain information about your topic. For example, the NASA site offers hundreds of pages about space exploration.

Since information on the Internet comes from a variety of people and places, you need to evaluate each source carefully. (See page 376 for guidelines.)

Points to Remember

- **Use the Web carefully.** Look for sites that have *.edu, .org,* or *.gov* in the address. These are educational, nonprofit, or government Web sites and will offer the most reliable information. If you are not sure about a site, check with your teacher or librarian.

- **Use a search site.** A search site such as www.google.com or www.yahoo.com is like a computer catalog for the Internet. You can enter keywords to find Web pages about your subject.

- **Look for links.** Often, a Web page includes links to other pages dealing with your topic. Take advantage of these links.

- **Be patient.** The Web is huge and searches can get complicated. New pages are added all the time, and old ones may change addresses or even disappear completely.

- **Know your school's Internet policy.** To avoid trouble, be sure to follow your school's Internet policy. Also follow whatever guidelines your parents may have set up for you.

Using the Library

Libraries provide a variety of resources for people seeking information, including books, periodicals, CD's, and much more.

1 **Books** are usually divided into three sections.

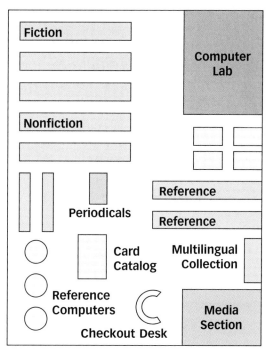

- The **fiction** section includes stories and novels. These books are arranged in alphabetical order by the authors' last names.

- The **nonfiction** section contains books that are based on fact. They are arranged according to the Dewey decimal system. (See page 370.)

- The **reference** section has encyclopedias, atlases, dictionaries, directories, and almanacs.

2 The periodicals section includes magazines and newspapers.

3 The computer lab has computers, often connected to the Internet. You usually sign up to use a computer.

4 The media section includes music CD's, cassettes, DVD's, videotapes, and CD-ROM's. Computer software (encyclopedias, games, and so on) may be found in this section as well.

Try It Visit your school library and look around. Notice where each of the above areas is located. Then draw a map of the library and label each area.

REPORT

Searching a Computer Catalog

Every computer catalog is a little different. The first time you use a particular computer catalog, either check the instructions for using it or ask a librarian for help. With a computer catalog, you can find information on the same book in three ways:

1 If you know the book's **title**, enter the title.

2 If you know the book's **author**, enter the author's name. (When the library has more than one book by the same author, there will be more than one entry.)

3 Finally, if you know only the **subject** you want to learn about, enter either the subject or a keyword. (A *keyword* is a word or phrase that is related to the subject.)

If your subject is . . .	your keywords might be . . .
ethnic cooking in the United States,	Mexican meals, southwestern cooking, or Native American recipes.

Computer Catalog Screen

Author:	Dent, Huntley
Title:	The Feast of Santa Fe: Cooking of the American Southwest
Published:	Simon and Schuster, 2005
Subjects:	Southwestern Cooking Spanish, Mexican, Anglo, and Native American recipes
STATUS: Available	**CALL NUMBER:** 641.5979D
LOCATION: General collection	

 Create a computer catalog screen like the one above for a book you are reading.

Searching a Card Catalog

If your library has a card catalog, it will most likely be located in a cabinet of drawers. The drawers contain title, author, and subject cards, which are arranged in alphabetical order.

1 To find a book's **title card**, ignore a beginning *A, An,* or *The* and look under the next word of the title.

2 To find a book's **author card**, look under the author's last name. Then find the author card with the title of the book you want.

3 To find a book's **subject card**, look up an appropriate subject.

All three cards will contain important information about your book—most importantly, its call number. This number will help you find the book on the library's shelves.

REPORT

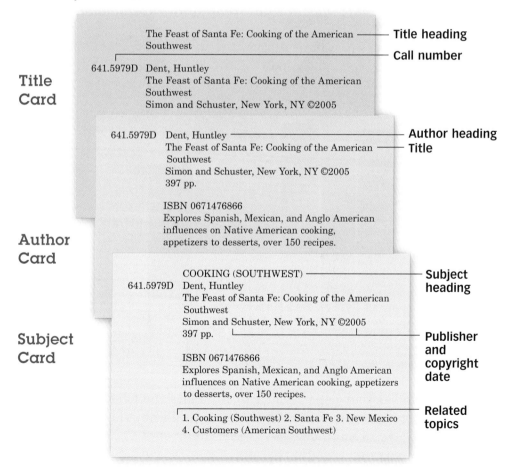

Title Card

The Feast of Santa Fe: Cooking of the American Southwest ——— **Title heading**
——— **Call number**
641.5979D Dent, Huntley
The Feast of Santa Fe: Cooking of the American Southwest
Simon and Schuster, New York, NY ©2005

Author Card

641.5979D Dent, Huntley ——— **Author heading**
The Feast of Santa Fe: Cooking of the American ——— **Title**
Southwest
Simon and Schuster, New York, NY ©2005
397 pp.

ISBN 0671476866
Explores Spanish, Mexican, and Anglo American influences on Native American cooking, appetizers to desserts, over 150 recipes.

Subject Card

COOKING (SOUTHWEST) ——— **Subject heading**
641.5979D Dent, Huntley
The Feast of Santa Fe: Cooking of the American Southwest
Simon and Schuster, New York, NY ©2005
397 pp. ——— **Publisher and copyright date**

ISBN 0671476866
Explores Spanish, Mexican, and Anglo American influences on Native American cooking, appetizers to desserts, over 150 recipes.

1. Cooking (Southwest) 2. Santa Fe 3. New Mexico ——— **Related topics**
4. Customers (American Southwest)

Finding Books

Each catalog entry for a book includes a **call number**. You can use this number to help you to find the book you are looking for. Most libraries use the Dewey decimal classification system to arrange books. This system divides nonfiction books into 10 subject categories.

000-099	**General Works**	500-599	**Sciences**
100-199	**Philosophy**	600-699	**Technology**
200-299	**Religion**	700-799	**Arts and Recreation**
300-399	**Social Sciences**	800-899	**Literature**
400-499	**Languages**	900-999	**History and Geography**

Using Call Numbers

A call number often has a decimal in it, followed by the first letters of an author's name. (See the illustration below.) Look first for the number when searching for a book, and then for the alphabetized letters.

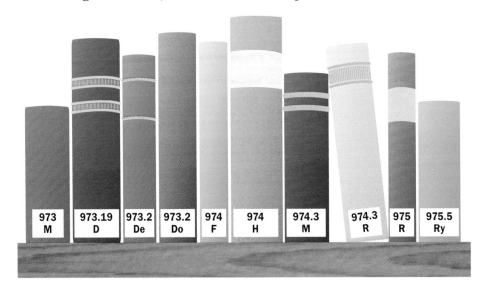

973	973.19	973.2	973.2	974	974	974.3	974.3	975	975.5
M	D	De	Do	F	H	M	R	R	Ry

Try It Number your paper from 1 to 10. Place the following call numbers in order as you would find them on a library shelf.

516.35 Ha	752 Be	516.35 T	980.1	603.99 Se
980.1 Al	610 Ce	516.35	610.1 C	980.1 Ad

Understanding the Parts of a Book

Understanding the parts of a nonfiction book can help you to use that book efficiently.

- The title page is usually the first page. It tells the title of the book, the author's name, and the publisher's name and city. (See illustration.)

- The copyright page comes next. It tells the year the book was published. This can be important. Some information in an old book may no longer be correct.

- An acknowledgement or preface may follow. It may tell what the book is about, why it was written, and how to use it.

- The table of contents shows how the book is organized. It gives the names and page numbers of the sections and chapters.

- A cross-reference sends the reader to another page for more information. *Example:* (See page 372.)

- An appendix has extra information, such as maps, tables, lists, and so on.

- A glossary explains special words used in the book. It's like a mini-dictionary.

- A bibliography lists books, articles, and other sources that the author used while writing the book. To learn more about the topic, read the materials listed in the bibliography.

- The index is an alphabetical list of all the topics in the book. It gives the page numbers where each topic is covered.

WRITE SOURCE

A PROGRAM FOR WRITING, THINKING, AND LEARNING

Written and Compiled by
Dave Kemper, Patrick Sebranek, and Verne Meyer

Illustrated by
Chris Krenzke

WRITE SOURCE.
GREAT SOURCE EDUCATION GROUP
a division of Houghton Mifflin Company
Wilmington, Massachusetts

RESEARCH

 Find the following information in this book.

1. What year was the book published?
2. Find a cross-reference and tell what is on the page you are referred to.
3. On what page does the index begin?

Using Reference Materials

The reference section in a library contains materials such as atlases, encyclopedias, and dictionaries.

Using Encyclopedias

An **encyclopedia** is a set of books or a CD with articles on almost every topic you can imagine. The topics are arranged alphabetically. The tips below can guide your use of encyclopedias.

- If the article is long, skim any subheadings to find specific information.
- Encyclopedia articles are written with the most basic information first, followed by more detailed information.
- At the end of an article, you may find a list of related topics. Look them up to learn more about your topic.
- The index lists all the places in the encyclopedia where you will find more information about your topic. (See the sample below.) The index is usually in the back of the last volume of a printed set.

Encyclopedia Index

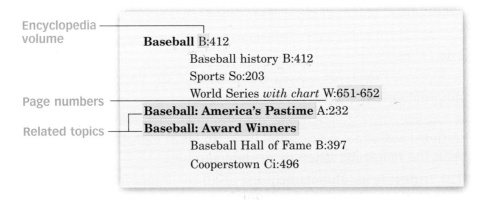

Encyclopedia volume

Baseball B:412
    Baseball history B:412
    Sports So:203
    World Series *with chart* W:651-652

Page numbers

Baseball: America's Pastime A:232
Baseball: Award Winners

Related topics

    Baseball Hall of Fame B:397
    Cooperstown Ci:496

Check the index entries above; then list the volume and page where you might find the following information.

1. A list of teams that have played in the World Series
2. A description of the first baseball game
3. The names of players in the Baseball Hall of Fame

Finding Magazine Articles

Periodical guides are found in the reference section of the library and list magazine articles about many different topics.

- **Locate the right edition** of the *Readers' Guide to Periodical Literature* (or a similar guide). The latest edition will have the newest information, but you may need information from an older edition.

- **Look up your subject.** Subjects are listed alphabetically. If your subject is not listed, try another word related to it.

- **Write down the information** about the article. Include the name of the magazine, the issue date, the name of the article, and its page numbers.

- **Find the magazine.** Ask the librarian for help if necessary.

REPORT

Readers' Guide Format

BAKE SALES	Subject Entry
Bake sale. S. Gandel. *Money* v32 no10 p32 O 2006.	
Fundraising: It's not just about the money. *Computers in Libraries* v23 no2 p32-35 Fe 2006.	Name, Volume, and Number of Magazine
BAKER, JACK	
Bebe Jodel Arf. *Back Yard Flyer* p60-65 My/Ag 2005.	Author Entry
BAKERY	
Appetite is growing for Parmalat's Archway cookie unit. R. Sidel. *Wall Street Journal* [Eastern] v242 no128 pC1 D 31 2006.	Name of Author
Bread reigns in France, where they say phooey to low-carb fads. *Nation's Restaurant News* v38 no1 Je 5 2006.	
Tainted food. D. Hawaleshka, B. Bethune and S. Ferguson. *Maclean's* v117 no4 p22-27 Je 26 2007.	Title of Article
Valentine's day treats from around the world. *Vanity Fair* no522 p64 Fe 2006.	Page Number/Date
BAKESHOP *See* Bakery	Cross-Reference

Internet-based databases are online subscription services that allow you to search for and read periodicals on the Internet.

 Using the above sample page, write answers to these questions.

1. In which magazine can you learn about the French diet?

2. Who wrote an article on bake sales?

3. On what page can you find out about Valentine's Day foods?

Checking a Dictionary

A dictionary is the most reliable source for learning the meanings of words. It offers the following aids and information:

- **Guide words** are located at the top of every page. They show the first and last entry words on a page, so you can tell whether the word you're looking up is listed on that page.

- **Entry words** are the words that are defined on the dictionary page. They are listed in alphabetical order for easy searching.

- **Parts of speech** labels tell you the different ways a word can be used. For example, the word *Carboniferous* can be used as a noun or as an adjective.

- **Syllable divisions** show where you can divide a word into syllables.

- **Spelling and capitalization** (if appropriate) are given for every entry word. If an entry is capitalized, capitalize it in your writing, too.

- **Spelling of verb forms** is shown. Watch for irregular forms.

- **Illustrations** are often provided to make a definition clearer.

- **Accent marks** show which syllable or syllables should be stressed when you say a word.

- **Pronunciations** are special spellings of a word to help you say the word correctly.

- **Pronunciation keys** give symbols to help you say or pronounce the entry words correctly.

- **Etymology** gives the history of a word [in brackets]. Knowing a little about a word's history can make it easier to remember.

Remember: Each word may have several definitions. It's important to read all of the meanings and select the one that is best for you.

 Open a dictionary to any page and find the following information.
1. Write down the guide words on that page.
2. Find a multisyllabic word and write it out by syllables. Jot down the word's part of speech. (There may be more than one.)
3. Find an entry that includes spelling of verb forms and write them down.

Dictionary Page

Guide words ——— **carbon dioxide | carburetor** 150

Entry word ———

carbon dioxide *n.* A colorless or odorless gas that does not burn, composed of carbon and oxygen in the pro-portion CO_2 and present in the atmosphere or formed when any fuel containing carbon is burned. It is ex- haled from an animal's lungs during respiration and is used by plants in photosynthesis. Carbon dioxide is used in refrigeration, in fire extinguishers, and in carbonated drinks.

Part of speech ———

carbonic acid *n.* A weak acid having the formula H_2CO_3. It exists only in solution and decomposes readily into carbon dioxide and water.

Syllable division ———

car·bon·if·er·ous (kär´bə-nĭf´ər-əs) *adj.* Producing or containing carbon or coal.

Spelling and capitalization ———

Carboniferous *n.* The geologic time comprising the Mississippian (or Lower Carboniferous) and Penn- sylvanian (or Upper Carboniferous) Periods of the Pa- leozoic Era, from about 360 to 286 million years ago. During the Carboniferous, widespread swamps formed in which plant remains accumulated and later hardened into coal. See table at **geologic time.—Car- boniferous** *adj.*

Spelling of verb forms ———

car·bon·ize (kär´bə-nīz´) *tr. v.* **car·bon·ized, car·bon ·iz·ing, car·bon·iz·es 1.** To change an organic com- pound into carbon by heating. **2.** To treat, coat, or combine with carbon.—**car´bon·i·za´tion** (kär´be-nĭ-zā´shən) *n.*

Illustration ———

air
air filter
choke valve
gas
gas and air mixture
float
venturi
throttle valve
float chamber

carburetor
cross section of a carburetor

carbon monoxide *n.* A colorless odorless gas that is extremely poisonous and has the formula CO. Car- bon monoxide is formed when carbon or a compound that contains carbon burns incompletely. It is present in the exhaust gases of automobile engines.

carbon paper *n.* A paper coated on one side with a dark coloring matter, placed between two sheets of blank paper so that the bottom sheet will receive a copy of what is typed or written on the top sheet.

Accent marks ———

carbon tet·ra·chlor·ide (tĕt´rə-klôr´īd´) *n.* A color- less poisonous liquid that is composed of carbon and chlorine, has the formula CCl_4, and does not burn although it vaporizes easily. It is used in fire extin-guishers and as a dry-cleaning fluid.

Pronunciation ———

Car·bo·run·dum (kär´bə-rŭn´dəm) A trademark for an abrasive made of silicon carbide, used to cut, grind, and polish.

Pronunciation key ———

ă	pat	ôr	core
ā	pay	oi	boy
âr	care	ou	out
ä	father	ŏŏ	took
ĕ	pet	ŏŏr	lure
ē	be	ōō	boot
ĭ	pit	ŭ	cut
ī	bite	ûr	urge
îr	pier	th	thin
ŏ	pot	*th*	this
ō	toe	zh	vision
ô	paw	ə	about

car·bun·cle (kär´bŭng´kəl) *n.* **1.** A painful inflamma- tion in the tissue under the skin that is somewhat like a boil but releases pus from several openings. **2.** A deep-red garnet.

car·bu·re·tor (kär´bə-rā´tər *or* kär´byə-rā´tər) *n.* A de- vice in a gasoline engine that vaporizes the gasoline with air to form an explosive mixture. [First written down in 1866 in English, from *carburet*, carbide, from Latin *carbō*, carbon.]

Etymology ———

RESEARCH

Evaluating Sources

Before you use any information in your writing, you must decide if it is trustworthy. Ask yourself the following questions to help judge the value of your sources.

Is the source a primary or a secondary source?

Firsthand facts are often more trustworthy than secondhand facts. However, secondary sources can also be trustworthy.

Is the source an expert?

An expert is an authority on a certain subject. You may need to ask a teacher, parent, or librarian for help when deciding how experienced a particular expert is.

Is the information accurate?

Sources that are well respected are more likely to be accurate. For example, a large city newspaper is much more reliable than a supermarket tabloid.

Is the information complete?

If a source of information provides some facts about a subject, but you still have questions, find another source.

Is the information current?

Be sure you have the most up-to-date information on a subject. Check for copyright dates of books and articles and for posting dates of online information.

Is the source biased?

A source is biased when it presents information that is one-sided. Some organizations, for example, have something to gain by using only some of the facts. Avoid such one-sided sources.

Research Writing
Summary Paragraph

How many times have you written a paragraph entitled, "What I Did on My Summer Vacation"? Each time, you condensed three months' worth of activities into a few sentences. You wrote a summary paragraph about your summery days!

Summaries get to the heart of information. They are short and clear. When you write a summary paragraph, you capture the main idea and key supporting facts.

In the next few pages, you'll learn how to read an article and uncover its main idea and most important information. Then you will be shown how to summarize the article. Once you've mastered writing summaries, you'll be ready to use this skill in all of your report writing.

Writing Guidelines

Subject: A research article

Form: Summary paragraph

Purpose: To express the main idea

Audience: Classmates

My Summer Vacation

Summary Paragraph

The following article tells of the eruption of Mount Saint Helens in 1980. The paragraph "Fire Mountain Roars" summarizes the article.

The Giant Awakens

The Native Americans near Mount Saint Helens had always called it "Fire Mountain," and for good reason. Between 1832 and 1857 the volcano had small eruptions. By the time most European settlers arrived, though, the mountain slept, and the stories of eruptions seemed like just legends.

On May 18, 1980, after two months of rumbling, the sleeping giant awoke. An earthquake shook loose the north face of the mountain, which poured down in a gigantic rock slide. The slide released an enormous cloud of rock, ash, and gas. The blast leveled huge trees, flattening them like matchsticks, killed thousands of animals, and left 57 people dead. Afterward came a devastating mud slide as the 9,677-foot mountain's ice cap melted and poured down the surrounding valleys.

Mount Saint Helens sleeps now, but it could erupt again. The blast in 1980 was actually small compared to some of the mountain's past eruptions. Three other peaks in the northern Cascades—Mount Rainier, Mount Hood, and Mount Shasta—all have the same explosive potential. Any of them could erupt, threatening communities from Seattle to San Francisco. Perhaps European settlers should have listened to the "Fire Mountain" legends after all.

Fire Mountain Roars

Topic Sentence (main idea)

On May 18, 1980, Mount Saint Helens erupted. Before that, most people near Mount Saint Helens thought that the Native American stories about "Fire Mountain" were just legends. Then, on that day, the volcano's north face slid off, and a huge cloud of ash, rock, and gas shot out. The forests were flattened, and thousands of animals and 57 people died. Mount Saint Helens has been quiet for a while, but it could blow again.

Body

Closing Sentence

Now people near other sleeping volcanoes like Mount Shasta, Mount Hood, and Mount Rainier know the "Fire Mountain" legends are true.

Respond to the reading. Answer the following questions.

☐ **Ideas** (1) What is the main idea of the summary?

☐ **Organization** (2) How is the paragraph organized?

☐ **Voice & Word Choice** (3) How does the summary writer describe the eruption in his own words?

Prewriting Selecting an Article

For this assignment, you must find an article to summarize. Choose one that . . .

- relates to a subject you are studying,
- discusses an interesting topic, and
- is fairly short (between three and six paragraphs).

Choose an article. Look through magazines and newspapers for an article to summarize. Choose one that has the three features listed above. Ask your teacher if the article will work for your summary paragraph.

Reading the Article

If possible, make a photocopy of your article so that you can underline important facts as you read. Otherwise, take brief notes on the article. The writer of the sample summary underlined the key facts.

> On May 18, 1980, after two months of rumbling, the sleeping giant awoke. An earthquake shook loose the north face of the mountain, which poured down in a gigantic rock slide. The slide released an enormous cloud of rock, ash, and gas. The blast leveled huge trees, flattening them like match sticks . . .

Read your article. First read through the article. Then reread it and identify the important facts.

Finding the Main Idea

The key to summarizing is finding the main idea of the article. Look over the material you underlined. What main idea do the facts suggest? The writer of the sample summary wrote this main idea: "On May 18, 1980, Mount Saint Helens erupted."

Write the main idea. Review the facts you identified. What main idea do they suggest? Write the main idea as a single sentence. This sentence (or a version of it) will be the topic sentence for your paragraph.

Writing Developing the First Draft

A summary paragraph includes a topic sentence, a body, and a closing sentence. As you write each part, follow these tips.

- **Topic sentence:** Introduce the main idea of the article.
- **Body:** Include just enough important facts to support or explain the main idea. As much as possible, use your own words and phrases to share these facts.
- **Closing sentence:** Restate the main idea of the summary in a different way.

 Write the first draft of your summary paragraph. Develop a topic sentence based on the main idea of the article. Add facts that support the main idea. Then end your paragraph with a closing sentence.

Revising Reviewing Your Writing

As you revise, check your first draft for the following traits.

- ☐ **Ideas** Does the topic sentence correctly identify the main idea? Do I include only the most important facts to support it?
- ☐ **Organization** Is all of the information in a logical order?
- ☐ **Voice** Does my voice sound confident and informative?
- ☐ **Word Choice** Do I use my own words? Do I define any difficult terms I use?
- ☐ **Sentence Fluency** Do I use a variety of sentence lengths and types?

 Revise your paragraph. First reread the article and your summary. Then use the questions above as a guide for your revising.

Editing Checking for Conventions

Focus on conventions as you edit your summary.

- ☐ **Conventions** Have I checked the facts against the article? Have I checked for errors in punctuation, spelling, and grammar?

 Edit your work. Use the questions above as your editing guide. Make your corrections, write a neat final copy, and proofread it for errors.

Research Writing

Research Report

Today, it is easier than ever to find answers to your questions. You might be wondering about new ways to treat some disease. Perhaps you're interested in learning about a strange-looking fish. You can find answers quickly by surfing the Internet. Of course, you can also find answers by talking to people or reading books, magazines, and newspapers. This question-and-answer work is called research.

In this unit, you will write a report about a natural event or formation that affects people. As you develop your report, you will *describe* the formation or event, *explain* some things about it, and *summarize* information from other sources. Then you will organize your ideas and facts into an interesting, informative report.

Writing Guidelines

Subject: **A natural event or formation that affects people**

Form: **Research report**

Purpose: **To research and share information about nature's effect on people**

Audience: **Classmates**

Research Report

The following research report is about an interesting geological area around the Pacific Ocean. Notice how important information is presented. The side notes point out key features in the report.

1/2"

Guerrero 1

Maria Guerrero

Mr. Shalhoub

Science

March 2, 2009

The entire report is double-spaced.

Exploring the Ring of Fire

Beginning

The opening gives important background information.

The earth is old, but it is always changing. Its outer crust is made of plates that float on its molten core. When the edges of these plates shift, volcanoes may erupt, earthquakes may destroy buildings, or giant ocean waves may flood the land. The Ring of Fire around the Pacific Ocean has more volcanoes, earthquakes, and tidal waves *right order* than any other place in the world.

The thesis (focus) statement identifies the topic (underlined).

The Ring of Fire actually circles the Pacific Ocean. The edge of the Ring of Fire runs north from New Zealand to Asia. Then it goes east to Alaska's Aleutian Islands. From there it runs

RESEARCH

Guerrero 2

south along the West Coast of North and South America. More than 75 percent of the world's 1,500 volcanoes exist on this ring (Ado and Dorsey 27).

2nd One of the most famous volcanoes on the Ring of Fire is Mount Saint Helens in the state of Washington.

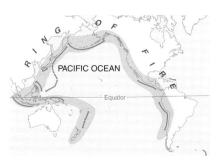

Carleton Ado and Robert Dorsey report that when it erupted on May 18, 1980, the blast was 50 times stronger than an atomic bomb. It flattened the forests in the area and shot out a dense cloud of ash, rock, and poisonous gas. Thousands of animals and 57 people died (31–32).

3rd Earthquakes are also a problem around the Ring of Fire. In 1906, an earthquake destroyed most of San Francisco, California. Another major quake hit Anchorage, Alaska, in 1964. In 2003, a powerful quake beneath the ocean near Hokkaido,

The writer's last name and page number go on every page.

A source and page number are provided in parentheses.

Only pages are listed in parentheses when the author is mentioned in the text.

Middle
Details are given about the topic, with each paragraph covering one main point.

Guerrero 3

Japan, caused terrible damage to the city and injured more than 300 people (Juranek 13).

4th When an earthquake occurs beneath the ocean, it causes huge waves. Sometimes those waves are big enough to cause destruction when they reach shore. A really gigantic wave is called a tsunami (pronounced tsoo-nä´-mē). A tsunami is so big that as it nears the shore it sucks the water away from the ocean floor. Then all this water crashes onto the land, destroying buildings and flooding whole cities. An average of five tsunamis occur each year in the Ring of Fire (Milburn).

Scientists study the Ring of Fire to predict when a volcanic eruption, an earthquake, or a tsunami may happen. By understanding these disasters, they hope to warn people ahead of time and save lives. Experts also use this knowledge to build safer buildings. Although people cannot control nature's Ring of Fire, they can study it in order to live more safely with it.

A difficult word is explained, and its pronunciation is shown.

Ending
The writer summarizes and expands upon the main idea.

Guerrero 4

Works Cited

Ado, Carleton C., and Robert E. Dorsey. Ring of
Fire: The Edge of the World. Philadelphia:
Countryside Press, 2007.

Juranek, Lucille. "When the Earth Moves."
Discover 16 May 2008: 12–14.

Milburn, Hugh B. "Volcanoes, Earthquakes, and
Tsunamis." Crystalinks.com. 6 June 2008.
Pacific Marine Environmental Laboratory in
Seattle, Washington. 28 March 2008 <http://
crystalinks.com/rof.html>.

The sources used in the report are listed alphabetically.

Respond to the reading. After reading the sample research report, answer the following questions about important traits of writing.

☐ Ideas **(1) What did you learn from reading the report? List at least two things.**

☐ Organization **(2) How are the middle paragraphs arranged? List the main idea for each of these paragraphs.**

☐ Voice **& Word Choice (3) List words and phrases that show the writer's interest in the topic.**

Prewriting

Selecting a Topic

Before you can begin doing research, you need to choose a topic—either a natural event or a natural formation. One way to do this is to create a cluster around the word "nature," as the writer of the following cluster has done.

Cluster

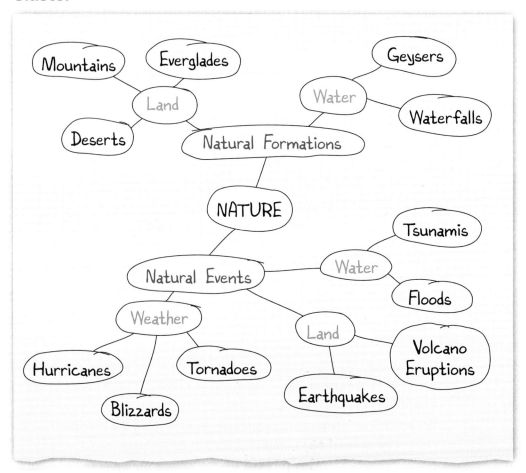

Create your cluster. Using the example above, create your own cluster. Fill in as many ideas as you can. Look at an atlas, a science book, or a geography book if you need help. Select a topic that interests you—one that you would like to learn more about.

Sizing Up Your Topic

Before beginning your research, it's important to have some sort of plan. Otherwise, you may end up with either too little or too much information for an effective report.

Start by writing a list of three to five questions that you want to answer. If you cannot think of at least three questions, you should choose a broader topic. On the other hand, if you have more than five, you should choose a narrower topic.

Lists

Too Narrow
SLEET
– What is sleet?
– How does it affect people?

Well–Focused
HURRICANES
– What are they?
– What causes them?
– How strong are their winds?
– How often do they occur?

Too Broad
WEATHER
– What causes wind?
– Where is it windiest?
– What are clouds?
– How many types of clouds are there?
– What causes rain?
– What places get the most rain?
– What places get the least rain?
– What causes snow?
– What places get the most snow?
– How is sleet different from rain or snow?
– How is hail different from sleet?
– How is an ice storm different from hail or sleet?
– What causes frost?

Size up your topic. Write a list of questions you want to answer about your topic. Do you have the right number of questions for a report?

Prewriting Using a Gathering Grid

One way to organize your research is to use a gathering grid. The following grid was created for a research report about hurricanes.

Gathering Grid

Hurricanes	National Geographic Kids (Internet)	Science World (magazine)	Hurricane Force (book)	World Almanac for Kids (encyclopedia)
What are they?				Largest type of storm
What causes them?		See note card number one. (See page 389.)		
How strong are their winds?		From 74 mph to more than 155 mph!		Up to 250 mph!
How often do they occur?	10 tropical storms each year; 6 become hurricanes		5 reach U.S. shore each year; only 1 is category 3 or higher	

Create a gathering grid. List the questions you wrote on page 387 down the left-hand margin. Across the top, list sources you will use. Fill in the squares with the answers you find.

Using Interviews

During your research, you may have the chance to interview someone who has experience with your topic. Before your interview, prepare a list of questions. Avoid questions that require only a "yes" or "no" answer. Keep careful notes so that you can accurately quote the person.

RESEARCH

Creating Note Cards

Sometimes the answer to a question won't fit on your gathering grid. Then you can use note cards to keep track of your research.

Number each card and write a question at the top. Underneath the question, write a quotation, a list, or an answer in the form of a paraphrase (see page 390). At the bottom, name the source of the information and the page number. Here are three sample note cards for the report about hurricanes.

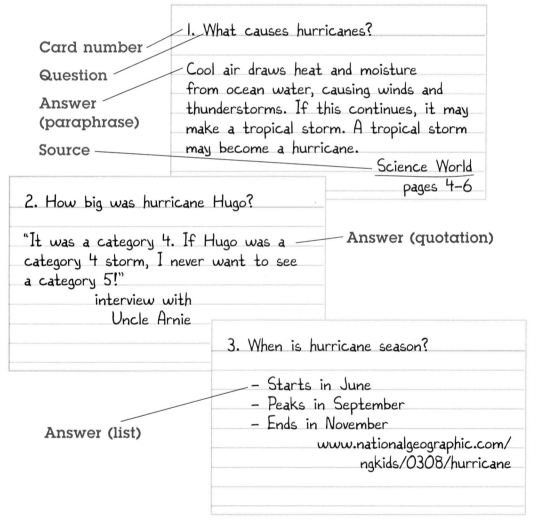

Card number
Question
Answer (paraphrase)
Source

1. What causes hurricanes?

Cool air draws heat and moisture from ocean water, causing winds and thunderstorms. If this continues, it may make a tropical storm. A tropical storm may become a hurricane.

Science World
pages 4-6

2. How big was hurricane Hugo?

"It was a category 4. If Hugo was a category 4 storm, I never want to see a category 5!"

interview with
Uncle Arnie

Answer (quotation)

3. When is hurricane season?

– Starts in June
– Peaks in September
– Ends in November

www.nationalgeographic.com/
ngkids/0308/hurricane

Answer (list)

Prewrite

Create note cards. Use note cards like those above whenever your answers are too long to appear on your gathering grid.

Prewriting Avoiding Plagiarism

As you do your research, you will find many interesting ideas, facts, and comments that will help you make your point. You **must not copy** these words and ideas and pretend they are yours. This is called *plagiarism,* and it is stealing. You can avoid plagiarism in one of two ways.

- **Quoting exact words:** If the exact words of a source capture an idea perfectly, you may include them in quotation marks and give credit to the source. (See page **395**.)

- **Paraphrasing:** You may also put the ideas from a source into your own words. This is called *paraphrasing.* However, you must still give credit to the original source.

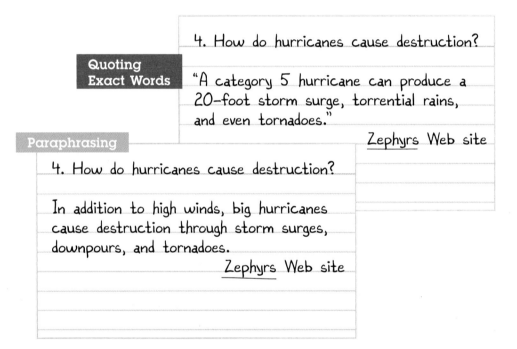

4. How do hurricanes cause destruction?

Quoting Exact Words

"A category 5 hurricane can produce a 20-foot storm surge, torrential rains, and even tornadoes."

Zephyrs Web site

Paraphrasing

4. How do hurricanes cause destruction?

In addition to high winds, big hurricanes cause destruction through storm surges, downpours, and tornadoes.

Zephyrs Web site

 Read the following material from the *Zephyrs* Web site. First decide which sentence from this passage would make the best quotation. Then paraphrase the entire passage as you would on a note card.

The storm surge is especially dangerous. It can arrive three to five hours before the center of the storm. A large surge can cause massive damage along shorelines and can flood low-lying escape routes.

Keeping Track of Your Sources

Whenever you find a source of information for your report, write down the following information. You'll need it for your works-cited page.

- **Encyclopedia entry:** Author's name (if listed). Entry title. Encyclopedia title. Edition (if given). Publication date.
- **Book:** Author's name. Title. Publisher. City. Copyright date.
- **Magazine:** Author's name. Article title. Title. Date published. Page numbers.
- **Internet:** Author's name (if listed). Page title. Site title. Date posted or copyright (if listed). Date found. Electronic address.
- **Interview:** Person's name. Type of interview (personal, telephone, mail, or e-mail). Date.

My Source Notes

Encyclopedia "Hurricane." World Almanac for Kids. 2004.

Book Michael C. Miles. Hurricane Force. Countryside Press. Philadelphia. 2002.

Magazine Libby Tucker. "Now That's Intense!" Science World. Nov. 27, 2003. Pages 4–6.

Internet Renee Skelton. "Flying into the Eye of a Hurricane." National Geographic Kids. March 12, 2004. <www.nationalgeographic. com/ngkids/0308/hurricane/>.

Interview Arnold Rasmussen. Personal interview. March 13, 2004.

Prewrite **List sources.** List the publication details from each of your sources. Update your list whenever you find new sources.

Prewriting Writing Your Thesis Statement

When you finish your research, you must find the best way to state your thesis, or focus. The thesis, which should remain the same throughout your report, is a special part of your topic that you emphasize. Remember this formula to help you write your thesis statement.

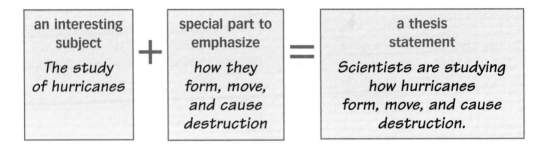

an interesting subject		special part to emphasize		a thesis statement
The study of hurricanes	**+**	how they form, move, and cause destruction	**=**	Scientists are studying how hurricanes form, move, and cause destruction.

Sample Thesis Statements

Deserts seem like lifeless stretches of sand (an interesting topic), but they are actually home to many plants and animals (special part to emphasize).

The Florida Everglades (an interesting topic) is truly one of North America's most unique environments (special part to emphasize).

Prewrite

Form your thesis statement. After reviewing your research notes, decide on two main points you could make about your topic. Write a separate thesis statement for each of these ideas, using the formula above. Finally, put a star (✱) next to the statement that says most clearly what you want to share about this topic.

Outlining Your Ideas

One way to plan your report is to make an outline. An outline is simply an organized list of ideas. A topic outline lists ideas as words or phrases; a sentence outline lists the ideas as full sentences. (Also see page 550.)

Sentence Outline

Below is the first part of a sentence outline for the report on pages 406–409. Notice that the outline begins with the thesis statement and then organizes ideas below it. Compare the outline with the opening paragraph and first middle paragraph of the report.

Thesis Statement	*THESIS STATEMENT: Scientists are studying how hurricanes form, move, and cause destruction.*
I. Topic Sentence (for first middle paragraph)	*I. Every hurricane forms because of heat, moisture, and wind.* *A. These combine to make a thunderstorm.* *B. If winds do not blow the storm apart, it grows into a tropical storm.* *C. When winds reach 74 miles per hour, the storm becomes a hurricane.*
A. B. C. Supporting Ideas	
Continue . . .	*II. Hurricanes move in a circular motion.* *A. . . .* *B. . . .*

Remember, in an outline, if you have a I, you must have at least a II. If you have an A, you must have at least a B.

Create your outline. Review your research notes and create a sentence outline for your report. Be sure that each topic sentence (I, II, III, . . .) supports your thesis statement and that each detail (A, B, C, . . .) supports the topic sentence above it. Use your outline as a guide when you write the first draft of your report.

Writing

Starting Your Research Report

The opening paragraph of your report should grab your reader's interest, introduce your topic, and share your thesis (focus) statement. Below are two possible ways that you could write the beginning of a hurricane report.

Beginning Paragraphs

This paragraph begins with interesting details and ends with the thesis (focus) statement.

Nature's most powerful storms are hurricanes. These huge, spinning storms build up over the ocean and sometimes move onto land. Hurricanes can cause a lot of damage before they weaken and turn into common thunderstorms. _To understand these storms, scientists are studying how hurricanes form, move, and cause destruction._

This paragraph begins with a question and ends with the thesis statement.

Should everyone be scared by the thought of a hurricane? Hurricanes cause a lot of damage every year, especially along the southeastern coast of the United States. _To understand these storms, scientists are studying how hurricanes form, move, and cause destruction._

Write your opening paragraph. Use one of the above samples as a guide to write your opening paragraph. Be sure to get your reader's interest, introduce your topic, and make a clear thesis statement.

Citing Sources in Your Report

As you write your report, remember to give credit to the sources of information that you quote directly or paraphrase.

When You Have All the Information

■ The most common type of credit (citation) lists the author's last name and the page number in parentheses.

> If the winds reach 74 miles per hour, the storm becomes a hurricane (Tucker 4).

■ If you already name the author in your report, just include the page number in parentheses.

> In Hurricane Force, Michael Miles explains that cool air draws heat and moisture from warm bodies of water to form a storm (22).

When Some Information is Missing

■ Some sources do not list an author. In those cases, use the title and page number.

> The winds of a hurricane are most violent around the eye ("Hurricane Season" 7).

■ Some sources do not use page numbers. In those cases, list just the author.

> Hurricanes in the Indian Ocean are called cyclones (Nealy).

■ If a source does not list the author or page number, use the title.

> In Southeast Asia, they are called typhoons ("Big Wind").

 Rewrite the following sentence giving credit to Libby Tucker's article "Now That's Intense!" from *Science World*, page 6.

Hurricanes in the Pacific Ocean are called typhoons and generally are limited to the coast of Southeast Asia.

Writing Developing the Middle Part

Beginning

▶ Middle

Ending

Once you have your reader's attention and have stated the thesis of your research report, you can begin writing the middle paragraphs. This part of your report should include facts, details, and examples that support your thesis statement.

Each middle paragraph should have a topic sentence covering one main idea, and everything you include in the paragraph should support that one idea. Be sure to arrange all your sentences so the reader can easily follow and understand the information. Use your sentence outline as a guide.

Middle Paragraphs

All the details support the topic sentences (underlined).

A personal memory is included.

Every hurricane forms because of heat, moisture, and wind. When cool air lies above a warm ocean, moisture begins to rise, causing a thunderstorm. If the thunderstorm gets strong enough, it is called a tropical storm. If the winds reach at least 74 miles per hour, the storm becomes a hurricane (Tucker 4).

Hurricanes move in a circular motion. The strongest winds of a hurricane are the closest to the center, or "eye." The weather is calm and clear in the eye. My uncle, Arnie Rasmussen, remembers when Hurricane Hugo hit Charleston, South Carolina, in 1989. "When that eye came after all the pounding wind and rain, the quiet was eerie. A high wall of clouds swirled around us. But we knew that when the eye passed, the pounding would begin again."

Hurricanes can destroy buildings, ruin crops, and cause serious injury and even death to people and animals. The sudden flood and high winds do most of the damage. Scientists use a 5-point scale to measure the strength of a hurricane. Category 1 is the weakest, with winds from 74 to 95 miles per hour and waves about 4 to 5 feet above normal tides. The category 5 hurricane is the strongest, with winds of at least 155 miles per hour and waves more than 18 feet above normal (Miles 26). Uncle Arnie said, "If Hugo was a category 4 storm, I never want to see a category 5!"

Sentences are arranged so that the reader clearly understands the main idea.

A graph makes an idea clearer.

Sources are included in parentheses.

Hurricane Categories

Categories	Wind Speed	Description
1	74–95 mph	Weak
2	96–110 mph	Moderate
3	111–130 mph	Strong
4	131–155 mph	Very Strong
5	greater than 155 mph	Devastating

However, only about five hurricanes form near the United States each year. Just two of those hurricanes reach land, and only one of those is a category 3 or stronger (Miles 30). In 1900, the worst hurricane in United States history hit Galveston, Texas. "A storm surge almost two stories high broke over the city, causing 20-foot floods and more than 8,000 deaths" (Skelton).

Write your middle paragraphs. At this point, don't worry about getting everything perfect. Just get your main ideas down in writing.

Writing **Ending Your Research Report**

Your ending paragraph should bring your report to a thoughtful close. Try one or more of the following ideas in your closing paragraph.

Beginning

Middle

▶ Ending

- ■ **Remind the reader about the thesis of the report.**
- ■ **Tell one last interesting fact about the topic.**
- ■ **Make a final observation about the topic.**

Ending Paragraph

The thesis is restated (underlined).

A final observation sums up the report.

Hurricanes are very dangerous storms. They can cause destruction, injury, and death over a very large area. <u>It's important to learn how these storms form and move, and that's why scientists spend so much time studying hurricanes.</u> Hurricanes cannot be stopped, so people must learn how to protect themselves and their belongings when one strikes.

Write your final paragraph. On your paper, write your final paragraph using the strategies above.

Look over your draft. Read your first draft, looking over your notes and outline to see if you included all the necessary details. Make notes about possible changes. You are now ready to begin revising.

Creating Your Works-Cited Page

The first step to creating a works-cited page is to format your sources according to proper style. The two following pages show formats for common types of sources.

Books

Author or editor (last name first). Title (underlined). City where the book was published: Publisher, copyright date.

Magazines

Author (last name first). Article title (in quotation marks). Title of the magazine (underlined) Date (day, month, year): Page numbers of the article.

Internet

Author (if available). Page title (if available, in quotation marks). Site title (underlined). Name of sponsor (if available). Date published (if available). Date found <electronic address>.

Books

Miles, Michael C. <u>Hurricane
     Force</u>. Philadelphia: Countryside
     Press, 2002.

Magazines

Tucker, Libby. "Now That's Intense!"
     <u>Science World</u> 17 Nov. 2003: 4–6.

Internet

Skelton, Renee. "Flying into the
     Eye of a Hurricane." <u>National
     Geographic Kids</u>. National
     Geographic. 12 Mar. 2004
     <http://www.nationalgeographic.com/
     ngkids/0308/hurricane/>.

Encyclopedia

 Author (if available). Article title (in quotation marks). Title of the encyclopedia (underlined). Edition (if available). Date published.

Interview

Person interviewed (last name first). Type of interview (personal, phone, mail, e-mail). Date.

Encyclopedia

"Hurricane." World Almanac for Kids. 2004.

Interview

Rasmussen, Arnold. Personal interview. 13 Mar. 2004.

Write

Format your sources. Check your report and your list of sources (page 391) to see which sources you actually used. Then follow these directions.

1 Write your sources using the guidelines above and on the previous page. You can write them on a sheet of paper or on note cards.

2 Alphabetize your sources.

3 Create your works-cited page. See the example below.

Works Cited

Miles, Michael C. Hurricane Force. Philadelphia: Countryside Press, 2002.

Rasmussen, Arnold. Personal interview. 13 Mar. 2004.

Skelton, Renee. "Flying into the Eye of a Hurricane." National Geographic Kids. National Geographic. 12 Mar. 2004 <http://www.nationalgeographic.com/ngkids/0308/hurricane/>.

Revising

A solid research report can rarely be written in one draft. Some ideas in the first draft may be incomplete or out of order. The voice may be boring in spots, and the word choice may be weak. Revision can turn your first draft into a clear and informative report.

Keys to Effective Revision

1. Read your entire draft to get an overall sense of your report.

2. Review your thesis statement to be sure that it clearly states your main point about the topic.

3. Make sure your beginning draws readers in. Then check that your ending brings your report to an interesting close.

4. Make sure you sound knowledgeable and interested in the topic.

5. Check for specific, colorful words and complete sentences.

6. Use the editing and proofreading marks inside the back cover of this book.

Aad Qotation

Revising Using a Checklist

Check your revising. On a piece of paper, write the numbers 1 to 12. If you can answer "yes" to a question, put a check mark after that number. If not, continue to work with that part of your report.

Ideas

____ 1. Have I written a clear thesis (focus) statement?
____ 2. Do I include one main idea in each topic sentence?
____ 3. Have I accurately quoted or paraphrased my sources?

Organization

____ 4. Do I have an effective beginning, middle, and ending?
____ 5. Have I put my middle paragraphs in the best order?
____ 6. Do I use transitions?

Voice

____ 7. Does my writing show my knowledge and interest?
____ 8. Does my voice sound formal?

Word Choice

____ 9. Do I define or explain any unfamiliar words?
____ 10. Do I use specific nouns and active verbs?

Sentence Fluency

____ 11. Do I vary the lengths and beginnings of my sentences?
____ 12. Do I avoid rambling sentences?

Make a clean copy. When you've finished revising your report, make a clean copy for editing.

Editing

After you've finished revising your report, it's time to edit your work for your use of conventions: spelling, punctuation, usage, and grammar.

Keys to Effective Editing

1. Use a dictionary, a thesaurus, your computer's spell checker, and the "Proofreader's Guide."

2. Read your essay out loud and listen for words or phrases that may be incorrect.

3. Look for errors in punctuation, capitalization, spelling, and grammar.

4. Check your report for proper formatting. (See pages 382–385 and 406–409 as guides.)

5. Edit on a printed computer copy. Then enter your changes on the computer.

6. Use the editing and proofreading marks inside the back cover of this book.

Editing **Using a Checklist**

Edit

Check your editing. On a piece of paper, write the numbers 1 to 12. If you can answer "yes" to a question, put a check mark after that number. If not, continue to edit for that convention.

Conventions

PUNCTUATION

_____ **1.** Do I use end punctuation after all my sentences?

_____ **2.** Have I correctly punctuated all direct quotations?

_____ **3.** Do I use commas in compound sentences?

_____ **4.** Do I use apostrophes to show possession *(boy's bike)*?

_____ **5.** Have I correctly punctuated my works-cited page?

CAPITALIZATION

_____ **6.** Do I start all my sentences with capital letters?

_____ **7.** Do I capitalize proper nouns and titles?

SPELLING

_____ **8.** Do I spell all my words correctly?

_____ **9.** Have I double-checked the spelling of names in my report?

GRAMMAR

_____ **10.** Do I use correct forms of verbs *(had gone,* not *had went)*?

_____ **11.** Do my subjects and verbs agree in number?
(Hurricanes *are* dangerous, not Hurricanes *is* dangerous.)

_____ **12.** Do I use the right words *(to, too, two)*?

Creating a Title

- Describe the main idea: **Exploring the Ring of Fire**
- Be creative: **Hurricane Havoc**

Publishing Sharing Your Report

After you have worked so hard to write and improve your report, you'll want to make a neat-looking final copy to share. You may also decide to prepare your report as an electronic presentation, an online essay, or an illustrated report.

Make a final copy. Use the following guidelines to format your report. (If you are using a computer, see page 60.) Create a clean final copy and carefully proofread it.

RESEARCH

Focus on Presentation

- Use blue or black ink and double-space the entire paper.
- Write your name, your teacher's name, the class, and the date in the upper left corner of page 1.
- Skip a line and center your title; skip another line and start your writing.
- Indent every paragraph and leave a one-inch margin on all four sides.
- Write your last name and the page number in the upper right corner of every page of your report.

Develop an Illustrated Report

Draw a diagram or prepare a model to illustrate an important part of your topic. (For example, if you wrote about geysers, you might draw a diagram showing how a geyser works.)

Make an Electronic Presentation

Prepare a multimedia presentation of your report. (See "Multimedia Presentations" on pages 411–415 for more information.)

Go Online

Look at the Write Source Web site www.thewritesource.com for information on publishing your work online.

Final Presentation of a Report

The research report begun on page 386 appears on the following pages. Note how careful formatting and helpful graphics give the report a polished look.

Greenberg 1

David Greenberg

Ms. Lin

Science

March 26, 2008

Hurricane Havoc

Does the thought of a hurricane scare you? It should. Hurricanes cause a lot of damage every year, especially along the southeastern coast of the United States. To understand these storms, scientists are studying how hurricanes form, move, and cause destruction.

Every hurricane forms because of heat, moisture, and wind. When cool air lies above a warm ocean, moisture begins to rise, causing a thunderstorm. If the thunderstorm gets strong enough, it is called a tropical storm. If the winds reach at least 74 miles per hour, the storm becomes a hurricane (Tucker 4).

Greenberg 2

Hurricanes move in a circular motion. The strongest winds of a hurricane are closest to the center, or "eye." The weather is calm and clear in the eye. My uncle, Arnie Rasmussen, remembers when Hurricane Hugo hit Charleston, South Carolina, in 1989. "When that eye came after all the pounding wind and rain, the quiet was eerie. A high wall of clouds swirled around us. But we knew that when the eye passed, the pounding would begin again."

Hurricanes can destroy buildings, ruin crops, and cause serious injury and even death to people and animals. The sudden flood and high winds do most of the damage. Scientists use a 5-point scale to measure the strength of a hurricane. Category 1 is the weakest, with winds from 74 to 95 miles per hour and waves about 4 to 5 feet above normal tides. The category 5 hurricane is the strongest, with winds of at least 155 miles per hour and waves more than 18 feet above normal (Miles 26). Uncle Arnie said, "If Hugo was a category 4 storm, I never want to see a category 5!"

HURRICANE CATEGORIES

Categories	Wind Speed	Description
1	74 – 95 mph	Weak
2	96 – 110 mph	Moderate
3	111 – 130 mph	Strong
4	131 – 155 mph	Very Strong
5	greater than 155 mph	Devastating

However, only about five hurricanes form near the United States each year. Just two of those hurricanes reach land, and only one of those is a category 3 or stronger (Miles 30). In 1900, the worst hurricane in United States history hit Galveston, Texas. "A storm surge almost two stories high broke over the city, causing 20-foot floods and more than 8,000 deaths" (Skelton).

Hurricanes are very dangerous storms. They can cause destruction, injury, and death over a very large area. It's important to learn how these storms form and move, and that's why scientists spend so much time studying hurricanes. Hurricanes cannot be stopped, so people must learn how to protect themselves and their belongings when one strikes.

Greenberg 4

Works Cited

Miles, Michael C. Hurricane Force. Philadelphia:

  Countryside Press, 2002.

Rasmussen, Arnold. Personal interview. 13 Mar. 2004.

Skelton, Renee. "Flying into the Eye of a Hurricane."

  National Geographic Kids. National Geographic.

  12 Mar. 2004 <http://www.nationalgeographic.com/

  ngkids/0308/hurricane/>.

Tucker, Libby. "Now That's Intense!" Science World

  17 Nov. 2003: 4–6.

Creating a Title Page

If your teacher requires a title page, follow his or her requirements. Usually you center the title one-third of the way down from the top of the page. Then go two-thirds of the way down and center your name, your teacher's name, the class, and the date on separate lines.

Hurricane Havoc

David Greenberg
Ms. Lin
Science
March 26, 2008

Research Report Checklist

Use the following checklist for your research report. When you can answer all of the questions with a "yes," your paper is ready to hand in.

Ideas

_____ **1.** Is my research report interesting and informative?
_____ **2.** Are my sources current and trustworthy?

Organization

_____ **3.** Does my report have a thesis statement in the opening paragraph and a topic sentence in each middle paragraph?
_____ **4.** Does my ending paragraph bring my report to a thoughtful close?

Voice

_____ **5.** Do I sound knowledgeable and interested in my topic?

Word Choice

_____ **6.** Have I explained any technical terms or unfamiliar words?
_____ **7.** Do I use quotations and paraphrasing effectively?

Sentence Fluency

_____ **8.** Do my sentences flow smoothly from one to another?

Conventions

_____ **9.** Does my first page include my name, my teacher's name, the class name, the date, and a title? (See page 382.)
_____ **10.** Do I correctly cite my sources? (See pages 383, 395, and 397.)
_____ **11.** Is my works-cited page set up correctly? Are the sources listed in alphabetical order? (See pages 385 and 399–400.)
_____ **12.** If my teacher requires a title page, is mine done correctly? (See page 409.)

Developing
Multimedia Presentations

If you've just written your best report or essay ever, you may want to share it with a larger audience. By creating a multimedia presentation using a computer, you'll be able to reach a larger audience, as well as add special effects to your report.

There are several kinds of software that you can use to produce multimedia presentations. Just add a little imagination, and you'll be connecting with your audience in a new, dynamic way.

What's Ahead

- Creating Multimedia Presentations
- Multimedia Presentation Checklist

Creating Multimedia Presentations

With the help of a computer, you can create a multimedia presentation that includes computer-generated slides with graphics and sound effects. These "extras" can make the important points of your presentation clearer and more interesting.

Prewriting Selecting a Topic and Details

For this presentation, you will want to use something you've already written, something that interests both you and your audience. After you've chosen your topic, make a list of the main ideas. Then find or create one or more of the following graphics or sound effects:

- **Pictures** such as photos or "click art"
- **Animations** that show a process or tell a story
- **Videos** of something you've filmed yourself
- **Sounds** and **music** to use as background or to make a point

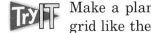 Make a plan and organize your ideas by creating a list or media grid like the one below.

Media Grid

Words on Slides	Pictures or Videos	Animations or Music	Sounds
1. Hurricanes cause a lot of damage each year.	photos	background music	
2. Scientists study the storms to understand them better.		hurricane animation	storm sound effects

 Gather details. Select ideas from your list or media grid for different graphics and sounds to include with each slide. Create them yourself or find them on the Internet. Save these images and sounds on your computer in a special folder created for this assignment.

Writing **Preparing the Presentation**

Make a *storyboard*. A storyboard is a "map" of the slides you plan to use in your presentation. (See the sample storyboard on the next page.) Use your list or media grid as a guide. Include one box in the storyboard for each main idea.

Use your computer software to design the slides. If you include words, choose a typestyle that is easy to read. Use the graphics and sounds you found earlier. Also consider using bulleted lists and graphs to organize your information. However, don't overdo the graphics.

Create a storyboard. Refer to your list or media grid to help you map out your storyboard. Include ideas for what your audience will see and hear. This will give you an idea of how the slides should look before you actually make them on the computer.

Revising **Improving Your Presentation**

Match the spoken parts of your presentation to the slides. To work well, everything in your presentation must be tied together so that it flows smoothly. Practice your presentation with family and friends and listen to any suggestions they may have for making your presentation even better.

Rehearse your report. As you rehearse, you may notice parts that don't work smoothly. Make whatever changes are necessary.

Editing **Checking for Conventions**

Check the text on each slide for spelling, punctuation, grammar, and capitalization errors. Consider asking an adult or a classmate to check your slides, too.

Make corrections. After you've made corrections, go through the presentation once more to make sure it works well.

You can save your presentation on a disk or CD to share with others. Make sure you copy all the necessary files.

REPORT

Interactive Report Storyboard

Here is the storyboard for a multimedia presentation based on the student research report "Hurricane Havoc." (See pages 406–409.) The author reads the report as the slides are presented.

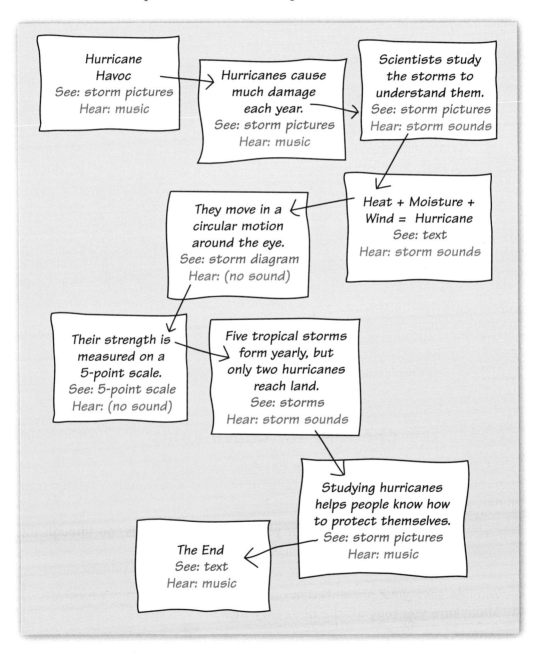

Presentation Checklist

Use the following checklist to make sure your presentation is the best it can be. When you can answer all of the questions with a "yes," you're ready to present!

Ideas

_____ **1.** Did I choose a strong essay or report for my presentation?
_____ **2.** Do my graphics help communicate my ideas clearly?
_____ **3.** Does each slide fit the audience and the purpose of the presentation?

Organization

_____ **4.** Did I introduce my topic clearly in the beginning?
_____ **5.** Did I include the important main points in the middle part?
_____ **6.** Did I end with a summary or wrap-up thought?

Voice

_____ **7.** Did I use an interesting, somewhat formal voice?
_____ **8.** Does my voice fit my audience and topic?

Word and Multimedia Choices

_____ **9.** Are the words on my slides easy to read?
_____ **10.** Did I choose the best pictures and sounds for my ideas?

Presentation Fluency

_____ **11.** Does my presentation flow smoothly from slide to slide?

Conventions

_____ **12.** Is my presentation free of grammar, spelling, and punctuation errors?

LISTEN
respect
clarify

The Tools
of Learning

observe
speak

Listening and Speaking

No matter where you are in school—in the classroom, in the gym, on the stage—you need to listen carefully. Why? For one thing, you don't want to miss anything. Teachers introduce new ideas, coaches explain new strategies, and directors give stage directions. Listening is one of the most important classroom skills you can master.

Speaking, which goes hand in hand with listening, is another key classroom skill. When you have mastered these two skills, you will be able to work better with others. You will also be more confident in your ability to learn and to succeed.

What's Ahead

- Listening in Class
- Participating in a Group
- Speaking in Class

Listening in Class

Listening involves more than just hearing. It means *paying attention, staying focused,* and *thinking about the speaker's ideas.* The following tips will help you become a better listener—in and out of school.

1 **Figure out your purpose for listening.** Is it to learn new information, understand an assignment, review for a test?

2 **Show that you are listening.** Let the speaker know that you are listening by looking at him or her and staying focused. Looking around the room tells the speaker that you don't care very much about what's being said.

3 **Listen carefully.** Hearing is not the same as listening. Hearing involves only your ears; listening involves your ears *and* your mind. To listen, you need to think about what you hear. Taking notes while you listen can help you think about what you hear.

4 **Listen and watch for signals.** Many speakers, especially teachers, will use signals to tell you what is important. Here are some common phrases to listen for.

And don't forget . . .	**This all means that . . .**
The two main reasons for . . .	**The bottom line is . . .**

> Sometimes speakers use their voice as a signal. Their voice gets higher or lower, louder or softer to help make a point. Speakers also use body language and facial expressions as signals.

 Keep a signal log. Make a chart like the one below for one of your classes. List the specific activities and what signals each teacher uses.

SIGNAL LOG

Class	Date	Activity	Signals
Spanish	Sept. 10	Reviewing for a test	The most important . . . Lo más importante . . .

A Closer Look at Listening

Good listening is one of the keys to successful learning. As you become a better listener, you will also become a better student. As you practice listening skills, you learn to . . .

- give your full attention to the speaker,
- notice the speaker's body language and tone of voice,
- consider how the speaker's message applies to you, and
- take notes and form questions.

 Test your speaking and listening skills by doing the activity below with a classmate.

1. Draw a simple picture using three or four different geometric shapes. (See the ***Original*** illustration below.)

2. Then have a classmate re-create your picture following your spoken directions. Do **not** let your classmate see the drawing!

3. After you have finished, compare the pictures. (See the ***Copy*** below.) How close are they? Why do you think they are not exactly alike?

4. Now switch and have your partner draw a picture and give you the directions. What did this activity teach you about speaking and listening?

LEARNING

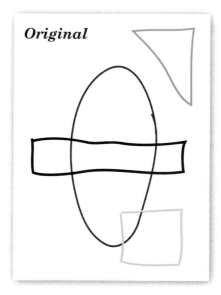

Original

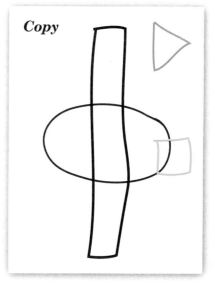

Copy

Participating in a Group

Nearly everything you say and do in a group is a response or reaction to what someone else has said or done. That's why it's important to follow basic rules of respect for yourself and for others.

Respect yourself by . . .

- believing that your own ideas are important.
- sharing your ideas clearly and politely.
- taking responsibility for what you say.

Respect others by . . .

- listening carefully to what others have to say.
- waiting for an opening before speaking, or interrupting politely by raising your hand and saying, "May I add something?"
- complimenting others when you can.
- encouraging everyone to participate.

> Remember, everyone is entitled to his or her opinion or idea.

 Sam is participating in a classroom group. Read about him below and then write a few sentences telling what you think Sam should do in each situation. Refer to the rules of respect above.

Situation 1

Sam has an idea to add, but he's not sure if he should share it immediately. What should Sam do?

Situation 2

Sam has been selected group leader. As the group brainstorms for project ideas, Sam notices that one of the students isn't saying anything. What should Sam do?

Group Skills

You now know why listening and speaking politely are so important to group work. Here are three skills you can use to make working in a group a truly positive experience. All members of a group need to use these skills: *observing, cooperating,* and *clarifying.*

Observe the speaker's . . .
- body language (facial expressions, eye contact, posture).
- tone of voice (for excitement, nervousness, shyness).

Cooperate by . . .
- staying positive and waiting your turn.
- avoiding put-downs.
- disagreeing in a polite way.

Clarify, or make something clearer, by . . .
- asking if there are any questions you can answer.
- restating a speaker's idea if necessary to be sure you understand everything.

LEARNING

 Read the statements and questions below about group skills. Then discuss your answers with a classmate.

   1. Latifah speaks very softly while looking down at her notes.
What message is Latifah sending with her tone of voice and body language? How could she improve her message?

   2. Ivan keeps saying that everything the group is doing is stupid.
What does Ivan need to learn about working in a group?

   3. Juan listens to his group, but he doesn't understand what he is supposed to do.
How can Juan make sure that he understands everything?

Speaking in Class

   To speak effectively in class or in small groups, follow the helpful guidelines listed below.

Pay attention. Listen carefully and limit your comments to the topic being discussed.

Think before you speak. Be sure your comments and ideas add to the discussion.

Be respectful. Respond politely to all speakers.

Make eye contact. Respect whomever you are talking to by looking at them. You can also listen more effectively when you watch a speaker's expressions and gestures.

Wait your turn. Show that you care about the opinions and ideas of others by listening until they are finished. Then they will be more willing to listen to you.

> Speak up so that everyone in class can hear your ideas.

Get to the point. Make your point quickly so that others have a chance to respond and join in the discussion.

Follow the rules. On your own paper, write down one of the six speaking rules above that you think is especially important.

1 List all the reasons why you think this is a good rule to follow.

2 Give examples of what might happen if this rule is not followed.

3 Share your responses in small groups.

Making Oral Presentations

You have probably already given lots of oral presentations—from your first show-and-tell in kindergarten to book reports, group projects, and demonstration speeches. Speaking in front of other people is an important lifelong skill, and the more you practice speaking now, the more your skill and confidence will grow.

In this chapter, you will learn how to present a report or an essay you have already written. You will also find some tips on effective speaking and how to apply them to your own presentation. Finally, you'll get some helpful hints on how to relax during your presentation.

What's Ahead

- **Preparing Your Presentation**
- **Organizing a Demonstration Speech**
- **Delivering Your Speech**

Preparing Your Presentation

When you are preparing a demonstration speech from an essay you have already written, you know your topic and the details you want to use. Here are some tips to get you started.

Start with an exciting opening to grab the audience's attention.

- Ask a question, tell a surprising fact, or make a strong statement.
- Share an interesting or a surprising story.
- Repeat a famous quotation.

Rewriting in Action

Below is the opening to the written essay "How to Give a Dog a Bath" (pages 163–164). Notice that the new beginning (on gold paper) is much more interesting for an oral presentation than the original opening.

If you or any of your friends have a dog, you know how much fun a pet can be. You also know that a dog can be a lot of work, especially if he is very active. It doesn't take long for a high-energy dog to look a mess and smell even worse. When that happens, it's time to gather up the dog shampoo and conditioner and freshen up your dog. If you follow these steps, bathing your dog can be easy and enjoyable.

Imagine this: You're relaxing, playing video games, when suddenly you notice a terrible smell that nearly makes you drop the remote control. You look down at Rover, who has just plopped down next to you. Shutting off the TV, you sigh, "Sorry, boy, time for you to have a bath!"

Rethink and rewrite your material. Select and review the essay or report you will use for your presentation. Rewrite parts that sound boring when you read them out loud. Use an exciting or interesting beginning.

Using Visual Aids

Once you have finished writing (or rewriting) your essay or report, you are ready to prepare your presentation. You may want to use visual aids like the ones listed below to make your presentation clear and interesting.

Posters	show words, pictures, or both.
Photographs	help your audience "see" who or what you are talking about.
Charts	compare ideas or explain main points.
Transparencies	highlight key words, ideas, or graphics.
Maps	show specific places being discussed.
Objects	allow your audience to see the real thing.

Here are some tips for preparing your visual aids.

1 **Choose them carefully.** Use visual aids that help explain or clarify a main point.

2 **Make them big.** Be sure your visual aids can be seen from the back of the room.

3 **Keep them clear.** Choose words and graphics that are to the point and easy to read at a glance.

4 **Use a good design.** Make visual aids colorful and attractive.

List visual aids. List a number of possible visual aids you could use in your presentation. Then select two that you think will work best.

> *List of visual aids*
> * *washtub and towels*
> * *shampoo*
> * *small bucket*
> * *stuffed dog*

Organizing a Demonstration Speech

If you are asked to give a demonstration speech in any of your classes, there are a few things you should know. When you give a demonstration, you don't just *tell* your audience how to do something, you *show* them. Follow these suggestions:

1 Use visual aids, props, and other materials to help your audience *see* what you are explaining.

2 Use an informal or conversational voice during your demonstration.

3 Present your main points and supporting details in an organized, step-by-step way.

Using Note Cards

One way to organize your details is to use note cards. Because you will be showing each step instead of simply reading it, you need to put your information in an easy-to-handle form.

For example, the writer of the how-to essay on pages 163–164, "How to Give a Dog a Bath," decided to present his essay as a demonstration. He rewrote his main ideas on note cards. Then, as he gave his demonstration, he was able to see his next point by simply glancing at the next card.

Note-Card Guidelines

- Write out your introduction word for word.
- Number your cards and use a separate card for each main step or idea.
- Write the main idea at the top of the card. Then add specific details for that idea underneath.
- At the appropriate points, list your visual aids with instructions for what to do with each one.
- Write out your ending word for word.

Create your note cards. Look over the note cards on the next page. Then create a note card for each step in your presentation. Be sure to add notes to yourself about visual aids.

1

Introduction

    Imagine this: You're relaxing, playing video games, when suddenly you notice a terrible smell that nearly makes you drop the control. You look down at Rover, who has just plopped down next to you. Shutting off the TV, you sigh, "Sorry, boy, time for you to have a bath!"

2

    To begin, get the bath ready and gather what you need. . . .
Mention warm water—not too hot or cold.
– Visual: Show shower hose and bucket.

3

Explain that animals need special shampoo and where to get it.
– Visual: Show how to work the shampoo into the dog's coat evenly.

4

5

Ending

    If you treat a dog calmly and gently, giving him a bath should be fun. Dogs that get used to taking baths learn to enjoy them. Remember, whenever your dog starts smelling too doggy, it's time to gather the supplies and wash him until he's clean and huggable again.

Delivering Your Speech

Every time you speak, you use both your voice and your body to communicate your message. The way you speak and move helps you connect with your listeners. This is especially important during an oral presentation. The following suggestions should be helpful.

Using Body Language

1 **Stand up straight.** Relax, but don't slouch. When you relax, it helps your audience to relax, too. They will enjoy your presentation more.

2 **Take a deep breath.** Breathe deeply to relax. Give yourself a moment to think about what you will say next.

3 **Look up.** Make eye contact with your audience. If looking at your audience is hard for you, look slightly over their heads.

4 **Look interested.** Use facial expressions to show the audience that you care about your topic.

5 **Use your hands.** Use simple hand gestures, such as pointing to a visual aid, to add emphasis and interest.

Using Your Voice

Along with your body, your voice helps you communicate clearly. The most important features of your speaking voice are *volume, tone,* and *speed.*

Volume	Practice speaking loudly enough so that everyone in the room will be able to hear you.
Tone	Stress certain words if you want to add feeling or emphasize an idea.
Speed	Practice your presentation. Remember that too slow is boring, but too fast can be confusing. Vary your speed of delivery depending on what you want to emphasize.

Practice and present. Practice your presentation using the tips and suggestions above and the checklist on the next page. Have a family member or friend listen to you practice and offer suggestions.

Overcoming Stage Fright

Most people feel nervous in front of a group. You may feel that way, too. Here are some ways to help you relax and reduce your "stage fright."

1 **Practice and be prepared.**

Know your presentation. That means you should practice every chance you get. Practice by delivering it in front of a mirror, family, or friends. Also consider videotaping your presentation to evaluate your delivery.

2 **Warm up.**

Before you begin your presentation, stretch your arms, neck, and shoulders. Breathe deeply.

3 **Focus.**

Often, nervousness or stage fright comes from losing your focus. When you are making your presentation, concentrate on what you are doing and on what comes next.

Using a Checklist

Whenever you practice your presentation, use the checklist below. If possible, record yourself with a camcorder or have someone else watch your presentation and offer suggestions.

_____ **1.** My posture is relaxed, but I don't slouch.

_____ **2.** I look up from my notes, have some eye contact with my audience, and move naturally.

_____ **3.** I speak clearly and loudly enough to be heard and understood by everyone.

_____ **4.** I look and sound like I'm interested in my topic.

_____ **5.** I control and vary my speed (not too fast, not too slow).

_____ **6.** I avoid unnecessary sounds and words: *um, er, like.*

_____ **7.** My visual aids are clear and large enough for all to see.

_____ **8.** I use my hands to hold my notes and to point out my visual aids.

LEARNING

Presentation Tips

Before your presentation . . .

- **Gather all the materials you will need.**
  Practice your demonstration as much as you can.
- **Time your presentation.**
  If it is too short, add information or personal stories.
- **Be prepared.**
  Put all your main ideas and important details on
  note cards.

During your presentation . . .

- **Hold up your materials as you explain the process.**
  Be sure that everyone can see what you are doing.
- **Speak up.** Be sure everyone can hear you.
- **Talk slowly.** You want your audience to understand you.
  Repeat important information if necessary.
- **Keep talking throughout the presentation.**
  If a step takes a little time, fill in with a story or
  personal experience related to the activity.
- **Show a finished product.**
  If your process takes too long to
  complete (such as baking a cake), have
  a finished product to show (a cake).

After your presentation . . .

- **Answer any questions.**
  Ask if anyone has a question
  about the topic.
- **Then collect your materials**
  and walk to your seat.

Practice and present. Have a final practice with a friend or someone at home. Ask for feedback and make changes. Then, after your classroom demonstration, listen to suggestions from your teacher and classmates.

Keeping Journals and Learning Logs

There are many ways to improve your writing and learning skills. Two of the best ways are writing regularly in a personal journal and keeping a learning log in your classes.

A personal journal is a place for you to record personal thoughts, feelings, and events. When you keep a journal, all your thinking and writing skills come into play, sharpening your mind and making you a better writer. In a learning log, you write about things you are studying. A learning log can help you understand tough subjects and make you a better student.

In the following chapter, you'll learn how to start your own personal journal and learning log.

What's Ahead

- Keeping a Personal Journal
- Writing in Other Journals
- Writing in a Learning Log
- Writing-to-Learn Activities

Keeping a Personal Journal

Keeping a personal journal can be a rewarding and enjoyable activity. You can write about things that happen to you (both good and bad). You can also write stories and poems without worrying about errors in your writing. All of this practice helps you become a better writer.

Getting Started

A personal journal is your own special place to write. Follow these steps to get started.

1 **Collect the proper tools.**

All you really need is a notebook and a supply of your favorite pens or pencils. Or you can use a computer if you have one available.

2 **Choose a time to write.**

Write early in the morning, late at night, or anytime in between.

3 **Write freely for at least 5 to 10 minutes at a time.**

If you regularly write for the same amount of time, count the number of words you get on paper. That number should increase little by little, which means you are learning to write freely and naturally.

4 **Write about things that are important to you.**

Here are some general subject areas to consider:
- important events,
- subjects you are studying,
- interesting things you see and hear, or
- thoughts and feelings you would like to explore.

5 **Keep track of your writing.**

Date your journal entries and read through them from time to time. Underline ideas that you would like to write more about in the future.

Start your journal writing. Write in a personal journal for two weeks for 5 to 10 minutes a day. At the end of the two weeks, put a star next to the entry that you would like to write more about some day. Tell a partner why you chose this entry.

Journal Entry

In the sample journal entry below, the student writes about what she's been doing lately and about her plans for the upcoming week.

April 16

We had our first track meet last night. I ran second in the half-mile relay and was really nervous about the handoffs. I did okay for my first time, and we placed third. All those practices paid off.

Cozzie slept over on Friday night. We played music and watched some TV and talked really late until my mom told us to quiet down. On Saturday morning, we made chocolate chip pancakes for everyone. I really enjoy cooking. Sometimes I even think I'd like to be a chef. Would it be as much fun if I did it every day as a job?

I've got a huge report in science to finish this week. I hope I can use the computer lab and get some help with adding the table to my report. Maybe Mr. Vernor can show me what to do. He helped me with my history report when I needed to create some graphs.

LEARNING

Asking questions and wondering are two ways to reflect in journal writing. (*Reflect* means "to think very carefully about something.")

Ask questions. As you write, ask yourself these questions:

What did I learn from the experience?
How do I feel about it now?

Wonder. Consider how the experience may affect your future. Compare your new experiences to others you have had.

Writing in Other Journals

Writing in a personal journal is one way to explore your thoughts and feelings. Here are four other types of journals you can try.

Dialogue Journal

In a dialogue journal, two people (you and a teacher, family member, or friend) talk to each other on paper over a period of time. A dialogue journal can help you and your partner learn more about each other or explore a common interest.

Specialized Journal

When you write in a journal about an ongoing event or experience, you are writing in a specialized journal. You may want to explore your thoughts while at summer camp, while participating in a team sport, while involved in a school play, or while working on a group project.

Travel Journal

One form of specialized journal is a travel journal. It preserves memories of a trip you've taken. You can write while riding on a bus, waiting in lines, or at the beginning or end of each day.

Reader-Response Journal

In a reader-response journal, you react to the books you are reading. Here are some questions that will help you write about literature.

1. What are you feeling after reading the opening chapter? After reading half of the book? After finishing the book?

2. Does the book make you laugh? Cry? Smile? Cheer? Explain.

3. How does the book connect with your life?

4. What about the writing is especially good?

5. Who else should read this book? Why?

 Respond to your reading. For the next short story or novel you read, keep a reader-response journal. Write at least one entry after each chapter. Use the questions above to get started.

Writing in a Learning Log

A learning log is a place to write down your thoughts, feelings, and questions about the subjects you are studying. Here are some tips to help get you started.

1 **Keep a learning log for any subject.**
It's especially helpful for the subjects that are hard for you.

2 **Keep your learning log well organized.**
Use a separate notebook for your learning log, date each entry, and leave space for adding information (in red below).

3 **Use graphic organizers and drawings.**
Pictures and illustrations can help you remember key ideas.

4 **Write freely about any of these ideas:**
- what you have learned from an assignment or class presentation,
- questions you have about new material, or
- how new material connects to other things you have learned.

LEARNING

Mar. 8

Key words:
heart   oxygen   oxygen = an odorless
pump   blood   gas in the air
life

Without blood pumping through our bodies, we would die. All our organs need whatever is in blood to live. Oxygen, for one thing. Mr. Chavez always calls good citizens the lifeblood of our nation. When I see all those cars going in and out of Chicago, well, they sure do look like blood cells rushing through arteries.

Science Log

Learning logs work for any subject. The sample log below was written following a discussion of mosquitoes in a science class. Keep in mind that a learning log works best if you put ideas in your own words.

Mosquitoes   Feb. 5

Key words: germs
            malaria

I thought mosquitoes were just summer pests. It turns out that mosquitoes can carry germs that cause serious diseases such as malaria. (Fortunately, mosquitoes in the United States almost never carry malaria.) Doctors think that, in all of history, more people have died of malaria than any other disease. That means that mosquitoes have had a pretty big part in history. It's funny because I don't ever remember reading about mosquitoes in history class!

History-making pest!

Log on in science. On your own paper, name the subject of the science unit you are currently studying. Then write a learning-log entry about something in the unit that you find interesting, surprising, or confusing.

Math Log

Many students keep learning logs in math class to help them think about math concepts. One way to set up a math log is to write a question related to the day's lesson and then answer it. Below are two examples.

MATH CLASS   Sept. 15

Question: Why do we need to show our work?
Answer: I know Mr. Manzo wants me to show my work so he knows that I did the problem myself. He can also see how I did it. If I get stuck, he can see how to help me.
      But sometimes it doesn't make sense. I can figure out some problems in my head. Why can't I just write the answer? Why should I write all the stuff about how I got the answer?

                                    Sept. 16
Question: What are two meanings of the minus sign?
Answer: The minus sign means "subtraction." Another meaning is "negative number."
      For example, the first minus sign in the equation below means "subtract 7." But the second minus sign on the right side means "negative 4."
      $3 - 7 = -4$

Log on in math. On your own paper, write a learning-log entry for math. First write down a question about a math concept you are studying. Then answer it. (Use the samples above as a guide.)

Social Studies Log

In the following sample, the student writes about a concept introduced in her social studies class. Writing about this idea helps the student explore her thoughts and feelings about it.

Social Studies   Nov. 17

Melting Pot

    Today in class we talked about the "melting pot." The United States is supposed to be a place where people from different races and backgrounds blend in or "melt" together. In one way, this idea makes sense because people from all over the world have settled here. And I know some "melting" has gone on, but then I think of this city. There still are definite neighborhoods. Most African Americans live in the central city and on the north side. Most Hispanic Americans live on the south side. Sure, some African Americans live in other places, but it seems to me that we still have a long way to go before we can really call ourselves a melting pot.

Log on in social studies. On your own paper, name the subject of the unit you are now studying in social studies. Then write a learning-log entry about something in the unit that you find interesting, surprising, or confusing.

Writing-to-Learn Activities

There are many ways to write in a learning log. Three basic ideas are described below, and five additional ideas are listed on the next page.

The Basic Three

Freewriting When you freewrite in a learning log, you write quickly about a subject you are studying. The act of writing freely and rapidly allows you to explore a subject from many different angles. Try to write for 5 to 10 minutes at a time. Don't stop to judge or correct your writing; just keep writing. (The learning-log entry on page 438 is an example of freewriting.)

Listing Listing is a simple form of freewriting. You make a list of the ideas, feelings, and questions that come to mind as you think about a subject.

Clustering Clustering also works well in a learning log. Place the subject you are studying in the center of the page and circle it. Then write words and phrases about the subject. Circle each one and draw a line connecting it to the closest related word.

LEARNING

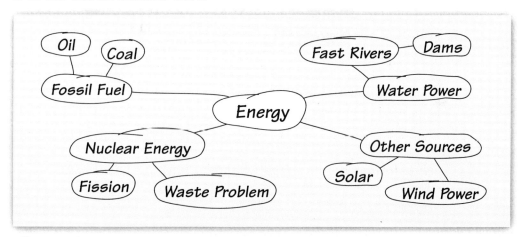

After clustering for 3 or 4 minutes, you may find it helpful to freewrite about the subject using one of the ideas in your cluster as a starting point.

 Make a cluster for a subject you are studying in one of your classes. Remember to write the subject in the middle of your paper. Keep clustering until you run out of ideas.

Special Writing Activities

Review the five learning-log activities on this page. Each one is quite different from the others and can be used for a special purpose.

First Thoughts When you begin to study something new in one of your classes, write what you think about it. Also write about where this particular subject may take you.

Stop 'n' Write In the middle of learning something new, take a moment to stop and write down what you are thinking. This will help you understand and remember what you are studying.

Picture Outlining A picture can be worth a thousand words. When you see something in class or in a book that will help you remember what you are learning, draw a picture of it and label it. The following picture outline quickly shows the different levels of organization in a person's body.

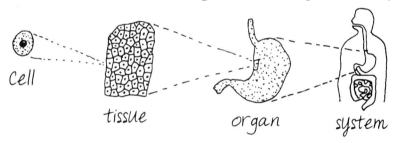

Cell   tissue   organ   system

Nutshelling After you learn something new, try putting it "in a nutshell." In other words, write a sentence that sums up what you have just learned.

Nutshelling summarizes what you have just learned.

Unsent Letters To think deeply about your learning, write a letter about it. You could write to someone real (like the author of a book you like) or to someone imaginary (like a friend in the Andromeda Galaxy). In your letter, describe what you have learned and what it means to you.

 Think about what you have learned so far about writing in a learning log. Then write an unsent letter to someone real or imaginary, explaining what you have learned.

Taking Notes

To become good at something, you need to roll up your sleeves and get involved. Fortunately, most of you are already involved in your learning. You listen in class and complete reading assignments. You do your homework and review for tests. However, to get totally involved, you must write about the subjects you are studying.

Research has shown that the best way to understand new material is to write about it. The writer of the following proverb appreciates the value of writing in the learning process: "I hear and I forget; I see and I remember; *I write and I understand.*"

Note taking is one of the most valuable writing skills you can develop. The information in this chapter will help you take useful classroom and reading notes.

What's Ahead

- Taking Classroom Notes
- Taking Reading Notes

Taking Classroom Notes

Taking notes can help you learn more effectively in class and do well on tests. It helps in three ways:

- Writing notes helps you pay attention.
- Reading over notes helps you understand.
- Studying notes helps you remember.

Guidelines for Note Taking

1 **Write the topic and date at the top of each page.**
You should also number each page of notes. Then, if a page gets out of order, you'll know exactly where it belongs.

2 **Listen carefully when the teacher introduces the topic.**
You may hear important clues. Your teacher may say, "I'm going to explain the three branches of the federal government." Then you can listen for those three branches.

3 **Listen for key words.**
Key words include *first, second, last, most important,* and so on.

4 **Use numbers or symbols to help organize your notes.**
For example, you can identify the steps in a process using 1st, 2nd, 3rd, and so on. A star or an asterisk can mark a key point.

5 **Write down the main ideas using your own words.**
Don't try to write down everything the teacher says.

6 **When you hear a word that is new to you, write it down.**
Don't worry about spelling. Just make your best guess, circle the word, and check a dictionary later.

7 **Copy whatever the teacher writes on the board.**
Usually, this information is important and often ends up on tests.

> The real secret to taking good notes is listening. Don't get so involved in taking notes that you forget to listen. If you listen carefully, you will hear details that you can add to your notes later.

Take class notes. Use the guidelines above and the sample set of notes on the next page to guide you the next time you take notes.

Setting Up Your Notes

Use a notebook or a three-ring binder for your notes. A three-ring binder allows you to add and remove pages when you need to. The side notes below give additional tips.

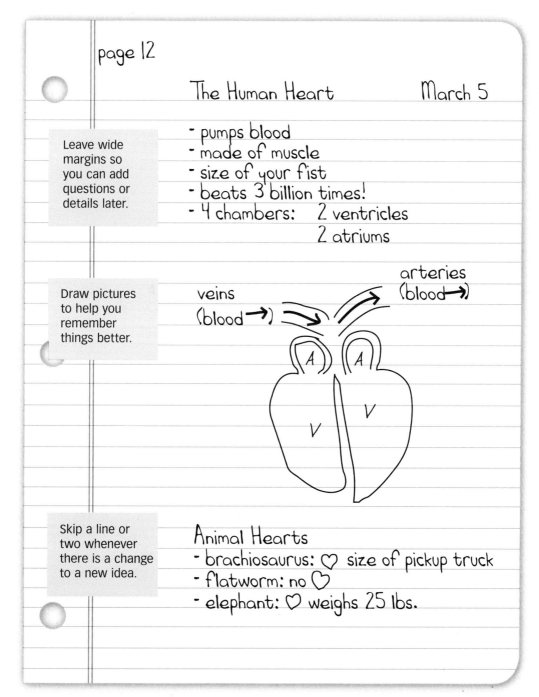

page 12

The Human Heart   March 5

- pumps blood
- made of muscle
- size of your fist
- beats 3 billion times!
- 4 chambers: 2 ventricles
                 2 atriums

Leave wide margins so you can add questions or details later.

veins
(blood →)

arteries
(blood →)

A   A

V   V

Draw pictures to help you remember things better.

Animal Hearts
- brachiosaurus: ♡ size of pickup truck
- flatworm: no ♡
- elephant: ♡ weighs 25 lbs.

Skip a line or two whenever there is a change to a new idea.

LEARNING

Reviewing Your Notes

Read over your notes at the end of each day.

- **Write any questions you have in the margins of your notes.** Talk over your questions with a classmate or your teacher.
- **Circle any words you don't understand.** Look up these words in a dictionary. Add the correct spelling and meaning to your notes.
- **Rewrite your notes if they are sloppy.** It's important to keep your notes organized and easy to read.
- **Cross-reference your notes.** Add the page numbers from your textbook that cover the same material to make reviewing easier.

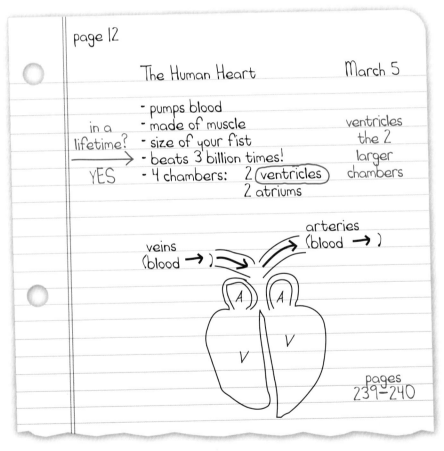

 Review your work. The next time you take notes, check them over using this page as a guide. Did you write any questions in the margins or circle any words?

Taking Reading Notes

Taking notes can help you understand what you are reading. As you read, you can stop anytime to write something down. Here are some tips for taking reading notes.

1 **Preview the assignment before reading it.**

Read the title, introduction, headings, and chapter summaries. Look at any pictures, charts, or other graphics. Each of these can give important information about the reading.

2 **Take notes as you read the material.**

Read carefully and think about what you are reading. (Use page 443 as a guide to set up your notes.)

- **Write down each heading or subtopic.**
  Then write the most important facts for each heading.
- **Try to write your notes in your own words.**
  Don't just copy from the book.
- **Take notes on any important graphics.** This includes pictures, charts, or maps. Make your own drawings if you wish.
- **Read difficult or important material out loud.**
  This "talking" will help you understand and remember the information better.
- **List each word that is new to you.**
  Look up each word in a glossary or dictionary. Choose the meaning that fits and write that meaning in your notes.
- **Review your notes.** Look over your notes and write down any questions you have for your teacher.

3 **Use graphic organizers whenever possible.**

Use any of the helpful organizers on the next three pages for taking notes—a time line, a table organizer, and a Venn diagram.

Try IT List three tips from this page that you could use the next time you take notes on your reading. Why did you choose these three tips?

LEARNING

Using a Time Line

Many types of writing are organized by time: first one thing happens and then another. Histories, biographies, and narratives are arranged in this way. When you want to keep track of the events you are reading about, you can use a **time line**.

Read the following short biography. Then look at the time line one student made to remember the details.

Shel Silverstein

The author, artist, and composer Shel Silverstein was born in 1930 in Chicago, Illinois. From an early age, he began to write. His first published work was a cartoon that appeared in 1950 in his college newspaper, *The Torch*. He went on to write classic books such as *The Giving Tree* (1963), *Where the Sidewalk Ends* (1974), *A Light in the Attic* (1982), and *Falling Up* (1996). He died in May of 1999.

Time Line

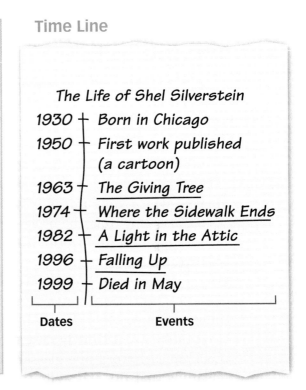

The Life of Shel Silverstein

1930	Born in Chicago
1950	First work published (a cartoon)
1963	The Giving Tree
1974	Where the Sidewalk Ends
1982	A Light in the Attic
1996	Falling Up
1999	Died in May

Dates   Events

 Read the following brief biography. Then create a time line that lists the important events.

1   Madeleine L'Engle was born on November 29, 1918, and
2   grew up in New York City. Her interest in writing began when
3   she was very young. In 1931, she and her parents moved to
4   the French Alps, where she attended a boarding school. She
5   published her first novel, *The Small Rain,* in 1945. Her best-
6   known work, *A Wrinkle in Time,* came out in 1962. It won the
7   Newbery Award in 1963. Madeleine has continued to write. She
8   has written more than 45 books.

Using a Table Organizer

Some types of writing are organized around main ideas. Each main idea is supported by details, the way a tabletop is supported by the legs. Essays, articles, feature stories, and textbook chapters are usually organized in this way.

Read the following short article. Then look at the **table organizer** to see how one student took notes on this reading.

Where Did English Come From?

The English language comes from many other languages. Many English words—such as *light, work,* and *good*—come from German. In fact, the word "English" was originally "Anglish," the language spoken by a German tribe called the Angles. Other English words come from French. Words like *courage, petite,* and *elephant* entered English when the French-speaking Normans invaded England. English also contains words from Latin and Greek. *Leopard* and *philosophy* are from these ancient languages.

Table Organizer

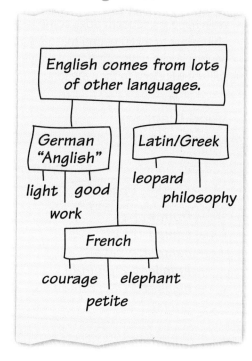

LEARNING

 Read the following paragraph. Then take notes on it using a table organizer. Put the main idea in the top box (the tabletop). Under it, put supporting details (the table legs).

1   There are three major types of writing. The first type is narrative
2   writing. Narratives tell a story and focus on what happens in a
3   certain place and time. The second type is expository writing. It gives
4   information by presenting main ideas and supporting them with
5   details. The third type is persuasive writing. It presents an opinion
6   and reasons for the opinion. A student who learns all three types will
7   be ready for most writing challenges.

Using a Venn Diagram

In some reading assignments, two topics are compared. You can take notes on this type of material by using a **Venn diagram**. It is two overlapping circles that shows similarities and differences between two things.

Dogs and Cats

Dogs and cats are both popular pets in the United States, but they are quite different. Early dogs were actually wolves 12,000 years ago, perhaps tamed as campsite pets. Early cats were wildcats 6,000 years ago, tamed to guard Egyptian grain supplies. Modern dogs come in all shapes and sizes, from a 2-pound Chihuahua to a 200-pound mastiff. Adult house cats weigh between 8 and 20 pounds. Since dogs came from wolves, they are social creatures. Cats came from solitary wildcats, so they are loners. Both creatures make good pets.

Venn Diagram

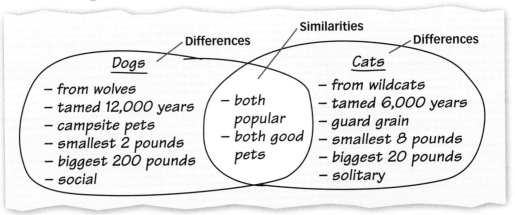

Similarities

Differences — Dogs / Cats — Differences

Dogs
- from wolves
- tamed 12,000 years
- campsite pets
- smallest 2 pounds
- biggest 200 pounds
- social

- both popular
- both good pets

Cats
- from wildcats
- tamed 6,000 years
- guard grain
- smallest 8 pounds
- biggest 20 pounds
- solitary

 Read the following paragraph. Then make a Venn diagram of your own, noting the similarities and differences between apples and oranges.

1   People say you can't compare apples and oranges, but you can.
2   Both fruits grow on trees and are sweet. They both provide juice that
3   has important vitamins in it. But apples have a thin
4   skin, while oranges have a thick rind. Under the skin, an apple is
5   crunchy and white, and its seeds are dark brown. The inside of an
6   orange has juicy pulp with white seeds. So, even though people may
7   say you can't compare apples and oranges, you can—and you can
8   enjoy eating them afterward.

Completing Writing Assignments

Writing is many things. Writing is expressing your feelings, connecting with other people, and telling stories. But more than anything else, writing is thinking on paper. Each time you put pen to paper or fingers to the keyboard, you must think about what you want to say. This is why your teachers give you writing assignments. They want you to *think* about the subjects you are studying.

The first step is to understand your assignment. If you start writing before you know what you are supposed to do, you might as well take a walk and forget the dog! This chapter will help you complete writing assignments by starting you out on the right foot.

What's Ahead

- **Understanding the Assignment**
- **Thinking Through Each Assignment**
- **Setting Up an Assignment Schedule**

Understanding the Assignment

Writing assignments come in all shapes and sizes, including the three types listed here.

Open-ended: Some writing assignments are open-ended. That means you get to select the topic. *(Recall a memorable experience in your life.)*

Specific: Other writing assignments are specific. They tell you exactly what to write about. *(Prove that the Battle of Gettysburg was a turning point in the Civil War.)*

In between: Still other assignments are somewhere in between. *(Compare Tom Sawyer to someone that you know well.)*

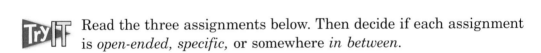 Read the three assignments below. Then decide if each assignment is *open-ended, specific,* or somewhere *in between.*

1. *Explain how photosynthesis works.*
2. *Describe an unforgettable place.*
3. *Contrast the cell phone with another method of communication.*

Assignment Checklist

Before you begin any writing assignment, make sure that you understand everything about it. Use the following checklist as a guide.

_____ 1. **Ask** how your writing will be assessed or graded.

_____ 2. **Find out** how much time you have to finish your work.

_____ 3. **Schedule** a time and place to work on your assignment.

_____ 4. **Read** the directions carefully to make sure you understand them.

_____ 5. **Look for** key words—*recall, prove, compare*—so you know exactly what your writing should do.

Thinking Through Each Assignment

Your writing assignments require you to think in different ways. These different levels of thinking include *recalling, understanding, applying, analyzing, synthesizing,* and *evaluating.* The chart below introduces the different levels, and the next six pages give you a closer look at each one.

Recalling means remembering information. Use this basic level of thinking when you are asked to . . .

- fill in the blanks.
- define terms.
- list facts or words.
- label parts of something.

Understanding means knowing what information means. Use understanding when you are asked to . . .

- explain something.
- choose the best answer.
- tell if something is true or false.
- summarize something.

Applying means using information. Use applying when you are asked to . . .

- follow directions.
- solve a problem.

Analyzing means breaking information down into different parts. Use analyzing when you are asked to . . .

- compare things.
- divide things into groups.
- give reasons for something.
- tell why something is the way it is.

Synthesizing means using information to create something new. Use synthesizing when you are asked to . . .

- create something.
- add new ideas.
- combine things.
- predict something.

Evaluating means using information to tell the value of something. Use this advanced level of thinking when you are asked to . . .

- assess something.
- give your opinion of something.

LEARNING

Recalling

When you *recall* information for an assignment, you are remembering what you have learned. To prepare for this type of thinking, listen carefully in class, read your assignments, and take careful notes.

You recall when you . . .

- write down facts, terms, and definitions.
- study the information until you can remember it.

The following test questions ask the student to recall information.

DIRECTIONS: Fill in the blanks below with the correct numbers.

1. Americans throw away __*195 million*__ tons of trash each year.

2. Almost __*55 million*__ tons of the total is packaging materials.

DIRECTIONS: Define each term by completing the sentence.

1. A *midden* is __*what scientists call a pit where*__

   __*Stone Age people threw their trash*__ .

2. The three R's of trash reduction are __*reduce*__ ,

   __*reuse*__ , and __*recycle*__ .

 Carefully review your notes about a topic that you are studying in class. After 10 minutes, put this information away. Then, on a clean sheet of paper, recall as many important facts as you can from your notes. Share your results with a classmate.

Understanding

When you *understand* information, you know what it means. If you can rewrite information in your own words, then you clearly understand it.

You understand when you . . .

- **explain something.**
- **tell how something works.**
- **summarize information.**

The following question asks the student to show understanding, and the answer does that.

ASSIGNMENT: Explain the three R's of trash reduction.

The three R's of trash reduction are reduce, reuse, and recycle. Reduce means cutting the amount of trash produced. (This is sometimes called precycling.) Reuse means using things again instead of throwing them away. Recycle means using paper, glass, aluminum, and other things to make new products, instead of throwing them away. Using the three R's is a good way to help the environment because all three help reduce the amount of trash produced.

understand

LEARNING

 Write a paragraph explaining your understanding of one of the following topics: thunderstorms, tornadoes, or earthquakes.

Applying

When you *apply* information, you use it. In order to apply something, you need to understand it completely.

You apply when you . . .

- use information to solve problems.
- follow directions to complete a task.

In this assignment, the writer applies information to her own life.

ASSIGNMENT: Make a trash-reduction plan for your family.

Family Trash-Reduction Plan

We can reduce trash by . . .

- *not using paper plates or Styrofoam cups.*
- *shopping for products that have little or no packaging.*

We can reuse by . . .

- *taking grocery bags back to the store to use again.*
- *saving boxes and wrapping paper to use again.*

We can recycle by . . .

- *taking our newspapers, plastic and glass jars, and soft-drink cans to the recycling center.*

 Write a journal entry showing how the problem of pollution relates to some part of your life. Write for at least 5 to 8 minutes.

recall *apply* **UNDERSTAND**
analyze synthesize evaluate
455
Completing Writing Assignments

Analyzing

When you *analyze* information, you break the information down into parts. There are many different ways to do this.

You analyze when you . . .

- tell how things are alike or different.
- tell which parts are most important.
- divide things into different groups.
- give reasons for something.

In this assignment, the writer analyzes what he knows.

ASSIGNMENT: In a paragraph, tell how a dump and a landfill are different.

> A landfill and a dump are quite different. A dump is just a place where trash is put. Garbage is left out in the open, and it attracts animals that may get sick and spread disease. Chemicals in trash (such as paint and insect killer) can leak into the ground and pollute the water. Landfills were invented to prevent these problems. In a landfill, trash is covered with dirt right away to keep animals away. Landfills are also lined with clay and plastic to keep chemicals from leaking into the water supply.

 Classify (break down into groups) the different types of meals served in your cafeteria or the different types of homework you are assigned. Share the results of your work with a classmate.

Synthesizing

When you *synthesize,* you create something new using information you have already learned.

You synthesize when you . . .

- add some new ideas to existing information.
- use information to make up a story or some other creative piece of writing.
- predict what may happen in the future because of this information.

In this assignment, the writer synthesizes a report using what she knows.

ASSIGNMENT: Write a title-down report about waste in America. Use the letters in the word "garbage" to begin each sentence.

Garbage is food waste, and trash is all other waste.

Americans make 195 million tons of trash a year.

Reducing, reusing, and recycling can cut down on trash.

Buying products with very little packaging is one good way to reduce trash.

All the packaging we throw away adds up to 55 million tons a year.

Garbage and trash take up a lot of room.

Everything we throw away adds to a mountain of trash somewhere.

synthesize

 Write your own title-down report using the letters from a topic you are studying in one of your classes *(erosion, Brazil, diagonal).*

Evaluating

When you *evaluate,* you tell the value of something (how good or bad it is). Before you can evaluate something, you must know a lot about it.

You evaluate when you . . .

- **tell your opinion about something.**
- **tell the good points and bad points about something.**

In this assignment, the writer evaluates something.

ASSIGNMENT: Explain the good points and the bad points about landfills.

Landfills are much better than dumps. Landfills keep chemicals from polluting the water. Also, when a landfill is full, the land can be covered with dirt and reused. Two big airports, JFK in New York and Newark in New Jersey, are built on landfills. But landfills are not perfect. They take up a lot of space that is often needed for homes, schools, and other things. Even though all people need a place to put their trash, none want a landfill in their neighborhood. They don't want the added traffic, noise, or smell. Obviously, landfills are both good and bad at the same time.

LEARNING

 Write a paragraph that explains the good and the bad points of homework, summer school, or study halls.

Setting Up an Assignment Schedule

Your teacher may give you a schedule to follow for completing your writing assignments. If not, you can set up your own. Let's say that you have been asked to write a persuasive essay. You have two weeks to complete your work. Here's a possible schedule that you could follow.

Day	Week One
1	**Prewriting:** • Review the assignment and assessment rubric. • Begin a topic search.
2	**Prewriting:** • Choose a writing topic. • Start gathering details.
3	**Prewriting:** • Gather and organize details. • Find a focus for the writing.
4	**Writing:** • Begin the first draft.
5	**Writing:** • Complete the first draft.

Day	Week Two
1	**Revising:** • Revise the completed draft for ideas and organization.
2	**Revising:** • Revise the draft for voice. • Ask a peer to review it.
3	**Revising:** • Check for word choice and sentence fluency.
4	**Editing:** • Check the writing for conventions; then write and proofread the final copy.
5	**Publishing:** • Share the final copy.

Change this schedule to fit your assignment. For example, if you have a week to do your work, you could focus on one step in the writing process per day.

Scheduling a Timed Writing

If you must complete a piece of writing in one class period (say 45 minutes), it is very important to plan your work. Try to set aside 5 to 10 minutes at the beginning of the period to plan your writing, 25 to 30 minutes for writing your first draft, and about 10 minutes at the end to make any necessary changes.

Taking Classroom Tests

Just the mention of the word "test" may cause your palms to sweat and your heart to pound. These are perfectly normal feelings. Taking tests can be very stressful because your performance can mean so much. Tests do, after all, show how well you are learning. Fortunately, you can reduce this stress by preparing properly for each test.

Start by keeping up with your daily work. Pay attention in each class, take good notes, and complete each assignment. It's also important that you understand the test-taking process. You need to know how to study for and how to take different types of classroom tests. This chapter can help you do that.

What's Ahead

- **Preparing for a Test**
- **Taking Objective Tests**
- **Taking Essay Tests**

Preparing for a Test

Use the information that follows to prepare for each test you take.

1 Ask questions.

- Ask what information the test will cover. Will it cover textbook chapters, class notes, experiments, or other material?
- Ask what types of questions will be on the test. Will it include multiple-choice, true/false, fill-in-the-blanks, or essay questions?
- Find out if you can use your textbook or notes for the test. Sometimes essay tests are "open book" tests.

2 Review the material.

- Begin reviewing at least a few days before the test.
- Look over all the test material once. Then make a list of the information that is especially challenging or important. Focus most of your reviewing time on this material.
- Continue reviewing your notes until you feel that you really understand everything.

3 Study carefully.

- Use lists, note cards, or graphic organizers to help you study.
- Say the material out loud. First read from your notes or text. Then explain the information to yourself in your own words.
- Write out the most important information from memory. Afterward, check your notes to see how well you did.
- Picture the information in your mind.
- Study with someone else or explain the material to a friend.

Try It Write a paragraph about the hardest test you have taken this year or last year.

1. What information did the test cover, and what type of questions were on the test?
2. How did you study for the test, and how well did you do on it?
3. How would you study for this test if you took it again?

Test-Taking Tips

- **Listen carefully.** Listen as your teacher gives directions. Don't try to get a head start while your teacher is talking, or you may miss important comments such as . . .

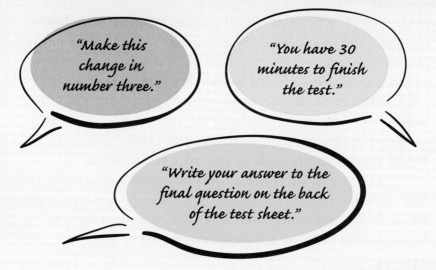

"Make this change in number three."

"You have 30 minutes to finish the test."

"Write your answer to the final question on the back of the test sheet."

- **Put your full name on the test right away.** Then you won't forget!

- **Take a quick look at the entire test.** This will help you decide how much time to spend on each question.

- **Begin the test.** Read the directions carefully before answering each set of questions. Do exactly what they tell you to do.

- **Read each question carefully.** Be sure you understand the question completely before answering it.

- **Answer the questions you are sure of first.** Then go back to the other questions and do your best to answer each one.

- **Check over your answers when you finish the test.** Do whatever double-checking you can in the time you have left.

Taking Objective Tests

There are four basic types of questions on objective tests: true/false, matching, multiple-choice, and fill-in-the-blanks.

True/False

For this type of test, you decide if a statement is true or false.

■ Read the statement carefully. If any part of the statement is false, the answer is "false."

False **Astronomers say that the sun is a giant planet.**
(The sun is a star, not a planet.)

■ Watch for words such as *always, all, every, never, none,* or *no.* Very few things are *always* true or *never* true.

False **All planets are made of solid rock and minerals.**
(The word "all" makes this statement false.)

■ Pay attention to words meaning "not": *doesn't, don't, isn't, wasn't.* Be sure that you understand what the statement means.

True **Jupiter isn't the last planet discovered by scientists.**

Matching

Matching consists of connecting an item in one list to an item in another.

■ Read both lists before beginning. Match the items you are sure of first. Then match the more difficult items using the process of elimination. Cross out each answer after you've used it.

   _C_ **1. A violent windstorm accompanied by a funnel-shaped cloud**
   _A_ **2. A severe snowstorm with cold winds**
   _B_ **3. A tropical storm with winds of 74 miles per hour or greater**

A. Blizzard
B. Hurricane
C. Tornado

■ Watch for items in each list that are very close in meaning since they may be the most difficult to match correctly.

 On your own paper, answer each of the following questions. Write at least three sentences for each answer.

1. Why can true/false questions be difficult to answer?

2. What is the best way to answer matching questions?

Multiple-Choice

A multiple-choice question gives you several possible answers to choose from. Follow the tips below.

- Read the directions carefully. There is usually only one correct answer, but sometimes you may have to mark more than one.

   1. Which of the following places are located in the United States?
   Ⓐ Utah   **Ⓒ New Mexico**
   B. Manitoba   **D. Jamaica**

- Look for words like *except, never,* and *unless.*

   2. These forms of government have never been used in the United States except
   A. a monarchy   **C. a dictatorship**
   B. a theocracy   **Ⓓ a democracy**

- Questions that include possible answers like "Both A and B" or "None of the above" can be hard to answer, so read carefully.

   3. Which states joined the Union during the 1800s?
   A. Pennsylvania   **D.   Minnesota**
   B. Nevada   **Ⓔ   Both B and D**
   C. Alaska   **F.   None of the above**

(Narrow your choices by eliminating answers you know are incorrect and then focus on the remaining answers.)

Fill-in-the-Blanks

A fill-in-the-blanks test is made up of sentences with some words left out. You have to fill in the missing words.

- Each blank usually stands for one missing word. If there are three blanks, you will have to write in three words.

   1. The three largest wild animals in the United States are
   ___elk___, ___bison___, **and** ___moose___.

- Look for clues in the sentence. For example, if the word before a blank is *an,* the word you have to fill in will begin with a vowel.

   2. A burrowing mammal with body armor is called an ___armadillo___.

 On your paper, explain which type of question you think can be more difficult to answer: multiple-choice or fill-in-the-blank. Why?

LEARNING

Taking Essay Tests

Answering an essay-test question is like writing an essay. You must understand what you have to do, organize your thoughts, write the essay, and check your work. The biggest difference is that you have a limited amount of time to complete your writing on a test. The information below and on pages 465–467 will help you write effective essay-test answers.

1 Understand the Question

- Read the question very carefully.
- Identify the key word that explains what you have to do. Here are some key words and an explanation of what each asks you to do.

Compare	. . . tell how things are alike.
Contrast	. . . tell how things are different.
Define	. . . give a clear, specific meaning of a term or an object.
Describe	. . . tell how something looks, sounds, and feels.
Diagram	. . . explain using lines, a web, or another graphic organizer.
Evaluate	. . . give your opinion about the value of a topic.
Explain	. . . tell what something means or how something works.
Identify	. . . answer the 5 W's and H about a topic.
Illustrate	. . . show how something works by using examples.
Prove	. . . present facts that show something is true.
Review	. . . give an overall picture of a topic.
Summarize	. . . tell just the key information about a topic.

 For each of the following essay-test questions, write the key word and explain what you need to do for each.

1. Summarize how the Central Pacific Railroad was built.
2. Describe a volcanic eruption.
3. Explain how to find the least common denominator.
4. Prove that recycling plastic and glass really makes a difference.

② Plan Your Answer

- Carefully study the question. Make sure that you understand the meaning of the key word.
- Write a topic sentence or a focus statement for your answer.
- Collect important supporting details. (You may be allowed to use your book or class notes.)
- Consider using a list, an outline, or a graphic organizer to organize the details. (See pages 548–550.)
- Double-check to make sure that your ideas answer the question.

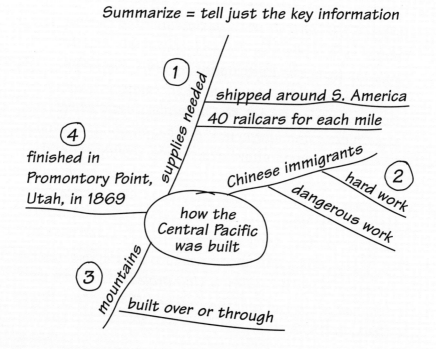

Summarize = tell just the key information

① supplies needed
shipped around S. America
40 railcars for each mile

④ finished in Promontory Point, Utah, in 1869

Chinese immigrants

how the Central Pacific was built

② hard work dangerous work

③ mountains
built over or through

LEARNING

Social Studies Test. Chapter 23

1. **Summarize how the Central Pacific Railroad was built.**

3 Write a One-Paragraph Answer

In a one-paragraph answer, remember to begin with your topic sentence and follow with the supporting details you have collected. Be sure to use your plan as a general writing guide.

Social Studies Test. Chapter 23

1. Summarize how the Central Pacific Transcontinental line was built.

The Central Pacific Railroad was built with a lot of hard work. First, supplies such as timber, metal rails, spikes, and even locomotives had to be sent from the East Coast by ship. The ships had to sail all the way around the southern tip of South America to get to California. That's where the Chinese immigrant workers began construction. The workers used shovels, pickaxes, dynamite, and their bare hands to build the railroad. For each mile of track the workers laid, they used 40 railcars full of supplies. When the workers came to a mountain, they either laid track over it or dug a tunnel through it. Many of the immigrant workers died in explosions or other accidents during this project. The work was finished when the railroad reached Promontory Point, Utah, in 1869.

Try IT Plan and write a one-paragraph answer to the following essay-test question:
Compare yourself to a main character in a story you have recently read.

④ Write an Essay Answer

Sometimes you will need to write an answer in the form of an essay. For example, the question below cannot be answered in one paragraph. You may use a graphic organizer such as a time line, a table organizer, or a Venn diagram to plan your essay answer.

The Union Pacific Railroad had an easier route but still faced many challenges. The company

Social Studies Test. Chapter 23

1. Summarize how the transcontinental railroad was built by the Central Pacific and Union Pacific Railroad Companies.

The transcontinental railroad was built by two different companies. The Central Pacific Railroad Company worked from Sacramento, California, and went east through the mountains. The Union Pacific Railroad Company went west from Omaha, Nebraska, across the plains. Both companies faced tough challenges along the way.

The Central Pacific Railroad had many challenges. First, supplies such as timber, metal rails, and even locomotives had to be sent from the East Coast by ship. The ships had to sail all the way around South America to get to California. That's where Chinese immigrants began building the Central Pacific Railroad. Using pickaxes, dynamite, and their bare hands, workers built the railroad. For each mile of track laid, they used 40 railcars full of supplies. When the workers came to a mountain, they either laid track over it or dug a tunnel through it.

LEARNING

compare

vary

Basic Grammar and Writing

CONNECT

modify

choose

Working with Words

Writing is like cooking. You have eight basic ingredients, called the parts of speech. Take a cupful of specific nouns and add a tablespoon of colorful adjectives. Then blend in a pint of action verbs, seasoned with adverbs. Finally, mix in the pronouns, interjections, prepositions, and conjunctions, and you'll be cooking with words!

Specific *nouns* will help you write clearly, and *pronouns* will help you write smoothly. Action *verbs* will add drama to whatever you are writing, and *conjunctions* will help by connecting the words in your writing.

Besides some basic information about each part of speech, this section answers the question,

"How can I use words effectively in my own writing?"

What's Ahead

- Using Nouns
- Using Pronouns
- Choosing Verbs
- Describing with Adjectives
- Describing with Adverbs
- Connecting with Prepositions
- Connecting with Conjunctions

Using Nouns

A noun is a word that names a person, a place, a thing, or an idea in your writing. (See page 702.)

Person	actor, Denzel Washington, students, President Adams
Place	state, Arizona, kitchen, San Diego, middle school
Thing	bird, Baltimore oriole, books, clock
Idea	holiday, Veterans Day, courage, thought

Try It On your own paper, rewrite the sentences below by filling in each blank with the type of noun shown.

1. _____*(a place)*_____ has spectacular fall colors.

2. The park contains hundreds of _____*(things)*_____.

3. _____*(a person)*_____ can spot wildlife throughout the park.

4. The destruction of wilderness areas may lead to the _____*(an idea)*_____ of certain animals.

Concrete, Abstract, and Collective Nouns

Concrete nouns name things that can be seen or touched.
Abstract nouns name things that you can think about but cannot see or touch.

Concrete	clown	valentine	school	heart
Abstract	happiness	February	education	love

Try It Write four concrete nouns and four related abstract nouns. For example, a *heart* (concrete) is a symbol of *love* (abstract).

Collective nouns name a collection of persons, animals, or things.

Persons	class	family	jury	audience	committee
Animals	herd	flock	pack	school	pod

Try It List two more collective nouns for both persons and animals. (See page 702.5 for help.) Share your words with a partner.

Proper and Common Nouns

You can use a **proper noun** in your writing to name a specific person, place, thing, or idea. Proper nouns are always capitalized. A **common noun** is any noun that is not a proper noun.

	Person	Place	Thing	Idea
Common	ranger	park	pet	holiday
Proper	Tom	Yosemite	Fido	Labor Day

Common The club visited the national park last weekend.

Proper The Dyer Biking Club visited Yosemite National Park last Saturday.

 Make a chart like the one above. Add your own common and proper nouns (four of each). Be sure to capitalize the proper nouns.

General and Specific Nouns

When you use **specific nouns** in your writing, you give the reader a clear picture of people, places, things, and ideas. The following chart shows the difference between **general nouns** and specific nouns.

General	actress	stadium	pants	emotion
Specific	Julia Roberts	Wrigley Field	blue jeans	happiness

 Read each pair of sentences below. Then, on your own paper, copy the sentence from each pair that uses nouns that are more specific.

1. The boy climbed the hill. Jamal climbed Prescot Hill.
2. Climbers like steep rock walls. People like challenges.
3. The girl scraped her leg. Josie scraped her knee and shin.
4. Look at that panorama of the Rocky Mountains.
   Look at that view.

 Rewrite the following sentences using more specific nouns in place of general nouns.

1. The student biked to a recreational area.
2. The girl painted a piece of art.
3. The storm blew things around the place.
4. The animal lapped up the liquid.

BASIC GRAMMAR

What can I do with nouns in my writing?

Identify People, Places, Things, and Ideas

You use nouns to identify the people, places, things, and ideas you are talking about in your writing. You can add variety to your writing by using these different types of nouns as subjects.

Yosemite National Park **is amazing.** (*a place*)

Ansel Adams **took many photographs in Yosemite.** (*a person*)

His pictures **captured** images **in black and white.** (*things*)

In the park, breathtaking beauty **surrounds you.** (*an idea*)

 Find the subject in each of the following sentences. Is it a person, a place, a thing, or an idea?

  In 1890, John Muir helped establish Yosemite National Park.
  John Muir, person

1. Muir wrote many magazine stories about the park's beauty.

2. The Sierra Club lists Muir as one of its founders.

3. His love of nature turned into a photography career.

Rename the Subject

A predicate noun follows a "be" verb (*am, is, are, was, were, will be*) and renames the subject of the sentence. Predicate nouns are useful for making simple, natural comparisons.

My favorite vacation **is a** visit **to the mountains.**
(The predicate noun "visit" renames the subject "vacation.")

 Write a sentence for each of the subjects and predicate nouns below using a "be" verb.

Predicate Noun	Subject
mountain hike	experience

A mountain hike is an invigorating experience.

1. walking and climbing	activities
2. fresh air	medicine
3. eagles and deer	companions

Complete the Action of the Verb

Readers may ask questions like *who?* and *what?* after many action verbs. You can use concise nouns to answer these questions and complete the action of the verb.

Campers must plan. (*What* must they plan?)

Yosemite offers an overnight permit. (*Who* gets a permit?)

See how the nouns below—*trips* and *visitors*—answer the questions *what?* or *who?* and complete the action of the verb.

Campers must plan overnight trips. (This answers *what?*)

Yosemite offers overnight visitors **a permit.** (This answers *who?*)

> Nouns that answer the question *what?* after a verb are called **direct objects**. Nouns that answer the question *who?* after a verb that has a direct object are called **indirect objects**. (See 692.4–692.5.)

 Number your paper from 1 to 4. Write a noun that answers each *what* and *who* question in the sentences below.

1. Long-distance hikers need good __(what?)__ for their feet.

2. The wilderness offers __(who?)__ sightings of rare birds.

3. Hikers can find __(what?)__ growing along the trail.

4. Maps give __(who?)__ specific trail information.

Add Specific Information

Prepositional phrases add information to your sentences. Using a specific noun as the **object of a preposition** makes your writing clearer. (See 742.1.) Notice how all of the nouns highlighted below add details to the passage.

A first-aid kit offers hikers medical supplies for minor problems like blisters. A new product, called "second skin," provides moist treatment for blisters and other wounds. Salt packets are also an important first-aid supply. They can prevent dehydration.

Object of Preposition

Direct Object

Indirect Object

Predicate Noun

Subject

BASIC GRAMMAR

Using Pronouns

A pronoun is a word used in place of a noun. The noun replaced, or referred to, by the pronoun is called the pronoun's **antecedent**. The arrows below point to each pronoun's antecedent. (Also see 706.1.)

Edgar Allan Poe rented a home in Philadelphia, and it is now a national historical site.

Amanda read a Poe story before she visited the site.

The personal pronouns listed below are used as subjects and objects. (For a complete list of personal pronouns, see page 710.)

Personal pronouns

I	you	he	she	it	we	they
me		him	her		us	them

Person and Number of a Pronoun

Pronouns show "person" and "number" in writing. The following chart shows which pronouns are used for the three different persons (*first, second, third*) and the two different numbers (*singular* or *plural*). (See 712.1–712.4.)

		Singular	Plural
First Person	(The person speaking)	I call.	We call.
Second Person	(The person spoken to)	You call.	You call.
Third Person	(The person or thing spoken about)	He calls. It calls.	They call.

 Number your paper from 1 to 4. Write sentences that use the pronouns described below as subjects.

first-person singular pronoun
I want to visit the White House.

1. third-person singular pronoun
2. third-person plural pronoun
3. second-person singular pronoun
4. first-person plural pronoun

Indefinite Pronouns

An indefinite pronoun refers to people or things that are not named or known. The chart below lists which indefinite pronouns are singular, which are plural, and which can be singular or plural.

Indefinite Pronouns					
Singular				**Plural**	**Singular or Plural**
another	either	nobody	someone	both	all
anybody	everybody	no one	something	few	any
anyone	everyone	nothing		many	most
anything	everything	one		several	none
each	neither	somebody			

When you use indefinite pronouns as subjects, the verbs and other pronouns used in the sentence must agree with the subject in number.

Singular
Everybody **needs to take** his or her **notebook on the field trip.**

Plural
Several **of the boys took notes on** their **trip to Lincoln's birthplace.**

Singular or Plural
Most **of the information is printed on handouts.** (singular)
Most **of the students are working on** their **research papers.** (plural)

 Number your paper from 1 to 5. Choose the correct pronoun to complete each of the following sentences.

1. Many of the boys will write about *(his, their)* favorite heroes.
2. Everyone posts *(his or her, their)* report on the school Web page.
3. All of the students will send *(his or her, their)* reports to the paper.
4. Someone named Leah sent *(their, her)* comments to the editor.
5. Both of my friends read *(his or her, their)* reports aloud.

If using *his or her* is clumsy, try changing the singular pronoun to a plural pronoun. For example, the first sample sentence above could be rewritten like this: **All** *of the students need to take* **their** *notebooks on the field trip.*

BASIC GRAMMAR

How can I produce better writing with pronouns?

Avoid Repeating Nouns

You can use pronouns in your writing to avoid repeating the same nouns over and over again. (See pages 706–714.) Read the sample paragraph below. How many times did the writer use "Mary Pickersgill"?

Without Pronouns

> Mary Pickersgill, a famous flag maker, is the subject of today's lesson. Mary Pickersgill made the flag that inspired "The Star-Spangled Banner." During the War of 1812, Mary Pickersgill made the flag that flew over Fort McHenry. The flag, which Mary Pickersgill's family helped Mary Pickersgill make, measured 30 feet by 42 feet.

Now read the revised sample below. The writer has replaced some of the nouns with pronouns. Which pronouns refer to Mary Pickersgill?

With Pronouns

> Mary Pickersgill, a famous flag maker, is the subject of today's lesson. She made the flag that inspired "The Star-Spangled Banner." During the War of 1812, she made the flag that flew over Fort McHenry. The flag, which her family helped her make, measured 30 feet by 42 feet.

 Read the following paragraph. On your own paper, rewrite the paragraph changing some of the underlined nouns to pronouns so that the paragraph reads more smoothly.

(1) Mary Pickersgill learned flag making from (2) Mary Pickersgill's mother, Rebecca Flower. (3) Mary Pickersgill and Mary Pickersgill's mother worked together to create the huge flag that flew over Fort McHenry during the Battle of Baltimore. This was (4) Mary Pickersgill's most famous flag. Francis Scott Key wrote a poem about the flag. (5) Francis Scott Key's poem became "The Star-Spangled Banner," the national anthem of the United States.

Improve Sentence Flow

Pronouns can be used to help the reader move easily from one sentence to the next. In the following paragraph, notice how the pronouns (in blue) improve the flow of the sentences. The arrows point to the antecedents (the words the pronouns replace).

Our class went on a field trip. We toured the two-story brick

Star-Spangled Banner Flag House in Baltimore, Maryland. It was

the home of Mary Pickersgill. In 1807, she moved there with her

mother and daughter. Later, they helped Mary sew the 30- by

42-foot flag that inspired "The Star-Spangled Banner." It was Mary's

most famous flag. She earned her living making flags to be flown

from the masts of ships. Our class wants to visit this site again.

Try IT Number your paper from 1 to 5. Add pronouns from the list below to help improve the sentence flow. (You may use some pronouns more than once.) Then write the antecedent for each pronoun.

| it you we them they us |

■ *pronoun: They antecedent: landmarks*

The students in my class studied national historic landmarks. _They_ represent the history of the United States in a very important way. **(1)** _____ discovered that landmarks are special buildings, sites, and structures, including Mount Vernon, Pearl Harbor, and Alcatraz. Becoming a national historic landmark is a long process. **(2)** _____ starts with filling out lots of forms and ends when the secretary of the interior gives approval. There are thousands of historic places in America. Only about 2,500 of **(3)** _____ are national historic landmarks. The Flag House in Baltimore, Maryland, is one of **(4)** _____. **(5)** _____ became a national historic landmark in 1969.

BASIC GRAMMAR

How can I use pronouns properly?

Avoid Agreement Problems

You can make your writing clearer by using pronouns properly. You must use pronouns that agree with their antecedents. (An antecedent is the noun or pronoun that a pronoun replaces or refers to. See 474 and 706.1.) Pronouns must agree with their antecedents in number, person, and gender.

The Henry Ford Museum and Greenfield Village are known for their **historic importance.**

Henry Ford is best known for his **automobiles.**

Agreement in Number

The **number** of a pronoun is either singular or plural. The pronoun must match the antecedent in number.

- A singular pronoun refers to a singular antecedent.

  Henry Ford invented his **own self-propelled vehicle—the quadricycle.**

- A plural pronoun refers to a plural antecedent.

  The Ford children grew up on their **family's farm in Dearborn, Michigan.**

Try It Number your paper from 1 to 3 and write the correct pronoun for each sentence. Then write the antecedent each pronoun refers to.

- Henry Ford changed the world when *(he, they)* built assembly-line automobiles.
  he, Henry Ford

1. So that people could learn more about *(his or her, their)* nation's history, Henry Ford also built a museum.

2. The chair Abraham Lincoln sat in at the time of *(their, his)* assassination is at the Henry Ford Museum.

3. The bus on which Rosa Parks refused to give up *(their, her)* seat is also on exhibit.

Agreement in Gender

The **gender** of a pronoun *(her, his, its)* must be the same as the gender of its antecedent. Singular pronouns can be feminine (female), masculine (male), or neuter (neither male nor female).

The Henry Ford Museum got its name in honor of Henry Ford.

Manuel went to Greenfield Village with his family.

Try IT Number your paper from 1 to 5. Correct each underlined pronoun so that it agrees with its antecedent in gender.

1   Manuel enjoyed her visit to Greenfield Village. He liked

2   his old buildings and the people in historical costumes. Manuel

3   visited Henry Ford's childhood home, and she saw a model of

4   the factory where Mr. Ford made its first automobile. At the

5   end of the tour, she even took a ride in a Model-T car.

Shift in Person

When you use pronouns, you must choose either first-, second-, or third-person pronouns. Using more than one "person" to express an idea, may cause an error called a pronoun shift.

Pronoun shift: If Jerry and I want to see whales, you must be patient.

Correct: If Jerry and I want to see whales, we must be patient.

Try IT In the sentences below, change each underlined pronoun so that it doesn't cause a shift in person. Use all first-person pronouns. (See the chart on page 714.)

1. My friend Jerry and I live near the ocean where you sometimes see whales.

2. When we know whales are migrating, you set up a telescope.

3. We wait and wait, watching through your telescope.

4. When we come home, Dad asks if they have seen any whales.

BASIC GRAMMAR

Choosing Verbs

Writers must constantly make choices, and one of their most important choices is which verb to use to express their thoughts clearly.

Action Verbs

An **action verb** tells what the subject is doing. Action verbs help bring writing to life. (Also see 718.1.)

During World War II, many women worked **in wartime industries.**
They built **tanks and** tested **airplanes to help win the war.**

Linking Verbs

A **linking verb** connects (links) a subject to a noun or an adjective in the predicate. (Also see 718.2.)

Common Linking Verbs	
Forms of "be"	be, is, are, was, were, am, been, being
Other linking verbs	appear, become, feel, grow, look, remain, seem, smell, sound, taste

Rosie the Riveter was **an imaginary** character.
(The linking verb "was" connects the subject "Rosie the Riveter" to the noun "character." "Character" is a *predicate noun*.)

She became popular **during World War II.**
(The linking verb "became" connects the subject "she" to the adjective "popular." "Popular" is a *predicate adjective*.)

 For each sentence below, write the linking verb and the predicate noun or predicate adjective. (One sentence has three predicate nouns.)

■ "Rosie Riveters" were women who got jobs during World War II.
   Linking verb: were   *predicate noun:* women

1. These women were skilled in a number of ways.
2. They became riveters, welders, and shipbuilders.
3. A park in Richmond, California, is a memorial to these women.
4. Richmond was home to four shipyards where the "Rosies" worked.

Irregular Verbs

Verbs in the English language can be either *regular* or *irregular*.

Regular Verbs

Most verbs in the English language are regular. A writer adds *ed* to regular verbs to show a past action. A writer can also use *has, have,* or *had* with the past participle to form other verb tenses. (See the chart below.)

Present	Past	Past Participle
I watch.	Yesterday I watched.	I had watched.
He watches.	Yesterday he watched.	He had watched.

Irregular Verbs

Irregular verbs do not follow the *ed* rule. Instead of adding *ed* to show a past action, the word might change. (See the two examples below.)

Present	Past	Past Participle
I speak.	Yesterday I spoke.	I have spoken.
She runs.	Yesterday she ran.	She has run.

Writers use the correct forms of irregular verbs by using them over and over. Since the 10 most common verbs in English are irregular, you should understand them first. The chart below gives the principal parts of these 10 irregular verbs. (See the list of irregular verbs on page **722**.)

 Choose three of these verbs and write a short sentence for each principal part *(present, past,* and *past participle).*

Present	Past	Past Participle
is	was	(has) been
come	came	(has) come
do	did	(has) done
get	got	(has) gotten
go	went	(has) gone
have	had	(has) had
make	made	(has) made
say	said	(has) said
see	saw	(has) seen
take	took	(has) taken

How can I use more effective verbs?

Show Powerful Action

You can use strong action verbs to help show the reader exactly what is happening (or has happened).

Ordinary Action Verbs

Louis Armstrong played a new kind of music—jazz.
He performed with many bands.

Powerful Action Verbs

Notes poured out of Louis Armstrong's horn.
When jazz became popular, Armstrong exploded into fame.

Try to avoid using linking verbs *(is, are, was, were)* too much. Often, a stronger action verb can be made from another word in the same sentence.

Joe "King" Oliver was Armstrong's trumpet teacher. (linking verb)

Joe "King" Oliver taught Armstrong to play the trumpet.
(The action verb "taught" is made from the word "teacher.")

Create Active Voice

A verb is in the active voice if the subject is doing the action. Use active voice more often than passive voice. (See pages 308 and 726.)

The trumpet was played by Louis Armstrong like no one else. (passive)

Louis Armstrong played the trumpet like no one else. (active)

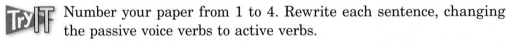 Number your paper from 1 to 4. Rewrite each sentence, changing the passive voice verbs to active verbs.

- Hit songs were recorded by Louis Armstrong for five decades.
  Louis Armstrong recorded hit songs for five decades.

1. Many music awards were also won by him.

2. The nickname "Satchmo" was given to Louis Armstrong by a group of musicians.

3. Dozens of famous jazz songs were composed by Mr. Armstrong.

4. His home, a national historic landmark in Queens, New York, can be visited by people.

Show When Something Happens

You can use different verb tenses to "tell time" in sentences. The three simple tenses are *present, past,* and *future.* (Also see page 720.)

The Three Simple Tenses of Verbs	Singular	Plural
Present	I dance. You dance. He or she dances.	We dance. You dance. They dance.
Past	I danced. You danced. He or she danced.	We danced. You danced. They danced.
Future	I will dance. You will dance. He or she will dance.	We will dance. You will dance. They will dance.

 Identify the tense of the underlined verbs in the sentences below.

■ Students <u>enjoy</u> reading books that Laura Ingalls Wilder <u>wrote</u>.
present, past

1. Laura <u>wrote</u> about many "little houses."
2. You <u>will enjoy</u> learning about one of the houses that <u>remains</u>.
3. It is the house where Laura <u>lived</u> in Burr Oak, Iowa.
4. Maybe someday it <u>will become</u> a national historic landmark.

 Find and correct the six incorrect verb tenses used in the following paragraph. (The first verb is correct.)

1 Laura Ingalls' adventures <u>began</u> in Pepin, Wisconsin, in the
2 1870s. Laura and her family are pioneers, and they move often
3 when Laura is a child. Many years later, Laura writes books
4 about her childhood adventures. Today, they were published
5 in America and in many foreign countries. In the future, new
6 "Little House" fans continue to read the stories.

 Choose verbs carefully to tell exactly when the actions in your writing happen.

What else can I do with verbs?

Show Special Types of Action

You need perfect tense verbs to express certain types of actions. (See page **724** in the "Proofreader's Guide.") There are three perfect tenses.

sing, sang, sung	Singular	Plural
Present perfect tense states an action that *began in the past but continues or is completed in the present.*		
Present perfect (use *has* or *have* + past participle)	I have sung. You have sung. He or she has sung.	We have sung. You have sung. They have sung.
Past perfect tense states an action that *began in the past and was completed in the past.*		
Past perfect (use *had* + past participle)	I had sung. You had sung. He or she had sung.	We had sung. You had sung. They had sung.
Future perfect tense states an action that *will begin in the future and will be completed by a specific time in the future.*		
Future perfect (use *will have* + past participle)	I will have sung. You will have sung. He or she will have sung.	We will have sung. You will have sung. They will have sung.

 Identify the tense of each underlined verb in the following paragraph. The first one has been done for you.

■ *present perfect*

Probably, you <u>have learned</u> of the midnight ride of Paul Revere. Once you read this paragraph, you **(1)** <u>will have learned</u> about Revere's house. His wooden home in Boston's North End **(2)** <u>has stood</u> since about 1680. Paul Revere and his family moved into the house in 1770. They **(3)** <u>had lived</u> there only 10 years when Revere decided to sell the house. By 1902, his great-grandson **(4)** <u>had seen</u> what bad condition the house was in and bought it. Today it is a national historic landmark. Over the years, many people **(5)** <u>have visited</u> Revere's house at 19 North Square, Boston, Massachusetts.

Share the Right Feeling

The verbs that you use should have the right connotation. (*Connotation* means "the feelings suggested by a word.") For example, you could say that a loud noise *alarmed* someone. But that word may not express the right feeling. Perhaps the word *terrified* or *excited* would better share your meaning.

Below are five words similar to *laugh,* but each of these words has a slightly different meaning.

Laugh	Definitions
giggle	to laugh with repeated, brief, soft sounds
snicker	to laugh slyly
chuckle	to laugh quietly to oneself
cackle	to laugh sharply and loudly
guffaw	to burst out in laughter

Try IT Complete a chart like the one above for the word *run, cry,* or *talk.* Use a thesaurus to help you create your list of five similar words. Then define each word with the help of a dictionary.

To get a specific feeling across, writers try to use verbs with the right connotation. In the paragraph below, the underlined verbs create a *rushed* feeling.

Paul Revere devoured his food and gulped from his cup. He then threw his napkin on the table before charging out the door. A sound in the yard caught his attention, and he dashed to the lighthouse. He tore up the stairs and grabbed a lantern.

Try IT Rewrite the paragraph above. Replace the underlined verbs in the paragraph with verbs that create a different feeling—*slow,* rather than *rushed.* Be sure that all your verbs match the new feeling you want to create.

Describing with Adjectives

Adjectives are words that describe or modify nouns or pronouns. Sensory adjectives help the reader see, hear, feel, smell, and taste what writers are describing. (Also see pages 732–735.)

Without Adjectives

> The world is full of landmarks. From the ring of Big Ben in England to the roar of Niagara Falls, landmarks are everywhere.

With Adjectives

> The world is full of mysterious and beautiful landmarks. From the deep-sounding ring of Big Ben in England to the thunderous roar of Niagara Falls, landmarks are everywhere.

Adjectives can answer three questions: *What kind? How many (much)? Which one?* Remember that proper adjectives can be made from proper nouns (England, *English;* Italy, *Italian*) and are capitalized.

What Kind?	Chinese **food**	pea **soup**	red **shoes**
How Many (Much)?	two **kittens**	a little **sugar**	some **bugs**
Which One?	this **book**	these **students**	those **cars**

 For each blank in the sentences below, write an adjective of the type called for in parentheses.

1. When you visit the historical site of the great Chicago fire, you can almost smell the *(what kind?)* blaze of 1871.

2. You'll hear *(how many?)* explosions as work continues on the Crazy Horse Memorial in South Dakota.

3. *(what kind?)* wildflowers cover *(how many?)* areas of the park.

4. The circle of stone called the Medicine Wheel, at Lovell, Wyoming, is a/an *(what kind?)* symbol of native civilization.

5. The Eiffel Tower in Paris is *(how many?)* landmark known around the world.

6. *(which one?)* structure is made of iron.

Comparative and Superlative Adjectives

You can use comparative adjectives to compare two things. For most one-syllable adjectives, add *er* to make the **comparative form**. To compare three or more things, add *est* to make the **superlative form**. (See 734.3–734.5.)

Positive	Comparative	Superlative
large	larger	largest

Comparative: **The Sears Tower is** taller **than the John Hancock Building.**
Superlative: **The Sears Tower is the** tallest **building in the United States.**

Add *er* and *est* to some two-syllable words and use *more* or *most* (or *less* or *least*) with others. Always use *more* or *most* with three-syllable adjectives.

Positive	Comparative	Superlative
joyful	more joyful	most joyful

Comparative: **The Chrysler Building is a** more complex **structure than other skyscrapers.**
Superlative: **The** most complex **structure in my town is a long bridge.**

Try It Write the comparative and superlative forms of the adjective in each of the following sentences.

1. While Washington, D.C., is an exciting city, New York is a _____ city. Javier thinks Rio de Janeiro is the _____ city in the world.

2. There was a long line to get into the Lincoln Memorial. There was a _____ line than that to get into the Capitol, but the _____ line was at the White House.

3. The Constitution is an important document. Some people think the Declaration of Independence is a _____ document than the Constitution, but I think the Constitution is our country's _____ document.

4. A beautiful park called Lafayette Square overlooks the White House. A _____ park than this one is located nearby in Great Falls, Virginia, and the _____ park I've ever visited is Great Smoky Mountains National Park.

5. The Postal Museum is a small part of the Smithsonian Institution. The American Indian Museum is a bit _____, and the Sackler Gallery is the _____.

BASIC GRAMMAR

How can I strengthen my writing with adjectives?

Create Stronger Descriptions

Strong adjectives help readers use their senses. For example, "Black Thunder is a cool waterslide" creates a basic picture of the slide, but "Black Thunder is a hair-raising, monster waterslide" creates a sharper picture.

> **Avoid ho-hum adjectives.** Some adjectives really don't provide a clear picture for the reader. Replacing vague words like *nice, good,* and *big* with vivid adjectives will make your writing more effective.

 Replace each underlined adjective in the sentences below with a stronger adjective. (A thesaurus can help you.)

1. Listen to the roar of Niagara Falls, a <u>big</u> waterfall.
2. The Liberty Bell is a <u>good</u> symbol of this country.
3. The <u>strong</u> Colorado River carved the Grand Canyon's <u>tall</u> cliffs.
4. San Francisco's cable cars are <u>different</u> landmarks.

Form "Extra-Strength" Modifiers

Compound adjectives are made of two or more words. Some are spelled as one word; others are hyphenated. (Use a dictionary to check spelling.)

Many natural but little-visited landmarks enjoy worldwide recognition.

 For each of the following sentences, write a compound adjective to fill in the blank. Make your compound adjectives by combining words from the following list.

earth	first	taking	wind	breath	rate	blown	shaking

■ There are _____ hiking trails in Glacier Park, Montana.
first-rate

1. Chicago could be called a _____ city.
2. You get a _____ view from the Statue of Liberty.
3. Mauna Loa in Hawaii has _____ volcanic eruptions.

Use Sensory Details

Writers often use adjectives to create sensory details. This kind of detail forms pictures in the reader's mind. As you read the paragraph below, think about the pictures formed by the sensory details. Then consider how the underlined adjectives help to create the sensory details.

> A thumping "rom-rom-rom" echoes across the muddy Mississippi River. I hurry on. My toes make squishing sounds in the sticky riverbank mud. The smell of rotting leaves and decaying fish doesn't bother me. I see an olive green lump at the edge of the river—a bullfrog! It sits still except for its vibrating yellow throat.

 Draw a chart like the one below and list all the sensory details that are underlined in the paragraph above.

sight	sound	smell	texture (feeling)
olive green lump			

> Try to get into the habit of using sensory details whenever you write. Practice focusing on one sense at a time. See if you can learn to be more aware of what is going on around you.

 List one or two sensory details in response to each of the following statements. (An example is provided for each.)

1. Identify the smells you like.
   Just-baked bread
2. Identify things you like to touch or feel.
   A gentle wind
3. Identify favorite tastes.
   A sour apple
4. Identify sights that you look forward to seeing.
   The fall colors
5. Identify the sounds that you like to hear.
   The 3:00 dismissal bell

Describing with Adverbs

Adverbs describe or modify verbs, adjectives, or other adverbs. You can use adverbs to answer *how? when? (or how often?) where?* or *how much?* (See pages 736–739.)

How?	slowly	**Kiet counts slowly to 20.**
When?	yesterday	**Tyisha went on a field trip yesterday.**
Where?	outside	**My classmates are waiting outside.**
How Much?	barely	**Falling debris barely missed the workers.**

For each of the following sentences, write the adverbs you find. (The number of adverbs is shown in parentheses.) Tell what word each adverb describes and what question it answers.

◼ Quietly, our class explored the Indian burial grounds. *(1)*
   quietly (explored, how)

1. I often go to Mexico City with my father. *(1)*

2. It may be hot outside, but Mammoth Cave is very cool. *(2)*

3. I never knew that Boston had landmarks everywhere. *(2)*

4. My uncle frequently travels to the East Coast. *(1)*

5. Recently we went to San Antonio, Texas, to see the Alamo. *(1)*

6. A famous battle was fought there. *(1)*

7. Our guide turned left and walked quickly away. *(3)*

8. Today I learned that Research Cave has been badly damaged. *(2)*

9. I instantly recognized the White House when I saw it for the first time. *(1)*

Comparative and Superlative Adverbs

You can use adverbs to compare two things. The **comparative form** of an adverb compares two people, places, things, or ideas. The **superlative form** of an adverb compares three or more people, places, things, or ideas.

 For most one-syllable adverbs, add *er* to make the comparative form and *est* to make the superlative form.

Positive	Comparative	Superlative
soon	sooner	soonest

Comparative: **I arrived** later **than Sheila did.**

Superlative: **Kayla arrived** latest **of all.**

While you add *er* and *est* to some two-syllable adverbs, you need to use *more* or *most* (or *less* or *least*) with others. Always use *more* or *most* with three-syllable adverbs.

Positive	Comparative	Superlative
quickly	more quickly	most quickly

Comparative: **Ed has visited the Sears Tower** more frequently **than I have.**

Superlative: **Of all of us, Ed visits the Sears Tower** most frequently.

 When you use the comparative form, make sure that you state a complete comparison: *I arrived later than Sheila did,* not *I arrived later than Sheila.*

 Write a sentence for each adverb below.

■ later (comparative)
I arrived at Marengo Cave later than the rest of my friends.

1. harder (comparative)
2. slowly (superlative)
3. more effectively (comparative)
4. fastest (superlative)

How can I use adverbs effectively?

Describe Actions

You can make your writing more descriptive by using adverbs. You can add *ly* to some adjectives to create adverbs.

> **bad** badly   **amazing** amazingly   **tight** tightly
>
> **The cat was lazy. / The cat stretched out** lazily **on the windowsill.**

When you add *ly* to form an adverb, you need to remember these three spelling rules.

- Add *ly* to some words: **neat** neatly
- Drop the *e* and add *ly* to others: **terrible** terribly
- Change the *y* to *i* and add *ly* to still others: **sleepy** sleepily

Try IT Rewrite the following sentences by changing the underlined adjectives to adverbs. (Change other words as needed.)

- The <u>swift</u> river ran under the bridge in the park.
  The river ran swiftly under the bridge in the park.

1. I was <u>happy</u> to walk over the bridge.

2. The woman heard a <u>sudden</u> cry.

3. Her <u>gentle</u> voice calmed the child.

Add Emphasis

You can stress the importance of something with adverbs. Generally, use adverbs of degree—those that answer *how much?*—for this job.

> **San Antonio's Riverwalk is** absolutely **beautiful.**
>
> I really **want to explore it.**

Try IT Rewrite the following sentences. Add emphasis by using adverbs to modify the underlined words.

- I <u>agree</u> with you.
  I completely agree with you!

1. I <u>suggest</u> that you visit the Riverwalk in the evening.

2. It is <u>scenic</u>.

3. We had an <u>exciting</u> time there last year.

Modify Adjectives

With adverbs, you can describe how often something is a certain way. Adverbs that tell how often include *sometimes, often, usually, occasionally, always,* and so on.

The Badlands are always **spectacular.**

A visit there is rarely **disappointing.**

 Rewrite the following sentences, using a *how often* adverb to modify each underlined adjective.

■ The Badlands' Fossil Exhibit Trail is <u>fascinating</u>.

The Badlands' Fossil Exhibit Trail is always fascinating.

1. The yucca plants are <u>interesting</u> to see.
2. Bison are <u>visible</u> on Sage Creek Rim Road.
3. Turkey vultures are <u>overhead</u>.
4. It is <u>rainy</u> in the Badlands.
5. People are <u>amazed</u> at the Badlands formations.

Be Precise

With adverbs, you can tell the reader exactly when *(then, yesterday, now)* or where *(there, nearby, inside)* something happens.

We are going to the Milwaukee Zoo tomorrow.

The buses will pick us up here **at 9:00.**

 Add an adverb that tells *when* or *where* to each one of the following sentences.

■ We need to turn in our permission slips.

We need to turn in our permission slips today.

1. I handed mine in.
2. Sheniqua wants to visit the primate house.
3. Carl spotted a bonobo, an African chimpanzee.
4. I will sit on this bench.

Connecting with Prepositions

A preposition is a word (or words) that shows how one word or idea is related to another. A preposition is the first word of a prepositional phrase like *over the hill* and *near the river*. (See page 742 for a complete list of prepositions.)

The Gila Cliff Dwellings National Monument is located in New Mexico.
(The preposition "in" shows the relationship between the verb "is located" and the object of the preposition "New Mexico." The prepositional phrase acts as an adverb telling "where.")

The monument in the Gila Wilderness **has 50,000 visitors annually.**
(The preposition "in" shows the relationship between the noun "monument" and the object of the preposition "Gila Wilderness." The prepositional phrase acts as an adjective telling "which one.")

> **Avoid confusing prepositions and adverbs.** If a word that can also be used as a preposition appears alone in a sentence, it is being used as an adverb.
> **Two students lagged** behind the group.
> ("Behind the group" is a prepositional phrase.)
> **Two students lagged** behind, **so we waited.**
> ("Behind" is an adverb that modifies the verb "lagged.")

 Identify each prepositional phrase in the sentences below. Then tell whether the phrase acts as an *adverb* or an *adjective*.

Next we went to the visitor center and watched a movie.
to the visitor center, adverb **(tells "where")**

1. Everyone climbed onto the bus and sat down.
2. "No fooling around during the movie," he warned.
3. "When the movie is over," he said, "meet in the lobby."
4. The movie about the monument was too long.
5. The driver of our bus pulled up immediately.
6. Everyone climbed aboard the bus and sat down.
7. The trip to Gila Wilderness had been fun.
8. As I thought about the trip, I was glad that I had brought my camera along.

What can I do with prepositions?

Add Information

You can use a prepositional phrase as an adjective to describe either a noun or a pronoun. Adjectives answer *what kind? how many?* or *which one?*

Which one? | What kind?

 The **Upper Geyser Basin** along the Firehole River **is home** to Old Faithful.

Write a prepositional phrase to describe each of the subjects listed below. Many prepositional phrases that are used as adjectives tell *which one* or *ones.* (See page 742.)

■ the flowers
   the flowers along the trail

1. my cousins
2. the buffalo
3. the river

4. several days
5. the camera
6. the dog
7. a camper

You can also use a prepositional phrase as an adverb to describe a verb, an adjective, or another adverb. Adverbs answer *how? when? where? how long? how often?* or *how much?*

Where? | When?

You can find Old Faithful in Yellowstone Park. **It erupts** on a regular basis.

 For each sentence below, write the prepositional phrase that is used as an adverb. Tell what question it answers.

■ At Yellowstone National Park, you can see Old Faithful.
   At Yellowstone National Park (where)

1. The geyser erupts on a regular schedule.
2. The water underground boils under pressure.
3. It erupts in a blast that sprays hot water and steam.
4. Yellowstone is located in Wyoming, Montana, and Idaho.
5. Old Faithful's eruptions can last for five minutes.

BASIC GRAMMAR

Connecting with Conjunctions

Conjunctions connect words, groups of words, and sentences. There are three kinds of conjunctions: *coordinating, subordinating,* and *correlative.* The following sentences show some of the ways to use conjunctions. (See page 744 for a list of common conjunctions.)

Coordinating Conjunctions Connect Words

Artists come to Crazy Horse near Mt. Rushmore in the Black Hills to sketch or paint the memorial.

Skilled crews shape the mountain with explosives and torches.

Connect Compound Subjects and Predicates

Today, a museum and a cultural center are part of the memorial.

Visitors view exhibits and meet Native American craftspeople there.

Connect Sentences

Work on Crazy Horse Memorial began in 1948, yet it is not finished.

The sculptor of Crazy Horse, Korczak Ziolkowski, died in 1982, so his family continues his work.

Subordinating Conjunctions Connect Dependent Clauses to Independent Clauses

For several years, Ziolkowski worked alone while he sculpted the memorial.

Before he started Crazy Horse, he worked as a sculptor on nearby Mt. Rushmore.

Correlative Conjunctions Connect Noun Phrases and Verb Phrases

Both foggy days and moonlit nights make Crazy Horse look mysterious.

People not only watch the work on Crazy Horse from a distance but also ride buses to the base of the huge project.

 Choose three of the sentences above to use as models. Write three sentences of your own imitating the three you've chosen. Underline the conjunctions you use.

What can I do with conjunctions?

Connect a Series of Ideas

You can use conjunctions to connect a series of three or more words or phrases in a row. Place commas between the words or phrases and place a conjunction before the final item.

People hike up the mountain, stand on the statue, and **enjoy the view.**
(The conjunction connects three verb phrases.)

Wild iris, pine trees, and **cone flowers greet the hikers.**
(The conjunction connects three noun phrases.)

 Copy the following sentences and place commas where they are needed. Underline the conjunctions.

1. I gaze out over the rocks trees and hills of the Black Hills.

2. I tilt my head back stare up at the face and feel very small.

3. Crazy Horse cared for the children the elderly and the sick.

Expand Sentences (with Coordinating Conjunctions)

You can use **coordinating conjunctions** *(and, but, or, nor, for, so, yet)* to make compound subjects and predicates and to write compound sentences.

Ziolkowski and **his sons carved stone for almost 36 years,** but **they didn't finish the sculpture.**
(In this sentence, "and" creates a compound subject, and the conjunction "but" creates a compound sentence.)

 For each blank, write a coordinating conjunction. Tell whether it connects a compound subject, a compound predicate, or a compound sentence.

Native Americans have lived in the Black Hills for 12,000 years,

(1) _____ several tribes consider the area to be sacred land.

Its noble history **(2)** _____ spiritual power are valued greatly. It

was fitting to honor Crazy Horse with a carving in the Black Hills,

(3) _____ the chosen sculptor was, surprisingly, not a Native

American. Korczak Ziolkowski, a sculptor of Polish descent, worked

on the mountain until his death **(4)** _____ did not finish the

sculpture. His family continues to work on the monument.

BASIC GRAMMAR

Expand Sentences (with Subordinating Conjunctions)

You can use a **subordinating conjunction** to connect a dependent clause to another sentence. A dependent clause (one that *cannot* stand alone as a sentence) must be connected to an independent clause (one that *can* stand alone as a sentence). In the expanded sentences below, the dependent clause is underlined, and the subordinating conjunction is in blue. (See page 517.)

Gutzon Borglum worked on Mt. Rushmore from 1927 until he died in 1941.

When he started his work on the mountain, he planned to include an area to keep historical documents.

Try IT Choose a subordinating conjunction *(before, although, because, while, when)* to complete each sentence in the paragraph below.

Borglum chose Mt. Rushmore **(1)** _____ he knew the granite would last for thousands of years. **(2)** _____ any carving was done, workers used dynamite to blast out large chunks of the mountainside. **(3)** _____ the sculptors got to work, they used jackhammers, drills, and chisels on the hard rock. Weather and financial problems halted the work several times **(4)** _____ the sculpture was in progress. **(5)** _____ it took 14 years to finish, sculptors actually worked on the monument for only 6 of those years.

Show a Relationship

You can use **correlative conjunctions** to show a relationship between two words, phrases, or clauses. Correlative conjunctions are always used in pairs: *both/and, not only/but also, neither/nor, either/or, whether/or.*

Either Gutzon Borglum or his son, Lincoln, supervised the people working on Mount Rushmore.

They weren't sure whether they would find skilled workers in South Dakota or they would have to train workers.

Try IT For each of the blanks in the sentences below, write the correlative conjunctions that make the most sense.

1. _____ bad weather _____ a lack of money could stop the work.

2. _____ the hard work _____ the tough conditions scared the workers away.

3. _____ were they paid well _____ they felt pride in their work.

Building Effective Sentences

Imagine eating the same thing every day, at every meal. Eventually, you would dislike even the cheesiest pizza or the most scrumptious cake. People just naturally like variety.

The same is true with writing. A story with one long sentence after another, or one short sentence after another, would soon become boring. Sometimes a short sentence expresses feeling in a way that a long sentence cannot, and a long sentence does a better job of explaining a complicated idea. One key to clear writing is using a variety of sentences.

What's Ahead

You will learn about . . .

- writing complete sentences.
- fixing sentence problems.
- adding variety to your sentences.
- combining sentences.
- using different types of sentences.
- expanding and modeling sentences.

Writing Complete Sentences

A sentence is a group of words that forms a complete thought. Writers use complete sentences in order to communicate clearly. Here is a group of words that does not form a complete thought:

The jumble of words above makes no sense. When these same words are rearranged into a sentence, however, they do make sense. They communicate a clear, complete thought:

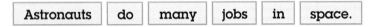

 On your own paper, unscramble the word groups below to create complete sentences. Some sentences can be arranged in more than one way. Remember to capitalize and punctuate each sentence correctly.

■ developed NASA the in 1970s the shuttle space
NASA developed the space shuttle in the 1970s.

1. a like shuttle a launches rocket

2. airplane an like lands it

3. used rockets be only can once most

4. be again shuttle can again a used and

5. 1981 first launched shuttle in was the

6. satellites orbit shuttles the to carried first

7. carry and now people shuttles cargo

8. is crew flown a flight by shuttle a

9. do to job member each crew has a special

 Write three or four sentences about space exploration. On another sheet, mix up the words and leave out punctuation and capitalization. Ask a classmate to rearrange the words so they form complete sentences.

Basic Parts of a Sentence

Every sentence has two basic parts: a complete subject—which tells who or what is doing something—and a complete predicate—which tells what the subject is doing. (See 690.3 and 692.3.)

Complete Subject	Complete Predicate
Who or what did something?	*What did the subject do?*
Scientists	explored the idea of flight.
George Cayley, an engineer,	studied flight for many years.

 Divide a piece of paper into two columns. For each of the sentences below, write the complete subject in the left column and write the complete predicate in the right column.

> In the following sentences, the words that come before the verb are the *complete subject*. The verb and all the words that follow it are the *complete predicate*.

■ Sir George Cayley discovered the principles of flight.
Sir George Cayley | discovered the principles of flight.

1. Cayley learned from birds soaring long distances.
2. A flying toy top was one of his first inventions.
3. It had a three-bladed propeller.
4. A model of the first glider flew successfully in 1804.
5. A small boy became the first person in history to fly.
6. He made a short flight in Cayley's glider.
7. Cayley prepared the way for other inventors.

Write **Write three or four sentences about what you think it was like to fly**
NOW **in Cayley's glider. Draw a line between the complete subject and the**
complete predicate in each of your sentences.

Simple Subjects and Predicates

A simple subject is the subject of a sentence without the words that modify it. A simple predicate is the verb without the words that modify it or complete the thought. In the sentences below, the simple subjects are orange and the simple predicates are blue. (See also 690.2 and 692.2.)

Complete Subject	Complete Predicate
Governments **in many countries**	developed **airplanes.**
Airplanes	changed **how people traveled.**

 Divide a piece of paper into two columns. For each of the sentences below, write the complete subject in the left column and write the complete predicate in the right column. Then underline the simple subjects and predicates.

⬛ Leonardo da Vinci drew designs of aircraft in the 1400s.
Leonardo da Vinci | *drew designs of aircraft in the 1400s.*

1. He gathered data about birds.
2. His first aircraft moved like a bird's wings.
3. Paul Cornu of France built a man-carrying helicopter in 1907.
4. Charles Lindbergh flew the first solo flight across the Atlantic.
5. Jumbo jets carry almost 500 passengers today.
6. These planes weigh nearly 460 tons!
7. The supersonic *Concorde* began passenger service in 1976.
8. It flew faster than the speed of sound.
9. Some airports need longer runways now.

 Write **NOW** Write three sentences about airplanes or airports. Ask a classmate to find and underline the simple subject and simple predicate in each sentence.

Compound Subjects and Predicates

Some sentences have compound subjects or compound predicates, and some have both.

- A compound subject includes two or more subjects that share the same predicate (or predicates).

- A compound predicate includes two or more predicates that share the same subject (or subjects).

Compound Subject	Compound Predicate
Hospitals and trauma centers	build and maintain heliports.

 Number your paper from 1 to 7. For each sentence below, write any compound subject and any compound predicate.

> Leonardo da Vinci, Louis Bréguet, and Paul Cornu designed and illustrated early helicopters.
>
> *Leonardo da Vinci, Louis Bréguet, and Paul Cornu designed and illustrated*

1. A huge whirling blade lifts a helicopter and keeps it in the air.
2. Helicopters carry seriously ill people to hospitals and save people from floods.
3. Radio reporters and television newspeople spot and describe traffic delays from helicopters.
4. The coast guard, police departments, and fire departments sometimes use helicopters in emergencies.
5. People explore wilderness areas and search for missing persons from helicopters.
6. Directors and photographers use helicopters for bird's-eye views of movie scenes.
7. A helicopter pilot can even find and track a whale.

 Write one sentence with a compound subject and another one with a compound predicate. Then write a sentence with both a compound subject and a compound predicate.

BASIC WRITING

How can I make sure my sentences are complete?

Check Your Subjects and Predicates

Sentence fragments are incomplete sentences. They may be missing a subject, a predicate, or both. You can learn how to fix sentence fragments by reading the examples below.

Fragment	Sentence
Is a place where airplanes take off and land. *(The subject is missing.)*	An airport **is a place where airplanes take off and land.**
In 2003, Atlanta's Hartsfield Airport, the world's busiest airport. *(The predicate is missing.)*	**In 2003, Atlanta's Hartsfield Airport** was **the world's busiest airport.**
At a small airport near Detroit. *(The subject and predicate are missing.)*	My uncle keeps his plane **at a small airport near Detroit.**

 Number your paper from 1 to 7. For each sentence, write "S" next to the number. For each fragment, write "F." Also tell which part or parts are missing: "subject," "predicate," or "both."

    Are like small cities.

    F – subject

1. Each year, more than 100 million people travel through large airports.
2. Most of the visitors to airports passengers.
3. At areas for ticketing, check-in, and baggage handling.
4. Some concourses hold restaurants and shops.
5. Can eat, shop, and relax.
6. Passengers are only one type of airport customer.
7. Airfreight companies as well.

 Rewrite the fragments above. Add the missing parts so that each fragment is now a complete sentence.

Edit Your Writing Carefully

Sentence fragments may be difficult to spot in your writing. At first glance, a fragment may look like a sentence. It starts with a capital letter, and it ends with a punctuation mark. Reading a sentence out loud can help you figure out if something is missing.

In the examples below, the writer found and underlined a number of fragments. Then she turned the fragments into complete sentences, some by combining the fragments with nearby sentences.

Fragment	Sentence
An airport is a busy place. <u>On the ground and in the air.</u> An airport doesn't have just planes and jets. <u>Cars, buses, and trains, too.</u>	An airport is a busy place both on the ground and in the air. An airport doesn't have just planes and jets. It has cars, buses, and trains, too.
You might see fire trucks and police cars. <u>Or motorized carts that carry luggage.</u>	You might see fire trucks, police cars, or motorized carts that carry luggage.

 Read the following paragraph and check for fragments. Then on your own paper, tell how many fragments you found. Rewrite the paragraph, correcting each of the fragments.

1 At an airport. You don't see just airplanes. Busy airports
2 also rely on ground vehicles. Like cars and buses. People drive
3 their cars to and from airports. Buses take passengers to local
4 hotels and car-rental offices. Also limousines and taxis. Trains
5 and subways, too. Ground transportation helps passengers get
6 to the airport on time. To catch their flights. It also helps them
7 get back home again.

 Write a short paragraph about an airport, a train or bus station, or a busy street in your town. Have a classmate check your writing for fragments.

Fixing Sentence Problems

Check for Run-On Sentences

Sometimes you may accidentally write a **run-on sentence**. A run-on sentence is two or more sentences that run together. Sometimes it is called a *comma splice* because it is connected with a comma instead of a period. Other run-ons may have no punctuation at all.

One way to fix run-on sentences is to divide them into two or more complete sentences. Another way is to add a comma and a conjunction.

Run-On Sentence	Corrected Sentences
This year, I learned what flight attendants do I think I might like to be one someday.	This year, I learned what flight attendants do. I think I might like to be one someday.
	This year, I learned what flight attendants do, and I think I might like to be one someday.

 On your own paper, correct the run-on sentences below by dividing them into two or more shorter sentences.

Flight attendants welcome passengers aboard they also help passengers find their seats.

Flight attendants welcome passengers aboard. They also help passengers find their seats.

1. First they check to see that seat belts are fastened then they check to make sure carry-on items are stored safely.
2. Flight attendants are trained for emergencies they know what to do if something unexpected happens.
3. They keep the passengers comfortable they serve food and beverages and supply blankets and pillows.
4. Flight attendants sometimes go to "career days" students can learn a lot by asking flight attendants questions.

 Write NOW Choose two of the above run-on sentences and correct them by using a comma and the conjunction "and."

Eliminate Rambling Sentences

A **rambling sentence** happens when you join too many sentences with the word *and*, as in the example below. Notice that there are two ways shown to correct a rambling sentence. (Also see page 310.)

 Of course, some *and*'s are necessary in sentences. See the blue and used in the following rambling sentence.

Rambling Sentence	Corrected Sentences
Air traffic controllers work in the control towers at airports and they have very important jobs and they must know where all the planes are, both in the air and on the ground.	Air traffic controllers work in the control towers at airports, and they have very important jobs. They must know where all the planes are, both in the air and on the ground. (Add a comma before the first *and*. Drop the second *and* to make two sentences.) Air traffic controllers work in the control towers at airports. They have very important jobs and must know where all the planes are, both in the air and on the ground. (Drop the first *and* to make two sentences. Drop *they* in the second sentence to make a compound predicate.)

 Correct the following rambling sentences on your own paper. (Watch for three *and*'s that are necessary.)

1. Controllers keep track of planes flying around the airport and they direct planes in and out of the airport and they even guide the planes on the ground.

2. Controllers warn pilots about weather changes and they also report on ground conditions and they tell pilots when and where to land.

3. Miles from the airport, the pilot contacts the tower and a controller in the tower watches the plane on radar and makes sure that the plane lands safely and once the plane lands, a ground controller directs it to its gate.

 Choose one of the rambling sentences above and correct it by rewriting it in a different way than you did at first.

BASIC WRITING

What can I do to write clear sentences?

Make Subjects and Verbs Agree

Writers must be careful to make the subjects and verbs in each of their sentences agree. That means a singular subject needs a singular verb, and a plural subject needs a plural verb. (Also see 728.1.)

Singular or Plural Subjects

A verb must agree with its subject in number.

■ If a subject is singular (refers to one person, place, thing, or idea), the verb must be singular, too.

   Luis enjoys **airport field trips.**

■ If a subject is plural (refers to more than one person, place, thing, or idea), the verb must be plural.

   My classmates enjoy **airport field trips.**

   (Don't forget that most nouns ending in *s* or *es* are plural, and most verbs ending in *s* are singular.)

 Number your paper from 1 to 7. For each of these sentences, write the correct verb (or verbs). Make sure each verb agrees with its subject.

■ Each May, the sixth graders goes on a field trip to Atlanta's Hartsfield International Airport.

   go

1. A plane arrive there every 40 seconds, 24 hours a day!

2. Almost 150 million passengers passes through the airport yearly.

3. People rides a "people mover" train to get around the airport.

4. The terminal buildings covers about 130 acres.

5. Shops, restaurants, and benches lines the long concourses.

6. Airplanes arrives and leaves from the 176 gates at Hartsfield.

7. People working at the airport helps keep passengers safe.

 Write one sentence using the subject "pilots" and another using the subject "airplane." Make sure your subjects and verbs agree.

Compound Subjects Connected by "And"

A compound subject connected by the word *and* needs a plural verb.

Miss Gonzales **and** Mr. Peet take **us on the field trip**.

Compound Subjects Connected by "Or"

A compound subject connected by the word *or* needs a verb that agrees in number with the subject nearest to it.

The teachers **or the** principal organizes **the field trip**.

(*Principal*, the subject nearer the verb, is singular, so the singular verb *organizes* is used.)

 Number your paper from 1 to 8. Write the correct verb choice for each of these sentences.

■ Airports and air travel *(is, are)* quite safe.
are

1. Airport rules and airline employees *(help, helps)* passengers stay safe.

2. Each passenger or airline employee *(carry, carries)* personal identification everywhere in the airport.

3. Metal detectors and X-ray scanners *(check, checks)* passengers and luggage.

4. An electronic game or a cell phone *(is, are)* not harmed by X-ray equipment.

5. Passengers or a lost kid *(sets, set)* off security detectors sometimes.

6. Even small scissors and nail files *(cause, causes)* alarms to go off.

7. Security guards or an airport police officer *(question, questions)* passengers who carry metal objects.

8. Checkpoints and security guards *(keep, keeps)* passengers and visitors safe.

 Rewrite sentence 5 above using a plural verb. Rewrite sentence 6 using a singular verb.

BASIC WRITING

What should I do to avoid nonstandard sentences?

Avoid Double Negatives

A **double negative** happens when two negative words are used together *(don't never, can't hardly)* in the same sentence. Using double negatives is incorrect in both spoken and written language. Your writing will seem careless—or even inaccurate—if you use double negatives.

Negative Words				
nothing	nowhere	neither	never	not
barely	hardly	nobody	none	no
Be Careful: Contractions that end in *n't* are also negative words.				
don't	can't	won't	shouldn't	
wouldn't	couldn't	didn't	hadn't	

Find the double negatives in the paragraph below. On your own paper, rewrite those sentences correctly. (There is usually more than one way to correct a double negative.)

Example: The family couldn't hardly wait to fly.
Corrected: The family could hardly wait to fly.
Corrected: The family couldn't wait to fly.

1   Almost since the beginning of time, people have wanted
2 to fly like the birds. None of the early inventions were no good.
3 They didn't fly at all. At first, the Wright brothers didn't have no
4 success either. Finally, they found a way to keep their plane in
5 flight. That changed things forever. Other inventors improved
6 on the Wright brothers' idea. Eventually, airplanes were
7 everywhere. Today, there aren't hardly any places that you
8 can't never reach by flying.

Write NOW   **Write a short paragraph about a time when you were frustrated. Use some negative expressions but avoid using any double negatives.**

Improving Your Sentence Style

There are a number of ways to add variety to your sentences and improve your writing style. Here are four of the most common ways.

1 **Combine short sentences.**

2 **Use different types of sentences.**

3 **Expand sentences by adding words and phrases.**

4 **Model sentences of other writers.**

What happens when too many sentences in a paragraph are the same length or follow the same pattern? Read the following paragraph to find out.

Little Variety

> I visited the Smithsonian's National Air and Space Museum. I saw part of the *Apollo 11* spacecraft. Three astronauts flew in this craft. Astronauts Armstrong, Aldrin, and Collins went to the moon in 1969. They worked, ate, and slept in the command module. They were there for eight days. The command module was very small.

Using a variety of sentences would keep this paragraph from sounding choppy. Read the following version, which has a better variety of sentences.

Good Variety

> When I visited the Smithsonian's National Air and Space Museum, I saw part of the *Apollo 11* spacecraft. In 1969, astronauts Armstrong, Aldrin, and Collins flew this craft to the moon. The command module was very small, but the astronauts worked, ate, and slept there for eight days.

 Read the paragraph below. Then, on your own paper, change the paragraph by creating more sentence variety.

1   I visited Kitty Hawk last summer. Kitty Hawk is in North
2 Carolina. That is where the Wright brothers first flew their
3 airplane. They flew it in 1903. I liked the museum. I loved walking
4 on the sand and climbing up Kill Devil Hill. I saw the memorial
5 tower up there.

BASIC WRITING

How can I make my sentences flow more smoothly?

Writers often combine sentences to help their writing flow more smoothly. If you have too many short sentences, your writing will sound choppy. Combining some of the sentences will add variety to your writing and improve your overall writing style.

Combine with Key Words or Phrases

One way to combine sentences is to use key words or phrases.

Moving a Key Word From One Sentence to Another	
Short Sentences	*Combined Sentences*
Katherine Stinson was a flier. She was a stunt flier.	**Katherine Stinson was a stunt flier.**

Moving a Key Phrase From One Sentence to Another	
Bessie Coleman, the first African American aviator, earned an international pilot's license. She earned it in 1922.	In 1922, **Bessie Coleman, the first African American aviator, earned an international pilot's license.**

 Combine each pair of sentences below by moving a key word or phrase from one sentence to another.

    Bessie Coleman wanted to open a school for young African Americans. She wanted to open a flight school.
    Bessie Coleman wanted to open a flight school for young African Americans.

1. In 1910, Blanche Stuart Scott flew solo in the United States. She became the first woman to do that.

2. Amelia Earhart was the first person to fly alone from Honolulu, Hawaii, to California. She made the flight in 1935.

3. Anne Morrow Lindbergh was a copilot for her husband, Charles Lindbergh. She was also a radio operator for him.

4. Many women are part of aviation history. They were brave.

 Write **NOW** Write a pair of sentences for a classmate to combine. Make sure your sentences can be combined using a key word or phrase.

Combine with a Series of Words

As you've already seen, sentences can be combined using a key word or phrase. Sentences can also be combined using a series of words or phrases.

Combining with a Series of Words or Phrases	
Short Sentences	*Combined Sentences*
Hot-air balloons can be made of nylon. They can be made of acrylic. They can be made of polyester.	**Hot-air balloons can be made of** nylon, acrylic, **or** polyester.
The hot-air balloon is an aircraft that has an envelope to hold hot air. It has a basket to carry people. It has a heating system to warm the air in the balloon.	**The hot-air balloon is an aircraft that has** an envelope **to hold hot air,** a basket **to carry people, and** a heating system **to warm the air in the balloon.**

Be sure to use commas between the words or phrases in your series. (See 582.1.) The items in any series must be alike (or parallel). For example, if the first item is a phrase, all the items must be phrases. The same is true for series containing words or clauses.

 Combine the following groups of sentences with a series of words or phrases. (You may need to change some words to make the sentences work.)

1. The mathematician Archimedes explored the idea of flying in balloons. The English scientist Roger Bacon did, too. So did the German philosopher Albertus Magnus.

2. In 1783, Joseph and Etienne Montgolfier powered the first hot-air balloon by burning straw in a fire pit attached to the bottom of the balloon. They burned wood in the fire pit, too. They also burned other materials in the fire pit.

3. When the brothers tested the balloon, a sheep went up in the balloon basket. A duck was on board. A rooster was also on board.

 Write three sentences for a classmate to combine. Make sure that your sentences can be combined using a series of words or phrases.

Combine with Subjects and Predicates

Another way to combine sentences is to move a subject or predicate from one sentence to another. When you do this, you create a compound subject or a compound predicate. (See page 503.)

Combining with Compound Subjects and Predicates	
Short Sentences	*Combined with a Compound Subject*
Orville Wright was a pilot. Wilbur Wright was a pilot, too.	Orville and Wilbur **Wright were pilots.**
Short Sentences	*Combined with a Compound Predicate*
The brothers owned a bicycle shop. They explored the idea of flying.	**The brothers** owned **a bicycle shop and** explored **the idea of flying.**

 Combine each set of sentences below by using a compound subject or a compound predicate (change the verb when necessary).

■ Orville Wright was an inventor. So was Wilbur Wright.
Orville and Wilbur Wright were inventors.

1. The brothers built the first airplane. They flew the first airplane.

2. The first flights covered short distances. The first flights lasted less than a minute.

3. Orville made changes to the design. Wilbur made changes to the design.

4. In 1908, the brothers demonstrated the plane. They set several records.

5. Americans were interested in the plane. Europeans were interested, too.

6. The United States government ordered Wright airplanes. Countries in Europe ordered them, too.

7. The Wright brothers formed a company. They built their planes.

8. The brothers earned awards. They received honors.

 Write two related sentences for your classmates to combine. Make sure they can be combined using a compound subject or a compound predicate.

What can I do to add variety to my writing?

Writers use different types of sentences to add variety to their writing and make it sound interesting. The three common types of sentences are **simple, compound,** and **complex**. By learning to write these three types of sentences effectively, you can create sentence variety in your writing.

Write Simple Sentences

A **simple sentence** is one independent clause. (An independent clause is a group of words that can stand alone as a sentence.) A simple sentence may contain a single or compound subject and a single or compound predicate.

> **Simple Sentence = One Independent Clause**
>
> **Simple Subject with a Simple Predicate**
> The early days of aviation had many heroes.
>
> **Simple Subject with a Compound Predicate**
> Pilots faced and overcame dangerous situations.
>
> **Compound Subject with a Simple Predicate**
> Amelia Earhart and Charles Lindbergh flew on heroic flights.

 Find the five simple sentences in the paragraph below and copy them. Underline the subjects once and the predicates twice.

1   Charles Lindbergh was a famous American pilot. Lindbergh flew
2   his airplane nonstop from New York City to Paris. The plane was
3   called the *Spirit of St. Louis*. Lindbergh made the flight because he
4   wanted to win a $25,000 prize. He flew across the Atlantic Ocean
5   and landed in Paris, France. Americans and Europeans cheered for
6   Lindbergh. He had made the first successful transatlantic flight, so
7   people called him a hero.

 Write three simple sentences about someone who is a hero to you.
  1 Write one with a simple subject and simple predicate.
  2 Write one with a simple subject and compound predicate.
  3 Write one with a compound subject and simple predicate.

Create Compound Sentences

A **compound sentence** is made up of two or more simple sentences joined together. Often, they are joined with a coordinating conjunction and a comma. (Coordinating conjunctions are words like *and, but,* and *so.*)

Compound Sentence = Two Independent Clauses

> **Yuri Gagarin was a Russian cosmonaut**, and **he became the first person to orbit Earth**. (A comma and the conjunction *and* join the two independent clauses.)
>
> **Russia was the first country to enter the "space race,"** but **the United States quickly followed**. (A comma and the conjunction *but* join the two independent clauses.)

 On your own paper, combine the pairs of simple sentences below to create compound sentences. Use commas and the coordinating conjunctions *and, but,* or *so.*

▪ The United States launched its first manned spacecraft in 1961. Alan Shepard became the first American astronaut in space.

The United States launched its first manned spacecraft in 1961, and Alan Shepard became the first American astronaut in space.

1. The first phase of space travel in this country used *Mercury* spacecraft. The second phase used bigger *Gemini* spacecraft.

2. The *Apollo* spacecraft were the third phase. They were created to explore the moon.

3. In 1969, Neil Armstrong stepped onto the moon. He said, "That's one small step for man, one giant leap for mankind."

4. Five more *Apollo* missions set out for the moon. *Apollo 13* had technical problems and returned to Earth.

5. Later, NASA launched its first space station. Astronauts could live and work in space for several months.

 Write two compound sentences that tell what you think it would be like to travel in space.

Develop Complex Sentences

A **complex sentence** has both an independent clause and at least one dependent clause. Because a dependent clause cannot stand alone as a sentence, it must be connected to an independent clause.

Complex sentences may contain a subordinating conjunction, such as *after, although, because, before, until, when,* and *while.* (See page **744** for more subordinating conjunctions.) Complex sentences may also contain a relative pronoun such as *that, which,* and *who.* (See page **710** for more.)

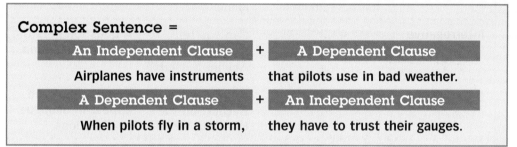

Complex Sentence =

An Independent Clause	+	A Dependent Clause
Airplanes have instruments		**that pilots use in bad weather.**

A Dependent Clause	+	An Independent Clause
When pilots fly in a storm,		**they have to trust their gauges.**

Try It Number your paper from 1 to 6. Then write the dependent clause found in each sentence below.

■ Since pilots can't always see where they are flying, they use flight instruments to get valuable information.

Since pilots can't always see where they are flying

1. If pilots study their instruments, they will know the plane's altitude, speed, and fuel supply.

2. A compass, which shows the airplane's direction, helps the pilot stay on course.

3. Another gauge measures cabin pressure because planes fly so high.

4. Before they land, pilots get directions from radio air controllers on the ground.

5. Unless planes have altimeters, pilots won't know how high they are above sea level.

6. Some people like to fly planes while others prefer being passengers.

Write **NOW** Write two complex sentences about an airplane or an airplane flight you've taken or heard about. (Be sure to use commas correctly.)

BASIC WRITING

Use Questions and Commands

Writers use a variety of sentences to make statements, ask questions, give commands, or show strong emotion. See the chart below.

Kinds of Sentences			
Declarative ▪	Makes a statement about a person, a place, a thing, or an idea	Amelia Earhart flew across the Atlantic Ocean alone.	This is the most common kind of sentence.
Interrogative ?	Asks a question	Can you tell me more about Amelia Earhart?	A question gets the reader's attention.
Imperative ▪	Gives a command	Read about Earhart on the FAA Web site.	Commands often appear in dialogue or directions.
Exclamatory !	Shows strong emotion or feeling	Amelia's plane disappeared!	Use these sentences for occasional emphasis.

 On a piece of paper, write the numbers 1 to 7. Identify each of the sentences shown below by writing "D" for declarative, "INT" for interrogative, "IMP" for imperative, or "EX" for exclamatory.

1. In 1932, Amelia Earhart flew across the Atlantic Ocean in 14 hours and 56 minutes.
2. Amelia Earhart had incredible courage!
3. In 1937, she began a flight around the world with her navigator, Frederick Noonan.
4. Imagine how she must have felt as that plane left the ground.
5. What happened to her and her navigator?
6. When her plane never arrived at Howland Island, southwest of Hawaii, a search found nothing.
7. Can you believe people are still looking for her plane?

 Write four sentences—one of each kind—about someone you feel showed courage.

What can I do to add details to my sentences?

Expand with Prepositional Phrases

Writers use prepositional phrases to add details and information to their sentences. The chart below shows how this is done. Prepositional phrases act like adjectives or adverbs. *Remember:* A prepositional phrase includes a preposition, the object of a preposition, and any words that modify the object. (See page 742 for a list of prepositions.)

Prepositional Phrase	Used in a Sentence
Early biplanes had two pairs of wings.	The phrase acts as an **adjective** to describe the noun "pairs."
Pilots took passengers on short flights.	The phrase acts as an **adverb** to modify the verb "took."

■ Prepositional phrases that are used as adjectives answer the adjective questions: *How many? Which one? What color? What size?*

■ Prepositional phrases used as adverbs answer the adverb questions: *When? How? How often? How long? Where? How much?*

 Number a piece of paper from 1 to 5. Write the prepositional phrase or phrases that you find in each of these sentences.

■ During the 1920s, the most popular planes were biplanes.

During the 1920s

1. These planes were made of wood and fabric.
2. Supports and wire between the wings gave the biplane strength.
3. Sometimes the front edge of the wooden propeller was covered with metal.
4. There were few airports, so pilots often landed in farm pastures.
5. Pilots called barnstormers flew in air shows across the country.

 Use one or two prepositional phrases to add information to each of the sentences below.

1 Biplanes were popular planes.

2 Pilots wore goggles.

3 The planes had wooden propellers.

Expand with Appositive Phrases

Writers sometimes make their sentences more interesting by adding appositive phrases. An **appositive phrase** renames the noun or pronoun before it and is set off from the rest of the sentence with commas.

Appositive Phrases

The Tuskegee Airmen, a group of fighter pilots, **helped win the war.**
(The appositive "a group of fighter pilots" renames the noun "Tuskegee Airmen.")

General Daniel "Chappie" James, a Tuskegee pilot, **became a hero.**
(The appositive "a Tuskegee pilot" renames the noun "General Daniel 'Chappie' James.")

 On your own paper, make a chart like the one below. Read the paragraph that follows the chart and list the appositive phrases you find. Also list the noun or pronoun each appositive renames. (The first one has been done for you.)

Appositive Phrase	Noun or Pronoun It Renames
a group of fighter pilots	Tuskegee Airmen

1 The Tuskegee Airmen, a group of fighter pilots, played an
2 important role in World War II. Beginning in 1941, they served
3 with the United States Army Air Force in Tuskegee, Alabama.
4 These men, all highly trained pilots, made up the first African
5 American flying unit in the U.S. military. The first group to train
6 at Tuskegee, the 99th Pursuit Squadron, was led by Lt. Col.
7 Benjamin O. Davis. The 99th was the only escort group not to
8 lose a bomber to enemy planes. The brave Tuskegee pilots, 992
9 men in all, flew 1,578 missions and won more than 850 medals.

 Write two or three sentences about what you think life would be like as a pilot. Use an appositive in each sentence.

How can I make my sentences more interesting?

Model Sentences

You can learn a great deal about writing by imitating, or modeling, the sentences of other writers. Studying these sentences can teach you how to punctuate and how to put parts together. When you come across sentences that you like, practice writing some of your own that use the same pattern.

Professional Model	Student Models
The mountains have been my lifelong companions, and I still make my home at their feet.	The gym has been my favorite hangout, but I sometimes ride my unicycle at the playground.
Marisa marveled at the open-air market with stalls of vegetables and cheese, people laughing and chatting, and music blaring. —*National Geographic*	My little sister clapped for the parade of clowns in huge shoes and curly red wigs, horses snorting and prancing, and bands marching.

Guidelines for Modeling

- Find a sentence or a short passage that you like and write it down.
- Follow the pattern of the sentence or passage as you write about your own subject. (You do not have to follow the model exactly.)
- Build each sentence one part at a time and check your work when you are finished. (Take your time.)
- Find other sentences to model and keep practicing. Share your sentences with a classmate.

Write NOW On your own paper, model the following sentences. Remember, you do not have to follow the model sentence exactly.

1 The hill was steep and slick, but I knew there was no turning back.

2 Having completed the work, Joshua carefully packed his toolbox and went home.

Develop a Sentence Style

Modeling sentences can help you make your writing more exciting, lively, and appealing. The following writing techniques will also help you improve your style. (Also see page 43.)

Varying Sentence Beginnings

Do too many of your sentences begin with a subject and a verb? Try beginning with a dependent clause or with a phrase, as in the sentences below. This adds variety to the subject-verb pattern.

When I awoke, **there were snowflakes on my eyes.**
                    —*True Grit* by Charles Portis

Hobbling on one foot, **Wanda opened the closet door and turned on the light.**   —*Summer of the Swans* by Betsy Byars

From the stable, **the pair of oxen bellowed and rolled their eyes in terror.**
                    —*The Book of Three* by Lloyd Alexander

Moving Adjectives

Usually, you write adjectives before the nouns they modify. Notice how these writers emphasized the adjectives by placing them after the nouns.

The children, shouting and screaming, **came charging back into their homeroom.**   —*The Friends* by Rosa Guy

Her brown face, upraised, **was stained with tears.**
                    —*The Red Badge of Courage* by Stephen Crane

Repeating a Word

You can repeat a word to emphasize a particular idea or feeling.

. . . **that government of** the people, **by** the people, **for** the people **shall not perish from the earth.**
                    —"Gettysburg Address" by Abraham Lincoln

Life is an exciting **business and most** exciting **when it is lived for others.**
                    —Interview with Helen Keller

 On your own paper, model one sentence from each of the three categories listed above.

Constructing Strong Paragraphs

If you can write a paragraph well, you can write anything. Writer Donald Hall calls a paragraph a "maxi-sentence" or a "mini-essay." Think of it as an important building block for all of your writing. If you can create strong, well-organized paragraphs, you can also create effective essays, book reviews, and reports.

A paragraph is made up of a group of sentences focused on one topic. Each sentence should add something to the overall picture. A paragraph can explain a process, share an opinion, describe something, or tell a story.

What's Ahead

You will learn about . . .
- the parts of a paragraph.
- types of paragraphs.
- writing effective paragraphs.
- adding details to paragraphs.
- gathering details.
- organizing your details.
- refining your details.
- turning paragraphs into essays.
- using a checklist.

The Parts of a Paragraph

Most paragraphs have three main parts: a topic sentence, a body, and a closing sentence. A paragraph usually begins with a *topic sentence* that tells what the paragraph is about. The sentences in the *body* share details about the topic, and the *closing sentence* brings the paragraph to a close.

Topic Sentence

Body

Closing Sentence

Striking It Rich

During the California gold rush, Levi Strauss invented blue jeans. In 1850, when so many gold diggers arrived in California, Strauss took bolts of canvas to San Francisco. He planned to make tents to sell to the miners. When that didn't work out, Strauss used the canvas to make pants that miners could wear for their rough work. Miners bought these pants as fast as Strauss could make them. These pants became the very first Levi jeans, and they changed the clothing world forever. Later, Strauss made the pants out of blue denim instead of canvas and added copper rivets. Since that time, blue jeans have become popular throughout the United States and around the world.

Respond to the reading. What common item of clothing is discussed in this paragraph? Based on the history of Levi jeans, what is the double meaning of the title?

A Closer Look at the Parts

The Topic Sentence

The topic sentence tells the reader what a paragraph is going to be about. A good topic sentence (1) *names the topic* and (2) *states a specific detail or a feeling* about it. Here is a simple formula for writing a topic sentence.

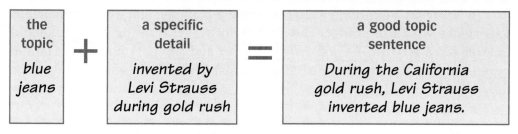

the topic		a specific detail		a good topic sentence
blue jeans	**+**	*invented by Levi Strauss during gold rush*	**=**	*During the California gold rush, Levi Strauss invented blue jeans.*

The topic sentence is usually the first sentence in a paragraph, although sometimes it comes later. It guides the direction of the sentences in the rest of the paragraph.

During the California gold rush, Levi Strauss invented blue jeans.

The Body

The sentences in the body of the paragraph include the details needed to understand the topic.

- **Use specific details to make your paragraph interesting.**
  The specific details below are shown in red.

  Later, Strauss made the pants out of blue denim instead of canvas and added copper rivets.

- **Organize your sentences in the best possible order.**
  Three common ways to organize sentences are chronological (time) order, order of location, and order of importance. (See page 551.)

The Closing Sentence

The closing sentence comes after all the details in the body. It will often restate the topic, give the reader something to think about, or provide a transition to the following paragraph.

Since that time, blue jeans have become popular throughout the United States and around the world.

BASIC WRITING

Types of Paragraphs

There are four types of paragraphs: *narrative, descriptive, expository,* and *persuasive.* Each type requires a different way of thinking and planning.

Compose Narrative Paragraphs

In a **narrative paragraph**, you share a personal story or an important experience with the reader. The details in a narrative paragraph should answer the 5 W's *(who? what? when? where?* and *why?).* A narrative is often organized according to time (what happened *first, next, then, finally).*

Topic Sentence

A Play Day

  It was Saturday morning, and I was ready for my first Service Day. Our school requires each student to volunteer for community service once a semester. My friends and I decided to

Body

work at Smith House, a place for families who need somewhere to stay. We walked inside the house, and before we could take off our coats, 10 little kids ambushed us and begged, "Please play with us!" We read books, played board games, and even went outside to shoot hoops.

Closing Sentence

When we left at noon, our new playmates hugged us and gave us loads of high fives. My friends and I agreed that a day of playing with young kids was the perfect service project for us.

Respond to the reading. Find the key word repeated in the topic sentence and the closing sentence. Does this paragraph answer the 5 W's?

Write your own paragraph. Write a paragraph that tells about an experience you've had recently. Be sure to include the 5 W's and whatever details are needed.

Create Descriptive Paragraphs

When you write a **descriptive paragraph**, you give a detailed picture of a person, a place, an object, or an event. Descriptive paragraphs include many sensory details *(sight, sound, smell, taste, touch)*. The following sample describes the sights, sounds, smells, and feelings of a local soup kitchen.

Topic Sentence

Body

Closing Sentence

Soup's On

One Friday night, my family decided to help at a local soup kitchen. By the time we arrived, the kitchen was filled with noisy people doing all sorts of things. Across the room beside the sink, some of them were washing vegetables, while others were peeling and chopping. Several people gathered around the stove that was in the middle of the kitchen. They added chopped vegetables to the steaming soup pots. Soon the smell of hot vegetable soup filled the room. On the counter between the kitchen and the dining area, another group worked like an assembly line putting together huge stacks of ham and cheese sandwiches. I set the paper plates, salt-and-pepper shakers, and butter plates on the tables. Finally, a stream of hungry people arrived. They seemed to really enjoy the meal and thanked us for everything.

BASIC WRITING

Respond to the reading. Which of the five senses are covered in the paragraph? Which two or three details are especially descriptive?

Write your own paragraph. Write a paragraph that describes a place with lots of sights, sounds, and so on.

Write Expository Paragraphs

In an **expository paragraph**, you share information. You can explain a subject, give directions, or show how to do something. Transition words like *first, next, then,* and *finally* are often used in expository writing.

Topic Sentence

Body

Closing Sentence

How to Start a Pet Pantry

A pet pantry is a place for citizens with low incomes to get free food and supplies for their pets. To create a pet pantry follow these steps. First, meet with the people at a local humane society. See if they will suggest a location for the pantry and a way to distribute food and supplies. Then talk with grocery-store managers and local veterinarians. Ask if they will allow donation containers in their stores and clinics. Next, contact local newspapers and television stations to get the word out. Also make posters and flyers to make sure that people know about the pet pantry. Finally, ask adults to help with the collection of pet food and supplies and to take them to the pantry. A well-run pet pantry can help keep people and their pets together.

Respond to the reading. List the transitions used between sentences in the paragraph above. How many transitions did the writer use? (See pages 572–573 for a list of transitions.)

Write an expository paragraph. Write a paragraph that explains how to do something—like play a game, make a snack, or plant a garden. Be sure to use transitions to connect your ideas.

Develop Persuasive Paragraphs

In a **persuasive paragraph**, you give your opinion (or strong feeling) about a topic. To be persuasive, you must include plenty of reasons, facts, and details to support your opinion. Persuasive writing is usually organized by order of importance or by logical order (as in the paragraph below).

Topic Sentence

Body

Closing Sentence

Get Involved in a Trash Bash

Participating in a trash bash or neighborhood cleanup is a great way to improve a community. First of all, it will help the city's trash collectors get rid of some of the garbage in places where it is hard to pick up. This will save the city time and money. In addition, cleaning up piles of trash will make a neighborhood a more pleasant place to live and play. Most importantly, participating in a cleanup will make a neighborhood safer. Piles of garbage can contain things like broken glass and dangerous chemicals. Germs produced by piles of garbage can make people sick. There are many good reasons to clean up the environment, and a trash bash is one way to do it.

BASIC WRITING

Respond to the reading. What is the writer's opinion in the paragraph? What reasons does she give to support her opinion? When is the most important reason given?

Prewrite

Give your opinion. Write an opinion about an environmental topic. Then list three strong reasons to support your opinion.

Writing Effective Paragraphs

Whenever you write paragraphs, use the following general guidelines.

Prewriting Selecting a Topic and Details

- Select a specific topic.
- Collect facts, examples, and details about your topic.
- Write a topic sentence that states what your paragraph is going to be about. (See page 525 for help.)
- Decide on the best way to arrange your details.

Writing Creating the First Draft

- Start your paragraph with the topic sentence.
- Write sentences in the body that support your topic. Use the details you collected as a guide.
- Connect your sentences with transitions. (See pages 572–573.)
- End with a sentence that restates your topic, leaves the reader with a final thought, or leads into the next paragraph.

Revising Improving Your Writing

- Add information if you need to say more about your topic.
- Move sentences that aren't in the correct order.
- Cut sentences that do not support the topic.
- Rewrite any sentences that are not clear.

Editing Checking for Conventions

- Check the revised version of your writing for capitalization, punctuation, grammar, and spelling errors.
- Then write a neat final copy and proofread it.

 When you write a paragraph, remember that readers want . . .
- original ideas. *(They want something new and interesting.)*
- personality. *(They want to hear the writer's voice.)*

How can I find interesting details?

No paragraph is complete without good supporting details. Here are some types of details you can use in expository and persuasive paragraphs: facts, explanations, definitions, reasons, examples, and comparisons. You might get these details from personal knowledge and memories or from other sources of information.

Use Personal Details

For narrative and descriptive writing, personal details can add interest. Personal details can include sensory, memory, and reflective details.

- **Sensory details** are things that you see, hear, smell, taste, and touch. (These details are important in descriptive paragraphs.)

  Soon the smell of hot vegetable soup filled the room.

- **Memory details** are things you remember from experience. (These details are important in narrative paragraphs.)

  When we left at noon, our new playmates hugged us and gave us loads of high fives.

- **Reflective details** are things you think about or hope for. (These details are often used in narrative and descriptive paragraphs.)

  I felt good about helping at the soup kitchen, and I hope my family decides to do it again soon.

Use Other Sources of Details

To collect details from other sources, use the following tips.

1. **Talk with someone you know.** Parents, neighbors, friends, or teachers may know a lot about your topic.

2. **Write for information.** If you think a museum, a business, or a government office has information you need, send for it.

3. **Read about your topic.** Gather details from books, magazines, and newspapers.

4. **Use the Internet.** The quickest source of information is the Internet. Remember to check Web sites carefully for reliability. (See page 376.)

BASIC WRITING

How do I know what kinds of details to gather?

Here are tips that will help you collect the right kinds of details when you write paragraphs about people, places, objects, and events—and also when you write definitions.

Writing About a Person

When writing about or describing a person, make sure you collect plenty of information. The following guidelines will help.

Observe ■ If possible, carefully watch the person. Maybe the person laughs in a special way or wears a certain type of clothing.

Interview ■ Talk with your subject. Write down words and phrases that the person uses.

Research ■ Use whatever sources are necessary—books, articles, the Internet—to find out more about this person.

Compare ■ Could your subject be compared to some other person?

Writing About a Place

When describing or writing about a place, use details that help the reader understand why the place is important to you.

Observe ■ Study the place you plan to write about. Use photos, postcards, or videos if you can't observe the place in person.

Remember ■ Think of a story (or an anecdote) about this place.

Describe ■ Include the sights, sounds, and smells of the place.

Compare ■ Compare your place to other places.

Writing About an Object

When writing about an object, tell your reader what kind of object it is, what it looks like, how it is used, and why this object is important to you.

Observe ■ Think about these questions: How is the object used? Who uses it? How does it work? What does it look like?

Research ■ Learn about the object. Try to find out when it was first made and used. Ask other people about it.

Define ■ What class or category does this object fit into? (See "Writing a Definition" on page 533.)

Writing About an Event

When writing about or describing an event, focus on the important actions or on one interesting part. Also include sensory details and answer the 5 W's. The following guidelines will help.

Observe ■ Study the event carefully. What sights, sounds, tastes, and smells come to mind? Listen to what people around you are saying.

Remember ■ When you write about something that happened to you, recall as many details connected with the event as you can.

List ■ Answer the *who? what? when? where?* and *why?* questions for facts about the event.

Writing a Definition

When you write a definition, you need to think about three things.

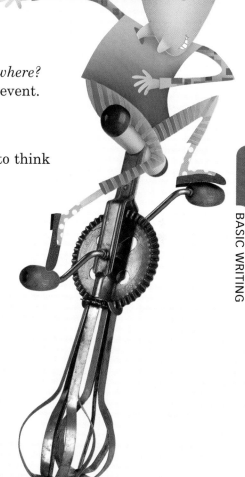

- First put the **term** you are defining *(coyote)* into a **class** or category of similar things *(wild member of the dog family)*.

- Then list special **characteristics** that make this individual different from others in that class *(like a wolf, only smaller)*.

> **Term**—*A coyote*
>
> **Class**—*is a wild member of the dog family*
>
> **Characteristic**—*that is like a wolf, only smaller.*

What can I do to organize my details effectively?

After you've gathered your details, you need to organize them in the best possible way. You can organize a paragraph by *time, location, importance,* or *comparison.* Graphic organizers can help you keep your details in order.

Use Chronological Order

Chronological means "according to time." Transition words and phrases that tell days, months, and years are often used in chronological paragraphs. So are words like *first, second, then,* and *finally.* A time line can help you organize your details.

Franklin's Kite		Faraday's generator	Morse's telegraph	Swan's lightbulb	Edison's lightbulb
1752		1831	1838	1878	1880

Topic Sentence

Body

Closing Sentence

From Kites to Lights

In 1752, Benjamin Franklin flew a kite in a thunderstorm and proved that lightning is a form of electricity. But there was no easy way to capture electricity. Almost 80 years after Franklin's discovery, the British inventor Michael Faraday created the first electric generator. It was simply a magnet moving inside a coil of copper wire. Seven years later, Samuel Morse put the new type of power to good use. He demonstrated his telegraph, which used electricity to send messages. Still, it took another 40 years before Sir Joseph Swan (in England) and Thomas Edison (in America) created the most famous electrical invention, the lightbulb.

Respond to the reading. How are dates given in the time line? How are they given in the paragraph?

Use Order of Location

Often, you can organize descriptive details by order of location. For example, a description may move from left to right, from top to bottom, or from one direction (north) to another (south). Words or phrases like *next to, before, above, below, east, west, north,* and *south* are used to show location. A drawing or map can help you organize your details.

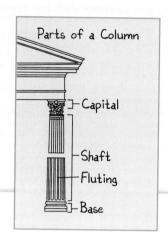

Parts of a Column

Capital

Shaft

Fluting

Base

Topic Sentence
....

Body

Closing Sentence
....

Parts of a Corinthian Column

A Corinthian column has three main parts: a base, a shaft, and a capital. The base is a large disk of stone that looks like rings stacked up. It has to be very strong to hold the weight of everything above it. The shaft stands on top of the base. This long cylinder is built from shorter sections of stone. Grooves called "flutes" run up and down its sides. On top of the column is the capital. It's shaped like an upside-down bell. Stone carvings of leaves surround the capital. All these parts come together to form a column that is both strong and beautiful.

BASIC WRITING

Respond to the reading. On the drawing, why is the column shown in two sections? In the paragraph, with what part of the column does the description begin? Where does it end?

Use Order of Importance

Persuasive and expository paragraphs are often organized by order of importance—from *most* to *least* important, or from *least* to *most* important.

Most important
1. _____
2. _____
3. _____
Least important

or

Least important
3. _____
2. _____
1. _____
Most important

Topic Sentence
············

Body

Closing Sentence
············

The Aztecs

Aztec civilization clearly was the most advanced culture in the Americas at one time. The Aztecs were the first people to make hot cocoa and other chocolate treats. They also wrote books and made colorful paintings. Aztec miners found gold, silver, and turquoise that artists used for jewelry and carvings. Engineers built a city named Tenochtitlan that had palaces, temples, and the world's largest pyramid. Astronomers watched the movements of the sun, the moon, and the stars to create calendars. If you still aren't sure that the Aztecs were the most advanced people of their time, here is one last fact: They could even predict the coming of comets!

Respond to the reading. How are the details organized in this paragraph? On your own paper, list them in reverse order (most to least, least to most). Which order works better?

Use Comparison-Contrast Order

When you write a comparison-contrast paragraph, you want to show how two subjects are both alike and different. A Venn diagram can be used to show differences (**A** and **B**) and similarities (**C**).

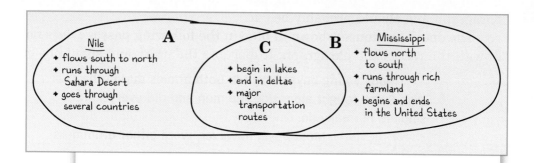

A **C** **B**

Nile
* flows south to north
* runs through Sahara Desert
* goes through several countries

* begin in lakes
* end in deltas
* major transportation routes

Mississippi
* flows north to south
* runs through rich farmland
* begins and ends in the United States

Topic Sentence

Body

Closing Sentence

Two Mighty Rivers

The Nile and the Mississippi Rivers are alike in many ways, but they are also very different. Each of these long rivers begins in a lake and ends in a delta, but they flow in different directions. The Mississippi flows from north to south in the United States, while the Nile flows from south to north through several countries. These rivers run through very different types of land. The Mississippi travels through rich farmland, while the Nile flows through the Sahara Desert. Both rivers are major transportation routes for business and wildlife. These two great rivers are truly wonders of nature.

BASIC WRITING

Respond to the reading. Find two body sentences that include contrasting details about the two rivers. What two words are used to show the contrast?

Write

Write a paragraph. Choose two rivers, lakes, or oceans to compare. Use a Venn diagram to list the details. Then write your paragraph.

How can I be sure all my details work well?

Create Unity in Your Writing

In a well-written paragraph, each detail tells something about the topic. If a detail does not tell something about the topic, it breaks the *unity* of a paragraph and should probably be cut.

The detail (sentence) shown in blue in the following passage does not fit in with the rest of the paragraph. It disrupts the unity and should be cut.

> **Many young boys served in both armies during the Civil War. Some fought alongside the men and did everything soldiers normally do.** One thing these soldiers didn't do was shave regularly. **Most boys, however, were either drummers or flag bearers.**

In the paragraph below, find three details (sentences) that do not support the topic sentence. Then read the paragraph aloud without those sentences. Did the unity of the paragraph improve?

1   Did you know that many famous writers played roles in
2 the Civil War? Probably other creative people also took part in
3 the war. Harriet Beecher Stowe wrote a novel called *Uncle Tom's*
4 *Cabin* that showed how slavery was wrong. My grandma has a
5 copy of that book. Louisa May Alcott, who wrote *Little Women*,
6 was a wartime nurse in an army hospital. Her novel was made
7 into a movie. Walt Whitman was a wartime nurse, too. After the
8 war, he wrote a poem about President Lincoln's death called
9 "O Captain! My Captain!" The poet Julia Ward Howe edited a
10 magazine that was against slavery. Each of these writers did
11 what they could to help with the war.

Look at your paragraph. Study the comparison-contrast paragraph you wrote on page 537. Do all your details support your topic? Would the unity of your paragraph be improved if you cut a detail or two?

Develop Coherence from Start to Finish

An effective paragraph reads smoothly and clearly. When all the details in a paragraph are tied together well, the paragraph has *coherence* and is easy for the reader to follow. One way to make your writing smooth and coherent is to use transitions.

 Number your paper 1 to 7. Use the transitions listed below to help tie the essay together. (Use each transition only once.) When you finish, read the paragraph. Does it read smoothly? If not, switch some transitions.

first	**in addition**	**besides**	**although**
then	**also**	**second**	

A well-trained dog has many career opportunities. _____ ,
                                                        (1)
there are jobs herding cattle and sheep. _____ , there are
                                            (2)
jobs in law enforcement. _____ tracking down criminals,
                            (3)
dogs can keep the suspects under control once they're caught.

_____ there are opportunities for dogs in the social services.
 (4)
Of course, dogs can be trained to guide people who are blind.

They can _____ pick up objects for people in wheelchairs or
            (5)
cheer up people in nursing homes. _____ , dogs are natural
                                     (6)
athletes and entertainers. The TV and movie industries are always

looking for a few good dogs. _____ dogs have so many career
                                (7)
opportunities, most dog owners are happy that their dogs are

content to be pets.

 Read your paragraph. Read your comparison-contrast paragraph from page 537. Underline any parts that don't flow smoothly. Then use transitions to make the writing smoother. (See pages 572–573.)

BASIC WRITING

How can I turn my paragraphs into essays?

Use an Essay Plan

Turning a group of paragraphs into an essay is not simply a matter of placing one after another. To begin with, each paragraph needs to be well written and well organized. Here are some additional tips to follow.

1 **Plan the organization.**

Organize your essay in a way that fits your topic—time order, order of importance, order of location, and so on.

2 **State the topic and focus in the first paragraph.**

Use an interesting fact, example, or story to catch the reader's interest. Then tell what your essay is about in a focus statement, which includes the topic and a main idea or feeling about it.

3 **Develop your writing idea in the middle paragraphs.**

Use each paragraph in the body of your essay to explain and support one part of your focus statement. Each paragraph must have a topic sentence that deals with one part of the focus, followed with supporting details.

4 **End with a concluding paragraph.**

The final paragraph is usually a review of the main points in the essay. Your ending may emphasize the importance of the topic, or it may leave the reader with something to think about.

5 **Use transition words or phrases to connect paragraphs.**

In the topic sentences below, the transitions are shown in red. For a complete list of transitions, see pages 572–573.

> **In addition to** jeans, athletic shoes and sports jerseys are worn in nearly every nation in the world.
>
> ....
>
> **For many reasons,** clothing trends have begun in the United States.

How do I know if I have a strong paragraph?
Use a Paragraph Checklist

You'll know that you have a strong paragraph if it gives the reader complete information on a specific topic. The first sentence should identify the topic and the other sentences should support it. Use the checklist below to help you plan and write effective paragraphs.

Ideas

_____ **1.** Do I focus on an interesting idea?

_____ **2.** Do I use enough specific details?

Organization

_____ **3.** Is my topic sentence clear?

_____ **4.** Have I organized the details in the best order?

Voice

_____ **5.** Do I show interest in—and knowledge of—my topic?

_____ **6.** Does my voice fit my audience? My purpose? My topic?

Word Choice

_____ **7.** Do I use specific nouns and active verbs?

_____ **8.** Do I use colorful adjectives and adverbs?

Sentence Fluency

_____ **9.** Have I written clear and complete sentences?

_____ **10.** Do I use a variety of sentence beginnings and lengths?

Conventions

_____ **11.** Do I use correct punctuation and capitalization?

_____ **12.** Do I use correct spelling and grammar?

BASIC WRITING

improve

support

A Writer's Resource

organize

REFERENCE

select

A Writer's Resource

If you're like most students, you often have questions when you are in the middle of a writing assignment. If a question pops up when you're in class, you can ask your teacher or a classmate. If, however, a question pops up when you're not in class, you need another source to ask or check. This "Writer's Resource" chapter can be a great source of information for answering many of your questions, like "How can I find the best topics to write about?" or "How can I make my voice more colorful?" or "What can I do to make my final copy look better?"

What's Ahead

You will learn how to . . .

- find topics and get started.
- collect and organize details.
- write terrific topic sentences.
- improve your writing style.
- use new forms and techniques.
- increase your vocabulary.
- improve your final copy.

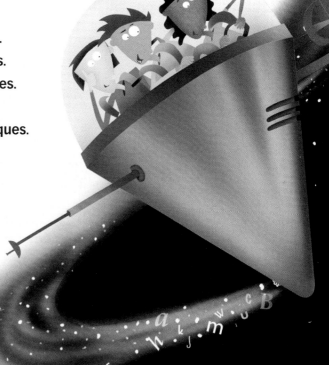

How can I find the best topics to write about?

Try a Topic-Selecting Strategy

A distinguished writer once said, "There are few experiences quite so satisfactory as getting a good writing idea. You're pleased with it, and feel good about it." Many writing assignments are related to a general subject area you are studying. Let's say, for example, you are asked to write a report about a current health issue as part of a science unit. Your job would be to select a certain part of that subject—a specific topic—to write about.

General Subject Area: Current health and medicine
Specific Writing Topic: Exercising to improve strength

The following strategies will help you select effective, specific topics that you can feel good about.

Journal Writing Write on a regular basis in a personal journal, recording your thoughts and experiences. Review your entries from time to time and underline ideas that you would like to write more about later. (See pages 431–434.)

Clustering Begin a cluster (also called a web) with a key word. Select a general term or idea that is related to your writing assignment. Then cluster related words around the key word, as in the model below.

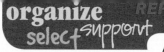

Listing Freely list ideas as they come to mind when you think about your assignment. Keep your list going as long as you can. Then look for words in your list that you feel would make good writing topics.

Freewriting Write nonstop for 5 to 10 minutes to discover possible writing ideas. Begin writing with a particular idea in mind (one related to your writing assignment). Underline ideas that might work as topics for your assignment.

Sentence Completion Complete an open-ended sentence in as many ways as you can. Try to word your sentence so that it leads you to a topic you can use for a particular writing assignment.

I wonder how . . .	I hope our school . . .	Television is . . .
Too many people . . .	I just learned . . .	Cars can be . . .
The good thing about . . .	One place I enjoy . . .	Grades are . . .

Review the "Basics of Life" List

The words listed below name many of the categories or groups of things that people need in order to live a full life. The list provides an endless variety of possibilities for topics. Consider the first category, *clothing*. You could write about . . .

- the wardrobe of a friend or a family member,
- your all-time favorite piece of clothing, or
- clothing as a statement (the "we are what we wear" idea).

clothing	machines	rules/laws
housing	intelligence	tools/utensils
food	history/records	heat/fuel
communication	agriculture	natural resources
exercise	land/property	personality/identity
education	work/occupation	recreation/hobby
family	community	trade/money
friends	science	literature/books
purpose/goals	plants/vegetation	health/medicine
love	freedom/rights	art/music
senses	energy	faith/religion

RESOURCE

What can I do to get started?

Use a List of Writing Topics

The writing prompts listed below and the sample topics listed on the next page provide plenty of starting points for writing assignments.

Writing Prompts

Every day is full of experiences that make you think. You do things that you feel good about. You hear things that make you mad. You wonder how different things work. You're reminded of a past experience. These common, everyday thoughts can make excellent prompts for writing.

Describe (Descriptive)

A bull moose, a fawn, a camel
A parrot, a guinea pig, a ferret
Newborn lambs, calves, chickens
Stalking cats, galloping horses
Pioneer days, wagon-train life
Life in ancient Egypt, Greece, or Rome
Solar or lunar eclipses, rainbows
Meteor showers, hailstorms, sun dogs

Tell Your Story (Narrative)

Meeting an unusual person
Learning something amazing, surprising
Visiting a special place
Overcoming a challenge
A sudden or a big change
Learning a lesson
Another person's triumph or determination

How-To (Expository)

Skateboard, snowboard, surf
Do a headstand, a flip, or a swan dive
Saddle a horse, show a dog, lift weights
Recognize constellations
Do origami, build a radio
Be patient, kind, brave, or helpful
Make or bake a favorite food
Get from one place to another

Parts of the Whole (Expository)

Types of workouts
Kinds of clouds, weather
Different games
Personality types
Variety of musical styles
Clothing styles

Promote (Persuasive)

Individual sports in school
An environment-friendly idea
Ways to help your community
Supporting a worthwhile cause
Ideas for avoiding boredom
Putting an end to something unfair
More field trips for students

Respond to . . .
(Response to literature)

A book that changed your thinking
A poem that helped explain something
A character that you identify with
The biography of someone you admire

Research (Report)

Aquifers, oil wells, salt mines
Hot springs, mud slides, droughts
Importance of natural forest fires
Deserts, tide pools, glaciers

Sample Topics

You come across many people, places, experiences, and things every day that could be topics for writing. A number of possible topics are listed below for descriptive, narrative, expository, and persuasive writing.

Descriptive

People: teacher, relative, classmate, coach, neighbor, bus driver, hero, someone you spend time with, someone you admire, brothers and sisters, someone with a special talent, someone from history

Places: hangout, garage, room, rooftop, historical place, zoo, park, hallway, barn, bayou, lake, cupboard, yard, empty lot, alley, valley, campsite, river, city street

Things: billboard, poster, video game, cell phone, bus, frostbite, boat, gift, drawing, rainbow, doll, junk drawer, flood, mascot, movie

Animals: dolphin, elephants, snake, armadillo, eagle, deer, toad, spoonbill, squirrel, pigeon, pet, coyote, catfish, octopus, beaver, turtle

Narrative

just last week, a big mistake, a reunion, a surprise, getting hurt, learning to _____, getting wet, getting caught, cleaning up, being a friend, a scary time, solving a problem, an important lesson, making a decision

Expository

How to . . . make a taco, improve your memory, care for a pet, entertain a child, impress your teacher, earn extra money, get in shape, overcome fear, get organized, plan a party

The causes of . . . sunburn, acne, hiccups, tornadoes, dropouts, rust, computer viruses, arguments, success, failure

Kinds of . . . crowds, friends, commercials, dreams, neighbors, pain, clouds, joy, stereos, heroes, chores, homework, frustration

Definition of . . . a good time, a conservative, "soul," a grandmother, loyalty, one type of music, advice, courage, hope, strength, fun, freedom, pride

Persuasive

dieting, homework, testing, air bags, teen centers, something that needs improving, something that deserves support, something that's unfair, something that everyone should see, need for more or less of something, healthful habits, dangerous situations, education issues, protecting the environment, preserving historical places, preventing accidents

RESOURCE

How can I collect details for my writing?

Try Graphic Organizers

Graphic organizers can help you gather and organize your details for writing. Clustering is one method. (See page 544.) These two pages list other useful organizers.

Cause-Effect Organizer

Use to collect and organize details for cause-effect essays.

Subject: _____

Causes	Effects
•	•
•	•
•	•
•	•
•	•

Problem-Solution Web

Use to map out problem-solution essays.

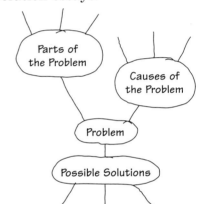

Parts of the Problem

Causes of the Problem

Problem

Possible Solutions

Time Line

Use to collect details for personal narratives and how-to essays.

Subject: _____

(Chronological Order)

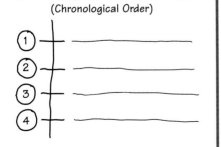

1
2
3
4

Before-After Organizer

Use to collect details for a before-after essay.

Subject: _____

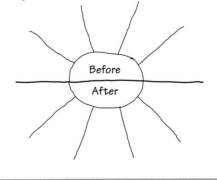

Before

After

Venn Diagram

Use to collect details to compare and contrast two subjects.

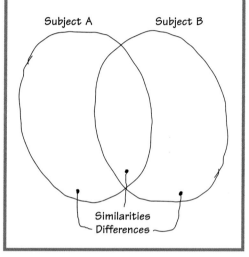

5 W's Chart

Use to collect the *Who? What? When? Where?* and *Why?* details for personal narratives and news stories.

Subject: _____

Who?	What?	When?	Where?	Why?

Sensory Chart

Use to collect details for descriptive essays and observation reports.

Subject: _____

Sights	Sounds	Smells	Tastes	Feelings

Process (Cycle)

Use to collect details for science-related writing, such as how a process or cycle works.

Subject: _____

(Chronological Order)

RESOURCE

What can I do to organize my details better?

Make Lists and Outlines

List Your Details

You can use a variety of ways to organize details as you prepare to write an essay or a report. For most writing, you can make a simple list.

Manatees
— eat 80 to 120 lbs. of water plants a day
— grow to 10 feet in length and live for 60 years
— are fun to watch in tropical areas
— can get caught in locks and dams
— are endangered—about 3,000 in U.S.

People hurt manatees
— drive boats that hit, injure, and kill manatees
— destroy manatee habitat

People help manatees
— enforce slow boat speeds in manatee areas
— install safety devices on locks and dams
— pass laws to protect manatee habitat

Outline Your Information

After gathering facts and details, select two or three main points that best support your focus. Write an outline to organize your information.

I. Manatees worth saving
    A. Keep rivers clear of plants
    B. Fun for people to watch these gentle giants
    C. Save an endangered animal
II. People harming manatees
    A. Injuring and killing in boating collisions
    B. Trapping in locks and dams
    C. Destroying habitat
III. People rescuing manatees
    A. Enforcing boat speed laws
    B. Installing lock and dam safety devices
    C. Protecting habitat

Use Patterns of Organization

■ **Chronological (Time) Order** or **Step-by-Step** You can arrange your details in the order in which they happen (*first, then, next,* and so on). Use these patterns for narratives, history reports, directions, how-to essays, and explaining a process. (See pages 38 and 534.)

> You can make a delicious omelet even if you've never cooked before. First, break the eggs into a bowl and add the milk. Second, mix everything with the beater until it is foamy. Next, heat . . .

■ **Order of Location** You can arrange details in the order in which they are located (*above, below, beside,* and so on). Use order of location for descriptions, explanations, and directions. (See pages 38 and 535.)

> From my mom's office window, I can see the west and south sides of the city. The town hall with its square clock tower is directly in front of me. To my left I see the top of the oldest church in town. . . .

■ **Order of Importance** You can arrange details in your writing from the most important to the least—or from the least important to the most. Persuasive and expository essays are often organized this way. (See pages 38 and 536.)

> Participating in a neighborhood cleanup is a great way to improve your community. First of all, you will help the city get rid of some of the garbage. In addition, if you help clean up piles of trash, you will make your neighborhood cleaner. Most importantly, if you . . .

■ **Comparison-Contrast** You can write about two or more subjects by showing how they are alike and how they are different. Compare subjects by talking about each separately or by talking about both, point by point, as in the following example. (See page 537.)

> The Nile and the Mississippi Rivers are alike in many ways, but they are also very different. Each of these long rivers begins with a lake and ends in a delta, but they flow in different directions. The Mississippi flows from north to south, while the Nile flows from . . .

■ **Logical Order** Use this pattern to organize information in a way that makes sense. Begin with a main idea followed by details, or lead up to a main point. (See page 38.)

> Hurricanes are very dangerous storms. They can cause destruction, injury, and death over a very large area. It's important to learn how these storms form and move. That's why scientists spend so much time studying hurricanes. . . .

RESOURCE

How can I write terrific topic sentences?

Try Eight Special Strategies

Writing a good topic sentence is a key to writing a great paragraph. A good topic sentence names the topic and states a specific feeling about it. Use the following strategies the next time you need to write a terrific topic sentence. (Also see page 525.)

Use a Number

Topic sentences can use number words to tell what the paragraph will be about.

Each cell has three **main parts.**

Ms. Chen should change the menu for several **reasons.**

Number Words		
two	couple	a pair
few	three	a number
several	four	many
a variety	five	a list

Create a List

A topic sentence can list the things the paragraph will talk about.

Egyptians built step pyramids, bent pyramids, **and** straight pyramids.

To stay healthy and alert, get **eight hours of sleep,** eat **a good breakfast, and** walk **a mile every day.**

Start with To and a Verb

A topic sentence that starts with "to" and a verb helps the reader know why the information in the paragraph is important.

To learn **a one-and-a-half flip, divers first need to learn a single flip.**

To understand **rock and roll, people should first learn about the blues.**

Use Word Pairs

Conjunctions that come in pairs can help organize a topic sentence.

Connelly Middle School needs not only **a new track** but also **new bleachers.**

Some scientists debate whether **T. rex was a hunter** or **a scavenger.**

Word Pairs
if . . . then
either . . . or
not only . . . but also
both . . . and
whether . . . or
as . . . so

Join Two Ideas

A topic sentence can state two equal ideas. You can do this by writing a compound sentence. (See page 516.)

A tree fort is easy to build, and **even beginning carpenters can lend a hand.**

The principal wants to ban hats in school, but **some students don't think that's a good idea.**

Use a "Why-What" Word

A "why-what" word is a subordinating conjunction that shows how ideas are connected.

So that **everyone can hear the candidates' ideas, the student council should hold a debate.**

Because **you want a smooth texture, use a mixer or blender.**

"Why-What" Words	
So that	Once
Before	Since
Until	Whenever
Because	While
If	As long as
As	After
In order that	When

Use a "Yes, But" Word

A "yes, but" word is a subordinating conjunction that tells how two ideas are different.

Instead of **just complaining about it, students should help clean up roadside litter.**

Even though **the writers' group is small, the members have written lots of material.**

"Yes, But" Words
However
Instead of
Although
Even though
Even if
Unless
Whether
Whereas

Quote an Expert

Sometimes the best way to start a paragraph is to quote someone who knows about your topic.

Michael Jordan once said, "You have to expect things of yourself before you can do them."

Amelia Earhart put it best: "It is far easier to start something than to finish it."

RESOURCE

What other forms can I use for my writing?

Try These Forms of Writing

Finding the right *form* for your writing is just as important as finding the right topic. When you are selecting a form, be sure to ask yourself who you're writing for (your audience) and why you're writing (your purpose).

Anecdote	A brief story that makes a point
Autobiography	A writer's story of his or her own life
Biography	A writer's story of some other person's life
Book review	A brief essay giving a response or an opinion about a book (See pages 287–322.)
Character sketch	Writing that describes a specific character in a story
Composition	A longer piece of writing, such as a story or an essay
Descriptive writing	Writing that uses details to help the reader clearly imagine a certain person, place, thing, or idea (See pages 71–91.)
Editorial	Newspaper letters or articles giving an opinion
Essay	A piece of writing in which ideas are presented, explained, argued, or described in an interesting way
Expository writing	Writing that explains by presenting the steps, the causes, or the kinds of something (See pages 157–217.)
Fable	A short story that often uses talking animals as the main characters and teaches a lesson or moral
Fantasy	A story set in an imaginary world in which the characters usually have supernatural powers or abilities
Freewriting	Writing whatever comes to mind about any topic
Historical fiction	A made-up story based on something real in history in which fact is mixed with fiction
Myth	A traditional story intended to explain a mystery of nature, religion, or culture
Narrative	Writing that tells about an event, an experience, or a story (See pages 93–155.)

organize
select support
REFERENCE
improve
555
A Writer's Resource

Novel	A book-length story with several characters and a well-developed plot
Personal narrative	Writing that shares an event or experience in the writer's personal life (See pages 97–134.)
Persuasive writing	Writing that is meant to persuade the reader to agree with the writer about someone or something (See pages 219–281.)
Play	A form that uses dialogue to tell a story and is meant to be performed in front of an audience
Poem	Writing that uses rhythm, rhyme, and imagery (See pages 353–361.)
Proposal	Writing that includes specific information about an idea or a project that is being considered for approval
Research report	An essay that shares information on a topic that has been researched well and organized carefully
Response to literature	Writing that is a summary or a reaction to something the writer has read (novel, short story, poem, article, and so on)
Science fiction	Writing based on real or imaginary science and often set in the future
Short story	A short piece of literature with only a few characters and one problem or conflict (See pages 343–349.)
Summary	Writing that presents only the most important ideas from a longer piece of writing (See pages 377–380.)
Tall tale	A humorous, exaggerated story (often based on the life of a real person) about a character who does impossible things
Tragedy	Literature in which the hero is destroyed because of some serious flaw or defect in his or her character

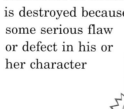

RESOURCE

How can I make my voice more colorful?

You can make your writing voice more colorful by using strong dialogue and by "showing" instead of "telling."

Use Dialogue

Each person you write about has a unique way of saying things, and well-written dialogue lets the reader *hear* the speaker's personality and thoughts. For example, notice how the following message can be spoken in several different ways.

> *Message:* Your new car is impressive.
>
> *Speaker 1:* "Whoa, Dad! Cool new wheels!"
>
> *Speaker 2:* "Nice coupe, Bill. I've always been a sedan man myself."
>
> *Speaker 3:* "Such a fancy car, Son! Hope you didn't spend too much."

Each of these speakers delivers the same message in a unique way. The dialogue tells as much about the speaker as it does about the topic.

One way to improve your dialogue is to think about the speaker and his or her personality. Look at the three personality webs below and try to decide which one is *Speaker 1, Speaker 2,* or *Speaker 3* from above. How does the dialogue show their personalities?

Tips for Punctuating Dialogue

- Indent every time a different person speaks.
- Put the exact words of a speaker in quotation marks.
- Set off the quoted words from the rest of the sentence by using a comma.
- At the end of quoted words, put a period or comma inside the quotation marks.

(For more information and examples on how to punctuate dialogue, see 588.1, 598.1, and 600.1 in the "Proofreader's Guide.")

Show, Don't Tell

The old saying "Seeing is believing" is especially true in writing. Writing that tells the reader is not as strong as writing that shows the reader something, allowing him or her to decide how to feel about it. Notice the difference between the two paragraphs below.

Telling: **I rode on the roller coaster. It was frightening but fun.**

Showing: As the roller coaster topped the first big hill, I could see my mom down below. She looked so small. Then the coaster began to surge down the hill. My hands went up, my heart jumped into my throat, and I let out a sound that was half laugh and half scream.

The first paragraph *tells* the reader that the roller coaster ride was "frightening but fun." The second paragraph *shows* just how "frightening but fun" it really was.

Key Strategies for Showing

Next time you realize your writing is telling rather than showing, try one of these strategies.

- **Add sensory details.** Include sights, sounds, smells, tastes, and touch sensations. That way, the reader can "experience" the event.

  Telling: **Swimming was refreshing.**

  Showing: All morning the sun beat down on us as we painted the garage, but we escaped all afternoon in the cool, refreshing water of Watkins Pond.

- **Explain body language.** Write about facial expressions and the way people stand, gesture, and move.

  Telling: **Sharissa was upset with me.**

  Showing: Sharissa glared at me, tapped her foot, pursed her lips, and snorted.

- **Use dialogue.** Let the people in your writing speak for themselves.

  Telling: **Sharon Whitecloud wanted to go to the Art Institute.**

  Showing: Sharon Whitecloud piped up, "You're not going to the Art Institute without me!"

RESOURCE

What can I do to improve my writing style?

Learn Some Writing Techniques

Writers put special effects in their stories and essays in different ways. Look over the following writing techniques and then experiment with some of them in your own writing.

Analogy	A comparison of similar objects to help clarify one of the objects **Personal journals are like photograph albums. They both share personal details and tell a story.**
Anecdote	A brief story used to illustrate or make a point **Abe Lincoln walked two miles to return several pennies he had overcharged a customer.** (This anecdote shows Lincoln's honesty.)
Exaggeration	An overstatement or a stretching of the truth used to make a point or paint a clearer picture (See *overstatement.*) **After getting home from summer camp, I slept for a month.**
Foreshadowing	Hints or clues that a writer uses to suggest what will happen next in a story **Halfway home, Sarah wondered whether she had locked her locker.**
Irony	A technique that uses a word or phrase to mean the opposite of its normal meaning **Marshall just loves cleaning his room.**
Local color	The use of details that are common in a certain place or local area (A story taking place on a seacoast would contain details about the water and the life and people near it.) **Everybody wore flannel shirts to the Friday fish fry.**
Metaphor	A figure of speech that compares two things without using the word *like* or *as* (See page 360.) **In our community, high school football is king.**
Overstatement	An exaggeration or a stretching of the truth (See *exaggeration.*) **When he saw my grades, my dad hit the roof.**

Parallelism	Repeating similar words, phrases, or sentences to give writing rhythm (See page 522.)
	We will swim in the ocean, lie on the beach, and sleep under the stars.
Personification	A figure of speech in which a nonhuman thing (an idea, object, or animal) is given human characteristics (See page 360.)
	Rosie's old car coughs and wheezes on cold days.
Pun	A phrase that uses words in a way that gives them a humorous effect
	The lumberjack logged on to the site to order new boots.
Sarcasm	The use of praise to make fun of or "put down" someone or something (The expression is not sincere and is actually intended to mean the opposite thing.)
	Micah's a real gourmet; he loves peanut butter and jelly sandwiches. (A *gourmet* is a "lover of fine foods.")
Sensory details	Specific details that help the reader see, feel, smell, taste, and/or hear what is being described (See page 489.)
	As Lamont took his driver's test, his heart thumped, his hands went cold, and his face began to sweat.
Simile	A figure of speech that compares two things using the word *like* or *as* (See page 360.)
	Faye's little brother darts around like a water bug.
	Yesterday the lake was as smooth as glass.
Slang	Informal words or phrases used by particular groups of people when they talk to each other
	chill out hang loose totally awesome
Symbol	An object that is used to stand for an idea
	The American flag is a symbol of the United States. The stars stand for the 50 states, and the stripes stand for the 13 original U.S. colonies.
Understatement	Very calm language (the opposite of exaggeration) used to bring special attention to an object or an idea
	These hot red peppers may make your mouth tingle a bit.

RESOURCE

How can I expand my writing vocabulary?

Study Writing Terms

This glossary includes terms used to describe the parts of the writing process. It also includes terms that explain special ways of stating an idea.

Antonym	A word that means the opposite of another word: *happy* and *sad; large* and *small* (See page 563.)
Audience	The people who read or hear what has been written
Body	The main or middle part in a piece of writing that comes between the *beginning* and the *ending* and includes the main points
Brainstorming	Collecting ideas by thinking freely about all the possibilities
Closing	The ending or final part in a piece of writing (In a paragraph, the closing is the last sentence. In an essay or a report, the closing is the final paragraph.)
Coherence	Tying ideas together in your writing (See page 539.)
Connotation	The "feeling" a word suggests (See page 485.)
Denotation	The dictionary meaning of a word
Dialogue	Written conversation between two or more people
Figurative language	Special comparisons, often called figures of speech, that make your writing more creative (See page 360.)
Focus statement	The statement that tells what specific part of a topic is written about in an essay (See *thesis statement* and page 35.)
Form	A type of writing or the way a piece of writing is put together (See pages 554–555.)
Grammar	The structure of language; the rules and guidelines that you follow in order to speak and write acceptably
Jargon	The special language of a certain group, occupation, or field **Computer jargon: byte digital upload**
Journal	A notebook for writing down thoughts, experiences, ideas, and information (See pages 431–434.)

Limiting the subject	Taking a general subject and narrowing it down to a specific topic

General subject   Specific topic
sports → **golf** → **golf skills** → **putting**

Modifiers	Words, phrases, or clauses that describe another word Our black **cat** slowly **stretched and** then **leaped** onto the wicker chair. (Without the blue modifiers, all we know is that a "cat stretched and leaped.")
Point of view	The angle from which a story is told (See page 352.)
Purpose	The specific reason that a person has for writing **to describe** **to narrate** **to persuade** **to explain**
Style	How an author writes (choice of words and sentences)
Supporting details	Facts or ideas used to tell a story, explain a topic, describe something, or prove a point
Synonym	A word that means the same thing as another word (*dog* and *canine*) (See page 563.)
Theme	The main point, message, or lesson in a piece of writing
Thesis statement	A statement that gives the main idea of an essay (See *focus statement*.)
Tone	A writer's attitude toward his or her subject **serious** **humorous** **sarcastic**
Topic	The specific subject of a piece of writing
Topic sentence	The sentence that contains the main idea of a paragraph (See page 525.) **Blue jeans are a popular piece of American clothing.**
Transition	A word or phrase that connects or ties two ideas together smoothly (See pages 572–573.) **also** **however** **lastly** **later** **next**
Usage	The way in which people use language (*Standard usage* generally follows the rules of good grammar. Most of the writing you do in school will require standard usage.)
Voice	A writer's unique, personal tone or feeling that comes across in a piece of writing (See page 40.)

What can I do to increase my vocabulary skills?

Try Vocabulary-Building Techniques

Technique	Description	Why It Works
Learn common roots, prefixes, and suffixes.	**If you know common word parts, you will be able to figure out many new words.**	Tens of thousands of English words come from Greek and Latin word parts. (See pages 564–569.)
Use context.	**Look at the passage surrounding the word you don't know. (See page 563.)**	Words and ideas around a word often give hints as to what the word means.
Look up words in the dictionary.	**Read the dictionary meaning. Also read the history of the word. (See pages 374–375.)**	Sometimes the word history helps you connect the new word with one you already know.
Keep a vocabulary notebook.	**Write down words you don't know. Include the pronunciation and meaning. Use each word in a sentence.**	Writing reinforces your learning. The notebook is also a handy study guide.
Say your new words out loud.	**Read your new words out loud and look for places in your writing where you can use them effectively.**	Saying new words out loud means you hear them. Using that extra sense helps you remember.
Use your new words often.	**Concentrate on using new words whenever possible in your writing.**	Research shows that you need to use a new word to make it your own.

Use Context

When you come across a word you don't know, you can often figure out its meaning from the other words in the sentence. The other words form a familiar context, or setting, for the unfamiliar word. Looking closely at these surrounding words will give you clues to the meaning of the new word.

When you come to a word you don't know . . .

▪ Look for a synonym—a word or words that have the same meaning as the unknown word.

> Sara had an ominous feeling when she woke up, but the feeling was less threatening when she saw she was in her own room.
> (An *ominous* feeling is a threatening one.)

▪ Look for an antonym—a word that has the opposite meaning from the unknown word.

> Boniface had always been quite heavy, but he looked gaunt when he returned from the hospital.
> (*Gaunt* is the opposite of *heavy.*)

▪ Look for a comparison or contrast.

> Riding a mountain bike in a remote area is my idea of a great day. I wonder why some people like to ride motorcycles on busy six-lane highways.
> (A *remote* area is out of the way, in contrast to a busy area.)

▪ Look for a definition or description.

> Manatees, large aquatic mammals (sometimes called sea cows), can be found in the warm coastal waters of Florida.
> (An *aquatic* mammal is one that lives in the water.)

▪ Look for words that appear in a series.

> The campers spotted sparrows, chickadees, and indigo buntings on Saturday morning.
> (An *indigo bunting,* like a *sparrow* or *chickadee,* is a bird.)

▪ Look for a cause-and-effect relationship.

> The amount of traffic at 6th and Main doubled last year, so crossing lights were placed at that corner to avert an accident.
> (*Avert* means "to prevent.")

RESOURCE

How can I build my vocabulary across the curriculum?

On the next several pages, you will find many of the most common prefixes, suffixes, and roots in the English language. Learning these word parts can help you increase your writing vocabulary.

Learn About Prefixes

A **prefix** is a word part that is added before a word to change the meaning of the word. For example, when the prefix *un* is added to the word *fair (unfair),* it changes the word's meaning from "fair" to "not fair."

ambi *[both]*
   ambidextrous (skilled with both hands)

anti *[against]*
   antifreeze (a liquid that works against freezing)
   antiwar (against wars and fighting)

astro *[star]*
   astronaut (person who travels among the stars)
   astronomy (study of the stars)

auto *[self]*
   autobiography (writing that is about yourself)

bi *[two]*
   bilingual (using or speaking two languages)
   biped (having two feet)

circum *[in a circle, around]*
   circumference (the line or distance around a circle)
   circumnavigate (to sail around)

co *[together, with]*
   cooperate (to work together)
   coordinate (to put things together)

ex *[out]*
   exhale (to breathe out)
   exit (the act of going out)

fore *[before, in front of]*
   foremost (in the first place, before everyone or everything else)
   foretell (to tell or show beforehand)

hemi *[half]*
   hemisphere (half of a sphere or globe)

hyper *[over]*
   hyperactive (overactive)

im *[not, opposite of]*
   impatient (not patient)
   impossible (not possible)

in *[not, opposite of]*
   inactive (not active)
   incomplete (not complete)

inter *[between, among]*
   international (between or among nations)
   interplanetary (between the planets)

macro *[large]*
   macrocosm (the entire universe)

mal *[bad, poor]*
   malnutrition (poor nutrition)

micro *[small]*
   microscope (an instrument used to see very small things)

mono [one]
  monolingual (using or speaking only one language)

non [not, opposite of]
  nonfat (without the normal fat content)
  nonfiction (based on facts; not made-up)

over [too much, extra]
  overeat (to eat too much)
  overtime (extra time; time beyond regular hours)

poly [many]
  polygon (a figure or shape with three or more sides)
  polysyllable (a word with more than three syllables)

post [after]
  postscript (a note added at the end of a letter, after the signature)
  postwar (after a war)

pre [before]
  pregame (activities that occur before a game)
  preheat (to heat before using)

re [again, back]
  repay (to pay back)
  rewrite (to write again or revise)

semi [half, partly)]
  semicircle (half a circle)
  semiconscious (half conscious; not fully conscious)

sub [under, below]
  submarine (a boat that can operate underwater)
  submerge (to put underwater)

trans [across, over; change]
  transcontinental (across a continent)
  transform (to change from one form to another)

tri [three]
  triangle (a figure that has three sides and three angles)
  tricycle (a three-wheeled vehicle)

un [not]
  uncomfortable (not comfortable)
  unhappy (not happy; sad)

under [below, beneath]
  underage (below or less than the usual or required age)
  undersea (beneath the surface of the sea)

uni [one]
  unicycle (a one-wheeled vehicle)
  unisex (a single style that is worn by both males and females)

Numerical Prefixes

deci [tenth part]
  decimal system (a number system based on units of 10)

centi [hundredth part]
  centimeter (a unit of length equal to 1/100 meter)

milli [thousandth part]
  millimeter (a unit of length equal to 1/1000 meter)

micro [millionth part]
  micrometer (one-millionth of a meter)

deca or dec [ten]
  decade (a period of 10 years)
  decathlon (a contest with 10 events)

hecto or hect [one hundred]
  hectare (a metric unit of land equal to 100 ares)

kilo [one thousand]
  kilogram (a unit of mass equal to 1,000 grams)

mega [one million]
  megabit (one million bits)

Study Suffixes

A **suffix** is a word part that is added after a word. Sometimes a suffix will tell you what part of speech a word is. For example, many adverbs end in the suffix *ly*.

able *[able, can do]*
  agreeable (able or willing to agree)
  doable (can be done)

al *[of, like]*
  magical (like magic)
  optical (of the eye)

ed *[past tense]*
  called (past tense of call)
  learned (past tense of learn)

ess *[female]*
  lioness (a female lion)

ful *[full of]*
  helpful (giving help; full of help)

ic *[like, having to do with]*
  symbolic (having to do with symbols)

ily *[in some manner]*
  happily (in a happy manner)

ish *[somewhat like or near]*
  childish (somewhat like a child)

ism *[characteristic of]*
  heroism (characteristic of a hero)

less *[without]*
  careless (without care)

ly *[in some manner]*
  calmly (in a calm manner)

ology *[study, science]*
  biology (the study of living things)

s *[more than one; plural noun]*
  books (more than one book)

ward *[in the direction of]*
  westward (in the direction of west)

y *[containing, full of]*
  salty (containing salt)

Comparative Suffixes

er *[comparing two things]*
  faster, later, neater, stronger

est *[comparing more than two]*
  fastest, latest, neatest, strongest

Noun-Forming Suffixes

er *[one who]*
  painter (one who paints)

ing *[the result of]*
  painting (the result of a painter's work)

ion *[act of, state of]*
  perfection (the state of being perfect)

ist *[one who]*
  violinist (one who plays the violin)

ment *[act of, result of]*
  amendment (the result of amending, or changing)
  improvement (the result of improving)

ness *[state of]*
  goodness (the state of being good)

or *[one who]*
  actor (one who acts)

Understand Roots

A **root** is a word or word base from which other words are made by adding a prefix or a suffix. Knowing the common roots can help you figure out the meaning of difficult words.

aster *[star]*
- **aster** (star flower)
- **asterisk** (starlike symbol [*])

aud *[hear, listen]*
- **audible** (can be heard)
- **auditorium** (a place to listen to speeches and performances)

bibl *[book]*
- **Bible** (sacred book of Christianity)
- **bibliography** (list of books)

bio *[life]*
- **biography** (book about a person's life)
- **biology** (the study of life)

chrome *[color]*
- **monochrome** (having one color)
- **polychrome** (having many colors)

chron *[time]*
- **chronological** (in time order)
- **synchronize** (to make happen at the same time)

cide *[the killing of; killer]*
- **homicide** (the killing of one person by another person)
- **pesticide** (pest [bug] killer)

cise *[cut]*
- **incision** (a thin, clean cut)
- **incisors** (the teeth that cut or tear food)
- **precise** (cut exactly right)

cord, cor *[heart]*
- **cordial** (heartfelt)
- **coronary** (relating to the heart)

corp *[body]*
- **corporation** (a legal body; business)
- **corpse** (a dead human body)

cycl, cyclo *[wheel, circular]*
- **bicycle** (a vehicle with two wheels)
- **cyclone** (a very strong circular wind)

dem *[people]*
- **democracy** (ruled by the people)
- **epidemic** (affecting many people at the same time)

dent, dont *[tooth]*
- **dentures** (false teeth)
- **orthodontist** (dentist who straightens teeth)

derm *[skin]*
- **dermatology** (the study of skin)
- **epidermis** (outer layer of skin)

fac, fact *[do, make]*
- **factory** (a place where people make things)
- **manufacture** (to make by hand or machine)

fin *[end]*
- **final** (the last of something)
- **infinite** (having no end)

flex *[bend]*
- **flexible** (able to bend)
- **reflex** (bending or springing back)

flu *[flowing]*
- **fluent** (flowing smoothly or easily)
- **fluid** (waterlike, flowing substance)

forc, fort *[strong]*
- **force** (strength or power)
- **fortify** (to make strong)

fract, frag *[break]*
- **fracture** (to break)
- **fragment** (a piece broken from the whole)

RESOURCE

Learn More Roots

gen *[birth, produce]*
congenital (existing at birth)
genetics (the study of inborn traits)

geo *[of the earth]*
geography (the study of places on the earth)
geology (the study of the earth's physical features)

graph *[write]*
autograph (writing one's name)
graphology (the study of handwriting)

homo *[same]*
homogeneous (of the same birth or kind)
homogenize (to blend into a uniform mixture)

hydr *[water]*
dehydrate (to take the water out of)
hydrophobia (the fear of water)

ject *[throw]*
eject (to throw out)
project (to throw forward)

log, logo *[word, thought, speech]*
dialogue (speech between two people)
logic (thinking or reasoning)

luc, lum *[light]*
illuminate (to light up)
translucent (letting light come through)

magn *[great]*
magnificent (great)
magnify (to make bigger or greater)

man *[hand]*
manicure (to fix the hands)
manual (done by hand)

mania *[insanity]*
kleptomania (abnormal desire to steal)
maniac (an insane person)

mar *[sea, pool]*
marine (of or found in the sea)
mariner (sailor)

mega *[large]*
megalith (large stone)
megaphone (large horn used to make voices louder)

meter *[measure]*
meter (unit of measure)
voltmeter (device to measure volts)

mit, miss *[send]*
emit (to send out; give off)
transmission (sending over)

multi *[many, much]*
multicultural (of or including many cultures)
multiped (an animal with many feet)

numer *[number]*
innumerable (too many to count)
numerous (large in number)

omni *[all, completely]*
omnipresent (present everywhere at the same time)
omnivorous (eating all kinds of food)

onym *[name]*
anonymous (without a name)
pseudonym (false name)

ped *[foot]*
pedal (lever worked by the foot)
pedestrian (one who travels by foot)

phil *[love]*
Philadelphia (city of brotherly love)
philosophy (the love of wisdom)

phobia *[fear]*
acrophobia (a fear of high places)
agoraphobia (a fear of public, open places)

phon *[sound]*
phonics (related to sounds)
symphony (sounds made together)

photo *[light]*
photo-essay (a story told mainly with photographs)
photograph (picture made using light rays)

pop *[people]*
population (number of people in an area)
populous (full of people)

port *[carry]*
export (to carry out)
portable (able to be carried)

psych *[mind, soul]*
psychiatry (treatment of the mind)
psychology (science of mind and behavior)

sci *[know]*
conscious (being aware)
omniscient (knowing everything)

scope *[instrument for viewing]*
kaleidoscope (instrument for viewing patterns and shapes)
periscope (instrument used to see above the water)

scrib, script *[write]*
manuscript (something written by hand)
scribble (to write quickly)

spec *[look]*
inspect (to look at carefully)
specimen (an example to look at)

spir *[breath]*
expire (to breathe out; die)
inspire (to breathe into; give life to)

tele *[over a long distance; far]*
telephone (machine used to speak to people over a distance)
telescope (machine used to see things that are very far away)

tempo *[time]*
contemporary (from the current time period)
temporary (lasting for a short time)

tend, tens *[stretch, strain]*
extend (to stretch and make longer)
tension (stretching something tight)

terra *[earth]*
terrain (the earth or ground)
terrestrial (relating to the earth)

therm *[heat]*
thermal (related to heat)
thermostat (a device for controlling heat)

tom *[cut]*
anatomy (the science of cutting apart plants and animals for study)
atom (a particle that cannot be cut or divided)

tract *[draw, pull]*
traction (the act of pulling)
tractor (a machine for pulling)

typ *[print]*
prototype (the first printing or model)
typo (a printing error)

vac *[empty]*
vacant (empty)
vacuum (an empty space)

vid, vis *[see]*
supervise (to oversee or watch over)
videotape (record on tape for viewing)

vor *[eat]*
carnivorous (flesh-eating)
herbivorous (plant-eating)

zoo *[animal or animals]*
zoo (a place where animals are kept)
zoology (the study of animal life)

What can I do to write more effective sentences?

Study Sentence Patterns

Sentences in the English language follow the basic patterns below. Use a variety of patterns to add interest to your writing. (Also see page 571.)

1 Subject + Action Verb

> S   AV
> **Gus giggles.** (Some action verbs, like *giggles,* are intransitive. This means that they *do not need* a direct object to express a complete thought. See 728.3.)

2 Subject + Action Verb + Direct Object

> S   AV   DO
> **Jesse tells ghost stories at camp.** (Some action verbs, like *tells,* are transitive. This means that they *need* a direct object to express a complete thought. See 728.2.)

3 Subject + Action Verb + Indirect Object + Direct Object

> S   AV IO   DO
> **Mom gave me this book.**

4 Subject + Action Verb + Direct Object + Object Complement

> S   AV   DO   OC
> **We named Jamaal the best storyteller.**

5 Subject + Linking Verb + Predicate Noun

> S   LV   PN
> **Christina is a beautiful singer.**

6 Subject + Linking Verb + Predicate Adjective

> S   LV PA
> **My teacher was terrific.**

(In the patterns above, the subject comes before the verb. In the patterns below, the subject (called a *delayed subject*) comes after the verb.)

> LV S   PN
> **7** **Is Larisa a poet?** (A question)

>   LV   S
> **8** **There was a meeting.** (A sentence beginning with *there* or *here*)

Practice Sentence Diagramming

Diagramming sentences can help you understand how the parts of a sentence fit together. Here are the most common diagrams. (See page 570.)

1
    S   AV
Gus giggles.

Gus | giggles

2
   S   AV   DO
Jesse tells ghost stories at camp.

Note: Place a preposition on a diagonal line under the word it modifies, with its object on an attached line (*at camp*).

Jesse | tells | stories
    at camp   *ghost*

3
   S   AV IO   DO
Mom gave me this book.

Mom | gave | book
    me *this*

4
   S   AV   DO   OC
We named Jamaal the best storyteller.

We | named | Jamaal \ storyteller
    the *best*

5
   S   LV   PN
Christina is a beautiful singer.

Christina | is \ singer

Note: Place an adjective or adverb on a diagonal line under the word it modifies.

    a *beautiful*

6
   S   LV PA
My teacher was terrific.

teacher | was \ terrific
  My

How can I connect my sentences and paragraphs?

Use Transitions

Transitions can be used to connect one sentence to another sentence or one paragraph to another within a longer essay or report. The lists below show a number of transitions and how they are used.

Note: The **colored lists** are groups of transitions that could work well together in a piece of writing.

Words that can be used to show location

above	around	between	inside	outside
across	behind	by	into	over
against	below	down	near	throughout
along	beneath	in back of	next to	to the right
among	beside	in front of	on top of	under

Above	In front of	On top of
Below	Beside	Next to
To the left	In back of	Beneath
To the right		

Words that can be used to show time

about	during	yesterday	until	finally
after	first	meanwhile	next	then
at	second	today	soon	as soon as
before	to begin	tomorrow	later	in the end

First	To begin	Now	First	Before
Second	To continue	Soon	Then	During
Third	To conclude	Later	Next	After
Finally			In the end	

Words that can be used to compare two things

likewise	as	in the same way	one way
like	also	similarly	both

In the same way	One way
Also	Another way
Similarly	Both

Words that can be used to contrast things (show differences)

| but | still | although | on the other hand |
| however | yet | otherwise | even though |

On the other hand Although
Even though Yet
Still Nevertheless

Words that can be used to emphasize a point

| again | truly | especially | for this reason |
| to repeat | in fact | to emphasize | |

For this reason Truly In fact
Especially To emphasize To repeat

Words that can be used to conclude or summarize

| finally | as a result | to sum up | in conclusion |
| lastly | therefore | all in all | because |

Because As a result To sum it up Therefore
In conclusion All in all Because Finally
  Therefore

Words that can be used to add information

again	another	for instance	for example
also	and	moreover	additionally
as well	besides	along with	other
next	finally	in addition	

For example For instance Next Another
Additionally Besides Moreover Along with
Finally Next Also As well

Words that can be used to clarify

| in other words | for instance | that is |

For instance For example
In other words Equally important

What can I do to make my final copy look better?

Add Graphics to Your Writing

You can add information and interest to essays and reports by using diagrams, tables, and graphs.

Diagrams are drawings that show the parts of something. A diagram may leave out some parts to show only the parts you need to learn.

Picture diagrams show how something is put together.

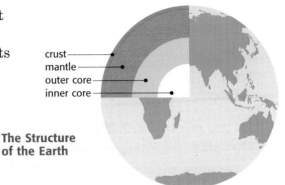

crust
mantle
outer core
inner core

The Structure of the Earth

Line diagrams also show how something is put together, but they show something you can't really see. Instead of objects, line diagrams show ideas and relationships.

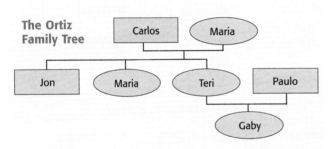

The Ortiz Family Tree

Carlos — Maria

Jon — Maria — Teri — Paulo

Gaby

Tables have two parts: rows and columns. Rows go across and show one kind of information or data. Columns go up and down and show a different kind of data.

To read a table, find where a row and a column meet. In the table to the right, if the wind speed is 15 and the air temperature is 20, the windchill factor is 6.

Windchill Chart												
Temperature (°F)												
Calm	40	35	30	25	20	15	10	5	0	-5	-10	-15
5	36	31	25	19	13	7	1	-5	-11	-16	-22	-28
10	34	27	21	15	9	3	-4	-10	-16	-22	-28	-35
15	32	25	19	13	6	0	-7	-13	-19	-26	-32	-39
20	30	24	17	11	4	-2	-9	-15	-22	-29	-35	-42
25	29	23	16	9	3	-4	-11	-17	-24	-31	-37	-44
30	28	22	15	8	1	-5	-12	-19	-26	-33	-39	-46

Wind Speed (mph)

organize
select support
REFERENCE
improve
575
A Writer's Resource

Graphs are pictures of information. **Bar graphs** show how things compare to one another. The bars on a bar graph may be vertical or horizontal. (*Vertical* means "up and down." *Horizontal* means "from side to side.") Sometimes the bars on graphs are called *columns*. The part that shows numbers is called the *scale*.

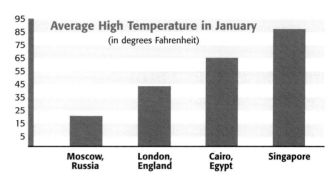

Average High Temperature in January
(in degrees Fahrenheit)

Pie graphs show how all the parts of something add up to make the whole. A pie graph often shows percentages. (A percentage is the part of a whole stated in hundredths: 35% = 35/100.) It's called a pie graph because it is usually in the shape of a pie or circle.

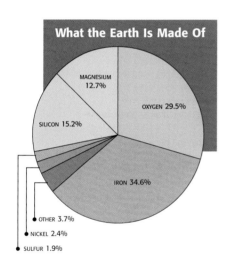

What the Earth Is Made Of

MAGNESIUM 12.7%
OXYGEN 29.5%
SILICON 15.2%
IRON 34.6%
OTHER 3.7%
NICKEL 2.4%
SULFUR 1.9%

Line graphs show how something changes as time goes by. A line graph always begins with an L-shaped grid. One line of the grid shows passing time; the other line shows numbers.

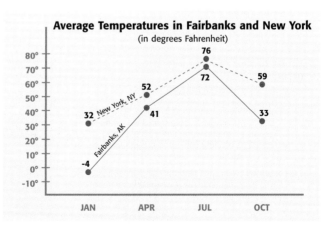

Average Temperatures in Fairbanks and New York
(in degrees Fahrenheit)

New York, NY: 32, 52, 76, 59
Fairbanks, AK: -4, 41, 72, 33

JAN APR JUL OCT

How should I set up my practical writing?

Use the Proper Format

Memos

A memo is a brief written message that you can share with a teacher, a coach, or a principal. Memos create a flow of information—asking and answering questions, giving instructions, describing work to be done, or reminding people about meetings.

Date: March 16, 2010

To: Mr. Ortega

From: Rebecca Ehly

Subject: Mid-Project Report on Training Rats

The goal of my science fair project is to train my rat Carmel to play basketball. I want to teach him to do four things:

1. Go to the rubber ball (about 1″ in diameter).
2. Push the ball with his nose across the basketball court that I made in his cage.
3. Pick up the ball with his forepaws.
4. Put the ball through the hoop (about 2″ above the floor of the cage).

Carmel has learned two steps: (1) go to the ball and (2) push it. I taught him how to do these things by luring him with pieces of cheddar cheese (extra sharp).

Unfortunately, I haven't been able to get Carmel to do ...ers 3 and 4. He won't lift the ball. I'm not sure what ...next. Do you have any suggestions?

Castle Construction for History Project

Description: For my history project on medieval life, I plan to build a scale model (2′ x 2′ x 2′) of an English castle and write an essay on the construction of castles for protection.

Materials:

1. Books on medieval life and on castles
2. 3′ x 3′ plywood board (for base)
3. Clay (for walls)
4. Toilet paper rolls (for frame of towers)
5. Toothpicks and glue (for ladders, gates)
6. Popsicle sticks and string (for drawbridge)
7. Cloth (for banners and tapestries)

Deadlines:

1. Jan. 25   Research medieval castles
2. Feb. 1   Choose a castle to build
3. Feb. 3   Design my model on paper as a blueprint
4. Feb. 10   Construct a scale model of castle
5. Feb. 16   Plan and write first draft of paper
6. Feb. 22   Complete paper and present project to class

Outcome: My project will help the class understand how a castle was built and how it was used.

Proposals

A proposal is a detailed plan for doing a project, solving a problem, or meeting a need.

Follow Guidelines

Letters

A letter is a written message sent through the mail. Letters follow a set format, including important contact information, a salutation or greeting, a body, and a closing signature. (See pages 276–277 for more information.)

> 1414 Johnson Street
> Walvan, WI 53000
> April 20, 2009
>
> Mayor Phillip Smith
> Walvan City Hall
> 111 Main Street
> Walvan, WI 53000
>
> Dear Mayor Smith:
>
> I am a student at Parker Lane Middle School. At a city council meeting last October, I asked the council to put up a stoplight at the intersection of 34th Avenue and Cottage Street. Six months later, cars are still going by too fast on 34th Avenue.
>
> I am not the only one who thinks this corner is dangerous. I passed around a petition asking for the stoplight, and more than 400 students, teachers, parents, and neighbors signed it. I have enclosed my petition. Mayor Smith, please vote for putting a traffic light at 34th Avenue and Cottage Street.
>
> Sincerely,
>
> *Ruby Keast*
>
> Ruby Keast

Envelope Addresses

Place the return address in the upper left corner, the destination address in the center, and the correct postage in the upper right corner.

> RUBY KEAST
> 1414 JOHNSON ST
> WALVAN WI 53000
>
>
>
> MAYOR PHILLIP SMITH
> WALVAN CITY HALL
> 111 MAIN ST
> WALVAN WI 53000

U.S. Postal Service Guidelines

1. Capitalize everything and leave out ALL punctuation.
2. Use the list of common abbreviations found on 634.1. Use numerals rather than words for numbered streets and avenues (9TH AVE NE, 3RD ST SW).
3. If you know the ZIP + 4 code, use it.

capitalize
SPELL
punctuate

Proofreader's Guide

improve
edit

Marking Punctuation

Periods

Use a **period** to end a sentence. Also use a period after initials, after abbreviations, and as a decimal point.

579.1
At the End of Sentences

Use a period to end a sentence that makes a statement or a request. Also use a period for a mild command, one that does not need an exclamation point. (See page 518.)

The Southern Ocean surrounds Antarctica. (statement)

Please point out the world's largest ocean on a map. (request)

Do not use a laser pointer. (mild command)

NOTE It is not necessary to place a period after a statement that has parentheses around it if it is part of another sentence.

The Southern Ocean is the fourth-largest ocean (it is larger than the Atlantic).

579.2
After Initials

Place a period after an initial.

J. K. Rowling (author)

Colin L. Powell (politician)

579.3
After Abbreviations

Place a period after each part of an abbreviation. Do not use periods with acronyms or initialisms. (See page 636.)

Abbreviations: Mr. Mrs. Ms. Dr. B.C.E. C.E.

Acronyms: AIDS NASA

Initialisms: NBC FBI

NOTE When an abbreviation is the last word in a sentence, use only one period at the end of the sentence.

My grandfather's full name is William Ryan James Koenig, Jr.

579.4
As Decimal Points

Use a period to separate dollars and cents and as a decimal point.

The price of a loaf of bread was $1.54 in 1992.

That price was only 35 cents, or 77.3 percent less, in 1972.

Question Marks

A **question mark** is used after an interrogative sentence and also to show doubt about the correctness of a fact or figure. (See page 518.)

580.1
At the End of Direct Questions

Use a question mark at the end of a direct question (an interrogative sentence).

Is a vegan a person who eats only vegetables?

580.2
At the End of Indirect Questions

No question mark is used after an indirect question. (An indirect question tells about a question you or someone else asked.)

Because I do not eat meat, I'm often asked if I am a vegetarian.

I asked the doctor if going meatless is harmful to my health.

580.3
To Show Doubt

Place a question mark within parentheses to show that you are unsure that a fact or figure is correct.

By the year 2020 (?) the number of vegetarians in the United States may approach 15 percent of the population.

Exclamation Points

An **exclamation point** may be placed after a word, a phrase, or a sentence to show emotion. (The exclamation point should not be overused.)

580.4
To Express Strong Feelings

Use an exclamation point to show excitement or strong feeling.

Yeah! Wow! Oh my!

Surprise! You've won the million-dollar sweepstakes!

Caution: Never use more than one exclamation point in writing assignments.

Incorrect: **Don't ever do that to me again!!!**

Correct: **Don't ever do that to me again!**

Grammar Practice

End Punctuation

On your own paper, write whether each of the following sentences needs a period, a question mark, or an exclamation point at the end.

Example: Wow, listen to that alarm ringing
exclamation point

1. Uh-oh, it's a fire drill

2. How many fire drills do you have at your school

3. Drills are held to make sure everyone knows how to get out of the building in an emergency

4. What can you do to make sure you will safely get out of a burning building

5. Should you take all of your books and belongings with you

6. You should simply get up and quickly walk out without taking anything with you

7. To prevent confusion and panic, everyone needs to exit calmly

8. Absolutely no pushing is allowed

9. Make sure those with a disability are assisted to the exit

10. Close the door on your way out to prevent a fire from spreading

11. Would you know another way out if the first exit was blocked

12. Meet at a chosen place to make sure everyone got out

13. Firefighter Jim asked us if we should go back into a burning building for any reason

14. The answer was a loud no

Next Step: Write about a fire drill you remember. End at least one sentence with a period, one with a question mark, and one with an exclamation point.

Commas . . .

Use a **comma** to indicate a pause or a change in thought. This helps to keep words and ideas from running together, so writing is easier to read. For a writer, no other form of punctuation is more important to understand than the comma.

582.1
Between Items in a Series

Use commas between words, phrases, or clauses in a series. (A series contains at least three items.) (See page 513.)

Chinese, English, and Hindi are the three most widely used languages in the world. (words)

Being comfortable with technology, working well with others, and knowing another language are important skills for today's workers. (phrases)

My dad works in a factory, my mom works in an office, and I work in school. (clauses)

582.2
To Keep Numbers Clear

Use commas to separate the digits in a number in order to distinguish hundreds, thousands, millions, and so on.

More than 104,000 people live in Kingston, the capital of Jamaica.

The population of the entire country of Liechtenstein is only 29,000.

NOTE Commas are not used in years.

The world population was 6.1 billion by 2003.

582.3
In Dates and Addresses

Use commas to distinguish items in an address and items in a date.

On August 28, 1963, Martin Luther King, Jr., gave his famous "I Have a Dream" speech.

The address of the King Center is 449 Auburn Avenue NE, Atlanta, Georgia 30312.

NOTE No comma is placed between the state and ZIP code. Also, when only the month and year are given, no comma is needed.

In January 2029 we will celebrate the 100th anniversary of Reverend King's birth.

Grammar Practice

Commas 1

■ Between Items in a Series
■ To Keep Numbers Clear
■ In Dates and Addresses

 For each sentence below, write the series, date, address, or number that should include a comma. Add the comma.

Example: A democracy, as Abraham Lincoln said, is a government of the people by the people and for the people.

of the people, by the people, and for the people

1. The first democracy was created in ancient Greece over 2000 years ago.

2. When colonial Americans declared independence from England on July 4 1776, they created a democracy.

3. Benjamin Franklin Thomas Jefferson and George Washington were men who worked to create an independent country.

4. Jefferson wrote the Declaration of Independence Franklin edited it and they both signed it.

5. The reasons for declaring independence included complaints about the king of England a wish to give power to the people and the desire for individual freedoms.

6. The people wanted the right to "life liberty and the pursuit of happiness."

7. The Declaration was signed on August 2 1776 in Philadelphia, which had a population at the time of about 25000.

8. The original document is kept in the National Archives Building 700 Pennsylvania Avenue Washington DC 20408.

Next Step: Write a sentence telling what you think your world would be like if the Declaration of Independence had not been adopted. Include commas between items in a series.

Commas . . .

Use commas to set off nonrestrictive phrases and clauses—those not necessary to the basic meaning of the sentence.

> **People get drinking water from surface water or groundwater, which makes up only 1 percent of the earth's water supply.**
> (The clause *which makes up only 1 percent of the earth's water supply* is additional information; it is nonrestrictive—not required. If the clause was left out, the meaning of the sentence would remain clear.)

Restrictive phrases or clauses—those that are needed in the sentence—restrict or limit the meaning of the sentence; they are not set off with commas.

> **Groundwater that is free from harmful pollutants is rare.**
> (The clause *that is free from harmful pollutants* is restrictive; it is needed to complete the meaning of the basic sentence and is not set off with commas.)

Use commas to set off a title, a name, or initials that follow a person's last name. (Use only one period if an initial comes at the end of a sentence.)

> **Melanie Prokat, M.D., is our family's doctor. However, she is listed in the phone book only as Prokat, M.**

NOTE Although commas are not necessary to set off "Jr." and "Sr." after a name, they may be used as long as a comma is used both before and after the abbreviation.

Use commas to set off a word, phrase, or clause that interrupts the main thought of a sentence. These interruptions usually can be identified through the following tests:

1. You can leave them out of a sentence without changing its meaning.

2. You can place them other places in the sentence without changing its meaning.

> **Our school, as we all know, is becoming overcrowded again.** (clause)
>
> **The gym, not the cafeteria, was expanded a while ago.** (phrase)
>
> **My history class, for example, has 42 students in it.** (phrase)
>
> **There are, indeed, about 1,000 people in my school.** (word)
>
> **The building, however, has room for only 850 students.** (word)

Grammar Practice

Commas 2

- ■ To Set Off Nonrestrictive Phrases and Clauses
- ■ To Set Off Titles or Initials
- ■ To Set Off Interruptions

 Rewrite each of the following sentences, placing commas where they are needed.

Example: Dr. Martin Luther King Jr. was originally named Michael.

Dr. Martin Luther King, Jr., was originally named Michael.

1. His parents Alberta and Martin Luther King Sr. renamed their son Martin when he was about six years old.

2. Benjamin Mays Ph.D. convinced Martin to begin a religious career when he finished college in 1948.

3. Reverend King became a very important leader as you may already know in the civil rights movement.

4. He believed that all people no matter what race or gender should be able to live and work together.

5. His nonviolent efforts toward peace which won him the Nobel Peace Prize in 1964 made him unpopular with some people.

6. His home for instance was bombed, and he was arrested several times.

7. King's assassination in 1968 however did not end his work.

8. His birthday in fact is a national holiday that is celebrated on the third Monday of January.

9. George Washington and Abraham Lincoln whose birthdays are also celebrated as national holidays are two other Americans who are honored in this way.

Next Step: Write a short paragraph describing what your school does for Presidents' Day or Martin Luther King, Jr., Day. Use sentences with commas that set off nonrestrictive phrases or clauses, titles or initials, and interruptions.

Commas . . .

586.1
To Set Off Appositives

Commas set off an appositive from the rest of the sentence. An appositive is a word or phrase that identifies or renames a noun or pronoun. (See page 520.)

> **The capital of Cyprus, Nicosia, has a population of almost 643,000.** (*Nicosia* renames *capital of Cyprus,* so the word is set off with commas.)

> **Cyprus, an island in the Mediterranean Sea, is about half the size of Connecticut.** (*An island in the Mediterranean Sea* identifies *Cyprus,* so the phrase is set off with commas.)

Do not use commas with appositives that are necessary to the basic meaning of the sentence.

> **The Mediterranean island Cyprus is about half the size of Connecticut.** (*Cyprus* is not set off because it is needed to make the sentence clear.)

586.2
To Separate Equal Adjectives

Use commas to separate two or more adjectives that equally modify the same noun.

> **Comfortable, efficient cars are becoming more important to drivers.** (*Comfortable* and *efficient* are separated by a comma because they modify *cars* equally.)

> **Some automobiles run on clean, renewable sources of energy.** (*Clean* and *renewable* are separated by a comma because they modify *sources* equally.)

> **Conventional gasoline engines emit a lot of pollution.** (*Conventional* and *gasoline* do not modify *engines* equally; therefore, no comma separates the two.)

Use these tests to help you decide if adjectives modify equally:

1. Switch the order of the adjectives; if the sentence is clear, the adjectives modify equally.

> **Yes: Efficient, comfortable cars are becoming more important to drivers.**

> **No: Gasoline conventional engines emit a lot of pollution.**

2. Put the word *and* between the adjectives; if the sentence is clear, use a comma when *and* is taken out.

> **Yes: Comfortable and efficient cars are becoming more important to drivers.**

> **No: Conventional and gasoline engines emit a lot of pollution.**

Grammar Practice

Commas 3

■ **To Set Off Appositives**

For each sentence below, write the appositive phrase and the noun it renames. Set off the appositive with commas.

Example: "Mexamerica" the region between Houston and Los Angeles is the location of choice for many people.
"Mexamerica," the region between Houston and Los Angeles,

1. San Diego California's second-largest city boasts some of the best weather in the country.

2. Austin the capital of Texas has a strong Tejano music scene.

3. San Antonio another Texas city hosts the annual Fiesta San Antonio to remember its war heroes.

4. Las Cruces, New Mexico, was ranked by *Forbes* a financial newsmagazine as the best small city to live and work in.

■ **To Separate Equal Adjectives**

For each numbered sentence below, write the adjectives that need commas between them. Add the commas.

Example: Los Angeles is located along the rugged sandy coast of southern California.
rugged, sandy

(1) Considered the "capital" of Mexamerica by some, Los Angeles is an exciting spread-out city. **(2)** It is full of lively unique neighborhoods. **(3)** Although many people live an enjoyable rewarding life in Los Angeles, the city also has its problems. **(4)** Everyone seems to know about the slow-moving congested traffic and the very high cost of living. **(5)** Despite the city's troubles, many people still like living in golden sunny Los Angeles.

Commas . . .

588.1
To Set Off Dialogue

Use commas to set off the exact words of a speaker from the rest of the sentence. (Also see page 556.)

> The firefighter said, "When we cannot successfully put out a fire, we try to keep it from spreading."

> "When we cannot successfully put out a fire, we try to keep it from spreading," the firefighter said.

NOTE Do not use a comma or quotation marks for indirect quotations. The words *if* and *that* often signal dialogue that is being reported rather than quoted.

> The firefighter said that when they cannot successfully put out a fire, they try to keep it from spreading. (These are not the speaker's exact words.)

588.2
In Direct Address

Use commas to separate a noun of direct address from the rest of the sentence. (A noun of direct address is a noun that names a person spoken to in the sentence.)

> Hanae, did you know that an interior decorator can change wallpaper and fabrics on a computer screen?

> Sure, Jack, and an architect can use a computer to see how light will fall in different parts of a building.

588.3
To Set Off Interjections

Use commas to separate an interjection or a weak exclamation from the rest of the sentence.

> No kidding, you mean that one teacher has to manage a class of 42 pupils? (weak exclamation)

> Uh-huh, and that teacher has other classes that size. (interjection)

588.4
To Set Off Explanatory Phrases

Use commas to separate an explanatory phrase from the rest of the sentence.

> English, the language computers speak worldwide, is also the most widely used language in science and medicine.

> More than 750 million people, about an eighth of the world's population, speak English as a foreign language.

Grammar Practice

Commas 4

- ■ **To Set Off Dialogue**
- ■ **In Direct Address**
- ■ **To Set Off Interjections**
- ■ **To Set Off Explanatory Phrases**

 Rewrite each of the following sentences, placing commas where they are needed.

Example: Whales are warm-blooded mammals breathing air through their blowholes and are found in all oceans.

Whales are warm-blooded mammals, breathing air through their blowholes, and are found in all oceans.

1. While most whales swim in groups, others like fin whales swim alone or in pairs.

2. Ms. Smith asked "Laticia did you know the longest dive by a sperm whale lasted more than an hour?"

3. Laticia replied "Uh-uh but I know sperm whales can dive to depths of more than a mile."

4. Jeremy said "Well that's hard to believe. Ms. Smith how do they do that?"

5. "Fish swim by moving their tails from side to side, but whales swim by pumping their tails up and down" she said.

6. Some of the sea creatures we know as dolphins are actually whales such as the killer whale and the pilot whale.

7. Humpback whales named for the hump behind the dorsal fin are an endangered species.

8. Laticia said "Other whales including the right and blue whales are also endangered."

Next Step: Write a brief, imagined conversation between whales. Use commas correctly to set off dialogue and nouns of direct address.

Commas

590.1
To Separate Introductory Clauses and Phrases

Use a comma to separate an adverb clause or a long phrase from the independent clause that follows it.

If every automobile in the country were a light shade of red, we'd live in a pink-car nation. (adverb clause)

According to some experts, solar-powered cars will soon be common. (long modifying phrase)

590.2
In Compound Sentences

Use a comma between two independent clauses that are joined by a coordinating conjunction (such as *and, but, or, nor, for, so,* and *yet*), forming a compound sentence. An independent clause expresses a complete thought and can stand alone as a sentence. (Also see page 516.)

Many students enjoy working on computers, so teachers are finding new ways to use them in the classroom.

Computers can be valuable in education, but many schools cannot afford enough of them.

Avoid Comma Splices: A comma splice results when two independent clauses are "spliced" together with only a comma—and no conjunction. (See page 506.)

SCHOOL DAZE

Grammar Practice

Commas 5

- ■ To Separate Introductory Clauses and Phrases
- ■ In Compound Sentences

 For each sentence below, write the word or words that should be followed by a comma. Add the comma.

Example: I sat down to eat lunch and I began to slurp my soup.
lunch,

1. Aunt Marianna wanted me to improve my table manners so she enrolled me in a class.

2. After the teacher, Ms. Wyatt, introduced herself she said, "The main thing to remember is to be polite."

3. If you are a guest at someone else's house don't sit down at the table or begin eating before the host does.

4. Along with Ms. Wyatt we sat at a beautifully set table.

5. Ramón wanted to sip some of his water but he didn't know which glass was his.

6. Your glass is always placed to the right of your plate and your bread plate goes on the left.

7. Before doing anything else put your napkin on your lap.

8. When you want to butter your bread put some butter on your bread plate first.

9. Since there was more than one fork at each place setting Ms. Wyatt said that we should use the utensils from the outside in.

10. Then she said, "While you're eating take your time yet try to keep pace with the other guests."

Next Step: Write two sentences telling how your table manners could be improved. Include an introductory phrase or clause in one sentence; the other should be a compound sentence. Use commas correctly.

Test Prep!

Number your paper from 1 to 12. For each underlined part of the paragraphs below, write the letter (from the next page) of the best way to punctuate it.

Our science <u>teacher Ms. Hewlitt</u> told us that the word *robot* comes
(1)
from a Czech word that means "tedious labor." What is a <u>robot It is</u>
(2)
a machine that works for people.

There are almost five million robots in the world <u>today and</u>
(3)
16 percent of them work in factories. Every day, these robots do the same

thing over and over again. In other <u>words they</u> do boring tasks. Robots
(4)
also do work that is <u>too faraway too dangerous or even impossible</u> for
(5)
people to perform.

In the late 1950s, one of the first modern <u>robots the Unimate</u> was
(6)
set up at a factory. In the '80s, better computers made more powerful

robots <u>possible</u> At the same <u>time, the</u> automotive industry started using
(7) **(8)**
robots on its assembly lines. <u>Today in fact</u> robots can make cars faster
(9)
than people ever could. As a result, all that's left for people to do is

<u>supervise maintain and repair</u> the machines.
(10)
In the future, robots may be programmed to do more complex tasks.

Robots will probably always be part of our <u>world but</u> it is unlikely that
(11)
they'll ever take over. <u>Whew</u>
(12)

1 (A) teacher Ms. Hewlitt,
   (B) teacher, Ms. Hewlitt,
   (C) teacher, Ms. Hewlitt
   (D) correct as is

2 (A) robot?
   (B) robot.
   (C) robot!
   (D) correct as is

3 (A) today and,
   (B) today, and
   (C) today, and,
   (D) correct as is

4 (A) words they,
   (B) words, they
   (C) words, they,
   (D) correct as is

5 (A) too faraway, too
      dangerous, or even
      impossible
   (B) too faraway, too dangerous
      or even impossible
   (C) too faraway too dangerous,
      or even impossible
   (D) correct as is

6 (A) robots, the Unimate,
   (B) robots the Unimate,
   (C) robots, the Unimate
   (D) correct as is

7 (A) possible?
   (B) possible.
   (C) possible!
   (D) correct as is

8 (A) time the
   (B) time. The
   (C) time the,
   (D) correct as is

9 (A) Today in fact,
   (B) Today, in fact,
   (C) Today, in fact
   (D) correct as is

10 (A) supervise, maintain,
       and repair
   (B) supervise, maintain,
       and repair,
   (C) supervise, maintain
       and repair
   (D) correct as is

11 (A) world, but
   (B) world but,
   (C) world, but,
   (D) correct as is

12 (A) Whew.
   (B) Whew!
   (C) Whew?
   (D) correct as is

PUNCTUATION

Semicolons

Use a **semicolon** to suggest a stronger pause than a comma indicates. A semicolon may also serve in place of a period.

594.1
To Join Two Independent Clauses

In a compound sentence, use a semicolon to join two independent clauses that are not connected with a coordinating conjunction. (See page 744.)

> The United States has more computers than any other country; its residents own more than 164 million of them.

594.2
With Conjunctive Adverbs

A semicolon is also used to join two independent clauses when the clauses are connected by a conjunctive adverb (such as *as a result, for example, however, therefore,* and *instead*). (See 738.1)

> Japan is next on that list; however, the Japanese have only 50 million computers.

> You might think that the billion people of China own a lot of computers; instead, the smaller country of Germany has twice as many computers as China.

594.3
To Separate Groups That Contain Commas

Use a semicolon between groups of words in a series when one or more of the groups already contain commas.

> Many of our community's residents separate their garbage into bins for newspapers, cardboard, and junk mail; glass, metal, and plastic; and nonrecyclable trash.

SCHOOL DAZE

It's true that I have only a few minutes to finish this; **however,** I am not worried.

Well, that makes one of us.

Grammar Practice

Semicolons

For each of the following sentences, write the word or words that should be followed by a semicolon. Add the semicolon.

Example: Go to the library first then do your homework.
          first;

1. Mom said I could go to Jean's house however, I have to do the dishes before I go.

2. Cam must be an artist this drawing is fantastic!

3. Sanjay is sick therefore, he can't go to Manny's party.

4. I have already read this book it's about a two-headed monster.

The following directions will help you create a sentence that uses semicolons. The semicolons will separate groups of words that already contain commas.

1. Think of three toys that involve imagination and write down their names.

2. Next write a list of three games.

3. Finally, write three toys a child would use outside.

4. Now copy and complete the following sentence. Fill in the blanks with your own toy lists. Make sure to include both the commas and the semicolons to separate your lists.

   My little sister Keisha's favorite toys are her _____, _____, and _____; her _____ game, _____ game, and _____ game; and her _____, _____, and _____ _____.

Next Step: Write a sentence about your favorite foods. Think of plenty of choices. Use semicolons between groups of words in a series, as in the sentence above.

Colons

A **colon** may be used to introduce a list or an important point. Colons are also used in business letters and between the numbers in time.

596.1
To Introduce Lists

Use a colon to introduce a list. The colon usually comes after words describing the subject of the list (as in the first example below) or after summary words, such as *the following* or *these things*. Do not use a colon after a verb or preposition.

> Certain items are still difficult to recycle: foam cups, car tires, and toxic chemicals.

> To conserve water, you should do the following three things: fix drippy faucets, install a low-flow showerhead, and turn the water off while brushing your teeth.

> Incorrect: To conserve water, you should: install a low-flow showerhead, turn the water off while brushing your teeth, and fix drippy faucets.

596.2
To Introduce Sentences

A colon may be used to introduce a sentence, a question, or a quotation.

> This is why air pollution is bad: We are sacrificing our health and the health of all other life on the planet.

> Answer this question for me: Why aren't more people concerned about global warming?

> Joaquin shared this with us: "Iceland is the world's leader in the use of renewable energy."

596.3
After Salutations

A colon may be used after the salutation of a business letter.

> Dear Ms. Manners: Dear Dr. Warmle: Dear Professor Potter:
> Dear Captain Elliot: Dear Senator:

596.4
For Emphasis

Use a colon to emphasize a word or phrase.

> The newest alternative energy is also the most common element on earth: hydrogen.

> Here's one thing that can help save energy: a programmable thermostat.

596.5
Between Numbers in Time

Use a colon between the parts of a number that indicate time.

> My thermostat automatically sets my heat to 60 degrees between 11:00 p.m. and 6:00 a.m.

PUNCTUATION

Grammar Practice

Colons

The following letter needs colons placed correctly. Write the words or numbers that need colons. Then add them.

Example: These are a few reasons to go to the dentist to have your teeth cleaned, to relieve a toothache, and to get a cavity filled.
dentist:

1 Dear Dr. Meyer

2   It was 330 p.m. last Thursday, almost time to have my cavity

3 filled. I was a bit nervous. As I was gnawing on my fingernails, I

4 thought of a question What are these things made of, anyway?

5   I remember hearing that fingernails are made of the same stuff

6 as these other things horses' hooves, birds' feathers, and bulls' horns.

7 They're also made of the same substance as another thing hair.

8   One great thing about nails and hair is that it doesn't hurt to

9 cut into them. By 400, as the drill was making the hole in my tooth

10 even bigger, I had this thought It would be fantastic to have teeth

11 like nails and hair, too! Just think, Dr. Meyer—without using any

12 anesthetic, you could do any of these procedures fill a cavity, fix a

13 broken tooth, or file a chipped tooth.

14   Well, Dr. Meyer, it doesn't hurt to dream! Thanks for helping

15 me take care of something very important to me my teeth.

16 Sincerely,

17 James Ormon

Next Step: Write a sentence containing a colon; after the colon, list all the different ways a colon can be used.

Quotation Marks . . .

Quotation marks are used in a number of ways:
- to set off the exact words of a speaker,
- to punctuate material quoted from another source,
- to punctuate words used in a special way, and
- to punctuate certain titles.

598.1
To Set Off a Speaker's Exact Words

Place quotation marks before and after a speaker's words in dialogue. Only the exact words of the speaker are placed within quotation marks.

> Marla said, "I've decided to become a firefighter."

> "A firefighter," said Juan, "can help people in many ways."

598.2
For Quotations Within Quotations

Use single quotation marks to punctuate a quotation within a quotation.

> Sung Kim asked, "Did Marla just say, 'I've decided to become a firefighter'?"

When titles occur within a quotation, use single quotation marks to punctuate those that require quotation marks.

> Juan said, "Springsteen's song 'The Rising' really inspired her."

598.3
To Set Off Quoted Material

When quoting material from another source, place quotation marks before and after the source's exact words.

> In her book *Living the Life You Deserve,* Tess Spyeder explains, "Choose a job you'll enjoy doing day after day over one that will fatten your bank account."

598.4
To Set Off Long Quoted Material

If more than one paragraph is quoted from a single source, quotation marks are placed before each paragraph and at the end of the last paragraph.

Quotations that are more than four lines are usually set off from the rest of the paper by indenting each line 10 spaces from the left. Quotations that are set off in this way require no quotation marks either before or after the quoted material.

Grammar Practice

Quotation Marks 1

■ **To Set Off a Speaker's Exact Words**
■ **For Quotations Within Quotations**

Rewrite the following conversation, using quotation marks correctly.

Example: Ms. Green said, Don't forget that your book reports are due next week.

Ms. Green said, "Don't forget that your book reports are due next week."

1 Reneé asked, What book will you use for your book report?

2 Fadi said, I've always liked the first Harry Potter book, so I'll

3 probably use that.

4 I just read a new book called *Hoot,* Reneé said. That's what I'm

5 going to report on.

6 I haven't heard of that book. What's it about? asked Fadi.

7 It's about three kids who help save some endangered miniature

8 owls. See, this big company wants to build a pancake house where

9 the owls' nest is, she said.

10 When you say, build a pancake house, do you mean they want

11 to build a house out of pancakes? Fadi asked.

12 Very funny, said Reneé. I think you know what I mean. It's a

13 restaurant that sells pancakes.

14 And so the kids stop this restaurant from being built? Fadi

15 asked.

16 I'm not going to tell you, Reneé said. You'll have to read the

17 book yourself if you want to find out!

Next Step: Imagine a conversation you have with a friend about a book you've read recently. Write a few lines of this dialogue. Make sure you use quotation marks correctly.

Quotation Marks

Always place periods and commas inside quotation marks.

> "I don't know," said Lac.

> Lac said, "I don't know."

Place an exclamation point or a question mark inside the quotation marks when it punctuates the quotation.

> Ms. Wiley asked, "Can you actually tour the Smithsonian on the Internet?"

Place it outside when it punctuates the main sentence.

> Did I hear you say, "Now we can tour the Smithsonian on the Internet"?

Place semicolons or colons outside quotation marks.

> First I will read the article "Sonny's Blues"; then I will read "The Star Café" in my favorite music magazine.

Quotation marks also may be used (1) to set apart a word that is being discussed, (2) to indicate that a word is slang, or (3) to point out that a word or phrase is being used in a special way.

> 1. Renny uses the word "like" entirely too much.
> 2. Man, your car is really "phat."
> 3. Aunt Lulu, an editor at a weekly magazine, says she has "issues."

Use quotation marks to punctuate titles of songs, poems, short stories, lectures, episodes of radio or television programs, chapters of books, and articles found in magazines, newspapers, or encyclopedias. (Also see 602.3.)

> "21 Questions" (song)
> "The Reed Flute's Song" (poem)
> "Old Man at the Bridge" (short story)
> "Birthday Boys" (a television episode)
> "The Foolish and the Weak" (a chapter in a book)
> "Science Careers Today" (lecture)
> "Teen Rescues Stranded Dolphin" (newspaper article)

NOTE When you punctuate a title, capitalize the first word, last word, and every word in between—except for articles (*a, an, the*), short prepositions (*at, to, with,* and so on), and coordinating conjunctions (*and, but, or*). (See 624.2.)

Grammar Practice

Quotation Marks 2

■ Placement of Punctuation

Rewrite the following sentences, placing commas and end punctuation where needed.

Example: "We're learning some new songs in chorus" said Ryan.
"We're learning some new songs in chorus,"
said Ryan.

1. "I hear that's a fun class" said Elisa.

2. "Who is the new teacher" she asked.

3. Ryan said, "Mr. Pescados"

4. "Did you say 'Mr. Pescados' If you did, that's funny" Elisa said.

5. She continued, "*Pescados* means 'fish' in Spanish"

■ To Punctuate Titles

For each of the following sentences, write the title that needs quotation marks. (Be careful to place commas or periods correctly.)

Example: The article Remember When talks about pleasant childhood memories.
"Remember When"

1. When I was little, I've Been Workin' on the Railroad was my favorite song.

2. I also remember learning the poem One, Two, Buckle My Shoe.

3. Mom read short bedtime stories from *Grimms' Fairy Tales,* and I never got tired of listening to Rapunzel.

4. I must have watched Day of the Dumpster, the pilot episode of *Mighty Morphin' Power Rangers,* a dozen times!

5. The recent *Time for Kids* magazine article Having a Blast in the Past made me think of all these memories.

Italics and Underlining

Italics is slightly slanted type. In this sentence, the word *happiness* is typed in italics. In handwritten material, each word or letter that should be in italics is **underlined**. (See an example on page 400.)

(See an example on page 400.)

602.1
In Printed Material

Print words in italics when you are using a computer.

> In *Tuck Everlasting,* the author explores what it would be like to live forever.

602.2
In Handwritten Material

Underline words that should be italicized when you are writing by hand.

> In <u>Tuck Everlasting,</u> the author explores what it would be like to live forever.

602.3
In Titles

Italicize (or underline) the titles of books, plays, book-length poems, magazines, newspapers, radio and television programs, movies, videos, cassettes, CD's, and the names of aircraft and ships.

> *Walk Two Moons* (book)   *Teen People* (magazine)
>
> *Fairies and Dragons* (movie)   *Everwood* (TV program)
>
> *The Young and the Hopeless* (CD)   *U.S.S. Arizona* (ship)
>
> *Columbia* (space shuttle)   *Daily Herald* (newspaper)

Exception: Do not italicize or put quotation marks around your own title at the top of your written work.

> A Day Without Water (personal writing: do not italicize)

602.4
For Scientific and Foreign Words

Italicize (or underline) scientific and foreign words that are not commonly used in everyday English.

> *Spinacia oleracea* is the scientific term for spinach.
>
> Many store owners who can help Spanish-speaking customers display an *Hablamos Español* sign in their windows.

602.5
For Special Uses

Italicize (or underline) a number, letter, or word that is being discussed or used in a special way. (Sometimes quotation marks are used for this same reason.)

> Matt's hat has a bright red *A* on it.

PUNCTUATION

Grammar Practice

Italics and Underlining

Write the word or words that should be italicized in each sentence. Underline the words.

Example: I just finished reading an article in Teen People.
Teen People

1. In the article, it says that one of the singers in Coldplay has 007 on his license plate.

2. Yes, he's a James Bond fan—his favorite movie is Thunderball.

3. You might say some of the characters in this movie, featuring some amazing underwater action, are benthic (they're bottom-dwellers).

4. James Bond, introduced in Ian Fleming's novel Casino Royale, first appeared on film in the television series Climax! in 1954.

5. Bond works for the British Secret Service; an actual British navy ship, the Devonshire, was used in the Bond movie Tomorrow Never Dies.

6. Two of Bond's associates have the letters M and Q for their names.

7. His boss used the word prism in telegrams as a sign of approval.

8. Did Bond's enemies ever say non, merci (no, thanks) to him?

9. A French media company publishes James Bond Magazine, and 007 Magazine is available to members of the James Bond International Fan Club.

10. Almost all the Bond movies have a soundtrack available on CD, and my favorite is The World Is Not Enough.

Next Step: Write some sentences that include the names of your favorite CD, movie, and book or magazine. Use italics (underlining) correctly.

Apostrophes . . .

Use **apostrophes** to form contractions, to form certain plurals, or to show possession.

604.1
In Contractions

Use an apostrophe to form a contraction, showing that one or more letters have been left out of a word.

Common Contractions

can't (cannot)	**couldn't** (could not)	**didn't** (did not)
doesn't (does not)	**don't** (do not)	**hasn't** (has not)
haven't (have not)	**isn't** (is not)	**I'll** (I will)
I'd (I would)	**I'm** (I am)	**I've** (I have)
they'll (they will)	**they'd** (they would)	**they've** (they have)
they're (they are)	**won't** (will not)	**wouldn't** (would not)
you'll (you will)	**you'd** (you would)	**you've** (you have)
you're (you are)		

604.2
In Place of Omitted Letters or Numbers

Use an apostrophe to show that one or more digits have been left out of a number, or that one or more letters have been left out of a word to show a special pronunciation.

class of '99 (*19* is left out)

g'bye (the letters *ood* are left out of *good-bye*)

NOTE Letters and numbers should not be omitted in most writing assignments; however, they may be omitted in dialogue to make it sound like real people are talking.

604.3
To Form Some Plurals

Use an apostrophe and *s* to form the plural of a letter, a sign, a number, or a word being discussed as a word.

A's   8's   +'s   to's

Don't use too many *and*'s in your writing.

604.4
To Form Singular Possessives

To form the possessive of a singular noun, add an apostrophe and *s*.

the game's directions	Dr. Mill's theory
Ross's bike	Roz's hair

NOTE When a singular noun with more than one syllable ends with an *s* or *z* sound, the possessive may be formed by adding just an apostrophe.

Texas' oil (or) **Texas's oil   Carlos' mother** (or) **Carlos's mother**

Grammar Practice

Apostrophes 1

■ **In Contractions**
■ **In Place of Omitted Letters or Numbers**

 In the following sentences, apostrophes are missing from numbers or words. Write the words or numbers with their apostrophes.

> **Example:** Comets arent solid rock, but when Grandpa was in school (the class of 65), people thought they were.
>
> *aren't   '70*

1. Jermaine enjoys reading his science book, published in 98.

2. The book says that space travelers wouldnt be able to take enough food and fuel for a trip to the stars.

3. Theyd run out of supplies long before they reached Pluto.

4. Back in 79, astronomers saw Pluto cross Neptune's orbit.

5. For the next 20 years, Pluto wasnt the most distant planet in our solar system—Neptune was.

■ **To Form Some Plurals**
■ **To Form Singular Possessives**

 In the following sentences, apostrophes are missing from some words. Write the words with their apostrophes.

> **Example:** A rocket must travel 25,000 miles per hour or about 7 miles per second, to escape Earths gravity.
>
> *Earth's*

1. How many 0s are needed to show the distance already covered by the space probe *Voyager 2?*

2. *Voyagers* cameras took pictures around Jupiter and Neptune.

3. In 2005, the Hubbles powerful telescope helped astronomers photograph the Carina Nebula maelstrom.

4. Today, the worlds most powerful telescopes allow us to see galaxies that are 13 billion light-years away.

Apostrophes

606.1
To Form Plural Possessives

The possessive form of plural nouns ending in *s* is usually made by adding just an apostrophe.

> students' homework teachers' lounge

For plural nouns not ending in *s*, an apostrophe and *s* must be added.

> children's book people's opinions

Remember: The word immediately before the apostrophe is the owner.

> student's project (*student* is the owner)
> students' project (*students* are the owners)

606.2
To Show Shared Possession

When possession is shared by more than one noun, add an apostrophe and *s* to the last noun in the series.

> Uncle Reggie, Aunt Rosie, and my mom's garden
> (All three own the garden.)
> Uncle Reggie's, Aunt Rosie's, and my mom's gardens
> (Each person owns a garden.)

606.3
To Form Possessives with Compound Nouns

The possessive of a compound noun is formed by placing the possessive ending after the last word.

> her sister-in-law's hip-hop music (singular)
> her sisters-in-law's tastes in music (plural)
> the secretary of state's husband (singular)
> the secretaries of state's husbands (plural)

606.4
To Form Possessives with Indefinite Pronouns

The possessive of an indefinite pronoun is formed by adding an apostrophe and *s*.

> no one's anyone's somebody's

NOTE In pronouns that use *else,* add an apostrophe and *s* to the second word.

> somebody else's anyone else's

606.5
To Express Time or Amount

Use an apostrophe with an adjective that is part of an expression indicating time (month, day, hour) or amount.

> In today's Spanish class, we talked about going to Spain.
> My father lost more than an hour's work when that thunderstorm knocked out our power.
> I bought a couple dollars' worth of grapes at the roadside stand.

Grammar Practice

Apostrophes 2

- To Form Plural Possessives
- To Show Shared Possession
- To Form Possessives with Compound Nouns
- To Form Possessives with Indefinite Pronouns
- To Express Time or Amount

 In each of the following sentences, one or more words are missing an apostrophe. Write the words with the apostrophes placed correctly.

Example: James Madison and Alexander Hamiltons report called for revising the Articles of Confederation.
Hamilton's

1. More than four years work was needed to create the new Constitution of the United States.

2. Our forefathers first ideas for a United States government were written in 1781 as the Articles of Confederation.

3. George Washington had accepted the commander in chiefs role in the Continental Army.

4. By 1787, however, he was not sure that the Articles truly represented everyones best interests.

5. Twelve of the original thirteen states delegates met to discuss the country's future, and Washington was named president of this Constitutional Convention.

6. It was an opportunity for everybodys ideas to be heard.

7. The delegates new document, called the Constitution of the United States, was the product of the convention.

8. George Washingtons, Benjamin Franklins, and Alexander Hamiltons signatures all appeared on that document.

9. The summers efforts had been successful.

10. In 1788, two final states votes for the Constitution meant that nine states had ratified it, and it became law.

Hyphens . . .

Use a **hyphen** to divide words at the end of a line and to form compound words. Also use a hyphen between the numbers in a fraction and to join numbers that indicate the life span of an individual, the scores of a game, and so on.

608.1
To Divide Words

Use a hyphen to divide a word when you run out of room at the end of a line. A word may be divided only between syllables. Here are some additional guidelines:

- Never divide a one-syllable word: *raised, through.*
- Avoid dividing a word of five letters or less: *paper, study.*
- Never divide a one-letter syllable from the rest of the word: *omit-ted,* **not** *o-mitted.*
- Never divide abbreviations or contractions: *NASA, wouldn't.*
- Never divide the last word in more than two lines in a row or the last word in a paragraph.
- When a vowel is a syllable by itself, divide the word after the vowel: *epi-sode,* **not** *ep-isode.*

NOTE Refer to a dictionary if you're not sure how to divide a word.

608.2
In Compound Words

A hyphen is used in some compound words, including numbers from twenty-one to ninety-nine.

about-face	warm-up	time-out
down-to-earth	ice-skating	high-rise
thirty-three	seventy-five	

608.3
To Create New Words

A hyphen is often used to form new words beginning with the prefixes *self, ex, all,* and *great.* A hyphen is also used with suffixes such as *elect* and *free.*

self-cleaning	ex-friend	all-natural	germ-free
self-esteem	ex-president	great-aunt	mayor-elect

608.4
Between Numbers in a Fraction

Use a hyphen between the numbers in a fraction. Do not, however, use a hyphen between the numerator and denominator when one or both are already hyphenated.

four-tenths   five-sixteenths   seven thirty-seconds (7/32)

Grammar Practice

Hyphens 1

- **To Divide Words**
- **In Compound Words**

 If the underlined words are presented correctly, write "correct." If not, write the correct form. Check a dictionary if you are not sure.

Example: <u>Twenty-one</u> gym students went outside just as a <u>po-werful</u> storm soaked the playing field.

correct, power-ful or pow-erful

1. <u>Fifty five</u> minutes of exercise is required each week, and that doesn't include a <u>warm-up</u>.

2. A <u>top-notch</u> physical-education teacher instructs students <u>a-bout</u> the value of regular exercise.

3. We'd rather play a game than do calisthenics, but that <u>would-n't</u> make us sweat enough, I guess.

4. Still, playing <u>volleyball</u> is more fun than doing <u>pushups</u>.

- **To Create New Words**
- **Between Numbers in a Fraction**

 For each of the following sentences, write the correct form of the underlined words.

Example: The coach was surprised that <u>three fourths</u> of his students were very fast runners.

three-fourths

1. Jamal saw that <u>two thirds</u> of his class ran faster than he could.

2. Since the coach was an <u>exrunner</u>, he knew that Jamal might be a better sprinter.

3. Jamal ran the 50-yard dash and beat <u>ninetenths</u> of the class.

4. Now Jamal is <u>self motivated</u> to improve his running skills.

5. He told his <u>greatgrandmother</u> about his new goal.

Hyphens

Use a hyphen to join two or more words that work together to form a single-thought adjective before a noun. Generally, hyphenate any compound adjective that might be misread if it is not hyphenated—use common sense. (See page 488.)

smiley-face sticker   dress-up clothes   fresh-breeze scent

Use the tests below to determine if a hyphen is needed.

1. When a compound adjective is made of a noun plus an adjective, it should be hyphenated.

    microwave-safe cookware   book-smart student

2. When the compound adjective is made of a noun plus a participle (*ing* or *ed* form of a verb), it should be hyphenated.

    bone-chilling story   vitamin-enriched cereal

3. Hyphenate a compound adjective that is a phrase (includes conjunctions or prepositions).

    heat-and-serve meals   refrigerator-to-oven dishes

Do *not* hyphenate compound adjectives in these instances:

1. When words forming the adjective come after the noun, do not hyphenate.

    This cookware is microwave safe.
    The cereal was vitamin enriched.

2. If the first of the two words ends in *ly,* do not hyphenate.

    newly designed computer   rarely seen species

3. Do not use a hyphen when a number or letter is the final part of a one-thought adjective.

    grade A milk   level 6 textbook

Use a hyphen to join a capital letter to a noun or participle.

U-turn   Y-axis   T-bar   A-frame
PG-rated movie   X-ray

Use a hyphen with prefixes or suffixes to avoid confusion or awkward spelling.

Re-collect (not recollect) **the reports we handed back last week.**
It has a shell-like (not shelllike) **texture.**

Grammar Practice

Hyphens 2

■ To Form Adjectives
■ To Join Letters to Words

 For each of the following sentences, write the word or words that should be joined by a hyphen.

Example: Truc found his T shirt rolled up in a ball under his bed.
T-shirt

1. The tie dyed shirt was all wrinkled, but he didn't have time to iron it.

2. Truc put the shirt on and looked for his acid washed jeans.

3. He raced from his fifth floor apartment to the sidewalk in front of the building.

4. It was early October, and he could smell a burning leaves odor in the air.

5. He ran back up to the apartment and grabbed his V neck sweater.

6. He decided to take his fleece lined jacket, too, just in case it got colder.

7. Truc was meeting Matt, and they were going to see a G rated, animated movie at the new theater in town.

8. Matt said it looked like a color blind designer had painted the lobby of the theater.

9. Truc and Matt sat in the top row seats of the balcony and settled in to watch the movie.

Next Step: Write two sentences about the movie Truc and Matt saw. Include a hyphenated adjective in each sentence.

Dashes

The **dash** can be used to show a sudden break in a sentence, to emphasize a word or clause, and to show that someone's speech is being interrupted. There is no space before or after a dash.

612.1
To Indicate a Sudden Break

A dash can be used to show a sudden break in a sentence.

> The three of us came down with colds, lost our voices, and missed the football game—all because we had practiced in the rain.

612.2
For Emphasis

A dash may be used to emphasize or explain a word, a series of words, a phrase, or a clause.

> Vitamins and minerals—important dietary supplements—can improve your diet.

> The benefits of vitamin A—better vision and a stronger immune system—are well known.

612.3
To Indicate Interrupted Speech

Use a dash to show that someone's speech is being interrupted by another person.

NOTE In typed material, if you don't know the keyboard shortcut for a dash, you can type two hyphens without a space before or after.

> Well—yes, I understand—no, I remember—oh—okay, thank you.

Parentheses

Parentheses are used around words that are included in a sentence to add information or to help make an idea clearer.

612.4
To Add Information

Use parentheses when adding information or clarifying an idea.

> Cures for diseases (from arthritis to AIDS) may be found in plants in the rain forest.

> Only about 10 percent (27,000) of the plant species in the world have been studied.

Grammar Practice

Dashes

The following sentences use dashes in different ways. Using each as a model, write your own sentence.

Example: Yes, Dara, I know that green is your favorite color—it's mine, too!

Why, Evan, I thought that green was a natural color—it's organic, man!

1. Dara, you really should—wait, listen—what?—never mind.

2. Yellow—the color of happiness—is often used for decorations at celebrations.

3. A person who feels blue—as in sad—would probably not wear bright red.

4. Hey, Maurice, how did—no, I didn't know—okay, no shorts.

5. She wants to paint her room—why, I'll never understand—purple and red.

6. Maybe she thinks purple and red will make her feel "royal"—like a queen.

Parentheses

Write the "added information" in the following sentences, enclosing it in parentheses.

Example: Ancient people Egyptians, Chinese, and Greeks believed in healing with colors.

(Egyptians, Chinese, and Greeks)

1. Warm colors red, yellow, and orange remind people of excitement and activity, while cool colors blue, green, and violet are calming.

2. Our reactions to color are based on our experiences both cultural and emotional.

Ellipses

Use an **ellipsis** (three periods) to show a pause in dialogue or to show that words or sentences have been left out. Leave one space before, after, and between each period.

614.1
To Show Pauses

Use an ellipsis to show a pause in dialogue.

> "My report," said Reggie, "is on . . . ah . . . cars of the future. One place that I . . . uh . . . checked on the Internet said that cars would someday run on sunshine.

614.2
To Show Omitted Words

Use an ellipsis to show that one or more words have been left out of a quotation. Read this statement about hibernation.

> Some animals, such as the chipmunk and the woodchuck, hibernate in winter. During this time, the animal's heart beats very slowly—only a few times per minute. Its body cools down so much that it nearly freezes, and this is called going into torpor.

Here's how you would type part of the above quotation, leaving some of the words out. If the words left out are at the end of a sentence, use a period followed by three dots.

> Some animals . . . hibernate in winter. During this time, the animal's heart beats very slowly . . . and this is called going into torpor.

SCHOOL DAZE

Grammar Practice

Ellipses

■ To Show Pauses

Rewrite the following brief conversation, inserting ellipses where appropriate to show a pause in dialogue.

Example: "Please open your books to um page 23."

"Please open your books to . . . um . . . page 23."

"Mr. O'Dell, why is it like so *important* to learn about civil rights?"

"Hmm well, we need to know how unfair life was how hard it was for people who were denied their civil rights, so we can make sure that it doesn't happen again."

"I see. That uh makes sense."

■ To Show Omitted Words

Rewrite the following paragraph, leaving out words in three places. Use ellipses to show where you have left out words.

Some civil rights, such as freedom of speech, freedom of the press, the right to vote, and the right to equality, can be taken for granted. It is important for these rights to be spelled out in our laws so that our nation can avoid discrimination. The United States Constitution, with a number of amendments, makes sure that people's rights are protected. Under the Civil Rights Act of 1964, discrimination based on race, color, or religion against any person in a public place is illegal.

Next Step: Write two sentences about why freedom of speech is important. Trade papers with a classmate and rewrite each other's sentences, omitting words in two places.

Test Prep!

 For each sentence below, write the letter of the line that contains a mistake. If there is no mistake, choose "D."

1
- (A) Art asked, "Why can't
- (B) we go see the new Harry
- (C) Potter movie today"?
- (D) correct as is

2
- (A) Franco's new book,
- (B) "Portable Poetry," was a
- (C) gift from his grandma.
- (D) correct as is

3
- (A) Mr. Roire is'nt very
- (B) happy about the class's
- (C) English test scores.
- (D) correct as is

4
- (A) Three fourths of
- (B) my friends have read the
- (C) poem "September."
- (D) correct as is

5
- (A) The three boy's dogs
- (B) don't have tags on
- (C) their collars.
- (D) correct as is

6
- (A) Mom wrote an article
- (B) called *Finding Treasures*
- (C) for *Antiques* magazine.
- (D) correct as is

7
- (A) Seth says two-thirds
- (B) of his dads' garage is
- (C) full of car parts.
- (D) correct as is

8
- (A) Did you just say,
- (B) "I won't be at band
- (C) practice today?"
- (D) correct as is

9
- (A) The song *Mandy*
- (B) was actually about
- (C) the writer's dog.
- (D) correct as is

10
- (A) Deshawn said, "You
- (B) should'nt be watching
- (C) television right now."
- (D) correct as is

11
- (A) It's a sad fact that
- (B) four fifths of teen girls
- (C) get too little calcium.
- (D) correct as is

12
- (A) Ms. Gray's niece got
- (B) a part in the play
- (C) "Hansel and Gretel."
- (D) correct as is

For each line, write the letter of the correct way (see choices below) to write the underlined part.

1. According to the <u>popular monthly magazine</u>

2. <u>"Telephone Users News,"</u> research shows that

3. about <u>seven eighths</u> of phone users prefer cordless phones.

4. In an article titled <u>"Cordless Rules,"</u> writer Margaret Pyle

5. says, "People <u>don't want</u> to be tied to a twisted, tangled

6. phone cord <u>any longer".</u> She continues, "Research shows

7. that most phone <u>user's choices</u> are based on experience."

8. Twisted phone cords are a minor annoyance compared to the serious accidents caused by careless <u>cell-phone users.</u>

1 Ⓐ popular monthly magazine,
Ⓑ popular, monthly magazine
Ⓒ popular monthly, magazine
Ⓓ correct as is

2 Ⓐ "Telephone Users News",
Ⓑ *Telephone Users News,*
Ⓒ telephone users news
Ⓓ correct as is

3 Ⓐ seven-eighths
Ⓑ 7 eighths
Ⓒ seven 8ths
Ⓓ correct as is

4 Ⓐ "Cordless Rules",
Ⓑ *Cordless Rules,*
Ⓒ Cordless rules
Ⓓ correct as is

5 Ⓐ dont want
Ⓑ dont' want
Ⓒ do'nt want
Ⓓ correct as is

6 Ⓐ any longer."
Ⓑ any longer.".
Ⓒ any longer"
Ⓓ correct as is

7 Ⓐ users choices
Ⓑ users' choices
Ⓒ user's choice's
Ⓓ correct as is

8 Ⓐ cell's phone users.
Ⓑ cell phone's users.
Ⓒ cell phones users.
Ⓓ correct as is

Editing for Mechanics

Capitalization . . .

618.1
Proper Nouns and Adjectives

Capitalize all proper nouns and all proper adjectives. A proper noun is the name of a particular person, place, thing, or idea. A proper adjective is an adjective formed from a proper noun.

Common Noun:	country, president, continent
Proper Noun:	Canada, Andrew Jackson, Asia
Proper Adjective:	Canadian, Jacksonian, Asian

618.2
Names of People

Capitalize the names of people and also the initials or abbreviations that stand for those names.

Samuel L. Jackson   **Aung San Suu Kyi**

Mary Sanchez-Gomez

618.3
Titles Used with Names

Capitalize titles used with names of persons; also capitalize abbreviations standing for those titles.

President Mohammed Hosni Mubarak   **Dr. Linda Trout**

Governor Michael Easley   **Rev. Jim Zavaski**

Senator John McCain

618.4
Words Used as Names

Capitalize words such as *mother, father, aunt,* and *uncle* when these words are used as names.

Uncle Marius **started to sit on the couch.** (*Uncle* is a name; the speaker calls this person "Uncle Marius.")

Then Uncle **stopped in midair.** (*Uncle* is used as a name.)

"So, Mom, **what are you doing here?" I asked.** (*Mom* is used as a name.)

Words such as *aunt, uncle, mom, dad, grandma,* and *grandpa* are usually not capitalized if they come after a possessive pronoun (*my, his, our*).

My aunt **had just called him.** (The word *aunt* describes this person but is not used as a name.)

Then my dad **and** mom **walked into the room.** (The words *dad* and *mom* are not used as names in this sentence.)

Grammar Practice

Capitalization 1

■ Proper Nouns and Adjectives
■ Names of People
■ Titles Used with Names
■ Words Used as Names

 Number your paper from 1 to 10. In one column, capitalize the words in each sentence that should be capitalized. In the other column, change the words that are incorrectly capitalized.

Example: Edgar Rice burroughs wrote science Fiction Books.

Burroughs   fiction, books

1. Jules verne began writing science fiction in 1851.

2. Science fiction is a mix of Reality and the imagination.

3. H. G. wells became a famous science-fiction writer in 1898 when he published *War of the Worlds*.

4. In 1938, orson welles broadcast *War of the Worlds* on the Radio.

5. Because mr. Welles used a real american town in New jersey as the setting for the broadcast, it caused people to panic.

6. Douglas Adams, Author of *The Hitchhiker's Guide to the Galaxy,* wrote science fiction in a humorous way.

7. *Jurassic Park,* by michael crichton, was published in 1990 and released as a Movie in 1993.

8. In the science-fiction Movie *The Empire Strikes Back,* the villain Darth vader told commander Luke Skywalker, "I am your Father."

9. *The Matrix* introduced the villain agent smith to the world.

10. In *i, robot,* will smith plays the part of a detective who believes robots will take over the world.

Next Step: Think about a science-fiction book you have read or a science-fiction movie you have seen. List three proper nouns, three proper adjectives, and a title used with a name from the work you have chosen.

Capitalization . . .

Capitalize the name of a specific educational course, but not the name of a general subject. (Exception—the names of all languages are proper nouns and are always capitalized: *French, English, Hindi, German, Latin.*)

Roberto is studying accounting at the technical college. (Because *accounting* is a general subject, it is not capitalized.)

He likes the professor who teaches Accounting Principles. (The specific course name is capitalized.)

Capitalize the names of businesses and the official names of their products. (These are called trade names.) Do not, however, capitalize a general word like "toothpaste" when it follows the trade name.

Old Navy	Best Buy	Microsoft	Kodak
Sony Playstation	Tombstone pizza	Mudd jeans	

Capitalize the names of languages, races, nationalities, and religions, as well as the proper adjectives formed from them.

Arab	Spanish	Judaism	Catholicism
African art	Irish linen	Swedish meatballs	

Capitalize the names of days of the week, months of the year, and special holidays.

Thursday	Friday	Saturday
July	August	September
Arbor Day	Independence Day	

Do not capitalize the names of seasons.

winter, spring, summer, fall (autumn)

Capitalize the names of historical events, documents, and periods of time.

World War II	the Bill of Rights	the Magna Carta
the Middle Ages	the Paleozoic Era	

Grammar Practice

Capitalization 2

- School Subjects
- Days, Months, Holidays
- Historical Events

 For each numbered sentence below, write the word or words that should be capitalized.

Example: What is armistice day?
Armistice Day

(1) Last friday Mr. Allis, who teaches biology II, told us that veterans day was celebrated on the fourth monday of october between 1968 and 1978. (2) In world history, we learned that veterans day was originally called armistice day. (3) The holiday was a remembrance of the day in 1918 when world war I ended. (4) That day, in the eleventh hour of the eleventh day of the eleventh month (november), a truce was signed to end the fighting. (5) Now we remember veterans of all wars, including world war II, the vietnam war, and the gulf war, on november 11 every year.

- Official Names
- Races, Languages, Nationalities, Religions

 Write the word or words that should be capitalized in each sentence.

1. Textiles are an important part of Pakistan's economy; proline footbags are made there, as are nizam tents.

2. A pakistani company supplies jeans to american companies such as wal-mart and the gap.

3. Pakistan was established in 1947 by indian muslims.

4. Only 3 percent of pakistanis are christian or hindu.

5. Only 8 percent of the population speaks urdu, the official language, but 48 percent speak punjabi.

Capitalization . . .

Capitalize the following geographic names.

Planets and heavenly bodies . . . . Venus, Jupiter, Milky Way

Lowercase the word "earth" except when used as the proper name of our planet, especially when mentioned with other planet names.

What on earth are you doing here?

Sam has traveled across the face of the earth several times.

Jupiter's diameter is 11 times larger than Earth's.

The four inner planets are Mercury, Venus, Earth, and Mars.

Continents . . . . **Europe, Asia, South America, Australia, Africa**

Countries . . . **Morocco, Haiti, Greece, Chile, United Arab Emirates**

States . . . . . **New Mexico, Alabama, West Virginia, Delaware, Iowa**

Provinces . . . . **Alberta, British Columbia, Quebec, Ontario**

Counties . . . . **Sioux County, Kandiyohi County, Wade County**

Cities . . . . **Montreal, Baton Rouge, Albuquerque, Portland**

Bodies of water . . . . **Delaware Bay, Chickamunga Lake, Indian Ocean, Gulf of Mexico, Skunk Creek**

Landforms . . . . **Appalachian Mountains, Bitterroot Range**

Public areas . . . . **Tiananmen Square, Sequoia National Forest, Mount Rushmore, Open Space Park, Vietnam Memorial**

Roads and highways . . . . **New Jersey Turnpike, Interstate 80, Central Avenue, Chisholm Trail, Mutt's Road**

Buildings . . . **Pentagon, Paske High School, Empire State Building**

Monuments . . . . **Eiffel Tower, Statue of Liberty**

Capitalize words that indicate particular sections of the country. Also capitalize proper adjectives formed from names of specific sections of a country.

Having grown up on the hectic East Coast, I find life in the South to be refreshing.

Here in Georgia, Southern hospitality is a way of life.

Words that simply indicate a direction are not capitalized; nor are adjectives that are formed from words that simply indicate direction.

The town where I live, located east of Memphis, is typical of others found in western Tennessee.

Grammar Practice

Capitalization 3
■ Geographic Names
■ Particular Sections of the Country

 Write the word or words that should be capitalized in each sentence.

Example: The united states, canada, and mexico have many
national parks.
United States, Canada, Mexico

1. One of the most famous parks is yellowstone national park, located in wyoming, idaho, and montana.

2. Just south of yellowstone, on rockefeller parkway, is grand teton national park.

3. The park's string lake is reserved for nonmotorized boats.

4. There are many national parks in the west, but the midwest has some interesting parks, too.

5. Sleeping bear dunes national lakeshore is located on the eastern shore of lake michigan.

6. The appalachian national scenic trail runs from katahdin, maine, to springer mountain in the northern part of georgia.

7. You might see polar bears at wapusk national park in manitoba, canada.

8. Some islands in a national park located on the saint lawrence river in ontario, canada, can be reached only by boat.

9. El chico was the first national park in mexico.

10. Copper canyon in chihuahua, mexico, is deeper than the grand canyon.

Next Step: Use complete sentences to answer the following questions. Be sure to use proper capitalization.
● In what section of the country is your state found?
● What large city is closest to your home?

MECHANICS

Capitalization . . .

Capitalize the first word of every sentence and the first word in a direct quotation.

> **In many families, pets are treated like people, according to an article in the *Kansas City Star*.** (sentence)

> **Marty Becker, coauthor of *Chicken Soup for the Pet Lover's Soul,* reports, "Seven out of ten people let their pets sleep on the bed."** (direct quotation)

> **"I get my 15 minutes of fame," he says, "every time I come home."** (Notice that *every* is not capitalized because it does not begin a new sentence.)

> **"It's like being treated like a rock star," says Becker. "Now I have to tell you that feels pretty good."**

Do not capitalize the first word in an indirect quotation.

> **Becker says that in the last 10 years, pets have moved out of kennels and basements and into living rooms and bedrooms.** (indirect quotation)

Capitalize the first word of a title, the last word, and every word in between except articles *(a, an, the),* short prepositions, and coordinating conjunctions. Follow this rule for titles of books, newspapers, magazines, poems, plays, songs, articles, movies, works of art, pictures, stories, and essays. (See **600.3**.)

> ***Locked in Time*** (book)

> ***Boston Globe*** (newspaper)

> ***Dog Fancy*** (magazine)

> **"Roses Are Red"** (poem)

> ***The Phantom of the Opera*** (play)

> ***Daddy Day Care*** (movie)

> **"Intuition"** (song)

> **Mona Lisa** (work of art)

Grammar Practice

Capitalization 4

■ First Words
■ Titles

 Number your paper from 1 to 3. As you read the following paragraphs, write the words that should be capitalized in each.

Example: *The Natural History book of dinosaurs says the Tyrannosaurus rex died out 65 million years ago.*
    Book   Dinosaurs

1.   Because dinosaurs lived long before people, no one really knows how they behaved. for example, scientists have long thought that *Tyrannosaurus rex* was a fierce, meat-eating predator. In the movie *jurassic park,* the *T. rex* chases other dinosaurs and people.

2.   Recently, however, Dr. Jack Horner determined that *T. rex* was actually a scavenger. In an article in *national geographic* magazine, Dr. Horner compared the teeth of *T. rex* with those of other hunters. He also studied the dinosaur's leg bones and compared them with those of modern predators. he thinks that *T. rex* could not move fast enough to be a predator. in addition, he points to its tiny arms, which could not hold a struggling animal.

3.   Another expert, Dr. Angela Milner, says that more information is needed to be sure that *T. rex* was only a scavenger. here is what we do know: a *T. rex* could grow to be over 40 feet long, stand 15 feet tall, and weigh about 6 tons. would *the mysterious Tyrannosaurus rex* make a good title for a book on this subject?

Next Step: Write a short paragraph about a book, movie, or poem you like. Exchange papers with a classmate. Are first words and titles capitalized correctly?

MECHANICS

Capitalization

626.1
Abbreviations

Capitalize abbreviations of titles and organizations.

Dr. (Doctor) **M.D.** (Doctor of Medicine)

Mr. (Mister) **UPS** (United Parcel Service)

SADD (Students Against Destructive Decisions)

626.2
Organizations

Capitalize the name of an organization, an association, or a team.

New York State Historical Society	**the Red Cross**
General Motors Corporation	**the Miami Dolphins**
Republicans	**the Democratic Party**

626.3
Letters

Capitalize the letters used to indicate form or shape.

T-shirt **U-turn** **A-frame** **T-ball**

Capitalize	Do Not Capitalize
American	un-American
January, February	winter, spring
Missouri and Ohio Rivers	the rivers Missouri and Ohio
The South is humid in summer.	Turn south at the stop sign.
Duluth Middle School.	a Duluth middle school
Governor Bob Taft	Bob Taft, our governor
President Luiz Lula Da Silva	Luiz Lula Da Silva, Brazil's president
Nissan Altima	a Nissan automobile
The planet Earth is egg shaped.	The earth on Grandpa's farm is rich.
I'm taking World Cultures.	I'm taking social studies.

Grammar Practice

Capitalization 5

■ Abbreviations
■ Organizations
■ Letters

 Write the words or abbreviations that should be capitalized in each sentence below.

Example: Dad took me to see dr. Zani Patell.
Dr.

1. The two major political parties in this country are the democrats and the republicans.

2. One of the most successful professional football teams in the country is the Dallas cowboys.

3. When a tornado hits a community, the red Cross sends help.

4. Our new social studies teacher is ms. Kenal.

5. An organization of mothers who try to prevent people from driving after drinking alcohol is called madd.

6. The b-pillar on a car is located right behind the front door.

7. America's space program is run by nasa.

8. The city building code says steel i-beams must be used in new skyscrapers.

9. Some of the biggest companies in the world include GE, ibm, AT&T, and gm.

10. The washing machine repairman replaced an o-ring.

Next Step: Write a sentence about a teacher you have now. Use an abbreviated title (such as *Ms., Dr.,* and so on) for this person in your sentence. Check your capitalization.

628

Test Prep!

 For each underlined part of the paragraphs below, choose the letter (on the next page) that shows the correct capitalization. If the underlined part is correct, choose "D."

Paragraph I

My dad is a mechanic at the local <u>toyota dealer. of course,</u> he
(1)
says <u>the japanese cars</u> are superior. <u>but mrs. Weiler,</u> who has had her
(2)   (3)
car repaired there many times, might disagree.

Paragraph II

Today in one of my classes (<u>Cultures in everyday life</u>), we had a
(4)
surprise visitor: <u>governor Consuela Jones. She</u> told us that when her
(5)
family first lived in <u>the United States</u>, they spoke <u>only spanish (no</u>
(6)   (7)
<u>English</u>).

Paragraph III

My new friend <u>Aziza is egyptian.</u> She and her family practice
(8)
<u>islam, so</u> they needed to find a mosque where they could worship.
(9)
They found that, compared to <u>the Eastern states</u>, there aren't many
(10)
<u>mosques in the Southwest.</u>
(11)

Paragraph IV

Grandma was a member of the <u>Women's Army Corps, or wac,</u>
(12)
during <u>world war II. Lately</u> she's been reading <u>Battle Of The WAC,</u> the
(13)   (14)
story of one woman's experience in the army.

punctuate *edit* capitalize
SPELL
improve
629

Editing for Mechanics

MECHANICS

1
- (A) Toyota Dealer. of course
- (B) Toyota dealer. Of course
- (C) Toyota Dealer. Of course
- (D) correct as is

2
- (A) The Japanese cars
- (B) The Japanese Cars
- (C) the Japanese cars
- (D) correct as is

3
- (A) but Mrs. Weiler
- (B) But Mrs. Weiler
- (C) But mrs. Weiler
- (D) correct as is

4
- (A) Cultures In everyday Life
- (B) Cultures in everyday Life
- (C) Cultures in Everyday Life
- (D) correct as is

5
- (A) Governor Consuela Jones. She
- (B) governor Consuela Jones. she
- (C) governor consuela Jones. She
- (D) correct as is

6
- (A) the united States
- (B) The united States
- (C) The United States
- (D) correct as is

7
- (A) only spanish (no english)
- (B) only Spanish (no english)
- (C) only Spanish (no English)
- (D) correct as is

8
- (A) Aziza Is Egyptian
- (B) aziza is Egyptian
- (C) Aziza is Egyptian
- (D) correct as is

9
- (A) islam, So
- (B) Islam, so
- (C) Islam, So
- (D) correct as is

10
- (A) the eastern states
- (B) The Eastern States
- (C) the Eastern States
- (D) correct as is

11
- (A) mosques in the southwest
- (B) Mosques in the southwest
- (C) mosques in The Southwest
- (D) correct as is

12
- (A) Women's Army Corps, or WAC
- (B) women's army corps, or WAC
- (C) women's Army corps, or wac
- (D) correct as is

13
- (A) world war II. lately
- (B) World war II. Lately
- (C) World War II. Lately
- (D) correct as is

14
- (A) *Battle of The WAC*
- (B) *Battle of the WAC*
- (C) *Battle of the wac*
- (D) correct as is

Plurals . . .

The **plurals** of most nouns are formed by adding *s* to the singular.

cheerleader — **cheerleaders**   wheel — **wheels**

bubble — **bubbles**

630.2
Nouns Ending
in *ch, sh, s,
x,* and *z*

The plural form of nouns ending in *ch, sh, s, x,* and *z* is made by adding *es* to the singular.

lunch — **lunches**   dish — **dishes**   mess — **messes**

buzz — **buzzes**   fox — **foxes**

The plurals of nouns ending in *o* with a vowel just before the *o* are formed by adding *s.*

radio — **radios**   studio — **studios**   rodeo — **rodeos**

The plurals of most nouns ending in *o* with a consonant just before the *o* are formed by adding *es.*

echo — **echoes**   hero — **heroes**   tomato — **tomatoes**

Exceptions: Musical terms and words of Spanish origin always form plurals by adding *s.*

alto — **altos**   banjo — **banjos**   taco — **tacos**

solo — **solos**   piano — **pianos**   burro — **burros**

The plurals of nouns that end with *ful* are formed by adding an *s* at the end of the word.

three **platefuls**   six **tankfuls**   four **cupfuls**   five **pailfuls**

The plurals of nouns that end in *f* or *fe* are formed in one of two ways: If the final *f* sound is still heard in the plural form of the word, simply add *s*; if the final sound is a *v* sound, change the *f* to *ve* and add *s.*

roof — roofs   **chief — chiefs**   **belief — beliefs**
(plural ends with *f* sound)

wife — wives   **loaf — loaves**   **leaf — leaves**
(plural ends with *v* sound)

Grammar Practice

Plurals 1

- Nouns Ending in *ch, sh, s, x,* and *z*
- Nouns Ending in *o*
- Nouns Ending in *ful*
- Nouns Ending in *f* or *fe*

 For each of the following sentences, write the plural form of the word or words in parentheses.

Example: Tawon and Richard grabbed *(handful)* of popcorn.
handfuls

1. Every fall, as the *(leaf)* change colors, football season begins.

2. People can see the games on their *(television)* or at *(stadium)*, or they can listen to the games on their *(radio)*.

3. At high school and college football games, marching *(band)* play during halftime.

4. At one game, a trumpet player in the band played two *(solo)*.

5. That made him so thirsty that he drank two *(glassful)* of water.

6. A few football *(stadium)*, called domes, have *(roof)*.

7. Some professional football *(player)* are like *(hero)* to their fans.

8. Even when these guys end up with *(helmetful)* of mud and grass, *(echo)* of adoration from their fans can be heard on the field.

9. For many of the *(player)*, their professional *(life)* are rather short—many end up playing for only a few *(year)*.

10. I wonder what some of these men think when they look back on their short *(career)*.

Next Step: Write two sentences about an outdoor activity. Use plurals in your sentences. Then double-check to make sure all the plural words are correct.

MECHANICS

Plurals

632.1 Nouns Ending in y

The plurals of common nouns that end in *y* with a consonant letter just before the *y* are formed by changing the *y* to *i* and adding *es*.

> fly — **flies**   baby — **babies**   cavity — **cavities**

The plurals of common nouns that end in *y* with a vowel before the *y* are formed by adding only *s*.

> key — **keys**   holiday — **holidays**   attorney — **attorneys**

The plurals of proper nouns ending in *y* are formed by adding *s*.

> There are three **Circuit Citys** in our metro area.

632.2 Compound Nouns

The plurals of some compound nouns are formed by adding *s* or *es* to the main word in the compound.

> **brothers-in-law**   **maids of honor**   **secretaries of state**

632.3 Plurals That Do Not Change

The plurals of some words are the same in singular and plural form.

> **deer   sheep   trout   aircraft**

632.4 Irregular Spelling

Some words (including many foreign words) form a plural by taking on an irregular spelling; others are now acceptable with the commonly used *s* or *es* ending.

> child — **children**   woman — **women**   man — **men**
>
> goose — **geese**   mouse — **mice**   ox — **oxen**
>
> tooth — **teeth**   octopus — **octopuses** or **octopi**
>
> index — **indexes** or **indices**

632.5 Adding an 's

The plurals of letters, figures, symbols, and words discussed as words are formed by adding an apostrophe and an *s*.

> Dr. Walters has two **Ph.D.'s**.
>
> My dad's license plate has three **2's** between two **B's**.
>
> You've got too many *but*'s and *so*'s in that sentence.

For information on forming plural possessives, see 606.1.

Grammar Practice

Plurals 2

- Nouns Ending in *y*
- Compound Nouns
- Plurals That Do Not Change
- Irregular Spelling
- Adding an *'s*

 For each of the following sentences, write the plural form of the word or words in parentheses. You may need to use a dictionary.

Example: There are about a dozen *(fish)* in Ashlee's tank.
fish

1. Have you heard the story of Santa and his eight tiny *(reindeer)*?

2. I got one A, three *(B)*, and two *(C)* on my report card.

3. The *(monkey)* escaped from the lab and ran down the *(hallway)*.

4. I have many *(ability)*, but writing *(essay)* is one skill that I definitely need to work on.

5. Nishan broke one of his *(foot)* and chipped two *(tooth)*.

6. A few *(Kennedy)* have held political office.

7. We're not supposed to use any *(&)* or *(#)* in our final papers.

8. Fresh foods do not have *(bar code)* printed on them.

9. Aunt Patti's job is to take customer satisfaction *(survey)* for different *(company)*.

10. Many *(African American)* become *(attorney-at-law)*.

11. It's not uncommon to see *(moose)* in northern Maine.

Next Step: Write sentences using the plurals of the following words: *chin-up, toy, child,* and *city.*

MECHANICS

Abbreviations . . .

An **abbreviation** is the shortened form of a word or phrase. The following abbreviations are always acceptable in any kind of writing:

Mr.   **Mrs.**   **Ms.**   **Dr.**   **a.m., p.m.** (A.M., P.M.)

B.C.E. (before the Common Era)   **C.E.** (Common Era)

B.A.   **M.A.**   **Ph.D.**   **M.D.**   **Sr.**   **Jr.**

Caution: Do not abbreviate the names of states, countries, months, days, or units of measure in formal writing. Also, do not use signs or symbols (%, &) in place of words.

Common Abbreviations

AC alternating current	**kg** kilogram	**pd.** paid
a.m. ante meridiem	**km** kilometer	**pg.** (or p.) page
ASAP as soon as possible	**kW** kilowatt	**p.m.** post meridiem
COD cash on delivery	**l** liter	**ppd.** postpaid, prepaid
DA district attorney	**lb.** pound	**qt.** quart
DC direct current	**m** meter	**R.S.V.P.** please reply
etc. and so forth	**M.D.** doctor of medicine	**tbs., tbsp.** tablespoon
F Fahrenheit	**mfg.** manufacturing	**tsp.** teaspoon
FM frequency modulation	**mpg** miles per gallon	**vol.** volume
GNP gross national product	**mph** miles per hour	**vs.** versus
i.e. that is (Latin *id est*)	**oz.** ounce	**yd.** yard

Address Abbreviations

	Standard	Postal		Standard	Postal		Standard	Postal
Avenue	Ave.	AVE	Lake	L.	LK	Route	RT.	RTE
Boulevard	Blvd.	BLVD	Lane	Ln.	LN	South	S.	S
Court	Ct.	CT	North	N.	N	Square	Sq.	SQ
Drive	Dr.	DR	Park	Pk.	PK	Station	Sta.	STA
East	E.	E	Parkway	Pky.	PKY	Street	St.	ST
Expressway	Expy.	EXPY	Place	Pl.	PL	Terrace	Ter.	TER
Heights	Hts.	HTS	Plaza	Plaza	PLZ	Turnpike	Tpke.	TPKE
Highway	Hwy.	HWY	Road	Rd.	RD	West	W.	W

Grammar Practice

Abbreviations 1

For each of the following sentences, write the correct abbreviation for the underlined word or words.

Example: Last week I talked to <u>Doctor</u> Wesley Brown.
Dr.

1. He earned his <u>doctor of medicine</u> degree from Franklin University.

2. The electric appliances in most homes and apartments use <u>alternating current</u> electricity.

3. Flashlights and other battery-operated items use <u>direct current</u> electricity.

4. This fan will use about one <u>kilowatt</u> of electricity every day.

5. Next week the city will elect a new <u>district attorney</u>.

6. <u>Mister</u> Hawthorn expects his science students to do their best.

7. He asked me to bring in my extra-credit project <u>as soon as possible</u>.

8. Our assignment was to convert 15 degrees <u>Fahrenheit</u> to its metric equivalent.

9. The <u>gross national product</u> of the United States in 2000 was $10.5 trillion.

10. My mom's hybrid car is supposed to get 60 <u>miles per gallon</u>.

11. The top speed for an electric car is 100 <u>miles per hour</u>.

12. Some fast-food places offer 32-<u>ounce</u> soft drinks.

13. The recipe includes a cup of flour, a <u>tablespoon</u> of cinnamon, and a <u>teaspoon</u> of salt.

Next Step: Write the words for these postal abbreviations: AVE, CT, EXPY, and RD. Now write the postal abbreviations for your own state or province and one near it.

Abbreviations

An **acronym** is an abbreviation that can be pronounced as a word. It does not require periods.

WHO — World Health Organization   **ROM** — read-only memory

FAQ — frequently asked question

An **initialism** is similar to an acronym except that it cannot be pronounced as a word; the initials are pronounced individually.

PBS — Public Broadcasting Service

BLM — Bureau of Land Management

WNBA — Women's National Basketball Association

Common Acronyms and Initialisms

AIDS	acquired immune deficiency syndrome	**ORV**	off-road vehicle
CETA	Comprehensive Employment and Training Act	**OSHA**	Occupational Safety and Health Administration
CIA	Central Intelligence Agency	**PAC**	political action committee
FAA	Federal Aviation Administration	**PIN**	personal identification number
FBI	Federal Bureau of Investigation	**PSA**	public service announcement
FCC	Federal Communications Commission	**ROTC**	Reserve Officers' Training Corps
FDA	Food and Drug Administration	**SADD**	Students Against Destructive Decisions
FDIC	Federal Deposit Insurance Corporation	**SSA**	Social Security Administration
FHA	Federal Housing Administration	**SUV**	sport-utility vehicle
FTC	Federal Trade Commission	**SWAT**	special weapons and tactics
HTML	Hypertext Markup Language	**TDD**	telecommunications device for the deaf
IRS	Internal Revenue Service	**TMJ**	temporomandibular joint
MADD	Mothers Against Drunk Driving	**TVA**	Tennessee Valley Authority
NAFTA	North American Free Trade Agreement	**VA**	Veterans Administration
NASA	National Aeronautics and Space Administration	**VISTA**	Volunteers in Service to America
NATO	North Atlantic Treaty Organization	**WAC**	Women's Army Corps
OEO	Office of Economic Opportunity	**WAVES**	Women Accepted for Volunteer Emergency Service
OEP	Office of Emergency Preparedness		

Grammar Practice

Abbreviations 2

■ Acronyms
■ Initialisms

Number your paper from 1 to 15. For each name or phrase on the left, write the letter of the abbreviation on the right that matches it.

1. all-terrain vehicle
2. telecommunications device for the deaf
3. magnetic resonance imaging
4. special weapons and tactics
5. Federal Bureau of Investigation
6. computer-aided design
7. World Health Organization
8. parental guidance
9. North Atlantic Treaty Organization
10. light amplification by stimulated emission of radiation
11. Organization of Petroleum Exporting Countries
12. personal identification number
13. master of business administration
14. attention deficit disorder
15. certified public accountant

A. ADD
B. ATV
C. CAD
D. CPA
E. FBI
F. LASER
G. MBA
H. MRI
I. NATO
J. OPEC
K. PG
L. PIN
M. SWAT
N. TDD
O. WHO

Next Step: Make up an organization name that can be abbreviated as an acronym. Share your new abbreviation—and what it stands for—with the class.

Numbers . . .

638.1
Numbers Under 10

Numbers from one to nine are usually written as words; all numbers 10 and over are usually written as numerals.

two   seven   nine   10   25   106

638.2
Numerals Only

Use numerals to express any of the following forms:

money **$2.39**

decimals **26.2**

percentages . . . . **8 percent**

chapters . . . . **chapter 7**

pages . . . . **pages 287–289**

time (with "a.m." or "p.m.") . . . . **4:30 p.m.**

telephone numbers **1-800-555-1212**

dates . . . . **44 B.C.E.; July 6, 1942**

identification numbers . . . . **Highway 36**

addresses . . . . **2125 Cairn Road**

ZIP codes **60004**

statistics . . . . **a vote of 23 to 4**

When abbreviations and symbols are used (for instance, in science or math), always use numerals with them.

12° C   7%   33 kg   9 cm   55 mph

638.3
Very Large Numbers

You may use a combination of numerals and words for very large numbers.

Of the 17 million residents of the three Midwestern states, only 1.3 million are blondes.

You may spell out a large number that can be written as two words. If more than two words are needed, use the numeral.

More than nine thousand people attended the concert.

About 3,500 people missed the opening act.

Grammar Practice

Numbers 1

- ■ **Numbers Under 10**
- ■ **Numerals Only**
- ■ **Very Large Numbers**

 Each sentence below has a choice of how a number should be written. Write the answers that make the sentences correct.

Example: There are *(nine, 9)* planets in our solar system.

nine

1. The sun is one of more than *(100 billion, 100,000,000,000)* stars in our galaxy.

2. The sun's diameter is *(one million three hundred ninety thousand, 1.39 million)* kilometers.

3. The sun contains more than *(99 percent, ninety-nine percent)* of the total mass of the solar system.

4. Is Earth about *(4 billion, 4,000,000,000)* years old?

5. While Mars has *(two, 2)* moons, Earth has only *(one, 1)*.

6. On July *(twentieth, 20)*, 1969, the first humans landed on the moon.

7. Just six hours after *Apollo 11* landed at *(4:17, four-seventeen)* p.m. eastern daylight time, the astronauts stepped onto the moon's surface.

8. That summer, you could buy a model of *Apollo 11* for only $*(2.50, two-fifty)*.

9. The last astronauts to land on the moon were those in *Apollo 17* in December *(nineteen seventy-two, 1972)*.

Next Step: Use complete sentences to answer the following questions. Be sure to use numbers correctly.

- ● On what day and in what year were you born?
- ● What time is it right now?

Numbers

640.1
Comparing Numbers

If you are comparing two or more numbers in a sentence, write all of them the same way: as numerals or as words.

Students from 9 to 14 years old are invited.

Students from nine to fourteen years old are invited.

640.2
Numbers in Compound Modifiers

A compound modifier may include a numeral.

The floorboards come in 10-foot lengths.

When a number comes before a compound modifier that includes a numeral, use words instead of numerals.

We need five 10-foot lengths to finish the floor.

Ms. Brown must grade twenty 12-page reports.

640.3
Sentence Beginnings

Use words, not numerals, to begin a sentence.

Nine students had turned in their homework. Fourteen students said they were unable to finish the assignment.

640.4
Time and Money

When time or money is expressed with a symbol, use numerals. When either is expressed with words, spell out the number.

6:00 a.m. (or) **six o'clock**

$25 (or) **twenty-five dollars**

SCHOOL DAZE

Jerry, haven't you finished your paper yet?

No, it's not due until **three o'clock**, and Mrs. Wright told me to add a few new twists and wrinkles.

Grammar Practice

Numbers 2

■ Comparing Numbers

Rewrite the underlined parts of the following sentences so that they are correct.

Example: Depending on which staircase I use, I have to climb <u>eight or 11</u> stairs on my way to our apartment.
8 or 11 (or) *eight or eleven*

1. The renters of the top-floor apartment sometimes have <u>five to 15</u> guests at once.

2. The children in that apartment are from <u>nine to 18</u> years old.

3. Apartments may have from <u>two to 10</u> windows.

4. They usually have <u>nine to 20</u> electrical outlets.

5. Our building has <u>seven</u> furnished <u>and 11</u> unfurnished units.

■ Sentence Beginnings
■ Time and Money

Rewrite the following sentences so that the numbers are correct.

Example: 9 apartments will be rented for 825 dollars per month.
Nine apartments will be rented for $825 per month.

1. The manager has agreed to show the apartment at eight p.m. tonight.

2. 60 people have already called about the new apartment complex.

3. Some people are interested in the smaller units renting for $6 hundred a month.

4. Three apartments were rented by 9 o'clock this morning.

5. 20 units remain available for rent.

Improving Spelling

Write *i* before *e* except after *c*, or when sounded like *a* as in *neighbor* and *weigh*.

Some Exceptions to the Rule: *counterfeit, either, financier, foreign, height, heir, leisure, neither, science, seize, sheik, species, their, weird.*

If a word ends with a silent *e*, drop the *e* before adding a suffix that begins with a vowel. There are exceptions, for example, *knowledgeable* and *changeable.*

state—stating—statement	**use—using—useful**
like—liking—likeness	**nine—ninety—nineteen**

NOTE You do not drop the e when the suffix begins with a consonant. Exceptions include *truly, argument,* and *ninth.*

When *y* is the last letter in a word and the *y* comes just after a consonant, change the *y* to *i* before adding any suffix except those beginning with *i.*

fry—fries—frying	**happy—happiness**
hurry—hurried—hurrying	**beauty—beautiful**
lady—ladies	

When forming the plural of a word that ends with a *y* that comes just after a vowel, add *s.*

toy—toys	**play—plays**	**monkey—monkeys**

When a one-syllable word ends in a consonant *(bat)* preceded by one vowel *(bat)*, double the final consonant before adding a suffix that begins with a vowel *(batting).*

sum—summary	**god—goddess**

When a multisyllable word ends in a consonant preceded by one vowel *(control)*, the accent is on the last syllable *(contról)*, and the suffix begins with a vowel *(ing)*—the same rule holds true: double the final consonant *(controlling).*

prefer—preferred	**begin—beginning**

Grammar Practice

Spelling 1

- *i* before *e*
- Silent *e*

If the underlined word is spelled correctly, write "correct." If it is spelled incorrectly, spell the word the right way.

Example: Jorge's family enjoys <u>dineing</u> out now and then.
dining

1. Jorge can't hide his <u>excitment</u> at seeing flan on the menu.

2. He likes <u>useing</u> lots of chocolate sauce on his dessert.

3. Jorge says he could eat <u>nineteen</u> scoops of chocolate.

4. We don't <u>beleive</u> that's possible.

5. But Jorge's best <u>friend</u> saw him eat that much once.

6. We're surprised he doesn't gain a lot of <u>wieght</u>!

- Words Ending in *y*
- Consonant Endings

If the underlined word is spelled correctly, write "correct." If it is spelled incorrectly, spell the word the right way.

Example: Buses are an important means of transportation in many <u>cityes</u>.
cities

1. Although buses must stop often, they always seem to be <u>hurrying</u> along city streets.

2. During the evening, some routes are <u>omited</u> from the schedule.

3. On most <u>holidaies</u>, buses run on a reduced schedule.

4. One passenger was <u>carriing</u> four bags of <u>groceries</u> on a bus.

5. When he asked if he was on the right bus, the driver <u>refered</u> him to another bus route.

Grammar Practice

Spelling 2

- *i* before *e*
- Silent *e*

Find the misspelled word or words in each sentence and write the words the right way.

Example: The largeest state in the union is Alaska.

largest

1. Hawaii recieves the most rainfall of all the states, so umbrellas are quite usful for its residents.

2. Niether Connecticut nor Delaware is the smallest state.

3. In Wyoming, Yellowstone Park is part of an anceint volcano.

4. Ohio and New York are loseing many older people who prefer liveing in warmer states like Florida or Arizona.

- Words Ending in *y*
- Consonant Endings

If the underlined word is spelled correctly, write "correct." If it is spelled incorrectly, spell the word the right way.

Example: The mountains and <u>valleies</u> in the Smoky Mountains of Tennessee attract tourists.

valleys

1. A volcanic explosion, which <u>occured</u> a long time ago, formed Crater Lake in Oregon.

2. Squirrels <u>burying</u> nuts are a common sight in the Midwestern states of Iowa and Missouri.

3. In North Dakota, you can see jackrabbits <u>hoping</u> across the fields.

4. The new governor of California is <u>planing</u> next year's budget.

5. The warm sun on the plains of Montana <u>dryed</u> our rain-soaked tent.

Yellow Pages Guide to Improved Spelling

Be patient. Becoming a good speller takes time.

Check your spelling by using a dictionary or list of commonly misspelled words (like the list that follows). And, remember, don't rely too much on computer spell-checkers.

Learn the correct pronunciation of each word you are trying to spell. Knowing the correct pronunciation of a word will help you remember how it's spelled.

Look up the meaning of each word as you are checking the dictionary for pronunciation. (Knowing how to spell a word is of little use if you don't know what it means.)

Practice spelling the word before you close the dictionary. Look away from the page and try to see the word in your mind's eye. Write the word on a piece of paper. Check the spelling in the dictionary and repeat the process until you are able to spell the word correctly.

Keep a list of the words that you misspell.

Write often. As noted educator Frank Smith said, "There is little point in learning to spell if you have little intention of writing."

SPELLING

A

	account	after	almost
	accurate	afternoon	already
	accustom (ed)	afterward	although
abbreviate	ache	again	altogether
aboard	achieve (ment)	against	aluminum
about	acre	agreeable	always
above	across	agree (ment)	amateur
absence	actual	ah	ambulance
absent	adapt	aid	amendment
absolute (ly)	addition (al)	airy	among
abundance	address	aisle	amount
accelerate	adequate	alarm	analyze
accident	adjust (ment)	alcohol	ancient
accidental (ly)	admire	alike	angel
accompany	adventure	alive	anger
accomplice	advertise (ment)	alley	angle
accomplish	advertising	allowance	angry
according	afraid	all right	animal

anniversary
announce
annoyance
annual
anonymous
another
answer
Antarctic
anticipate
anxiety
anxious
anybody
anyhow
anyone
anything
anyway
anywhere
apartment
apiece
apologize
apparent (ly)
appeal
appearance
appetite
appliance
application
appointment
appreciate
approach
appropriate
approval
approximate
architect
Arctic
aren't
argument
arithmetic
around
arouse
arrange (ment)
arrival
article
artificial

asleep
assassin
assign (ment)
assistance
associate
association
assume
athlete
athletic
attach
attack (ed)
attempt
attendance
attention
attitude
attorney
attractive
audience
August
author
authority
automobile
autumn
available
avenue
average
awful (ly)
awkward

B

baggage
baking
balance
balloon
ballot
banana
bandage
bankrupt
barber
bargain
barrel

basement
basis
basket
battery
beautiful
beauty
because
become
becoming
before
began
beggar
beginning
behave
behavior
being
belief
believe
belong
beneath
benefit (ed)
between
bicycle
biscuit
blackboard
blanket
blizzard
bother
bottle
bottom
bough
bought
bounce
boundary
breakfast
breast
breath (n.)
breathe (v.)
breeze
bridge
brief
bright
brilliant

brother
brought
bruise
bubble
bucket
buckle
budget
building
bulletin
buoyant
bureau
burglar
bury
business
busy
button

cabbage
cafeteria
calendar
campaign
canal
cancel (ed)
candidate
candle
canister
cannon
cannot
canoe
can't
canyon
capacity
captain
carburetor
cardboard
career
careful
careless
carpenter
carriage

carrot	colossal	cooperate	deceive
cashier	column	corporation	decided
casserole	comedy	correspond	decision
casualty	coming	cough	declaration
catalog	commercial	couldn't	decorate
catastrophe	commission	counter	defense
catcher	commit	counterfeit	definite (ly)
caterpillar	commitment	country	definition
catsup	committed	county	delicious
ceiling	committee	courage	dependent
celebration	communicate	courageous	depot
cemetery	community	court	describe
census	company	courteous	description
century	comparison	courtesy	desert
certain (ly)	competition	cousin	deserve
certificate	competitive (ly)	coverage	design
challenge	complain	cozy	desirable
champion	complete (ly)	cracker	despair
changeable	complexion	cranky	dessert
character (istic)	compromise	crawl	deteriorate
chief	conceive	creditor	determine
children	concerning	cried	develop (ment)
chimney	concert	criticize	device (n.)
chocolate	concession	cruel	devise (v.)
choice	concrete	crumb	diamond
chorus	condemn	crumble	diaphragm
circumstance	condition	cupboard	diary
citizen	conductor	curiosity	dictionary
civilization	conference	curious	difference
classmates	confidence	current	different
classroom	congratulate	custom	difficulty
climate	connect	customer	dining
climb	conscience	cylinder	diploma
closet	conscious		director
clothing	conservative		disagreeable
coach	constitution		disappear
cocoa	continue		disappoint
cocoon	continuous	daily	disapprove
coffee	control	dairy	disastrous
collar	controversy	damage	discipline
college	convenience	danger (ous)	discover
colonel	convince	daughter	discuss
color	coolly	dealt	discussion

SPELLING

disease
dissatisfied
distinguish
distribute
divide
divine
divisible
division
doctor
doesn't
dollar
dormitory
doubt
dough
dual
duplicate

 E

eager (ly)
economy
edge
edition
efficiency
eight
eighth
either
elaborate
electricity
elephant
eligible
ellipse
embarrass
emergency
emphasize
employee
employment
enclose
encourage
engineer
enormous
enough

entertain
enthusiastic
entirely
entrance
envelop (v.)
envelope (n.)
environment
equipment
equipped
equivalent
escape
especially
essential
establish
every
evidence
exaggerate
exceed
excellent
except
exceptional (ly)
excite
exercise
exhaust (ed)
exhibition
existence
expect
expensive
experience
explain
explanation
expression
extension
extinct
extraordinary
extreme (ly)

 F

facilities
familiar
family

famous
fascinate
fashion
fatigue (d)
faucet
favorite
feature
February
federal
fertile
field
fierce
fiery
fifty
finally
financial (ly)
foliage
forcible
foreign
forfeit
formal (ly)
former (ly)
forth
fortunate
forty
forward
fountain
fourth
fragile
freight
friend (ly)
frighten
fulfill
fundamental
further
furthermore

 G

gadget
gauge
generally

generous
genius
gentle
genuine
geography
ghetto
ghost
gnaw
government
governor
graduation
grammar
grateful
grease
grief
grocery
grudge
gruesome
guarantee
guard
guardian
guess
guidance
guide
guilty
gymnasium

 H

hammer
handkerchief
handle (d)
handsome
haphazard
happen
happiness
harass
hastily
having
hazardous
headache
height

hemorrhage
hesitate
history
hoarse
holiday
honor
hoping
hopping
horrible
hospital
humorous
hurriedly
hydraulic
hygiene
hymn

icicle
identical
illegible
illiterate
illustrate
imaginary
imaginative
imagine
imitation
immediate (ly)
immense
immigrant
immortal
impatient
importance
impossible
improvement
inconvenience
incredible
indefinitely
independence
independent
individual
industrial

inferior
infinite
inflammable
influential
initial
initiation
innocence
innocent
installation
instance
instead
insurance
intelligence
intention
interested
interesting
interfere
interpret
interrupt
interview
investigate
invitation
irrigate
island
issue

jealous (y)
jewelry
journal
journey
judgment
juicy

kitchen
knew
knife
knives

knock
knowledge
knuckles

label
laboratory
ladies
language
laugh
laundry
lawyer
league
lecture
legal
legible
legislature
leisure
length
liable
library
license
lieutenant
lightning
likable
likely
liquid
listen
literature
living
loaves
loneliness
loose
lose
loser
losing
lovable
lovely

M

machinery
magazine
magnificent
maintain
majority
making
manual
manufacture
marriage
material
mathematics
maximum
mayor
meant
measure
medicine
medium
message
mileage
miniature
minimum
minute
mirror
miscellaneous
mischievous
miserable
missile
misspell
moisture
molecule
monotonous
monument
mortgage
mountain
muscle
musician
mysterious

N

naive
natural (ly)
necessary
negotiate
neighbor (hood)
neither
nickel
niece
nineteen
nineteenth
ninety
ninth
noisy
noticeable
nuclear
nuisance

O

obedience
obey
obstacle
occasion
occasional (ly)
occur
occurred
offense
official
often
omission
omitted
operate
opinion
opponent
opportunity
opposite
ordinarily
original
outrageous

P

package
paid
pamphlet
paradise
paragraph
parallel
paralyze
parentheses
partial
participant
participate
particular (ly)
pasture
patience
peculiar
people
perhaps
permanent
perpendicular
persistent
personal (ly)
personnel
perspiration
persuade
phase
physician
piece
pitcher
planned
plateau
playwright
pleasant
pleasure
pneumonia
politician
possess
possible
practical (ly)
prairie
precede
precious

precise (ly)
precision
preferable
preferred
prejudice
preparation
presence
previous
primitive
principal
principle
prisoner
privilege
probably
procedure
proceed
professor
prominent
pronounce
pronunciation
protein
psychology
pumpkin
pure

Q

quarter
questionnaire
quiet
quite
quotient

R

raise
realize
really
receipt
receive
received

recipe
recognize
recommend
reign
relieve
religious
remember
repetition
representative
reservoir
resistance
respectfully
responsibility
restaurant
review
rhyme
rhythm
ridiculous
route

S

safety
salad
salary
sandwich
satisfactory
Saturday
scene
scenery
schedule
science
scissors
scream
screen
season
secretary
seize
sensible
sentence
separate
several

sheriff
shining
similar
since
sincere (ly)
skiing
sleigh
soldier
souvenir
spaghetti
specific
sphere
sprinkle
squeeze
squirrel
statue
stature
statute
stomach
stopped
straight
strength
stretched
studying
subtle
succeed
success
sufficient
summarize
supplement
suppose
surely
surprise
syllable
sympathy
symptom

 T

tariff
technique
temperature
temporary
terrible
territory
thankful
theater
their
there
therefore
thief
thorough (ly)
though
throughout
tired
tobacco
together
tomorrow
tongue
touch
tournament
toward
tragedy
treasurer
tried
tries
trouble
truly
Tuesday
typical

 U

unconscious
unfortunate (ly)
unique
university
unnecessary
until
usable
useful
using
usual (ly)
utensil

 V

vacation
vacuum
valuable
variety
various
vegetable
vehicle
very
vicinity
view
villain
violence
visible
visitor
voice
volume
voluntary
volunteer

 W

wander
wasn't
weather
Wednesday
weigh
weird
welcome
welfare
whale
where
whether
which
whole
wholly
whose
width
women
worthwhile
wouldn't
wreckage
writing
written

 Y

yellow
yesterday
yield

SPELLING

Using the Right Word

652.1
a, an

A is used before words that begin with a consonant sound; *an* is used before words that begin with any vowel sound except long "u."

a heap, a cat, an idol, an elephant, an honor, a historian, an umbrella, a unicorn

652.2
accept, except

The verb *accept* means "to receive"; the preposition *except* means "other than."

Melissa graciously accepted defeat. (verb)

All the boys except Zach were here. (preposition)

652.3
affect, effect

Affect is almost always a verb; it means "to influence." *Effect* can be a verb, but it is most often used as a noun that means "the result."

How does population growth affect us?

What are the effects of population growth?

652.4
allowed, aloud

The verb *allowed* means "permitted" or "let happen"; *aloud* is an adverb that means "in a normal voice."

We aren't allowed to read aloud in the library.

652.5
allusion, illusion

An *allusion* is a brief reference to or hint of something (person, place, thing, or idea). An *illusion* is a false impression or idea.

The Great Dontini, a magician, made an allusion to Houdini as he created the illusion of sawing his assistant in half.

652.6
a lot

A lot is not one word, but two; it is a general descriptive phrase meaning "plenty." (It should be avoided in formal writing.)

652.7
all right

All right is not one word, but two; it is a phrase meaning "satisfactory" or "okay." (Please note, the following *are* spelled correctly: *always, altogether, already, almost.*)

Grammar Practice

Using the Right Word 1

■ a, an; **accept, except;** affect, effect; **allowed, aloud**

For each of the following sentences, write a word from the list above to fill in the blank.

Example: Louis Braille had _____ accident that left him blind when he was three years old.

an

1. At the school he attended, everyone _____ Louis Braille could see.

2. Not being able to read can _____ anyone's life dramatically.

3. Louis Braille was _____ to become a teacher in 1926, when he was only 15 years old.

4. He created _____ alphabet of raised dots to make teaching easier.

5. It was _____ marvelous invention.

6. These dots _____ a blind person to read and write.

7. The Braille alphabet had quite an _____ on the blind population.

8. Most sight-impaired students _____ the challenge of learning the Braille system.

9. Today, people can also hear many books read _____ on cassettes or CD's.

10. This has had an _____ on my mom (who is not blind) because now she can "read" while driving her car!

Next Step: Write a brief paragraph about learning a new skill. Use the words *a lot* and *all right* correctly.

RIGHT WORD

654.1
already,
all ready

Already is an adverb that tells when. *All ready* is a phrase meaning "completely ready."

We have already eaten breakfast; now we are all ready for school.

654.2
altogether,
all together

Altogether is always an adverb meaning "completely." *All together* is used to describe people or things that are gathered in one place at one time.

Ms. Monces held her baton in the air and said, "Okay, class, all together now: sing!"

Unfortunately, there was altogether too much street noise for us to hear her.

654.3
among, between

Among is used when speaking of more than two persons or things. *Between* is used when speaking of only two.

The three friends talked among themselves as they tried to choose between trumpet or trombone lessons.

654.4
amount, number

Amount is used to describe things that you cannot count. *Number* is used when you can actually count the persons or things.

The amount of interest in playing the tuba is shown by the number of kids learning to play the instrument.

654.5
annual,
biannual,
semiannual,
biennial,
perennial

An *annual* event happens once every year. A *biannual* (or *semiannual*) event happens twice a year. A *biennial* event happens once every two years. A *perennial* event happens year after year.

The annual PTA rummage sale is so successful that it will now be a semiannual event.

The neighbor has some wonderful perennial flowers.

654.6
ant, aunt

An *ant* is an insect. An *aunt* is a female relative (the sister of a person's mother or father).

My aunt is an entomologist, a scientist who studies ants and other insects.

654.7
ascent, assent

Ascent is the act of rising or climbing; *assent* is agreement.

After the group's ascent of five flights of stairs to the meeting room, plans for elevator repairs met with quick assent.

Grammar Practice

Using the Right Word 2

■ already, all ready; **altogether, all together;** among, between; **amount, number;** ant, aunt

 For each of the following sentences, write the correct choice from each set of words in parentheses.

Example: We *(already, all ready)* have plans for the holiday.
already

1. Every Memorial Day my family meets at my *(ant's, aunt's)* house for a family picnic.

2. Many members of the family *(all ready, already)* live in the same town she lives in.

3. When the out-of-town people arrive, there are 53 of us *(all together, altogether)*.

4. Last year, as we were *(all ready, already)* to start eating our food, a large *(amount, number)* of *(ants, aunts)* invaded the picnic area.

5. The family was *(all together, altogether)* disappointed in that year's picnic.

6. As the adults talked *(among, between)* themselves, I heard them say we should get together more often.

7. All my cousins expressed a strong *(amount, number)* of interest when they heard this idea.

8. Maybe we can squeeze in another family gathering sometime *(among, between)* Independence Day and Labor Day.

Next Step: Write three sentences that show your understanding of these words: *amount, among,* and *between.*

656.1
bare, bear

The adjective *bare* means "naked." A *bear* is a large, heavy animal with shaggy hair.

Despite his bare feet, the man chased the polar bear across the snow.

The verb *bear* means "to put up with" or "to carry."

Dwayne could not bear another of his older brother's lectures.

656.2
base, bass

Base is the foundation or the lower part of something. *Bass* (pronounced like "base") is a deep sound or tone.

The stereo speakers are on a base so solid that even the loudest bass tones don't rattle it.

Bass (rhymes with "mass") is a fish.

Jim hooked a record-setting bass, but it got away . . . so he says.

656.3
beat, beet

The verb *beat* means "to strike, to defeat," and the noun *beat* is a musical term for rhythm or tempo. A *beet* is a carrot-like vegetable (often red).

The beat of the drum in the marching band encouraged the fans to cheer on the team. After they beat West High's team four games to one, many team members were as red as a beet.

656.4
berth, birth

Berth is a space or compartment. *Birth* is the process of being born.

We pulled aside the curtain in our train berth to view the birth of a new day outside our window.

656.5
beside, besides

Beside means "by the side of." *Besides* means "in addition to."

Besides a flashlight, Kedar likes to keep his pet boa beside his bed at night.

656.6
billed, build

Billed means either "to be given a bill" or "to have a beak." The verb *build* means "to construct."

We asked the carpenter to build us a birdhouse. She billed us for time and materials.

656.7
blew, blue

Blew is the past tense of "blow." *Blue* is a color and is also used to mean "feeling low in spirits."

As the wind blew out the candles in the dark blue room, I felt more blue than ever.

Grammar Practice

Using the Right Word 3

■ bare, bear; **base, bass**; beat, beet; **billed, build**; blew, blue

 For each pair of words in parentheses below, write the line number and the correct choice.

Example: 1   The city decided to *(billed, build)* a skateboard
2   park near the baseball diamond.
1   *build*

1   In 1958, ocean surfers became frustrated by small waves

2 and bad weather. They couldn't *(bare, bear)* being off their boards

3 for long, so they took to the streets with skateboards. Soon

4 skateboarding became a craze on the West Coast.

5   The first contest to see who could *(beat, beet)* all the other

6 competitors was held in Hermosa, California, in 1963. Some guided

7 their skateboards with their *(bare, bear)* feet, but most wore gym

8 shoes. However, it would be almost 10 years before boarders could

9 *(billed, build)* up the sport's popularity nationwide. By this time,

10 better wheels and trucks (the metal parts that hold the wheels to

11 the board) made jumps and other tricks possible. Skateboarders

12 now seemed to sail right into the *(blew, blue)* sky as their boards

13 climbed up specially built, steep walls.

14   A strong *(base, bass)* of support among the real competitors

15 kept the sport going. In 2003, skateboarding *(blew, blue)* past

16 artificial wall climbing and paintball to become the fastest growing

17 extreme sport in the country.

Next Step: Write three sentences that show your understanding of
these words: *bare, billed,* and *bass.*

RIGHT WORD

658.1
board, bored

A *board* is a piece of wood. *Board* also means "a group or council that helps run an organization."

The school board approved the purchase of 50 pine boards for the woodworking classes.

Bored means "to become weary or tired of something." It can also mean "made a hole by drilling."

Dulé bored a hole in the ice and dropped in a fishing line.
Waiting and waiting for a bite bored him.

658.2
borrow, lend

Borrow means "to *receive* for temporary use." *Lend* means "to *give* for temporary use."

I asked Mom, "May I borrow $15 for a CD?"
She said, "I can lend you $15 until next Friday."

658.3
brake, break

A *brake* is a device used to stop a vehicle. The verb *break* means "to split, crack, or destroy"; as a noun, *break* means "gap or interruption."

After the brake on my bike failed, I took a break to fix it so I wouldn't break a bone.

658.4
bring, take

Use *bring* when the action is moving toward the speaker; use *take* when the action is moving away from the speaker.

Grandpa asked me to take the garbage out and bring him today's paper.

658.5
by, buy, bye

By is a preposition meaning "near" or "not later than." *Buy* is a verb meaning "to purchase."

By tomorrow I hope to buy tickets for the final match of the tournament.

Bye is the position of being automatically advanced to the next tournament round without playing.

Our soccer team received a bye because of our winning record.

658.6
can, may

Can means "able to," while *may* means "permitted to."

"Can I go to the library?"
(This actually means "Are my mind and body strong enough to get me there?")
"May I go?"
(This means "Do I have your permission to go?")

Grammar Practice

Using the Right Word 4

■ board, bored; **brake, break**; bring, take; **by, buy**; can, may

 For each numbered sentence below, write the word "correct" if the underlined word is used correctly. If it is incorrect, write the right word.

Example: A tornado can drive a <u>bored</u> into a tree.

board

(1) A tornado is a powerful, twisting windstorm that <u>can</u> destroy just about anything in its path. **(2)** A tornado will easily <u>brake</u> a wooden house into many pieces. **(3)** A tornado <u>takes</u> destruction wherever it touches down.

(4) <u>Buy</u> the time a storm has passed, relief workers are on their way to the scene. **(5)** Usually, only residents or relief workers <u>may</u> enter an area damaged by a tornado.

 For each of the following sentences, write the correct choice from each set of words in parentheses.

Example: An elevator has a special *(break, brake)* to prevent accidents.

brake

1. Would you please *(bring, take)* that garbage out to the dumpster?

2. Dad, *(can, may)* I use your set of wrenches?

3. Leander plans to *(by, buy)* a new CD next week.

4. Someone bumped the table, causing the glass to *(brake, break)*.

5. Pablo has to walk *(by, buy)* an abandoned building every day.

6. Mrs. Serbins said we *(can, may)* stay inside for recess today.

7. Johar is always complaining that he is *(board, bored)* and has nothing to do.

8. Felipe said, "Please *(bring, take)* me a glass of water."

RIGHT WORD

660.1
canvas, canvass

Canvas is a heavy cloth; *canvass* means "ask people for votes or opinions."

Our old canvas tent leaks.

Someone with a clipboard is canvassing the neighborhood.

660.2
capital, capitol

Capital can be either a noun, referring to a city or to money, or an adjective, meaning "major or important." *Capitol* is used only when talking about a building.

The capitol building is in the capital city for a capital (major) reason: The city government contributed the capital (money) for the building project.

660.3
cell, sell

Cell means "a small room" or "a small unit of life basic to all plants and animals." *Sell* is a verb meaning "to give up for a price."

Today we looked at a human skin cell under a microscope.

Let's sell those old bicycles at the rummage sale.

660.4
cent, sent, scent

Cent (1/100 of a dollar) is a coin; *sent* is the past tense of the verb "send"; *scent* is an odor or a smell.

After our car hit a skunk, we sent our friends a postcard that said, "One cent doesn't go far, but skunk scent seems to last forever."

660.5
chord, cord

Chord may mean "an emotion or a feeling," but it is more often used to mean "the sound of three or more musical tones played at the same time." A *cord* is a string or rope.

The band struck a chord at the exact moment the mayor pulled the cord on the drape covering the new statue.

660.6
chose, choose

Chose (chōz) is the past tense of the verb *choose* (chōoz).

This afternoon Mom chose tacos and hot sauce; this evening she will choose an antacid.

660.7
coarse, course

Coarse means "rough or crude." *Course* means "a path" or "a class or series of studies."

In our cooking course, we learned to use coarse salt and freshly ground pepper in salads.

Grammar Practice

Using the Right Word 5

■ capital, capitol; **cell, sell;** sent, scent; **chose, choose;**
coarse, course

**For each of the following sentences, write the correct choice from each
set of words in parentheses.**

Example: Carlos's Coffee Shops *(sell, cell)* the world's best
breakfast burritos.

sell

1. If I had lots of *(capital, capitol)* to spend, I'd buy a big-screen
   TV.

2. Is your state's *(capital, capitol)* building located on the highest
   ground in your *(capital, capitol)* city?

3. Johnson City's old jailhouse, which had only three *(cells, sells)*,
   is now a small restaurant.

4. Rigid walls surround the *(cells, sells)* of most plants, bacteria,
   fungi, and algae.

5. Reggie's older sister is taking a creative writing *(course, coarse)*
   at the community center.

6. We often smell the *(sent, scent)* from the Bread Factory drifting
   up to our second-floor apartment.

7. I even *(sent, scent)* my cousin Cade an e-mail to tell him how
   good it smells!

8. On Monday, Rhea *(chose, choose)* to color her hair pink, but
   tomorrow she may *(chose, choose)* to make it bright green.

9. Did Leroy and Tamra use fine or *(course, coarse)* sandpaper to
   make the sand dunes for their geography project?

Next Step: Write four sentences that show your understanding of the
following words: *choose, scent, capitol,* and *sell.*

RIGHT WORD

662.1
complement, compliment

Complement means "to complete or go with." *Compliment* is an expression of admiration or praise.

> Aunt Athena said, "Your cheese sauce really complements this cauliflower!"

> "Thank you for the compliment," I replied.

662.2
continual, continuous

Continual refers to something that happens again and again; *continuous* refers to something that doesn't stop happening.

> Sunlight hits Peoria, Iowa, on a continual basis; but sunlight hits the earth continuously.

662.3
counsel, council

When used as a noun, *counsel* means "advice"; when used as a verb, *counsel* means "to advise." *Council* refers to a group that advises.

> The student council asked for counsel from its trusted adviser.

662.4
creak, creek

A *creak* is a squeaking sound; a *creek* is a stream.

> I heard a creak from the old dock under my feet as I fished in the creek.

662.5
cymbal, symbol

A *cymbal* is a metal instrument shaped like a plate. A *symbol* is something (usually visible) that stands for or represents another thing or idea (usually invisible).

> The damaged cymbal lying on the stage was a symbol of the band's final concert.

662.6
dear, deer

Dear means "loved or valued"; *deer* are animals.

> My dear, old great-grandmother leaves corn and salt licks in her yard to attract deer.

662.7
desert, dessert

A *desert* is a barren wilderness. *Dessert* is a food served at the end of a meal.

> In the desert, cold water is more inviting than even the richest dessert.

The verb *desert* means "to abandon"; the noun *desert* (pronounced like the verb) means "deserving reward or punishment."

> A spy who deserts his country will receive his just deserts if he is caught.

Grammar Practice

Using the Right Word 6

■ counsel, council; **creak, creek;** cymbal, symbol;
dear, deer; desert, dessert

For each of the following sentences, write the correct choice from each set of words in parentheses.

Example: My dad's shed door *(creaks, creeks)* every time it opens.
creaks

1. I heard a fish splash in the *(creek, creak)*.

2. Sometimes we see *(deer, dear)* drinking water from a nearby pond.

3. Last year when we were in the *(dessert, desert)*, we saw vultures flying overhead.

4. The bald eagle is our country's *(cymbal, symbol)* of freedom.

5. Our family dinners at Grandma's are always followed by *(dessert, desert)*.

6. After such a big meal, Grandpa's old wooden chair begins to *(creek, creak)*.

7. The leader of the band *(councils, counsels)* students to store their instruments properly.

8. After the school concert, Janelle put her *(cymbal, symbol)* away.

9. Her *(deer, dear)* grandfather was so proud of her performance.

10. The student *(counsel, council)* decided that another concert should be scheduled.

11. If the floodwaters continue to rise, we will be forced to *(dessert, desert)* our house.

Next Step: Write three sentences that show your understanding of these words: *symbol, dessert,* and *counsel.*

RIGHT WORD

664.1 die, dye

Die (dying) means "to stop living." *Dye* (dyeing) is used to change the color of something.

The young girl hoped that her sick goldfish wouldn't die.

My sister dyes her hair with coloring that washes out.

664.2 faint, feign, feint

Faint means "feeble, without strength" or "to fall unconscious." *Feign* is a verb that means "to pretend or make up." *Feint* is a noun that means "a move or an activity that is pretended in order to divert attention."

The actors feigned a sword duel. One man staggered and fell in a feint. The audience gave faint applause.

664.3 farther, further

Farther is used when you are writing about a physical distance. *Further* means "additional."

Alaska reaches farther north than Iceland. For further information, check your local library.

664.4 fewer, less

Fewer refers to the number of separate units; *less* refers to bulk quantity.

I may have less money than you have, but I have fewer worries.

664.5 fir, fur

Fir refers to a type of evergreen tree; *fur* is animal hair.

The Douglas fir tree is named after a Scottish botanist.

An arctic fox has white fur in the winter.

664.6 flair, flare

Flair means "a natural talent" or "style"; *flare* means "to light up quickly" or "burst out" (or an object that does so).

Jenrette has a flair for remaining calm when other people's tempers flare.

664.7 for, four

The preposition *for* means "because of" or "directed to"; *four* is the number 4.

Mary had grilled steaks and chicken for the party, but the dog had stolen one of the four steaks.

Grammar Practice

Using the Right Word 7

◼ die, dye; **farther, further;** fewer, less; **fir, fur;** for, four

 For each of the following sentences, write the correct choice from each set of words in parentheses.

Example: Yesterday I spent *(fewer, less)* money at the mall than I did last time I was there.
less

1. An elephant separates itself from the rest of the herd when it is about to *(dye, die)*.

2. Leona walks six blocks *(further, farther)* to school than Tomei does.

3. I spend *(less, fewer)* time studying than my brother does, so I have *(less, fewer)* A's on my report card than he does.

4. Sometimes, when cattle and horses rub against *(fur, fir)* trees, bits of their *(fur, fir)* get stuck in the rough bark.

5. Do you want to *(dye, die)* your shoes orange or chartreuse for "Crazy Shoe Day"?

6. Sloan wants to trade her lunch *(four, for)* yours.

7. Sloan's lunch is a day-old sandwich, soggy potato chips, and *(four, for)* rock-hard chocolate chip cookies.

8. Ramón is helping his dad plant some Douglas *(furs, firs)* in their yard.

9. Does Seattle, Washington, or Portland, Oregon, have *(less, fewer)* sunny days?

10. If you need *(further, farther)* help with the assignment, call me after dinner.

Next Step: Show your understanding of the words *dye, further,* and *fewer* by using each of them correctly in a sentence.

666.1 good, well

Good is an adjective; *well* is nearly always an adverb.

The strange flying machines flew well. (The adverb *well* modifies *flew*.)

They looked good as they flew overhead. (The adjective *good* modifies *they*.)

When used in writing about health, *well* is an adjective.

The pilots did not feel well, however, after the long, hard race.

666.2 hare, hair

A *hare* is an animal similar to a rabbit; *hair* refers to the growth covering the head and body of mammals and human beings.

When a hare darted out in front of our car, the hair on my head stood up.

666.3 heal, heel

Heal means "to mend or restore to health." *Heel* is the back part of a human foot.

I got a blister on my heel from wearing my new shoes. It won't heal unless I wear my old ones.

666.4 hear, here

You *hear* sounds with your ears. *Here* is the opposite of *there* and means "nearby."

666.5 heard, herd

Heard is the past tense of the verb "to hear"; *herd* is a group of animals.

The herd of grazing sheep raised their heads when they heard the collie barking in the distance.

666.6 heir, air

An *heir* is a person who inherits something; *air* is what we breathe.

Will the next generation be heir to terminally polluted air?

666.7 hole, whole

A *hole* is a cavity or hollow place. *Whole* means "entire or complete."

The hole in the ozone layer is a serious problem requiring the attention of the whole world.

666.8 immigrate, emigrate

Immigrate means "to come into a new country or area." *Emigrate* means "to go out of one country to live in another."

Martin Ulferts immigrated to this country in 1882. He was only three years old when he emigrated from Germany.

Grammar Practice

Using the Right Word 8

◼ good, well; **hare, hair;** hear, here; **heard, herd;** heir, air; **hole, whole**

 For each of the following sentences, write the correct choice from each set of words in parentheses.

Example: Mammals are animals covered with *(hare, hair).*
hair

1. A wood duck looks for a *(hole, whole)* in a tree to build a nest.

2. Although you can't see turtles' ears, they can *(hear, here)* very *(good, well).*

3. The peregrine falcon can dive through the *(heir, air)* at 200 miles per hour.

4. I'd say that's a pretty *(good, well)* speed!

5. Caribou always travel in a large *(heard, herd).*

6. The sounds a whale makes underwater can be *(heard, herd)* for miles.

7. A *(hare, hair)* has long ears and very long hind legs.

8. The sailfish can swim from *(hear, here)* to there faster than any other fish.

9. While humans grow *(hare, hair)* in just a few places, most mammals are covered with it.

10. As an *(heir, air)* of his uncle, Rashid was given the scarlet macaw.

11. Listen! The *(hole, whole)* forest is filled with singing birds.

12. They sound *(good, well),* don't they?

Next Step: Write three sentences about animals. Show your understanding of these words: *herd, whole,* and *hair.*

668.1
imply, infer

Imply means "to suggest indirectly"; *infer* means "to draw a conclusion from facts."

"Since you have to work, may I infer that you won't come to my party?" Guy asked.

"No, I only meant to imply that I would be late," Rochelle responded.

668.2
it's, its

It's is the contraction of "it is." *Its* is the possessive form of "it."

It's a fact that a minnow's teeth are in its throat.

668.3
knew, new

Knew is the past tense of the verb "know." *New* means "recent or modern."

If I knew how to fix it, I would not need a new one!

668.4
know, no

Know means "to recognize or understand." *No* means "the opposite of yes."

Phil, do you know Cheri?

No, I've never met her.

668.5
later, latter

Later means "after a period of time." *Latter* refers to the second of two things mentioned.

The band arrived later and set up the speakers and the lights. The latter made the stage look like a carnival ride.

668.6
lay, lie

Lay means "to place." (*Lay* is a transitive verb; that means it needs a word to complete the meaning.) *Lie* means "to recline." (*Lie* is an intransitive verb.)

Lay your sleeping bag on the floor before you lie down on it. (*Lay* needs the word *bag* to complete its meaning.)

668.7
lead, led

Lead (lēd) is a present tense verb meaning "to guide." The past tense of the verb is *led* (lĕd). The noun *lead* (lĕd) is the metal.

Guides planned to lead the settlers to safe quarters. Instead, they led them into a winter storm.

Peeling paint in old houses may contain lead.

668.8
learn, teach

Learn means "to get information"; *teach* means "to give information."

I want to learn how to sew. Will you teach me?

Grammar Practice

Using the Right Word 9

■ it's, its; **knew, new;** know, no; **lay, lie;** lead, led; **learn, teach**

 For each numbered sentence below, write the correct choice from each set of words in parentheses.

> **Example:** Ancient stone carvings show that the Egyptians *(new, knew)* about swimming 5,000 years ago.
> *knew*

(1) Doctors *(no, know)* that swimming is good exercise. **(2)** All children should *(learn, teach)* how to swim, but parents need to make sure they *(lie, lay)* down the ground rules about water safety.

Some kids take swimming lessons. **(3)** After a short talk, the swimming instructor will *(led, lead)* students to the pool and *(learn, teach)* them basic strokes. The most common stroke is called the front crawl. **(4)** *(Its, It's)* how most people swim. **(5)** Some people like to *(lie, lay)* on their backs when they swim—this is called the backstroke. **(6)** Some Olympic swimmers have *(lead, led)* the race doing the butterfly stroke. **(7)** A *(new, knew)* swimmer might think that this stroke is too difficult to do, but *(no, know)* stroke is impossible to learn.

(8) Many people have tried to swim the English Channel; *(it's, its)* water is very cold. **(9)** Although the swimmers *(new, knew)* what a difficult task it would be, I'm sure they looked forward to going home to *(lie, lay)* down in a nice, warm bed!

Next Step: Lay and lie are challenging words to use correctly. Write two or more sentences that show you know the meanings of those words.

670.1 leave, let

Leave means "fail to take along." *Let* means "allow."

Rozi wanted to leave her boots at home, but Jorge wouldn't let her.

670.2 like, as

Like is a preposition meaning "similar to"; *as* is a conjunction meaning "to the same degree" or "while." *Like* usually introduces a phrase; *as* usually introduces a clause.

The glider floated like a bird. The glider floated as the pilot had hoped it would.

As we circled the airfield, we saw maintenance carts moving like ants below us.

670.3 loose, lose, loss

Loose (lüs) means "free or untied"; *lose* (looz) means "to misplace or fail to win"; *loss* (lôs) means "something lost."

These jeans are too loose in the waist since my recent weight loss. I still want to lose a few more pounds.

670.4 made, maid

Made is the past tense of "make," which means to "create," "prepare," or "put in order." A *maid* is a female servant; *maid* is also used to describe an unmarried girl or young woman.

The hotel maid asked if our beds needed to be made.

Grandma made a chocolate cake for dessert.

A maid strolled in the garden before the concert.

670.5 mail, male

Mail refers to letters or packages handled by the postal service. *Male* refers to the masculine sex.

My little brother likes getting junk mail.

The male sea horse, not the female, takes care of the fertilized eggs.

670.6 main, mane

Main refers to the most important part. *Mane* is the long hair growing from the top or sides of the neck of certain animals, such as the horse, lion, and so on.

The main thing we noticed about the magician's tamed lion was its luxurious mane.

670.7 meat, meet

Meat is food or flesh; *meet* means "to come upon or encounter."

I'd like you to meet the butcher who sells the leanest meat in town.

Grammar Practice

Using the Right Word 10

■ leave, let; **like, as;** loose, lose, loss; **main, mane;** meat, meet

 For each of the following sentences, write the correct choice from each set of words in parentheses.

Example: Emme and James swim *(as, like)* fish.
like

1. They glide across the surface *(as, like)* water bugs *(as, like)* we sit and watch.

2. Your tomcat's *(mane, main)* makes him look like a miniature lion.

3. Don't *(leave, let)* the dog eat cake anymore.

4. The straps on Brad's backpack are very *(loose, lose)*.

5. If he's not careful, he may *(loose, lose)* it.

6. The *(lose, loss)* of his valuable art supplies would be a disaster!

7. Mom wouldn't *(leave, let)* me go to Jule's party until 6:30.

8. At this weekend's *(main, mane)* event, Vegan Fest, no one will be eating any *(meat, meet)*.

9. At the stable, a woman was braiding her horse's *(main, mane)*.

10. *(As, Like)* a ballerina, Marta pranced across her room, twirling and hopping.

11. I don't want to *(lose, loss)* my ring while I'm swimming, so I'll *(leave, let)* it at home.

12. "I'm happy to finally *(meat, meet)* you," said Rocco's pen pal.

13. "You look *(as, like)* your picture," he said.

Next Step: Write two sentences that show your understanding of the words *leave* and *let*.

RIGHT WORD

672.1
medal, metal, meddle, mettle

A *medal* is an award. *Metal* is an element like iron or gold. *Meddle* means "to interfere." *Mettle,* a noun, refers to quality of character.

Grandpa's friend received a medal for showing his mettle in battle. Grandma, who loves to meddle in others' business, asked if the award was a precious metal.

672.2
miner, minor

A *miner* digs in the ground for valuable ore. A *minor* is a person who is not legally an adult. *Minor* means "of no great importance" when used as an adjective.

The use of minors as miners is no minor problem.

672.3
moral, morale

Moral relates to what is right or wrong or to the lesson to be drawn from a story. *Morale* refers to a person's attitude or mental condition.

The moral of this story is "Everybody loves a winner."

After the unexpected win at football, morale was high throughout the town.

672.4
morning, mourning

Morning refers to the first part of the day (before noon); *mourning* means "showing sorrow."

Abby was mourning her test grades all morning.

672.5
oar, or, ore

An *oar* is a paddle used in rowing or steering a boat. *Or* is a conjunction indicating choice. *Ore* refers to a mineral made up of several different kinds of material, as in iron ore.

Either use one oar to push us away from the dock, or start the boat's motor.

Silver-copper ore is smelted and refined to extract each metal.

672.6
pain, pane

Pain is the feeling of being hurt. A *pane* is a section or part of something.

Dad looked like he was in pain when he found out we broke a pane of glass in the neighbor's front door.

672.7
pair, pare, pear

A *pair* is a couple (two); *pare* is a verb meaning "to peel"; *pear* is the fruit.

A pair of doves nested in the pear tree.

Please pare the apples for the pie.

Grammar Practice

Using the Right Word 11

■ medal, metal; **miner, minor;** oar, ore, or; **pain, pane;**
pair, pare, pear

**For each of the following sentences, write the correct choice from each
set of words in parentheses.**

Example: *(Miners, Minors)* work underground to find *(oar, ore)*
used in manufacturing.
Miners, ore

1. Should I use my *(oar, or)* on the left side of the boat *(ore, or)*
   on the right side?

2. We are required to wear a *(pare, pair)* of blue socks with our
   uniforms.

3. A first-place winner in the Olympic Games receives a
   (metal, medal) made of a precious *(metal, medal)*—gold.

4. Do you know that some states still call people between the
   ages of 18 and 21 *(minors, miners)*?

5. When Abe stumbled and fell, he felt a sharp *(pane, pain)* as his
   arm went through a *(pane, pain)* of glass in the patio door.

6. Juan received our school's *(metal, medal)* of excellence during
   the graduation ceremony.

7. If you are going to put that *(pare, pear)* in the fruit salad, you
   have to *(pare, pear)* it first.

8. Huge barges carry iron *(oar, ore)* to steel mills along the
   Mississippi River.

9. Most fine jewelry is made of *(metal, medal)*.

10. A *(pare, pair)* of red-handled scissors and a *(pare, pear)*-shaped
    pincushion are on Grandma Delora's sewing table.

Next Step: Write a short paragraph in which you correctly use four
of the italicized words above.

RIGHT WORD

674.1 past, passed

Passed is always a verb; it is the past tense of *pass*. *Past* can be used as a noun, as an adjective, or as a preposition.

> A motorcycle passed my dad's 'Vette. (verb)
>
> The old man won't forget the past. (noun)
>
> I'm sorry, but I'd rather not talk about my past life. (adjective)
>
> Old Blue walked right past the cat and never saw it. (preposition)

674.2 peace, piece

Peace means "harmony, or freedom from war." A *piece* is a part or fragment of something.

> In order to keep peace among the triplets, each one had to have an identical piece of cake.

674.3 peak, peek, pique

A *peak* is a "high point" or a "pointed end." *Peek* means "brief look." *Pique*, as a verb, means "to excite by challenging"; as a noun, it means "a feeling of resentment."

> Just a peek at Pike's Peak in the Rocky Mountains can pique a mountain climber's curiosity.
>
> In a pique, she marched away from her giggling sisters.

674.4 personal, personnel

Personal means "private." *Personnel* are people working at a job.

> Some thoughts are too personal to share.
>
> The personnel manager will be hiring more workers.

674.5 plain, plane

A *plain* is an area of land that is flat or level; it also means "clearly seen or clearly understood" and "ordinary."

> It's plain to see why the early settlers had trouble crossing the Great Plains.

Plane means "a flat, level surface" (as in geometry); it is also a tool used to smooth the surface of wood.

> When I saw that the door wasn't a perfect plane, I used a plane to make it smooth.

674.6 pore, pour, poor

A *pore* is an opening in the skin. *Pour* means "to cause a flow or stream." *Poor* means "needy."

> People perspire through the pores in their skin. Pour yourself a glass of water. Your poor body needs it!

Grammar Practice

Using the Right Word 12

■ past, passed; **peace, piece;** peak, peek; **personal, personnel;** plain, plane

 For each of the following sentences, write the correct choice from each set of words in parentheses.

Example: Imaginative wrapping on a gift box can make it more *(personal, personnel).*
personal

1. Uleasha's mom said to her friends, "I like the *(personal, personnel)* gifts Uleasha gives me."

2. She can make even a simple *(peace, piece)* of *(plain, plane)* paper into a work of art.

3. As Janet *(past, passed)* the group of women, she stopped to listen.

4. Janet took a *(peak, peek)* at one of Uleasha's origami cranes.

5. She could see how it would give Uleasha's mom a feeling of *(peace, piece).*

6. In the *(past, passed)*, origami was practiced only in the Far East.

7. Still a Japanese tradition, origami is now created everywhere— from the Great *(Plains, Planes)* to Greenland.

8. At the scene of the accident, the driver said he hadn't had a ticket in the *(past, passed)* 10 years.

9. Then the driver admitted he had been looking at a nearby mountain *(peak, peek).*

10. "We'll need more *(personal, personnel)* to get this mess cleaned up," said the officer.

Next Step: Write three sentences in which you use the word *past* in these different ways: as an adjective, as a noun, and as a preposition.

RIGHT WORD

676.1
principal,
principle

As an adjective, *principal* means "primary." As a noun, it can mean "a school administrator" or "a sum of money." *Principle* means "idea or doctrine."

> My mom's principal goal is to save money so she can pay off the principal balance on her loan from the bank.

> Hey, Charlie, I hear the principal gave you a detention.

> The principle of freedom is based on the principle of self-discipline.

676.2
quiet, quit, quite

Quiet is the opposite of "noisy." *Quit* means "to stop." *Quite* means "completely or entirely."

> I quit mowing even though I wasn't quite finished.
> The neighborhood was quiet again.

676.3
raise, rays, raze

Raise is a verb meaning "to lift or elevate." *Rays* are thin lines or beams. *Raze* is a verb that means "to tear down completely."

> When I raise this shade, bright rays of sunlight stream into the room.

> Construction workers will raze the old theater to make room for a parking lot.

676.4
real, very, really

Do not use the adjective *real* in place of the adverbs *very* or *really*.

> The plants scattered throughout the restaurant are not real.

> Hiccups are very embarrassing.

> Her nose is really small.

676.5
red, read

Red is a color; *read*, pronounced the same way, is the past tense of the verb meaning "to understand the meaning of written words and symbols."

> "I've read five books in two days," said the little boy.

> The librarian gave him a red ribbon.

Grammar Practice

Using the Right Word 13

■ quiet, quit, quite; **raise, rays, raze;** real, very, really; **red, read**

 For each of the following sentences, write the correct choice from each set of words in parentheses.

Example: It's *(quiet, quite)* nice to read a good book on a *(really, real)* rainy afternoon.
quite, really

1. Max's sister has beautiful *(read, red)* hair.

2. Have you ever seen the colors and patterns formed when *(raze, rays)* of sunlight pass through a prism?

3. Mom pleaded, "*(Quit, Quiet)* playing that CD so loudly and be *(quite, quiet)* for a while."

4. "That would make me *(quiet, quite)* happy!" she added.

5. The city will *(rays, raze)* the old water tower a week before the new one goes up.

6. A huge crane will *(raise, raze)* the new water tank to the top of the new tower.

7. I *(read, red)* an article about miniature horses.

8. It's *(real, really)* hard to believe that they are horses since they are not *(very, real)* tall.

9. I saw one in a parade once, and it definitely was a *(real, really)* horse.

10. I think it would be an interesting hobby to *(raise, rays)* these animals.

Next Step: Write a few sentences about a hobby that you find interesting. Use at least four of the italicized words above in your sentences. Then exchange papers with a classmate and read about each other's hobby.

RIGHT WORD

678.1
right, write, rite

Right means "correct or proper"; *right* is the opposite of "left"; it also refers to anything that a person has a legal claim to, as in "copyright." *Write* means "to record in print." *Rite* is a ritual or ceremonial act.

> We have to write an essay about how our rights are protected by the Constitution.
>
> Turn right at the next corner.
>
> A rite of passage is a ceremony that celebrates becoming an adult.

678.2
scene, seen

Scene refers to the setting or location where something happens; it also means "sight or spectacle." *Seen* is a form of the verb "see."

> The scene of the crime was roped off. We hadn't seen anyone go in or out of the building.

678.3
seam, seem

A *seam* is a line formed by connecting two pieces of material. *Seem* means "appear to exist."

> Every Thanksgiving, it seems, I stuff myself so much that my shirt seams threaten to burst.

678.4
sew, so, sow

Sew is a verb meaning "to stitch"; *so* is a conjunction meaning "in order that." The verb *sow* means "to plant."

> In Colonial times, the wife would sew the family clothes, and the husband would sow the family garden so the children could eat.

678.5
sight, cite, site

Sight means "the act of seeing" or "something that is seen." *Cite* means "to quote or refer to." A *site* is a location or position (including a Web site on the Internet).

> The Alamo at night was a sight worth the trip. I was also able to cite my visit to this historical site in my history paper.

678.6
sit, set

Sit means "to put the body in a seated position." *Set* means "to place." (*Set* is a transitive verb; that means it needs a direct object to complete its meaning.)

> How can you just sit there and watch as I set up all these chairs?

Grammar Practice

Using the Right Word 14

■ right, write, rite; **scene, seen;** sight, cite, site; **sit, set**

For each numbered sentence below, write the correct choice from each set of words in parentheses.

Example: A student needs to *(sight, cite)* sources used for a research report.

cite

(1) Mali will *(rite, write)* about the history of bicycles. **(2)** Several Web *(sites, cites)* about it can be found on the Internet. According to one Web page, Baron von Drais invented the first bike, a wooden one without pedals, in 1817. **(3)** He would *(sit, set)* on the bike and use his feet on the ground to make the bike move. **(4)** Men riding these bikes were quite a *(sight, site)* to see!

(5) For a long time, women were only *(scene, seen)* riding tricycles. **(6)** It was not considered *(right, rite)* for a woman to ride a bicycle. **(7)** If a woman rode a bike, she'd cause a *(scene, seen)*! **(8)** Now people see learning to ride a bike as a *(write, rite)* of growing up.

For each of the following sentences, write the correct choice from each set of words in parentheses.

Example: Is it *(write, right)* that I always have to take the garbage out?

right

1. Maybe you'd prefer to *(sit, set)* the table for dinner every evening.

2. Allow me to *(site, cite)* my mother: "Life is not fair."

3. James said he had already *(scene, seen)* that movie.

4. Just the *(sight, site)* of a skunk makes its enemies run.

5. Please *(write, rite)* a thank-you note to Grandma.

680.1 sole, soul

Sole means "single, only one"; *sole* also refers to the bottom surface of a foot or shoe. *Soul* refers to the spiritual part of a person.

Maggie got a job for the sole purpose of saving for a car.

The soles of these shoes are very thick.

"Who told you dogs don't have souls?" asked the kind veterinarian.

680.2 some, sum

Some means "an unknown number or part." *Sum* means "the whole amount."

The sum in the cash register was stolen by some thieves.

680.3 sore, soar

Sore means "painful"; to *soar* means "to rise or fly high into the air."

Craning to watch the eagle soar overhead, we soon had sore necks.

680.4 stationary, stationery

Stationary means "not movable"; *stationery* is the paper and envelopes used to write letters.

Grandpa designed and printed his own stationery.

All of the built-in furniture is stationary, of course.

680.5 steal, steel

Steal means "to take something without permission"; *steel* is a metal.

Early ironmakers had to steal recipes for producing steel.

680.6 than, then

Than is used in a comparison; *then* tells when.

Since tomorrow's weather is supposed to be nicer than today's, we'll go to the zoo then.

680.7 their, there, they're

Their is a possessive pronoun, one that shows ownership. (See **714.2**.) *There* is an adverb that tells where. *They're* is the contraction for "they are."

They're upset because their dog got into the garbage over there.

680.8 threw, through

Threw is the past tense of "throw." *Through* means "passing from one side to the other" or "by means of."

Through sheer talent and long practice, Nolan Ryan threw baseballs through the strike zone at more than 100 miles per hour.

Grammar Practice

Using the Right Word 15

■ some, sum; **sore, soar;** steal, steel; **their, there, they're**

 For each of the following sentences, write the correct choice from each set of words in parentheses.

Example: Hearing such beautiful music makes my spirits *(sore, soar)*.

soar

1. The rummage sale earned us the *(sum, some)* of $62.45.

2. There's a little *(sore, soar)* on my dog's paw.

3. Little League coaches spend hours teaching baseball players how to *(steal, steel)* a base.

4. Only *(sum, some)* of my teammates were able to save enough money for baseball camp.

5. *(Their, They're)* parents are helping them out.

6. Watching a kite *(sore, soar)* in the afternoon sky, Rubi felt peaceful.

7. Blueprints often call for *(steel, steal)* I-beams to support large buildings.

8. Linc's legs grew *(sore, soar)* as he struggled to finish the marathon.

9. Ms. Ramsay pointed to room 102 and whispered, "Shhh! *(Their, They're)* taking a test in *(they're, there)*."

10. *(They're, Their)* jackets, books, and papers were scattered here, *(their, there)*, and everywhere.

11. Robin Hood would *(steel, steal)* from the rich and give to the poor.

Next Step: See if you can, in one sentence, use the words *their, there,* and *they're* correctly.

RIGHT WORD

682.1
to, too, two

To is the preposition that can mean "in the direction of." (*To* also is used to form an infinitive. See 730.4.) *Too* is an adverb meaning "very or excessive." *Too* is often used to mean "also." *Two* is the number 2.

> Only two of Columbus's first three ships returned to Spain from the New World.

> Columbus was too restless to stay in Spain for long.

682.2
vain, vane, vein

Vain means "worthless." It may also mean "thinking too highly of one's self; stuck-up." *Vane* is a flat piece of material set up to show which way the wind blows. *Vein* refers to a blood vessel or a mineral deposit.

> The weather vane indicates the direction of wind.

> A blood vein determines the direction of flowing blood.

> The vain mind moves in no particular direction and thinks only about itself.

682.3
vary, very

Vary is a verb that means "to change." *Very* can be an adjective meaning "in the fullest sense" or "complete"; it can also be an adverb meaning "extremely."

> Garon's version of the event would vary from day to day. His very interesting story was the very opposite of the truth.

682.4
waist, waste

Waist is the part of the body just above the hips. The verb *waste* means "to wear away" or "to use carelessly"; the noun *waste* refers to material that is unused or useless.

> Don't waste your money on fast-food meals. What a waste to throw away all this food because you're concerned about the size of your waist!

682.5
wait, weight

Wait means "to stay somewhere expecting something." *Weight* is the measure of heaviness.

> When I have to wait for the bus, the weight of my backpack seems to keep increasing.

682.6
ware, wear, where

Ware means "a product to be sold"; *wear* means "to have on or to carry on one's body"; *where* asks the question "in what place or in what situation?"

> Where can you buy the best cookware to take on a campout—and the best rain gear to wear if it rains?

Grammar Practice

Using the Right Word 16

■ to, too, two; **waist, waste;** wait, weight; **wear, where**

For each of the following sentences, write the correct choice from each set of words in parentheses.

Example: I am not sure what costume I will *(wear, where)* to Alberto's Halloween party.
wear

1. I thought about being a knight, but then I'd have the *(wait, weight)* of all that armor.

2. Perhaps if I just wrap a grass skirt around my *(waist, waste)*, I'll look like a hula dancer.

3. I do have a wig that I can *(wear, where)*.

4. I got it last year, but I didn't use it—what a *(waist, waste)*!

5. I will *(wait, weight)* until this weekend *(to, too, two)* make my costume.

6. I hope making it won't be *(to, too, two)* much work.

7. I'll have *(to, too, two)* days to work on it, but I can't *(waist, waste)* any time because the party is on Monday.

8. Mom and Dad will drive me *(to, too, two)* the party, but they don't want me out *(to, too, two)* late on a school night.

9. I must look at a map to see *(wear, where)* Alberto's house is.

10. He said it's close to the public library; in fact, it's just *(to, too, two)* houses away.

11. It sounds like so much fun—I can't *(wait, weight)*!

Next Step: Write three sentences that show your understanding of the words *where, waste,* and *weight.*

RIGHT WORD

684.1
way, weigh

Way means "path or route" or "a series of actions." *Weigh* means "to measure weight."

What is the correct way to weigh liquid medicines?

684.2
weather,
whether

Weather refers to the condition of the atmosphere. *Whether* refers to a possibility.

The weather will determine whether I go fishing.

684.3
week, weak

A *week* is a period of seven days; *weak* means "not strong."

Last week when I had the flu, I felt light-headed and weak.

684.4
wet, whet

Wet means "soaked with liquid." *Whet* is a verb that means "to sharpen."

Of course, going swimming means I'll get wet, but all that exercise really whets my appetite.

684.5
which, witch

Which is a pronoun used to ask "what one or ones?" out of a group. A *witch* is a woman believed to have supernatural powers.

Which of the women in Salem in the 1600s were accused of being witches?

684.6
who, which,
that

When introducing a clause, *who* is used to refer to people; *which* refers to animals and nonliving beings but never to people (it introduces a nonrestrictive, or unnecessary, clause); *that* usually refers to animals or things but can refer to people (it introduces a restrictive, or necessary, clause).

The idea that pizza is junk food is crazy.

Pizza, which is quite nutritious, can be included in a healthful diet.

My mom, who is a dietician, said so.

684.7
who, whom

Who is used as the subject in a sentence; *whom* is used as the object of a preposition or as a direct object.

Who asked you to play tennis?

You beat whom at tennis? You played tennis with whom?

NOTE To test for who/whom, arrange the parts of the clause in a subject–verb–direct-object order. *Who* works as the subject, *whom* as the object. (See page 570.)

Grammar Practice

Using the Right Word 17

■ way, weigh; **weather, whether;** week, weak; **which, witch;** who, which, that

 For each of the following sentences, write the correct choice from each set of words in parentheses.

Example: Ms. Sebastian asked, *"(Which, Witch)* one of you can watch the news tonight?"
Which

1. "We need to know what the *(weather, whether)* is going to be like for our field trip to the zoo on Friday," she said.

2. Rain will determine *(weather, whether)* we go or not.

3. Quentin, *(who, which, that)* had already watched the news, said it might rain for the rest of the *(week, weak)*.

4. I hoped that *(weather, whether)* forecast, *(who, which, that)* was on channel 13, was wrong.

5. I think the weather forecast *(who, which, that)* is on channel 29 is the best.

6. Once the weather reporter there dressed as a *(which, witch)* on Halloween.

7. I like the *(way, weigh)* she explains things.

8. So I watched her report, and she said there was only a *(week, weak)* chance of rain on Friday.

9. When I *(way, weigh)* the facts, I trust her report the most.

10. So it looks like our field trip, *(who, which, that)* we planned months ago, will happen after all!

Next Step: Write two sentences using the words *which* and *that* correctly. *Hint:* If the clause you're introducing is not required to understand the meaning of the sentence, use *which* and set the clause off with commas. Otherwise, use *that*—without commas—to introduce the clause.

686.1
who's, whose

Who's is the contraction for "who is." *Whose* is a possessive pronoun, one that shows ownership.

> Who's **the most popular writer today?**
>
> Whose **bike is this?**

686.2
wood, would

Wood is the material that comes from trees; *would* is a form of the verb "will."

> **Sequoia trees live practically forever, but** would **you believe that the** wood **from these giants is practically useless?**

686.3
your, you're

Your is a possessive pronoun, one that shows ownership. *You're* is the contraction for "you are."

> You're **the most important person in** your **parents' lives.**

SCHOOL DAZE

David, you know **you're** supposed to be doing **your** homework.

I am, Mom. I'm doing firsthand research on energy conservation.

Grammar Practice

Using the Right Word 18

■ who's, whose; **wood, would;** your, you're

 For each of the following sentences, write the correct choice from each set of words in parentheses.

Example: Dentists say you should floss *(your, you're)* teeth every day.

your

1. *(Whose, Who's)* going to the dentist next month?

2. *(Whose, Who's)* dentist is the friendliest?

3. George Washington's false teeth were not really made of *(wood, would)*.

4. It's important to take care of *(your, you're)* teeth if *(your, you're)* going to keep them.

5. *(Wood, Would)* you be willing to brush twice a day?

Using the Right Word Review

 For each of the following sentences, write the correct choice from each set of words in parentheses.

1. The teacher *(accepted, excepted)* *(a, an)* award from the school *(board, bored)*.

2. Please use *(coarse, course)* sandpaper for this project.

3. Death Valley is a vast *(desert, dessert)*.

4. Randall managed to run *(among, between)* the *(to, two)* fences.

5. After some *(miner, minor)* surgery, Will's foot looks *(good, well)*.

6. I'd like a *(peace, piece)* of the cake *(which, that)* Dad made.

7. A semi *(can, may)* carry a huge *(amount, number)* of grain.

8. I *(heard, herd)* Mom say, "Please don't *(brake, break)* that vase."

9. Did you *(know, no)* that *(it's, its)* my birthday today?

RIGHT WORD

Test Prep!

For each sentence below, write the letter of the line in which the underlined word or words are used incorrectly. If there is no mistake, choose "D."

1
(A) The prices at <u>two</u> stores
(B) will determine <u>whether</u>
(C) we <u>by</u> a new oven.
(D) correct as is

2
(A) I <u>sent</u> a letter to my
(B) <u>dear</u> great-grandmother,
(C) <u>who's</u> 100 years old.
(D) correct as is

3
(A) When Mom was <u>billed</u>
(B) for the lawyer's <u>council</u>,
(C) I <u>heard</u> her gasp.
(D) correct as is

4
(A) The <u>whole</u> school was
(B) not <u>allowed</u> to tour the
(C) <u>capital</u> building at once.
(D) correct as is

5
(A) Terry, is this the <u>right</u>
(B) <u>weigh</u> to make tonight's
(C) ice-cream cake <u>dessert</u>?
(D) correct as is

6
(A) With a <u>pare</u> of binoculars,
(B) Grandpa can see <u>farther</u>
(C) than anyone I <u>know</u>.
(D) correct as is

7
(A) Iron <u>ore</u> is turned
(B) into <u>steel</u> in a
(C) <u>real</u> complicated process.
(D) correct as is

8
(A) Maria failed to <u>break</u> in
(B) time, and she <u>passed</u> right
(C) by her <u>aunt</u>.
(D) correct as is

9
(A) We are <u>all ready</u> to
(B) taste a <u>piece</u> of that
(C) barbequed <u>meet</u>.
(D) correct as is

10
(A) Do you know <u>which</u>
(B) <u>bear</u>—grizzly or panda—
(C) has white and black <u>fur</u>?
(D) correct as is

11
(A) I just can't <u>except</u> the idea
(B) that you would <u>choose</u> a
(C) <u>plain</u> donut over an eclair!
(D) correct as is

12
(A) Twice a <u>week</u>, Dad does
(B) <u>weight</u>-bearing exercises
(C) to tone his <u>waste</u>.
(D) correct as is

13
Ⓐ In order to give <u>you're</u>
Ⓑ <u>hair</u> a new look, use
Ⓒ some temporary <u>dye</u>.
Ⓓ correct as is

14
Ⓐ A <u>cymbal</u> makes such a
Ⓑ loud noise because <u>it's</u>
Ⓒ made of <u>medal</u>.
Ⓓ correct as is

15
Ⓐ I have <u>scene</u> that even
Ⓑ minor <u>pain</u> has a big effect
Ⓒ on people's <u>personal</u> lives.
Ⓓ correct as is

16
Ⓐ That mountain <u>peak</u> looks
Ⓑ <u>as</u> a big red triangle
Ⓒ <u>between</u> two gray ones.
Ⓓ correct as is

17
Ⓐ The twins will put <u>four</u>
Ⓑ of <u>they're</u> paintings
Ⓒ here and <u>two</u> over there.
Ⓓ correct as is

18
Ⓐ Marcus, please <u>set</u> the
Ⓑ <u>bass</u> level on the stereo
Ⓒ <u>to</u> a lower number.
Ⓓ correct as is

19
Ⓐ Uncle Ted won't <u>let</u> her
Ⓑ out of his <u>site</u>, so Angie
Ⓒ says that she's <u>bored</u>.
Ⓓ correct as is

20
Ⓐ If you <u>bring</u> balloons to
Ⓑ my party, I'll have <u>fewer</u>
Ⓒ work to do this <u>week</u>.
Ⓓ correct as is

Understanding Sentences

Sentences

A **sentence** is a group of words that expresses a complete thought. A sentence must have both a subject and a predicate. A sentence begins with a capital letter; it ends with a period, a question mark, or an exclamation point.

I like my teacher this year.

Will we go on a field trip?

We get to go to the water park!

Parts of a Sentence . . .

690.1 Subjects

A subject is the part of a sentence that does something or is talked about.

The kids on my block play basketball at the local park.

We meet after school almost every day.

690.2 Simple Subjects

The simple subject is the subject without the words that describe or modify it. (Also see page 502.)

My friend Chester plays basketball on the school team.

690.3 Complete Subjects

The complete subject is the simple subject and all the words that modify it. (Also see page 501.)

My friend Chester plays basketball on the school team.

690.4 Compound Subjects

A compound subject has two or more simple subjects. (See page 503.)

Chester, Malik, and Meshelle play on our pickup team.

Lou and I are the best shooters.

Grammar Practice

Parts of a Sentence 1

- ▪ Simple Subjects
- ▪ Complete Subjects

 For each sentence below, write the complete subject. Circle the simple subject.

Example: A group of people in one neighborhood wanted to make a difference in society.

A (group) of people in one neighborhood

1. A special week for doing good things was announced.
2. The positive actions of some kids were reported in the paper.
3. One boy in the neighborhood carried groceries for someone in a wheelchair.
4. Two strong, young men cleaned the hallway in their apartment building.
5. A teenage girl cleaned the kitchen in her home for her mother.
6. Kindness can be something easy to do.
7. Many people doing good things will change the world.

- ▪ Compound Subjects

 Write the compound subject in each of the following sentences.

Example: My cousin and his friends went to the movies.

cousin, friends

1. The big black box and the gray snake belong to me.
2. Did Bill or Sophia buy balloons for the party?
3. Students, teachers, and school staff enjoy good school assemblies.
4. Simone, Alister, Ramona, Shaleen, and Leia donated canned goods for the hunger drive.
5. Hoping to catch the bus, Raul and Malcolm raced across the lawn.

SENTENCES

Parts of a Sentence . . .

The predicate, which contains the verb, is the part of the sentence that shows action or says something about the subject.

Hunting has reduced the tiger population in India.

The simple predicate is the predicate (verb) without the words that describe or modify it. (See page 502.)

In the past, poachers **killed** too many African elephants.
Poaching is illegal.

The complete predicate is the simple predicate with all the words that modify or describe it. (See page 501.)

In the past, **poachers** killed too many African elephants.
Poaching is illegal.

The complete predicate often includes a direct object. The direct object is the noun or pronoun that receives the action of the simple predicate—directly. The direct object answers the question *what* or *whom*. (See page 570.)

Many smaller animals need **friends** who will speak up for them.

The direct object may be compound.

We all need **animals, plants, wetlands, deserts,** and **forests.**

If a sentence has a direct object, it may also have an indirect object. An indirect object is the noun or pronoun that receives the action of the simple predicate—indirectly. An indirect object names the person *to whom* or *for whom* something is done. (See page 570.)

I showed the **class** my multimedia report on endangered species. (*Class* is the indirect object because it says *to whom* the report was shown.)

Remember, in order for a sentence to have an indirect object, it must first have a direct object.

A compound predicate is composed of two or more simple predicates. (See page 503.)

In 1990 the countries of the world **met** and **banned** the sale of ivory.

Grammar Practice

Parts of a Sentence 2

■ Simple Predicates
■ Compound Predicates

For each numbered sentence below, write the simple or compound predicate.

Example: Henry "Hank" Aaron hit 755 home runs during his career.

hit

(1) Henry Aaron was born in Mobile, Alabama, on February 5, 1934, and became a great baseball player. **(2)** For a long time, segregation kept him from the major leagues. **(3)** Finally, he joined the Milwaukee Braves baseball team. **(4)** Hank was one of the most dependable and valuable players on the team. **(5)** He played 3,298 games and batted in 2,297 runs.

■ Complete Predicates
■ Direct and Indirect Objects

For each numbered sentence below, write the complete predicate. Underline the direct object once. If there's an indirect object, underline it twice.

Example: Hank Aaron's career spanned 23 years.

spanned 23 <u>years</u>

(1) Hank won the Most Valuable Player award for 1957. **(2)** He gave baseball a very memorable moment in 1974. **(3)** "Hammerin' Hank" hit his 715th home run in the fourth inning. **(4)** That hit broke Babe Ruth's record. **(5)** Hank Aaron showed the world his determination during his successful career.

SENTENCES

Parts of a Sentence . . .

694.1
Understood Subjects and Predicates

Either the subject or the predicate (or both) may not be stated in a sentence, but both must be clearly understood.

> [You] **Get involved!** (*You* is the understood subject.)
>
> **Who needs your help? Animals** [do]. (*Do* is the understood predicate.)
>
> **What do many animals face?** [They face] **Extinction.** (*They* is the understood subject, and *face* is the understood predicate.)

694.2
Delayed Subjects

In sentences that begin with *there* followed by a form of the "be" verb, the subject usually follows the verb. (See page 570.)

> **There are** laws **that protect endangered species.** (The subject is *laws; are* is the verb.)

The subject is also delayed in questions.

> **How can we preserve the natural habitat?** (*We* is the subject.)

SCHOOL DAZE

John, I've got all the projects. Now which one is yours?

I'm not sure. See if there's one with a missing piece.

694.3
Modifiers

A modifier is a word (adjective, adverb) or a group of words (phrase, clause) that changes or adds to the meaning of another word. (See pages 486–493.)

> **Many North American zoos and aquariums voluntarily participate in breeding programs that help prevent extinction.**

The modifiers in this sentence include the following: *many, North American* (adjectives), *voluntarily* (adverb), *in breeding programs* (phrase), *that help prevent extinction* (clause).

Grammar Practice

Parts of a Sentence 3

■ Understood Subjects and Predicates
■ Delayed Subjects

 For each of the sentences below, write down the part or parts named in parentheses.

Example: Study for the math test. *(understood subject)*
You

1. When will we have the test? *(delayed subject)*

2. Tomorrow. *(understood subject and predicate)*

3. Get some help with your homework. *(understood subject)*

4. What is the lesson on page 244? *(delayed subject)*

5. Long division. *(understood predicate)*

6. Be sure to read it carefully. *(understood subject)*

■ Modifiers

 Rewrite the following simple sentences, adding modifiers to expand them.

Example: Lalita talks.
Lalita talks endlessly on her cordless phone.

1. Dominic runs.

2. She read a book.

3. Brigitte plays basketball.

4. Theo listened.

5. Habib writes.

6. I will walk.

7. Prem asked a question.

8. Shaquana paints.

Test Prep!

 Number your paper from 1 to 14. For each underlined part in the following paragraphs, choose the letter or letters from the list below that best describe it.

- Ⓐ simple subject
- Ⓑ complete subject
- Ⓒ compound subject
- Ⓓ simple predicate
- Ⓔ complete predicate
- Ⓕ compound predicate

Today, <u>one in eight people in the United States</u> is Hispanic.
(1)
Grocery <u>stores</u> now offer more Hispanic foods than ever before.
(2)
This <u>is changing</u> the buying habits of the rest of the U.S.
(3)
population. Americans <u>are exploring foods from other cultures,</u>
(4)
and Hispanic foods top the list of favorites.

Not long ago, <u>tomatillos, serrano peppers, and other</u>
(5)
<u>Hispanic items</u> were not easy to find. Then, in the early 1990s,

more people were trying Latino cooking. They <u>enjoyed</u>

<u>traditional Latin food such as black beans and rice, mangoes,</u>
(6)
<u>and avocados.</u> Now most of these ingredients can be found in

just about any grocery store.

Much Hispanic food is spicy. <u>Hundreds of kinds of chile</u>
(7)
<u>peppers</u> add a kick to plain food. <u>Americans</u> like hot foods. In
(8)
fact, people across the country now <u>buy and eat</u> more salsa
(9)
than ketchup.

The avocado and the plantain, a couple of other traditional
(10)
Hispanic foods, are also becoming more popular. Plantains look
(11)
like bananas. They can be boiled, baked, or fried, and served as
(12)
a vegetable or as a sweet dessert. Avocados are the main

ingredient in guacamole. Lately, they are also showing up in

salads and on sandwiches.

The largest Hispanic food company in the U.S., Goya
(13)
Foods, employs 2,500 people in seven states, Puerto Rico,

Spain, and the Dominican Republic. Many other food

companies are also beginning to supply Hispanic products.

With so many fans, Hispanic food is surely here to stay.
(14)

Parts of a Sentence . . .

698.1
Clauses

A clause is a group of related words that has both a subject and a verb. (Also see pages 515–517.)

a whole chain of plants and animals is affected
(*Chain* is the subject, and *is affected* is the verb.)

when one species dies out completely
(*Species* is the subject; *dies out* is the verb.)

698.2
Independent Clauses

An independent clause presents a complete thought and can stand alone as a sentence.

This ancient oak tree may be cut down.

This act could affect more than 200 different species of animals!

Why would anyone want that to happen?

698.3
Dependent Clauses

A dependent clause does not present a complete thought and cannot stand as a sentence. A dependent clause *depends* on being connected to an independent clause to make sense. Dependent clauses begin with either a subordinating conjunction (*after, although, because, before, if*) or a relative pronoun (*who, whose, which, that*). (See pages 710 and 744 for complete lists.)

If this ancient oak tree is cut down, it could affect more than 200 different species of animals!

The tree, which experts think could be 400 years old, provides a home to many different kinds of birds and insects.

SCHOOL DAZE

Grammar Practice

Parts of a Sentence 4

■ Clauses

 Write the dependent clause in each numbered sentence below. If the sentence does not contain a dependent clause, write "none."

Example: Spiral notebooks, which are held together with strong wire, can be dangerous in the wrong hands.
which are held together with strong wire

(1) One day in eighth grade, I learned to be more careful around my spiral notebooks. (2) During science class, an end of the wire that was sticking out managed to corkscrew its way into my thumb. (3) Because I couldn't get it out, Mr. Gibson, my teacher, saw what had happened. (4) He clipped the wire from the notebook and tried unsuccessfully to pull the other part out of my thumb. (5) Then Mr. Zold, who was the gym teacher, had a go at it. (6) Since he couldn't get it out either, I went to the office. (7) As the secretary looked at my thumb, she decided right then to call my mother. (8) When my mother picked me up, she rushed me to the emergency room at St. Luke's Hospital. (9) I didn't have much pain through all of this, but the wire, which was still sticking out of my thumb, sure made me feel foolish. (10) After the doctor examined my injury, she froze my thumb and twisted the wire out with some kind of medical pliers. (11) From that day on, I always covered the spiral part of my notebooks with tape.

Next Step: Read the dependent clauses that you wrote. Circle the clauses that begin with a subordinating conjunction and underline those beginning with a relative pronoun.

SENTENCES

Parts of a Sentence

A phrase is a group of related words that lacks either a subject or a predicate (or both). (See pages **519–520**.)

guards the house (The predicate lacks a subject.)

the ancient oak tree (The subject lacks a predicate.)

with crooked old limbs (The phrase lacks both a subject and a predicate.)

The ancient oak tree with crooked old limbs guards the house. (Together, the three phrases form a complete thought.)

Phrases usually take their names from the main words that introduce them (prepositional phrase, verb phrase, and so on). They are also named for the function they serve in a sentence (adverb phrase, adjective phrase).

The ancient oak tree (noun phrase)

with crooked old limbs (prepositional phrase)

has stood its guard, (verb phrase)

very stubbornly, (adverb phrase)

protecting the little house. (verbal phrase)

For more information on verbal phrases, see page **730**.

SCHOOL DAZE

Give me an example of a **verbal phrase** used as a subject.

Hanging upside down refreshes my brain.

Grammar Practice

Parts of a Sentence 5

■ Phrases

Write whether each of the following phrases is missing a subject, a predicate, or both. Then use the phrase in a sentence.

Example: won a prize

missing a subject

My brother won a prize at the school science fair.

1. in Kansas

2. her parents

3. ran her first race

4. was the librarian

5. at a summer festival

6. other kids in the class

7. is not feeling well

8. writes letters to his grandchildren

9. Zack's blond hair

10. between the fence and the oak tree

11. lived in Chicago

Next Step: Go back to the phrases above and identify each as a noun phrase, a verb phrase, or a prepositional phrase.

Using the Parts of Speech

Nouns . . .

A **noun** is a word that names a person, a place, a thing, or an idea.

Person: **John Ulferts** (uncle)   Thing: **"Yankee Doodle"** (song)
Place: **Mississippi** (state)   Idea: **Labor Day** (holiday)

Kinds of Nouns

702.1
Common Nouns

A common noun is any noun that does not name a specific person, place, thing, or idea. These nouns are not capitalized.

woman   museum   book   weekend

702.2
Proper Nouns

A proper noun is the name of a specific person, place, thing, or idea. Proper nouns are capitalized.

Hillary Clinton   Central Park   *Maniac McGee*   Sunday

702.3
Concrete Nouns

A concrete noun names a thing that is physical (can be touched or seen). Concrete nouns can be either proper or common.

space station   pencil   Statue of Liberty

702.4
Abstract Nouns

An abstract noun names something you can think about but cannot see or touch. Abstract nouns can be either common or proper.

Judaism   poverty   satisfaction   illness

702.5
Collective Nouns

A collective noun names a group or collection of persons, animals, places, or things.

Persons: **tribe, congregation, family, class, team**
Animals: **flock, herd, gaggle, clutch, litter**
Things: **batch, cluster, bunch**

702.6
Compound Nouns

A compound noun is made up of two or more words.

football (written as one word)
high school (written as two words)
brother-in-law (written as a hyphenated word)

Grammar Practice

Nouns 1

■ **Common and Proper Nouns**

For each line of the following paragraph, write the nouns and label them either "C" for common or "P" for proper.

Example: In Iraq, date-palm trees are a source of wealth.

Iraq – P, trees – C, source – C, wealth – C

1   The trees are passed down from one generation to the next. In

2   Europe, families often pass down jewelry or art. In America, families

3   may save fine furniture or dishes for future generations. Wherever

4   families live, most people are interested in giving their children

5   keepsakes from their past.

■ **Concrete and Abstract Nouns**

For each line of the following paragraph, write the underlined nouns and label them either "C" for concrete or "A" for abstract.

Example: Grandpa said he doesn't know his true age.

Grandpa – C, age – A

1   Research shows that the life span of people is increasing in

2   most countries of the world. Georgia, a country that used to be part

3   of the Soviet Union, has many people who are more than 110 years

4   old. When one old man was asked for the secret to his long life, he

5   replied, "I sleep with my hat on."

Next Step: Write two sentences about your family. Use an abstract noun in one sentence and a proper noun in the other.

Nouns

Number of Nouns

The number of a noun is either singular or plural.

704.1

Singular Nouns

A singular noun names one person, place, thing, or idea.

boy　　group　　audience　　stage　　concert　　hope

704.2

Plural Nouns

A plural noun names more than one person, place, thing, or idea.

boys　　groups　　audiences　　stages　　concerts　　hopes

Gender of Nouns

704.3

Noun Gender

Nouns are grouped according to gender: *feminine, masculine, neuter,* and *indefinite.*

Feminine (female): **mother, sister, women, cow, hen**

Masculine (male): **father, brother, men, bull, rooster**

Neuter (neither male nor female): **tree, cobweb, closet**

Indefinite (male or female): **president, duckling, doctor**

Uses of Nouns

704.4

Subject Nouns

A noun that is the subject of a sentence does something or is talked about in the sentence.

The roots of rap can be traced back to West Africa and Jamaica.

704.5

Predicate Nouns

A predicate noun follows a form of the *be* verb *(am, is, are, was, were, being, been)* and renames the subject.

In the 1970s, rap was a street art.

704.6

Possessive Nouns

A possessive noun shows possession or ownership.

Early rap had a drummer's beat but no music.

The rapper's words are set to music.

704.7

Object Nouns

A noun is an object noun when it is used as the direct object, the indirect object, or the object of the preposition.

Some rappers tell people their story about life in the city. (indirect object: *people*; direct object: *story*)

Rap is now a common music choice in this country. (object of the preposition: *country*)

Grammar Practice

Nouns 2

■ **Number and Gender of Nouns**

For each of the following sentences, write the correct singular or plural noun from the choices in parentheses. Then write whether it is masculine, feminine, neuter, or indefinite.

Example: Hanukkah is a happy Jewish *(holiday, holidays)*.
holiday (neuter)

1. It usually falls during the *(month, months)* of December.

2. The holiday includes eight *(day, days)* of celebration.

3. All the *(member, members)* of the family take part.

4. My *(aunt, aunts)* makes a huge dinner.

5. My *(brother, brothers)* like to light the candles on the menorah.

■ **Subject, Predicate, Possessive, and Object Nouns**

Identify each underlined noun in the sentences below as a subject noun, a predicate noun, a possessive noun, or an object noun.

Example: One of Hanukkah's symbols is a dreidel.
possessive noun, predicate noun

1. The dreidel is a square-shaped top with letters on each side.

2. The letters on the dreidel stand for the words "A Great Miracle Happened There."

3. In ancient times, the study of the Jewish holy books was forbidden in some countries.

4. Soldiers checking Jewish homes would find people playing with the dreidel.

5. The dreidel's meaning is that freedom is a miracle.

Pronouns . . .

A **pronoun** is a word used in place of a noun. Some examples are *I, you, he, she, it, we, they, his, hers, her, its, me, myself, us, yours,* and so on.

> Without pronouns: Kevin said Kevin would be going to Kevin's grandmother's house this weekend.
>
> With pronouns: Kevin said he would be going to his grandmother's house this weekend.

706.1
Antecedents

An antecedent is the noun that the pronoun refers to or replaces. All pronouns (except interrogative and indefinite pronouns) have antecedents. (See page 474.)

> Jamal and Rick tried out for the team, and they both made it.

(*They* refers to *Jamal* and *Rick*; *it* refers to *team.*)

NOTE Pronouns must agree with their antecedents in number, person, and gender.

Types of Pronouns

There are several types of pronouns. The most common type is the personal pronoun. (See the chart on page 710.)

706.2
Personal Pronouns

A personal pronoun takes the place of a specific person (or thing) in a sentence. Some common personal pronouns are *I, you, he, she, it, we,* and *they.*

> Suriana would not like to live in Buffalo, New York, because she does not like snow.

706.3
Relative Pronouns

A relative pronoun is both a pronoun and a connecting word. It connects a dependent clause to an independent clause in a complex sentence. Relative pronouns include *who, whose, which,* and *that.* (See 684.6.)

> Buffalo, which often gets more than eight feet of snow in a year, is on the northeast shore of Lake Erie.
>
> The United States city that gets the most snow is Valdez, Alaska.

706.4
Interrogative Pronouns

An interrogative pronoun helps ask a question.

> Who wants to go to Alaska?
>
> Which of the cities would you visit?
>
> Whom would you like to travel with?
>
> What did you say?

punctuate *edit* capitalize
improve SPELL 707
Using the Parts of Speech

Grammar Practice

Pronouns 1

■ Antecedents and Personal, Relative, and Interrogative Pronouns

The type of pronoun that's missing is indicated at the end of each sentence. First write the antecedent of the missing pronoun and then write a pronoun that agrees with it. (See the chart on page 710.)

NOTE An interrogative pronoun doesn't have an antecedent, so write "none" in place of the antecedent.

Example: Kathryn says _____ favorite holiday is Labor Day. *(personal)*

        Kathryn – her

1. Holidays have been celebrated for a long time, and _____ were originally known as "holy days." *(personal)*

2. Because many people traveled during the holy days, tradesmen along the way were there to meet _____. *(personal)*

3. Fairs and bazaars, _____ became part of many holiday celebrations, encouraged spending. *(relative)*

4. Now that spending is a big part of these holidays, many products are associated with _____. *(personal)*

5. _____ can guess what my favorite holiday is? *(interrogative)*

6. It is a holiday _____ is celebrated each January. *(relative)*

7. Sunee, if _____ guessed New Year's Day, _____ are correct. *(personal, personal)*

8. Aunt Fabiola wishes New Year's Day were celebrated in March; _____ thinks that's when the earth is new again. *(personal)*

9. _____ of the holidays is your favorite? *(interrogative)*

Next Step: Write two sentences about a holiday. Use pronouns in both sentences. Exchange papers with a classmate and circle the antecedents in each other's sentences.

Pronouns . . .

Types of Pronouns

A demonstrative pronoun points out or identifies a noun without naming the noun. When used together in a sentence, *this* and *that* distinguish one item from another, and *these* and *those* distinguish one group from another. (See page 710.)

> This is a great idea; that was a nightmare.

> These are my favorite foods, and those are definitely not.

NOTE When these words are used before a noun, they are *not* pronouns; rather, they are demonstrative adjectives.

> Coming to this picnic was fun—and those ants think so, too.

An intensive pronoun emphasizes, or *intensifies,* the noun or pronoun it refers to. Common intensive pronouns include *itself, myself, himself, herself,* and *yourself.*

> Though the chameleon's quick-change act protects it from predators, the lizard itself can catch insects 10 inches away with its long, sticky tongue.

> When a chameleon changes its skin color—seemingly matching the background—the background colors themselves do not affect the chameleon's color changes.

NOTE These sentences would be complete without the intensive pronoun. The pronoun simply emphasizes a particular noun.

A reflexive pronoun refers back to the subject of a sentence, and it is always an object (never a subject) in a sentence. Reflexive pronouns are the same as the intensive pronouns—*itself, myself, himself, herself, yourself,* and so on.

> A chameleon protects itself from danger by changing colors. (direct object)

> A chameleon can give itself tasty meals of unsuspecting insects. (indirect object)

> I wish I could claim some of its amazing powers for myself. (object of the preposition)

NOTE Unlike sentences with intensive pronouns, these sentences would *not* be complete without the reflexive pronouns.

punctuate *edit* capitalize
SPELL   **709**
improve
Using the Parts of Speech

Grammar Practice

Pronouns 2

■ **Demonstrative Pronouns**

Write whether the underlined word is a demonstrative adjective or a demonstrative pronoun. *Extra challenge:* Rewrite any sentence that contains a demonstrative adjective so that the word is used as a pronoun instead.

Example: <u>This</u> pie is good!
demonstrative adjective   This is good pie!

1. Is <u>that</u> ring valuable?

2. <u>Those</u> cars are the finest available.

3. <u>That</u> was useful two years ago, but not now.

4. <u>These</u> apples are expensive.

■ **Intensive Pronouns**
■ **Reflexive Pronouns**

For each sentence below, write whether the underlined pronoun is intensive or reflexive.

Example: Although Elijah McCoy <u>himself</u> was not a slave, he was the son of former slaves.
intensive

1. In 1858, Elijah McCoy traveled from Canada to Scotland to better <u>himself</u> with a college education.

2. McCoy earned a degree in engineering and then moved to Michigan, where he went into business for <u>himself</u>.

3. Elijah believed that he <u>himself</u> could invent products that would save companies both time and money.

4. He invented a tool that allowed a machine to oil <u>itself</u>.

5. Over time, the oiling tool <u>itself</u> became so popular that people would ask whether it was the "real McCoy."

Pronouns . . .
Types of Pronouns

710.1
Indefinite Pronouns

An indefinite pronoun is a pronoun that does not have a specific antecedent (the noun or pronoun it replaces). (See page 475.)

Everything **about the chameleon is fascinating.**

Someone **donated a chameleon to our class.**

Anyone **who brings in a live insect can feed our chameleon.**

Types of Pronouns

Personal Pronouns

I, me, mine, my, we, us, our, ours, you, your, yours, they, them, their, theirs, he, him, his, she, her, hers, it, its

Relative Pronouns

who, whose, whom, which, what, that, whoever, whomever, whichever, whatever

Interrogative Pronouns

who, whose, whom, which, what

Demonstrative Pronouns

this, that, these, those

Intensive and Reflexive Pronouns

myself, himself, herself, itself, yourself, yourselves, themselves, ourselves

Indefinite Pronouns

all	both	everything	nobody	several
another	each	few	none	some
any	each one	many	no one	somebody
anybody	either	most	nothing	someone
anyone	everybody	much	one	something
anything	everyone	neither	other	such

punctuate *edit* capitalize
improve SPELL **711**
Using the Parts of Speech

Grammar Practice

Pronouns 3

■ Indefinite Pronouns

Write the indefinite pronoun in each of the following sentences.

Example: Rodeo events offer entertainment for everybody.
everybody

1. Most are designed to showcase a person's skill and strength.
2. Calf roping is enjoyed by many.
3. Nothing harmful is done to the animals.
4. Each must be lassoed, thrown down, and tied.
5. None are hurt, and riders earn points for speed.
6. No one can deny that bull riding is an exciting event.

Pronoun Review

For each numbered sentence below, identify the underlined pronoun as "personal," "relative," or "indefinite."

Example: In a rodeo, even the clowns have their own event.
personal

(1) Rodeo events can be dangerous, and sometimes someone gets hurt. (2) Bull riding, which is the most dangerous event, is very exciting. (3) The rider must stay on a bucking bull for eight seconds, holding on to a rope that is tied around the bull's middle.

Women riders enjoy the rodeo as well. (4) They have their own events, including barrel racing. (5) The contestants ride around a series of three barrels as fast as possible without knocking any over.

Those are just a couple of the many events featured at a rodeo. (6) Anyone may take part, but he or she had better know how to ride!

PARTS OF SPEECH

Pronouns . . .

Number of a Pronoun

712.1
Singular and Plural Pronouns

Pronouns can be either singular or plural in number.

Singular: I, you, he, she, it   Plural: we, you, they

NOTE The pronouns *you, your,* and *yours* may be singular or plural.

Person of a Pronoun

The person of a pronoun tells whether the pronoun is speaking, being spoken to, or being spoken about. (See page 474.)

712.2
First Person Pronouns

A first-person pronoun is used in place of the name of the speaker or speakers.

I am speaking.   We are speaking.

712.3
Second Person Pronouns

A second-person pronoun is used to name the person or thing spoken to.

Eliza, will you please take out the garbage?

You better stop grumbling!

712.4
Third Person Pronouns

A third-person pronoun is used to name the person or thing spoken about.

Bill should listen if he wants to learn the words to this song.

Charisse said that she already knows them.

They will perform the song in the talent show.

Uses of Pronouns

A pronoun can be used as a subject, as an object, or to show possession. (See the chart on page 714.)

712.5
Subject Pronouns

A subject pronoun is used as the subject of a sentence (*I, you, he, she, it, we, they*).

I like to surf the Net.

A subject pronoun is also used after a form of the *be* verb (*am, is, are, was, were, being, been*) if it repeats the subject. (See "Predicate Nouns," 704.5.)

"This is she," Mom replied into the telephone.

"Yes, it was I," admitted the child who had eaten the cookies.

punctuate *edit* capitalize SPELL **713**
improve
Using the Parts of Speech

Grammar Practice

Pronouns 4

■ Number of a Pronoun
■ Person of a Pronoun

 For each of the following sentences, write the pronouns and identify them as first, second, or third person. (See the chart on page 714.)

Example: We studied the Civil War in my history class.
We (first person), my (first person)

1. Abraham Lincoln was elected president of the United States in 1860; he was the sixteenth president.

2. In January of 1861, South Carolina decided it would leave the United States of America.

3. In class, we learned that 11 states decided to leave the United States, and they created the Confederate States of America.

4. In February of 1861, the Confederate States elected Jefferson Davis as their new president.

5. He became the first—and last—president of the Confederacy.

6. Our teacher said, "I will test you on the Civil War next week."

7. I said, "José, I am sure you can pass the test easily."

8. "Your study habits are better than mine."

9. The night before the test, we reviewed the study sheets together.

10. Dad gave us three agates and a fossil that he had found.

11. José told me, "You could try rereading each chapter carefully, Joanne."

12. He was right; it helped me get a passing grade.

Next Step: Look at your answers for the exercise above. Underline the pronouns that are singular and circle those that are plural.

Pronouns
Uses of Pronouns

714.1
Object Pronouns

An object pronoun *(me, you, him, her, it, us, them)* can be used as the object of a verb or preposition. (See 692.4, 692.5, and 742.1.)

> I'll call **her** as soon as I can. (direct object)

> Hand **me** the phone book, please. (indirect object)

> She thinks these flowers are from **you**. (object of the preposition)

714.2
Possessive Pronouns

A possessive pronoun shows possession or ownership. These possessive pronouns function as adjectives before nouns: *my, our, his, her, their, its,* and *your.*

> School workers are painting **our** classroom this summer. **Its** walls will look much better.

These possessive pronouns can be used after verbs: *mine, ours, hers, his, theirs,* and *yours.*

> I'm pretty sure this backpack is **mine** and that one is **his**.

NOTE An apostrophe is not needed with a possessive pronoun to show possession.

Uses of Personal Pronouns

	Singular Pronouns			Plural Pronouns		
	Subject Pronouns	Possessive Pronouns	Object Pronouns	Subject Pronouns	Possessive Pronouns	Object Pronouns
First Person	I	my, mine	me	we	our, ours	us
Second Person	you	your, yours	you	you	your, yours	you
Third Person	he	his	him	they	their, theirs	them
	she	her, hers	her			
	it	its	it			

Grammar Practice

Pronouns 5

■ Subject, Object, and Possessive Pronouns

For each numbered sentence in the paragraphs below, identify the underlined pronoun as a subject, an object, or a possessive pronoun.

Example: Roberto Clemente liked many sports, but <u>his</u> favorite sport was baseball.
possessive pronoun

(1) Roberto Clemente was born in Puerto Rico in 1934; <u>he</u> was the youngest of four children. **(2)** As a young boy, Roberto discovered sports were easy for <u>him</u>. **(3)** He played baseball for several teams, but <u>his</u> big break came when he signed with the Brooklyn Dodgers. **(4)** At first, <u>they</u> sent Roberto to play on a minor-league team. **(5)** In 1954, the Pittsburgh Pirates drafted him, and he spent 17 years with <u>them</u>. **(6)** Roberto was named the most valuable player in a World Series, and <u>it</u> was a great honor for him.

(7) For many years, Clemente helped <u>those</u> in need. **(8)** When a devastating earthquake hit Nicaragua in 1972, Clemente helped arrange relief for Nicaragua and <u>its</u> people. **(9)** Determined to see that food and other supplies got to the people, <u>he</u> chartered a plane and accompanied four others on the flight. **(10)** Before the flight, Roberto's wife said <u>she</u> was worried about his safety. **(11)** On December 31, 1972, the plane flew into storm winds that caused <u>it</u> to crash, leaving no survivors. **(12)** Today, many people remember Roberto Clemente not only for <u>his</u> baseball skills but also for his desire to help others.

Next Step: Go back to the "Colons" exercise on page 597. Identify the pronouns in the last paragraph of the letter as subject, object, or possessive pronouns.

Test Prep!

Number your paper from 1 to 18. For each underlined word in the paragraphs below, write the letter of the best description from the following list.

Ⓐ subject noun   Ⓓ subject pronoun
Ⓑ object noun   Ⓔ object pronoun
Ⓒ predicate noun   Ⓕ possessive pronoun

My <u>aunt</u> is a <u>nurse</u>. <u>She</u> works in a doctor's office. Aunt
   (1)   **(2)**   **(3)**

Margy made a <u>decision</u> a few years ago to finish college and get
           (4)

<u>her</u> nursing degree. <u>I</u> really admire <u>her</u> for that because she is a
(5)   **(6)**   **(7)**

busy <u>wife</u> and mother who took the time to improve herself.
    (8)

   <u>Aunt Margy</u> knew that she would need her family's
     (9)

support while she was in school. She asked <u>Uncle Tim</u>, her
                    (10)

husband, to spend a little more time with the kids. <u>They</u> all
                               (11)

agreed to help out more around the <u>house</u>.
                      (12)

   <u>My</u> aunt went to school part-time for her degree, and she
 (13)

worked hard for <u>it</u>. She studied her <u>books</u> and practiced her
          (14)   **(15)**

skills. <u>Uncle Tim</u> helped her review for tests. The whole <u>family</u>
    (16)   **(17)**

went to the graduation ceremony, where Aunt Margy saw <u>our</u>
                                      (18)

great pride in her achievement.

punctuate *edit* capitalize
improve SPELL 717
Using the Parts of Speech

 Number your paper from 19 to 28. Write the letter of the answer that correctly completes each of the following sentences.

19 Mari and _____ went to the movies yesterday.
(A) me   (B) I   (C) her

20 On the way, Mari lost _____ new wallet.
(A) hers   (B) she   (C) her

21 Luckily, Mom gave _____ some extra money.
(A) me   (B) I   (C) he

22 It was enough for both of _____.
(A) we   (B) us   (C) ours

23 _____ passed the park on the way back home.
(A) We   (B) Us   (C) Ours

24 A woman said that _____ had found a wallet.
(A) us   (B) her   (C) she

25 The woman asked Mari if it was _____.
(A) hers   (B) her   (C) they

26 Mari excitedly said, "Yes, it is _____!"
(A) it   (B) me   (C) mine

27 Mari asked the woman, "May I offer _____ a reward?"
(A) you   (B) yours   (C) she

28 It was such a relief for both Mari and _____.
(A) me   (B) I   (C) we

Verbs . . .

A **verb** is a word that shows action or links a subject to another word in a sentence.

Tornadoes cause tremendous damage. (action verb)

The weather is often calm before a storm. (linking verb)

Types of Verbs

718.1
Action Verbs

An action verb tells what the subject is doing. (See page 480.)

Natural disasters hit the globe nearly every day.

718.2
Linking Verbs

A linking verb connects—or links—a subject to a noun or an adjective in the predicate. The most common linking verbs are forms of the verb *be* (*is, are, was, were, being, been, am*). Verbs such as *smell, look, taste, feel, remain, turn, appear, become, sound, seem, grow,* and *stay* can also be linking verbs. (See page 480.)

The San Andreas Fault is an earthquake zone in California. (The linking verb is connects the subject to the predicate noun *zone.*)

Earthquakes there are fairly common. (The linking verb are connects the subject to the predicate adjective *common.*)

718.3
Helping Verbs

A helping verb (also called an auxiliary verb) helps the main verb express tense and voice. The most common helping verbs are *shall, will, should, would, could, must, might, can, may, have, had, has, do, did,* and the forms of the verb *be*—*is, are, was, were, am, being, been.* (See pages 482–484.)

It has been estimated that 500,000 earthquakes occur around the world every year. (These helping verbs indicate that the tense is present perfect and the voice is passive.)

Fortunately, only about 100 of those will cause damage. (*Will* helps express the future tense of the verb.)

punctuate *edit* capitalize SPELL
improve
Using the Parts of Speech
719

Grammar Practice

Verbs 1 ■ Action Verbs, Linking Verbs, and Helping Verbs

Number your paper from 1 to 10. Then identify the underlined verbs as action, linking, or helping verbs.

Example: The Baldwin Locomotive Works <u>built</u> 75,000 locomotives.
action

1 Matthias Baldwin <u>founded</u> the Baldwin Locomotive Works in
2 1831. His company <u>built</u> train locomotives to fit the needs of his
3 customers. Baldwin technicians <u>designed</u> powerful steam engines,
4 and buyers <u>were</u> pleased. The company <u>grew</u> bigger.
5 Steam engines eventually <u>were challenged</u> by diesel engines.
6 One steam locomotive <u>was</u> more powerful than one diesel
7 locomotive, but the train engineers <u>used</u> several diesel engines
8 hooked together to pull more freight. The Age of Steam <u>was coming</u>
9 to an end. After more than 120 years, Baldwin Works <u>closed</u> its
10 doors in 1954.

Write the linking verb in each of the following sentences. Then write the word it links the subject to and tell whether it is a noun or an adjective.

Example: Railroads were the fastest transportation in the 1800s.
were, transportation (noun)

1. The South Carolina Railroad was the first company to have a passenger train.

2. In 1852, the Pacific Railroad of Missouri became the first railroad in the West.

3. To some people, trains seemed scary.

4. Today, automobiles are the most common form of passenger travel.

5. However, many people remain fans of train travel.

PARTS OF SPEECH

Verbs . . .

Tenses of Verbs

A verb has three principal parts: *present, past,* and *past participle.* (The part used with the helping verbs *has, have,* or *had* is called the past participle.)

All six of the tenses are formed from these principal parts. The past and past participle of regular verbs are formed by adding *ed* to the present tense. The past and past participle of irregular verbs are formed with different spellings. (See the chart on page 722.)

720.1
Present Tense Verbs

The present tense of a verb expresses action (or a state of being) that is happening now or that happens continually or regularly. (See page 483.)

> The universe **is** gigantic. It **takes** my breath away.

720.2
Past Tense Verbs

The past tense of a verb expresses action (or a state of being) that was completed in the past. (See page 483.)

> To most people many years ago, the universe **was** the earth, the sun, and some stars. The universe **reached** only as far as the eye could see.

720.3
Future Tense Verbs

The future tense of a verb expresses action that *will* take place. (See page 483.)

> Maybe I **will visit** another galaxy in my lifetime.
>
> Somebody **will find** a way to do it.

SCHOOL DAZE

I **know** the answer!

Okay, but I **said** you **will have** to sing the answer . . . go ahead!

punctuate *edit* capitalize
improve SPELL   721
Using the Parts of Speech

Grammar Practice

Verbs 2

■ Present Tense Verbs
■ Past Tense Verbs
■ Future Tense Verbs

 For each of the following sentences, write the verb or verbs and identify them as "present tense," "past tense," or "future tense."

Example: The "Great War" started in Europe more than 90 years ago.

started (past tense)

1. Now we call that war World War I.

2. The conflict began in the summer of 1914.

3. The Central Powers (Germany and Austria-Hungary) fought against the Allies.

4. England and France, two countries on the Allied side, sent more than 2 million soldiers to the battlefields.

5. England and France are still allies (friends) to this day.

6. Both countries also maintain a friendly relationship with the United States.

7. These three nations probably will remain allies for years to come.

8. Leaders of these countries meet together often.

9. These nations depend on one another economically.

10. They will support one another during times of crisis.

11. It is good to have political friends!

Next Step: Whom do you depend on? Write three sentences about this person. Write one sentence for each of the verb tenses: *past, present,* and *future.*

Common Irregular Verbs and Their Principal Parts

The principal parts of the common irregular verbs are listed below. The part used with the helping verbs *has, have,* or *had* is called the **past participle**. (Also see page 481.)

Present Tense:	I write.	She hides.
Past Tense:	Earlier I wrote.	Earlier she hid.
Past Participle:	I have written.	She has hidden.

Present Tense	Past Tense	Past Participle	Present Tense	Past Tense	Past Participle
am, is, are	was, were	been	lead	led	led
begin	began	begun	lie (recline)	lay	lain
bid (offer)	bid	bid	lie (deceive)	lied	lied
bid (order)	bade	bidden	make	made	made
bite	bit	bitten	ride	rode	ridden
blow	blew	blown	ring	rang	rung
break	broke	broken	rise	rose	risen
bring	brought	brought	run	ran	run
burst	burst	burst	see	saw	seen
buy	bought	bought	set	set	set
catch	caught	caught	shake	shook	shaken
come	came	come	shine (polish)	shined	shined
dive	dived, dove	dived	shine (light)	shone	shone
do	did	done	shrink	shrank	shrunk
draw	drew	drawn	sing	sang, sung	sung
drink	drank	drunk	sink	sank, sunk	sunk
drive	drove	driven	sit	sat	sat
eat	ate	eaten	sleep	slept	slept
fall	fell	fallen	speak	spoke	spoken
fight	fought	fought	spring	sprang, sprung	sprung
flee	fled	fled	steal	stole	stolen
fly	flew	flown	strive	strove	striven
forsake	forsook	forsaken	swear	swore	sworn
freeze	froze	frozen	swim	swam	swum
get	got	gotten, got	swing	swung	swung
give	gave	given	take	took	taken
go	went	gone	tear	tore	torn
grow	grew	grown	throw	threw	thrown
hang (execute)	hanged	hanged	wake	woke, waked	woken, waked
hang (dangle)	hung	hung	wear	wore	worn
hide	hid	hidden, hid	weave	wove	woven
know	knew	known	wring	wrung	wrung
lay (place)	laid	laid	write	wrote	written

Grammar Practice

Verbs 3

■ Present Tense Verbs
■ Past Tense Verbs
■ Past Participle Verbs

 For each sentence below, write the correct form of the irregular verb or verbs in parentheses.

Example: I have always _____ a roller-coaster fan. *(am)*
          been

1. Mom _____ us to the amusement park last Saturday. *(take)*

2. Alberto and Jim _____ along. *(come)*

3. They had _____ at my house the night before, and we nearly _____ with excitement. *(sleep, burst)*

4. On Saturday morning, Mom _____ us up at 7:00, and we _____ a light breakfast. *(wake, eat)*

5. As soon as we arrived at the park, we _____ in line for the super roller coaster. *(get)*

6. If we had _____ that we would wait more than an hour, we wouldn't have _____ in line. *(know, get)*

7. After we _____ the roller coaster, we _____ from the water fountain. *(ride, drink)*

8. Dad had _____ me money to purchase a souvenir. *(give)*

9. Just as I _____ my money on the counter, a gust of wind _____ it away. *(lay, blow)*

10. I _____ after it, and, luckily, I _____ it. *(run, catch)*

11. You have never _____ someone so relieved! *(see)*

12. I _____ a cap with the park's name on the front. *(buy)*

Next Step: Write three sentences using the present tense, past tense, and past participle of the word begin.

PARTS OF SPEECH

Verbs . . .
Tenses of Verbs

The present perfect tense verb expresses action that began in the past but continues or is completed in the present. The present perfect tense is formed by adding *has* or *have* to the past participle. (Also see page 484.)

I have wondered for some time how the stars got their names.

A visible star has emitted light for thousands of years.

The past perfect tense verb expresses action that began in the past and was completed in the past. This tense is formed by adding *had* to the past participle. (Also see page 484.)

I had hoped to see a shooting star on our camping trip.

A future perfect tense verb expresses action that will begin in the future and will be completed by a specific time in the future. The future perfect tense is formed by adding *will have* to the past participle. (Also see page 484.)

By the middle of this century, we probably will have discovered many more stars, planets, and galaxies.

A present continuous tense verb expresses action that is not completed at the time of stating it. The present continuous tense is formed by adding *am, is,* or *are* to the *ing* form of the main verb.

Scientists are learning a great deal from their study of the sky.

A past continuous tense verb expresses action that was happening at a certain time in the past. This tense is formed by adding *was* or *were* to the *ing* form of the main verb.

Astronomers were beginning their quest for knowledge hundreds of years ago.

A future continuous tense verb expresses action that will take place at a certain time in the future. This tense is formed by adding *will be* to the *ing* form of the main verb.

Someday astronauts will be going to Mars.

This tense can also be formed by adding a phrase noting the future *(are going to)* plus *be* to the *ing* form of the main verb.

They are going to be performing many experiments.

punctuate *edit* capitalize
SPELL
improve
Using the Parts of Speech
725

Grammar Practice

Verbs 4

- ■ **Present Perfect Tense Verbs**
- ■ **Past Perfect Tense Verbs**
- ■ **Future Perfect Tense Verbs**

 For each of the sentences below, write the verb and identify the tense as "present perfect," "past perfect," or "future perfect."

Example: Students in the ecology club had thought quite a bit about the environment.
had thought (past perfect)

1. Progress has caused some negative effects on our world.

2. As early as the 1970s, research scientists in Antarctica had noticed the growth of a hole in our atmosphere's ozone layer.

3. Some argue that the hole had grown due to pollution.

4. This discovery has worried researchers.

5. Scientists have suggested ways to protect the ozone layer.

6. Some countries have banned the use of chlorofluorocarbons.

7. Environmental groups hope all pollution will have stopped by 2020.

8. The ecology club students had wanted to help in some way.

9. They have worked to spread the word about saving the ozone.

10. They will have made 100 posters by the end of the week.

11. The club members have promised to put the posters up this weekend.

Next Step: Write two sentences about what your community is doing to reduce pollution. Use a perfect tense verb in each sentence.

Verbs . . .
Forms of Verbs

The voice of a verb tells you whether the subject is doing the action or is receiving the action. A verb is in the active voice (in any tense) if the subject is doing the action in a sentence. (See page 482.)

I dream of going to galaxies light-years from Earth.

I will travel in an ultrafast spaceship.

A verb is in the passive voice if the subject is not doing the action. The action is done *by* someone or something else. The passive voice is always indicated with a helping verb plus a past participle or a past tense verb.

My daydreams often are shattered by reality. (The subject *daydreams* is not doing the action.)

Of course, reality can be seen differently by different people. (The subject *reality* is not doing the action.)

Tense	Active Voice		Passive Voice	
	Singular	**Plural**	**Singular**	**Plural**
Present Tense	I find	we find	I am found	we are found
	you find	you find	you are found	you are found
	he/she/it finds	they find	he/she/it is found	they are found
Past Tense	I found	we found	I was found	we were found
	you found	you found	you were found	you were found
	he found	they found	he/she/it was found	they were found
Future Tense	I will find	we will find	I will be found	we will be found
	you will find	you will find	you will be found	you will be found
	he will find	they will find	he/she/it will be found	they will be found
Present Perfect	I have found	we have found	I have been found	we have been found
	you have found	you have found	you have been found	you have been found
	he has found	they have found	he/she/it has been found	they have been found
Past Perfect	I had found	we had found	I had been found	we had been found
	you had found	you had found	you had been found	you had been found
	he had found	they had found	he/she/it had been found	they had been found
Future Perfect	I will have found	we will have found	I will have been found	we will have been found
	you will have found	you will have found	you will have been found	you will have been found
	he will have found	they will have found	he/she/it will have been found	they will have been found

punctuate edit capitalize SPELL 727
improve
Using the Parts of Speech

Grammar Practice

Verbs 5

■ Active or Passive Voice

For each sentence below, write the verb and tell whether it is active (doing the action) or passive (receiving the action).

Example: William Shakespeare has been called the greatest writer of the English language.

has been called (passive)

1. People feel his influence in many ways.

2. Many words and phrases were invented by Shakespeare.

3. He created the words "moonbeam," "elbow," and "buzzer."

4. Most people know Shakespeare best for his plays.

5. He wrote 37 plays in his lifetime.

6. Additional plays might have been written by Shakespeare and another writer.

7. Shakespeare also created beautiful poems, including many sonnets.

Rewrite each of the following sentences in the active voice. Add or delete words as necessary.

Example: Shakespeare's plays have been enjoyed by millions of people.

Millions of people have enjoyed Shakespeare's plays.

1. His plays have been explained in different ways by different audiences.

2. The play *The Taming of the Shrew* was made by Gil Junger into the movie *10 Things I Hate About You.*

3. The part of the "shrew" was played by Julia Stiles.

4. Whatever you think about the play, it will be enjoyed by you.

5. Shakespeare's plays are loved by people who have read them.

PARTS OF SPEECH

Verbs . . .
Forms of Verbs

A singular subject needs a singular verb. A plural subject needs a plural verb. For action verbs, only the third-person singular verb form is different: *I wonder, we wonder, you wonder, she wonders, they wonder.* Some linking verbs, however, have several different forms.

First Person   **Singular:** I am (or was) a good student.
                     Plural: We are (or were) good students.

Second Person   **Singular:** You are (or were) a cheerleader.
                     Plural: You are (or were) cheerleaders.

Third Person   **Singular:** He is (or was) on the wrestling team.
                     Plural: They are (or were) also on the team.

A transitive verb is a verb that transfers its action to a direct object. The object makes the meaning of the verb complete. A transitive verb is always an action verb (never a linking verb). (See page 570.)

> An earthquake shook San Francisco in 1906. (*Shook* transfers its action to the direct object *San Francisco.* Without *San Francisco,* the meaning of the verb *shook* is incomplete.)

> The city's people spent many years rebuilding. (Without the direct object *years,* the verb's meaning is incomplete.)

A transitive verb transfers the action directly to a direct object and indirectly to an indirect object.

> Fires destroyed the city. (direct object: *city*)

> Our teacher gave us the details. (indirect object: *us;* direct object: *details*)

See 692.4 and 692.5 for more on direct and indirect objects.

An intransitive verb does not need an object to complete its meaning. (See page 570.)

> Abigail was shopping. (The verb's meaning is complete.)

> Her stomach felt queasy. (*Queasy* is a predicate adjective describing *stomach*; there is no direct object.)

> She lay down on the bench. (Again, there is no direct object. *Down* is an adverb modifying *lay.*)

punctuate edit capitalize
improve SPELL 729
Using the Parts of Speech

Grammar Practice

Verbs 6

■ Singular and Plural Verbs

For each sentence below, write the correct choice from the verb forms in parentheses and identify it as "singular" or "plural."

Example: She *(was, were)* the perfect actress for the role.
was—singular

1. I *(am, are)* going to try out for the next play.

2. We *(am, are)* fine actors.

3. We *(was, were)* in the last play.

4. She *(love, loves)* to be the star.

5. They *(are, is)* in the chorus.

6. You must *(shine, shines)* the spotlights on Kim.

■ Transitive Verbs
■ Intransitive Verbs

For each of the following sentences, write whether the underlined verb is transitive or intransitive.

Example: Nigel <u>threw</u> a forward pass to Manuel.
transitive

1. Manuel <u>turned</u> sideways to catch it.

2. Suddenly, Roger ran up to Manuel and <u>grabbed</u> the football.

3. Roger <u>carried</u> it all the way down the field for a touchdown.

4. He <u>spiked</u> the ball onto the artificial turf.

5. Then he <u>danced</u> around the end zone.

6. Unfortunately, the referee had <u>blown</u> his whistle.

7. Roger <u>looked</u> surprised that he hadn't scored the touchdown.

8. The team gloomily <u>walked</u> back up the field.

Verbs

Forms of Verbs

Some verbs can be either transitive or intransitive.

> Transitive: **She reads my note. Albert ate an apple.**
>
> Intransitive: **She reads aloud. Albert ate already.**

Verbals

A **verbal** is a word that is made from a verb but acts as another part of speech. Gerunds, participles, and infinitives are verbals.

A gerund is a verb form that ends in *ing* and is used as a *noun.* A gerund often begins a gerund phrase.

> **Worrying is useless.** (The gerund is the subject noun.)
>
> **You should stop worrying about so many things.** (The gerund phrase is the direct object.)

A participle is a verb form ending in *ing* or *ed.* A participle is used as an *adjective* and often begins a participial phrase.

> **The idea of the earth shaking and splitting both fascinates and frightens me.** (The participles modify *earth.*)
>
> **Rattling in the cabinets, the dishes were about to crash to the floor.** (The participial phrase modifies *dishes.*)
>
> **Why doesn't this tired earth just stand still?** (The participle modifies *earth.*)

An infinitive is a verb form introduced by *to.* It may be used as a *noun,* an *adjective,* or an *adverb.* It often begins an infinitive phrase.

> **My need to whisper is due to this secret.** (The infinitive is an adjective modifying *need.*)
>
> **I am afraid to swim.** (The infinitive is an adverb modifying the predicate adjective *afraid.*)
>
> **To overcome this fear is my goal.** (The infinitive phrase is used as a noun and is the subject of this sentence.)

punctuate *edit* capitalize SPELL **731**
improve
Using the Parts of Speech

Grammar Practice

Verbs 7

■ Gerunds, Participles, and Infinitives

 In each numbered sentence below, identify the underlined verb form as a gerund, a participle, or an infinitive.

Example: A Michigan man, J. Sterling Morton, worked
to improve agricultural practices in Nebraska.
infinitive

(1) Arbor Day began in 1872 when Morton decided to settle in Nebraska. (2) He came up with a plan to get more trees growing in his adopted state. (3) Working as a newspaper editor, he wrote articles that encouraged people to plant more trees. (4) He said the trees would be good for blocking the winds, preventing soil erosion, and making the prairie lands more beautiful. (5) Morton proposed that people observe a special day dedicated to tree planting, and in 1885, Arbor Day was named a legal holiday in Nebraska. (6) In the beginning, April 22 (Morton's birthday) was the selected date. (7) Today, the date for Arbor Day varies by state, depending on the best time for planting trees locally. (8) Improving the look of a community is a great result of Arbor Day. (9) The success of the holiday in the United States has caused the idea to spread to other countries, as well.

 For each of the following sentences, write the infinitive phrase and label how it is used: noun, adjective, or adverb.

Example: To improve the natural environment is the ecology
club's cause.
To improve the natural environment (noun)

1. Our efforts to plant trees will result in a more scenic landscape.

2. A local business offered to supply seedlings.

3. We are eager to make a difference in our community.

4. Would you be willing to help us?

Adjectives . . .

An **adjective** is a word used to describe a noun or a pronoun. Adjectives tell *what kind, how many (how much),* or *which one.* They usually come before the word they describe. (See pages 486–489.)

ancient **dinosaurs**   800 **species**   that **triceratops**

Adjectives are the same whether the word they describe is singular or plural.

small **brain**—or—small **brains**   large **tooth**—or—large **teeth**

732.1
Articles

The articles *a, an,* and *the* are adjectives.

A **brontosaurus was an animal about 70 feet long.**

The **huge dinosaur lived on land and ate plants.**

732.2
Proper Adjectives

A proper adjective is formed from a proper noun, and it is always capitalized. (See 618.1.)

A **Chicago museum is home to the skeleton of one of these beasts.** (*Chicago* functions as a proper adjective describing the noun *museum.*)

732.3
Common Adjectives

A common adjective is any adjective that is not proper. It is not capitalized (unless it is the first word in a sentence).

Ancient **mammoths were** huge, woolly **creatures.**

They **lived in the** ice **fields of Siberia.**

Special Kinds of Adjectives

732.4
Demonstrative Adjectives

A demonstrative adjective points out a particular noun. *This* and *these* point out something nearby; *that* and *those* point out something at a distance.

This **mammoth is huge, but that mammoth is even bigger.**

NOTE When a noun does not follow *this, these, that,* or *those,* these words are pronouns, not adjectives. (See 708.1.)

732.5
Compound Adjectives

A compound adjective is made up of two or more words. (Sometimes it is hyphenated.)

Dinosaurs were egg-laying **animals.**

The **North American Allosaurus had sharp teeth and powerful jaws.**

punctuate *edit* capitalize
improve SPELL 733
Using the Parts of Speech

Grammar Practice

Adjectives 1

- Articles
- Proper Adjectives
- Common Adjectives

 Label the underlined adjectives in the following sentences by writing "article," "proper," or "common."

Example: In 1957, Althea Gibson was <u>the</u> first <u>African American</u> <u>tennis</u> player to win at Wimbledon.

article, proper, common

1. As a <u>young</u> woman, Althea set out to be <u>the</u> best woman tennis player of all time.

2. This goal motivated her to win <u>a</u> girls' <u>singles</u> championship in New York in 1942 when she was 15 years old.

3. Ms. Gibson was the <u>first</u> African American to enter the <u>American Lawn Tennis Association</u> championships in 1950.

4. After college, she entered a <u>French</u> competition in 1956, and that tournament became her first <u>major</u> victory.

5. Althea also won <u>the</u> singles competition of the U.S. Open <u>two</u> years in a row.

6. Trophies from these championships lined a <u>broad</u> glass shelf.

7. After retiring from tennis, she toured America with the <u>Harlem Globetrotters</u> basketball team.

8. Later, Althea tried <u>professional</u> golf, and she became <u>an</u> athletic advisor for the state of New Jersey.

9. Ms. Gibson enjoyed those duties for <u>several</u> years.

10. Althea Gibson died on September 28, 2003, in a <u>New Jersey</u> hospital.

Next Step: Read the sentences above again, this time looking for demonstrative adjectives (not underlined). Write them down as you find them. (There are four.)

Adjectives
Special Kinds of Adjectives

734.1
Indefinite Adjectives

An indefinite adjective gives approximate, or indefinite, information (*any, few, many, most,* and so on). It does not tell exactly how many or how much.

Some mammoths were heavier than today's elephants.

734.2
Predicate Adjectives

A predicate adjective follows a linking verb and describes the subject.

Mammoths were once abundant, but now they are extinct.

Forms of Adjectives

734.3
Positive Adjectives

The positive form describes a noun or pronoun without comparing it to anyone or anything else.

The Eurostar is a fast train that runs between London, Paris, and Brussels.

It is an impressive train.

734.4
Comparative Adjectives

The comparative form of an adjective *(er)* compares two persons, places, things, or ideas. (See page 487.)

The Eurostar is faster than the Orient Express.

Some adjectives that have more than one syllable show comparisons by their *er* suffix, but many of them use the modifiers *more* or *less.*

It is a speedier commuter train than the Tobu Railway trains in Japan.

This train is more impressive than my commuter train.

734.5
Superlative Adjectives

The superlative form *(est* or *most* or *least)* compares three or more persons, places, things, or ideas. (See page 487.)

In fact, the Eurostar is the fastest train in Europe.

It is the most impressive commuter train in the world.

734.6
Irregular Forms

Some adjectives use completely different words to express comparison.

good, better, best   **bad, worse, worst**

many, more, most   **little, less, least**

punctuate *edit* capitalize
improve SPELL **735**
Using the Parts of Speech

Grammar Practice

Adjectives 2

■ Indefinite Adjectives
■ Predicate Adjectives

For each of the following sentences, identify and label the indefinite adjectives and the predicate adjectives.

Example: Many homes were destroyed during the great
Chicago fire of 1871.
many (indefinite)

1. Before the fire, most buildings were wooden.

2. Few buildings escaped the fire.

3. Wooden sidewalks were flammable and added fuel to the fire.

4. Almost 100,000 city residents became homeless due to the fire.

5. Some residents rebuilt their homes after the fire.

■ Positive, Comparative, and Superlative Adjectives

Write the correct form of the underlined adjectives in the following sentences.

Example: The Panama Canal was one of the expensive
projects ever to be built.
most expensive

1. The <u>bad</u> problem affecting the construction workers was disease caused by mosquito bites.

2. The engineers had to make the canal 100 feet <u>wide</u> than they originally planned in order to let large ships through.

3. The *Jahre Viking*, currently the <u>large</u> ship in the world, is too wide to pass through the canal.

4. The first toll (in 1914) of 90 cents per ton was <u>cheap</u> than today's rate, which is almost three dollars per ton.

5. The <u>quick</u> travel time through the canal is eight hours.

Adverbs . . .

An **adverb** is a word used to modify a verb, an adjective, or another adverb. It tells *how, when, where, how often,* or *how much.* Adverbs can come before or after the words they modify. (See pages 490–493.)

Dad snores loudly. (*Loudly* modifies the verb *snores.*)

His snores are really **explosive.** (*Really* modifies the adjective *explosive.*)

Dad snores very **loudly.** (*Very* modifies the adverb *loudly.*)

Types of Adverbs

There are four basic types of adverbs: *time, place, manner,* and *degree.*

736.1 Adverbs of Time

Adverbs of time tell *when, how often,* and *how long.*

tomorrow   often   never   always

Jen rarely **has time to go swimming.**

736.2 Adverbs of Place

Adverbs of place tell *where, to where,* or *from where.*

there   backward   outside

We'll set up our tent here.

736.3 Adverbs of Manner

Adverbs of manner often end in *ly* and tell *how* something is done.

unkindly   gently   well

Ahmed boldly **entered the dark cave.**

Some words used as adverbs can be written with or without the *ly* ending. When in doubt, use the *ly* form.

slow, slowly   deep, deeply

NOTE Not all words ending in *ly* are adverbs. *Lovely,* for example, is an adjective.

736.4 Adverbs of Degree

Adverbs of degree tell *how much* or *how little.*

scarcely   entirely   generally   very   really

Jess is usually **the leader in these situations.**

punctuate edit capitalize
improve SPELL
737
Using the Parts of Speech

Grammar Practice

Adverbs 1

■ Adverbs of Time
■ Adverbs of Place
■ Adverbs of Manner
■ Adverbs of Degree

The number of adverbs in each sentence below is indicated in parentheses at the end of the sentence. Write the adverbs and identify them as adverbs of "time," "place," "manner," or "degree."

Example: We are going to see a Chicago Cubs game tomorrow. *(1)*
tomorrow (time)

1. The Chicago Cubs always play home games at Wrigley Field, generally during the day. *(2)*

2. Cubs fans really like to watch games there. *(2)*

3. People even stand outside of the stadium, waiting patiently for home runs that completely clear the fence. *(4)*

4. The last time the Cubs were world champions was 1908; now the Cubs rarely make it to the play-offs. *(2)*

5. Their fans often say, "Wait till next year," and they faithfully attend as many games as they can. *(2)*

6. Some of them openly complain that the Cubs will never win a World Series again. *(3)*

7. Although the Cubs may be a very poor team in some critics' opinions, their fans love them deeply. *(2)*

8. The fans eagerly purchase Cubs T-shirts and caps. *(1)*

9. They support their team enthusiastically. *(1)*

10. Occasionally, their hopes are rewarded, as it was when the Cubs actually made it to the 2003 play-offs. *(2)*

Next Step: Write a short paragraph about a favorite sport or team. Include one of each type of adverb in the paragraph.

PARTS OF SPEECH

Adverbs
Special Kinds of Adverbs

738.1
Conjunctive Adverbs

A conjunctive adverb can be used as a conjunction and shows a connection or a transition between two independent clauses. Most often, a conjunctive adverb follows a semicolon in a compound sentence; however, it can also appear at the beginning or end of a sentence. (Note that the previous sentence has an example of a conjunctive adverb.)

also	besides	however	instead
meanwhile	nevertheless	therefore	

Forms of Adverbs

Many adverbs—especially adverbs of manner—have three forms: *positive, comparative,* and *superlative.*

738.2
Positive Adverbs

The positive form describes but does not make a comparison.

Juan woke up late.

He quickly ate some breakfast.

738.3
Comparative Adverbs

The comparative form of an adverb *(er)* compares two things.

Juan woke up later than he usually did. (See page 491.)

Some adverbs that have more than one syllable show comparisons by their *er* suffix, but many of them use the modifiers *more* or *less.*

He ate his breakfast more quickly than usual.

738.4
Superlative Adverbs

The superlative form *(est* or *most* or *least)* compares three or more things. (See page 491.)

Of the past three days, Juan woke up latest on Saturday.

Of the past three days, he ate his breakfast least quickly on Saturday.

738.5
Irregular Forms

Some adverbs use completely different words to express comparison.

Positive	Comparative	Superlative
well	better	best
badly	worse	worst

Grammar Practice

Adverbs 2

■ **Conjunctive Adverbs**

Number your paper from 1 to 3 and write the three conjunctive adverbs that appear in the following paragraph.

Example: When money was invented, it made buying and selling easier. Thus, one coin could replace a basketful of vegetables.

Thus

Many people like to pay with cash; others, however, prefer to barter for goods. Buying from these people may be more difficult. A lot of shoppers today prefer to buy what they want at a mall instead. Meanwhile, the computer age and its electronic money are steering us toward a cashless economy. Electronic credit may eventually be all that people use to buy and sell.

■ **Comparative Adverbs**

For each sentence below, write the correct comparative form of the underlined adverb.

Example: A computer can solve a difficult arithmetic problem <u>fast</u> than a human can.

faster

1. Some students think the computer in Ms. Stowe's room works <u>well</u> than the one in the library.

2. The new word processor program actually runs <u>slowly</u> than the old one.

3. This green mouse moves <u>smoothly</u> than that red one.

4. The keys on Kayla's keyboard stick <u>badly</u> than mine do.

Test Prep!

Number your paper from 1 to 12. For each underlined part of the paragraphs below, write the letter (from the next page) of the best choice.

Have you <u>seed</u> any news about the future of dentistry?
      (1)
Cavities and gum disease won't be problems. Tiny robots in your

mouth <u>will brush and flossed</u> your teeth for you. Artificial
        (2)
materials <u>maked</u> of teeth and bone cells will rebuild the teeth,
      (3)
gum tissue, and jawbone. People will have <u>fewer</u> worries about
           (4)
losing their teeth than they do now.

Actually, humans <u>had began</u> to work at keeping their teeth
       (5)
clean a <u>long</u> time ago than you might think. The ancient Egyptians
   (6)
<u>chew</u> twigs so the ends would fray, and—presto!—they had a
(7)
toothbrush. Europeans rubbed their teeth with cloth after they

<u>eated</u>. Sometime during the 1700s, man-made toothbrushes
(8)
<u>will be invented</u>; the brush part was created from hog bristles.
    (9)
Today, dental products can keep teeth <u>healthy and white</u> than
           (10)
in the past. To make sure your teeth are <u>taken</u> care of, brush twice
        (11)
a day, floss daily, eat a balanced diet, and see a dentist regularly.

Technology has not <u>bringed</u> us carefree dentistry yet!
      (12)

1
(A) saw
(B) seen
(C) sawed
(D) correct as is

2
(A) will brush and floss
(B) will brushed and flossed
(C) will brushed and floss
(D) correct as is

3
(A) make
(B) made
(C) maded
(D) correct as is

4
(A) few
(B) fewest
(C) the fewest
(D) correct as is

5
(A) began
(B) beginned
(C) begun
(D) correct as is

6
(A) longest
(B) more longer
(C) longer
(D) correct as is

7
(A) chewing
(B) will chew
(C) chewed
(D) correct as is

8
(A) eaten
(B) ate
(C) had ate
(D) correct as is

9
(A) were invented
(B) are invented
(C) was invented
(D) correct as is

10
(A) healthier and white
(B) healthier and whiter
(C) healthiest and whiter
(D) correct as is

11
(A) took
(B) taked
(C) takened
(D) correct as is

12
(A) bring
(B) brought
(C) broughted
(D) correct as is

Prepositions

Prepositions are words that show position, direction, or how two words or ideas are related to each other. Specifically, a preposition shows the relationship between its object and some other word in the sentence.

> **Raul hid under the stairs.** (*Under* shows the relationship between *hid* and *stairs.*)

742.1
Prepositional Phrases

A preposition never appears alone; it is always part of a prepositional phrase. A prepositional phrase includes the preposition, the object of the preposition, and the modifiers of the object. (See pages 494–495.)

> **Raul's friends looked in the clothes hamper.** (preposition: *in*; object: *hamper*; modifiers: *the, clothes*)

A prepositional phrase functions as an adjective or as an adverb.

> **They checked the closet with all the winter coats.** (*With all the winter coats* functions as an adjective modifying *closet.*)

> **They wandered around the house looking for him.** (*Around the house* functions as an adverb modifying *wandered.*)

NOTE If a word found in the list of prepositions has no object, it is not a preposition. It is probably an adverb.

> **Raul had never won at hide 'n' seek before.** (*Before* is an adverb that modifies *had won.*)

Prepositions

aboard	apart from	beyond	from	like	outside	under
about	around	but	from among	near	outside of	underneath
above	aside from	by	from between	near to	over	until
according to	at	by means of	from under	next	over to	unto
across	away from	concerning	in	of	owing to	up
across from	back of	considering	in addition to	off	past	up to
after	because of	despite	in front of	on	prior to	upon
against	before	down	in place of	on account of	regarding	with
along	behind	down from	in regard to	on behalf of	since	within
along with	below	during	in spite of	on top of	through	without
alongside	beneath	except	inside	onto	throughout	
alongside of	beside	except for	inside of	opposite	to	
amid	besides	excepting	instead of	out	together with	
among	between	for	into	out of	toward	

punctuate *edit* capitalize
improve SPELL **743**
Using the Parts of Speech

Grammar Practice

Prepositions

For each sentence below, write the prepositional phrase or phrases. (The number of phrases in each sentence is in parentheses.) Circle the prepositions.

Example: The first issue of the *Cherokee Phoenix* newspaper was printed in English and in Cherokee. *(3)*

(of) the Cherokee Phoenix newspaper, (in) English, (in) Cherokee

1. For many years, Cherokee history was told from memory. *(2)*

2. No written form of their language existed at the time. *(2)*

3. A Native American named Sequoya was a silversmith and a trader in Georgia. *(1)*

4. His name was given to him by missionaries. *(2)*

5. Until his creation of a symbol for each sound in Cherokee, none of the Cherokee could read or write. *(5)*

6. Sequoya wrote a story in Cherokee on some paper, and his daughter read it. *(2)*

7. He traveled throughout Arkansas so he could teach other Cherokee. *(1)*

8. Then he moved with the whole tribe to Oklahoma. *(2)*

9. Without his assistance, the Cherokee might not have become such a strong, united people. *(1)*

10. On account of Sequoya's achievement, the Cherokee people became leaders among Native Americans. *(2)*

11. The giant California trees called *sequoias* are named after him. *(1)*

12. He is remembered, along with other great Americans, for his contributions. *(2)*

Next Step: Pick five prepositions from the list on the facing page. Write several sentences using those prepositions correctly. Exchange papers with a classmate and circle each other's prepositional phrases.

Conjunctions . . .

A **conjunction** connects individual words or groups of words. There are three kinds of conjunctions: *coordinating, correlative,* and *subordinating.* (See pages 496–498.)

744.1
Coordinating Conjunctions

A coordinating conjunction connects a word to a word, a phrase to a phrase, or a clause to a clause. The words, phrases, or clauses joined by a coordinating conjunction must be equal, or of the same type.

Polluted rivers and streams can be cleaned up. (Two nouns are connected by *and.*)

Ride a bike or plant a tree to reduce pollution. (Two verb phrases are connected by *or.*)

Maybe you can't invent a pollution-free engine, but you can cut down on the amount of energy you use. (Two equal independent clauses are connected by *but.*)

NOTE When a coordinating conjunction is used to make a compound sentence, a comma always comes before it.

744.2
Correlative Conjunctions

Correlative conjunctions are conjunctions used in pairs.

We must reduce not only pollution but also excess energy use.

Either you're part of the solution, or you're part of the problem.

Conjunctions

Coordinating Conjunctions
and, but, or, nor, for, so, yet

Correlative Conjunctions
either, or   neither, nor   not only, but also   both, and   whether, or   as, so

Subordinating Conjunctions
after, although, as, as if, as long as, as though, because, before, if, in order that, provided that, since, so, so that, that, though, till, unless, until, when, where, whereas, while

punctuate *edit* capitalize
SPELL
improve   **745**
Using the Parts of Speech

Grammar Practice

Conjunctions

■ Coordinating Conjunctions

Combine the following pairs of sentences by using a coordinating conjunction to connect the sentence parts given in parentheses.

Example: Every country has a flag. Each flag is different. *(clauses)*

Every country has a flag, but each flag is different.

1. Sonja likes the Canadian flag. Sanjeev likes the Canadian flag. *(words)*

2. Displaying a flag can be patriotic. Carrying a flag can be patriotic. *(words)*

3. You can buy a cotton flag. You can buy a nylon flag. *(phrases)*

4. The school flag got very wet. The janitor dried it. *(clauses)*

5. Does this flag belong to Sweden? Does this flag belong to Denmark? *(words)*

6. Citizens honor their flag. A flag represents the country. *(clauses)*

■ Correlative Conjunctions

Use a different set of correlative conjunctions to combine each sentence pair below. Underline the conjunctions.

Example: Jaguars live in rain forests. Tapirs live in rain forests.
Both jaguars and tapirs live in rain forests.

1. Elephants do not live in South America. Tigers do not live in South America.

2. In a rain forest, people walk. They also ride in boats.

3. The Amazon is one of the longest rivers in the world. It flows through one of the largest rain forests in the world.

4. If we want to use rain-forest plants for medicines, we must save the rain forests. If we want to use rain-forest plants for food, we must save the rain forests.

Conjunctions

746.1
Subordinating Conjunctions

A subordinating conjunction is a word or group of words that connects two clauses that are not equally important. A subordinating conjunction begins a dependent clause and connects it to an independent clause to make a complex sentence. (See page 517 and the chart on page 744.)

Fuel-cell engines are unusual **because** they don't have moving parts.

Since fuel-cell cars run on hydrogen, the only waste products are water and heat.

As you can see in the sentences above, a comma sets off the dependent clause only when it begins the sentence. A comma is usually not used when the dependent clause follows the independent clause.

NOTE Relative pronouns and conjunctive adverbs can also connect clauses. (See 706.3 and 738.1.)

Interjections

An **interjection** is a word or phrase used to express strong emotion or surprise. Punctuation (a comma or an exclamation point) is used to separate an interjection from the rest of the sentence.

Wow, would you look at that!   **Oh no!** He's falling!

Grammar Practice

Conjunctions and Interjections

- Subordinating Conjunctions
- Interjections

 Write the subordinating conjunction that connects the clauses in each of the sentences below. (The chart on page 744 will help.)

Example: The buffalo became a symbol of the Native Americans because it was vital to their survival.

because

1. After the Native Americans killed the huge animals they needed, they used every part of the buffalo, from horns to tail hairs. Wow!

2. Before the settlers moved into Native American areas, millions of buffalo roamed through the prairies.

3. Because buffalo herds were deliberately overhunted during the 1800s, the herds declined in the United States.

4. Oh dear, the buffalo was almost extinct when President Ulysses S. Grant created Yellowstone National Park.

5. Although the buffalo no longer rules the prairies, many tribes of Native Americans are working to increase the herd numbers.

6. Gee, more than 55 tribes have joined together to help restore the buffalo herds since the Intertribal Bison Cooperative was formed in 1990.

7. While Native Americans no longer need food from the buffalo to survive, selling buffalo meat has become a huge industry.

8. Whereas the buffalo once meant food and clothing to the Native Americans, today the meat can be sold to help support the tribes.

9. Well, the Native Americans can still make use of the majestic animal as long as the buffalo herds continue to grow.

Next Step: Find the interjections in the sentences above and write them on your paper. You should find four of them.

Quick Guide: Parts of Speech

In the English language, there are eight parts of speech. Understanding them will help you improve your writing skills. Every word you write is a part of speech—a noun, a verb, an adjective, and so on. The chart below lists the eight parts of speech.

Noun

A word that names a person, a place, a thing, or an idea

Alex Moya   Belize   ladder   courage

Pronoun

A word used in place of a noun

I   he   it   they   you   anybody   some

Verb

A word that shows action or links a subject to another word in the sentence

sing   shake   catch   is   are

Adjective

A word that describes a noun or a pronoun

stormy   red   rough   seven   grand

Adverb

A word that describes a verb, an adjective, or another adverb

quickly   today   now   bravely   softer

Preposition

A word that shows position or direction and introduces a prepositional phrase

around   up   under   over   between   to

Conjunction

A word that connects other words or groups of words

and   but   or   so   because   when

Interjection

A word (set off by commas or an exclamation point) that shows strong emotion

Stop! Hey, how are you?

punctuate *edit* *capitalize* SPELL **749**
improve
Using the Parts of Speech

Grammar Practice

Parts of Speech Review

For each numbered sentence below, write whether the underlined word is a noun, a pronoun, a verb, an adjective, an adverb, a preposition, a conjunction, or an interjection.

Example: <u>Wow</u>, it took months for an immigrant to travel across the ocean in the 1800s.

interjection

(1) Ellis Island was the first <u>stop</u> for many immigrants seeking a better life in the United States. **(2)** Between 1892 and 1954, the island was the country's <u>main</u> immigration center. **(3)** More than 12 million immigrants <u>passed</u> through its gates during that time.

(4) In its first year of operation, nearly 450,000 people stepped <u>on</u> American soil for the first time at Ellis Island. **(5)** <u>It</u> welcomed 11,747 immigrants, the most in a single day, on April 17, 1907. **(6)** About 40 percent of all Americans have an ancestor who arrived at Ellis Island, <u>but</u> it accepted its last immigrant in November 1954.

(7) After the center closed, the great limestone walls of the Main Arrival Building <u>slowly</u> began to crumble. **(8)** Then, in 1965, Ellis Island <u>became</u> part of the Statue of Liberty National Monument. **(9)** Through <u>generous</u> private donations, the building was restored to its original state. **(10)** The <u>cost</u> was more than $156 million. **(11)** <u>Wow</u>! **(12)** In 1990, the doors of the old building, now a museum, <u>finally</u> reopened.

(13) Today, museum visitors research <u>their</u> ancestors. **(14)** Exhibits <u>and</u> hundreds of photographs honor this country's immigrant heritage. **(15)** Every U.S. citizen should make a trip <u>to</u> Ellis Island.

Next Step: Write a two-word sentence (noun and verb). Exchange papers with a classmate and keep adding words to each other's sentences until they have all eight parts of speech.

Credits

Photos:

comstock.com: pages vi, ix, xi, xii, 1, 5, 9, 29, 32, 57, 60, 93, 96, 97, 101, 107, 113, 125, 129, 135, 140, 143, 157, 161, 165, 171, 174, 177, 186, 189, 193, 198, 199, 223, 227, 233, 235, 239, 251, 255, 261, 264, 266, 274, 283, 291, 295, 301, 313, 323, 329, 363, 365, 366, 381, 401, 403, 405, 411, 417, 420, 423, 430, 441, 449, 464, 469, 499, 521, 523, 533, 750

Getty Images: pages iii, v, x, xi, xviii, 10, 11, 33, 44, 45, 60, 65, 68, 75, 83, 97, 105, 129, 143, 157, 161, 169, 193, 205, 219, 261, 266, 267, 276, 287, 317, 321, 343, 349, 363, 368, 376, 377, 381, 405, 411, 459, 466, 523, 547, 555

Hemera: page 71
istockphoto.com: page 398
Ulead Systems: pages 300, 353, 354, 356, 359, 431
www.jupiterimages.com: page 361

Credits:

Page 375: Copyright © 2007 by Houghton Mifflin Company, Adapted by permission from *The American Heritage Student Dictionary.*

Acknowledgements

We're grateful to many people who helped bring *Write Source* to life. First we must thank all the teachers and students from across the country who contributed writing models and ideas.

In addition, we want to thank our Write Source/Great Source team for all their help:

Steven J. Augustyn, Laura Bachman, Ron Bachman, April Barrons, William Baughn, Colleen Belmont, Lisa Bingen, Evelyn Curley, Sandra Easton, Chris Erickson, Jean Fischer, Sherry Gordon, Mariellen Hanrahan, Kathy Henning, Tammy Hintz, Mary Anne Hoff, Kathy Kahnle, Rob King, Lois Krenzke, Mark Lalumondier, Joyce Becker Lee, Ellen Leitheusser, Kevin Nelson, Douglas Niles, Sue Paro, Pat Reigel, Jason C. Reynolds, Susan Rogalski, Janae Sebranek, Lester Smith, Richard Spencer, Julie Spicuzza, Thomas Spicuzza, Jean Varley, Sandy Wagner, and Claire Ziffer.

Index

The **index** will help you find specific information in the handbook. Entries in italics are words from the "Using the Right Word" section. The colored boxes contain information you will use often.

process BASICS resource
forms proofreader's guide
753
Index

F

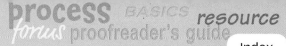

process BASICS resource
forms proofreader's guide
763
Index

Underlining, as italics, 602
Understanding information, 451, 453
Understanding assignments, 450
Understanding the writing process, 5–10
Understatement, 559
Understood subject and predicate, 694.1
Unity in writing, 538
Unnecessary details, 303, 538
Unsent letters, 440
Usage, 561, 652–686
Using the right word, 315, 652–686

Vain/vane/vein, 682.2
Vary/very, 682.3
Venn diagram, 448, 537, 549
Verbs,
    718–730
    Action, 41, 185, 480, 482, 718.1
    Active, 308, 482, 726.1
    Agreement with subject, 508–509, 728.1
    "Be" verbs, 472, 480, 704.5, 718.2
    Helping, 718.3
    Intransitive, 570, 728.3, 730.1
    Irregular, 481, 720, 722
    Linking, 480, 718.2
    Passive, 308, 482, 726.1
    Perfect tense, 484, 724
    Phrase, 700.2, 730
    Plural, 508, 509, 728.1
    Predicate in a sentence, 501–503, 514
    Principal parts of, 481, 722
    Regular, 481
    Singular, 508, 509, 728.1
    Specific, 41, 185, 485
    Tense, 297, 314, 483–484, 720–726
    Transitive, 570, 728.2, 730.1
    Vivid, 41

Verbals, 730
Very/vary, 682.3
Visual aids, 425
Vocabulary,
    Building techniques, 562
    Context, 562–563
    Improving, 564–569
    New words, 563
    Prefixes, suffixes, roots, 564–569
    Using a dictionary, 374–375

Voice (trait), 12, 16, 34, 40
    Descriptive writing, 72, 77, 82
    Expository writing, 158, 162, 164, 169, 182–183, 188, 194–195, 201, 204, 215
    Multimedia presentation, 415
    Narrative writing, 94, 98, 100, 105, 118–119, 124, 130–131, 137, 141, 153
    Paragraph, 541
    Persuasive writing, 220, 224, 226, 232, 244–245, 250, 256–257, 263, 266, 279
    Poems, 354, 357
    Research writing, 378, 380, 385, 402, 410, 415
    Response to literature, 284, 288, 290, 293, 306–307, 312, 318–319, 325, 328, 339
    Stories, 345, 348

Voice, 561
    Active/passive, 308, 482, 726.1
    Engaging, 80
    Formal, 182–183, 307
    Revising for, 118–119, 182–183, 244–245, 250, 306–307, 556–557
    Using your, 428
    Verb, 41, 482, 726
Volume, voice, 428

W

Waist/waste, 682.4
Wait/weight, 682.5
Ware/wear/where, 682.6

Way/weigh, 684.1
Weather/whether, 684.2
Web diagram, see *Clustering*
Web pages, making, 63
Web site, Write Source, 64, 405
Week/weak, 684.3
Weekly planner, 458
Well/good, 666.1
Wet/whet, 684.4
Which/witch, 684.5
Who/which/that, 684.6
Who/whom, 684.7
Whole/hole, 666.7
Who's/whose, 686.1
Why write?, 1–3
Wood/would, 686.2
Words, 469–498, 702–748
    Division of, 374, 375, 608.1
    Linking, see *Transitions*
    Parts of, 564–569
    Using the right, 315, 652–686

Word choice (trait), 12, 20, 34, 41
    Descriptive writing, 72, 77, 82
    Expository writing, 158, 162, 164, 184–185, 188, 194–195, 204
    Multimedia presentation, 415
    Narrative writing, 94, 98, 100, 120–121, 124, 130–131, 137, 141, 153
    Paragraph, 541
    Persuasive writing, 220, 224, 226, 246–247, 250, 256–257, 263, 266
    Poems, 357
    Research writing, 378, 380, 385, 402, 410, 415
    Response to literature, 284, 288, 290, 308–309, 312, 318–319, 325, 328, 339
    Stories, 345, 348

Word choice,
    Connotation, 485, 560
Workplace writing,
    Business letters, 274–277, 577
    Memos, 576
    Practical, 150–151, 212–213, 334–335
    Proposals, 576